3RD Edition

INFANT AND TODDLER DEVELOPMENT AND RESPONSIVE PROGRAM PLANNING

A Relationship-Based Approach

Donna S. Wittmer
University of Colorado Denver

Sandra H. Petersen
ZERO TO THREE: The National Center for
Infants, Toddlers, and Families

Boston   Columbus   Indianapolis   New York   San Francisco   Upper Saddle River
Amsterdam   Cape Town   Dubai   London   Madrid   Milan   Munich   Paris   Montréal   Toronto
Delhi   Mexico City   São Paulo   Sydney   Hong Kong   Seoul   Singapore   Taipei   Tokyo

Vice President and Editorial Director: Jeffery W. Johnston
Senior Acquisitions Editor: Julie Peters
Editorial Assistant: Andrea Hall
Vice President, Director of Marketing: Margaret Waples
Senior Marketing Manager: Krista Clark
Senior Managing Editor: Pamela D. Bennett
Production Project Manager: Carrie Mollette
Production Manager: Fran Russello
Senior Art Director: Jayne Conte
Cover Designer: Suzanne Behnke
Cover Art: Vanessa Davies/Getty Images
Full-Service Project Management: George Jacob/Integra Software Services Pvt. Ltd.
Printer/Binder: Courier Companies, Inc.
Text Font: 10/12, Meridien LT Std

Credits and acknowledgments for material borrowed from other sources and reproduced, with permission, in this textbook appear on the appropriate page within the text.

Every effort has been made to provide accurate and current Internet information in this book. However, the Internet and information posted on it are constantly changing, so it is inevitable that some of the Internet addresses listed in this textbook will change.

Photo Credits: Deanna Wittmer Clauson, p. iii (FM); Dennis Wittmer, p. 61; Donna Wittmer, pp. 70, 248; Barbara Melinkovich, pp. 194, 408; Donna Easton Brooks, p. 332; All remaining photos by Carla Mestas.

Copyright © 2014, 2010, 2006 by Pearson Education, Inc. All rights reserved. Manufactured in the United States of America. This publication is protected by Copyright, and permission should be obtained from the publisher prior to any prohibited reproduction, storage in a retrieval system, or transmission in any form or by any means, electronic, mechanical, photocopying, recording, or likewise. To obtain permission(s) to use material from this work, please submit a written request to Pearson Education, Inc., Permissions Department, One Lake Street, Upper Saddle River, New Jersey 07458, or you may fax your request to 201-236-3290.

Library of Congress Cataloging-in-Publication Data
Wittmer, Donna Sasse.
    Infant and toddler development and responsive program planning: a relationship-based approach/
Donna S. Wittmer, University of Colorado Denver, Sandra H. Petersen, Zero to Three, the National
Center for Infants, Toddlers, and Families.—Third edition.
        pages cm
    ISBN-13: 978-0-13-286994-2
    ISBN-10: 0-13-286994-2
    1. Child development—Study and teaching.   2. Infants—Development—Study and teaching.
    3. Toddlers—Development—Study and teaching.   I. Petersen, Sandra H.   II. Title.
    RJ131.W56 2014
    649'.68—dc23
                                                                                2012047293

10 9 8 7 6 5 4 3

ISBN 10:   0-13-286994-2
ISBN 13: 978-0-13-286994-2

We would like to dedicate the third edition to John Clauson, who died on July 25, 2012, of acute myeloid leukemia at the age of 41. John, husband of Deanna and father to Kai, 5 years old, and son-in-law of Donna Wittmer, exemplified what it means to be a wonderful, caring father. At all times, he demonstrated his love for Kai, while supporting him to be prosocial, kind, curious, and love learning. As exclaimed at the celebration of life for John, fathers not only noticed his devotion to Kai but also wanted to emulate John's enthusiasm to be the best father he could be to his child. We miss him greatly.

Donna Wittmer
Sandy Petersen

Preface

This new edition of a comprehensive, applied text not only covers, but *celebrates*, infant and toddler development from prebirth through age 36 months, curriculum and program planning, and guidance using a relationship-based model. In addition, it focuses on the importance of families' and teachers' relationships and responsiveness in interactions with children; the latest developmental research; an emphasis on child-centered planning; a particularly strong coverage of infants and toddlers with special needs; and an emphasis on the effects of culture, families, and quality programs on infant-toddler development and interactions. It is research based *and* written so that the information is accessible and highly motivating to a wide range of readers.

What Is a Relationship-Based Approach?

Infants and toddlers have emotional and social needs to feel safe, valued, loved, and appreciated for their individuality and to be deeply connected with their family, culture, important adults, and peers. Supportive and positive relationships meet these needs and create the environment in which development proceeds.

Infant and Toddler Development and Responsive Program Planning uses a relationship-based model as a framework for understanding how infants and toddlers grow and learn with the support of their families and teachers. A relationship-based model respects the effects of an individual child's characteristics and the child's environment on the quality of the child's relationships. These relationships then become the filter and the catalyst for children's sense of well-being and development. As you use the relationship-based model to discover the importance of the infant and toddler years, we hope that you will gain a sense of enthusiasm and excitement about the influence that infant and toddler professionals can have on the quality of experiences and programs for young children and their families.

What This Book Provides for Our Readers

Our text provides a foundation in how infants and toddlers develop, in typical and atypical ways, and in program planning.

Why and How of Developmental Practice

We present all aspects of development within the context of brain development and the foundational structure of emotional development and early relationships. We want students to understand *why*, according to the science of child development, certain practices support or hinder an infant's or toddler's optimal development—and *how* to provide responsive, high-quality care. This book integrates theory, research, and practice in usable language for teachers.

Program Planning

In addition to including developmental content, it also uniquely includes program planning, which highlights the following components:

1. developing the foundation of a program
2. the teacher's roles
3. the importance of relationships with families and how to provide culturally sensitive care
4. a responsive planning process
5. conducting sensitive transitions and routines
6. creating responsive and relationship-based environments
7. providing responsive experiences and opportunities for children
8. a relationship-based approach to guidance

An Emphasis on Culture and Children with Disabilities

To fully respect the impact of culture on early development, information on this and on the importance of inclusion of children with disabilities in early education and development programs is included throughout the book. These topics are presented as they relate to the major content of each chapter, such as how disabilities may affect learning or how people from different cultures approach learning. Many of the scenarios in italic type are about children who develop atypically as well as on a more typical trajectory.

New to This Edition

1. **Video links have been embedded in this new edition's Pearson eText**. Several videos relevant to the chapter content have been embedded in each chapter of this edition's Pearson eText. Look for the "Play" icon button and click to observe infants, toddlers, teachers, and family members to learn about development, program planning, and professionalism.
2. Readers who care about infants and toddlers will experience close-up experiences with cultural and family beliefs and goals concerning how infants and toddlers are cared for and educated. This edition includes *Culture Close Up* features that identify a real-life cultural opportunity that infant and toddler professionals encountered in their work with coworkers, families, and communities. The Culture Close Up includes creative thinking that contributes to relationship building and culturally sensitive practice and usually includes an inquiry that leads to group problem solving.
3. **Learning Outcomes** are added to each chapter to identify the primary objectives for learning in the chapter. These assist the reader in reflecting, self-assessing, and assimilating the knowledge base in each chapter. In the Pearson eText, they aid in navigation by linking the Learning Outcome to the relevant section heading in the text.
4. **More information on ethical dilemmas** has been added to encourage readers to identify ethical situations and develop ethical solutions to

challenges that infant-toddler professionals face each day in their work with children, families, and communities.

5. *All new* **color photos and *Observation Invitations*** in the Pearson eText clearly represent the content of each chapter, reinforce important concepts, contribute to the readers' understanding of the importance of relationships, and add to an enriched learning experience of the reader.

6. **The research information has been updated and new concepts are discussed.** Each year, exciting, innovative research on brain development, infants, toddlers, families, and culture contributes to our understanding of young children's growth, development, and learning as well as family dynamics and teacher practices.

7. **The new color design** in the Pearson eText makes it easier for readers to access the important information and to comprehend the material.

SPECIAL PEDAGOGICAL FEATURES

The special features of this text include the following:

Observation Invitations

Observation Invitations in the development chapters (Chapters 6 through 10) invite readers to enter the world of a child to reflect on what a photo or written observation reveals about the child's development and goals.

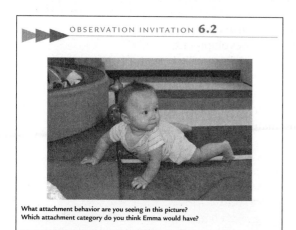

OBSERVATION INVITATION **6.2**

What attachment behavior are you seeing in this picture?
Which attachment category do you think Emma would have?

Strategies to Support

At the end of each development chapter, a **Strategies to Support** box summarizes specific strategies for teachers and other adults that facilitate the child's development in that domain.

STRATEGIES TO SUPPORT EMOTIONAL DEVELOPMENT AND LEARNING

1. Comfort young babies who are stressed or unhappy by swaddling, holding them close to you, rocking them, and speaking or singing quietly.
2. Help young babies learn to regulate themselves by letting them suck on their hands, feeding them on demand, and helping them fall asleep and awaken calmly.
3. Be available for interaction when babies are awake and alert; talk quietly and gaze into their eyes when they are interested; allow them to turn away and collect themselves when they need a break.
4. Mirror a baby's facial expressions, adding words that describe the feeling with a congruent tone of voice.

5. Express your own feelings honestly and clearly.
6. Allow infants and toddlers to express the full range of emotions. There are no "bad" feelings. Babies need to learn socially acceptable ways to express their feelings.
7. Use your facial expressions and language to let infants and toddlers know whether or not a situation is safe from a small distance.
8. Be responsive and reassuring when infants and toddlers are fearful about exploring. Let them know you are watching them and will keep them safe.
9. Encourage infants and toddlers to explore and play, while you remain available when they return to you for moments of contact.

- **Observation and planning forms** for individuals and groups in Chapter 13 and Appendix D.
- Each development chapter presents a comprehensive chart, **Developmental Trends and Responsive Interactions,** which describes the capacities of the child as well as developmental milestones. It includes examples of development to help students connect theory with practice; lists teacher or parent interaction strategies to support development and learning; and provides a list of toys, materials, equipment, and other environmental supports that enhance development. These tables also appear in Spanish in Appendix C.

Culture Close Up

Culture Close Up a feature that identifies a real-life opportunity that infant and toddler professionals encountered in their work with coworkers, families, and communities.

Other Learning Features

- ***Reflections and Resources for the Reader*** at the end of each chapter provide follow-up questions and reinforcing material to correspond with the chapter's content. Relevant Web links are provided as well.
- ***Vignettes*** are woven throughout the chapters to illustrate how theories and concepts look in real settings where infants and toddlers are cared for and educated.
- ***Glossary terms*** are defined in the margin of the page where the term is used. Glossary definitions also appear when glossary terms are clicked on in the Pearson eText.
- ***Quotes*** from a variety of early childhood education and child development authors are highlighted throughout the text to illuminate specific points of interest.
- A complete ***Summary*** at the end of each chapter highlights the major points of that chapter.

CULTURE CLOSE UP

A Japanese family moved to Minneapolis for the father to spend a semester as a visiting professor at the university. After several weeks in an apartment, alone all day with her 2- and 4-year-old daughters, the mother enrolled them in a neighborhood child care program. Although the girls spoke no English, they enjoyed playing when they visited with their mother. After a few visits, the mother decided to leave them. They had never been away from her before. Together, they ran to the big glass door of the church, sobbing and looking down the sidewalk where their mother had disappeared. The 4-year-old kept repeating some words in Japanese. The director looked them up in a phonetic dictionary: "My mother is dead! My mother is dead!"

Organization

Chapters 1 through 3 set the stage by focusing on early experiences, family relationships, and theoretical perspectives. Chapter 1 describes the current status of the infant and toddler field. Powerful research informs us that the early years matter. Science is establishing that the child's attitudes, knowledge, and skills developed during the first 3 years provide a foundation for a lifetime of learning and loving. Families, as the primary influence on their child's development, build this foundation, and the factors that influence how families function are explored in Chapter 2. Infant and toddler professionals also have a strong influence on whether babies thrive, and it is important that professionals build their practice on knowledge of theoretical perspectives. In Chapter 3, the theories that guide teachers to become purposeful about their work, understand how infants and toddlers develop, know what they need, and appreciate how they learn are described. The observation and documentation strategies highlighted in Chapter 4, provide methods for teachers to learn about children—how they develop and think and what they need to thrive.

The second section of this book describes the remarkable development of children in the prenatal period (Chapter 5), and in the emotional (Chapter 6), social (Chapter 7), cognitive (Chapter 8), language (Chapter 9), and physical or motor (Chapter 10) domains. Each domain of development is explored on several levels that relate to the relationship-based model presented in the first chapter. We describe the capacities that each child brings to that domain and then explore individual attributes such as gender or temperament. Early disabling conditions and intervention strategies are included in "Children with Special Needs." The development of the child within his or her family, culture, and an infant and toddler program is emphasized, along with strategies for supporting that aspect of development. At the end of these chapters, we describe components of programs that support and enhance the development of infants, toddlers, and their families.

The third section of the book (Chapters 11 through 16) takes you, the infant and toddler professional, into the world of responsive program planning that happens day to day, the relationship way. Equipped with the knowledge of the importance of the early years, theoretical perspectives, and the amazing development of infants and toddlers, you will learn how to plan a program that meets their needs and supports them as they learn. This process includes *respecting* the child's experience, *reflecting* on his or her intentions and your own reactions, and *relating* to the child through your response.

Nurturing and responsiveness are key elements of being an infant and toddler professional, and you will learn ways to promote the emotional development of young children within a program setting. With an emphasis on responsive interactions and relationships, you will discover how to set up an enriched environment full of learning opportunities (Chapter 13). The guidance strategies recommended (Chapter 14) respect the child's culture and individuality, require reflection on the part of the professional, and build infants' and toddlers' capacity to be in constructive relationships with others. Because programs include children with disabilities as well as children with diverse interests, needs, and abilities, Chapter 15 discusses how to individualize programs for children with special needs and how to work with the early intervention system.

The quest for quality experiences for very young children leads us to focus on what it means to be a professional who works with infants, toddlers, and their families. Chapter 16 describes the professional's journey toward developing an identity as an infant and toddler professional; becoming reflective; creating and nurturing relationships for professional development; and advocating for teachers, children, families, programs, and the community to move the profession forward.

We hope this book inspires you to promote the well-being, competence, and quality of life for infants and toddlers and their families. We also hope that it is the beginning of a new or renewed journey to develop a community of caring that recognizes the importance of the infant and toddler years. Infants and toddlers are depending on it.

Instructor Resources

The following ancillaries can be downloaded from www.pearsonhighered.com by instructors who adopt this text. Click on "Educators" and then "Download Instructor Resources."

Instructor's Resource Manual. An extensive *Online Instructor's Resource Manual* includes discussion points, a multitude of active learning strategies, and an annotated bibliography of resources such as videos, DVDs, manuals, articles, and books to accompany each chapter of the text.

Online Test Bank. The Test Bank contains multiple-choice and essay items for every chapter.

Online PowerPoint Slides. These slides cover the major points and strategies of each chapter.

Online Test Generator Software. Known as TestGen, this test-generator software permits instructors to create and customize exams.

Course Management. The assessment items in the Test Bank are available in a variety of learning management system formats.

Acknowledgments

No book is written without affecting the lives of the friends and families of the authors. We especially want to thank our husbands, children, and sons-in-law for their never-ending support and encouragement. They, and our grandchildren, provide a secure and joyous base from which to explore this field. We thank Deanna, Donna's daughter, for an excellent first edit of the first edition of this book.

We have shared numerous professional and personal experiences, and we have been influenced by many of the same individuals and programs. Together, we gratefully acknowledge and thank Dr. Ron Lally and Dr. Peter Mangione for their mentorship, friendship, and untiring leadership in their efforts to improve the quality of early care and development programs for young children. Because they embrace their Fellows as family, we thank everyone at ZERO TO THREE who has led to the promotion of relationship-based practice. These people have deepened our understanding of the infant family field and have been a constant source of support for us.

To our friend Jo Koehn, we offer deep respect, affection, and gratitude. Her wisdom and fortitude have provided us with endless opportunities to deepen and refine our understanding of infant and toddler care through the Colorado Department of Education's statewide infant and toddler training, Expanding Quality for Infants and Toddlers. We offer our heartfelt appreciation to the faculty, community teachers, and participants across the state who are endlessly supporting quality care.

Special thanks to Julie Peters, our editor at Pearson, who strives for quality in all she does. She is insightful, knowledgeable, and wise. We definitely could not have completed this book without her positive regard and constant encouragement. We sincerely and gratefully thank Carrie Mollete for her production work. They are key to the ongoing and finished project. Their humor, excellence, and guidance are indispensable.

We would also like to thank Carla Mestas, who took most of the excellent new photos in the book that represent relationship-based care and education; Janelle, a wonderful family child care provider; and all of the parents who provided the photographs of loving and skilled teachers and beautiful children throughout this text.

We would like to say a special thank you to Dr. Alice Honig, professor emeritus at Syracuse University, and a mentor and friend of Donna's since graduate school, for her continuous warm support and her infinite wisdom about infants and toddlers. For their influence on our visions of quality for infants, toddlers, and families, we also offer our gratitude and affection to Rose Bromwich, Jeree Pawl, Judith Pekarsky, Lillian Sugarman, Judie Jerrald, and Tammy Mann.

Finally, we would like to acknowledge the following third edition reviewers for their insight and comments: Sheila Brookes, University of Southern Mississippi; Janice L. Hendrix, University of Cincinnati; Marla Michelsen, Owens Community College; and Claire Vallotton, Michigan State University. They greatly improve the content because of their experience with adult learners and their knowledge of infants, toddlers, and families.

Brief Contents

Contents

11 Responsive Programs: Quality, Health, Safety, and Nutrition 250

12 Creating a Relationship-Based Curriculum 276

Routines, Environments, and Opportunities: Day to Day the Relationship Way   312

Respect, Reflect, and Relate: The 3 R Approach to Guidance   348

Including Infants and Toddlers with Disabilities in Child Development and Education Programs   382

The Infant-Toddler Professional: Identity, Relationships, and Resources   402

INFANT AND TODDLER DEVELOPMENT
AND RESPONSIVE PROGRAM PLANNING

1

A Relationship-Based Model and the Importance of the Infant and Toddler Years

LEARNING OUTCOMES

After reading this chapter, you will be able to:

- Promote the well-being, competence, good developmental outcomes, and quality of life of infants and toddlers and their families
- Define a relationship-based model
- Describe the importance of the infancy period (prenatal to 3 years of age)
- Discuss the core concepts of prenatal, infant, and toddler development
- Explain the changes in demographics that affect infants and toddlers and their families
- List and describe programs that serve infants, toddlers, and families

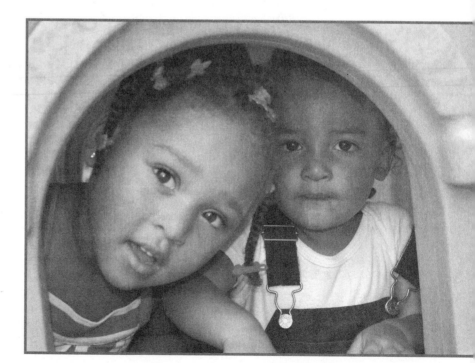

Infants and toddlers are remarkable, delightful, and engaging human beings who require sensitive and responsive families and teachers in order to develop into capable and caring adults. Connections with others—family, care teachers, and peers—support infants and toddlers as they figure out who they are, sustain meaningful relationships, and gain knowledge about their world. As you walk through the incredible developmental journey taken by infants and toddlers, you will appreciate how children influence their families and teachers—and in turn how families, cultural perspectives, and the larger world influence whom these infants and toddlers become.

In this book, our goal is that you gain an appreciation for how vitally important the prenatal period and the first 3 years of life are. Our hope is that you will become knowledgeable about and gain a passion for promoting the (1) well-being, (2) competence, (3) good developmental outcomes, and (4) quality of life of infants and toddlers and their families. To better understand these goals for infants and toddlers, we will define each one.

Well-being refers to "how a child feels and thinks about him- or herself and the joy and satisfaction that the child experiences in regard to his or her relationships and accomplishments" (Erickson & Kurz-Riemer, 1999, p. 26). *Competence* refers to how effectively the child adjusts to day-to-day changes, how adaptable and flexible a child is. This is the outward manifestation of "*good developmental outcomes*" (p. 26, italics added). *Developmental outcomes* include the increasing abilities in learning, language, motor, emotional, and social skills. *Quality of life* refers to the child's feelings about the value, worth, living conditions, and relationships that he or she experiences. We hope that your enthusiasm and excitement about these four goals will grow and guide you in your interactions with, beliefs about, and support for infants and toddlers.

The theoretical basis for this book is a relationship-based model that promotes infants' and toddlers' optimal *mental health* in the context of the children's family, culture, community, and world. When toddlers reach age 3, they will be mentally healthy if they (1) feel competent and confident, (2) enjoy intimate and caring relationships, (3) feel safe, (4) have basic trust in others, (5) regulate and express emotions in healthy ways, (6) communicate and are understood, (7) feel valued for their unique personalities, (8) have the energy and curiosity to learn, and (9) enjoy excellent health and nutrition. The term **mental health** describes infants' and toddlers' social and emotional well-being.

mental health
The emotional and social well-being of a person.

A Relationship-Based Model

This book focuses on a relationship-based model for understanding infant and toddler development and responsive program planning.

A **relationship-based model** (see Figure 1.1) recognizes that constructive, caring relationships are fundamental to the human experience. As adults we know that intimate relationships and worthwhile friendships are a source of joy. Relationship-building skills such as initiating interactions, maintaining congenial associations with others, and social problem solving are often the key to success at home, as well as in the workplace. Positive relationships are vital for infants and toddlers as well. They need loving adults to protect them, nurture them, and help them learn. When adults respond to children respectfully, they promote the child's strengths. In fact, respectful responses from others are *essential* to infants' and toddlers' sense of security, self-worth, self-confidence, and motivation to learn. Infants' and toddlers' experience of healthy relationships is the foundation for their ability to love and learn.

Infants and toddlers exist within a network of relationships: mother–child, father–child, mother–father, mother–grandmother, father–neighbor, mother–employer, and

relationship-based model
A model whereby constructive, caring relationships are fundamental to infant and toddler development.

FIGURE 1.1   **Relationship-based model for infant and toddler development and program planning**

many more that are influenced by and in turn influence infants' well-being (see Figure 1.1). A relationship-based model predicts that the quality of the relationship in one dyad (two people who interact with each other) affects the quality of relationships in other dyads (Hinde & Stevenson-Hinde, 1987). For example, a parent's positive relationship with the infant can affect the expectations that the infant has for a relationship with an infant teacher. Both of these relationships can then have an impact on the nature of the child's peer interactions. The array and quality of children's relationships exist within and throughout a web of interconnected circles, with each relationship influencing the other.

Both the *ecology* (environment), including culture, and the child's individual characteristics influence the features of the relationships that a child experiences. We discuss the theories supporting this in detail in Chapter 3; however, here we briefly discuss how first the ecology and then a child's individual attributes and capacities influence the child's relationships with parents, families, and teachers.

How the Ecology Affects Relationships

When infants and toddlers are physically, emotionally, and cognitively healthy and experiencing positive relationships, it is because of a support system that involves family, culture, the neighborhood, community, and a society that knows and cares deeply about the importance of the first 3 years of life. According to **bioecological systems theory** (Bronfenbrenner, 1979, 1986, 2004), the ecology—the personal and physical environment—influences the nature of the relationships that the child experiences. These relationships are most influenced by the immediate settings: namely, family, community, and the early care and education program that the child is experiencing.

> **bioecological systems theory**
> How the settings in which a developing child lives interact with the child's biological characteristics to influence development.

Families are also influenced by their culture—the values and beliefs about what is important in life, including traditions, celebrations, languages, and styles of interacting with others (Gonzalez-Mena, 2008). According to Haviland, culture includes "the abstract values, beliefs, and perceptions of the world that lie behind people's behavior, and which are reflected in their behavior" (Barrera, Corso, & Macpherson, 2003). For example, a family's culture may value a child who is quiet, whereas other parents might encourage their child to be assertive and vocal. These values and beliefs guide the decisions about how to respond to the child's behavior. The importance of cultural perspectives, as a key part of the ecological model, is highlighted in this book.

> **culture**
> The beliefs, way of life, abilities, and arts of a particular group of people that are held and/or passed along to future generations.

National and international laws and policies are a part of the ecology that influences the quality of a child's relationships with parents, family, and teachers. For example, how a nation's citizens view families in poverty, welfare reform, or the importance of quality child care intensely affects life's possibilities for infants and toddlers.

In addition to being influenced by the environment, infants and toddlers influence the relationships they have with their parents and families. Infants and toddlers are born with unique characteristics, attributes, and capacities that have an effect on how we, as adults, interact and relate to them.

How Children's Attributes and Capacities Affect Relationships

Transactional theory highlights how the feelings and reactions of families and teachers are affected by their children's *attributes*—age, biological makeup, gender, temperament, appearance, and actions (Sameroff & Feise, 2000) (see Figure 1.1). These attributes influence how the family or teacher treats the infant or toddler. Not all babies within the same family or program are treated the same. For example, a toddler who reminds the family of a favorite uncle has a different impact than a child who resembles a relative who isn't liked by the family.

> **transactional theory**
> Emphasizes the ongoing reciprocal nature of the effects of the child's and the environments characteristics and behavior on each other.

How much a child's characteristics influence a family, however, may depend on the ecology of the particular family and how the ecology affects the relationships within the family. A family under stress that has outside support from relatives, friends, or a community program may do well with a fussy baby. A family that is isolated from relatives or friends may have a difficult time with the same type of baby, who cries often and requires sensitive adult responses. When families perceive that they have social support from a shared community, the family and the children in that family are more likely to thrive (Child Welfare Information Gateway, 2008; Runyan et al., 1996).

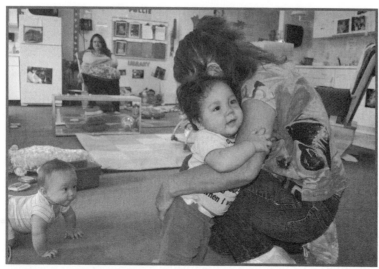

Beginning in infancy, create the capacity to love and nurture.

Infants and toddlers come into this world with many capacities. They have the ability to be social, express emotions, learn, communicate, and move. These capacities blossom throughout the infant and toddler years within loving relationships with family members and other caring adults and peers.

In a relationship-based model of infant and toddler development, there is a constant interplay between children's attributes and capacities and the ecology, and all of these—together and separately—influence the quality of children's relationships. The quality of the relationships then affects the experiences and development of the children—their development in the emotional, social, cognitive, language, and motor **domains** (see Figure 1.1).

domains

The specific areas of development that include emotional, social, cognitive, language, and motor development.

In the **video**, Infant Feeding, observe how the care teacher is sensitive and responsive to the infant's needs and communication cues. What are the infant's communication cues? How does the care teacher understand what the infant is communicating?

self-regulation

The process of adapting reactions to sensory experiences, feelings, the environment, and people.

responsiveness

Adult sensitivity and reaction to a child's facial expression, body postures, gestures, and words.

Research on the Importance of Relationships for Children, Families, and Infant-Toddler Professionals

The research on the importance of infants' and toddlers' positive, caring relationships with family members, teachers in centers and child care homes, and early interventionists (who work with children with special needs) is clear. Research conducted in the United States found that young infants and toddlers who feel safe and secure with their mother, father, and other family members feel less stressed (Gunnar & Cheatham, 2003) and can express and control emotions in healthy ways (**self-regulation**) (Feldman, Greenbaum, & Yirmiya, 1999; Gunnar & Quevedo, 2007) compared to young children who experience fearful or anxious relationships. The quality of the parent-child relationship also influences the quality of children's peer relationships. For example, children with secure attachments to their fathers at age 2 haSd more reciprocal and diverse friendships in preschool (Verissimo et al., 2011).

How do parents help young children feel secure? Children feel secure when parents are responsive and affectionate (de Wolff & van IJzendoorn, 1997; Harel & Scher, 2003), and also when adults support the children's self-directed activities and autonomy (NICHD Early Child Care Research Network, 2004). Parents' sensitivity to their children's needs and distress is important. Parents' sensitivity to infant distress at 6 months relates to infants feeling secure (McElwain & Booth-LaForce, 2006). Ziv, Aviezer, Gini, Sagi, and Koren-Karie (2000), researchers in Israel, reported that among 687 Israeli mother-infant dyads, higher mother *emotional availability* scores predicted young children's feelings of security. Also, support for families to help them become responsive influences children's sense of security. When mothers of adopted 6-month-old children were given video feedback to become more sensitively responsive, their children were more likely to be secure at 12 months than were children of mothers who did not receive the intervention (Jeffer, Bakermans-Kranenburg, & van IJzendoorn, 2005).

Responsiveness is a key term that is used frequently in this book. Babies communicate through their facial expressions, body postures, gestures, and words. **Responsiveness** refers to both how well the adult understands what the infant or toddler is trying to communicate (the child's cues) and how effectively (promptly, contigently, and appropriately) the adult acts in response to the child (Eshel, Daelman, de Mello, Cabral, & Martines, 2006). Responsiveness occurs moment to moment in an interaction with the child and over time as the adult plans future interactions, an environment, and experiences that meet the child's needs and interests. Adult responsiveness influences how infants and toddlers expect others to treat them. For example, in one study mothers' warm and contingent (based on the child's cues) responsiveness influenced infants' expectations for positive social interactions and a sense of self-efficacy (a belief in their ability to interact effectively; Mcquaid, Bibok, & Carpendale, 2009). In another study the authors found that toddlers' social-emotional competence was related to the contingent responsiveness of the mother (Brophy-Herb, et al., 2011).

Infants' and toddlers' secure relationships with care teachers in child care and education programs also are vital for the children's development. When children feel secure within caring relationships with teachers, they are more socially competent (Howes, Phillips, & Whitebook, 1992), have better language development, can regulate their emotions, and participate more in problem-solving activities (Howes & Smith, 1995). What do care teachers do that helps infants and toddlers feel secure?

Classic research found that young children feel secure to love and learn when care teachers are highly involved with the children—hold them, hug them for comfort, and engage them in conversations (Howes & Hamilton, 1992). The more sensitive (warm, attentive, and engaged) the teacher is with children as compared to harsh (critical, threatening, and punitive) or detached (low levels of interaction), the more secure the child feels with the teacher (Howes & Hamilton, 1992).

Recent research shows that not only the quality of the teacher-child interactions is important, but also the quantity: "In center day care, children not only need sensitive caregivers but, more importantly, they need sensitive caregivers who find the time to display their sensitivity frequently enough to create a sense of confidence in their availability as a safe haven and a secure base" (De Schipper, Tavecchio, Van IJzendoorn, 2008, p. 648). It is critical, then, to consider how the young child is experiencing the sensitivity and responsiveness of the teacher.

Teachers can also promote security by providing many opportunities for the infants and toddlers to make choices in an interesting environment (NICHD Early Child Care Research Network, 2004).

Continuity of care in child care and education programs is important for infants' and toddlers' feelings of security. Helen Raikes (1993) observed infants and toddlers in child care centers and found that 91% of the children who stayed with a teacher more than 1 year felt secure, whereas only about 50% of those children who were with a teacher for a shorter period of time felt secure. A more recent study of more than 1,000 toddlers found that when at least one care teacher "moves up" with the group or all care teachers stay with the group as they age, the following occurs:

- Children and teachers develop close trusting affectionate relationships.
- At child care, children are more positive with peers.
- At home, children are less negative and less aggressive.
- Children have increased cognitive and language skills. (NICHD, 2001b)

Continuity of care
providing children in programs with one or more care teachers who stay with the children throughout their first three years

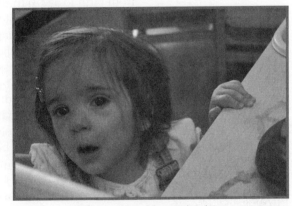
Children can live in a state of fear and sadness.

When care teachers do not move with the children and the children experience the loss, the results are not as positive. The more caregiver losses infants and toddlers have experienced by the time they are preschoolers, the more likely they are to be socially withdrawn and aggressive with peers (Howes & Hamilton, 1993). Infants and toddlers learn to trust adults and learn *how* to be in quality relationships with continuous care.

In this book, stories of children, families, and communities are shared to bring to life the attributes and capacities, the relationships, and the ecology of infants and toddlers in the first 3 years of life. Our intention is to share these stories; the results of research; information on development and responsive care; ideas about relationship-based programs; and how to help infants love, laugh, and learn in such a way that you, too, will become an advocate for the importance of the early years.

The Importance of the Infancy Period (Prenatal to 3 Years of Age)

While you have been reading this, a newborn baby has opened her eyes for the first time and sensed the closeness of her mother gazing lovingly into her eyes, and a toddler, seeking nurturing, has reached up for his father's hand. In this moment, a mobile infant is learning to walk, falling down every 5 seconds but quickly getting up to master the task. Who are we talking about when we use terms like *infants, mobile infants,* and *toddlers*?

> The word infant *derives from Latin words meaning "not yet speaking." It emphasizes what the child cannot do and reflects the baby's total dependence on adults. The word* toddler, *however, demonstrates our change in perspective, for it focuses on the child's increasing mobility and burgeoning independence. (Kutner)*

infants
Birth to approximately 18 months of age.

toddlers
18 months to 36 months of age.

prenatal
The time period (usually 9 months) prior to birth or during pregnancy.

infant and toddler professional
The broad range of specialists who teach in or administer child development and education programs.

care teacher
A professional who has received specialized training to work with young children.

The general term *infants and toddlers* refers to children from birth to 36 months of age. An **infant** is a baby from birth to approximately 18 months of age. At 8 months, the baby is crawling and some babies are even beginning to walk; it is then that infants are often referred to as mobile infants. From age 18 to 36 months, infants become **toddlers**, walking and even running in a straight-legged manner that causes them to toddle—sometimes wobble, weave, and bobble—as their physical and mental abilities develop at lightning speed. The infancy period refers to development from birth to age 3. In this textbook, the terms *babies, infants and toddlers,* and *infancy* are used to refer to children from birth to age 3. **Prenatal** development occurs prior to birth. From the prenatal period to age 3, babies grow from helpless dependency to children with a rich collection of relationships, skills, attitudes, and behaviors.

Who are the professionals who work with infants, toddlers, and their families? We use the term **infant and toddler professional** to refer to the broad range of specialists who teach or administer child development and education programs, which include *center child care* and *family (home) child care* programs. *Infant and toddler professionals* also refers to professionals who support families in the care and education of their children through home visits, early intervention, and family support programs. (These types of programs are defined and discussed later in the chapter and book.) The term **care teacher** refers to a professional who has received specialized training to work with young children individually and/or in groups and/or is in a position of responsibility with infants and toddlers in a classroom or home setting. We have chosen to use the word care *teacher* rather than the more commonly used term *caregiver* because of the mistaken notion that caregivers give care but do not teach. The reality is that with infants and toddlers, *teaching* is (1) taking care of infants' and toddlers' physical needs, (2) interacting with them in ways that meet their emotional and social needs and facilitate their development, (3) setting up an environment that promotes learning in all domains, and (4) working closely with the families of the children to build trusting relationships with them. In this book when the term **caregiver** is used, it is in the context of any adult who takes care of and cares about young children. Caregivers include parents, teachers, grandparents and others.

caregiver
Any adult who takes care of and cares about young children; includes parents, teachers, grandparents and others.

Recent Understanding of the Importance of the Infant and Toddler Years

It is easier to build a child than to rebuild an adult. (Author unknown)

No other stage of human development requires as much learning and results in as many changes as the first 3 years of life. Some infants and toddlers are healthy, have enough to eat, feel safe and loved, are talked to in responsive ways, and feel like valued members of their families and cultures. Sadly, other infants and toddlers are hungry, fearful, surrounded by violence, or abused and neglected. Do these early experiences make a difference? Yes, without a doubt. What happens during this time period may largely determine the well-being of not only children and their families but also their communities and the world in which they live. Educators and parents now know, definitely, that what happens during the first 3 years of a child's life has a long-lasting effect on who that person is and will become. It is worth repeating that infants' and toddlers' early experiences will influence their ability to learn, feelings of self-worth, sense of competence, and capacity to love and care for others. The infancy years do matter—and you can make a difference in promoting the health, wellness, quality of life, and happiness of children and families in these important years of development. The work of parenting, caring for, and educating young children from birth to age 3, during this time of rapid growth and development, is among the most important work that exists.

Early childhood is both the most critical and the most vulnerable time in any child's development. (Brazelton & Greenspan)

Parents and professionals are learning more each day about how the kind of environment in which an infant or toddler lives has a strong and lasting influence on that baby's development. Sammy, age 2, opens his eyes after a nap and cries out for his mother. As she comes to the side of the crib, she says soothingly, "Hello, you're awake? How are you feeling?" He wiggles around and then turns over and gradually stands up to see her better. His face relaxes and he smiles as she asks, "Are you ready to get out of your crib?" He answers by reaching up with his hands, getting ready for her to reach in the crib and pick him up. In this short but important interaction, Sammy is learning that he is important enough to be responded to quickly, that he can make things happen in this world, and that adults can be trusted to meet his needs most of the time. He is learning about who he is, how to be a generous partner in a relationship, and important concepts about the world in which he was born. These are the most important things for him to be learning at this time in his life, and these lessons will serve him well in years to come. If Sammy consistently receives this kind of responsive care, he will continue to thrive.

The latest scientific discoveries concerning prenatal, infant, and toddler development have significantly influenced the renewed interest concerning how babies think and what they need not only to survive, but also to thrive. The landmark publication *From Neurons to Neighborhoods: The Science of Early Childhood Development* (Shonkoff & Phillips, 2000) highlights important research and practice that illustrates the significance of these early life experiences. This book focuses on the central role of positive and loving relationships in a child's life and the powerful capabilities of young children. On the other hand, the authors express concern about the features of modern life that contribute to the stress of families: The potential damage to developmental outcomes from **risk factors** such as poor quality of child care, poverty, stresses, trauma, and violence is emphasized. The authors, following rigorous scientific scrutiny of the research and writings of infant and toddler specialists, strongly and with certainty recommend that families, teachers, communities, advocates, policy makers, businesses, government officials, and scientists come together to ensure an environment that facilitates "a rewarding childhood and a promising future for all children" (p. 15). As we move into the 21st century, research results, particularly the astounding new knowledge of brain development, have changed the way parents and professionals view the importance of the early years.

risk factors

Personal, environmental, and relationship features that are threats or a danger to the optimal development of a child.

Research on Brain Development

Brain development is covered in detail in Chapter 5 of this book. Here we highlight how research on brain development has influenced parents' and professionals' beliefs about the importance of the early years.

A ray of sunlight dances across 6-month-old Tamara's line of vision. Her dad talks warmly to her about the bright light, her eyes, and what she is seeing. We can't see inside of Tamara's head as new signals race along neural pathways in her brain. If we look closely, though, we can see it in her eyes, as they show curiosity, wonder, and joy.

In another home, the stresses of life have caused Jo's parents to reach the end of their coping skills. As Jo, barely 1 year old, reaches for a forbidden cookie, her hands are slapped hard, as they are frequently. We can't see how hormones of fear surge in her brain, and how development is hindered by the constant fear and vigilance that Jo must maintain to protect herself, but if we look closely, we can see it in her eyes, as they show sadness, panic, anger, and pain.

The discoveries about the brain development of Tamara, Jo, and other infants and toddlers have been remarkable. For Tamara everyday experiences evoke a healthy bath of hormones in her brain, helping build strong circuitry and creating a platform for learning. For Jo a bath of harmful, stress-induced hormones bathe her brain, which is being built to be vigilant to danger rather than other information around her. As a mom, dad, or teacher talks to a baby, a song is sung, or the baby is positioned

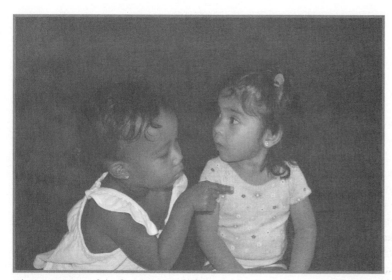

The importance of the first 3 years of life cannot be disputed.

on the parent's body where he can see the playing dog, the baby reacts to these events, taking in information, processing it, and storing it. The synapses and the pathways formed actively create a web of learning in the brain. This is why early responsive experiences are so crucial: Those synapses that have been activated many times by virtue of repeated early experience tend to become permanent to ensure optimal emotional, social, language, and thinking development.

Let's examine how the study of sensitive periods of development and windows of opportunity has made a remarkable difference in how we view the importance of the early years.

Sensitive Periods and Windows of Opportunity

There is always one moment in childhood when the door opens and lets the future in. (Graham Greene)

There are windows of opportunity for learning that nature seems to fling open. These **windows of opportunity** are periods in the development of the brain when specific types of learning take place. Later, like windows stuck with age, they are more difficult to open and use. For example, the learning window for language is from birth to 10 years. However, circuits in the auditory section of the brain are wired by age 1, and the more words used in meaningful ways that a child hears by age 2, the larger her vocabulary will grow. Early-life windows of opportunity have been discovered for vision, hearing, math and logic, cognition, problem solving, and emotional development.

windows of opportunity
Periods in the development of the brain when specific types of learning take place.

Sensitive periods also occur early in a child's life. **Sensitive periods**, also known as *prime times* (Shore, 1997; Thomas & Johnson, 2008), are periods of development when positive or negative experiences are more likely to have serious and sustained effects.

sensitive periods
Periods of development when positive or negative experiences are more likely to have serious and sustained effects.

We must remember, however, that all is not lost if the infant, toddler, or preschooler has a less than optimal start. Many competent adults have overcome difficult and challenging starts in life. The human brain has a remarkable capacity to change, but timing is essential. Time and effort are often required to help older children or adults compensate for negative and damaging experiences in their lives. For example, a child whose world has been mostly silent during the first 2 years of life because of a hearing loss or lack of responsive language talk with an adult will likely be delayed in language development. This child will need intensive support to learn how to use language to communicate in a variety of ways. In the future, brain-imaging techniques may help unravel the mysteries of when sensitive periods occur and how intervention can remediate losses (Spelke, 2002; Stanford University Medical Center, 2007).

The brain power developed during the first 3 years is a foundation for the child to build on for learning and loving, just as a house must have a strong foundation to continue standing. Will the foundation be strong and sturdy, upon which one can build solidly, or will the foundation crumble easily under the weight of future challenging times—the emotional windstorms, sleet, hail, and drought that may occur in a person's life? The exciting research on the early years, brain development, windows of opportunity, and sensitive periods has led to a better understanding of human development and the importance of the first 3 years of life. Ten core concepts of development during the infancy period summarize the findings of all of the latest and best research.

Core Concepts of Prenatal, Infant, and Toddler Development

After analyzing what is known about the brain, early experiences, and child development, the Committee on Integrating the Science of Early Childhood Development from the National Research Council Institute of Medicine (Shonkoff & Phillips, 2000) proposed that 10 core concepts frame our current understanding of early development. These core concepts of human development are based on clinical and research findings from 1925 to 2000 and "help to organize what is known about infants and families and to suggest what is yet to be discovered or understood" (p. 13). These concepts provide a framework for thinking about what is important for infants and toddlers to develop optimally, how and when infants and toddlers best learn, and how problems in development can be prevented. Parents and professionals can use these core concepts as guides for interacting with very young children; for developing quality programs that support infant development and families; and for creating systems, laws, and public policies that value the amazing early years. These concepts are briefly introduced here and will be revisited numerous times throughout the text. We have rewritten the titles of the core concepts to capture the primary meaning expressed in the concept (see Figure 1.2), followed by information that supports the concept.

1. Both Nature and Nurture Affect Children's Development

nature
Genetic influences on the growth and development of a child.

nurture
The influences of the environment, experiences, and education on the growth and development of the child.

epigenetics
changes resulting from external influences.

It has often been asked which has more effect on a child's development: **nature** (genetic influences on growth and development) or **nurture** (environment, experiences, and educational influences on growth and development). This is no longer a controversy in the early childhood field. There is a complex interplay between these two in the development of an infant (Gottlieb, 1992). Both play their parts in shaping whom the infant will become. The impact of the child's experiences is dramatic and specific; experience actually affects whether some genes will be activated, as we know from the new science of **epigenetics** (National Scientific Council on the Developing Child, 2010).

FIGURE 1.2   **Ten core concepts of human development**

1. Both nature and nurture affect children's development.
2. Culture influences development and child-rearing beliefs and practices.
3. Self-regulation is an important indicator of development.
4. Children contribute to their own development through active exploration.
5. Human relationships, and the effects of relationships on relationships, are the building blocks of healthy development.
6. There is a broad range of individual differences.
7. The development of children is both continuous and discontinuous.
8. Infants and toddlers are both vulnerable and resilient.
9. The timing of early experiences can matter and children are open to change.
10. Early intervention can make a difference.

Source: Shonkoff and Phillips (2000), pp. 23–32.

2. Culture Influences Development and Child-Rearing Beliefs and Practices

All families and cultures have different backgrounds, experiences, and dreams for their children, as well as habits and customs that guide their thinking about raising children (Coll & Magnuson, 2000; Gonzalez-Mena, 2008). All people see the world through the lens of their own culture (Small, 1998), and these beliefs about development, child-rearing practices, and family and community customs and routines continually influence the child's and the family's thinking and feeling. A rich and valuable array of beliefs and practices define who children and families are, how they interact with and care for others, their traditions, and their ways of life.

This video helps us think about the meaning of the term culture. How would you define "culture"?

3. Self-Regulation Is an Important Indicator of Development

When infants begin to recognize when they are hungry or sleepy, focus on what is important, and tune out extraneous noise, they are regulating their reactions to the world. When toddlers begin to express sadness or happiness without falling apart, attend without often becoming distracted, wait a few minutes for lunch, touch a flower gently, and process information without becoming overwhelmed, they are demonstrating **self-regulation**. One can see how these behaviors provide the foundation for all further learning. The ability to self-regulate is the backdrop of capabilities that allow the child to concentrate on a task, focus on another person's feedback in a social situation, and control emotions in positive ways (Boyer, 2009; Bronson, 2000a, 2000b; Kopp, 2000).

4. Children Contribute to Their Own Development Through Active Exploration

Infants don't need lessons to learn to walk, or drill practice to learn to talk. Rather, babies desire to walk and talk; they practice on their own and with responsive peers and adults. They act on their environment; they put objects in containers to figure out where they go. They shake, bang, roll, and stack objects to see what will happen. They make all kinds of funny sounds to get a response from a laughing sibling. They have goals, such as getting a favorite adult to look at them or opening a door, and they experiment with different strategies to make these events happen. When all is going well, infants and toddlers are curious, energetic, and motivated to figure things out. They are communication partners who need to take a turn in a conversation, even if the communication turn is a sneeze or a soft cooing sound. When given the opportunity (and this is how they learn best), they pursue their interests with adults who keep them safe, talk to them, nurture them, and support their learning. They are *motivated* to learn about themselves, others, and the world in which they live.

5. Human Relationships, and the Effects of Relationships, Are the Building Blocks of Healthy Development

Relationships have an effect on relationships (Hinde & Stevenson-Hinde, 1987). This concept means that what infants learn in their first relationships is how to *be* in relationships. If the initial relationships are satisfying and enjoyable, then young children learn to trust, communicate, negotiate, show empathy, and cooperate with parents, peers, and others they meet—the building blocks of satisfying relationships.

When relationships are comfortable, stable, and constant rather than anxiety producing, confusing, or frightening, then babies have the emotional energy and feelings of safety to focus on exploring and investigating—important aspects of learning.

6. There Is a Broad Range of Individual Differences

There are many normal variations in motor, language, and adaptive development. However, whereas some children who aren't saying clear words by 2 years of age may eventually start to talk, others may have a hearing impairment or auditory disorder that must be diagnosed early in the infant's life so that appropriate intervention can occur. Because of the broad range of individual differences, it is sometimes difficult to distinguish between an *individual difference* in development and what might be a *developmental delay* that requires intervention. When there are questions about a child's development, adults can review developmental sequences as found in this book at the end of Chapters 6 through 10.

7. The Development of Children Is Both Continuous and Discontinuous

As an infant goes from reflexively holding a rattle, to sucking on it, to banging it, throwing it, and looking at it closely, she is demonstrating a *continuous* trajectory of development. She seems to progress forward in her acquisition of skills that help her learn about objects such as rattles. Each skill seems to build on the previous one. Discontinuity occurs at significant points of development when the child's behavior seems very different from the age before. For example, 7-month-olds (as opposed to 2-month-olds) have a cluster of skills that propel them to be social partners who "act as if they understand that their thoughts, feelings, and actions can be understood by another person" (Zeanah, Boris, & Larrieu, 1997, p. 166). Toddlers also seem worlds apart from infants because they have developed a whole constellation of skills that contribute to their emerging independence, a marked contrast to only a year before. These points of rapidly increasing skills in development are considered transition points, as they have an effect on both how the baby views the world and how the teachers and caregivers interact with the infant or toddler. For example, when a baby begins to walk, she views the world differently and the caregiver views her as more capable.

8. Infants and Toddlers Are Both Vulnerable and Resilient

Every person has sources of vulnerability and sources of resilience. Shana, a 1-year-old, has experienced much anguish in her short life: excessive hunger, hours of crying for someone to come to her crib to take her out, and bouts of severe diarrhea. She feels **vulnerable** (helpless and defenseless) and open to further trauma. What are her sources of vulnerability? They may be parent alcoholism, mental illness, criminality, or poverty that contributes to overwhelming stress in the family, or maternal/paternal abuse. These are just a few of the risk factors that increase the likelihood that something negative will happen to Shana's well-being in the future—her own drug abuse, dropping out of school, or social problems. Yet, there are sources of **resilience** (ability to thrive despite risk factors) in Shana's and in many children's lives that contribute to **positive turnarounds** (Werner, 2000). The source of resilience may be within the child—an easygoing, engaging temperament, for example, or a curious mind. Resilience may come from the child's

vulnerable

The state of being helpless, defenseless, or open to criticism or danger.

positive turnarounds

The resilience of a person to recover from challenging life experiences.

family—a loving grandfather or a mother who is at first neglectful of her child but then goes to school or gains support for new, positive ways of interacting with her baby. The source of competence for Shana could come later in life in the form of a caring circle of friends, counseling, or an adult mentor. Every person has sources of vulnerability and sources of resilience (Werner, 1993, 2000).

Let's explore the topic further. "Risks to development can come both from direct threats and from the absence of normal, expectable opportunities" (Garbarino & Ganzel, 2000, p. 77). Risk conditions (see Figure 1.3) can influence current and later outcomes for children in learning, language, social, and emotional development. The most serious detrimental effects occur when multiple **risk factors** are present in a child's life (Appleyard, Egeland, Manfred, van Dulment, & Sroufe, 2005; Garbarino & Ganzel, 2000; Sameroff, 1998. There are, however, personal and environmental characteristics that contribute to resilience in children who are experiencing risk factors.

"Resilience is the ability to thrive, mature, and increase competence in the face of adverse circumstances" (Rouse, 1998, p. 47). Resilient children have aspects within themselves or their environment that help them withstand more stress and cope better than many other children. Breslin (2005) notes that it is not helpful to label a child "at risk," but rather to focus on the strengths and competencies in each child that can help him thrive—the resiliency factors. Resiliency factors (see Figure 1.4), or features that contribute to the resiliency in the child, can be divided into three groups: personal, environmental, and relationship based.

Just as many threads woven tightly together hold up well against outside forces, the more threads of resiliency there are for a child, the more likely that they will create a durable tapestry that resonates strength and transformation despite risk and adversity. Werner (2000) demonstrated the importance of **protective factors** (factors that shield and protect the child) in forming resiliency in a study of 698 multiethnic children born into high-risk environments in 1955. In a follow-up report when those children were 45 years old, Werner found that primarily positive caregiving during

> **protective factors**
> Characteristics that shield the child from harmful effects of the environment or relationships and support the child's development.

FIGURE 1.3   **Risk conditions**

- Poor nutrition
- The child's own biological risks—such as injury, low birth weight, or health
- Living in poverty or near poverty
- Parents who are addicted to drugs or alcohol
- Negative and abusive parenting
- Parents' use of harsh physical punishment
- Lack of social support for the family
- Living in a community with a high rate of violence
- Unemployed parents
- Low-wage jobs for parents
- Lack of quality child care
- Lack of access to health and medical care
- Low parent-education levels
- Moving frequently (transience)
- Parent in jail or prison

Sources: Hodgkinson (2003); Werner (2000).

FIGURE 1.4   **Resiliency factors**

1. *Personal factors*—characteristics of the infant or toddler
   - Energetic
   - Tolerant of frustration
   - Cooperative
   - Internal locus of control
   - Strong social skills
2. *Environmental factors*—characteristics of the environment
   - Social support for the mother
   - Social support for the family
   - Caregiver with education
   - A safe community
3. *Relationship factors*—characteristics of the child's relationships with others
   - Strong caregiver–child bond
   - Nurturing adults in the child's life
   - Responsive caregiver
   - Parents and teachers who allow ample exploration time within a safe environment
   - Peers
   - Adults who give positive feedback about strengths

the first years of life is a protective factor that results in better adjusted adults. Also, the emotional support of close friends, spouses, adult mentors, and parent education classes contributed to the resiliency of the adults. Werner's work inspires us to think about the importance of personal, environmental, and relationship factors when planning policy and redesigning programs for infants, toddlers, and their families. When adults recognize risk and resiliency factors for young children and their families, then they can make important decisions in community and business practices that recognize the significance of loving, responsive adults for infants and toddlers.

9. The Timing of Early Experiences Can Matter and Children Are Open to Change

The importance of a responsive, caring environment during the first 3 years of life cannot be disputed. However, a wonderful infancy is not a magical immunization against later troubles in life. A 3-year-old may be bright, full of zip, caring, and engaging and yet face unbelievable trauma as a 4-year-old or as a teenager. A result of stress and trauma could be an erosion of the child's trust in others and her own sense of self-worth. The developing child remains vulnerable to risks at all ages. Conversely, a child is still open to protective factors after age 3. For example, a child who has an emotionally difficult first 3 years and has challenging behaviors may respond beautifully to a loving adult who sincerely believes in the child's positive characteristics and supports the child by providing a consistent caring environment that promotes the child's competence (Luthar, 2006; Masten & Motti-Stefanidi, 2008; Sapienza & Masten, 2011).

10. Early Intervention Can Make a Difference

Early intervention includes services and programs for children at risk and children with disabilities and their families. We discuss these types of programs later in the chapter. Early intervention with children and support for families can reduce the risk factors, ameliorate vulnerabilities, and increase protection factors and resiliency (Cicchetti & Curtiss, 2007).

Conclusion of the 10 Core Concepts

Clearly, the main ideas represented in these 10 core concepts are that positive, responsive, mutual, and protective adult-infant and adult-toddler relationships promote a child's development and have sustaining effects on the young child's ability to be in a relationship. Very young children need adults to help them become an important part of their community and culture, and support them in learning how to become healthy, caring, and constructive members of society.

Changes in Demographics that Affect Infants and Toddlers and Their Families

Two demographic factors (characteristics of a population) that influence the vulnerabilities, protective factors, and character of relationships for infants and toddlers—an increasingly diverse population and the increase in families and children experiencing poverty—are discussed next. Let's start with information on how the population of the United States is becoming more diverse.

A Changing Population in the United States

As illustrated in Figure 1.5, there is great diversity in the United States. Approximately 74 million children are under the age of 17 in the United States (The Annie E. Casey Foundation, 2012). Based on the 2010 census, 73.7% of children under age 17 years are White, 15.2% are Black, 5% are Asian, 2% are American Indian, Alaska Native, or Native Hawaiian and Other Pacific Islander, and 5% are two races. Of these children 23.6% are Hispanic and 76.4% are Non-Hispanic. (ChildStats, n.d.). Approximately 20% of people in the United States 5 years or older speak a language other than English at home and approximately 5% speak English less than "very well" (The Annie Casey Foundation, 2008).

FIGURE 1.5   **Diversity of total census population in the United States**

Race: For the 2010 census, Hispanic origins are not a separate race		
One Race		
White	75.1%	72.4%
Black or African American	12.3%	12.6%
Asian	3.6%	4.8%
American Indian and Alaska Native	.9%	.9%
Native Hawaiian and Other Pacific Islander	.1%	.2%
Some Other Race	5.5%	6.2%
Two or More Races	2.4%	2.9%
Hispanic or Latino Origin		
Not Hispanic or Latino	87.5%	83.7%
Hispanic or Latino	12.5%	16.3%

Source: Retrieved from census.gov. Overview of Race and Hispanic Origin: 2010. Table 1. Population by Hispanic or Latino Origin and by Race for the United States: 2000 and 2010.

An increase in the numbers of children and families from diverse cultures has an impact on public policy, health systems, and education systems. Thoughtful consideration must be given to several questions posed by this change in demographics. One question involves the type of training that infant and toddler professionals should receive to help them become culturally competent, in order to respectfully create a menu of responsive services. A second question relates to how communities, child development and education centers, and family support programs can demonstrate how they appreciate and embrace people of many cultures and races (Barrera & Corso, 2003). The United States truly is a **kaleidoscope of cultures** with different values, customs, and languages (Lynch & Hanson, 1998, p. 492) that are interconnected, and when this diversity of cultures and races is respected by professionals, children benefit. Both teachers and children must become **culturally competent** in our diverse world in order to thrive.

kaleidoscope of cultures

A society with a variety of values, customs, and languages.

culturally competent

Possessing skills that enable a person to interact effectively with people from a variety of different cultures.

Poverty

Another issue that affects the quality of children's relationships with their families and teachers is poverty, which affects everyone either through experience or through the effects that it has on a nation. Poverty in the United States is defined by income. According to the 2010 U.S. census figures, 25% of children under age 5 live in poverty, defined as an annual income of $22,113 or less for a family of four (Child Trends, 2011). Furthermore, according to Children's Defense Fund (2011), almost 10% percent of U.S. children under age 5 live in extreme poverty, with household incomes less than 50% of the poverty line. For children under age 5, approximately 15% of white children, 42.7% of African American children, and 36% of Hispanic children live in poverty. According to the U.S. Census Bureau (2010a) of children under age 5 in families with a single mother, 58.7% live in poverty and in families with a single father 32.3% live in poverty. Every 35 seconds, a baby in the United States is born into poverty (Children's Defense Fund, 2006).

Poverty is a global concern (Penn, 2005). From a basic needs approach to defining poverty, seven elements that children need have been identified: "drinking water, sanitation, nutrition, health, shelter, education, [and] information" (Delamonica & Minujin, 2007). When a child lacks one of the seven elements in his life, he is considered as living in poverty. Delamonica and Minujim report that in 46 developing countries, 1 billion children—one-half of the population—are deprived of at least one of these elements. An organization of the United Nations—the United Nations Children's Fund, or UNICEF (UNICEF, 2008) in its publication *The State of the World's Children 2008* reports that although vast improvements have been made in reducing the number of newborns who do not live to see their fifth birthday, an estimated almost 10 million children worldwide still do not as a result of the lack of one or more of the seven elements children need to survive.

 CULTURE CLOSE UP

Chris is a toddler teacher in a large child care and education center that has an ethnically diverse population. Chris knew when she was hired that the staff and parents were questioning how to celebrate holidays in the classroom. One proposal under discussion was to eliminate the celebration of *all* holidays in the program. She wasn't sure what to think about not celebrating Halloween, Christmas, and Easter because she had many materials from working at a previous center that she wanted to use, and she thought it was fun to celebrate those holidays. Parents of different ethnic and religious groups had mixed feelings as well. Some parents and teachers asked if the major holidays that the children celebrated at home could also be celebrated at school, while helping each child gain self-respect and learn about cultural differences. Each year would be different for each classroom based on who was in the classroom that year. One teacher, however, thought that even if there wasn't much cultural/ethnic diversity in a classroom, the children should learn that there are many different holidays and ways to celebrate them. What do you think the program should do?

FIGURE 1.6   **Reducing poverty**

Reducing child poverty is one of the smartest investments that Americans can make in their nation's future. Fewer children in poverty will mean:

- More children entering school ready to learn
- More successful schools and fewer school dropouts
- Better child health and less strain on hospitals and public health systems
- Less stress on the juvenile justice system
- Less child hunger and malnutrition, and other important advances

Source: Child Poverty Fact Sheet (2001).

Living in poverty, whether defined as low income or lack of basic rights, is difficult and challenging, to say the least, for families of infants and toddlers. Families that are in or near poverty face challenges that include the need for well-paying jobs, access to high-quality affordable child care and health care, adequate nutrition, decent housing, and basic services provided by the community (e.g., see the National Center for Children in Poverty Web site (www.nccp.org). These stresses for families in poverty can negatively affect children's academics, health, and social outcomes. The information in Figure 1.6 emphasizes how reducing child poverty is one of the smartest investments that nations can make in the future.

In summary, many parents and professionals, legislators, and policy makers are working hard toward building a nation and world that can do something about racial and ethnic injustice and poverty and eliminating risk factors, but we can do more. We each have a part to play to support infants, toddlers, and their families as they strive for a meaningful life. They deserve our best efforts.

Early Development and Education Programs

Early development and education programs are an important part of the lives of infants and toddlers and their families in the United States. Quality programs that support parents can reduce infants' and toddlers' exposure to risk factors and build resiliency and positive relationships (Wittmer & Petersen, 2009). Let's examine three types of early development and education programs available to families of infants and toddlers and a few of the issues related to these programs: (1) child care, (2) early intervention for children at risk, and (3) early intervention for children with disabilities.

early development and education programs
Programs for children from birth to age 5 that include, but are not limited to, child care, early intervention for children at risk, and early intervention for children with disabilities.

Child Care

Child care programs offer varying hours of care for infants and toddlers, usually during the day while parents are at work. The number of families utilizing child care is continually increasing. In 2011, more than 9 million mothers with children under age 3 were in the workforce, one-third of those with children under age 1 (Bureau of Labor Statistics, 2012). As the need for infant and toddler child care increases, so does the urgent need for public and private resources to improve the quantity and quality of child care. Parents often use an assortment of child care services that may change and blend with one another to create an array of experience for infants and toddlers. These choices include child care provided in private homes (family child care) or in child care centers. Family child care homes may be of the following types:

- Small, family child care (or a few children in the home of the care provider)
- Large, family, or group child care homes (typically no more than 7 to 12 children in the home of the care provider, who has a full-time assistant)
- In-home care (by a nonrelative in the family home)
- Kith and kin care (provided by a relative, friend, or neighbor)

Center child care includes the following:

- Nonprofit (community or agency supported)
- Local for-profit (privately owned)
- National chain for-profit (centers found across a region or nationally or internationally owned by one company)
- Church supported (sponsored by and usually located in a church)
- On-site business (child care operated by a company, on-site for its employees)

National policies concerning the importance of parental care versus child care outside the home contribute significantly to parents' choices. For example, an employed mother in the United States usually must use her accumulated sick and personal days to stay home with her newborn baby for approximately 6 to 12 weeks. In the United States, the Family and Medical Leave Act provides family members with 3 months of *unpaid* leave; however, in 128 other countries mothers are provided an average of 16 weeks *paid* and job-protected leave to be used before and/or after the birth of their baby with benefits provided by a combination of sources—government, employers, and health insurance. For example, Sweden provides full parental leave at 80% of the previous salary for 18 months. Leave in some countries may be extended if the father stays home with the child for a period of time, as in Austria, where 3 years of extended leave are provided, but only if the father takes 6 months of the leave. Several countries—for example, the United Kingdom and Sweden—also provide parents with choices as to how the leave is spread out over the first 18 months after the birth of the child ("Mother's Day," 2002). Parents in the United States, because of work leave policies, may not have as many choices about how and when they use child care services.

Parents want a setting where their children will be safe and where teachers show they care about their children (Gable & Cole, 2000). The challenge is to find infant-toddler child care that has adequately trained teachers, low child-to-teacher ratios, and small group sizes that make nurturing, relationship-based care possible. Unfortunately, parents have difficulty locating care for their children that is both affordable and excellent.

In a classic study concerning the availability of affordable and quality care of 400 child care centers located in four states, only 8% of infant classrooms were judged to be of good or excellent quality. An astonishing 40% of the centers observed were rated poor on the Infant/Toddler Environment Rating Scale (ITERS), a widely used measure of the physical and emotional characteristics of a child care environment (Helburn, 1995). The other 52% were deemed mediocre.

The Early Child Care Research Network of the National Institute of Child Health and Human Development (NICHD) (NICHD, 1996) conducted a longitudinal study of more than 1,000 children to determine the characteristics and quality of child care for infants, toddlers, and preschoolers. Researchers conducting the study reported in 2000 that among infants and toddlers who attend child care, the ones who attend higher-quality facilities develop better language, intellectual, and social skills (NICHD Early Child Care Research Network, 2000a, 2000b). Higher-quality care emphasizes the importance of an adult's gentle and considerate responsive interactions, well-organized learning toys and materials, language development, and friendly and reciprocal program-family relationships. And it has a positive effect on the development of infants and toddlers.

Because the quality of early development and education settings is so important, we devote five chapters (Chapters 11 through 16) to the development of programs for infants and toddlers that are responsive to babies' and families' needs, promote learning, and are relationship based.

A Web site (www.childcare.gov) has been created to bring together in one place all of the federal agency resources concerning child care. Parents, professionals, and providers will benefit from information on this site on health, safety, family child care, staff training, regulations, and funding. The results of research studies, news, and publications are also included at the site.

Early Intervention Programs for Children at Risk pg. 15

Early intervention programs for children at risk comprise a second type of resource for families and children. One such program is Early Head Start (EHS), which has been said to mark "a turning point in America's commitment to our youngest children and their families" ("Shalala Calls," 1995). An example of a nationally supported intervention program that provides support to families living in poverty, EHS reduces infants' and toddlers' risk factors, builds resiliency, and provides child and family development services. As Donna Shalala, former secretary of the Department of Health and Human Services, described it, "Early Head Start is about giving our youngest and most disadvantaged children a chance to grow up healthy, to learn, and to prepare for school" (U.S. Department of Health and Human Services, 2001). The federally funded program provides services to families that are expecting a child or have a child age 3 or younger and helps parents support their children's development. The program includes child development services, family involvement and parent education, health and nutrition, and prevention and early intervention. These services may take place as a home-based option, as family child care services, as center-based programs, or in some combination. The detailed and comprehensive Head Start Program Performance Standards (HSPPS), which EHS programs must meet, are often used as a basis of comparison as individual states develop their own program standards.

Each of the 1,007 EHS programs that exists across the United States emphasizes collaboration with community agencies to provide services. Specific services that EHS provides, in collaboration with its community partners, include prenatal and postpartum education, counseling services, infant and toddler child development programs, family education and engagement, health and nutrition education, medical and dental services, and referrals and assistance to families to access comprehensive prenatal and postpartum care and in some cases child care services. These services are also provided through home visits planned collaboratively with the family, infant and toddler group socialization experiences, family support groups, and a multitude of other creative initiatives.

The results of a comprehensive national study (Early Head Start Research and Evaluation Project [EHSRE], 1996–Current) of the effectiveness of EHS that included

This center-based program offers inviting environments.

approximately 3,000 infants and toddlers from 17 sites demonstrate that EHS is making a difference for children and families. Half of the 3,000 children who participated in the study were enrolled in EHS (the experimental group) and half were not (the control group). EHS children scored higher than the control group on measures of cognition (thinking) and language (vocabulary and use of complex sentences), had better attention with play objects, were more emotionally engaged with their parents, and scored lower in aggressive behavior at age 3 (Love et al., 2005). Only 50%, though, of the EHS children moved into formal programs at age 3, and those who did had higher reading-related skills at age 5. At age 5, the EHS children had significantly fewer behavior problems and scored higher on approaches to learning.

The program is making a difference for families as well as children. When the EHS children were 3 years old, the EHS families were observed to have more supportive attitudes toward learning than the control group families; were more likely to read to their children; were more emotionally supportive of their children; and scored higher on measures of the quality of home environment, parenting behavior, and knowledge of infant-toddler development. Parents who attended EHS reported that they spanked their children less and were more likely to resolve problems by using distraction, explanation, or mild responses rather than physical punishment. EHS families reported lower levels of parenting stress and family conflict and were more likely to attend school or a job training program (EHSRE, 1996–Current; Love et al., 2005). When the EHS children were 5 years old, their parents read more to their children, provided a more enriched home environment, and were at lower risk for depression (EHSRE, 1996–Current, 2006). This longitudinal study highlights the benefits of EHS as well as the importance of the EHS children attending a formal preschool, but unfortunately, because of limited federal funding, fewer than 4% (120,433) (CLASP, 2011) of the poorest infants and toddlers in the United States attend EHS. The major Web site providing additional information and resources for families and professionals on Early Head Start is the Early Childhood Knowledge and Learning Center (ECLKC) at eclkc.ohs.acf.hhs.gov/.

Early Intervention for Children with Disabilities

Early intervention services for children with disabilities and their families are the third type of early development and education program we will discuss. All infants and toddlers in the United States are entitled to a comprehensive assessment to determine whether or not they have a disability. A disability may include a developmental delay in how the child communicates and relates with others, moves, thinks, or perceives. This comprehensive assessment is provided by the school district in which the family lives. If a child qualifies for services, then the family and the professionals involved develop a plan for the child and family that builds on the family's strengths, priorities, concerns, and resources. The early intervention program may offer home visits and family support to "enhance the ability of families to work toward their own goals and deal effectively with their own concerns" about their child and family (Blasco, 2001, p. 159). Infants and toddlers may also receive special help from professionals while attending a child development and education center or family child care home.

The Individuals with Disabilities Education Act (IDEA; www.idea.ed.gov/) provides federal funds, paired with a high proportion of state funds, for special education services for children with disabilities. Part C of IDEA provides funds and directives for providing early intervention services to infants and toddlers

with disabilities. The act specifies which intervention services must be available for children but
also sets policies that ensure that parents function
as active members of the team and determine the
goals for their own children. A high value is placed
on the full inclusion of individuals with disabilities
in their communities by specifying that early intervention services must be offered in natural settings,
to the extent possible—homes, parks, child care
programs, and other places where very young children without disabilities would be spending time.
The final regulations of the current act were published in 2011 and available at www.idea.ed.gov/.

*Infants and toddlers have irreducible needs for good health,
belonging and love.*

The number of children identified with disabilities and served under Part C of IDEA has increased
from a total of 165,351 in 1994 (the first year that
state-reported data are considered reliable) to
342,821 in 2010 (NECTAC, 2012). Children's disabilities will be discussed in many
of the following chapters and will receive special attention in Chapter 15.

Infants' and Toddlers' Irreducible Needs

Meeting young children's irreducible needs is the thread that ties these three
types of early development and education programs together. **Irreducible needs**
are the needs of children that are absolutely necessary for them to survive and
thrive (see Figure 1.7). Brazelton and Greenspan (2000) emphasize that when
these seven needs are met, a child will grow, learn, and flourish. We can think of
these from the child's perspective and imagine what it must feel like to the infant
or toddler whose irreducible needs are met compared to the infant or toddler
whose irreducible needs are not met. This text contains research and descriptions
of practice that will provide strategies to meet children's irreducible needs. It is
our hope that all adults, including those who read this book, can work together
to meet infants' and toddlers' needs so that they can thrive—feel secure, be able
to relate (feel warm and close) to others, communicate, solve problems, express
feelings in culturally appropriate ways, appreciate their own and others' individuality, and have a sense of self-worth.

irreducible needs

The needs of children that are
absolutely necessary for them to
survive and thrive.

FIGURE 1.7   **Infants' and toddlers' irreducible needs**

1. Ongoing nurturing relationships
2. Physical protection, safety, and regulation
3. Experiences tailored to individual differences
4. Developmentally appropriate experiences
5. Limit setting, structure, and expectations
6. Stable communities and cultural continuity
7. Adults to protect the future

Source: Brazelton and Greenspan (2000).

Summary

The goal of this text is that you will become knowledgeable about and gain a passion for promoting the well-being, competence, and good developmental outcomes of infants and toddlers and their families.

- The prenatal period and the first 3 years of life are vitally important for children and for the adults they will become.
- A relationship-based model of infant and toddler development informs and influences the content and organization of this book.
- The ecology of the child and the individual attributes and capacities of the child influence the quality of the relationships that the child experiences.
- The quality of the child's relationships influences the experiences and the development of the child.
- Research on brain development has influenced the way parents and professionals view the significance of the first 3 years of life.

- Two demographic trends that affect both infants and toddlers and those who care for them are a changing population and the number of children experiencing poverty.
- Early development and education programs are available for infants and toddlers.
- There is a strong need for quality in early development and education programs—programs that have adequately trained teachers, responsive and affectionate adult interactions with children, and mutually beneficial relationships with families.

When we see the sparkle in an infant's eyes and the curiosity of a healthy toddler, then we know that the focus on healthy relationships and ecological factors that influence these relationships is a very worthwhile endeavor.

Key Terms

bioecological systems theory
caregiver
care teacher
continuity of care
culturally competent
culture
domains
early development and education
    programs
epigenetics

infant and toddler professional
infants
irreducible needs
kaleidoscope of cultures
mental health
nature
nurture
positive turnarounds
prenatal
protective factors

relationship-based model
resilience
responsiveness
risk factors
self-regulation
sensitive periods
toddlers
transactional theory
vulnerable
windows of opportunity

Reflections and Resources for the Reader

REFLECTIONS

1. Why do infants and toddlers need responsive, continuous caring relationships with parents, families, and teachers?
2. Create a list of why the first 3 years of life are so important for the well-being of infants and toddlers.
3. How are children's irreducible needs met in your community?
4. How has the research on brain development influenced the way parents and teachers think about the importance of the first 3 years of life?

OBSERVATION AND APPLICATION OPPORTUNITIES

1. Choose one of the 10 core concepts and discuss how that concept plays out in your life.
2. Discuss how your individual attributes influence the relationships in your life.
3. Brianna lives in a family that is experiencing poverty. What are some of the risk and resiliency factors that may influence the quality of the relationships that she is experiencing?
4. Choose one of the irreducible needs of children and discuss what would happen to a child, from the child's perspective, if this need is or is not met.

SUPPLEMENTARY ARTICLES AND BOOKS TO READ

Copple, C., & Bredekamp, S., with Gonzalez-Mena, J. (2011). *Basics of developmentally appropriate practice: An introduction for teachers of infants and toddlers.* Washington, DC: NAEYC.

Gopnik, A. (2010). *The philosophical infant: What children's minds tell us about truth, love, and the meaning of life.* New York: Picador Publishing.

Gopnik, A. (2012). Nurturing brain development from birth to 3. *Zero to Three, 32*(3), 12–17.

Koralek, D., & Gillespie, L. G. (2011). *Spotlight on infants and toddlers.* Washington, DC: NAEYC.

INTERESTING LINKS

www.childrensdefense.org/
Children's Defense Fund The mission of the CDF is to Leave No Child Behind® and to ensure every child a healthy start, a head start, a fair start, a safe start, and a moral start in life and successful passage to adulthood with the help of caring families and communities.

www.childtrends.org/
Child Trends Child Trends is an organization that seeks to impact policy decisions and programs that affect children through conducting and disseminating research, collecting and analyzing data, and sharing this information with those who set policy and provide services.

www.csrees.usda.gov/nea/family/part/childcare_part_nccic.html
The National Child Care Information Center (NCCIC), a project of the Child Care Bureau, Administration for Children and Families (ACF), U.S. Department of Health and Human Services (HHS), is a national resource that links information and people to complement, enhance, and promote the child care delivery system, working to ensure that all children and families have access to high-quality comprehensive services.

www.csrees.usda.gov/nea/family/part/childcare_part_nccic.html
The National Child Care Information Center (NCCIC), a project of the Child Care Bureau, Administration for Children and Families (ACF), U.S. Department of Health and Human Services (HHS), is a national resource that links information and people to complement, enhance, and promote the child care delivery system, working to ensure that all children and families have access to high-quality comprehensive services.

www.naccrra.org/
Child Care Aware of America is a leading voice for child care. This organization works with resource and referral agencies nationwide to ensure that families have access to high-quality child care. It also leads projects that support professionals, conduct research, and advocate child care policies.

www.nccp.org/
National Center for Children in Poverty NCCP highlights 25 initiatives in the United States that improve the lives of infants and toddlers.

www.parentsaction.org/
This Web site (I Am Your Child) has several articles on emotional development and some video clips, as well as a national public awareness and engagement campaign to make early childhood development a top priority for the country and show the importance of the first 3 years of life.

www.unicef.org/
UNICEF (United Nations Children's Fund) UNICEF was created by the United Nations after World War II. It works in 190 countries and focuses on children's rights to protection, education, health care, shelter, and good nutrition. Its work depends entirely on voluntary contributions of time and money. UNICEF published *The State of the World's Children 2012*, which can be accessed on its Web site.

www.zerotothree.org/
ZERO TO THREE ZERO TO THREE is an organization that develops publications dedicated to advancing the healthy development of infants and toddlers. This Web site offers cutting-edge research, demonstrated best practices, parenting tips, publications, and conference information.

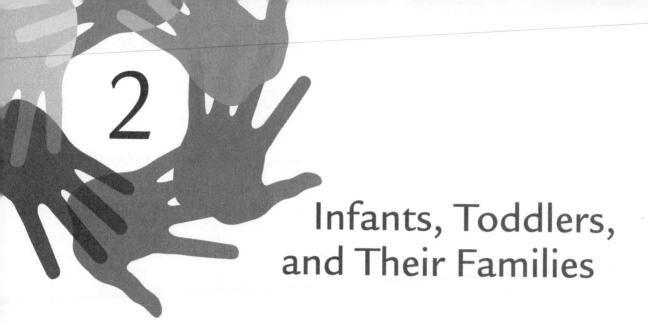

2

Infants, Toddlers, and Their Families

LEARNING OUTCOMES

After reading this chapter, you will be able to:

- Describe the effects of biology and culture on the family's experience of birth
- Describe elements that may cause variations in the experience of parenting
- Reflect on parenting styles
- Consider implications for teachers in the diversity of family structures
- Relate aspects of programs that support parents
- Articulate resources available for parents of children with special needs

Looking around the room at the parent meeting, Sammie was impressed with the diversity of the group they served at the Metro Infant-Toddler Center. Some of the differences were racial. Some were cultural. Given their neighborhood, they tended to serve people of many backgrounds and religions. Nevertheless, there was more depth to the diversity. Susan was a single physician who had adopted a baby from Cambodia. Jewel was raising her grandbabies. Mare and Ernesto were adjusting from being a young married couple to becoming parents. Brooke and Tara were a lesbian couple raising Tara's baby. Each family seemed to have a unique situation regarding parenting, unique needs for support and information, and unique—and very strongly held—beliefs about parenting!

As Sammie understands, families come in all shapes and sizes—and all kinds of families have happy, healthy, well-developing babies. All families are similar in some ways and each is unique in some ways. There are vast differences in size and composition, the roles of parents and children, the beliefs and values of their different cultures regarding infants and parents, even the rituals and processes surrounding birth itself. While we explore the basic similarities and differences, we also look beyond the immediate family to the support it receives from programs and agencies as family members utilize health care, child care, and other services. These services, in turn, are affected by policies and regulations made by state and federal legislators. Although these policies may seem far removed from any one family's daily life, they may have great effect on access to resources, services, and information, as reflected in bioecological theory (see Chapter 3).

Biological and Cultural Effects on the Family

All humans share common beginnings. The very biology of conception, birth, and early development that will be described in Chapter 5 is much the same for all human babies. However, even within this basic prototype of early development, each beginning is different. Some mothers welcome the birth of their child; some fear birth or don't want the child. Some biological fathers are present and active participants in the pregnancy and birth; some are not. Like birth, parenting is always an intensely personal experience. Each family creates its own, unique identity while responding to or incorporating its culture, current societal norms, personal history and characteristics, resources, stresses, and family structure.

Our Biology Affects Our Parenting

Biology and evolution have determined some of our parenting patterns. Because babies are born so dependent, parents around the world have developed ways to closely care for and protect their infants. Humans are born with large but not fully developed brains. The baby cannot stay in the mother's womb long enough for the brain to fully develop, as both the mother's body and the placenta can support the developing baby's needs only until the baby reaches a certain size. The baby's size is also an important factor in the birth process; the woman's pelvic structure was better suited to childbirth before humans became upright and started walking on two feet. Birth is now a long and arduous process for many mothers and babies, and in most cultures the event is planned for and helpers attend the mother, whether they are medical professionals, doulas, midwives, or family members.

Along with these biological aspects of reproduction, human mothers and fathers react to newborns similarly across the world. Upon seeing their newborn for the first time, mothers and fathers hold the baby so that they can gaze into each other's eyes. They touch the baby's fingers, the palms, the arms and legs, and then the trunk (Goodnow, Cashmore, Cotton, & Knight, 1984). Babies, in turn, are born ready to participate in human interactions (Gopnik, Meltzoff, & Kuhl, 1999; Nash & Hay, 2003; Shonkoff, 2011).

The long gestation, difficult birth process, dependency of the infant, and predictable responses of the parents to the newborn are constant factors across humanity. Together, they promote long-term, closely attentive, highly invested parenting. However, the exact nature of that parenting varies widely across cultures.

Cultural Effects on Parenting

Our parenting decisions today may be based in part on human biology, but they are also based on cultural adaptations made by our ancestors. The following definition of *culture* can help clarify this idea:

> Each member of a group lives by a set of social rules, operates within a particular spiritual belief system, and adheres to an ideology that helps the society run smoothly. Each group can be described relative to the subsistence pattern, the production of goods and their distribution, the interpersonal interactions and social rules, and the history of its society. (Small, 1998, p. 74)

So, for example, consider a spiritual belief system that "babies are godlike" versus one that believes "babies must be trained to be god-serving members of the community." These cultural beliefs would result in very different parenting practices. The first might cause parents to quickly and responsively meet every expressed need of their children; in the latter, parents might actively teach infants patience and generosity from the beginning. Economics also affects our view of children and parenting. If a society depends on its children to watch the livestock on the farm or to care for the infants while the parents work, the expectations of the children (and the ways they are treated) will be very different from an industrialized country where we generally see the "work" life beginning in adulthood.

Differing Cultural Values

individualist cultures

Emphasize the importance of the individual over the group.

collectivist cultures

Emphasize cooperation and interdependent relationships over individuality.

Values concerning the relationships among people differ by culture. **Individualist cultures**, such as many in the United States, emphasize the importance of each individual over the whole group. They tend to value independence, competition, production, and personal responsibility. **Collectivist cultures**, such as Latino, African, and Asian cultures, value cooperation, process (rather than production), and interdependent relationships. The individual is primarily responsible to the harmony and well-being of the group, setting aside individual interests (Keller, 2002; Keller et al., 2006).

These basic cultural belief systems about people are transmitted to babies through their earliest interactions with their caregivers as they help babies become members of their family and community. In one study of 214 families from nine cultural communities around the world, the researchers proposed that the very earliest interaction patterns used by parents with their infants contributed to the child learning the values of their culture. They described two major patterns of interaction. The *proximal* style involves ongoing body contact and body stimulation. The proximal style is most often used by "traditional subsistence societies, in which socialization goals that embody relatedness, obedience, and hierarchy are preferred" (Keller et al., 2009, p. 412). The *distal* style is characterized by face-to-face eye contact and object stimulation. The distal style is most often used by industrialized, educated societies that value "autonomy and separateness which have been demonstrated as precursors of independent agency" (Keller et al., 2009, p. 412).

In fact, parents from educated, industrial societies that valued independence spent a great deal of time showing infants toys that encouraged the child's sense of himself or herself as an individual. However, parents often held the infant during these interactions so there was also body contact. Parents from societies that valued interdependence carried their babies against their bodies most of the time, presumably preparing them for a sense of closeness and shared responsibilities. Well-educated urban parents from highly interdependent cultures tended to use both styles of interaction (Keller et al., 2009).

Cultural Questions in Infant and Toddler Child Care

Cultural differences create many questions for teachers and others who study child development. Care Teachers and parents may have different opinions on how they want an infant handled in feeding, sleeping, being helped, developing language, or many other issues. When this happens, it is important to consider if the differences are grounded in each person's own invisible, cultural beliefs about babies. If so, respectful negotiations may lead to everyone agreeing on how these issues will be handled in group care. For example, consider a mother who always carried her baby son because, within her culture, carrying your baby signifies your love and protection of the baby. If the baby were allowed to play and crawl on the floor in child care, how would he know he was loved? The care teacher believed equally strongly that floor time was good for physical development, and it was impossible for her to care for four babies when she was constantly carrying one. When the mother and care teacher took time to discuss their positions, trying to respect and listen to each other, they were able to resolve their differences. The care teacher assured the mother the teacher could sit by and play with the baby on a clean surface to help him feel protected. The care teacher also agreed to more holding and carrying of the baby than she would do naturally, as a way of providing the kind of care the baby had come to expect.

Even when differences may be seen as cultural, some areas cannot be negotiated. An example that often arises is a parent who insists: "I was spanked as a child and I'm fine. I want you to spank my child if she gets out of line." Spanking, or any form of corporal punishment, may go against or be part of your cultural beliefs—but it is definitely not allowed under child care licensing regulations. No discussion of cultural differences is required with this one. A simple "our licensing does not allow us to spank children" should end that discussion. Providing information as to why licensing would have such a rule would be a useful parent education effort.

Variations in the Experience of Parenting

Teachers meeting very young infants in child care are often fascinated by the quick pace of change and development they are able to observe. Sometimes it seems as though a baby is changing before your very eyes. The

Wyatt's parents hold and carry him much of the time, but they also believe he needs time to experience his own body.

In this **video**, Sue Bredekamp, who has done extensive work with NAEYC, NAEYC talks about why it is so important that teachers work closely with families.

CULTURE CLOSE UP

A New York City home visiting program served a growing community of Chinese immigrants, all from the same province. A home visitor had been working with a woman throughout her pregnancy. When the baby was born, the home visitor was looking forward to meeting him. She needed to see the mother within 2 weeks of birth—a protocol of her program and a rule of its funder. When the home visitor called to set a time, she was told that people from their province believe that a new mother and her baby should stay in bed and be cared for only by family for 100 days. How can the home visitor fulfill her funder's rules and respect the family's cultural beliefs?

huge changes the parents are experiencing within themselves are not always as obvious, but they are equally profound and teachers can be very helpful as people make the transition to parenthood.

Our common biological and evolutionary heritage and our cultural variations, although each a huge factor in parenting, barely begin to describe the many influences on how people act as parents. An ecological approach to parenting describes a number of factors that account for the variation we find across families and that have a significant influence on how the family forms and functions (Susman-Stillman, Appleyard, & Siebenbruner, 2003). These factors include attitudes, early experiences, and current circumstances.

The impact of childhood and attachment experience. The structure of one's own family growing up may have a significant influence on whether young men and women become parents outside of marriage. Hofferth and Goldscheider (2010) found that young women who grew up in single-parent homes are more likely to have a baby as a single parent. Young men who grew up in unstable households with many transitions in their lives are more likely to become a father early and less likely to live with the mother. However, although family structure is important, the quality of early relationships is also a significant factor on marital satisfaction. The translation of early attachment relationships into marital relationships has not been widely studied. Nonetheless, attachment theory suggests that the early parent-child relationship becomes the child's mental representation of all relationships (Bretherton, 1985). It appears that when an adult has a history of secure attachment, he or she is more likely to handle potentially upsetting disagreement supportively (Crowell, Treboux, & Brockmeyer, 2009). If both adults had secure relationships as children, they report less ambivalence about their marriage and more competence in parenting (Volling, Notaro, & Larsen, 1998). and they experience fewer divorces during their first six years of marriage, even if their parents were divorced (Crowell et al., 2009).

The influence of a single parent's other adult relationships. Single parents and their children benefit when the parents have other helpful adult relationships. Strong social networks of friends and/or family can increase the success of single parents in their ability to maintain strong, positive relationships with their children.

A research brief (Bandy, Andrews, & Moore, 2012) reports "emotional support matters, even when you take into account…family structure, income, gender, race/ethnicity, and child age" (p. 1). Particularly in disadvantaged families, when mothers report having emotional support, the children were less likely to act out, be depressed, or be retained a grade. They were more likely to be socially competent and engaged in school than children of mothers without emotional support.

Economics as a factor affecting parent–child interactions. Economics may have more impact on children's socioemotional development than does family structure (Kesner & McKenry, 2001). Fathers in higher socioeconomic levels who are employed and have good jobs tend to be more involved with their children, but work schedules can interfere with consistent parenting opportunities (Yeung, Sandberg, Davis-Kean, & Hofferth, 2001). Flexible work arrangements are associated with increased father involvement with their children (Castillo, Welch, & Sarver, 2012) whereas "increased stability at work without increased flexibility is negatively related to involvement" (p. 120).

The relative economic opportunities of the two adults affect their relationship and their willingness to marry. If a woman sees the man as having the potential to raise her economic state, she is more likely to marry. If her economic status seems more secure if she is single, she is more likely to want to live separately or cohabit, rather than marry (Edin, 2000).

Becoming a Mother

Nan woke up each morning feeling she could barely face the day. She had always wanted children and thought this should be the happiest time of her life. Her husband, Roy, had been increasingly distant since she announced her pregnancy and now he was out playing basketball almost every evening. Her family called and sent flowers when the baby was born but lived too far away to help. Friends from work seemed a lifetime away. She felt very much alone, and felt like a very bad mother for not just being grateful and happy that she had a baby. She was worried that she didn't know enough, or care enough, to ever be the kind of mother her baby deserved.

Becoming a mother is both "a natural progression and a major transition" as Redshaw and Martin (2011) so aptly put it. It is both a universal experience and a deeply personal, individual one. As a woman's body changes, as she sees the growth of the fetus in sonograms, and as she begins to think about herself caring for a baby, the process of becoming a mother is taking place. It can occur joyously or in despair. So much depends on the mother's health, her resources, her supports, and her relationship with the father and with her own mother.

In a fascinating qualitative study, a small group of pregnant women in Sweden shared their thoughts on many topics. Twelve women around the end of their first trimester talked about feeling that they had a secret only they and their partners knew, which felt good but it also felt lonely as they wanted to share this joyous news. The women talked about being happy to be able to give their parents a grandchild while also bringing up memories of their own upbringing and parental losses (Sevon, 2012). A study of conversations with pregnant women in New Zealand showed the more they felt they would be in charge of the birthing process, the better they felt about the birth itself (Howarth, Swain, & Treharne, 2011). A study of women after the birth of the child looked at the causes of marital dissatisfaction from the women's point of view. Dew and Wilcox (2011) found that women felt worst about having less time alone with their partner and their sense of unfairness in the distribution of housework, although they also struggled with exhaustion, loss of identity as a working person, a changed social life, and no time for themselves.

The term *high-intensity mothering* is being used to describe the high standards mothers expect of themselves and the external pressures they feel for doing everything right—and believing there is a right way to do things. High-intensive mothering attitudes include the belief that mothers are the most essential parent, that mothers should provide consistent intellectual stimulation for their child, that parenting is challenging, and that parents' lives should totally revolve around their children. These intensive mothering beliefs were found to be associated with greater depression and feelings of stress (Rizzo, Schiffrin, & Liss, 2012).

Implications for Care Teachers

Care Teachers need to understand that becoming a mother—or becoming a mother again—can have an enormous effect on a woman's sense of herself, her satisfaction with her marriage, or her need for a social support network. Teachers can be sympathetic listeners and help mothers within the program get to know one another.

Craig grew up thinking he wanted to have children someday, but he really believed that being a parent was something special between mothers and babies. Now he is the head-over-heels-in-love dad to 6-month-old Caitlin. When he picks up Caitlin from child care every day, her care teacher always greets him saying, "Just look at how excited she is to see you. She just lights up when you enter the room!"

Becoming a Father

Care teachers also have an important role in welcoming and valuing the child's father. The National Fatherhood Initiative (2012) has collected a fascinating array of facts regarding the numbers of children living or not living with their fathers and the effects of father absence or presence. The numbers are staggering. Twenty-four million children (one out of three) live without their biological father even though there has been an increasing understanding and emphasis on the importance of fathers, not just as providers for the family but also for their unique contributions to positive development in their children (Bretherton, 2010; Lamb, 2010; Tamis-Lemonda & Cabrera, 2002).

The guys who fear becoming fathers don't understand that fathering is not something perfect men do, but something that perfects the man. The end product of child raising is not the child but the parent. (Frank Pittman)

Men struggle with the changes in their lives, dealing with the biological, cultural, and personal aspects of becoming fathers. For many men, the concept of paternity has enormous meaning, in both a biological and a cultural context. Fathers' perceptions of their role will differ based on culture and social group. Bronte-Tinkew, Carrano, and Guzman (2006), based on an Early Childhood Longitudinal Study, found that the more fathers perceived that they had important roles to play, the more they were involved in caregiving activities, nurturing activities, physical care, and cognitively stimulating activities and the more paternal warmth they provided.

Fathers play an important role in a child's life, even in prenatal health. If the father is involved, the likelihood that a woman will receive prenatal care in her first trimester increases by 40% and reduces a pregnant woman's cigarette consumption by 36%. Expectant fathers can be influential advocates for breast-feeding by playing a critical role in encouraging a mother to breast-feed the newborn infant. Fathers who accompanied the mother on a prenatal visit were more likely to engage in father-child activities later in the child's life (Association of Maternal and Infant Health Programs, 2009).

A study that looked at whether the level of father engagement with their infants was affected by race found that African American fathers had a higher level of physical play, whereas white men used more verbal stimulation. African

This uncle and nephew clearly take great pleasure in each other's company.

American women suffering with postpartum depression reported that their children's fathers had more physical play with the child; this was not true for white women (Cabrera, Hofferth, & Chae, 2011). This may reflect the collectivist African American culture that promotes closeness, with the fathers compensating for the mother's depression. In another study, father engagement was measured by quality and quantity of fathering, attachment remaining relatively stable, and sensitivity over time. Infants had secure attachments to the more sensitive fathers and when the attachments stayed stable (Brown, Mangelsdorf, & Neff, 2012).

The mother's positive attitude toward the father and her support of the father's involvement are important factors in both married and unmarried families (Carlson & McLanahan, 2002). In a study looking at different influences on non-resident fathers' involvement with their children, the parents' positive relationship was the strongest determining factor predicting the level of the father's involvement (Sano, Smith, & Lanigan, 2011). Mothers draw fathers into involvement with their children by having child-centered conversations, encouraging fathers to take on caregiving tasks, and having a harmonious mother-father relationship (Coley & Chase-Lansdale, 1999).This has implications for care teachers.

Implications for Care teachers

Infant-toddler care teachers should be aware of their own attitudes in making fathers feel welcome and appreciated for their relationship with the baby. Including posters of fathers with babies as part of the room decor, offering pamphlets and brochures specifically for fathers, and even including a few sports magazines in the foyer can help fathers feel welcome. It is also helpful for new fathers to hear from their child's teacher that they are doing a good job as a dad, that they have a wonderful baby, and that it is clear that the baby loves them very much. Parent education for first-time fathers can be effective in teaching interaction skills if active learning strategies are used (Magill-Evans, Harrison, Benzies, Gierl, & Kimak, 2007).

The Transition from Couples to Parents

The essential acceptance of cohabitation without marriage, use of effective contraception, and women earning as much or more than their husbands in the workplace have all been game changers in how couples experience the shift to parenthood. We cannot even begin to know what effects the current economic stresses are having on couples becoming new parents.

When marriage and cohabitation are no longer tied to traditional intentions of raising a family, the union is sometimes described as *expressive*—the, couple feels stronger in expressing themselves as individuals and as a couple together. (Sevón, 2012). There is value to the romantic and sexual partnership but also to the companionship, shared interests, and activities. When these couples do have a child, excitement is often shared about having a baby and about the birth itself. However, the months of the following the birth often bring a declining satisfaction for the union as both the partners miss time to be together, their roles take on more traditional gender traits, and they struggle with sleep deprivation and insecurity about handling the baby. For basically strong relationships, this dissatisfaction begins to dissipate when the baby is around 6 months old (Barnes, 2011; Dew & Wilcox, 2011; Milkie, 2011).

Implications for Care Teachers

Although care teachers are primarily responsible for the children in their care, providing opportunities for parents to meet other parents and explore both personal and practical issues of parenting can be very valuable. Merely understanding and appreciating the huge impact that becoming a parent has on the individuals and on the couple can make the baby's teacher a great source of support for the entire family.

The Imagined Baby and the Real Baby

Long before we become parents, long before we experience pregnancy, early in our own childhoods, we play at being parents. In our play, during teen years of babysitting, watching younger siblings or cousins growing up, we form ideas about what babies are like. During pregnancy, parents wonder about their baby and imagine what she will look like and how she will be. Mental health providers who specialize in the relationships between babies and their parents believe that expectant parents use the months of pregnancy to imagine the ideal child they hope to have (attractive, smart, athletic, happy) as well as deal with their fears of who the child might be (malformed, weak, ugly—or ultimately violent, alcoholic, or mean, like some disliked member of the family). Part of the process of becoming a parent after the birth is getting to know and accept the real baby (Stern, 2000). This may involve letting go of some imagined attributes while having the time to learn who this new baby really is. Infant teachers need to be aware that new parents are vulnerable to the thoughts and comments of others during the early infancy of their child, and their comments about each baby's character should be both true and positive.

Parenting Styles

Even with considerable appreciation for the importance that nurturing, involved mothers and fathers have in the lives of children, it is important to recognize that mere presence does not ensure a positive contribution. The parent's emotional availability, mental health, and reasonableness all affect what it feels like for the child to be with the parent. Even the good effects of having an involved, nurturing father disappear if the father is also highly restrictive, authoritarian disciplinarian (Radin, 1982).

The term *parenting styles* describes the normal variation in patterns of how parents try to control their children (Baumrind, 1991). Parenting style includes both parent responsiveness and parent demands (Maccoby & Martin, 1983). Four parenting styles are commonly identified in the literature: *indulgent* (or *permissive*), *authoritarian, authoritative,* and *uninvolved.*

indulgent (or permissive) parents
Responsive but seldom demand mature behavior from their child, relying instead on the child's self-regulation.

authoritarian parents
Unresponsive, but demand obedience from their child.

authoritative parents
Responsive, but also demanding, holding high standards for the child while being supportive in their discipline.

uninvolved parents
Neither responsive nor demanding, although not to the point of being neglectful.

Indulgent (or permissive) parents are highly responsive but seldom demand mature behavior from their child, depending instead on the child's self-regulation.

Authoritarian parents are demanding but not responsive. They demand obedience to an extensive set of rules.

Authoritative parents are demanding and responsive. They hold high standards for their children but are supportive in their discipline.

Uninvolved parents are neither responsive nor demanding but not to the point of being neglectful (Baumrind, 1991).

In Western cultures, parenting styles are related to child outcomes, especially in adolescence. Children of indulgent parents have higher self-esteem but are more likely to have problems in school and in their behavior. Children from highly authoritarian families do well in school but tend toward poor self-esteem, depression, and poor social skills. Children whose parents are authoritative are rated more socially and intellectually competent than those of other parents. Children of uninvolved parents do most poorly in all areas (Darling, 1999).

However, parenting style is also related to culture. In America, with a predominant emphasis on individualism and freedom, authoritarian parents seem restrictive and constraining. However, children of Chinese families with highly authoritarian styles develop very well, possibly reflecting the cultural attitude toward authority as serving the harmony of the group (Chao, 1994), and because strict and extensive rules are usually paired with great warmth and closeness, making the parenting style more of a mix between authoritative and authoritarian. The emphasis on effort and hard work over talent may seem authoritarian but really be authoritative (Dewar, 2011).

Implications for Care Teachers

Infant-toddler care teachers may find it helpful to share this information on parenting styles with the families they serve. However, this may also be useful information for self-reflection. As an infant-toddler teacher, you have a relationship with the children that is similar to that of a parent. Reflection on whether your style of relating to the children is permissive, authoritarian, authoritative, or uninvolved could be very enlightening.

Family Structure

As we continue to wrestle with the complexity of understanding families, one large task would be simply defining the word *family*. A **family** may meet the traditional image of two married, biological parents and their children—or it may mean single parents, grandparents raising children, same-sex couples raising children, adoptive parents, blended families, or foster parents. Parents may be of the same or different religions and of the same or different races or cultures. The changing composition of the family does not change what is important to the child about being a member of a family, however. A report from the American Academy of Pediatrics states, "Children's optimal development seems to be influenced more by the nature of the relationships and interactions within the family unit than by the particular structural form it takes" (Perrin, 2002, p. 341).

> **family**
> Individuals related by birth, marriage, or choice.

In the recent past, we considered the two-biological-parent family as "normal" and regarded any other family structure as having deficits. The many changes in the structure of families have caused us to look at this differently. We currently view all families as having both risk factors and protective factors (Seifer, Sameroff, Baldwin, & Baldwin, 1992). As defined in Chapter 1, *risk factors* are those life events or personal characteristics that threaten a child's or family's well-being. *Protective factors* are the events and characteristics that act against risk factors (Donahoo, 2003).

Care teachers may become part of a single parent's support network.

For example, a calm, nurturing single-parent home would provide more protection than a two-biological-parent home affected by alcohol and violence.

Children can grow up happily, healthy, and without serious problems in all kinds of families, but children in two-parent households are more likely to escape poverty, teenaged unmarried childbearing, and school and mental health issues (Child Trends, 2002; Weitoft, Hjern, Haglund, & Rosén, 2003). The majority of American children live in two-parent households; however, according to census reports, that percentage has been steadily decreasing since the 1960s. About 66% of children live with two parents (biological or stepparents), 23% live with only their mother, 3% live with only their father, and 4% live with neither parent (ChildStats, 2011). In order to work effectively with extremely diverse families and their infants and toddlers, it is helpful to understand some of the issues that may be related to family structure. There are so many variations to the American family, and the issues surrounding them are so complex, that the following discussion should be considered a brief introduction to a topic worthy of deeper study.

Divorce

Parents of infants and toddlers have particular issues to consider when they divorce. Infants and toddlers may not be able to understand the difficulties their parents are experiencing, but they are very aware of the emotional tone of their environment. The sadness, tension, and anger of divorce can be stressful to even very young infants (George & Soloman, 2011). The baby's ability to develop a sense of trust in others depends on the adults' predictability and consistent emotional availability. Custody issues concerning parenting time are quite complex when it comes to infants and toddlers. (George, Soloman, & McIntosh, 2011) suggest that overnight visitation with fathers in divorced or separating families is very stressful to young infants who are still establishing the rhythms of their days. After decades of research in this area, they conclude that overnight visits with the non-custodial parent not take place until the child is an older toddler.

Implications for Care Teachers

An infant-toddler care teacher needs to be sure that she relates fairly to both divorced parents, supporting each parent's relationship with the child. She must remain neutral in a situation that can be fraught with difficult feelings. In supporting the child's relationship with each parent, the care teacher must keep both parents well informed about the child and find ways, when necessary, to describe the effect that the parent's relationship or the custody situation is having on the child.

Single Parents

Some of the issues for infants and toddlers concerning divorce are also relevant for children raised by a single, never-married parent. The percentage of children born to women who have never married is increasing dramatically: In the early 1960s, less than 1 percent of children lived with a never-married parent. By 2000, nearly one in 10 children lived with a never-married parent….In 2009, 41% of all births occurred to unmarried women (Martinez, Daniels, & Chandra, 2012).

Implications for Care Teachers

Care teachers need to be particularly sensitive to infants and toddlers who are growing up with only one parent, as these children need and long for safe, nurturing contact with adults of both sexes. Because child care providers are predominantly female, it is easier to provide female experiences to children being raised by fathers than male experiences to children of single mothers.

Same-Sex Parents

Same-sex parents are estimated to be raising as many as 9 million of America's children, but accurate statistics are impossible to find. Gay and lesbian parents share the same concerns and worries of all parents but face additional issues unique to their situation. If the child was not originally conceived within an earlier heterosexual relationship, there are questions of adoption, artificial insemination, or surrogate

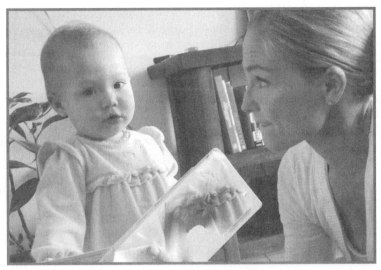

Many early childhood programs serve families through home visits, working with the parent and child together.

mothers. Legal issues arise wherein the biological or adoptive parent may have full parental rights, but the same-sex partner may not be allowed to adopt the child as an equal parent.

A study of the well-being of adult children raised by same-sex parents showed that two factors seemed most influential in supporting their development. The adults with the best outcomes were raised in a community that had several similar families and a social climate that included voting Democratic, having more accepting religious beliefs, and school rules against bullying (Lick, Tornello, Riskind, Schmidt, & Patterson, 2012). Patterson (2006) summarized the research in this way: "More than two decades of research has failed to reveal important differences in the adjustment or development of children or adolescents reared by same-sex couples compared to those reared by other-sex couples. Results of the research suggest that qualities of family relationships are more tightly linked with child outcomes than is parental sexual orientation" (p. 241).

Implications for Care Teachers

The care teacher's primary responsibility is to support the relationship between the infant and the parents. When same-sex couples bring an infant or toddler to a program, they may share the questions anyone may bring to the experience of being a new parent. The teacher should, as always, be ready to share information on development and early parenting practices. However, same-sex parents may face more complicated questions about each person's new role. How does a baby have two mommies or two daddies? How does each person understand sharing this role? The teacher should listen to these questions with the same compassion and acceptance as she would with any other parent issues about adjusting to the role.

A bigger question for same-sex couples may be whether they and their child will be genuinely welcomed into the program or will staff or families have animosity toward the couple based on religious or personal objections. These are issues that may also arise when families of a different race or religion enter an otherwise homogeneous program. As in dealing with any feelings of discomfort based on differences, the teacher should begin by examining her own feelings, perhaps in supervision or with the mental health consultant. The care teacher may also want to practice with that person how to politely, but firmly, put a stop to cruel remarks from other parents. For example, "I can see you have strong feelings about Jami having two mommies, but this is not the time or place to talk about it. Our director will be happy to have a conversation with you, but we keep this room calm for the babies."

Although no one is free of bias toward others, each care teacher is expected to behave in a professional manner and always work to support the relationship between the child and his family. Many baby board books illustrate homes with two daddies or two mommies and will help the child from such a home feel represented.

Grandparents

Grandparents raising grandchildren is an increasing phenomenon in America (Williams, 2011). Parents may or may not live in the same household, but grandparents are increasingly providing primary care for grandchildren. According to the U.S. Census Bureau, in 2010, 7 million children were living in homes maintained by their grandparents, up from 3.9 million in 1997 (U.S. Census Bureau, 2012). The steady increases are due to a variety of factors: substance abuse by parents, teen pregnancy, family violence, illness, and incarceration. Grandparents are sometimes able to offer a stable home to their grandchildren; however, they often care for their grandchildren without any legal rights. This leaves them in precarious conditions for accessing health care or other social supports for the children (Minkler, 2002).

Implications for Care Teachers

Both the grandparents and the infant or toddler will need sensitive understanding from educators: "While the home-school connection is critical for every young child, it is especially crucial in grandparent-headed households. Education professionals need unique insight and information about custodial grandparents' particular circumstances" (Smith, Dannison, & Vach-Hasse, 1998, p. 16). The infants and toddlers may be grieving for the loss of a parent, and grandparents may be struggling with transforming their role of doting grandparent into one of parent with multiple responsibilities for their grandchildren.

Adoptive Parents

Adoption is another subgroup of parenting with so many variables that it is tempting to say it can be understood only on a family-by-family basis. Given that in 2008, 135,813 adoptions occurred in the United States and about 1 million children live with adoptive parents, there are endless differences (Child Welfare Information Gateway, 2011). Infants may be adopted at birth from parents who relinquish their rights immediately, they may be adopted by family members, or they may be removed from their birth parents because of abuse or neglect and spend years in foster care without a permanent home. They may have been exposed to drugs or alcohol in utero. Obviously, the circumstances leading up to the adoption will have considerable effect on the child's outcomes.

For infants and toddlers, the work of developing relationships and establishing trust is highly dependent on consistent, responsive caregiving. Achieving a balance between a secure attachment to a caregiver and a healthy ability to move out into the world to explore can be challenging for any baby. Infants and toddlers who have experienced many disruptions in early relationships may have particular difficulties in establishing trust and in feeling safe enough to explore the world (2004).

Implications for Care Teachers

Care Teachers may also need to support adoptive parents as they struggle with particular issues. In an earlier section of this chapter, we described some of the issues men and women struggle with as they become parents. Although the process of adoption is very time-consuming, many adoptive parents have only a few days between being notified that their child is available and actually receiving the child. In contrast to a 9-month pregnancy, this can leave little time for emotional preparation. In order to protect themselves from disappointment, the adoptive parents may not dream and fantasize about parenting as much as the pregnant couple. They may be afraid at first to become too attached to the baby. They may worry whether they will love the baby or whether the baby can love them, given the lack of genetic connection. They may also need help in determining whether issues that arise are typical behavioral issues for infants and toddlers or whether they are related to the adoption.

Foster Parents

When children are abused or neglected, they enter the child welfare system and often are placed in foster homes. More than 43% of all children in foster care are under age 5 (U.S. Department of Health and Human Services (2012). Thirty-one percent of the children who entered foster care in 2011 were under 3 years old (U.S. Department of Health and Human Services, 2012). These children are possibly the most vulnerable in our country. In order to be placed in foster care in the first months or years of life, they have already experienced deficient or dangerous parenting. Their mothers may not have received prenatal care, and they may have been poorly nourished and exposed to substances in utero.

Nearly 80% of these children are at risk for medical and developmental problems as a result of prenatal exposure. They may have witnessed or been victims of physical or sexual violence. More than 40% of foster children were born prematurely and/or were of low birth weight. More than half have serious health problems and developmental delays—4 to 5 times the rate of children in the general population. With all of these problems, children in foster care are also unlikely to receive basic health care such as immunizations and are highly unlikely to receive early intervention or mental health services because of fragmented systems and record keeping (Stacks & Partridge, 2011).

Implications for Care Teachers

Participation in high-quality early childhood programs is included as one of five strategies to promote the healthy development of young children in foster care proposed by the National Council on Poverty. High-quality early childhood programs provide stimulating, engaging, and nurturing environments that can be inherently supportive of development. Early childhood teachers can also provide information, strategies, ideas, and emotional support to foster parents.

▶ Watch the video *A Conference with Kayla's Mom.* How does Kayla's teacher prepare for the conference with Kayla's mother?

parent education

The array of government and private programs that provide informational services to young children and their families.

family support programs

Provide and coordinate a variety of services and supports for families, including prenatal care; assessment for special needs; and other medical, educational, and social services.

Care and Education Programs that Support Families

Parent Education

In addition to child care, many programs are available to support parents. In a broad sense, all programs that provide informational services to young children and their families might be called **parent education**. The specific purpose of the program may lie anywhere along what the National Parenting Information Network (NPIN) calls the "parenting education spectrum." This includes an increasing intensity of services and supports, such as resources and referrals, suggestions or strategies, informal community programs or groups, formal instruction through classes, and counseling and one-on-one support for parents (Robertson, 1998). All families need support at various stages of family life and at select times. **Family support programs** provide and coordinate a variety of services and supports for families—such as prenatal care for the mother, health services for children, quality child care and child care options, assessment and services for special needs, education, and social services. Different agencies in a city, county, or state may collaborate to provide the services and supports in a coordinated way that creates a strong infrastructure to support families and children prenatally to age 5.

In 2010, the Patient Protection and Affordable Care Act established the Maternal Infant Early Childhood Home Visiting (MIECHV) program. The MIECHV program is designed to improve coordination of services for at-risk communities, to strengthen and improve the activities of the Maternal and Child Health Block Grant, and to identify and provide comprehensive services to improve outcomes for families in high-risk communities. States were invited to apply for the funding to support one of seven evidence-based home visiting models: Early Head Start, Parents as Teachers, Family Checkup, Healthy Families American, Healthy Steps, Home Instruction Program for Preschool Youngsters (HIPPY), and the Nurse Family Partnership. This is a $1.5 billon investment in serving families through the highly effective model of home visiting—another employment opportunity for early care and education professionals. Home visitors develop close relationships with families while providing child development information, emotional support, and connections to many community resources.

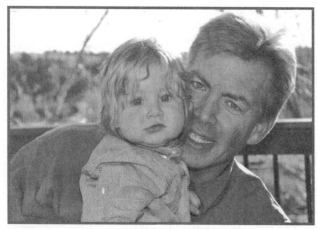

Personality, culture, and the experiences of one's own childhood will influence the parenting styles each parent adopts.

Programs for Parents of Children with Special Needs

Perhaps there is no other group of parents for whom such a variety of education and support services are available as parents of children with disabilities. These parents represent every race, culture, economic status, and family structure. Assisting them are programs that provide information about legal, developmental, financial, and medical aspects of disabilities, as well as parent-to-parent connections and advocacy.

When infants or toddlers are identified with disabilities, parents may have any number of reactions, influenced by many factors including their personal history with disabilities, their religious or cultural beliefs about disability, the nature or severity of the particular disability, and their own capacity to be open to someone other than the wished-for perfect child.

Despite a prevailing societal assumption that the discovery of a disability in one's child is a tragedy for the parent, parents describe many kinds of reactions. One study reported parents as describing themselves in a constant state of tension between feelings such as "joy and sorrow," "hope and no hope," and "defiance and despair." Parents also identified their own optimism and resourcefulness in meeting the ongoing challenges of their child's disability (Kearney & Griffin, 2001). Other parents have less positive experiences and describe their reactions as including fear over the child's future ability to live a satisfying life or guilt over having possibly caused the disability through a physical or spiritual act. Some parents feel confusion over the new situation, often trying to understand complex medical information at a time when anxiety and lack of sleep make understanding anything difficult. Parents may feel powerless to control their own lives, may feel disappointed by the child they have produced, and even have feelings of rejection of the child or the professionals who carry this image of the child (Smith, 2003). Many parents describe themselves as having all of these feelings at different times—sometimes even having contradictory feelings at the same time!

The only disability is having no relationships. (Judith Snow)

Each state has at least one parent training and information center (PTIC) to provide parents with training and information about disabilities; information about parents' and children's rights under the relevant laws; and resources in the community, state, and nation (Müller, 2007). These centers are funded through the Individuals with Disabilities Education Act (IDEA), which mandates special education services for children with disabilities. The parent center staff members are often parents of children with disabilities themselves. They provide information over the phone, through workshops, and through conferences, helping parents understand their own child's needs and learn about available options. They encourage parents to actively participate in making decisions about their child's services and in negotiating with providers and intervention systems to ensure that their child's legal rights to services are fulfilled.

Parent-to-Parent support programs are also available all over the country and through national clearinghouses. Parent-to-Parent is a program that matches parents of children with similar needs to provide support and information to each other. A parent whose child is newly identified as having a disability may contact a Parent-to-Parent program and be matched with an experienced parent trained to discuss the new parent's concerns. Parent-to-Parent may provide an understanding friend with whom the parent can share experiences of stress, confusion, or optimism. Strategies for utilizing resources, making decisions, and simply gaining confidence in trusting one's own feelings and understandings may be shared. Lifelong friendships sometimes begin in Parent-to-Parent matches (Santelli, 2003).

Care teachers should be considered part of the early intervention team serving an infant or toddler with disabilities and should have a good knowledge of the resources and programs in the local community. However, the role of the child care provider as a partner to the parent may be even more important in day-to-day life. Care teachers can contribute ongoing observations and information about a child's new interests and accomplishments. They can help parents sort out what new behaviors may be related to the disability and what is typical toddler behavior. Most importantly, teachers can provide a genuine welcome to and true affection for a child whose acceptance in other settings may be of great concern to parents.

Summary

Many aspects of life affect how families form and function in their parenting:

- Human families all over the world share a common biology of reproduction that determines some aspects of their parenting—attending births, caring for vulnerable young infants, and valuing the bonds between parents and their children.
- Cultural beliefs about how people relate to each other and the role of children within the culture directly, if sometimes invisibly, determine the guidance parents offer their children.
- The transition to parenthood is a powerful and significant life change for the individual and for the couple, which can be supported or undermined by factors such as personal history, support from the partner, social support, and economic stability.
- Personality, culture, and the experiences of one's own childhood will influence the parenting styles each parent adopts—indulgent (or permissive), authoritarian, authoritative, or uninvolved.

- Families created through marriage, divorce, nonmarried individuals, same-sex couples, grandparents raising grandchildren, adoption, and foster care may each provide different experiences for the family members. Nonetheless, the quality of caring, responsiveness, and relationship will have a greater impact on the child's mental health and overall developmental well-being than the configuration of the family.
- Finally, many early childhood programs provide information and support to help parents do the best jobs they can with their children. These programs include parent education, family support programs, and early intervention parenting programs.

Every early childhood program must respect the primacy of the family in the lives of infants and toddlers. Parents are our best partners, our best sources of information and guidance concerning their own children, and often our real reason for existence.

Key Terms

authoritarian parents
authoritative parents
collectivist cultures

family
family support programs
individualist cultures

indulgent (or permissive) parents
parent education
uninvolved parents

Reflections and Resources for the Reader

REFLECTIONS

1. In your own family, do you think your parents believed their job was basically to teach you to be independent and self-sufficient or to be interdependent? How did they communicate these messages to you?
2. In reading about different family structures, did you think that some kinds of families might be harder for you to accept than others? How would you manage that challenge, if it occurred? Discuss with a partner in class.

OBSERVATION AND APPLICATION OPPORTUNITIES

1. As you observe parents with their young children at child care, in a store, or on a bus, what do you see parents do that suggests to you that they might be authoritative, authoritarian, indulgent (permissive), or uninvolved?
2. Children are able to grow and develop well in all sorts of families. What unique strengths have you seen in families of different structures such as grandparents

raising children, single parents, divorced parents sharing custody, or others?

3. Visit a parenting class in your community. Evaluate how useful the class appears to be to the families.

SUPPLEMENTARY ARTICLES AND BOOKS TO READ

Barrera, I., Kramer, L., & Macpherson, T. D. (2012). *Skilled dialogue* (2nd ed.). Baltimore, MD: Paul H. Brooks.

Dozier, M., Bick, J., & Bernard, K. (2012). Intervening with foster parents to enhance biobehavioral outcomes among infants and toddlers. *ZERO TO THREE, 31*(3), 17–22.

Parlakian, R., & Lerner, C. (2012) Practical tips and tools—sharing the caring: Considerations for co-parenting arrangements when there is a separation or divorce, *ZERO TO THREE, 32*(5), 40–42.

Pruett, K., & Pruett, M. K. (2012). Sustaining parent-young child relationships during and after separation and divorce. Or not. *ZERO TO THREE, 32*(5), 33–40.

INTERESTING LINKS

www.childwelfare.gov
Child Welfare Information Gateway. This government Web site provides research briefs, statistics, and issue papers.

www.fatherhood.gov
The *National Responsible Fatherhood Clearinghouse* is a resource of the U.S. Department of Health and Human Services Administration for Children and Families' (ACF) Office of Family Assistance (OFA).

npen.org/
National Parenting Education Network The National Parenting Education Network is a national organization that promotes parenting education. The Web site has many articles and resources on parenting education.

www.parentcenternetwork.org/national/aboutus.html
Parent Technical Assistance Center The Web site provides an array of data about parent training and information centers (PTICs) and community parent resource centers. PTICs are funded by the federal government to support parents of children with disabilities.

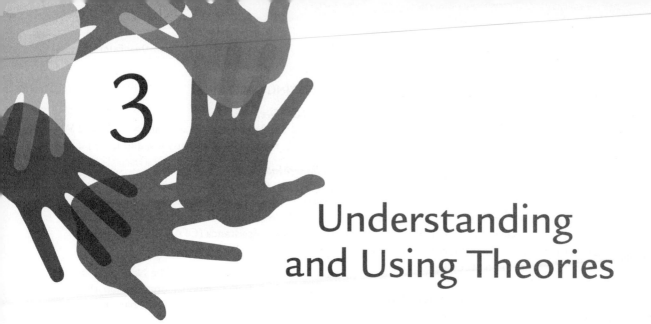

3

Understanding and Using Theories

LEARNING OUTCOMES

After reading this chapter, you will be able to:

- Define "theories"
- Describe the major points of the developmental theories
- Describe the major points of emotional development theories
- Describe the major points of cognitive development theories
- Describe the major points of language development theories
- Describe the major points of motor development theories
- Explain how theories would look applied in a program

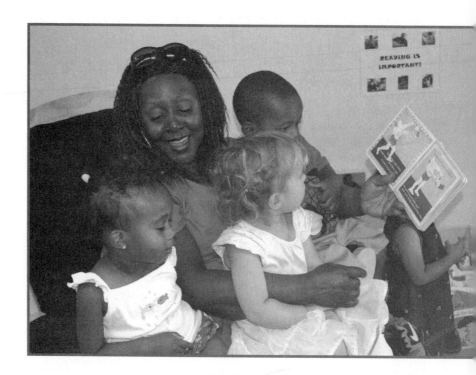

It is not unusual for the new care teacher or parent to discover contradictory information on child development. One book instructs adults to let babies cry themselves back to sleep if they awaken in the night; another tells them to respond with a comforting pat on the back. Still others advocate for a "family bed" where the children sleep with the parents. Women who are told by their mothers to keep babies on a strict feeding schedule—regardless of their cries of hunger, even during growth spurts—may be told by their pediatricians to feed their babies on demand. Parents and care teachers alternately are seen as too strict or too lenient in guiding children's behavior. It is not surprising that people feel frustration in trying to sort out what, if anything, is really known about supporting development in children.

What Are Theories?

Child development is similar to any other body of knowledge. From early in history, people have had a desire to understand how the world works (a desire we see reflected in even the youngest infants). In trying to make sense of human development, just as in trying to understand the changing seasons or the patterns of stars in the skies, people developed ideas about how things *might* work. Some of those ideas may have been scoffed at and lost to history. Others were recognized, acknowledged, and adopted by thinking people of their day. These ideas were developed into theories. *Theories* are explanations of information, observations, and life experiences. They are attempts to provide continuity and meaning between past and present events and to provide a way of thinking about, or anticipating, future events. Theories are based on the thoughts and studies of one person or one group of people. Sometimes the theorist has been primarily interested in one area of development and proposes ideas about that area without trying to encompass every aspect of development. The limits of the theory depend on those who first proposed it or those who follow—taking the idea, adding new information, examining it from new perspectives, and testing its application to reality. The benefit of a theory is that it helps us understand the possible relationship between separate events. The limitation of a theory is that reality is so complex that a single theory is unlikely to explain anything entirely.

Our Theoretical Framework

Theories of child development have been proposed throughout all of recorded history. This chapter does not provide a history of theories or even an overview of recent theories. Instead, we introduce the theories that inform the beliefs and values expressed throughout this book. This theoretical framework derives from many important developmental theorists. Each of these theories is described here, but a major common theme among them is that infants and toddlers achieve their development within relationships with responsive, caring adults. This book is based on these beliefs:

- Optimal growth and development for children, families, and communities occurs within nurturing relationships.
- Children influence the relationships within their families, and families influence the children's relationships.

- Experiences prenatally and in the early years affect the course of development across the life span—the brain becomes wired to expect stress or to thrive within relationships, to learn or to be challenged by learning.
- Children are able to learn when they feel safe enough to explore, when they feel they can have a responsive effect on the people and objects in their environment, and when they have an adult partner who listens, talks and reads to them.
- Early developing attachment relationships may be disturbed by parental histories or relationships such as unresolved losses and traumatic life events or current events that change the parent's circumstances.
- The relationships that parents have with other adults affect their ability to build positive, secure relationships with their children.
- A child is part of a family, which is part of a culture, which is part of a community, which is part of a country, and each of these elements affects the others.
- Service delivery models, community programs, and public policy can and should build strong relationships and reduce the risk of relationship failure.

The clear emphasis on the importance of quality relationships for the well-being of infants and toddlers and their families reflects the neuroscience-based *ecobiodevelopmental theory of development* (Shonkoff & Garner, 2012), *relationship-based theory* of child development (Emde & Robinson, 2000; Hinde, 1992b), *transactional theory* (Sameroff & Chandler, 1975), and *bioecological systems theory* (Bronfenbrenner, 2004). Each of these theories acknowledges the power of the cultural lens through which people make decisions, as well as the family and individual differences that exist within that person's particular culture (Barrera, Kramer, & Macpherson, 2012; Howes, 2009). Each of these complements and, to some extent, includes the others. Among these theories, the relationship-based theory most clearly describes the individual child's experience while simultaneously considering the social network in which he lives, as described by Hinde (1992b):

> A relationships approach involves the recognition that children must be seen not as isolated entities, but as forming part of a network of social relationships; and requires a delicate balance between conceptions of the child as an individual and as a social being. (p. 1019)

Relationship-Based Theory

When Tara, the infant-toddler teacher, welcomes Jaime into her arms in the morning, her warmth, the meeting of their eyes, and the sound of pleasure in her voice all make Jaime feel that Tara remembers him and is happy to see him. As Tara is welcoming Jaime, however, her words also address her relationship with his mother: "Have a good day. I'll take good care of Jaime today. We'll be fine, and then he'll be very happy when you come and get him after work."

Recall from Chapter 1 that **relationship-based theory** offers an understanding of development that is consistent with our current knowledge about brain development, our experience with the effects of adverse relationships such as abuse and neglect, and—perhaps most importantly—with our own personal experiences. We understand the power of a loving relationship to support us through difficulties.

Jeree Pawl (1995), an infant-parent psychotherapist, wrote a wonderful description of the power of the infant's relationship with a trusted adult:

> *A two-month-old held facing outward will drop his head back to look at the holder from time to time, if he's well nurtured. By the time you are a sitting baby, with good enough ordinary experiences, your very back feels safe, held. You know you are watched—that is, that you exist, are held, in someone's mind. You feel secure, and secured....*
>
> *But this only develops if you truly are consistently in the mind of someone, so that you are noted, noticed, spoken to over distance, rescued, protected, appreciated, and tethered across space and out of mutual sight. It is the teacher that creates and confirms this, by her continual surveillance and by holding the child in continual existence in her mind. This becomes a crucial part of a child's internal sense and experience. (p. 5)*

The infant-toddler care teacher's relationship with each baby, holding the baby in her mind, is very important. Her relationship with each parent and other family members is also important because the adults' relationships may affect their relationships with the baby. So much of each baby's ability to develop well depends on the availability of a responsive, meaningful relationship, on the capacities of the adult to hold the infant in her mind, on the surrounding social and physical environments to support the adult in the relationship, and on the condition of the society in which they live.

> *Care for your children as you wish them to care for your grandchildren. (Al Solnit and Sally Provence)*

Relationship-based theory explicitly defines relationships. Within this construct, *relationship* is not a general word used to describe casual contacts or moments of interaction. Relationship-based theory says that relationships are effective as the organizing force of development, the element that gives an action or a feeling greater meaning and importance. According to this theory, relationships can differ depending on the following dimensions: (Hinde, 1992b)

relationship-based theory

A model whereby constructive, caring relationships are fundamental to infant and toddler development.

- *Content of the interactions.* The content of infant-adult interactions may include established routines, play, affection, guidance, and sharing interests and experiences. The content may have a predominantly positive or negative affective tone.
- *Diversity of the interactions.* Infant-adult interactions could be composed only of routine caregiving, such as diapering and feeding. Other adults and babies may share a wide range of interactions including conversation, singing, walks, play, and household activities.
- *Qualities of the interactions.* Relationships vary in how well the behavior of one partner coordinates with that of the other. A sensitive adult perceives the infant's signal, correctly interprets it, selects an appropriate response, and delivers the response in a timely, contingent fashion (Ainsworth, Bell, & Stayton, 1971).
- *Qualities that emerge from the relative frequency and patterning of different types of interactions.* Behaviors are meaningful in a relationship not because they occur a certain number of times, but because the *pattern of frequency* of touching, smiling, and nuzzling amid the more neutral behaviors comes to have meaning. If touching occurs relatively often but only when the parent feels like it, it may be less satisfying to the baby than if it occurs less frequently but always in response to his signal that he desires contact.

Teachers develop real affection for the children.

- *Complementarity versus reciprocity of the interactions.* Complementary interactions are a negotiation of different behaviors in the two partners. Reciprocal interactions are characterized by both partners using similar behaviors. When parents cooperate with and facilitate the baby's behavior, they establish the foundation of a reciprocal relationship whereby the partners can adjust their actions for the benefit of the infant or toddler in reaching his goal (comfort, food, a toy, a friend) (Bowlby, 1969).
- *Intimacy.* An intimate relationship provides a warm emotional tone, a desire for closeness, a sense of security in the close presence of the other, and a willingness to act on behalf of the well-being of the other.
- *Interpersonal perception.* Relationships are also characterized by how each partner feels the relationship affects him- or herself. This assessment of the effect of the relationship may depend on the emotional availability and cognitive understanding of self and of the other person.
- *Commitment.* The final dimension is the willingness to act on the other's behalf and work for the other's well-being, in a relationship that endures over time. It is this aspect of endurance that elevates another person's importance so that one would act supportively and empathically for the other person's good. Hinde (1988) described the importance of endurance:

> At the behavioral level, a relationship involves a series of interactions between two individuals, each interaction being relatively limited in duration but affected by past interactions between the same individuals and affecting future ones. But a relationship can persist in the absence of interactions, and involves also subjective aspects—including especially memories of past interactions and expectations of future ones, which have both cognitive and affective aspects. (p. 1)

Care teachers utilizing the relationship-based theory of development commit to deep, meaningful relationships that endure over time with infants, toddlers, and families. They are capable of incorporating intimate relationships within their professional role.

Ecobiodevelopmental Theory

Two days a week, Dr. Westmore worked in a public health clinic in the inner city. He was very familiar with the disparities between the children he saw there and the children he saw in his affluent, suburban practice. The inner-city children had little prenatal care, poor nutrition, and stressful home lives. The current science of neurobiology and epigenetics told him the children were at risk of challenges to their brain development.

ecobiodevelopmental theory
A theory that puts together all aspects of health, an understanding of the effects of stressful environments and interventions to relieve them, and the new information from science about neurobiology.

The American Association of Pediatrics issued a paper (Shonkoff & Garner, 2012) introducing a new theory of lifelong health. The **ecobiodevelopmental** theory puts together all aspects of health, an understanding of the effects of stressful environments and interventions to relieve them, and the new information from science about neurobiology and **epigenetics**. We now know that early experiences (prenatal and in the first years of life) actually affect the architecture of the brain—the way neural connections are made and strengthened or lost. This theory takes our current scientific knowledge and applies it to development.

The ecobiodevelopmental theory proposes that a new approach to providing health and intervention services could make a significant difference in the lives and health of children whose background has traditionally contributed to poor health, poor relationships, and poor performance in school and work. By concentrating on all aspects of health and providing parenting and learning supports, we could change the evolving structure of the brain within our poorest children.

> epigenetics
>
> The process by which a gene is "told" whether or not to turn on (express itself).

Transactional Theory

> *A professional football player whose entire life is dedicated to rough physical contact becomes a father to a baby girl. This little girl is very sensitive about how she is handled and fusses unless treated gently. Her daddy does not want her to cry, and he adjusts his handling of her so that she feels safe and comfortable in his arms. Over time, being close to her daddy becomes a high priority for this baby, and she learns to tolerate play that is more active because she feels his pleasure in it.*

These silent, instantaneous transactions are negotiated in each moment between infants and toddlers and those around them. As discussed in Chapter 1, *transactional theory*, as first proposed by Sameroff and Chandler (1975), emphasizes characteristics of both the child and the environment, and their dynamic interplay over time. For example, the child is seen as bringing certain biological and genetic characteristics such as gender, temperament, physical health, and genetic predispositions toward intellectual and other abilities—or in the previous story, a desire to be handled gently. The environmental influences include the psychological resources and behaviors of the most important people in the child's life: parents, siblings, extended family, peers, friends, schools, and neighborhood communities. In the previous example, one influence was the dad's ability to be responsive but another was the dad's pleasure in active, physical sports.

Transactional theory was first developed as a way of understanding why children with similar biological risk factors at birth could have very different courses of development. Sameroff and Chandler (1975) proposed that the child's biological status is only one contribution to development. The parent's understanding of the child and the appropriateness or helpfulness of the parent's response also have enormous impact.

> *Children affect their environment and environments affect children. Children are neither doomed nor protected by their characteristics or by the characteristics of their caregivers alone. (Sameroff and MacKenzie)*

The transactional theory identifies the "bi-directional, reciprocal relationships between infants and their caregivers" as providing several points as the basis for intervention (Sameroff & MacKenzie, 2003, p. 19). Transaction is seen as a three-part sequence, offering three points at which to intervene. First, the baby stimulates the parents, either through his appearance or through

FIGURE 3.1   **Transactional theory of development and points of intervention**

Source: Based on Sameroff and MacKenzie (2003).

his behavior. The parents then attribute some meaning to the baby's message. Finally, the parents react with some form of caregiving. As seen in Figure 3.1, the dynamic between infant and parent (or teacher) could be changed at any of these three points, changing the child through remediation, the parents' meaning through redefinition, and the parents' caregiving reaction through reeducation or increasing skills and knowledge (Sameroff & Fiese, 2000).

Bioecological Systems Theory

Perry loved being a home family provider. She had close relationships with the children and their families. But her city council was putting new restrictions on home businesses, and she was worried about meeting the new requirements. Other providers were also concerned, and they were meeting with the state child care administrator, hoping for some help.

The many levels that affect Perry's child care program are addressed within bioecological systems theory (Bronfenbrenner, 2004). Bioecological systems theory projects beyond the interpersonal relationships into the effects of the community and society on the child. Bronfenbrenner begins with his belief that the primary relationship needs to be with someone who can provide a sense of caring for a lifetime, and that children need stable families that provide constant mutual interaction with their children; he then looks to the structure of society to determine whether society supports this level of relationship.

CULTURE CLOSE UP

As the bioecological system demonstrates, culture permeates development—and our thinking about development. A study compared the understanding of theory of mind (ToM; the understanding that other people have thoughts, feelings, and values that may differ from yours) of Iranian preschoolers to Australian preschoolers. The scale the researchers used assumed that ToM was developed in five sequential steps: diverse desires (DD), then diverse beliefs (DB), then knowledge access (KA), then false beliefs (FB), and finally hidden emotions (HE). The children all had a solid understanding of ToM by age 6, but they did not follow the same sequence of skill acquisition. The Iranian children had KA before DB. The Australian children had DB and then KA. The researchers theorize that the Iranian children are growing up in an interdependent, collectivist society that greatly values knowledge and academic ideas but discourages diverse ideas. The Australian children, on the other hand, are growing up in a society in which people talk about their feelings, discuss events from different perspectives, and generally value independence and autonomy. Culture determines how one thinks about the world (Shahaeian, Peterson, Slaughter, & Wellman, 2011).

FIGURE 3.2   **Bioecological systems theory of development, adapted to child care**

Source: Adapted from Feldman Robert S., *Child Development*, 4th Edition, copyright 2007, Electronically adapted by permission of Pearson Education, Inc., Upper Saddle River, NJ. Based on concepts developed by Urie Bronfenbrenner in his books (Bronfenbrenner, 1979, 1994, & 2004).

The bioecological systems model is usually portrayed as a series of concentric circles emanating from the child, as seen in Figure 3.2.

The innermost circle is the microsystem that describes the child's direct relationships with his family, and which relates most closely to relationship-based theory. In echoes of the transactional theory, the family members, friends, and care teachers in the microsystem affect the child—but the child affects them as well. The next circle is the mesosystem; this includes relationships among the microsystems, also relating closely to transactional theory. For example, the child care providers and parents have a relationship with each other that can affect the parent-child relationship or the teacher-child relationship.

The exosystem consists of settings that do not include children but that affect them. In Perry's case, it is the city council's new restrictions that are about to have an impact on her caregiving. She is hoping that the state administrator might be a more helpful part of this exosystem. Other exosystem examples would include the policies of the parent's workplace concerning flexible work hours or staying home with a sick child.

ecobiological theory

A model combining our knowledge of health, the effects of the environment, and interventions to support development.

microsystem

The child's most immediate relationships.

mesosystem

The relationships among the people within the child's microsystem.

exosystem

The local social settings that indirectly affect the child.

macrosystem

The culture, values, beliefs, and public policies of the society in which the child lives.

chronosystem

The changes in all of the systems over time, including aging, structure of the family, moving, death, or shifting social attitudes and public policies.

The next circle is the **macrosystem**, which refers to the values and laws of the society (Bronfenbrenner, 2004). A society that does not believe in women working will not support policies that give women equal wages and flexibility concerning their responsibilities to their children. In Perry's case, if the city values the service of home family providers and understands that the economics of this business are quite different from those of other businesses, the city council might exempt child care from its new requirements.

The encompassing circle is the **chronosystem**, which addresses the element of time as it affects the child. Time elements might mark external events such as the parents' divorce or the birth of a sibling, or they may be internal, describing the growth and maturation of the child.

The model obliges us to be aware that the well-being of any child is dependent on events and forces far beyond the child's own daily experiences. Programs will use a family-centered approach and also become aware of community resources for families. The care teacher utilizing the bioecological systems theory would participate in professional organizations such as the National Association for the Education of Young Children or the Family Child Care Association.

Theories of Emotional Development: A Sense of Self and Relationships with Others

Emotional development, our feelings, our loves, our motivations and desires, our fears and feelings of safety, and our ability to reflect on our experiences all proceed within the context of our relationships. The theories of emotional development that follow are congruent with the previous theories, but they focus our attention on how we develop a sense of self and relationships with others. These are brief descriptions of complex theories, each of which has a rich literature of studies and papers. Although each of the following theories has a different focus, each has contributed to our understanding of how the infant and toddler discover and form an identity through a primary relationship with one or more adults.

Theory of Psychosocial Development

Cecil had worked with infants and toddlers for 15 years. When he had newborns, he often thought, "This is my favorite stage!" Then he would have older toddlers and wonder at their competence, thinking, "This is my favorite stage!" Part of what Cecil likes is that at each stage, not only are the children different, but they seem to need different things from him.

theory of psychosocial development

Human development is a series of eight stages characterized by psychosocial crises that derive from physiological development and the demands made on the individual by family and society.

Cecil doesn't know it, but his thinking in terms of stages is very much like that of Erik Erikson, a psychologist who created a framework of stages to explain development from birth through adulthood, which he called the **theory of psychosocial development**. Erikson proposed that individuals go through eight distinct, predictable stages as they develop their sense of self and their relationships with others, as shown in Table 3.1 (Erikson, 1950). At each stage, as a child experiences different biological, social, and cognitive needs, a sort of developmental crisis provides an opportunity for that child to discover whether her family, society, and culture can meet those needs.

TABLE 3.1   Erikson's psychosocial stages

Age Range	Basic Conflicts	Developmental Tasks
Birth to 18 months	Trust vs. Mistrust	Infants learn that teachers can be trusted to meet their needs and that the world is a safe, pleasant place to grow up.
18 months to 3 years	Autonomy vs. Doubt, Shame	Toddlers discover that their actions are their own and enjoy independence, but they experience shame and doubt when corrected or criticized.
3 to 6 years	Initiative vs. Guilt	Children work hard to be responsible for their bodies, their toys, and their actions. When they are irresponsible or criticized, they may experience guilt.
6 to 12 years	Industry vs. Inferiority	Children do schoolwork, sports, household chores, and work toward achievement while fighting feelings of inferiority.
Adolescence	Identity vs. Role Confusion	Adolescents work to solidify a sense of identity.
Young adulthood	Intimacy vs. Isolation	Young adults struggle to form intimate relationships within which they can maintain their own identity. Failure to create intimate relationships results in isolation.
Middle age	Generativity vs. Stagnation	Generativity means helping the next generation become productive; stagnation means contributing little to the next generation.
Old age	Integrity vs. Despair	As older people look back on their lives, they either believe that the various crises were resolved well and that the whole picture of their lives has integrity or cohesion, or they believe that the crises were not resolved well and they experience feelings of despair and doom.

Source: Based on Erikson (1950).

As you can see in Table 3.1, each crisis or dilemma is an opportunity for increased potential and healthy development and decreased vulnerability. Each stage's crisis reflects a sense of struggle; in the resolution of each crisis, both of the options should be represented. For example, the infant should not feel that everyone could be trusted in every moment to meet every need. The toddler, while achieving increasing independence, must develop an understanding that his actions may have consequences that are hurtful or dangerous and that the feelings of shame and doubt can be good warning signals. The infant-toddler care teacher must be responsive while respecting that there is potential for growth in children's tolerable levels of struggle.

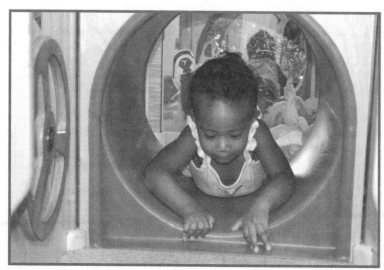

Toddlers enjoy challenges they can master alone.

The Hierarchy of Human Needs

Selma was a perceptive observer of the children in her care. She knew that trying to teach a crying 2-year-old was never a good idea. So when Joseph screamed over being wet and hungry after his nap, she comforted him. Later, in a quiet moment, she talked to him about how he might get up from his nap more comfortably tomorrow.

Selma is intuitively responding to Joseph through the **hierarchy of human needs** (Maslow, 1968). In an explanation of development that is somewhat different from Erikson's, Abraham Maslow looked at the research on human motivation and suggested that people are motivated to further their development because of needs that arise from deficiencies and desire for growth.

In the hierarchy of human needs, as shown in Figure 3.3, the needs that are lower in the figure, forming the foundation, must be met before the person even experiences the needs that are higher in the figure. So Joseph, experiencing physiological discomfort, had to achieve comfort in that area, which led him to feel safe again. Selma used her own ability to comfort him before she even began to appeal to his need for mastery—a way to consider waking up from nap tomorrow without screaming. In one way, the hierarchy does follow a path of human development. Young infants must first regulate their physiological needs, and then they develop a sense of safety in the world. As that sense of safety evolves, they feel a sense of love and belonging with the adult who keeps them safe. During preschool and school years, children work on mastery, gaining the skills and knowledge they will need in life. As people mature, they find self-fulfillment in marital relationships, in work and productivity, and in passing on their legacy to another generation.

hierarchy of human needs

Development proceeds in human beings in response both to basic needs being met and to needs for growth, the more basic needs having the priority.

Attachment Theory

Aurelia was always fascinated by the differences among her little toddler group in how they played. Ethan was calm and played well alone or with others, as long as she checked in periodically. Meredith was clingy but also resisted being comforted. Alicia seemed to play very independently, rarely looking at Aurelia—but she was distraught if Aurelia ever moved out of her line of sight. What was so interesting to Aurelia was that when these children greeted their parents in the evening, she saw echoes of this behavior.

attachment theory

Children need a relationship that provides safety and security in order for them to attend to learning and exploration.

Aurelia is seeing the three classic forms of behavior described in **attachment theory** (Ainsworth, Blehar, Waters, & Wall, 1978; Bowlby, 1982). These three children demonstrate how they use her presence to feel safe enough to play and explore. At the same time, they are showing her that they have had very different experiences with being kept safe by the adults in their lives. Attachment theory is further described in Chapter 6.

FIGURE 3.3 | **Maslow's hierarchy of human needs**

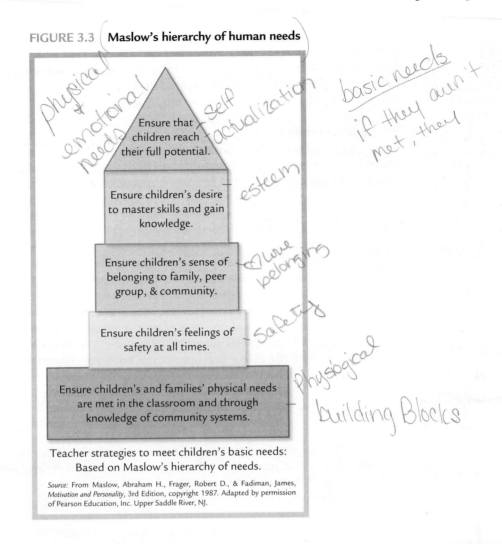

Ensure that children reach their full potential.

Ensure children's desire to master skills and gain knowledge.

Ensure children's sense of belonging to family, peer group, & community.

Ensure children's feelings of safety at all times.

Ensure children's and families' physical needs are met in the classroom and through knowledge of community systems.

Teacher strategies to meet children's basic needs: Based on Maslow's hierarchy of needs.

Source: From Maslow, Abraham H., Frager, Robert D., & Fadiman, James, *Motivation and Personality*, 3rd Edition, copyright 1987. Adapted by permission of Pearson Education, Inc. Upper Saddle River, NJ.

[Handwritten annotations: physical + emotional needs; self actualization; esteem; love belonging; safety; physiological; building blocks; basic needs if they aren't met, they]

Care teachers utilizing attachment theory in their work are responsive to infants and toddlers in ways that help them feel safe. They help young infants manage their own feelings and reactions to difficulties and help toddlers feel free to explore while gently assuring them of their safety.

Interpersonal Development Theory

At 6 months, Eli looks from his mother to his infant care teacher, clearly knowing each of them. On some level, he has an ongoing sense of what it is to be Eli with these two people he knows so well.

Stern (2000), a psychoanalyst and developmental psychologist, offers a theory of emotional development based on the past several decades of infancy research. Stern asserts that infants experience themselves as separate beings from birth, always working toward greater connection. He believes the child experiences moments in which he is aware of an internal and/or external experience. These moments become linked as memories or mental images. This *experience of being* occurs with a sense of self-agency (an ability to make things happen), a sense of

Watch this **video**, and consider how the infant is aware of internal and/or external experiences. How is the baby experiencing self-agency, a sense of self-coherence, and a sense of continuity?

self-coherence (awareness of being a complete, contained entity), and a sense of continuity (sensation of going-on-being). At the same time, the infant is aware of *being with other*—managing a sense of being a separate self with another person. Stern suggests that these are layered experiences that support one another. Rather than having stages of emotional development, he calls this *layered development*.

The infant-toddler care teacher utilizing the interpersonal development theory would understand the importance of each moment's experience to the infant. She would be responsive to his cues and know that he is building his model of being with people, in part, from his moments with her (Stern, 2000).

Theories of Cognitive Development: Learning About the World

Just as we have many perspectives on emotional development, many theories describe how children learn about the world. Many of these theories echo aspects of the theories of emotional development. They describe a developmental process, they divide that process into stages, and they recognize the importance of interested, available adults in supporting learning. The learning theories most closely aligned with the theoretical basis of this book are constructivist theory and sociocultural theory, each of which is briefly described here.

Constructivist Theory of Learning

constructivist theory
Children construct an understanding of the world through their play and interactions.

Over and over, 6-month-old Jeremiah would bang his little trucks together, suck on them, look at them, and toss them aside. He was always happy to see them on the play mat but didn't appear to look for them when his tossing landed them behind a larger toy and out of sight. At 9 months, however, if one of Jeremiah's trucks rolled out of his sight, he would crawl after it and retrieve it.

schema
A combination of ideas and actions that babies create in order to learn and explore.

assimilation
Using existing schemas to explore and understand new experiences.

accommodation
Developing new schemas to understand information when the established schemas are not adequate.

equilibrium
The point at which the mental image of the world seems to adequately explain the environmental information.

disequilibrium
The point at which the child's existing schemas or mental images are not adequate for understanding the environment.

Infant-toddler care teachers have many opportunities to observe how very young children keep making new discoveries about how the world works. In his **constructivist theory**, Swiss developmental psychologist Jean Piaget depicted infants and children as actively constructing their understanding of the world through their play and exploration (Piaget & Inhelder, 1969, 2000). The child develops **schemas**, mental structures of his current understanding of the world.

Piaget suggested that children first try to use their existing schemas to understand new information and new experiences. He called this process **assimilation**. At 6 months, Jeremiah uses the schemas of sucking, shaking, banging, and tossing with almost every object. If the schemas are not adequate to explain the information, the child creates new schemas to use in a process called **accommodation**. For example, when a child who is using grasping and looking as a way of understanding the world is given a small drum and a rounded stick, he may decide to try banging as a new method of exploring the two items together. Piaget used the term **equilibrium** to describe the moments when the child's schemas and the information presented are in balance. When the current schemas are not adequate for exploring or explaining new information, the child's mental organization is thrown into **disequilibrium**. The child then modifies his mental structures to accommodate the new information (Flavell, 1996).

TABLE 3.2   **Piaget's stages of cognitive development**

Stage	Age Range	Characteristics
Sensorimotor	Birth to 2 years	Child moves from using reflexes to using simple motor actions as means of exploration. Motor actions become increasingly intentional, they are combined into a series of actions, and the child increasingly develops expectations about the effect of his actions.
Preoperational	3 to 7 years	Children replace their earlier sensorimotor actions with symbols such as language and pretend play. The way children think about the world can be magical and illogical—for example, thinking they could float away down the bathtub drain just as the water in the tub does.
Concrete operations	7 to 11 years	Children develop logical understandings of concrete things.
Operational thinking	Early adolescence	A child can imagine a variety of solutions to a problem, can understand the abstractions of higher mathematics, and can begin to grapple with theoretical questions concerning deity or the meaning in life.

Source: From Piaget and Inhelder (1969, reprinted 2000).

Like several of the emotional development theorists, Piaget described cognitive development as a series of stages, as shown in Table 3.2. Each stage is a very different way of seeing and understanding the world.

The impact of Piaget's work on American early childhood education cannot be overstated. Piaget's image of children busily constructing their knowledge of reality has been the driving force in early childhood programs concentrating on creating learning environments to be explored. The assumption that children learn through exploration derives directly from his work. Interest in Piaget's basic theory of cognitive development has led researchers to more closely observe how children begin to think about themselves, how they think about relationships, and how they use different strategies to complete their goals.

Although his work far preceded the current research on brain development and early learning, Piaget did a great deal to establish the image of infants and toddlers as active learners. In fact, he broke down the first two years of life into six distinct substages of learning processes, describing the progression of infant learning from the first reflexive reactions to the world at birth, through the use of language and **symbolic representations** by age 2. As impressive as Piaget's contribution is to our understanding of children, his work is criticized on two points. First, research on learning and brain development in infancy suggests that Piaget greatly underestimated the young infant's ability to think—even to hypothesize about the possible outcomes of her actions. Second, the children Piaget writes about seem to discover all of their knowledge through their own exploration and construction. The role of culture and the impact of the other people in the children's lives are not identified within the learning process (Sutherland, 1992).

symbolic representation
The ability to use a symbol to stand for something else.

Despite these criticisms, constructionist theory continues to be a strong force in American education. Bruner extends Piaget's idea that learning is an active process in which learners construct new ideas or concepts based upon their current and past knowledge. Bruner's work incorporates the infancy research showing that the

mental model

Bruner's term for the cognitive schema, or mental image held by the child to organize and give meaning to information in the environment.

child selects and transforms information, constructs hypotheses, and makes decisions by relying on a cognitive structure to do so. The cognitive structure, whether called a schema or a **mental model**, provides meaning and organization to experiences and allows the individual to go beyond the information given. For Bruner, the role of the teacher is to provide opportunities for children to discover basic principles by themselves, although social and cultural influences are also at play. The teacher structures the information in ways that allow children to grasp it, understanding that they will continuously revisit the same information in greater depth as their capacity to understand deepens (Bruner, 1966, 1996b).

The infant-toddler care teacher who utilizes the constructivist theory of learning will provide a variety of interesting materials for infants and toddlers to manipulate and explore. She will understand that the child is motivated to learn, actively building an understanding of how people relate, and figuring out how the objects in the world work. She will support these discoveries through her relationship with the child.

Sociocultural Theory

Morris, at 7 months, enjoyed playing with trucks. He still sometimes mouthed them and threw them—but he also watched the older toddlers "driving" their trucks on a carpet with roads marked on it. Sophie, his care teacher, talked with him about his trucks. "Look at all your trucks Morris! Let's make sounds like trucks—rrrrr, rrrrr. This truck carries food to the store. Oh, look out the window—there are trucks on the street!"

The addition of the adult partner, or even the other children to watch, adds an important element to how children construct their knowledge about the world. Morris may be using schemas to learn about trucks, but he is also using the language of his care teacher. Vygotsky believed that adults and more knowledgeable peers teach culture, language, beliefs, customs, and highly valued activities to younger children. In fact, full cognitive development could not occur without social interaction. He describes how learning happens when children get *just enough* help and information from adults to allow them to figure out solutions to problems that are just beyond their reach independently, problems he describes as being in the **zone of proximal development**. For example, a 10-month-old baby who is playing with sounds becomes hungry and makes complaining noises to her teacher. Her teacher knows the baby is not ready to use words, but she is nearly ready. Word use is in her zone of proximal development. So the teacher supplies the word: "Bottle? You want a bottle?" The baby then makes a "Ba-ba" sound, demonstrating more skill in language with help (or **scaffolding**, to use Vygotsky's term) than she could do alone.

zone of proximal development

The difference between what the child can do with help and what the child can do without guidance.

scaffolding

The social and instructional guidance for students learning new concepts.

A second important contribution from Vygotsky was attention to the role of language in learning. Young children use the language of others—parents, care teachers, and peers—to help them develop new concepts. He believed that children also used language to guide and teach themselves in a way similar to that used by adults with children—for example, by naming objects and using words such as *dog* to classify and organize information.

A third, and perhaps most important, contribution from Vygotsky was his awareness of how knowledge is created, first in a cultural context on an interpersonal level and then on a personal level. A child's culture influences his belief, use of language, social attitudes and skills, and priorities.

The infant-toddler care teacher who utilizes a sociocultural approach will study the cultures of the children in his program and discuss cultural beliefs with the families. He will observe children to determine the children's zone of proximal development and will scaffold children's learning to guide them to learn the tools for how to solve problems. He will use rich, descriptive language to support children's ability to communicate and to organize their world.

Social Learning/ Cognitive Theory

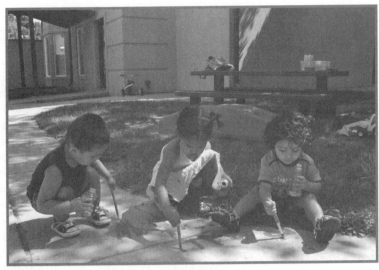

Children learn from their peers as well as from adults.

Social learning theory (Bandura, 1977) is now often referred to as social cognitive theory (Bandura, 1989, 2001) to recognize the importance of children's thinking abilities. Imitation is a primary way that young children learn and cultures are transmitted from one generation to another. Bandura emphasized how children decide who and when to imitate, showing that imitation is not a rote action but rather a decision-making process. Children learn through imitation, with reasons for imitating some people over others or objects. For example, 18-month-olds will not imitate an adult's actions if that adult says "Oh, no" after completing the task, as this indicates to the infant that the behavior is not one to imitate. Bandura (1997) emphasizes self-efficacy, the ability of humans to set goals, problem solve, and reflect. He also emphasizes that what children believe about how effective they are influences how they act.

This ability to make decisions about who and what to imitate is referred to by Gergely, Bekkering, and Király (2002) as "rational imitation." Gergely and Csibra (2006) also emphasize that "human infants are equipped with specialized cognitive resources that enable them to learn from infant-directed teaching" (p. 9). They tune into the cues of an adult; for example, by 15 months, they can imitate what an adult intended to do but failed (for some reason) to do (Bellagamba, Camaioni, & Colonnesi, 2006; Meltzoff, 1995).

An infant-toddler care teacher who knows social cognitive theory will observe how and what the children in the program observe and imitate. The care teacher will recognize that infants and toddlers can imitate adults' and peers' *goals* and *actions*. They will understand that a child's belief about his capabilities will influence how he behaves.

Core Knowledge Theory

Elizabeth Spelke, a cognitive psychologist, bases her core knowledge theory on the research on infant learning. This theory proposes that humans have evolved with inborn systems or brain structures ready to learn about those things necessary to survival. The four core knowledge systems address how infants learn about objects, agents, number, and geometry. The idea of separate knowledge systems refutes the belief that learning happens through one "general purpose device" (Spelke & Kinzler, 2007, p. 91). Core knowledge also emphasizes the importance of social interactions that provide the content of what and how much children learn in the different systems.

The core system of *object representation* allows human infants to "perceive object boundaries, to represent the complete shapes of objects that move partly or fully out of view, and to predict when objects will move and where they will come to rest" (Spelke & Kinzler, 2007, p. 89). For example, young babies (4 to 5 months old) will react as an object approaches, demonstrating an understanding that objects that move toward them may hit them (Schmuckler, Collimore, & Dannemiller, 2007). The core system of *agents* (persons and animals) allows infants to recognize goal-directed actions of living things. For example, at 10 to 11 months of age, an infant will follow an adult's head turning if the adult has her eyes open, but not if the adult's eyes are closed (Brooks & Meltzoff, 2005). The core system of *number* has its own limits and principles. An infant will look surprised if two objects move behind a curtain but only one object comes out the other side (Wynn, 1992). Jordan and Brannon (2006) found that 6- to 8-month-olds looked at a video with the number of adults that matched the number of voices they were hearing. The fourth system is *geometry of the environment*. It allows children and adults to orient themselves in relation to places in the environment. We've all seen infants who quickly learn how to crawl down a hallway, into the bedroom through one door and out the other, confidently orienting themselves in the environment.

The core knowledge theory suggests an inborn ability to learn about what is most important for survival. It suggests that different information is needed for different aspects of survival and that humans have developed structures in the brain to attend to that information.

Theories of Language Development

Kuhl's Perceptual Mapping Model

perceptual mapping

Capacity for figuring out (mapping) the rules of language.

Today, Patricia Kuhl, a leading researcher in language acquisition, proposes a model of language acquisition called **perceptual mapping**. This theory is consistent with a constructionist theory of learning and a relationship-based theory of development. The basic premise of how infants learn language is that infants are able to figure out the structure of language in the first year of life before they can speak (Kuhl, 2000).

Kuhl emphasizes that in the first year of life, infants are more capable then many have thought. They can break down the language they hear to determine the critical aspects of that language and determine patterns. They are able to predict which sounds in their primary language generally follow each other. Infants are able to figure out the likelihood of when words will start and end by attending to how often certain combinations of sounds are likely to occur within words or between words. They learn which syllables in words in the language they are hearing are usually stressed and by 9 months prefer the patterns they hear in their language to patterns in other languages. They "map" the major components of language—sounds, words, intonation, and rules for how language is constructed. Infants can also discriminate non-language-related sounds, so this ability may not have evolved specifically for speech.

According to Kuhl (2000), experience with hearing language changes *how* infants hear language. Infants map the most commonly heard language sounds in their brain. When they hear similar sounds, these are drawn (as though by a magnet) to that same part of the brain to be stored. As infants, they are able to hear and discriminate the sounds (auditory processing) of every language in the world, but by 12 months they hear only the differences between sounds they have heard frequently.

Learning to speak a language requires hearing it spoken and hearing oneself making the sounds of the language. Many parents around the world use a high-pitched, exaggerated, simplified form of language called "parentese" in speaking directly to young infants. It includes using new words repeatedly and with many examples. This exaggerated form of language is also called "child-directed speech" (Thiessen, Hill, & Saffran, 2005) because it is directed at the child and functions to help the child learn speech and language. Young children need this experience with responsive adults to learn to speak a language.

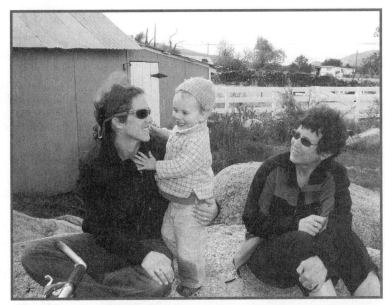

Infants and toddlers learn language through pleasant and interesting social interactions.

The infant-toddler care teacher utilizing the perceptual mapping theory will recognize that for the infant, learning language is an active, relationship-based process. She will use parentese with young infants, speak to the infant or toddler frequently throughout the day, and read to the child, providing rich language experiences.

Social Interaction Theory

Other language researchers emphasize how the social environment interacts with biology to influence language development rather than emphasizing specific innate language structures (Johnson, 2005). *Social interaction theory* of language development incorporates Vygotsky's **sociocultural theory** and emphasizes that infants and toddlers need (1) responsive interactions with adults to learn a language and (2) opportunities to communicate. This theory argues that it is important not only for a child to hear language but also that the adults speaking the language are responsive and engage infants in baby conversations—responding to sounds, wiggles, and words as an infant's contribution to a conversation. This helps infants learn *how* to engage in a conversation—with turn taking, pauses, and listening.

sociocultural theory

Learning is embedded within social events and occurs as a child interacts with people, objects, and events in the environment.

Care Teachers who emphasize *social interaction theory* will recognize that infants are active learners who co-construct language with adults, as they adjust their language in order to be understood. Care Teachers will constantly listen for children's yawns, sounds, and words and respond in order to engage a young child in a conversation. They will give the child many opportunities to express herself, making mistakes but constantly learning how to engage in human communication.

A Theory of Motor Development: Learning to Move

Niko was a good crawler. He safely crawled around the room, up and down the three steps to the little climbing structure and even up and down the low slide. His care teacher was surprised, when he first started walking, that he would step right off the 5-inch platform of the cozy area and fall on his nose! What happened to his good judgment about moving in space?

The traditional theory of motor development proposes an ages and stages progression of locomotor abilities that flow as the child's neuromuscular system matures (Gesell, 1946). Today, however, movement is understood as a process of learning, or as Karen Adolph (2008) puts it, "learning to learn to move" (p. 217). Movement requires the infant or toddler to overcome gravity, have the strength to support her own weight, and balance and coordinate body parts. It also requires the child to readjust to constantly changing skills, size, and environments. Adolph suggests that the skills and judgment needed moment to moment in movement require the child to "learn to learn" rather than to learn one particular solution. For instance, knowing how to maneuver down a small slope while *crawling* does not give the child the knowledge of how to *walk* down that same slope a month later. Niko, in the previous vignette, cannot call upon his knowledge of crawling and slopes to keep him safe as a new walker. He has to take in new information, adjusting it to his current posture and mode of locomotion and learn how to solve the problem of walking down a slope.

The infant-toddler care teacher who utilizes the learn to learn to move theory understands that each new posture requires new learning on the part of the infant or toddler as to how to move in the world. She would provide lots of opportunities for movement but understands that with each new posture, the child would need to learn again how to move in the environment. She would offer opportunities and encouragement but know that she needs to be vigilant about safety as infants and toddlers are constantly learning new ways to move.

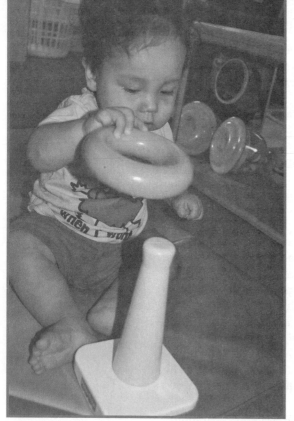

Find toys for young children that encourage a child to "learn to learn."

Applying Theories in Programs

Although most early childhood development and education programs in America are based on the theoretical approaches described in this chapter, we are more likely to know them by names such as *developmentally based* or *relationship based*. Most of these programs use the stage models of development and the constructionist and sociocultural theories, although their applications differ in terms of environments, learning activities, and the role of the care teacher.

Child Development Programs

Most infant and toddler programs would identify themselves as being developmentally based and would reflect an understanding of attachment theory; of child development theories derived from Erikson, Piaget, and Vygotsky; and of the brain research of the past two decades. If you visited a high-quality, developmentally based program, you would see many things happening. Attachment theory would be evident in that each care teacher would have primary responsibility for a small group of babies and would provide their care for a long period of time, preferably the first 3 years of life. The care teacher and parents would have a close partnership in which each would support the other's understanding of and affection for the baby. Erikson's theory would be most evident in how teachers support the early development of a sense of self. With infants, the care teachers would be highly responsive as they support the child's development of trust. With toddlers, teachers may consciously pull back, encouraging children to explore their environment and develop autonomy while still being physically and emotionally available to meet the toddlers' needs.

Piaget's theory of cognitive development would be evident in how care teachers follow the interests of the child and provide a variety of books, small toys, mirrors, and appropriate large motor experiences for the infant or toddler to explore. The materials would be likely to offer information on basic cognitive concepts such as object permanence or cause and effect. Vygotsky's theory of sociocultural development would be evident in the way the teacher interacts with the children and families and in the many symbols of the culture in the room. There would be posters showing "our community" and dramatic play materials that replicate the kitchen and workroom equipment used in the children's own households. Teachers would adjust the language they use and the type and amount of help they give children according to the child's ability to accomplish the task at hand.

Relationship-Based Programs

Although every early care and development program probably values relationships, programs based on relationship theory would have some recognizable features. A relationship-based program would create a structure of care teachers schedules and group sizes that would provide opportunities for relationships to develop over time. A primary caregiver would be assigned to each child, and small groups of children would stay together with the same teacher from infancy to preschool (Lally et al., 1995). Friendships between children would be nurtured and honored (Wittmer, 2008). Adults would model caring, responsive, thoughtful relationships with children and with other adults (Edwards & Raikes, 2002). Teachers and families would communicate regularly to ensure a consistent caregiving experience for each child.

Care and attention would be given to the development of secure, affectionate attachment relationships and to the expression and understanding of emotional experiences.

Summary

Theories are explanations of information, observations, and life experiences. The theoretical foundation of this book encompasses ecobiodevelopmental theory, relationship-based theory, transactional theory, and bioecological systems theory.

- Ecobiodevelopmental theory
  - Early experiences affect the architecture of the brain.
  - Chronic stress is damaging to the developing brain.
  - Interventions can support the developing brain.
- Relationship-based theory
  - Infants and toddlers do not exist as separate entities but as part of social networks.
  - Infants and toddlers require meaningful, supportive, enduring relationships.
  - Relationships differ on a number of dimensions, and intimacy, reciprocity, and commitment are important factors in determining the quality and usefulness of a relationship.
- Transactional theory
  - Relationships are bidirectional: Adults affect children and vice versa.
  - Transactions include the baby's behavior or appearance as a stimulus, the meaning given by the adult to the baby's behavior, and the adult's response.
  - Relationships that are troubled may be responsive to intervention at any of three points: the baby by remediation, the meaning by redefinition, and the response by reeducation.

- Bioecological systems theory
  - Development can be affected by many levels of relationships, from close family all the way to national policies.
  - All systems affect one another.

The theories of emotional development and cognitive development are constantly evolving. Some theories that are important today include the following:

- Theory of psychosocial development: Erikson's stages of emotional development characterized by crises that need to be resolved
- The hierarchy of human needs: Maslow's description of human motivation
- Attachment theory: Bowlby's and Ainsworth's descriptions of organizational systems that allow us to explore and learn while remaining safe and protected
- Interpersonal theory: Stern's description of how infants develop a sense of self and a sense of self with others
- Constructivism: Piaget's stages of cognitive development
- Sociocultural theory: Vygotsky's processes of learning through exploration, relationships, and culture
- Core knowledge: Spelke's theory of four innate systems of knowledge that form a foundation for learning
- Perceptual mapping: Kuhl's theory of language acquisition build on decoding the structure of language
- Learning to move: Adolph's theory of movement as a learning process

Key Terms

accommodation
assimilation
attachment theory
chronosystem
constructivist theory
disequilibrium
ecobiodevelopmental
epigenetics

equilibrium
exosystem
hierarchy of human needs
macrosystem
mental model
mesosystem
microsystem
perceptual mapping

relationship-based theory
scaffolding
schema
sociocultural theory
symbolic representation
theory of psychosocial
    development
zone of proximal development

Reflections and Resources for the Reader

REFLECTIONS

1. In your own life, using Bronfenbrenner's bioecological systems theory, fill in the circles of the system. It is probably obvious to you that your family and closest friends, your care teachers and your employers affect your life. However, you may see new connections between yourself and the people or groups in the exosystem and macrosystem of your own ecological system.
2. From your readings, observations, and experiences with infants and toddlers, can you describe your own theory of how children develop?

OBSERVATION AND APPLICATION OPPORTUNITIES

1. Visit an infant-toddler child care program. From your observation of the environment and the interactions, how would you describe the theory of child development being practiced? What do the people in this program believe influences the development of a child?
2. In observing adults and children together, you may see one adult treating children differently from one another. Transactional theory suggests the child's characteristics are affecting the interaction. Are you able to observe differences in infants or toddlers that are influencing the responses of adults?

SUPPLEMENTARY ARTICLES AND BOOKS TO READ

Capuozzo, R. M., Sheppard, B. S., & Uba, G. (2010). Boot camp for new dads: The importance of infant-father attachment. *Young Children 65* (3): 24–28.

Quan-McGimpsey, S., Kuczynski, L., & Brophy, K. (2011). Early education teachers' conceptualizations and strategies for managing closeness in child care: The personal domain. *Journal of Early Childhood Research, 9*, 232–246. (Example of transactional theory)

INTERESTING LINKS

www.childstudy.net/tutorial.php
The Child Development Website: *Classic Theories of Child Development* ChildStudy.net offers an overview of the classical child development theorists and a month-by-month description of child development, relating each month to the developmental phases proposed by the classic theorists—Freud, Mahler, and Erikson.

www.ncrel.org/sdrs/areas/issues/students/earlycld/ea7lk18.htm
Theories of Child Development and Learning The Web site of the North Central Regional Educational Laboratory includes a link to a short paper titled "Theories of Child Development and Learning," describing maturational, environmental, and developmental perspectives.

http://www.earlychildhoodnews.com/earlychildhood/article_view.aspx?ArticleID=411
Theories of Child Development: Building Blocks Blocks of Developmentally Appropriate Practice. Terri Jo Swim. Article in Early Childhood News describes the connection of theory and DAP.

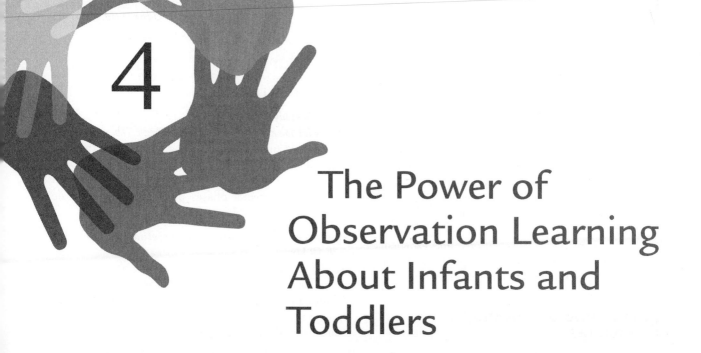

4

The Power of Observation Learning About Infants and Toddlers

LEARNING OUTCOMES

After reading this chapter, you will be able to:

- Explain why observation is an important skill for early childhood professionals
- Explain the ethical considerations of observation
- Describe on what a teacher might learn by observing an infant or toddler
- Use a variety of methods for observation and recording

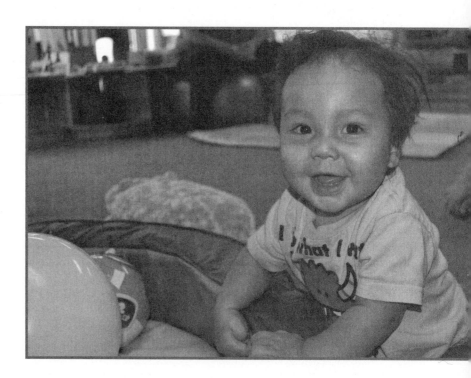

Patty thought to herself that if LaNita had one more tantrum she would throw herself on the floor and join her in the screaming! Patty felt as if LaNita had tantrums almost nonstop. When the behavior consultant from the Child Care Resource and Referral office came in to help, he began by observing and recording the tantrums. To Patty the day seemed like a typical one with LaNita tantruming many times, but to her amazement, there were only four tantrums. Patty realized that she spent the entire day dreading, tolerating, and recovering from the tantrums.

Sometimes our own reactions to events affect our ability to understand the meaning of the event for the child. Patty found LaNita's tantrums so upsetting that she felt they went on all day. An objective observation by the behavior consultant helped her see that LaNita had a limited number of tantrums and that each lasted less than 5 minutes. Together, Patty and the behavior consultant analyzed his notes and discovered that most of LaNita's tantrums occurred when both care teachers in the room were busy responding to the immediate needs of other children and couldn't help LaNita in the moment. When one of the care teachers was on the floor where the children were playing, LaNita rarely lost control. Patty and the behavior consultant used the observation to make a plan to ensure the children always had enough adult attention.

Observing—A Powerful Skill

This chapter covers how theories influence what is important to observe, ethical considerations, and many methods of observing and recording the observations that are available for students of child development, care teachers, and families, along with guidance on how to choose the best method for the purpose of the observation. We end the chapter with how effective observation also involves awareness of the observer's own reactions and biases. This chapter sets the stage for the use of strategies that readers can use as they move through the next 12 chapters—to see children in new ways and to be able to interpret their actions and reactions, the exciting ways they learn, their many emotions, and their individual interests.

Why Observation Is Important

Observation is one of the most powerful skills for learning more about infants and toddlers. Observation provides opportunities to learn about an individual child's interests, development, and perspectives. Families use this information to plan experiences at home, and care teachers use it to plan curriculum that is responsive to the child's interests and goals. Shared from observations at home and in a program, information guides how a care teacher, early interventionist, or family member interacts with a child as well as needed changes in the child's routines, guidance, and environment.

When teachers and families thoughtfully observe infants and toddlers and share their observations with each other, they deepen their awareness and appreciation of children's ongoing, meaningful discoveries. For example, when professionals and parents observe an infant's strategies for communicating, they may be in awe of the many gestures, sounds, and facial expressions that the infant uses to communicate. Adults not only begin to see *a* child differently, but they may also see the capabilities of *all children* differently. This knowledge may change the way adults value children's communication efforts and inspire the adults to respond to infants as budding communicators. Through observation, we understand the process of learning as well as how children may be challenged and when they need special support.

Most important, observation and documentation methods allow care teachers and other professionals to build relationships with children and families: "Observing helps you build relationships by revealing the uniqueness of every child—including the child's temperament, strengths, personality, work style, and preferred mode of expression" (Jablon, Dombro, & Dichtelmiller, 1999, p. 9). When a child feels understood, the relationship grows. When family members know that a teacher understands their child, teacher-family relationships develop as well.

The Ethics of Observing

Adults who are with young children want to do the right thing by behaving ethically. Ethical considerations influence observation and documentation, as they do every aspect of working with young children and families. These range from the professional guidance on ethical behavior from the National Association for the Education of Young Children (NAEYC) and the Division for Early Childhood (DEC) of the Council for Exceptional Children (CEC) to the basic common sense of being respectful. Ethical considerations include having permission to observe and record observations of a child, the parent's right to see records, maintaining confidentiality, and how the care teacher writes and talks about children.

Observation and recording by the care teacher is a solid tradition of early childhood education. NAEYC's Code of Ethical Conduct (2005) and DEC's Position Statement: Code of Ethics (2009) do not directly name observation, but specific statements should guide one's actions in doing observations. The overriding principle in NAEYC's Code of Ethical Conduct (2005) states:

> P-1.1—Above all, we shall not harm children. We shall not participate in practices that are emotionally damaging, physically harmful, disrespectful, degrading, dangerous, exploitative, or intimidating to children. This principle has precedence over all others in this Code.

How could observations be harmful? Observation recordings may attribute unkind intentions to a child's actions or ridicule or demean the child, her family, or her culture. The purpose of observation should always be to achieve a deeper understanding of the child: never to prove there is something wrong with the child.

Conducting observations and sharing them with families can serve the following principles from the NAEYC Code:

> P-1.5—We shall use appropriate assessment systems, which include multiple sources of information, to provide information on children's learning and development.
> P-1.7—We shall strive to build individual relationships with each child; make individualized adaptations in teaching strategies, learning environments, and curricula; and consult with the family so that each child benefits from the program.

This principle goes on to describe the possible need for additional supports or another placement. In addition, the DEC Code of Ethics (2008) states:

> III. 7. We shall be responsible for protecting the confidentiality of the children and families we serve by protecting all forms of verbal, written, and electronic communication.

During a program's enrollment process, teachers should inform families that observations are part of the program and explain which recordings will be kept confidential and which might be shared publicly. For example, an observation method called *time sampling* to track biting would be kept confidential, but photo panel documentations with photos and captions are often posted on the wall for the children, families, and visitors to enjoy and appreciate what and how children are learning. The purpose of observation and documentation may be explained through a permission to observe form as seen in Figure 4.1.

FIGURE 4.1   Sample permission form

Observation Permission Form

Date: _____

Name of Child: _____

*Name of Program, Agency, or Person Requesting Permission: _____

_____

Dear Parent or Guardian, Please complete the remainder of this form and return it to

_____

I give permission for my child _____
to be observed for educational purposes. These observations can be written, photographic, or electronic (video or computer). I understand that these observations may be displayed or used in the program or in educational settings to provide insight to teachers, parents, family members, and children into how children think and learn. My child's first name may be used unless I refuse by writing a note to that effect at the bottom of this page.

I understand that I may decide to refuse permission at any time and I understand that all observations will be available for me to review at any time.

Date Signed _____

Name of Parent/Guardian (print) _____

Signature of Parent/Guardian _____

Address _____

City_____

Zip Code _____

Phone (Home) _____ (Work or Cell) _____

*Review the legality of this form with the program or agency for which you are doing the observation.

What Can We Learn?

In the book *The Power of Observation*, Jablon and colleagues (1999) define observation as "watching to learn." They go on to say, "We learn about children by watching them, listening to them, and studying their work. Watching and listening to children helps us understand what they are feeling, learning, and thinking" (p. 1).

What else can we learn by watching and listening to children? We can learn about how the child behaves and feels within different relationships. We learn about the stages of development (e.g., how a child coos before he says words), but we also learn about the *quality* of development (how a specific child uses communication, to whom he talks, the words he says, and the feelings expressed). We also learn the following:

- How infants and toddlers think and learn
- What they are feeling and how they regulate their emotions
- How they use their bodies
- Their interests and what they especially enjoy
- How they relate to others
- Their challenges
- Their many skills
- The strategies children use to accomplish their goals
- The interactions, materials, equipment, and toys to make available to children to encourage engagement, participation, and relationships

As can be seen from the list, you might choose to observe many areas. Sometimes it is helpful to try to capture everything that a child says and does for a time period, and at other times to choose a behavior, such as smiling, and record evidence of only that behavior. At other times, you may want to observe what the children in a group are learning from playing with certain materials such as water. As you observe, you will begin to see infants' and toddler's behavior and interests in new ways.

Observers who study child development learn to observe the intricacies of infants' and toddlers' attitudes and behavior. For example, a classic study demonstrated how toddler hitting may have different meanings depending on how the toddler hits (Brownlee & Bakeman, 1981). An open or low-intensity hit or a swipe at the body of another toddler might mean "Leave me alone." When a toddler hits another child with an object in the hand in a low-intensity way, the behavior could mean "Hey, wanna play?" A hard hit, on the other hand, seems to mean "I don't like that" and is more likely than other hits to provoke a negative response from the other toddler. Once an observer knows that toddlers may understand hitting differently than adults do, the adults see toddler hitting differently.

The observant teacher sees moments of kindness.

How to Observe and Record Observations

There are many established methods of conducting and recording an observation. This section presents the steps for the use of anecdotal records and running records, event sampling, charts and diagrams, and documentation with infants and toddlers. Observation may also be used to create a portfolio for each child—a collection of care teacher and family observations and the child's own creations such as scribbles on a piece of paper.

With each of the following methods, you will want to begin recording the observation with a cover page that has space for

- The child's name
- Age
- Date of observation
- Setting
- The name of the person conducting the observation

If the observations are placed in a portfolio, then families and other team members will appreciate the additional information.

Anecdotal Records and Running Records

Anecdotal records and running records are written accounts of children's actions and typically include comments that are written after reviewing a number of the observations.

Anecdotal Records

Anecdotal records are short accounts of children's behavior written while or soon after the behavior occurs. They describe what happened in a factual way and include when and where it happened. They are usually brief descriptions that the care teacher writes in an objective manner. Descriptions that are objective are factual and do not include the observer's opinions or feelings about the child's behavior. With practice, the adult captures the child's behavior with words that help someone who is reading the record visualize what the child was doing. Often, after capturing the child's actions objectively in the left-hand column of a page, the comments based on the observation, called interpretations or **inferences**, are written in the right-hand column.

Inferences are conclusions that the observer draws from the objective observation. For example, if a toddler was observed throwing dandelions into a stream and watching the current carry them away, the observer might *infer* that the child was learning about the properties of water and movement. She could objectively observe his motions, but she is inferring the intentions and mental processes that drive his motions. As a care teacher records an observation, he may ask, "Is the child watching the current or is he just enjoying the movement of the flowers?" "Is he experimenting or are his actions random?" The teacher may write his questions and/or several possible inferences in the right-hand column. After several observations, the teacher might see a pattern in the child's behavior.

Anecdotal records may focus on behavior that represents the concepts explored by the child, such as how objects fit into containers; specific domains of development, such as the social domain; or behavior that is of special

anecdotal records
Short accounts of children's behavior written while or soon after the behavior occurs that describe what happened in a factual way.

inferences
Conclusions that an observer draws from interpretation of objective observation.

FIGURE 4.2 **Sample anecdotal record**

Anecdotal Observation of Nicholas (2y–9m)
Observer: Michelle
Date: 6/1/13
Place: Play yard

Sequence	Inference
Nicholas and the other toddlers in my group took off their socks and shoes to wade in our stream.	
Nicholas watched the water moving downstream in a little current.	Nicholas appeared to notice the movement of the water.
He dropped a dandelion from his hand into the stream and watched as the current took it away.	Dropping the dandelion looked accidental and he seemed surprised by the water carrying it away.
He picked a few more and threw them into the water that was carrying the dandelions.	He seemed to be trying to understand how the water carried the dandelions.
Picked up a plastic container and splashed water with it.	
Took container onto grass and half-filled it with dandelion flowers.	He seemed to be very purposeful in collecting the flowers.
Returned to stream and emptied dandelions into stream, watching current take them away. Smiled, pointed, and yelled, "Look. Look."	He seems to be testing his hypothesis about water, currents, and dandelions. His "Look" was a toddler "Eureka!"

interest, such as challenging behavior. See Figure 4.2 for an example of an anecdotal record. Note how the actions in Figure 4.2 that are written in the left column are objective and the notes in the right column are interpretations of the records.

To use anecdotal records to focus on a particular area of development of a child, such as fine motor development, record a number of short observations over a time period, such as 4 months. See Figure 4.3 for an example of a series of anecdotal records of a toddler's ability to grasp that was observed during lunchtime once a month for 4 months and the inferences drawn from these observations. After sharing the information with the family, both the care teacher and the mother expressed surprise at how LaDon's fine motor abilities had developed in such a short time.

Watch the **video**, *Mobile Infant with a Stacking Toy.* Write an anecdotal record or running record, paying attention to how the child changes strategies to accomplish his goal of placing the ring on the spool.

running records

Observations that require recording a child's behavior as it happens with descriptive language. They are generally longer and more detailed than anecdotal records.

Running Records

Running records are written observations that capture the details and sequence of children's behavior. They are typically longer than anecdotal records. Running records could be used, for example, if the observer wants to capture a child's behavior for 10 minutes on the playground. A care teacher used the running record in Figure 4.4 to learn more about Paul's level of play, when he interacted with peers, and how he interacted with them.

When writing running records, try to write exactly what the children are doing and saying. Try to describe movements, facial expressions, and gestures.

FIGURE 4.3 **Sample anecdotal record of a child's fine motor development**

Anecdotal Record
Name of Child: LaDon
Age of Child: See below
Setting: Fine motor development—several observations
Observer: Marvin

Behavior	Inference
7/15/12 (7m) High chair Picks up softened cereal "O's" with raking motion—using all of her fingers without much help from the thumb.	She has an intent look as if she is really working hard.
8/14/12 (8m) High chair Picks up softened cereal "O's" with a scissors grasp—using her thumb with her fingers.	In one month she moved from using a raking grasp to a scissors grasp. She still looks very intent when she is accomplishing a task.
9/15/12 (9m) High chair Picks up cereal "O's" with a pincer grasp—using her thumb and first finger only.	Again, in a month she has progressed to using a pincer grasp. She seems to like fine-motor and hand-eye coordination tasks.
10/15/12 (10m) High chair Picks up cereal "O's" with a pincer grasp. She picks up the cereal "O's" one by one and puts each one in her mouth.	She easily picks up the "O's" and as she picks them up, she often smiles as if she is really enjoying herself. We will need to provide safe eye-hand coordination activities each day as she really seems proud of herself and very interested.

Describe exactly what the children say to each other without making inferences. Inferences are written after reviewing one or more running records.

Running records require practice to write a continuous stream of behavior. Immediately after the observation, the observer can review the record and add more details.

After reading several running records on Paul, the teachers recognized how important active play and movement are to him. They expanded the large motor area in the room and the time outdoors. The teachers also noticed that Paul had a great interest in Derrick (and Derrick in Paul), so the care teachers sat them beside each other at lunch.

Care teachers, early interventionists, and students have developed creative ways of observing with anecdotal and running records. They

- Use sticky notes or index cards kept in a pocket of an apron or clothing.
- Use a sheet of address labels on a clipboard, writing an anecdote on one or more labels.
- Schedule times during the day when one teacher will observe while other teachers interact with the children.

FIGURE 4.4   **Sample running record**

Name of Child: Paul
Date: 12/17/12
Age of Child: 20 months
Setting: Outdoors

Sequence	Inference
At outdoor time, Paul ran out the door to the play yard.	Paul seems intent on running the minute he is outside. He can hardly wait to get through the door.
For 3 minutes, Paul ran all around the yard, looking at his feet or just ahead of his feet as he ran.	He seems to need to run—maybe to burn off energy.
	Paul looks content but serious as he is running.
Derrick (about 2 feet away) called "Paul" as Paul ran by him. Paul did not look at Derrick. After 3 minutes, with a smile on his face, Paul ran back to Derrick. He said "Trucks" to Derrick and sat on the hill, joining Derrick. Paul pushed a truck for approximately 2 feet using both hands while he kneeled on the ground. He then turned to Derrick and said "Trucks" again. Derrick looked at Paul and began pushing his truck.	He joins his friend after he runs, while still enjoying active play.

We need to continue observing Paul to see whether active play helps him self-regulate and focus. |

Watch the first minute ten seconds of the video, *Designing Developmentally Appropriate Days*. Create an event sampling to record the number and types of social interactions of children.

event sampling

Observation of an event that has been defined in advance and what happens before and after, recorded briefly while it is taking place.

Event Sampling

Observers, such as care teachers and parents, use **event sampling** to record and analyze the nature of certain events. The collection of information about events, such as hitting incidents, usually begins with a question, such as "When, where, and how does the child hit others?" (see Figure 4.5). Observers may also question the frequency, or how *often*, a child exhibits a particular behavior. Next, an observer decides when to observe the behavior. Perhaps the hitting behavior primarily occurs when the toddler is outside in a family child care setting. An observer might begin to observe in that setting. The observer then describes the incident as soon as possible after a hitting event with detailed information to answer the question (after responding to the situation of course).

After several of these events, the observer(s) might see a pattern of the child hitting when other children are moving in too closely to the child or when he is tired or before lunch when he is hungry. As shown in Figure 4.5, a teacher concluded that Grace, who doesn't have language yet, doesn't like it when another child moves in too closely to her and doesn't have words to tell the other child. A care teacher stayed close to Grace for several days to try to support her to use sign language for STOP when another child came too close. The teacher continued conducting event sampling to see if the intervention worked to decrease hitting. Observing before, during, and after an intervention is planned and implemented gives adults valuable information about which intervention might be helpful to the child and would reduce the number of aggressive behaviors.

FIGURE 4.5   **Sample event sampling focusing on hiting events**

Event Sampling					
Child's Name: Grace Child's Age: 19 months Observer/teacher: Tom Behavior to observe: Hitting Define the behavior: Bringing a hand or tool in contact with someone in a way that causes harm or distress					
Date Time	**Setting**	**What Happened Prior to the Event?**	**Event**	**What Happened Following the Event?**	**Duration**
2/18/13 9:10 a.m.	Breakfast	Sam pushed his chair close.	Grace hit him on arm.	Tom checked Sam's arm—talked to Grace.	1 min
2/19/13 10:05 a.m.	Play time	Sarah sat on Grace's legs.	Grace hit Sarah's arm.	Tom checked Sarah. Talked firmly to Grace.	1.5 min
2/22/13 11:06 a.m.	Play time	Matt took Grace's toy.	Grace hit Matt's arm.	Tom took care of Matt. Laura talked to Grace.	1 min

A second type of event sampling is shown in Figure 4.6. An observer may want to study a class of behaviors such as those that intentionally hurt others—often called aggressive behavior—to determine how often they occur (a frequency count). First, the observer (or observers) defines the term *aggressive behavior* in specific terms. An observer might discuss the following questions with teammates:

- Does *aggressive behavior* include hitting, biting, and yelling at another child?
- Does it include the child biting teachers as well as peers?
- Does the behavior need to seem intentional?

To obtain accurate observations, observers must be clear about these definitions.

The care teachers who studied this event sampling learned that the child uses aggressive behaviors with peers rather than teachers (at this time); hits, bites, and pushes; and hits with a closed fist, which is more likely to cause the victim to retaliate. The next step would be to observe with the event sampling demonstrated in Figure 4.5 to learn what might be triggering the behaviors in the immediate context. The care teacher can observe further and discuss the observations with the child's parents concerning the child's experience with trust and feelings of security (Erikson), the child's thinking about how to interact with peers (Piaget), whom the child may be imitating (Bandura), the child's sociocultural experiences (Vygotsky), and what strategies scaffold the child's success in social situations (Vygotsky). Event sampling can be repeated before and after care teachers and families implement strategies that increase prosocial behavior and decrease aggressive behavior to determine whether the strategies used are successful.

Charts

An interesting way to observe and document children's choice of activity and their behavior is the use of charts. Care teachers and others interested in observing children often use time sampling.

FIGURE 4.6 **Sample event sampling of aggressive behavior**

Child's Name: Melikia
Child's Age: 22 months
Date: 9/10/12
Observer: Mia

Behavior/Time Event Occurs	Tally (Object of Behavior)
Hit with open hand	Peer: II
	Teacher:
Hit with closed fist	Peer: I
	Teacher:
Hit with an object	Peer: II
	Teacher:
Bite	Peer: II
	Teacher:
Push	Peer: I
	Teacher:

Time sampling involves developing a chart that is used to observe children's behavior at designated times (see Figure 4.7). For example, a care teacher might want to observe to determine how many children are using particular areas of the room and if there are any areas that are not being used by the children. The information will help the teacher develop an environment that infants and toddlers truly enjoy.

After studying the **time sampling** in Figure 4.7, the care teachers could see that the housekeeping/dramatic play area was not used and the toddlers did not engage in any games that they or the teacher created from 9:00 to 9:30 a.m. Also, a child or several children were wandering in four out of the seven observations. After several time samplings with similar results, the teachers began to watch for children who were wandering to try to help them make a choice of an activity or be with the teacher, and they added empty boxes of food to the housekeeping area to see if that sparked any children's interest. Observing provided important information to the care teachers on patterns of behavior that were not easily observed while the teachers were naturally very busy staying near or being with the toddlers. Figure 4.8 provides an example of time sampling with a focus on a child.

After reviewing Figure 4.8, the care teachers realized how often Letty is isolated from both peers and teachers. The teachers asked whether this behavior occurs because the child chooses to play away from others or because the child is being rejected by others. This led to further investigation with running records and event sampling. Note that the time sampling did not reveal how many minutes the child played beside another child or alone. It did reveal what Letty was doing at the designated times she was observed.

time sampling

Developing a chart that is used to observe children's behavior at designated times.

FIGURE 4.7   **Time sampling of toddlers: 8 toddlers/2 care teachers**

Activity/Time	9:00	9:05	9:10	9:15	9:20	9:25	9:30
Wandering—no obvious aim				1	1	1	1
Moving from one area/teacher to another	1	2		1			
Water			2	3	3	1	1
Painting	2	2	1	1	2	2	2
Housekeeping							
Manipulative	2	3	2		1	1	1
Construction							
Active Area	2	1	2		1	3	2
With a Care Teacher	1		1				1
Involved with game—such as musical chairs—created by the children or teacher							

FIGURE 4.8   **Time sampling: Focus on a child**

Activity/Time	10:00	10:15	10:30	10:45	11:00	11:15	11:30
Playing beside another child	1						
Playing alone—no child within 3 feet			1	1		1	1
With a care teacher with other children		1					
With a care teacher without other children					1		

Documentation

Documentation is more than record keeping. It is a special way of observing that records children's experiences through a variety of media for use in analyzing and understanding their construction of knowledge (Gandini & Goldhaber, 2001). Often documentation includes a series of photos, video recordings, and other *visual* means that are displayed to communicate the remarkable process of

documentation

Recording of children's experiences through a variety of media for use in analyzing and understanding their construction of knowledge.

how infants and toddlers learn. Documentation frames your understanding of children and your work as a care teacher. When photos or children's drawings are displayed, for example, the children's learning becomes visible to teachers and parents.

Our current interest in documentation has its origins in Reggio Emilia, an Italian approach to young children's care and education. In the Reggio approach, respect for young children's ability to construct knowledge is central to the organization of the early childhood programs. The key tool used by teachers to understand the child's construction of knowledge is purposeful observation and documentation of the children's activities. This documentation process is not simply recording activities or accomplishments; it is a method of coming to thoughtful, reflective understanding of the children's activities and thinking. It is the basis of the teacher's planning for introducing new activities or materials into the program. The documentation process consists of observing and collecting supporting information (e.g., pictures and samples of a child's language), thinking about and talking with the other teachers and the families about the observations, and then planning and responding from one's understanding of the children's knowledge, goals and interests (Gandini & Goldhaber, 2001).

The documentation process usually begins with a question. It may be something general about many of the children in the group, such as "What are the children most interested in right now?" or "In what ways are children showing interest in mathematical concepts?" Or it may be quite specific and individual, such as "What is Mia learning as she takes her first steps?" or "What is Matt discovering when he plays with the blocks?" The question may be posed and one care teacher in a center or several may choose to work together on the same question with the same or different children.

Observation within this model is not aiming at objective, detached recording of the children's activities. Teachers are actively involved with the children, trying to "construct a shared understanding of children's ways of interacting with the environment, of entering into relationships with other adults and other children, and of constructing that knowledge" (Gandini & Goldhaber, 2001, p. 125). The recording of observations, then, includes thoughtful choices concerning what to record and the medium to use for creating the record. Pen and paper, still cameras, video cameras, audio recordings, and the artwork of the children are all used. However, the intention is rarely to capture an event in just one photo. These documented observations record the series of moments that comprise an event—and related events over time.

Note that "The intent of documentation is to explain, not merely to display" (Edwards, Gandini, & Forman, 1998, p. 241). The observations—as text, pictures, or artifacts—are reviewed and organized by the observer and shared with colleagues, parents, and the children themselves. The very act of reviewing the documentation and making choices regarding its organization provides the teacher an opportunity to reflect on the children's experience and on her own way of relating to the children. The observations then are shared with others to create a deeper and more complex understanding of the children's actions and ideas, as well as to plan which materials, environmental changes, and relationships could spark children's discoveries. Documentation can be used to demonstrate how an infant or toddler with special needs is progressing on the goals that were developed by the family and recorded on an individualized family service plan (IFSP).

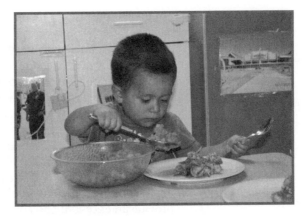

FIGURE 4.9   **Example of documentation**

Example of Documentation

In Figure 4.9, Anthony is sitting down for a family-style meal. In the first picture, he is scooping carrots from a bowl. In the second, he is serving the carrots onto his plate. This documentation tells the teacher about his motor development, how he plans and works toward goals, and his ability to attend to a task. What are you learning about Anthony by looking at this documentation?

Documentation can be used to plan curriculum that meets the interests and needs of a number of infants or toddlers in a group. If a care teacher provides opportunities for children to experience water and several children show an interest, the teacher will want to provide more opportunities related to water play.

Summary of Observation Methods

Anecdotal records, running records, event sampling, charts, and documentation strategies all lead to increased knowledge of individual children's development, thinking, and interests; a group of children's well-being or use of materials; and how children relate to adults' creations of enriched environments and responsive interactions. Another way to gather information about children's development is through developmental profiles and screening instruments. In these methods, observation skills are critically important.

Observation as Part of Assessment

Group care programs and early intervention programs often use developmental profiles to observe and record children's development and to *plan* for individual children and a group of children. As you read this book, you may want to observe children using the Developmental Trends and Responsive Interactions charts at the ends of Chapters 6 through 10 or a developmental profile discussed next as well as the other observation and documentation strategies described in this chapter.

Developmental Profiles

A **developmental profile** lists a sequence of behaviors in domains such as communication, emotional, social, thinking, and motor development.

A developmental profile outlines or profiles a child's development. Care teachers and other observers observe a child over time and in his home or program

> **Developmental profile**
>
> A document that lists a sequence of behaviors in domains such as communication, emotional, social, thinking, and motor development.

environment, using the information to learn about his development and, if in a program, to plan responsively for him.

Developmental profiles generally do not capture children's interests: for example, playing with water, dropping objects to see what will happen, fitting small bodies into small spaces, or making a friend. In addition, they often do not capture the nuances or qualities of a child's behavior—for example, the intensity with which a child expresses anger—although teachers' notes do. Nor do developmental profiles capture the variety of strategies that a child might use as he tries to fit objects into a container. These are all important aspects of a child's essence that adults want to observe and document to know a child well.

Developmental profiles do, however, provide valuable pieces of information about how the child is developing and, if completed in concert with the family, provide an excellent basis of conversation about the child. They also provide information that care teachers can use to plan an individualized program for the child and that early interventionists might use with the family during a home visit to discuss the strengths of the child and the next developmental steps. They also begin to give the family and care teacher an idea of whether the child is developing as a typical child does.

Let's examine a few of the most commonly used developmental profiles, how they are used, and the information they provide.

Developmental profiles help teachers plan an individualized and group responsive curriculum.

The OUNCE Scale

The OUNCE Scale is an assessment from birth to age 3½. The *User's Guide* (Marsden, Dombro, & Dichtelmiller, 2003) emphasizes that "it can be used with children who are at risk, those living in poverty, those with known disabilities, and those who are thriving and developing as expected" (p. iii). Three elements make up the OUNCE Scale: the Observation Record, a Family Album, and Developmental Profiles with associated learning standards. Each element is divided into eight age ranges: 0 to 4 months, 4 to 8 months, 8 to 12 months, 12 to 18 months, 18 to 24 months, 24 to 30 months, 30 to 36 months, and 36 to 42 months. For more information on the OUNCE Scale, go to the following Web site: www.pearsonassessments.com/ and search for the OUNCE Scale.

The OUNCE Scale is organized around six meaningful areas of development:

- Personal connections—how children show trust
- Feelings about self—how children express who they are
- Relationships with other children—how children act around other children
- Understanding and communicating—how children understand and communicate
- Exploration and problem solving—how children explore and figure things out
- Movement and coordination—how children move their bodies and use their hands (Meisels, Dombro, Marsden, Weston, & Jewkes, 2003)

The Observation Record provides a focus for center-based child care providers, Early Head Start teachers, home visitors, parent support group leaders, visiting nurses, teen parenting program providers, early interventionist specialists, family home providers, or pediatricians and health aides to observe and document children's behaviors in programs or in the home (Meisels et al., 2003).

The Family Album provides a means to learn about the child's development. It creates an opportunity for the teacher "to 'wonder' along with families so you [the teacher, early interventionists, etc.] can learn how they see or experience their child. This wondering and observing together is the foundation for building trusting relationships between caregivers and parents" (Marsden et al., 2003, p. 11).

Developmental Profiles are organized by social and emotional, communication and language, cognitive development, and physical development and give the rater an opportunity to summarize growth and development and compare the development to expectations for that age. Summaries of the results for individuals and groups can be obtained from a Web database.

The authors emphasize that this is a relationship-based tool that improves the teacher-child relationship, family-child relationship, and teacher-family relationship. Families report how the OUNCE has helped them learn about typical child development as well as how they can support their children's learning at home.

This seeing where the child is & provide extra support.

High/Scope COR for Infants and Toddlers

The purpose of the COR (Child Observation Record) is to provide care teachers a method for observing children's development and for determining "whether children are developing as they should be. They use the results to continue what is working and improve what is not; for example, to decide whether to provide more training to caregivers or to redesign infants' and toddlers' play areas" (High/Scope, 2008). The COR covers these developmental areas:

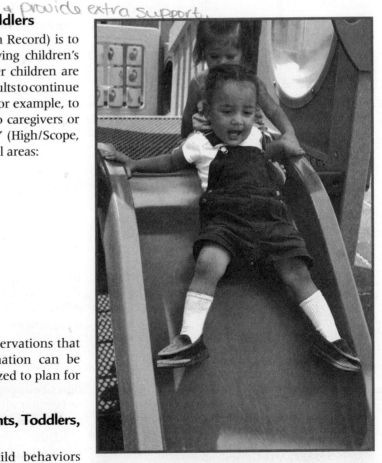

- Sense of Self
- Social Relations
- Creative Representation
- Movement
- Music
- Communication and Language
- Exploring Objects
- Early Quantity and Number
- Space
- Time

With the COR, care teachers write observations that describe children's behavior. The information can be entered into a Web database and summarized to plan for individual children and a group.

The Teaching Strategies GOLD for Infants, Toddlers, and Twos

This assessment provides sequential child behaviors in four areas: social/emotional, physical, cognitive, and language. The assessment system helps teachers

What could teachers from different cultures observe in this photo?

observe children intentionally and use what they learn to respond to children's interests, strengths, and needs; share information with families; and identify children's levels of development in reaction to 14 objectives in four goal areas (go towww.teachingstrategies.com and search for Teaching Strategies GOLD). The system is also designed to help teachers support the inclusion of children with disabilities.

These developmental continuum tools supplement the observation and documentation strategies discussed earlier in the chapter. In fact, the strategies described earlier are necessary in order to complete the developmental continuum tools in an accurate manner and to support the results with observations.

Screening Tools

Programs may also use screening instruments to find out if a discussion should occur between the care teacher(s) and a child's family about referral to an assessment team for a more comprehensive evaluation to determine if the child has a disability. This referral process is described in Chapter 15 of this book. One screening tool that is frequently used is the Ages and Stages Questionnaire (ASQ): A Parent-Completed, Child-Monitoring System, Third Edition. The ASQ is a widely used system developed by Bricker and Squires (2009). Parents answer questions at only one point in time or numerous times based on the age of their child. Because the measure is standardized, answers are scored and compared to cutoff scores to determine whether the child should be referred for more in-depth assessment. Chapter 15 describes the ASQ as well as the Denver Developmental Screening Test.

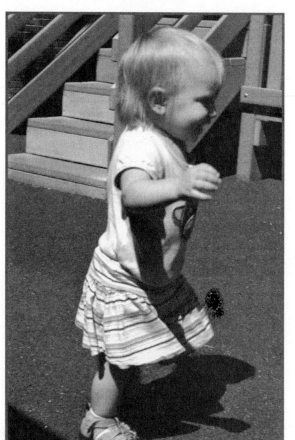

What Method to Use?

As we've discussed, there are many ways to observe and to record observations. These include anecdotal records, running records, event sampling, and time sampling. There are also a number of documentation strategies to use, for example, use of photos or video. Professionals and students of infant-toddler development also use developmental checklists and developmental screening tools. During assessments to determine whether a child has a disability, a team of professionals may use more formal assessments, but recommended practice advises using many of the described methods in this chapter to observe the child in familiar environments and involve families and care teachers in the assessment process.

How does an observer know when to use a particular method of observing? The left-hand column of Table 4.1 lists sample questions that care teachers and other professionals can ask themselves and discuss

TABLE 4.1   **Sample questions and methods of observation**

Sample Questions	Methods of Observation
What are the interests of each child and the children in the room?	Anecdotal records, running records
What concepts (space, time, object permanence, light, how to relate to peers) is a child or are the children exploring?	Anecdotal records, running records
When, where, and how frequently does a particular behavior occur, for example, biting?	Event sampling
How does each child spend his or her time when playing?	Time sampling, documentation
What does a child or what do the children in the group know about water, for example? What opportunities could be provided to help the children learn about the properties of water?	Anecdotal records of children's conversations, strategies, or concepts explored; documentation of children playing with water
How is a child or how are the children in the group developing?	Developmental checklists
How do we know if a child should be referred to an assessment team for a comprehensive evaluation to determine whether he or she is eligible for special support services?	Developmental screening

with team members and families. The right-hand column indicates methods that answer those questions. Each of these methods has been described in detail in this chapter.

Bring Information Together: Portfolios of Observations/Documentations

Care teachers and others who are interested in learning about development may compile individual children's observations and creations into individual portfolios. Often a notebook is organized by information about the child, photos of the child, family photos, dated observations, child creations planning forms (see Chapter 12), documentation, and results of assessments. Portfolios can be organized by age of child, by topic (drawing, playing blocks), or by domains (emotional, social, cognitive, language, and motor development) or placing artifacts in sequence throughout a certain time period.

What the Observer Brings to Observations

Observers bring themselves to an observation—their past experiences, beliefs, values, culture, knowledge about children; their skills in observing; and their relationships with the children they are observing.

CULTURE CLOSE UP

Assessments developed in one culture do not necessarily translate to another culture. One example is an American assessment that used the phrase "gets into everything." The exact translation into the Mandarin dialect was "want to sort everything." The direct translation changed the meaning, connoting a thoughtful approach. The translators settled on the phrase "want to participate in everything" (Liu, Leung, Sun, Li & Liu, 2012, p. 8)

Past Experiences, Beliefs, Values

Past personal experiences, beliefs, and values about child rearing or culture may affect the observer's perspective. Care teachers who believe that children should be heard and not just seen may focus on strategies that toddlers use to negotiate with adults. They may interpret a child saying no as a positive step in development, whereas others may see it as insubordination. To avoid this type of **bias**, observers can discuss their observations with team members and families before drawing conclusions from the behavior. Observers can give the objective piece of an observation to another person, ask for his or her interpretation, and then check to see how well the interpretations match (reliability).

Culture

> **bias**
>
> Basing conclusions on partial information or preconceived ideas.

Culture may provide a frame through which observers interpret behavior. A culture that promotes the independence of children will view a child's shy behavior differently than a culture that values interdependence or dependence of children. Awareness of all of the possible influences on an observer's choice of what, how, and when to observe; the interpretation of the observations; and the use of the observations are key to reducing bias, whether the observer is using more objective or subjective methods.

Presence

Observers try not to change the setting by their presence. If the observer knows the children, then observing is challenging because infants and toddlers have certain expectations for their care teachers to respond to them as they typically do. If observing in a group setting, observe only if the ratio of teachers to toddlers is adequate without counting you. If observing a child or children who do not know you, introduce yourself, encourage the parent or teacher to smile at you to show the children that you are safe, and sit among the children for a period before observing. Once observation begins, however, it is important for the observer to try to remain unobtrusive.

Deanna's early drawing and a later drawing can be placed in a portfolio to demonstrate changes in development.

Remaining unobtrusive while observing is not easy. One of the authors thought she was being a low-profile observer of a toddler group when one of the toddlers speedily ran to her sitting in a low chair and hit her as hard as he could on the leg with a long block. Obviously, the child had been quite aware that a stranger was present and either he wanted the observer to know that he was not comfortable with her presence or he wanted to check to see if she was alive. However, sitting back, staying low, and being quiet are still the best ways for an observer to create minimal changes in a setting. If a toddler approaches the observer, he can say, "I'm watching you play today" in an enthusiastic voice. After several observations with the same group, toddlers begin to ignore the observer.

Summary

Observing is a skill that a parent, care teacher, early interventionist, or someone who is studying about infants and toddlers can use to learn more about child development, children's interests and needs, and how to plan responsively. Many methods are available to observe and document children to support the learning of infants and toddlers in all domains of development—emotional, social, cognitive, communication, and motor.

Key Terms

anecdotal records
bias
developmental profile

documentation
event sampling
inferences

running records
time sampling

Reflections and Resources for the Reader

REFLECTIONS

1. What do you think is the most important aspect of a child to observe first to develop a positive relationship with the child?
2. Observation involves collaboration among you, the child, and the family. How will you improve your observation skills in a collaborative way? How will you build trust among the three participants?

OBSERVATION AND APPLICATION OPPORTUNITIES

1. Observe two children of approximately the same age using the Developmental Trends and Responsive Interactions charts at the end of Chapters 6 to 10 (or other observation technique). How are the two children alike? How are they different?
2. After observing two children of different ages, identify their interests and how they pursue those interests.

SUPPLEMENTAL ARTICLES AND BOOKS TO READ

Beaty, J. J. (2010). *Observing development of the young child* (7th ed.). Columbus, OH: Merrill Publishing Co.
Moreno, A. J., & Klute, M. M. (2011). Infant-toddler teachers can successfully employ authentic assessment: The learning through relating system. *Early Childhood Research Quarterly, 26*(4), 484–496.

INTERESTING LINKS

journal.naeyc.org/btj/200401/dichtel.pdf
NAEYC. Dichtelmiller, M. L., & Ensler, L. (2004, January) Infant/toddler assessment. One program's experience. *Beyond the Journal, Young Children on the Web*, 1–7.
This online article on infant/toddler assessment highlights the challenges and benefits of developmentally appropriate assessment.

http://www.educate.ece.govt.nz/learning/curriculumAndLearning/Assessmentforlearning/KeiTuaotePae/Book8.aspx
Early Childhood Education Teaching and Learning. Assessment for Infants and Toddlers.
This exquisite site sensitively discusses the meaning of assessment of infants and toddlers and provides specific examples of children's portfolio pages.

5

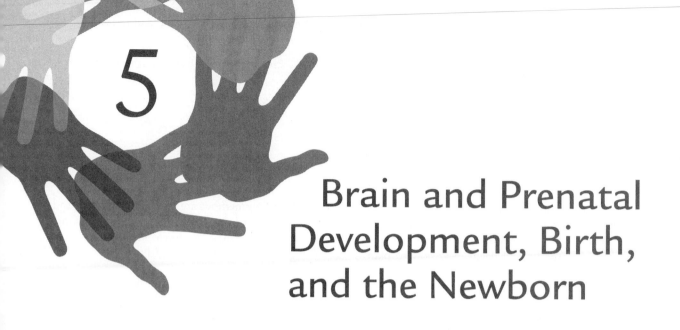

Brain and Prenatal Development, Birth, and the Newborn

LEARNING OUTCOMES

After reading this chapter, you will be able to:

- Describe early brain development
- Describe genetics and prenatal development
- Recount the development of the fetus
- Describe the womb as an environment for the fetus
- Explain the experience of the mother as an environment
- Explain the experience of the newborn
- Be aware of unique beginnings

LaShana smiled to herself as she remembered the morning. As a toddler teacher, she frequently was included in special moments in the lives of the children's families. This morning Alberto's mother was almost dancing as she brought him in. She pulled LaShana aside and whispered, "I'm pregnant!"

This really is beginning at the beginning.

In a book designed to help teachers understand infants and toddlers and care for them in groups, there are two very different reasons for including information on a period of life before infants can possibly be in group care. First, to appreciate the wonder and complexity of early development, it is helpful to be aware of the fascinating newly discovered details of how our brains develop, as well as the amazing information we now have on the journey from conception to birth. Development races forward from that first meeting of egg and sperm in ways that illustrate the developmental and ecological theories of our field. In essence, it helps us understand babies if we know about brain development, conception, gestation, and the first weeks after birth.

The second reason we need to understand pregnancy, prenatal development, and the earliest period of life is that either directly, as in home visiting programs, such as the Maternal Infant and Early Childhood Home Visiting programs, or indirectly through serving toddlers whose parents become pregnant with another child, we are often in a position of providing parent education around this very early period of development. Parents recognize teachers as having knowledge and experience with infants and toddlers and see teachers as a source of personal support in parenting issues. Everyone benefits by the teacher being grounded in the details of healthy pregnancy and prenatal development.

Brain Development: An Overview

The newborn responds to the feel of a nipple on his cheek with a reflex and begins to suck before the nipple even reaches his mouth. Four months later, the baby knows that when his caregiver moves from the cupboard to the sink, she is preparing a bottle for his snack. How much has been learned—and remembered—in these few months!

The development of the brain begins within the first days following conception and it continues to develop throughout our lifetimes. The course of brain development during **gestation** is generally predictable, but it is affected by the mother's nutrition, her emotional condition, and her exposures to toxins. Both the nutrients available to the developing brain and its experiences affect the structure of the brain.

gestation

The period of pregnancy when the fetus is carried in the uterus.

The Structure of the Brain

In the first weeks following conception, as cells are rapidly dividing and the amniotic sac and placenta are first developing, the embryo develops three layers of cells: (1) the ectoderm, which will become the brain, sensory organs, and nervous system; (2) the mesoderm, which will become the circulatory, skeletal, and muscular systems; and (3) the endoderm, which will become the digestive and glandular systems (see Figure 5.1). By 4 weeks following conception,

FIGURE 5.1 **Early development of the human embryo**

The cells rapidly multiply, the ball shape begins to flatten to a disk, and the embryo develops three layers of cells.

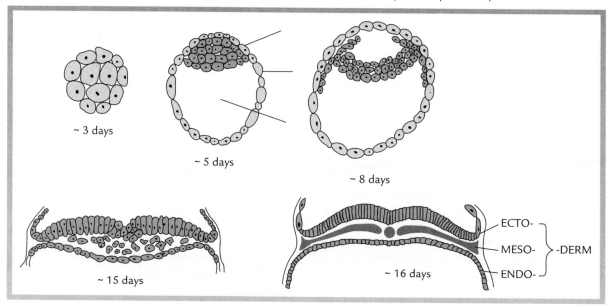

~ 3 days

~ 5 days

~ 8 days

~ 15 days

~ 16 days

ECTO-

MESO- }-DERM

ENDO-

the embryo is about one-fourth-inch long, curled into a crescent with little nubs sticking off the sides; a heart tube forms and begins pulsating; the internal organs are beginning to develop; and the future brain and nervous system become apparent as a spoon-shaped structure, only one cell thick, known as the neural plate. The neural groove runs the length of the neural plate, dividing it into right and left halves, a precursor of the future cerebral hemispheres (Restak, 2001, p. 2).

Over the next several weeks, fetal brain cells, or neurons, are generated at about 200,000 per minute and the brain develops three areas: the forebrain, the midbrain, and the hindbrain (Figure 5.2). These become larger and more differentiated in the womb and form the sections of the adult nervous system. The forebrain becomes the cerebrum, controlling thinking and language; the midbrain becomes the thalamus and hypothalamus, controlling the passage of sensory information; and the hindbrain becomes the cerebellum and the brain stem, controlling heartbeat, respiration, and motor development (Medline Plus, 2011).

At about 5 months gestation, the brain is growing rapidly, but it is relatively smooth. In the last 3 months of gestation, the brain continues to grow quickly, limited by the containing force of the skull. As the surface of the brain continues to grow, the cerebral hemispheres fold in on themselves, packing themselves efficiently into the available space. By the time a baby is born, the brain looks as furled and gnarled as that of an older child or adult, with a visible crease down the middle separating the two hemispheres (Shore, 1997).

It is the large size and complexity of the human brain that make us different from every other species. Babies are born with about 100 billion brain cells—twice the number they will have as adults. This abundance of cells helps ensure

FIGURE 5.2   **Prenatal brain development**

The brain begins to form at the end of the embryo, first as a thin plate. A groove develops, delineating the future hemispheres. The brain rapidly grows into its adult form and then creates many folds as it becomes increasingly differentiated.

Day 16   Day 22   3 weeks   4 weeks   5 weeks

7 weeks   11 weeks   4 months   6 months   8 months   Newborn

that babies will be born with healthy brains and will be able to learn whatever they need to survive in their unique environment (Restak, 2001, p. 5).

Creating Connections Between Neurons

The work of neurons is to make connections with other neurons, constantly exchanging information. The fetus's and then the baby's, experiences provide the information that causes the connections to form, therefore literally creating the physical structure moment by moment. Each neuron has an axon (transmitter), a thin fiber that carries information in the form of electrical signals out from the neuron to the dendrites (receivers) in other cells. Each neuron also has many dendrites, hairlike fibers that receive electrical information from other neurons (see Figure 5.3).

When an axon sends out information from one neuron, dendrites from one or more other neurons receive the information through a connection between axon and dendrite called a synapse (Debanne, et al., 2011). A neuron

Amy's synapses are firing as she drinks her milk and gazes at her family child care provider.

FIGURE 5.3 **The neuron**

A single neuron with one axon transmitting information and many dendrites receiving messages.

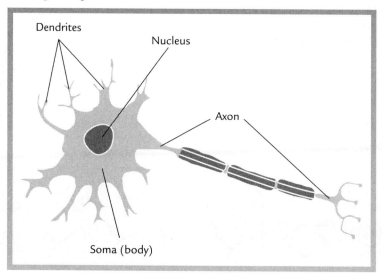

may connect to up to 15,000 other neurons, creating the phenomenon known as "wiring the brain" (Gopnik, Meltzoff, & Kuhl, 1999). In order for an electrical signal to be transmitted across the synapse, a neurotransmitter chemical such as serotonin, dopamine, or endorphins must be present (Chugani, 1998) (see Figure 5.4).

FIGURE 5.4 **A synaptic connection**

The axon and dendrite exchange information at a point of connection called a synapse, using chemical neurotransmitters.

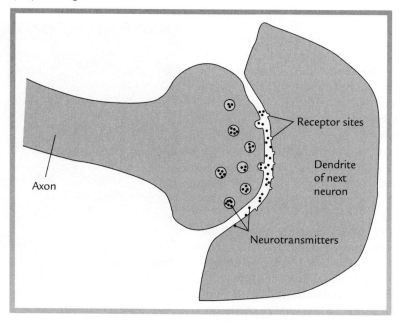

The synapses, or connections, that are used repeatedly in the infant's day-to-day life will be reinforced and strengthened. The synapses that form but are never reactivated will be eliminated in a process often called *pruning* (Low & Cheng, 2006). This profusion of synapses followed by a sort of weeding out of unused dendrites is a very efficient way of ensuring that the child learns what he or she needs to.

> *The genes are the bricks and mortar to build a brain. The environment is the architect. (Christine Hohmann)*

For example, say a very young infant is hungry and crying. He sees a familiar shape moving toward him in a familiar way. The shape is wearing something soft and light blue. It has a familiar smell and it is making familiar sounds: "It's OK, honey, I'm here. Are you sooo hungry?" Synapses begin firing all over the baby's brain: "What do I know about that shape? Sometimes it's Aunt Sherri or a stranger, but it's usually Mommy. It looks like something Mommy often wears. It smells like Mommy, it sounds like Mommy's words and voice."

The infant has information about all of these aspects of "Mommy" stored in synapses in his brain. When he is near Mommy, or probably even just thinking about her, these synapses carrying familiar information are set off and become strengthened. On the other hand, if a stranger passes the infant in the grocery store, the baby registers information but never "reactivates" it. Synapses that are formed in brief, one-time experiences but never reused tend to wither and be eliminated—or pruned. If synapses are activated frequently, they become stable and are preserved from pruning. So, connections that are made and strengthened in the brain in the early years create the physical wiring of the brain of the adult (Belsky & deHaan, 2011).

All learning, throughout one's life, follows this pattern of synaptic connection. We continue to have experiences—either physical or conceptual, immediately scan our synapses for stored information, and either pull up the relevant information or create new synaptic connections. In doing this, we continuously change the physical structure of our brains.

The Importance of Early Experiences for Brain Development

Some synapses are created in the brain while the fetus is still in the womb. In the last months of the pregnancy, the fetus is able to hear external sounds and see light. The sounds and light, in addition to the proprioceptive information of his own movement and possibly the sense of touch he feels when his mother rubs her expanded belly, all provide information that is conducted through the brain in synaptic connections (DeLoache, 2000). Even the process of pruning synapses begins in the womb. So it is no exaggeration to say that early experiences have enormous and lasting impact on the brain.

During the first year of life, an infant's brain grows to about 70% of its adult size; by age 3, the human brain develops to 90% of its full adult growth and establishes most of the structures that will guide all future emotional, behavioral, social, and psychological functioning later in life.

Newborns are dependent on adults for their survival and to help them have appropriate experiences with the world (Belsky & deHaan, 2011; Belsky & Pluess, 2009).

However, babies are not passive participants. They clearly express their need for nourishment and comfort and demonstrate interest in both sensory experiences (sounds, smells, sights, touch) and relational experiences (hugging, cooing, smil-ing, comforting). For most babies, these sensory and relational experiences occur simultaneously and become transformed into patterned neuronal activity that influences the ongoing formation of the brain in positive ways. An infant's brain is most likely to keep the synapses that are formed through experiences that are repeated *and* that occur within emotionally meaningful relationships.

Long before we knew the specifics of how our brains develop, researchers had understood the importance of an emotionally available adult partner for babies. In studies of very young children in hospitals, orphanages, and other institutions in the 1930s, it was clear that food, clothing, and a bed to sleep in are not enough for young children. Between 25% and 30% of these infants and toddlers, receiv-ing custodial care without human interaction, died. Many who survived were severely cognitively challenged (Skeels & Dye, 1939; Spitz, 1945). Bruce Perry (1999), a leading researcher in early brain development, puts it this way:

> The young child's undeveloped brain is trained in a "use dependent" way, mir-roring the pattern, timing, nature, frequency, and quality of experiences and interactions. Think of it in terms of nutrition. If an infant or toddler is not fed consistent, predictable messages of love and communication, then those areas of the brain are shut down and the child's capacity to function later in life [is] compromised. (p. 1)

The Effects of Stress and Violence on Brain Development

Of course, positive experiences are not the only experiences that have an impact on an infant's or toddler's brain development. Stressful experiences also occur. The National Scientific Council on the Child (2010a) suggests that there are three levels of physiological stress responses in young children—positive, tolerable, and toxic. Positive stress responses are mild and of short duration. Most importantly, a responsive adult with whom the child has a meaningful, ongoing relationship buffers the child's experience and helps calm him. Positive stress might occur with a vaccination or a loud, barking dog. Positive stress is helpful to the child's growing ability to deal with difficult situations. A tolerable stress response occurs when there is a drastic, life-changing event such as the death of a parent, divorce, a serious illness, or a natural disaster. The stress response will last longer but may not cause long-term damage to the brain if there is an adult helping the child through the experience.

Part of the biological response to stress is the increased secretion of the hormones cortisol and adrenalin. In situations of immediate threat, these hor-mones are useful in helping a person focus on survival. However, when these hormones are excessively high for long periods of time, they become toxic to the brain. As an evolutionary function of the brain, when survival is at stake people do not use the more thoughtful, reflective parts of their brain. Instead, cortisol, adrenalin, and other hormones activate the part of the brain that focuses on choosing a survival strategy: fight or flight, or in very young infants, freeze. As these neural connections are reinforced through use, they become the pre-dominant pathways the brain uses to assess situations. Every event is perceived as a life-or-death situation. Even neutral situations are perceived as threatening. Fetuses and very young children who live in homes with abuse, violence, mental illness, or substance abuse maintain their stress response much of the time. This chronic stress response is toxic to the developing brain and influences a child's ability to attend (Liston, McEwen, & Casey, 2009). Whether the fetus is exposed to these maternal hormones or the infant produces these hormones, the child builds a brain that is highly adaptive in abusive or neglectful situations, but it is inadequate for the work of healthy relationships (Shonkoff et al., 2012).

The brain that is growing in an atmosphere of toxic stress actually develops a different physical structure: "The result may be a child who has great difficulty functioning when presented with the world of kindness, nurturing, and stimulation. It is an unfamiliar world to him; his brain has not developed the pathways and memories to adapt to this new world" (CWIG, 2001). In a National Scientific Council on the Developing Child Working Paper (2005), the authors state that "Excessive stress disrupts the architecture of the developing brain."

Children who experience toxic stress in infancy have brains that work differently later in life (Roth, & Sweatt, 2011). They may be in a state of hyperarousal, always scanning the environment for signs of danger. These children may even evoke in others the abusive behavior that they fear, just to have some control over it. Therefore, a boy whose mother was raging and frightening may pick fights with other children, or a girl who was sexually abused may act seductively with a teacher. The opposite reaction to early frightening experiences is to feel so powerless that the child just freezes, or dissociates. Dissociation appears to be surrender to the situation, but the child feels as though she is not even present in the moment. During dissociation, the child may not even hear what is said to her, and so she does not attempt to respond. The child may have no memory of the experience. If children do not experience reliable responsiveness in their caregivers, they may later lack the neuronal pathways that would present adult assistance as a possible solution to problems. If children experience extreme deprivation in infancy, little contact with caregivers, and little stimulation from the environment, they will develop significantly smaller than normal brains (Gunnar, Herrera, & Hostinar, 2009; Perry, 1996; Perry & Pollard, 1997). The brain may incorporate the effects of chronic frightening or neglectful early experiences for a lifetime (Gunnar & Quevedo, 2007).

Genetics and Prenatal Development

The process of brain development begins with conception, and it continues throughout life. The brain is a good example of the value of understanding prenatal development as a foundation for understanding early development. Our knowledge of the brain has increased dramatically in the past decade, as has our knowledge of every aspect of development.

We know more about the composition of our bodies today than at any time in history, and more is being learned every day. For example, your body is composed of about 100 *trillion* cells. Your little toe is made of 2 or 3 billion cells. Each cell is smaller than the diameter of one strand of hair—and yet the material inside each cell makes us similar to all other human beings and, at the same time, our own, completely unique selves.

Our skin is made of skin cells, our liver made of liver cells; about 200 kinds of cells are needed to create our bodies. Each cell contains genetic information that directs it to be a specific kind of cell doing the work it needs to do in our body. (See Figure 5.5.)

Each cell is enclosed by a somewhat porous membrane. Within the cell membrane is a watery fluid called cytoplasm—a mixture of water, enzymes, amino acids, glucose, and other molecules. At the center of the cell is the nucleus.

FIGURE 5.5   **A cell**

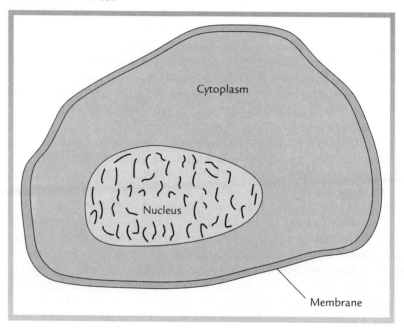

Protected by a nuclear membrane, the nucleus holds 6 feet of DNA (deoxyribonucleic acid) tightly packed into 46 chromosomes. Human beings inherit 23 chromosomes from their father and 23 from their mother. There are 22 pairs of autosomes and one pair of sex chromosomes, designated the X chromosome and the Y chromosome, which determine gender. Females have two X chromosomes and males have one X and one Y chromosome. (See Figure 5.6.)

The DNA of the chromosome is a pattern that tells the cell how to make its proteins. Each strand of DNA is a pattern of pairs of nucleotides that link together between two strands like rungs in a ladder. The strand of DNA then has the

FIGURE 5.6   **A chromosome, DNA, and genes**

Each chromosome is packed with long strands of DNA, carrying all of the body's genetic information.

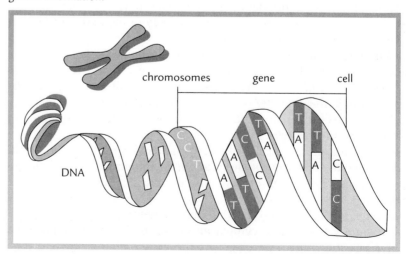

appearance of a double helix. Human beings have about 3 billion base pairs of nucleotides on their DNA (refer again to Figure 5.6).

About 2% of the DNA provides genetic information. Each little section of the pattern of DNA is marked by a starting point and an ending point. The material between those points is a gene. Genes carry the general information on how to create and maintain the body as well as specific information that tells your body to have hair color like your mother's or a nose like your grandfather's (Human Genome Project, 2008). However, genes do not automatically express themselves as intended. Just like the brain, genes are affected by early experiences. As previously noted in this book, *epigenetics* demonstrates how the hormones secreted in response to positive or negative experiences give genes directions about whether to turn on or express themselves. Toxic stress may also affect whether the genetic blueprint can be carried out (National Scientific Council on the Child, 2010b).

There are around 25,000 genes in the human genome. The Human Genome Project, described in Box 5.1, has mapped out the entire human genome. At this point, we have identified more than 5,000 genes, any one of which, if damaged or missing, can cause drastic changes in the human being. Missing genes are known to cause a variety of diseases and disabling conditions including lactose intolerance, albinism, cystic fibrosis, Tay-Sachs disease, sickle cell anemia, hemophilia, and muscular dystrophy. Disabilities caused by genetic issues are described in Chapter 15.

There is not necessarily a direct one-to-one, gene-to-disease correlation, however. Damage to one gene may cause a variety of problems, and many diseases are caused by damage to a set of genes. **Genetic counseling** can be helpful to families that have concerns about inherited diseases.

In sum, the foregoing has been a brief introduction to some of the newest, most complicated, and most compelling information science is currently providing. We are all complex and unique human beings—yet each of us is built of single cells that are predominantly exactly like the cells in all other human beings. Although the components and functioning of single cells are pretty impressive, when two cells meet and create a new human being, the picture of development is really thrilling!

genetic counseling

Informing parents of possible birth defects in their children on the basis of chromosomal tests and such medical procedures as amniocentesis.

The Fetus

The development of the baby from conception to birth takes about 40 weeks. In talking about gestation, or the period of pregnancy, we usually divide those weeks into three parts, or trimesters.

The First Trimester

Fetal development begins when the sperm cell from the father enters the ripe egg (ovum) of the mother. These two cells are different from all others in the human body. Whereas almost all cells have 46 chromosomes (23 pairs), the sperm and the ovum have only 23 each. This enables the genetic material from the mother and father to pair up and begin to create a whole new person.

BOX 5.1

The Human Genome Project

This study of the DNA in our cells was designed to tell us

- How many genes we have
- How cells work
- How living things evolved
- How single cells develop into complex creatures
- What happens when we become ill

The work includes

- Charting the sequence of the 3 billion letters of human DNA
- Mapping the human genes

Source: The Human Genome Project is funded by National Institutes of Health and the U.S. Department of Energy.

When the ovum and the sperm combine to create a new cell, this cell quickly multiplies as it travels down the fallopian tube to implant itself in the uterine wall on the 6th day after conception. The placenta develops to keep the fetus nourished and to supply oxygen. (See Figure 5.7.)

During these first 3 months of development, the first trimester, the cells rapidly multiply but they also begin to differentiate into blood cells, liver cells, nerve cells, and so forth. As you can see in Figure 5.7, the external features such as eyes, ears, arms and legs, and the internal organs have begun to form. Although less than 3 inches long, the fetus can make a fist; spontaneously move her arms and legs; begin a rudimentary sleep and waking cycle; and grasp, suck, and swallow ("Fetal Development," 2007; Solchany, 2001).

The Second Trimester

Months 4 through 6 of gestation are a time of growth and development. The fetus grows to about 15 inches and weighs about 2 pounds 11 ounces. (See Figure 5.8.) The fetus is active about half the time and the mother can

FIGURE 5.7   **First trimester of fetal development**

FIGURE 5.8   **Second trimester of fetal development**

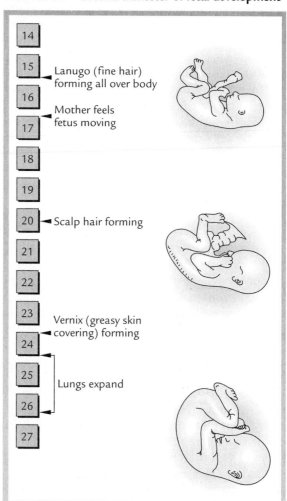

sometimes feel the movement. The heartbeat, and sometimes even crying, can be heard with a stethoscope.

The Third Trimester

By the beginning of the third trimester, the fetus could survive a premature birth, but the potential for complications is high. The brain is rapidly developing, perhaps in part stimulated by movement, light, temperature changes, and sounds. Listening through the noises of the womb to the voices of her family, she may be learning the sounds of her family's language. After birth, the baby will be able to recognize stories repeatedly read out loud during this gestational period. The fetus gains body fat and grows quickly to fill the entire uterus. (See Figure 5.9.)

Thus, the development of the human being is the predetermined work of the new cell formed by the egg and the sperm duplicating itself over and over. The genetic information encoded in the DNA tells each cell where to travel in the developing embryo and what sort of cell it should be. Over the course of 40 weeks, the human being grows from one cell into a complex, competent human being who is able to hear, react, and learn even while still inside the womb.

FIGURE 5.9   **Third trimester of fetal development**

28 ◄ Fetus hiccups
29 ◄ Fat layer forming
30
31
32 ◄ Organs maturing
33 ◄ Fetus growing rapidly
34
35
36 ◄ Kidneys mature
37 ◄ Lungs mature
38
39
40 ◄ Estimated date of delivery

The Womb as an Environment for Development

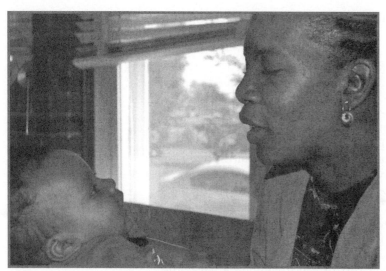

Casey's benefited from her mother's nutritional diet when Casey was in the womb.

As Peter entered the center to begin his shift as a toddler teacher, he passed by Trina, who seemed to be taking a minute in the doorway after dropping off her daughter for child care. Peter was surprised to see her smoking, as just a few weeks earlier she had happily announced that she was pregnant with her second child. Peter greeted her, paused, and said, "Trina, I'm a little startled to see you smoking. Do you know about the effects of smoking during pregnancy?" This time it was Trina's turn to be surprised. "No, is it a problem?" she asked. "I know not to drink beer or anything, but smoking…What's the problem?"

We used to think of the womb as a safe place for the developing fetus with the placenta as a barrier that kept dangerous things outside of the womb. Although the placenta is able to act as somewhat of a filter, we now know that the fetus can be compromised if the mother has inadequate nutrition, that the fetus may be affected by many substances that can harm it, that genetic and other congenital factors can cause the formation to go astray, that the birth process can be dangerous, and that maternal stress and anxiety may directly affect the baby's well-being. Without frightening expectant families, when infant-toddler teachers have ongoing contact with the expectant parents, they can provide information and resources that promote the best outcome for every pregnancy.

Nutrition

Women with a good nutritional diet before pregnancy probably don't need to make big changes in what they eat in order to provide themselves and their baby with the protein, vitamins, and minerals they need. According to the American College of Obstetricians and Gynecologists (ACOG), pregnant women should increase their usual servings of a variety of foods from the four basic food groups to include the following:

- Four or more servings of fruits and vegetables for vitamins and minerals
- Four or more servings of whole-grain or enriched bread and cereal for energy
- Four or more servings of milk or milk products for calcium
- Three or more servings of meat, poultry, fish, eggs, nuts, dried beans, and peas for protein

Eating a well-balanced diet while pregnant will help keep mother and baby healthy. Most physicians agree that the Recommended Daily Allowances (RDAs), except those for iron, can be obtained through a proper diet (National Women's Health Information Center, 2009).

There are some specific nutrients that pregnant women must be sure they are getting, either through diet or with supplements. Iron is needed in larger amounts, especially in the later stages of pregnancy, and it is difficult to consume enough of it through food. This mineral is essential to the formation of healthy red blood cells and will help the mother avoid anemia and being susceptible to infections.

A woman's need for folic acid doubles during pregnancy. Folic acid has been shown to be important in preventing neural tube defects, such as spina bifida and anencephaly, and is essential to the formation of red blood cells. Folic acid can be found in many foods, including kidney beans, leafy green vegetables, peas, and liver—or a doctor may prescribe a diet supplement.

Pregnant women need to increase their calcium and fluid intake. Pregnant and lactating adult women require an additional 40% of calcium a day (three extra servings of milk or dairy products). Almost all of the extra calcium goes into the baby's developing bones. Extra fluids, especially water, are needed to support pregnant women's increased blood volume. They should drink at least eight glasses of water each day to prevent dehydration and constipation (NWHIC, 2009).

Many cultures around the world have particular beliefs about nutrition during pregnancy. In India and many Asian countries, women are encouraged to "eat down"—eat less than before the pregnancy in order to keep the baby small and the delivery easier (Brems & Berg, 1988). Many Asian cultures also think generally about health, and particularly about food, in terms of being *hot* or *cold*—not literally hot or cold in how they are served, but as in adding heat or cold to the balance of the body's temperatures. Pregnancy is thought of adding heat, so cold foods are increased to provide balance (Nag, 1994). Young mothers in Latin America avoid hot foods during pregnancy but consume them in the postpartum period as a way of reestablishing heat lost in childbirth (Taylor, Ko, & Pan, 1999). Some cultures believe specific foods have specific effects on pregnancy. The Beng tribespeople in Africa avoid eating large bananas because they would create a fat baby, meat from the striped antelope because it would create striped or patchy skin, and boiled yams because they would make for a difficult delivery (Gottlieb, 2000). Middle Eastern Muslim customs include ensuring that the newly married woman eats foods that are rich in iron to ensure the baby is well nourished. These include a molasses-like grape drink and organ meats (Delaney, 2000). An aboriginal group in Australia's desert believes it is important to avoid meat from animals with sharp, pointed parts to avoid miscarriage (Pierroutsakos, 2000).

Cultural beliefs, habits, and access to healthy foods can all affect a woman's nutrition during pregnancy. Child care programs often keep pamphlets providing nutrition information in their parent information areas because they are helpful and of interest to pregnant women. It is also helpful to keep information handy on what may be harmful to the developing fetus. Women like Trina, at the beginning of this section, may not always know what to avoid during pregnancy.

Toxins and Teratogens

Many substances in the environment may threaten the positive development and cause disabling conditions in the fetus. Some of these conditions and their effect on development are described more thoroughly in Chapter 15. This section contains information that infant-toddler teachers may want to share with expectant families. For instance, although you may be a little uncomfortable bringing up the use of alcohol or drugs with a parent, general information about substances in the

—●●●● **CULTURE CLOSE UP**

The women of the Wind River Indian Reservation were very concerned about the poor pregnancy outcomes for their young mothers. American Indian/Alaska Native (AI/AN) women had the least access to prenatal care and the second highest infant mortality and prematurity rates in the country. Working with their Early Head Start program, the women wanted to support their young mothers in a more traditional manner. At the same time, the Cherokee Nation was surveying prenatal literature for the the March of Dimes, looking for culturally relevant materials. They found 49 items out of 500 that were culturally appropriate.

The March of Dimes brought together a committee of women representing the Shoshone, Cherokee, Nez Perce, Choctaw, Mayan, Navajo, Dakota, Chickasaw, Blackfeet, and Athabascan Nations to determine what was needed to address the health care disparity. The committee ultimately created a prenatal information booklet called *The Coming of the Blessing*. This booklet told the story of a healthy pregnancy the way a mother would to her daughter. The women created a medicine wheel on which the first trimester was called *the blessing has been planted*, the second *feel the blessing dance*, and the third *the blessing has arrived*. Traditional practices, information for the father, and the woman's circle of support accompany the medical information supplied by the March of Dimes.

The booklet was immensely successful and is now an ongoing part of the March of Dimes materials for Indian health educators (Arnold, Aragon, Shepherd, & Van Sell, 2011).

environment that may be harmful to a fetus or threatening to a pregnancy is important for expectant parents to know. Having this kind of information as part of ongoing parent education efforts is especially important because harm can occur before the mother even knows she's pregnant.

Because of the rapid division and replication of cells early in gestation, exposure to a toxic substance is likely to cause more damage the earlier it occurs in the pregnancy. Drinking alcohol during pregnancy can have severe effects on the child, including mental retardation, growth deficiency, and facial abnormalities (Jacobson & Jacobson, 2002; Paintner, Williams, & Burd, 2012; Riley, Alejandra, & Warren, 2011; Salihu, Kornosky, Lynch, Alio, August, & Marty, 2011). More than 40,000 babies a year are born with alcohol-related damage (Szalavitz, 2010).

Cocaine use appears to be related to premature births and smaller babies (Gouin, Murphy, Shah, & the Knowledge Synthesis Group on Determinants of Low Birth Weight and Preterm Births, 2011). Determining the effects of cocaine is complicated because of pregnant women's use of multiple drugs and alcohol. A contributing factor to possible negative effects of cocaine use is that mothers who used cocaine prenatally show less sensitivity and more negative affect with infants (Eiden, Schuetze, & Coles, 2011) and are more angry and aggressive with their toddlers (Eiden, Schuetze, Colder, & Veira, 2011).

An exhaustive review of studies of the effect of maternal smoking, looking at 12 million children including 173,000 with birth defects, showed that babies born to mothers who smoked had a

- 20% to 30 % increased risk of having shortened or missing arms and legs, cleft lips and cleft palates, and abnormally shaped heads or faces
- 27% increased risk of gastrointestinal abnormalities, including problems with the throat, esophagus, colon, intestine, bile ducts, gall bladder, and liver
- 50% increased risk of being born with their intestines hanging outside the body
- 20% increased risk of being born with a blocked or closed anus
- 9% increased risk of heart defects
- 13% higher risk that baby boys would be born with undescended testes

Although researchers are not exactly sure how smoking damages the fetus, it is assumed that cigarette smoke limits the available oxygen. Nicotine causes blood vessels to constrict, and carbon monoxide binds to hemoglobin, which carries oxygen through the body. It is estimated that 20% of pregnant women younger than age 25 in the United States smoke (Hackshaw, Rodeck, & Boniface, 2011).

Exposure during pregnancy to environmental toxins such as lead, mercury, arsenic, cleaning products, and chemical solvents may lead to miscarriage, premature birth, low birth weight, and developmental delays. Lead may be present in drinking water through old lead plumbing pipes. Mercury is stored in the fatty tissue of most fish. Arsenic exposure may occur through industrial workplaces and cleaning products and solvents often used in the home (Perera et al., 2002).

Pesticides pose similar hazards to the fetus; although unless women are in agricultural areas, the risk is not great. Recently, however, health care providers have voiced concerns about insect repellents containing DEET. However, in areas where there is the danger of West Nile virus or Lyme disease, it is suggested that a pregnant woman use small amounts of insect repellent on her clothing, socks, and shoes and that she wear gloves when applying it (OTIS, 2005).

Child care providers may want to keep informative brochures on hand to help expectant families be aware of substances that could be harmful to their unborn child. Such materials can often be obtained from the March of Dimes or the local public health agency. A program's nurse consultant could be helpful in obtaining these materials.

Structural/Metabolic Birth Defects and Maternal Infections

Of course, many prenatal problems are not anticipated. Sometimes, for reasons we do not yet understand, malformations occur during gestation. Missing chromosomes, abnormal genes carried by one or both parents, and inaccurate migrations of cells can cause a variety of malformations in the fetus. Cleft palate may be caused by a combination of these factors. Metabolic disorders (1 in 3,500 babies) such as Tay-Sachs or phenylketonuria (PKU) are generally genetic diseases and can be harmful or even fatal.

The term TORCH syndrome—an acronym for Toxoplasmosis, Other agents, Rubella, Cytomegalovirus, and Herpes simplex—refers to a set of maternal infections that can cause harm to a fetus. Maternal infections such as rubella (rare, due to vaccinations) and cytomegalovirus (3,000 to 4,000 babies a year) occurring early in the pregnancy may result in mental retardation, blindness, or deafness. Sexually transmitted diseases (1 in 2,000 babies) may result in stillbirth, newborn death, or bone defects (MOD, 2009e).

Prenatal Testing

Child care providers are increasingly likely to serve infants and toddlers who are medically complex or have disabilities. Understanding both the normal progression of gestation and birth and the difficulties that can occur in the process will help you be a resource and support to expectant and new parents.

Many problems that occur during gestation can be diagnosed through prenatal testing. Doctors are able to test for various conditions as well as the general well-being of the fetus through a variety of methods, from simple tests of the mother's blood to actually inserting a needle into the amniotic sac and removing fluid. The three-dimensional,

Marcus's mother was reassured by prenatal testing during her pregnancy.

TABLE 5.1 **Types of prenatal testing**

Prenatal Test	Purpose	Performed at
Doppler device	Ultrasound to hear fetal heartbeat	6 weeks to birth
Ultrasound	High-frequency sound waves to provide live-action picture of fetus; track growth and development	5 weeks to birth
Chorionic villus sampling (CVS)	Needle sampling to test for genetic disorders	10.5 to 13 weeks
Magnetic resonance imaging (MRI)	Creates images of soft tissue such as the brain	12 weeks to birth
Fetal echocardiography	Detailed ultrasound for babies at high risk for heart problems	14 weeks to birth
Alpha fetoprotein blood tests (AFP)	Part of the Triple Screen test. Screens mother's blood for alpha fetoprotein assessing risk of Down syndrome and neural tube defects	15 to 20 weeks
Triple screen test	A maternal blood test that that looks for AFP, human chorionic gonadotropin (hCG), and estriol. These test assess potential genetic and physical disorders	15 to 20 weeks
Amniocentesis	Tests amniotic fluid for chromosomal disorders	16 to 20 weeks

Source: American Pregnancy Association, 2012, http://www.americanpregnancy.org/index.htm

moving images of the fetus available through ultrasound are so fascinating that parents sometimes keep the still photographs or videos as their first pictures of their baby.

Table 5.1 contains a short description of the most common prenatal tests. Nearly every pregnant woman hears her baby's heartbeat through the Doppler device during regular prenatal checkups. Medical offices sometimes use ultrasound to create a visual image of the developing fetus.

The Mother's Experience as an Environment

Luisa came in at the end of the day to pick up her 2-year-old daughter, Anna. Harriet, Anna's teacher, commented on how tired she looked. "It's been hard just being a mom and working," Luisa said, "but being pregnant too—I'm so tired. I have to tell you, though, this morning I was just dragging, but you were so happy to see Anna, and I felt like you cared for me…it made my whole day better!"

Sometimes one moment of friendliness or kindness can completely change your attitude. You actually *feel* differently. That is because attitude and feelings have a chemical component. The experience of fear increases the presence of fear-fighting hormones such as cortisone; pleasurable experiences increase serotonin. If emotions are translated into hormonal activity, and hormones can cross the placenta and enter the fetal bloodstream, it is easy to understand that the mother's emotional experience is part of the baby's environment.

Maternal Stress, Anxiety, and Other Factors

Anxiety

Pregnancy can be a joyful time if a family is stable and financially secure, has a good support system, and wants the child. When any of these components are missing—and sometimes even when they are all present—pregnant women can experience stress and anxiety. When the mother is anxious, the baby's heart rate may increase, less blood flows to the uterus, and the result is a baby with decreased birth weight. When a mother has high levels of stress hormones such as cortisol in her bloodstream, the baby is likely to have low birth weight, a small head and poor brain development, and low **APGAR** ratings in the minutes after birth. Certainly home visitors need to be aware of the impact of maternal stress on the developing fetus. Child care providers would do well to attend to a mother's reports of stress and anxiety as well, providing information and emotional support as they are able.

APGAR

Scoring system of a newborn's well-being in the areas of activity (muscle tone), pulse, grimace (reactivity to irritation), appearance (skin color), and respiration.

Depression

Some situations during pregnancy are not well known but can be dangerous to the mother and the fetus (Davalos, Yadon, & Tregellas, 2012). Although postpartum depression is discussed in detail in Chapter 6, the less well-known condition of prenatal depression is described here because of its potential effects on the baby. Prenatal depression may be very difficult, even for professionals, to diagnose because physical symptoms of pregnancy are so similar to symptoms of depression; poor appetite, fatigue, difficulty sleeping, and mood swings are certainly common to both depression and pregnancy (Matthey, Barnett, Ungerer, & Waters, 2000). Home visitors, child care providers, and health providers should pay particular attention to pregnant women who speak of feeling flat and hopeless. Depression during pregnancy is a strong predictor of postpartum depression. Women who are depressed during pregnancy should be referred for mental health evaluations and counseling.

Domestic Violence

An even harder issue to think about during pregnancy is domestic violence and its impact on the fetus (Shad & Shad, 2010). The National Center for Chronic Disease Prevention and Health Promotion (CDC, 2006) warns that in addition to the immediate dangers, the presence of domestic violence during a pregnancy may result in

- Stress for the mother, with health implications for the baby
- Delays in seeking prenatal care, with health implications for the baby
- Unhappiness with being pregnant, with implications for the relationship between the mother and the child

Home visitors may deal with these issues more directly than child care providers. However, child development and education programs could provide staff training on domestic violence, know about community resources, provide parent information brochures, and have a plan in place for helping move a woman and her children to safety if necessary.

Simply reading about some of these issues may feel heavy and difficult. It may seem far out of the realm of working in a pleasant child development and education program and taking care of babies. Most teachers will never deal with these issues with pregnant mothers. Nonetheless, this is good information to tuck away. Simply being aware of these issues, knowing your community resources, and keeping information available to parents could make a significant difference in the lives of children and their families.

Pregnancy is such a natural part of life that it's easy to take it for granted. Reading through all the potential dangers can be a little distressing, especially if you are of childbearing age yourself. So, it is important to remember that most pregnancies proceed without alarm and result in wonderful, healthy, and amazingly capable newborns.

The Newborn

The evidence that very young infants are active learners is compelling. They are born able to find the nipple and suck, thanks to inborn reflexes. They like to look at human faces and hear human voices. They use facial expressions that adults can easily understand, even though they have never seen their own faces. Newborns are ready to learn and ready to engage in relationships.

The first days and weeks after birth are a time of great adjustment for the new infant and the family, especially the mother. The baby is adjusting to life outside the womb, managing breathing, eating, digestion, elimination, and temperature regulation. The newborn infant is experiencing an array of new sensory experiences—touch, sound, light, odors, and tastes. The newborn can see about 8 to 12 inches and is most interested in human faces and human voices.

Adults help the newborn manage these sensations by reading their facial expressions, cries, and gestures to help determine what the infant needs. Adults help the baby learn to coordinate swallowing and sucking, keep diapers clean, and stay comfortably warm. Adults help the newborn fall asleep and maintain short periods of being awake and alert. During this time, mothers are going through hormonal changes as their bodies adjust to a postpregnancy condition. Mother and child may both be discovering the fine points of breast-feeding. Newborns may sleep for very short periods, needing to eat every few hours, so mothers are likely to be extremely fatigued during this postpartum stage.

At 6 weeks, just as mother and infant are each beginning to get their bearings, many mothers have to return to work. The baby may not have sleep patterns established yet. Breast-feeding babies may have little experience with the bottle, and

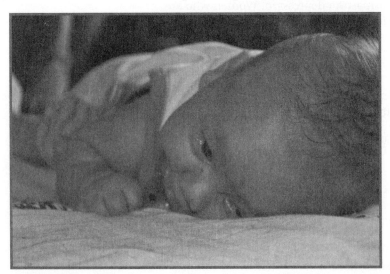

This infant is being comforted by a pacifier during adult supervised "tummy time."

their mothers may have difficulty expressing enough milk to send to child care. Babies often go through a growth spurt at 6 weeks, eating frequently and stimulating the production of more milk in the mother. Teachers need to be aware of how vulnerable these very young infants are when they enter group care.

Postnatal Brain Development

The food that is good for the heart is likely to be good for the brain. (Hippocrates)

The first 3 months of life are sometimes referred to as the fourth trimester of gestation. Human babies are born after 9 months in the womb, but they still have significant developmental tasks before them. Although the brain has been growing and becoming more complex, at birth it is only 25% of its adult weight. The lower parts of the brain (the spinal cord and cortex) are well developed, but the higher levels of the brain are quite immature. The lower brain then controls much of the newborn's activity through reflexes.

The newborn brain has all of its neurons, but there are few connections among them in the cortex, the higher level of the brain. Over the course of the first year, these synaptic connections will begin to form at an astounding rate peaking at 2 million per second (ZERO TO THREE, 2009). Adults protect the newborn brain by maintaining a quiet and calm environment and being responsive to the baby's needs. The messages the baby receives and processes must be given in ways the baby can understand. Touch and language are two important ways adults communicate with newborns.

Touch

Touch is one of the most powerful sensory experiences for a young infant. In fact, Bruce Perry has said in conference presentations that touch is vital to an infant's ability to grow and develop: "Biologically, it is as critical for a baby to be touched and held as it is to be fed." Very young infants benefit from being held and carried much of the time they are awake. Teachers and home caregivers may want to use a commercially available infant carrier such as a Snuggly to keep the young infant against their own body while keeping hands free to be with other children.

Infants use touch to learn about the world—sucking on objects, feeling them with their hands, and kicking at them with their feet. They respond with strong cries to physical discomforts such as hunger or wet diapers and are comforted by being held close to their caregiver's body or snug swaddling.

Language

Long before infants are able to utter a single word, they are learning language through their early experiences of listening to the language around them. In order to acquire a specific language, the infant brain has to develop a structure that emphasizes the distinctive sounds in the child's own language and ignores other sounds. A revealing long-term observational study (Hart & Risley, 1995) of infants and toddlers showed that children learn the language culture of their families. For example, some families' verbalizations to their children were composed of 80% negative comments. By age 3, the language used by these children was composed of about 80% negative comments to their parents and peers. Children also learn to talk about as much as their families talk. Children with the best verbal skills and highest intelligence scores were active partners in eliciting conversations with their parents and the parents were responsive, used a diverse vocabulary, had a positive tone, talked about the relationship between things and events, and often asked their children to do things rather than telling them what to do (Hart & Risley, 1995). Language learning, however, is a resilient process, meaning that even under adverse circumstances, children learn some communication strategies (Shonkoff & Phillips, 2000).

Developmental Milestones of the Newborn

In the first weeks of life, the newborn will move his arms and legs in small jerking movements or in wide flailing movements, but none of these actions appears to be intentional. Most babies will move their hands near their face and those who sucked their thumbs in the womb may recover that skill. The newborn keeps his hands fisted and will hold an asymmetrical posture on his back, with one arm down to his side and the other raised near his head.

His hearing is good and, as described, he will recognize his mother's voice and the sound of her language. Most of his actions, including rooting for the nipple, moving his head from side to side, and grasping his daddy's finger, are actually reflexes. If he is lifted into an adult's arms, his head will fall backward because he does not have control of his head, neck, or trunk.

In these first weeks, the infant depends entirely on responsive adults to help him regulate or manage his reactions to hunger, fatigue, and other discomfort. He needs help in learning how to suck and swallow and to burp up air from his tummy. He may need help to move from waking to sleeping, from sleeping to waking, and from crying to calm. Teachers and home caregivers who care for these very young infants will still be helping with these basic tasks of regulation throughout the day.

As the baby reaches 4 months, he will use his arms to raise his head and chest when lying on his stomach. He can bring his hands together to his mouth and use his hands to hold and shake lightweight toys. He will recognize familiar people and grace them with a smile. His vision is improving and he may recognize his family at a small distance. He is likely to watch faces intently and enjoy playing with people.

At 4 months, infants are likely to be much better regulated and easier to serve in group care. They are likely to be accomplished at bottle feeding, interested in others, and communicating their needs clearly. They are able to play alone for very short periods of time and may take longer naps. Mothers may be physically and emotionally better able to return to work.

Unique Beginnings

premature
Born less than 36 weeks gestation.

Not all babies remain in the womb for the full gestation of 40 weeks. Infants born before 37 weeks gestation are considered **premature.** There are many possible causes and outcomes of prematurity. However, medical intervention has improved so much that more than 90% of premature babies who weigh 800 grams or more (a little less than 2 pounds) survive. Those who weigh more than 500 grams (a little more than 1 pound) have a 40% to 50% chance of survival, although their chances of complications are greater (KidsHealth, 2009). Infants closer to full term and weighing more usually have better outcomes.

The cause of a premature birth is not always known, but common causes include external threats to maternal and fetal health including the mother's use of drugs, alcohol consumption, cigarette smoking, poor nutrition and low weight gain, obesity, physical stress, and lack of prenatal health care. Medical conditions that can cause premature birth include maternal hormone imbalances, problems with the uterus, or various illnesses including high blood pressure and diabetes. Women carrying twins or triplets are also at increased risk for premature birth (KidsHealth, 2009; MOD, 2009c). Premature births constitute about 12.5% of all births in the United States. About 25% of the more than half a million premature births are either induced or delivered by Caesarean (MOD, 2009d).

Babies born prematurely are at risk for a variety of problems. The least mature babies, those born at less than 28 weeks gestation, need intensive medical intervention in specialized hospital wards called neonatal intensive care units (NICU). They may stay in the hospital for many months, even beyond the original due date, as they learn to suck, swallow, and breathe on their own. These infants are at high risk for significantly disabling conditions such as cerebral palsy and serious learning and communication disorders.

All premature infants are at risk for these issues:

Respiratory Distress Syndrome **(RDS)** Babies born before 34 weeks gestation do not produce the protein **surfactant,** which helps the air sacs in the lungs stay open. Without the surfactant, these babies struggle to breathe. Now, mothers who are in premature labor are given medication to begin the production of surfactant in the baby. Artificial surfactant is then administered directly to the baby. Infants with RDS usually also require additional oxygen and, sometimes, a ventilator for breathing.

> **surfactant**
> A substance produced in the lungs that coats and lubricates the air spaces of the lungs. It prevents the lungs from collapsing between breaths.

Apnea Apnea is a condition in which the brain is too immature to regulate breathing and the infant stops breathing. Most babies born at less than 30 weeks experience apnea. Babies may wear an apnea monitor in the hospital and at home. They may be given medication or use a device that blows a steady stream of air into their nostrils to keep the airways open.

Intraventricular Hemorrage **(IVH)** IVH occurs most often in infants born before 32 weeks gestation. This bleeding in the brain may resolve without damage or may cause severe damage resulting in cerebral palsy or other problems. IVH may be treated with medication or the insertion of a tube to relieve the buildup of fluid.

Retinopathy of Prematurity **(ROP)** ROP is the abnormal growth of blood vessels in the eye, which can result in vision disorders or blindness. Severe cases can be treated with a laser.

Jaundice (Hyperbilirubinemia) Jaundice occurs when the liver is too immature to filter a waste product called bilirubin. Infants with jaundice are treated with special lights.

Chronic Lung Disease (Bronchopulmanory Displasia **[BPD])** BPD is a condition caused by extended use of oxygen, which causes a buildup of fluid, scarring, and lung damage. These children continue to suffer from a chronic lung disease that resembles asthma.

The following chapters will describe development in each of the domains in detail. The 9 months from conception to birth and the first 3 months of life are certainly a time of enormous growth and development. The next 3 years are even more exciting!

Summary

The journey from conception to birth is both hazardous and wondrous. The child and her brain are constantly moving toward increasing complexity and ability—vulnerable to assault but responsive to loving care, good nutrition, and a healthy environment. Early experiences, even within the womb, can have lifelong effects. In the first 3 months of life, the brain continues its rapid growth and the infant is gaining some control of her body. She is also becoming a relationship partner.

The brain develops early in gestation:

- The brain begins development within days of conception.
- Rapid cell division follows from the moment of conception.
- At 4 weeks, the neural groove appears, establishing the two cerebral hemispheres.
- Over the next weeks, thousands of neurons are generated, creating the forebrain, the midbrain, and the hindbrain.
- Neurons experience sensory information, transmitting that experience through an axon to dendrites on other neurons at a connection called a synapse.
- A human infant is born with more than 100 billion neurons, twice the number he will have as an adult.
- Synaptic connections develop rapidly in the first 3 months of life.

Early experiences create the structure of the brain:

- Experiences either reinforce the synapses of the brain or, through lack of use, cause them to be pruned.
- Touch, language, and responsive, loving care create strong, healthy circuits in the brain.

- In the first 3 months of life, infants begin to gain control of their head and trunk and to become more active relationship partners.
- Hormones associated with stress and violence change the structure of the brain, creating a brain that is attentive to danger but not to affection.

Fetal development is a time of tremendous growth and development:

- Fetal development is directed by the genetic information embedded in our DNA.
- The first trimester of gestation is marked by rapid cell division and differentiation as cells become skin cells, muscle cells, brain cells, and so forth. Internal organs and external features are formed.
- The second trimester is a period of growth and development. The mother can feel movement and, with a Doppler device, hear the baby's heartbeat.
- The third trimester is a period of rapid growth and the formation of synapses in the brain as the baby experiences movement, light, and sound.

Early experiences affect the fetus in the womb:

- Nutrition is key to healthy fetal development.
- Toxins from the environment are harmful to a fetus. These include tobacco smoke, alcohol, prescription and illegal drugs, and chemicals from common household and industrial products.
- Maternal experiences such as illness, anxiety, and domestic violence can affect the health of the fetus.

Key Terms

APGAR
genetic counseling

gestation
premature

surfactant

Reflections and Resources for the Reader

REFLECTIONS

1. The emphasis on the impact of early experiences on brain development has changed some ways we think about being with infants. What would you try to be aware of in a baby's environment because of your knowledge of brain development?
2. The womb is not as safe a place as we once thought. What might you do as an infant-toddler teacher to support parents in having healthy pregnancies?

OBSERVATION AND APPLICATION OPPORTUNITIES

1. Visit an infant-toddler program. What, if any, information is available for parents on healthy pregnancies? What could be provided?
2. Can you find information in newspapers and magazines that is readily available on having a healthy pregnancy?
3. Observe an infant-toddler program. In what ways are the environment and interactions supporting brain development? What would you change?

SUPPLEMENTARY ARTICLES AND BOOKS TO READ

Center on the Developing Child at Harvard University. (2011). Building the brain's "Air Traffic Control" system: How early experiences shape the development of executive function. (Working paper No. 11). Retrieved from www.developingchild.harvard.edu

Galinsky, E. (2010). *Mind in the making.* New York: HarperCollins Publishers.

Marshall, J. (2011). Infant neurosensory development: Considerations for infant child care. *Early Childhood Education Journal, 39*(3), 175–181.

Roth, T. L., & Sweatt, J. D. (2011). Annual research review: Epigenetic mechanisms and environmental shaping of the brain during sensitive periods of development. *Journal of Child Psychology & Psychiatry, 52*(4), 398–408.

Tierney, A. L., & Nelson, C. A. (2009). Brain development and the role of experience in the early years. *ZERO TO THREE, 30*(2), 9–13.

INTERESTING LINKS

http://www.parents.com/pregnancy/
Pregnancy The links on this site provide a week-by-week description of prenatal development and information on a vast variety of other pregnancy topics.

http://www.pbs.org/wnet/brain/
The Secret Life of the Brain This must-see series of video clips and text is taken from a PBS television series on the brain. Features include a 3-D brain anatomy and episodes titled "The Baby's Brain" and "The Child's Brain."

http://www.pbs.org/wgbh/nova/miracle/program.html
Life's Greatest Miracle This film originally aired on the PBS series *Nova* and is available for viewing online. It shows the development of a fetus from the moment of conception through birth and provides a wonderful overview of the information covered in this chapter.

http://www.zerotothree.org/baby-brain-map.html
Baby Brain Map This interactive Web-based tool shows the development of the brain in the womb and through the first three years.

http://www.sumanasinc.com/webcontent/animations/content/neuronal_development.html
Neuronal Development This animated PowerPoint® with notes explains the development of neurons, creating the brain. (Purves et al., *Neuroscience,* 4th ed., published by Sinauer Associates)

6

Attachment and Emotional Relationships

LEARNING OUTCOMES

After reading this chapter, you will be able to:

- Appreciate the uniqueness of each child's emotional development
- Describe the role of regulation
- Explain the history and importance of attachment
- Determine the cultural components of emotional expression
- Understand the role of relationships in forming an identity

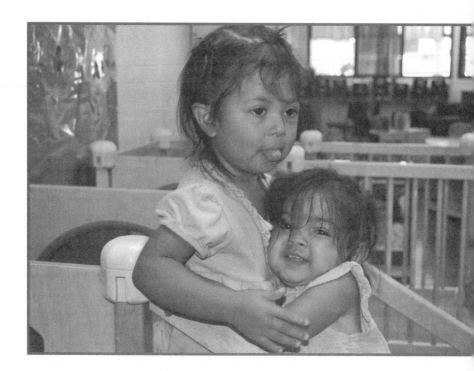

Nora had midwifed hundreds of births. As she watches babies, even in their first minutes out of the womb, she reacts to them as though she believes they have feelings. As the newborn cries out, feeling room temperature air and flailing in space, Nora is sure to say, "Oh, you don't like this, do you? You want to be warm."

The Uniqueness of Each Child

We react this way because from the first moments of life, babies are using the language of emotional expression to communicate with us. They don't need to be taught that quivering lips, a grimacing face, and a cry are ways to communicate; they are born as emotional communicators. We watch them and believe that we can understand their feelings from their expressions. We want to help them be calm and comfortable. Infants and toddlers use our responses to keep them feeling safe.

Capacities

Capacities refer to children's innate or biological potential and abilities. "Infants are born highly vulnerable and somewhat competent," said Ron Lally at a conference (Head Start Child Development Institute, 2000), adding, "And over the next few years, the balance changes and they become much less vulnerable and highly competent." Using their inborn abilities to engage with others through nonverbal communication, infants move quickly toward remarkable competency in emotional development. The significant capacities and accomplishments of emotional development are

- Learning to regulate one's reaction to the environment
- Learning to express emotions and understand the expression of emotions
- Developing an attachment relationship with a caring adult
- Developing a firm sense of self or identity

Regulation and attachment are described in this section. Emotional expression is described in the section on culture, and identity is described in the section on learning within relationships. As we explore the aspects of early emotional development, the emphasis on the child's emotional capacities developing within close and secure personal relationships will be clear.

Regulation

Regulation is the process that allows the baby to manage sensory and emotional experiences in order to develop interest in the world. Over the first 3 years of life, the child needs to learn to regulate his reactions and react only to the information most pertinent for survival.

   In order to survive life outside of the womb, the baby must learn to regulate breathing, body temperature, eating and digestion, elimination, waking, and sleeping—and, later, to regulate his reactions to both physical and emotional life experiences. Emotional self-regulation describes the activities used by the child "to tolerate frustration, curb aggressive impulses, delay gratification, and express emotions in socially acceptable ways" (Frankel et al., 2012). In infancy, it may include the actions of the infant (gaze aversion, finger sucking) or of the adult (soothing, rocking, swaddling) to reduce the baby's distress and help him maintain

How is this **video** an example of the child demonstrating self-regulation? What does the adult do to reduce the baby's distress and help her maintain a calm, alert level of arousal?

regulation

The ability to manage one's physical and emotional reactions to internal sensations or events in the environment.

OBSERVATION INVITATION **6.1**

Alijah is getting very distressed alone on a blanket. Then, a few minutes later, he is calm and peaceful. How did this care teacher help Alijah regulate his distress?

a calm, alert level of arousal (Rothbart & Derryberry, 1981). Although regulation is usually categorized under emotional development, it is now clear that there is a cognitive element as well. Regulation is closely tied to attention. In the second half of the first year, infants who have better self-regulation are also better able to focus their attention. Infants also use attention to a neutral object or moving their attention away from a distressing event to help calm themselves (Morash & Bell, 2012). Control of attention and regulation increases in the second half of the first year of life as the brain's cortical and subcortical regions develop. These regions control both attention and regulation and create a fundamental change in how the child relates to the world (Posner, 2011). The child's ability to achieve both regulation and attention during early childhood depends greatly on a responsive adult who mediates the child's experiences, but it is also influenced by the child's own temperament and physiology (Morash & Bell, 2012).

Hierarchy of Human Organization

To varying degrees, the very young infant must struggle with the immaturity of her own neurological system, her digestive tract, and her relatively unused muscles. The high level of relationship between systems regarding regulation is well illustrated by the image of the hierarchy of human behavioral systems (Als, Lester, Tronick, & Brazelton,1982) seen in Figure 6.1. Although the construct has been around for a long time, it continues to provide the framework for the Newborn Individualized Developmental Care and Assessment Program (www.nidcap.org), which provides guidance for neonatal nurseries.

In working with premature babies, Als et al. (1982) observed that stable functioning begins with the *autonomic system*: regulating body temperature, digestion, and breathing. If that system is not regulated, no other system will work smoothly. If the autonomic system is stable, the *motor system* involving muscle tone; the ability to resist gravity; and the capacity for graceful, controlled movement may function well. The next system in the hierarchy is the *state of alertness*

FIGURE 6.1   **Hierarchy of behavioral organization**

Self-Regulatory System
Signs of stress:
Sucking on hand, grasping, hand clasping

Attention System
Signs of stress:
Cannot stay focused, cannot look and listen at same time

State of Alertness System
Signs of stress:
Not resting quietly, sudden shifts from awake to sleep

Motor System
Signs of stress:
Limp, unable to resist gravity, flailing, spread fingers

Autonomic System
Signs of stress:
Heart rate, respiration, blood pressure, skin color, visceral responses—vomiting, gagging, hiccups, sneezing, yawning

Source: Based on Als, Lester, Tronick, and Brazelton (1982).

system, regulating whether the infant can achieve a deep restful sleep, an active REM sleep, and quiet and active alert states. A well-regulated state system allows the baby's *attention system* to focus and attend to information, to engage in excitement, to calm and rest—and to move between these states without too much difficulty. At the top of the hierarchy is the *self-regulatory system.*

Als et al. (1982) also described how babies lose their sense of organization system by system—first losing their ability to self-comfort; then crying or demonstrating other disorganized states of alertness; then exhibiting movements that are jerky and disorganized; and finally losing the organization of their autonomic system by hiccupping, drooling, or gasping for breath. A sensitive adult is more likely to respond when the infant is struggling with self-comforting or showing distress through a fussy state of alertness rather than waiting until the baby has completely fallen apart. The sensitive care teacher can quickly help the mildly disorganized baby recover, calm, and attend to the world.

Regulation and Relationships

Emphasizing the role of relationships in emotional development, Robinson and Acevedo (2001) suggest that moments of distress actually provide parents with opportunities to experience and understand the child's emotional cues. Infants who opt too quickly for self-comforting strategies may reduce the opportunities for adults to provide help and become their partners in understanding the world. Also, "not signaling adults for help may result in strategies such as aversion or **dissociation** when fear is aroused" (Robinson & Acevedo, 2001).

A study relating early emotional regulation to secure attachment suggested that "some infants may be naturally better able to regulate emotions than others" (Braungart-Rieker, Garwood, Powers, & Wang, 2001). However, it is possible that a care teacher who sensitively meets an infant's emotional needs is helping the baby develop regulation skills, whereas a disinterested or rejecting teacher may leave the infant struggling to find ways to self-comfort (Braungart-Rieker et al., 2001). Braungart-Rieker and colleagues suggest that at 4 months, some infants who are faced with a less sensitive mother may already be suppressing their emotions and highly regulating their own reactions, developing coping styles that derive in part from their temperament. Other infants faced with similarly less sensitive mothers respond differently, becoming highly emotionally reactive—perhaps reflecting more sensitive temperaments unable to tolerate distress and coping styles aimed at drawing in less responsive mothers.

The adult partner, whether parent or care teacher, helps the infant regulate her physical condition by ensuring that the baby is warm, dry, well fed, rested, and in a comfortable position. If a baby is crying, the adult soothes the baby by holding her upright against the shoulder, rocking, swaddling, or moving into another room or outdoors. When the baby is calm and awake, the adult can provide opportunities and support for the infant to focus her attention on interesting things. The quiet, alert infant is able to be an active partner in relationships.

The Attachment Relationship

There is probably no one concept that has been more influential in our field than that of attachment theory. A recent keyword search on Amazon.com for "attachment infancy" returned more than 13,000 current book titles on the topic. A Google search brought nearly 3 million hits. Attachment theory has been used to explain how we relate to others in our world, from infancy through our adult lives, and it is a serious consideration in the study of child care and parenting (NICHD, 2003).

Bowlby's Theory The concept of attachment was introduced by John Bowlby (1982). In a theory that described early development in terms of many active mental systems, Bowlby described an exploratory system that forwards the child's goal of learning about the world. However, the young, vulnerable child also has the goal of survival; the attachment system motivates the child to stay close enough to an adult who is invested in his well being that the child feels a sense of safety and security. The exploratory and attachment systems thus operate as balance to each other, with infants using the **attachment relationship** as a secure base from which to explore. As they venture out to play and explore, they carefully maintain enough proximity to remain in visual contact with their attachment figure. The current, casual use of the term *attachment* often refers to feelings of love and affection. Attachment really addresses basic feelings of trust, safety, and security (Bowlby, 1982).

Bowlby described children as developing an internal representation, a constant mental image, of themselves and their relationships to others. The child carries that mental image of his first relationship into all future relationships.

dissociation
The disconnection from full awareness of self, time, and/or external circumstances, causing a loss of memory or sense of identity.

The **videos** *Separation Anxiety* and *Stranger Anxiety* demonstrate how infants from approximately 9–18 months of age can become distressed when separated from their attachment partner.

attachment relationship
A relationship in which young children use an adult as a source of security when distressed or during exploration.

Mary Ainsworth's Patterns of Attachment   In naturalistic studies of infants and their mothers, Mary Ainsworth began to notice patterns in the behavior of mothers toward their infants, and a consistent pattern of responsive behavior from the infants toward certain maternal behaviors. The goal of the baby in the first year of life seemed to be to maintain a feeling of safety and security. Physical proximity to the mother seemed to be the most effective way of achieving this. However, Ainsworth saw babies going about this task with three basic, but differing, strategies, each of which related to the mother's usual pattern of being with the baby. These strategies were eventually described as three patterns of attachment: **secure attachment, anxious-ambivalent attachment, and anxious-avoidant attachment** (Ainsworth, Blehar, Waters, & Wall, 1978). These patterns of attachment are described in Table 6.1.

The Strange Situation following her naturalistic studies, Ainsworth found a way to evoke attachment behavior from babies in a laboratory setting. She developed a research protocol called the "Strange Situation," in which the situation becomes increasingly stressful as a stranger enters, the parent leaves and returns, until finally the baby is momentarily alone in a room. The behavior of the infant upon reunion with his mother most clearly illustrates the attachment category of the child. Securely attached children run to their mothers and allow themselves to be comforted. Children with anxious-ambivalent attachment run to their mothers but resist being comforted. Children with anxious-avoidant attachments will appear to ignore the mother's return while scrupulously regaining proximity to the mother (Ainsworth et al., 1978).

As researchers continued to work with attachment theory and the Strange Situation protocol, they observed children whose behavior did not fit into any of the three patterns. Although the three categories varied in their effectiveness as methods of healthy adaptation, each allowed the child ultimately to engage the adult to provide enough care and attention for the child to feel secure. Main and Cassidy (Main & Cassidy, 1988) call these the *organized* categories. However, not all attempts to elicit care work. These researchers (1988) introduced a fourth pattern—one in which the children couldn't seem to come up with or settle on

secure attachment
Children are able to use an adult as a secure base for exploration and can be comforted by their parents when distressed.

anxious-ambivalent attachment
Children have exaggerated preoccupation with their caregiver's attention but may both solicit and resist comforting when distressed.

anxious-avoidant attachment
Children seem to ignore the presence of their caregiver and concentrate on play and exploration but are really working at containing their distress.

TABLE 6.1   **Patterns of Attachment**

Attachment Category	Maternal Behaviors	Infant Behaviors
Secure	Sensitively reads child's cues for comfort and responds effectively	Can signal distress, be comforted, resume play and exploration
Anxious-ambivalent	Attends to infant when it serves her own needs; may ignore infant's signals of distress	Find it difficult to allow themselves to be comforted; usually anxious during play
Anxious-avoidant	Ignores or feels anger toward infant much of the time	Appears to be unusually independent in play but maintains proximity to mother without engaging her

OBSERVATION INVITATION **6.2**

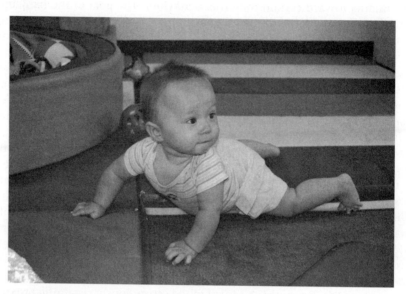

What attachment behavior are you seeing in this picture?
Which attachment category do you think Emma would have?

a strategy to help them feel secure. They labeled this one *disorganized attachment* (Main & Cassidy, 1988).

Children who demonstrated the disorganized pattern had parents whose behavior was violent, frightening, or frightened; whose own childhoods had been violent and frightening; or who had experienced an unresolved loss. These parents responded to their children's attachment cues in such confusing ways that these children simply could not come up with a strategy that would consistently work to give them a feeling of safety and security. There was no way for the baby to develop any feeling of control over a distressing situation.

Attachment Research in the Late 20th Century   Attachment theory writing and research exploded in the late 20th century. One aspect of Bowlby's early work generated particular interest. It was the idea that attachment behavior actually signified the mental representations the child held of relationships. If the child did indeed form a sort of mental template for understanding and even seeing relationships, all future encounters with people would be measured against the familiarity of this first relationship (Bretherton, 1985; Sroufe, 1990). Furthermore, because it is the only way an infant knows how to be with other people, the infant (or child or adult) may behave in ways that inspire the other person also to behave within the expectations of the attachment relationship.

For example, Sherri, a teacher, has a history of secure relationships. In caring for little Ben, who has a history of anxious-ambivalent attachment, she responds to his distress by picking him up and comforting him. Ben, not trusting that this comforting will really be available when he needs it, does not trust this moment

and arches away from her, crying harder. Sherri reads his cues and puts him back down, believing that is what he wants. Ben's idea that people are not there for you when you need them is reinforced by being put down when he is distressed. Ben's expectations and behavior essentially create behavior in other people that continually tell him that he is right to be ambivalent about his relationships with others.

Attachment categories are not permanently fixed once set, but they are likely to stay consistent if the overall stability of the family remains the same. Studies of preschool children and 6-year-olds show high correlations with attachment categories at 12 and 18 months. The secure preschoolers tend to have positive peer relationships and are well regarded by their teachers, who see them as resilient and likely to be leaders. They are neither victims nor victimizers in relationships (Troy & Sroufe, 1987; Weinfield, Sroufe, Egeland, & Carlson, 2002). Avoidant infants tend to harass and victimize their peers in preschool and their teachers tend to reject them—as though children rejected by their mothers elicited rejection by others (Troy & Sroufe, 1987; Weinfield et al., 1999). Children assessed as anxious-ambivalent at 12 months tend to be "babied" by their teachers, being treated as younger than they are, and they are often the victims of the anxious-avoidant bullies (Troy & Sroufe, 1987).

It is easier to build strong children than to repair broken men. (Frederick Douglass)

Working Models of Attachment   Main, working with colleagues in Berkeley, has investigated how the mother's working model of attachment relationships may be driving her own behaviors and creating an intergenerational pattern of attachment (Main & Goldwyn, 1994). Main developed the Adult Attachment Interview as a way of learning about the parent's own mental representation of attachment relationships (Main, 2000; Main & Goldwyn, 1994).

The three resulting organized classifications for adults are very similar to the three organized classifications of infant attachment. Secure/autonomous adults express "clear valuing of attachment figures and attachment-related experiences, together with an apparent objectivity in the descriptions and evaluations of particular relationships" (Main, 2000, p. 1078). They were parents of securely attached babies. Parents of avoidant babies presented themselves as dismissing of the importance of attachment relationships (Main, 2000, p. 1080). Insecure/preoccupied adults are continually preoccupied with their own early relationships with their parents—much like their own insecure/ambivalent babies who are so preoccupied with keeping track of their mothers, they cannot settle their attention on play (Main, 2000, p. 1080).

Attributes

Attributes are characteristics of a child that make that child unique. Temperament is an attribute. The following example illustrates how three children might react to a parent saying good-bye:

On entering the toddler room in the morning, Kevin sobs as though his heart is broken as his father leaves. After a moment of comforting, and full of energy, he enthusiastically plays with the rocking horse, leaps off, and runs to the easel. Faron enters the room quietly, kisses her mother good-bye, and settles into the housekeeping area. Terra clings to her mother's skirt, preventing her from leaving in the morning. When her mother finally is able to leave, Terra hangs back and watches the other children play while she sucks her thumb and holds her teddy bear.

Temperament

Each of these children is going through the experience of being welcomed into the child development and education program and separating from his or her parents. However, each of these children brings a different behavioral style and a different way of expressing emotion to the experience. Although adult behavior has an enormous effect on young children, in a transactional, relationship-based, and bioecological model of development, it is understood that infants and toddlers bring their own characteristics to expressing emotions and being in relationships.

Since the pioneering work of Thomas, Chess, Birch, Hertzig, and Korn (1963), these differences have been known as *temperament,* or **temperament style**. Early temperament research looked at the dynamic interaction between characteristics that were inherent to the child and characteristics of the child's environment. Thomas and colleagues identified nine *temperament traits,* defined in Figure 6.2: activity level, biological rhythms, approach/withdrawal, adaptability, intensity of reaction, mood, persistence, distractibility, and sensitivity. In children, these traits tend to appear in groupings that the researchers called *temperament types:* easy, difficult, and slow-to-warm-up. The "easy" or **flexible** child tends to have regular biological rhythms (eating, sleeping, and eliminating on a predictable schedule), a positive mood, easy adaptation to new experiences, moderate emotional reactions, and low sensitivity to sensory stimulation. The **slow-to-warm-up** or shy child tends to withdraw from new situations and adapt to them slowly. The "difficult" or **feisty** child is very active, emotional expressions are intense, and attention is easily distracted. These children are very sensitive to changes in light or sound; they tend to eat and sleep without regular patterns; and their moods can change frequently (Thomas et al., 1963; Thomas & Chess, 1977).

Temperament is an aspect of development that resonates for most people. We recognize these traits in ourselves and see them as the source of conflict or ease in our relationships. (It's annoying when someone plays music louder than you like it or comfortable when the lighting in a room is just as you like it.) However, some temperament traits may be more central than others to successful development. The trait of intensity of reaction, sometimes called emotional reactivity or vitality, combined with the abilities for self-regulation, is one trait that may

temperament style

A set of biological characteristics that influence how a child will react to the environment.

flexible temperament

Regular biological rhythms (eating, sleeping, and eliminating on a predictable schedule), a positive mood, easy adaptation to new experiences, moderate emotional reactions, and low sensitivity to sensory stimulation.

slow to warm-up temperament

Child tends to withdraw from new situations and adapt to them slowly.

feisty temperament

Irregular biological rhythms, swings in mood, high reactivity, and sensitivity to sensory experiences.

FIGURE 6.2   **Temperament traits**

- *Activity level:* Amount of physical movement
- *Biological rhythms:* Regularity of eating, sleeping, elimination
- *Approach/withdrawal:* Comfort in new situations
- *Mood:* Amount of time in pleasant, cheerful mood as opposed to fussing, crying, or resisting others
- *Intensity of reaction:* Energy level of emotional expressions
- *Sensitivity:* Response to sensory information, including light, sounds, textures, smells, tastes
- *Adaptability:* Ability to manage changes in routine or recover from being upset
- *Distractibility:* How easily the child's attention is distracted
- *Persistence:* How long a child will stay with a difficult activity before giving up

Source: Based on Thomas, Chess, Birch, Hertzig, and Korn (1963).

have enormous impact on a child's life (Rothbart, 1989). Emotional vitality or reactivity "can be defined as the lively expression of emotion that is shared with others" (Robinson & Acevedo, 2001). Infants with high emotional vitality are more expressive and more likely to recruit an adult's involvement into whatever interests them. These moments of interaction provide opportunities for babies to develop a relationship with the adult during which they may think, "I know you are interested in me—and you will help me when I need it. I know how to call on you for help."

Reactivity can also have negative effects for the child and the adult. It is the more highly reactive child who may have more negative reactions to experiences. For example, researchers sometimes restrain an infant's hands to produce a stressful situation. In a study looking at possible physiological components of reactivity, researchers found that some 6-month-old infants had a brief episode of bradycardia (significant slowing of the heart rate) at the beginning of the restraint. These infants also cried louder and longer, tried more often to escape, and looked less at their mothers than the non-bradycardia infants. There is clearly a physiological component to reactivity (Porter & Jones, 2011).

Another interesting line of research suggests looking at children and seeing who might be ill suited temperamentally for child care. A large body of literature defines quality in child care and suggests that children have better outcomes when they are in higher-quality programs. This essay, however, suggests that children who are more reactive—either more easily upset or shyer and more inhibited—may be physiologically unable to handle what is a tolerable level of stress for other children in group care (Phillips, Fox, & Gunnar, 2011).

In a relationship-based model, we think about the effect of the child's temperament on the adult and on the relationship. In their initial work on temperament, Thomas and Chess proposed the idea of "goodness of fit" between child and parents. They proposed that no one temperament was any easier or better, nor that any one parenting style was really better. They proposed that the ease of the relationship between parent and child would, at least in part, depend on how well matched the parent and child were on certain temperamental traits. For example, the highly active and emotionally expressive child would have a goodness of fit with a parent who was also active and expressive. That same child might be difficult for a very quiet, subdued parent. Or, it might not be the parent's own personality but his expectations about children derived from his own history or culture that would apply to the goodness of fit. Understanding that one's own perception of behavior is important begins to link the concepts of temperament and attachment.

Development and Learning Through Relationships

Lyssa is playing on a blanket when the teacher, Tinnaka, walks past. Lyssa feels pleasure at seeing Tinnaka and smiles at her. To Lyssa, Tinnaka's smile looks somehow similar to the way her own smile feels and assures her about the accuracy of her emotional response to this experience. Tinnaka adds language to the experience by saying, "Lyssa, are you happy to see me? I'm sooo happy to see you today!" as she picks her up and snuggles her. Lyssa's sense of self, in this moment, is of a well-loved, easily understood, and welcomed human being.

OBSERVATION INVITATION **6.3**

Francisco has been exploring his own image. He watches himself giving his mirror image a kiss. If you think of Francisco being in the process of developing a sense of who he is, how do you understand this moment? What might you say?

Identity Development

Every experience that a baby has occurs within a physical experience, a feeling state, and, generally, information from the environment that both inspires the moment and informs it. As memories of these experiences accumulate for the infant, he begins to develop a sense of himself, an internal picture of self, an identity: "This is me when I am happy and playing with my teacher—my body is active, my face is smiling, I am comfortable and safe." Developing an identity is a complex mixture of the baby's own temperament; physical, sensory, and processing abilities; and the physical, social, and emotional environment surrounding him.

In infancy research, the development of a sense of self is understood to occur during interactions with others, through moment-by-moment experiences of emotional communication. Babies learn about themselves as they learn about the feelings of others.

> *Children have never been very good at listening to their elders, but they have never failed to imitate them. (James Baldwin)*

self-fusion

young infants not knowing that they are separate beings from their mothers

Although some theorists believe that in early infancy babies exist in a state of **self-fusion**, not knowing that they are actually separate beings from their mothers

(Mahler, 1975), interpersonal development theory points out that from the moment of birth, babies are experiencing themselves as separate beings contained in a boundary of skin. From the first moments, the experience of being held by another person is different from being swaddled in a crib; seeing your own hand and simultaneously feeling the motor information of the movement of that hand are different from seeing another person's hand (Stern, 2000). As described in Chapter 3, Stern (2000) asserts that the infant's greatest task in emotional development is not learning that she is separate from others but learning to make connections with others.

Cultural Differences and Emotional Expression

All five major elements of emotional development discussed in this chapter—regulation, attachment, temperament, identity formation, and emotional expression—must be considered within a cultural context.

A number of studies suggest that infants around the world use the same facial expressions, with potentially the same meanings, in the same situation—but they may express emotion more or less quickly and more or less heartily. For example, one study looked at emotion regulation in two very different societies. One was an urban, middle-class, German group, whose members were well educated, individualistic, lived in a money-driven society, and organized by autonomy. Their patterns of attachment and emotional expression were assessed with the Strange Situation and found to be similar to those in American studies. The other group members, the Cameroonian Nso tribe, were subsistence farmers living in a highly interdependent society and organized by relatedness. Their children were never separated from their mothers. The Strange Situation was not considered culturally appropriate. Instead, an Nso female stranger came to the home, greeted the family, and picked up the child.

The three response patterns that emerged for the Nso had parallels to the Western secure, anxious-ambivalent, and anxious-avoidant patterns. One group of 1-year-olds was quiet and kept the same sober expressions throughout the interaction. The second group did not react to the stranger's entry but became distressed on contact. The third group became distressed at the woman's entry and remained distressed. Saliva tests of cortisol before and after the encounter showed the first group to have no change in cortisol, the second group to have increased cortisol demonstrating increased stress, and the third group had high levels of cortisol before and after the encounter. These children were distressed even before the woman arrived. The three sober, nonreactive infants were already well socialized to a society that valued hiding individual emotions to contribute to the harmony of the group. The other two groups would be characterized as anxious-avoidant and anxious-ambivalent in our taxonomy (Keller & Otto, 2009).

Emotional Expression and Understanding

Emotional expression is the primary form of communication for very young children. Infants make themselves known, and know about others, primarily through emotional expression. In early studies, some

CULTURE CLOSE UP

A Japanese family moved to Minneapolis for the father to spend a semester as a visiting professor at the university. After several weeks in an apartment, alone all day with her 2- and 4-year-old daughters, the mother enrolled them in a neighborhood child care program. Although the girls spoke no English, they enjoyed playing when they visited with their mother. After a few visits, the mother decided to leave them. They had never been away from her before. Together, they ran to the big glass door of the church, sobbing and looking down the sidewalk where their mother had disappeared. The 4-year-old kept repeating some words in Japanese. The director looked them up in a phonetic dictionary: "My mother is dead! My mother is dead!"

researchers believed that babies were born able to use a universally understandable set of facial expressions to demonstrate a few basic emotions, and that more complex emotions appeared in a predictable pattern over time (Izard & Malatesta, 1987). Others believed that emotional expression and understanding, inborn to some extent, were quickly learned through interactions with adults (Emde, 1998). Our current understanding of the development of emotional expression suggests that many elements are at play: innate reactions common to all humans, what is unique to the child physiologically (including temperament), and what is learned through actual interactions with parents and teachers in a particular culture (Colonnesi, Zillstra, Van der Zande, & Bogels, 2012).

Progression of Emotional Expression

In the **video** *Social Referencing*, watch how the toddler looks at her mother's reaction to determine if an unknown object is safe. Notice how, when the mother is encouraging, the child approaches the unknown object. When the mother looks fearful, the child is cautious.

The innate reactions are seen during the first months of life, but babies are also learning through their interactions with others. Infants begin to respond to others with big, genuine social smiles and to anticipate how their favorite adults will behave. They learn to expect certain patterns of interaction and are surprised when things go differently. They will coo and smile at toys that respond contingently to their actions (Watson, 1972). Emotions become more specific as joy becomes different from contentment, and anger and sadness emerge as separate experiences from distress (Lewis, 1993). Active games such as "I'm going to get you!" followed by blowing on the baby's tummy can bring chortles at 4 months, especially when little variations create the sense of suspense and surprise.

In the period from about 4 months through 7 months, there is a shift in emotional development, as infants begin to demonstrate that they are "falling in love" (Greenspan & Greenspan, 1994). They will brighten, smile, and reach for the beloved adult when they see her. A parent or consistent care teacher gets the feeling that the baby recognizes her, enjoys her, and calms and feels safe when she is near.

intersubjectivity

The perception of sharing an experience between two people.

social referencing

The way a baby makes use of an older child's or adult's signals to determine the safety of a situation.

At 9 to 12 months, babies go through a second shift in emotional development that Stern (2000) calls "the discovery of **intersubjectivity**—the knowledge that the baby's own thoughts and feelings can be known by others and that they can understand the thoughts and feelings of others." They begin to use the facial expressions and emotional tone of others as a way to interpret the meaning of events in their environment. This process, called **social referencing**, allows the baby to use a trusted adult to judge whether a stranger or a new experience is safe. The baby literally looks to the adult to see how to react. Although this visual checking in with an adult to clarify ambiguous events can be easily observed in everyday situations, researchers have also found creative ways to determine how babies use increasingly sophisticated strategies for social referencing. Klinnert (Klinnert, Emde, Butterfield, & Campos, 1986) investigated the idea of babies understanding that an adult's emotional expression had meaning tied to an object or an event. She created a smooth surface for a baby to crawl over, with the mother waiting on the other side. The middle of the surface, however, appeared to have a sudden drop-off; it was a "visual cliff." When the new crawler approached this apparent cliff edge, he would look to his mother for information. If she smiled and nodded reassuringly, the baby would continue crawling across the seemingly empty space. If she looked fearful, the baby would stay on his side of the "cliff" (Klinnert et al., 1986). (See Figure 6.3.)

FIGURE 6.3   **The visual cliff paradigm**

In the visual cliff study, an infant is seated on a table. In order to reach her mother, she must cross what appears to be a drop of more than 2 feet—although, in reality, the table is covered in a clear plastic. The mother either encourages the crossing with an inviting expression or discourages it with a terrified facial expression.

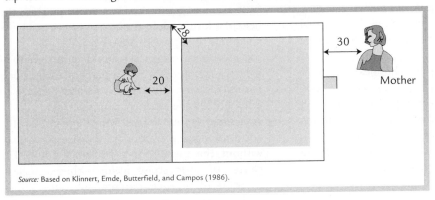

Source: Based on Klinnert, Emde, Butterfield, and Campos (1986).

OBSERVATION INVITATION **6.4**

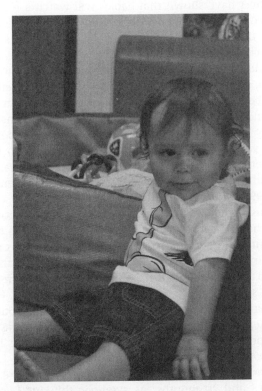

How do you think this boy is feeling? What does his body posture and facial expression tell you?

BOX 6.1

Toxic Stress

Stress causes the body to release hormones including cortisol, adrenaline, and norepinephrine. The internal organs and inflammatory systems react. This can be helpful in preparing the body to respond to the cause of the fear; but when an infant is in a chronically frightening environment, this response begins to wear the body down. The developing brain circuitry is disrupted, and the seeds of later physical and mental health problems are sown. The chronic, relentless stress is *toxic*.

The National Council on the Scientific Study of the Child proposes that infants and toddlers experience three kinds of stress responses:

- *Positive stress response* is brief and mild; a caring and responsive adult helps the child cope with the stressor. These are common life events such as frustration or getting an immunization. With the help of a loving adult, these experiences teach the child how to cope with adversity.
- *Tolerable stress response* is caused by an event of greater magnitude such as a parental divorce or a natural disaster. The stress is tolerable because an adult buffers the experience for the child.
- *Toxic stress response* comes from frequent, strong, and prolonged activation of the stress response without the benefit of a buffering adult. The causes of toxic stress include abuse, neglect, exposure to violence, parental substance abuse, and maternal depression. Toxic stress causes the brain to be hypervigilant in searching out danger and restricts the ability to learn.

Other researchers have shown that babies will watch a researcher's reactions to a toy or to the contents of two boxes and will willingly explore the objects that were targets of positive adult reactions and will avoid the objects that adults treated with disgust (Repacholi, 1998).

During this period, infants also use information from adults to learn which emotions can be expressed and how and when they can be expressed. These **emotional display rules** may be specific to a culture, a family, or even a member of a family. One parent may encourage the child to experience the full range of human emotions. Another may be uncomfortable with displays of love and intimacy and react in very restrained ways in comforting or showing approval to his baby. Another family may be extremely uncomfortable with the expression of sadness or anger and may teach the child to minimize or avoid expression of these emotions (Gottman, Katz, & Hooven, 1997).

Infants are constantly watching the adults in their world for genuine expressions of emotion that appear to be congruent with the events that inspire them. In fact, when infants are taught to suppress negative emotions they may become anxious, they experience physiological hyperarousal, and they may store the negative emotion and the maladaptive response they develop in their memory to be used in future, similar situations (Eisenberg, Cumberland, & Spinrad, 1998). Infants and toddlers who live in fear have brains that are built to detect danger. Then, even neutral situations can be seen as frightening and bring about an aggressive response (National Scientific Council on the Developing Child (2010b)). (See Box 6.1.)

The third major shift in emotional expression occurs as the infant becomes a toddler, between 18 and 20 months. As symbolic thinking becomes established, children are able to use language to organize their thinking. They remember past events and form representations of repeated events that help them anticipate what

emotional display rules

Culture-specific social rules about how and when to express certain emotions.

OBSERVATION INVITATION **6.5**

What is this toddler learning about what it is like to be in a relationship?

future events might be like. This is particularly true of the representations they form of what it is like to be in a relationship.

The increased ability to symbolize is accompanied by a more fully developed sense of self. Children begin to recognize themselves in a mirror, use personal pronouns to refer to themselves, and identify themselves as boys or girls. They express self-conscious emotions such as guilt, shame, embarrassment, and empathy. They are also beginning to control their own behavior in the service of maintaining relationships.

Impact of Maternal Depression

Brooke has just given birth to her third child. She took a leave from her job but is having trouble returning to it. She has always felt good about her life, her marriage, her children, and her work. Since this last birth, however, she can't seem to feel interested in anything. She is tired and bored. She can see her baby trying to have a relationship with her but just can't respond the way she wants to.

In the past several years, postpartum depression has been recognized as a major element impeding a mother's ability to care for her new baby and as having lasting effects on the baby's abilities.

It is estimated that approximately 50% to 80% of all new mothers experience postpartum blues in the first weeks after giving birth. This usually includes a few days of mild feelings of sadness, fatigue, tearfulness, and feeling overwhelmed. In a survey of new mothers (Brown University, 2006), 19% of mothers reported moderate to severe depression. This may include debilitating symptoms of low mood, sleep and appetite changes, lack of pleasure in daily life, poor concentration, fatigue, irritability, feelings of worthlessness, despair, and thoughts about harming herself or her child. In addition, a very small number of women experience postpartum psychosis, delusions, agitation, paranoia, and thoughts about suicide or infanticide (Clark & Fenichel, 2001). Early Head Start (EHS) national research reports that as many as 52% of women enrolling in EHS were depressed. For 12% of women, that depression was chronic and lasted through their child's third birthday (Early Head Start Research and Evaluation Project, 2006).

Although mothers suffering from postpartum psychosis are the ones we see on the news, the less dramatic postpartum depression is being recognized as a serious problem for the well-being of both mother and infant. Maternal depression often occurs within a cluster of other risk factors such as low income, marital dissatisfaction, prior episodes of depression, and mothers' negative perceptions of their neighborhoods (Campbell, 1995; Cooper & Murray, 1998; Murray & Cooper, 1999; Christie-Mizell, Andre, Peralta, & Laske, 2008), and it occurs in all socioeconomic groups. Colic in the baby and maternal depression have been found to be related, but it is not known whether infant colic might cause maternal depression or if depression might lead to infant colic (Maxted et al., 2005).

Maternal depression was found to have negative effects on babies as early as the neonatal period, suggesting that there may be effects from prenatal exposure to a biochemical imbalance in the mother's body. Babies of clinically depressed mothers were poorly regulated in their behavior, their physiology, and their biochemistry. Depressed mothers seem to offer one of two interactive styles. They withdraw or they become very intrusive. Each of these styles has deleterious effects on the infant's ability to organize his state of arousal, to interact, and to be responsive to the world. When mothers were treated with antidepressants and cognitive therapy, many had remission from their depression. The earlier the remission, the better the infant's behavioral and psychological outcomes will be (Wickramaratne et al., 2011).

Maternal depression is generally treatable, through both medication and therapeutic intervention (Cooper & Murray, 1998). Home visiting programs have been identified as particularly good avenues for helping depressed mothers get treatment (Golden, Hawkins, & Beardslee, 2011).

Children with Special Needs

autism

A disorder that affects a child's ability to engage in social interactions and to communicate. Child may engage in repetitive behavior. Symptoms begin before the child is 3 years old.

bipolar disorder

A disorder of the brain that affects energy, mood, and behavior.

The emotional system is so basic to the human body that the responders for pleasure and pain exist in the same part of the brain that regulates breathing and heart rate (Damasio, 2003). This may explain why infants and toddlers with even the most significant multiple disabilities still demonstrate a preference for being with their own family. However, although emotional experience is a common, even defining, aspect of our humanity, it is also the source of each person's completely unique sense of identity and unique relationships.

Because emotional development occurs within the brain, conditions that affect the brain may affect emotional development. **Autism** and **bipolar disorder** are two examples of biological aspects of the child that may result in poor emotional development. Autism, even in children of normal intelligence, is often characterized by an inability to understand that other people exist with their own point of view, feelings, and experiences (Gopnik, Meltzoff, & Kuhl, 1999). Bipolar disorder, an emotional illness characterized by severe, often out-of-control mood swings, has a biological basis and may be identified in infancy (Egeland, Weinfield, Bosquet, & Cheng, 2000). These biologically based issues may make it difficult to develop a mutual, loving, healthy relationship between a child and even the most committed parents or teachers. David Howes (2006) writes that although it may be challenging to parent some children with disabilities, if parents are supported in reflecting on their parenting and are emotionally tuned in to their children, the children are likely to feel secure.

It is important to remember, however, that in the infant and toddler years, the child's emotional development must always be understood within the context of relationships. Adults are expected to provide safety, to see and respond accurately to communication cues, and to be sensitive and responsive. Even when infants or toddlers bring very real challenges such as biologically based emotional illness, it is important to promote parenting relationships that can help the child achieve the best possible development. Further information about the progression of emotional development and how adults can create strong relationships is available in a chart called Developmental Trends and Responsive Interactions later in this chapter.

Programs That Enhance Emotional Development and Learning

Infant Mental Health

As the fields of child development and psychology have developed an increased appreciation for the powerful lifetime effects of early relationships, the field of **infant mental health** has been established. For some parents, instead of recognizing the message sent by the baby's expressions and actions, the parent attributes meaning and motivations to the baby that really generate from the parent's own life experiences (Fraiberg, 1996). For example, a woman who has been physically abused, first by her father and then by her husband, sees her baby son as physically threatening to her.

As should be clear from the rest of this chapter, in infants and toddlers, good mental health requires a partner who helps the baby regulate his reactions, express and understand expressions of emotions, and develop a secure base of attachment balanced by an autonomous sense of self. Unfortunately, for some babies a reciprocal relationship with a sensitive, responsive adult partner is not available. When adults are unable to "see" the infant, situations become confusing for the baby. Adults behave in ways that do not make sense and the child's development can be thrown off course.

Infant mental health is a growing field that promotes emotional health in children and intervenes in the relationship between parent and infant when there are relationship challenges, trying to support the parent in giving accurate, responsive care. By compassionately understanding and caring about the

> **infant mental health**
> Therapist intervenes in the relationship between parent and infant when there are relationship challenges, trying to support the parent in giving accurate, responsive care.

STRATEGIES TO SUPPORT EMOTIONAL DEVELOPMENT AND LEARNING

1. Comfort young babies who are stressed or unhappy by swaddling, holding them close to you, rocking them, and speaking or singing quietly.
2. Help young babies learn to regulate themselves by letting them suck on their hands, feeding them on demand, and helping them fall asleep and awaken calmly.
3. Be available for interaction when babies are awake and alert; talk quietly and gaze into their eyes when they are interested; allow them to turn away and collect themselves when they need a break.
4. Mirror a baby's facial expressions, adding words that describe the feeling with a congruent tone of voice.
5. Express your own feelings honestly and clearly.
6. Allow infants and toddlers to express the full range of emotions. There are no "bad" feelings. Babies need to learn socially acceptable ways to express their feelings.
7. Use your facial expressions and language to let infants and toddlers know whether or not a situation is safe from a small distance.
8. Be responsive and reassuring when infants and toddlers are fearful about exploring. Let them know you are watching them and will keep them safe.
9. Encourage infants and toddlers to explore and play, while you remain available when they return to you for moments of contact.

parent's immediate or earlier experiences, the therapist may provide a kind of relationship never before experienced by the parent. The actual therapeutic work includes seeing the parent and infant together. Although the parent's conversation and actions may dominate the session, the therapist is always watching and sometimes commenting on the relationship between the parent and the baby. If a mother is revealing a particularly sad and painful story from her own childhood, the therapist might acknowledge the mother with a comment such as, "I'm sorry, that is really more than such a little girl should have to experience," but she may then add, "I'm really taken with how your baby watched you as you talked about this. She can't understand your words but she seems very concerned about whether you are all right." A while later, the therapist might point out, "Your baby seems to watch you a lot. She's so interested in everything you do. And she really reacts to your feelings." The ability of the therapist to genuinely ally herself with a parent while still standing up for the baby may provide an entirely new kind of relational experience for the parent.

Respectful and consistent, the practitioner remains attentive to each parent's strengths and needs. Within the safety of this relationship, parents feel well cared for and secure, held by the therapist's words and in her mind (Pawl, 1995). The practitioner listens carefully, follows the parent's lead, remains attuned, sets limits, and responds with empathy. Within the context of the working relationship, the parent experiences possibilities for growth and change through the relationship with her own infant (Weatherston, 2001).

Insight-based psychotherapy emerges from exposure to the parent and infant together, as the therapist becomes aware of particularly conflicted moments of interaction. The therapist may ask the parent how she feels when her baby cries, or perhaps if she remembers how someone comforted her when she was little and crying. Questions designed to help parents remember and reflect on their own childhoods or their immediate feelings in this moment help them become aware of the discrepancy between their response and the baby's real needs.

Always be aware that you may also have issues in your relationship history that may play out in your caregiving relationships. Or a child's behavior may be so confusing that you will need support in understanding and responding to the child.

Child Care Experiences and Emotional Development

Given the tremendous importance of deep, meaningful, ongoing, responsive relationships in the first years of life, there has understandably been considerable concern about the effects on infants and toddlers of long hours each day in child care. In 1989 the National Institute of Child Health and Development (NICHD) launched a massive study of the effects of child care on child development. Although the study was a comprehensive look at aspects of quality and child outcomes, the effect of child care on the emotional development of young children was a primary question. The study does offer some significant information.

Major results of the study revealed that mothering was a stronger and more consistent predictor of child outcomes than child care. There is little evidence that early, extensive, and continuous care was related to problematic child behavior. Among the child care predictors, child care *quality* was the most consistent predictor of child functioning (NICHD, 1998). In terms of the child's attachment to the mother, the child care experience (quality, amount, age of entry, stability, or type of care) did not have a direct effect on attachment security or avoidance. As with children not in child care, maternal sensitivity and responsiveness did have the main effects on security of attachment. There were significant interaction effects when low maternal sensitivity was combined with poor-quality child care, heavy use of child care, and more than one child care arrangement. Boys with many hours of care and girls in minimal amounts of care were somewhat less likely to be securely attached (NICHD, 1997).

Some of the results reflected differences in the effect of child care on different groups of people. Children from minority and single-parent families were rated as less prosocial by their mothers when in low-quality child care (National Institute of Child Health and Development, 2002b). More child care experience across the first 3 years was associated with less maternal sensitivity and less positive engagement of the mother for White children, but greater maternal sensitivity and child positive engagement for non-White children through first grade. Positive associations of mother-child interaction with hours of child care were similar for both African American and Hispanic children (NICHD, 2003).

Quality of child care consistently related to differences in the children's outcomes. Early experience with higher-quality child care benefited children's positive engagement with their mothers through first grade when their mothers were depressed and seemed to have a positive effect on maternal sensitivity through first grade (NICHD, 2003). Maternal sensitivity and responsiveness and experience in child care both seem to contribute to prosocial skills with peers (NICHD, 2001b).

ATTACHMENT AND EMOTIONAL RELATIONSHIPS

Infants and toddlers develop a strong sense of who they are through increasing self-regulation, learning about effective emotional expression, and developing attachment relationships.

Development	Example
0–4 months (infant)	
• Infants are taking in a lot of information about the world. • Infants can get overwhelmed and begin to yawn, look away, or fuss. • Infants begin to calm themselves by sucking on their hands or listening to an adult talk quietly to them. • Infants gaze into their teacher's eyes as she feeds them. • Infants turn their heads toward a familiar voice. • Infants relax and allow themselves to be comforted by familiar people. • Infants cry when they are hungry, tired, or uncomfortable.	Carlos followed Karen with his eyes whenever she entered the room. When she came close to him, he looked at her as though he wanted her to join him. Accepting his invitation to play, she sat with him on the floor. As he began to tire and fuss, she swaddled him in a blanket, held him close, and spoke softly to him.
4–8 months (infant)	
• Infants like to look at their hands and feet. • Infants wave their arms and kick in excitement when they see a familiar person. • Infants will smile at a teacher, expecting her to smile back. • Infants use their faces and bodies to express many feelings: everything from frowning and crying to laughing out loud. • Infants express their feelings more clearly to familiar people and are more reserved with strangers.	Deborah loves being carried in her teacher's arms as they move around the room "talking" about the things they see. Her eyes are wide and bright, she smiles, and she makes cooing sounds as though taking her turn in the conversation. When a visitor enters the room, Deborah gets very quiet and serious and holds tightly to her teacher's shoulder as she looks at the visitor.
8–12 months (mobile infant)	
• Mobile infants may be fearful with strangers. • Mobile infants will call upon familiar adults to help them when they are upset. • Mobile infants will look at a familiar adult to determine whether a situation is safe or dangerous. • Mobile infants will cling to a familiar adult when they are in a strange situation. • Mobile infants will find humor in silly games and adults making big facial expressions.	Jamie is enjoying his new ability to quickly crawl anywhere he wants to go. He loves the little climber that lets him look out the window. But when another child joins him, he likes to look back at his teacher, Fred—just making sure he's still safe.
12–18 months (mobile infant)	
• Mobile infants will imitate the actions of familiar adults, such as using the phone or caring for a baby doll. • Mobile infants will seek an adult's attention by pulling on their leg or taking their hand. • Mobile infants will use a favorite blanket or stuffed animal to help calm themselves. • Mobile infants will protest loudly when their parents leave them. • Mobile infants will relax and be comforted by cuddling with a familiar adult. • Mobile infants will let their likes and dislikes be clearly known.	Amelia carries her teddy bear around all morning. Sometimes she copies her teacher Sophia's actions, patting its back or "feeding it a bottle." When she gets tired, she rubs the teddy against her ear and sucks her thumb.

Teacher or Parent–Child Interaction	Environment

0–4 months (infant)

- Keep young babies close to you, in your arms, in a snuggly, or on a blanket nearby.
- Recognize the signals that indicate a baby wants to be with you—intent gazing, reaching, a happy look—and respond with quiet, verbal and nonverbal turn taking.
- Recognize the signals that indicate a baby needs a break—yawning, drooling, looking away—and sit back quietly and wait while the baby regroups.
- Comfort babies whenever they cry.

- Being close to a familiar care teacher is best.
- A serene, quiet space with gentle lighting limits the information an infant needs to take in.
- Avoid playing background music all day.
- Limit the number of objects, sounds, color, and movements around a young infant.
- The care teacher is the most interesting thing for a baby to watch, but other babies, mirrors, and toys within the baby's visual range of focus are also interesting.

4–8 months (infant)

- Provide opportunities for babies to look in mirrors as they play.
- Mirror the emotional expressions of the infant and add appropriate words: "I'm so excited to see you today!"
- Respond to babies in a way that helps them be calm and active. If babies are crying, soothe them.

- Mount unbreakable mirrors on walls.
- Provide floor time when babies can play with their feet while on their backs, or move around on the ground.
- Books and posters of photographs of real faces with different emotional expressions are very interesting to infants.

8–12 months (mobile infant)

- Encourage mobile infants to move off and explore by reassuring them that you are watching and keeping them safe.
- Understand that mobile infants may become afraid of new situations that wouldn't have been frightening a few months ago. Be comforting and reassuring.

- Play peek-a-boo.
- Read stories about mothers and fathers who go away and come back.
- Read books with flaps to lift to find things.
- Keep room arrangements and routines predictable.

12–18 months (mobile infant)

- Demonstrate your interest in babies' activities.
- Show your pride in babies' accomplishments.
- Let babies use you as a secure base from which to explore the world.
- Let babies know you understand their feelings and respond with respect.
- These are still very young children who need lots of cuddling and holding.

- Provide child-size copies of tools adults use: telephones, dishes, keys, etc.
- Post photographs of the infants with their family on the wall.
- Laminate photos of the infants with their family for carrying around.
- Make photo albums of the children at your program and talk about the pictures.
- Have adult chairs and quiet, comfortable spaces for holding children.

DEVELOPMENTAL TRENDS AND RESPONSIVE INTERACTIONS (Continued)

Development	Example
18–24 months (toddler)	
• Toddlers begin to control some impulses, saying "no, no, no" as they begin to throw blocks.	Frankie climbs up onto the table, looking his disapproving teacher right in the eye, and says "no, no, no."
• Toddlers may stop their actions when told to by a teacher.	
• Toddlers may not want to stop playing when their parent comes to pick them up.	
• Toddlers may cry when they are unable to master what they are trying to do.	
• Toddlers know their own names and may use "me" and "mine."	
24–36 months (toddler)	
• Toddlers can sometimes be independent, but they like to know the care teacher is close by.	Kiki carried her baby doll over to the photos of her own family on the wall. She crooned to her baby while looking at her own mother's face.
• Toddlers like to study pictures of themselves, their friends, and their families.	
• Toddlers listen to your words and the tone of your voice when you talk about them. They want you to be interested in them and proud of their accomplishments.	
• Toddlers need clear and consistent limits. They will forget rules, or test rules, but feel secure when you remind them and help them follow the rules.	
• Toddlers may use words to express their feelings, or they may hit or bite.	
• Toddlers care about the feelings of others and will comfort someone who is sad or bring a Band-Aid to someone who is hurt.	

Teacher or Parent–Child Interaction	Environment

18–24 months (toddler)

- Keep your sense of humor. Understand that sometimes toddlers can stop themselves from doing things but other times they cannot.
- Respect the strong feelings of toddlers. Taking turns and sharing come later—now "me" and "mine" are an important part of developing a strong sense of self.

- Provide spaces that allow children to explore without ever being out of sight.
- Have enough copies of the same toy for several children to each have one without sharing or taking turns.
- Let children bring comfort items like blankets or stuffed animals to your program. Provide a quiet place where they can comfort themselves.

24–36 months (toddler)

- Establish clear and consistent rules. Be prepared to remind the toddlers frequently of how to follow the rules: "We don't bite. Biting hurts."
- Give toddlers enough of your time and attention so that they feel understood.
- Echo the enthusiasm toddlers can bring to their play.
- Notice and comment on the interactions that toddlers are watching and thinking about.

- Provide many photographs of the children with their family: on the walls, in little books, and laminated to carry around.
- Provide protected spaces for quiet play.
- Maintain predictable routines and room arrangement.
- Provide books that tell simple stories of coming and going, of families, and of friendship.
- Sing songs about feelings such as "When you're happy and you know it" and "When you're sad, angry…"

Summary

Self-regulation, emotional expression, and an attachment relationship create the core of the healthy development of a sense of self and a sense of oneself with others. It provides the attentional and motivational foundations for later relationships, learning, and motor development.

- Each infant and toddler must find a balance between reacting to his experiences and regulating his reactions so that he can be relaxed, alert, and attentive. Adults help babies learn to self-regulate first with swaddling, rocking, and sucking, but later by helping them control their own reactions.
- Responsive adults build their relationship with infants through moments of regulation. Whether they take the opportunity to comfort a baby's distress or engage in interaction when a baby is alert, this sensitivity to regulation is an opportunity for the relationship.
- Temperament traits are inborn characteristics influencing how a child responds to the world. There are nine traits: activity level, biological rhythms, approach/withdrawal, mood, intensity of reaction, sensitivity, adaptability, distractibility, and persistence.
- Temperament traits are often found in groupings called difficult or feisty; slow-to-warm-up, shy, or fearful; and easy or flexible.
- Within the first year of life, infants learn their cultural norms regarding how intensely people express emotions and the nature of the attachment in infant-parent relationships.
- Infants and toddlers have active emotional lives. They express emotions in similar ways around the world and generally understand emotional expressions, although their ability to interpret expressions is influenced by their early experiences.
- Infants and toddlers use the facial expressions of those they trust to help them judge the safety of a situation through a process called social referencing.
- Over time, through repeated interactions, infants develop an attachment relationship with the important adults in their life. They use the adult as a source of safety and security as they venture out to explore their world.
- Aspects of the level of security a child feels in the attachment relationship (secure, anxious-ambivalent, anxious-avoidant, or disorganized) may provide the mental model for later relationships in the child's life.
- Many women experience postpartum depression to the extent that they are emotionally unavailable to their babies. Postpartum depression is often not identified, and it can have serious effects on the baby and on the mother-child relationship.
- Some parents are unable to establish a relationship with their infants because they have never had close relationships or because of traumatic losses or experiences in their own past. Infant-parent psychotherapy can be effective during the early years of a child's life.
- Child care can be neutral, beneficial, or harmful to the parent-child relationship. The greatest factor in the effect of child care on the parent-child relationship is the quality of the child care program.

Key Terms

anxious-ambivalent attachment
anxious-avoidant attachment
attachment relationship
autism
bipolar disorder
dissociation

emotional display rules
feisty temperament
flexible temperament
infant mental health
intersubjectivity
regulation

secure attachment
slow-to-warm-up temperament
social referencing
temperament style
self-fusion

Reflections and Resources for the Reader

REFLECTIONS

1. How do you see self-regulation as being a foundation of healthy development?
2. How could you meet the emotional needs of three or four infants and toddlers in your care at one time?

OBSERVATION AND APPLICATION OPPORTUNITIES

1. Observe a young baby with an adult. Do the baby's facial expressions become part of his or her language?
2. Visit a library or bookstore and look at some picture books for infants and toddlers. Can you find books that teach babies about emotional expression? About adults who keep them safe in attachment relationships? Share these books in class.

SUPPLEMENTARY ARTICLES AND BOOKS TO READ

Center on the Developing Child at Harvard University. (2010). The foundations of lifelong health are built in early childhood.Retrieved from www.developing-child.harvard.edu

Center on the Developing Child at Harvard University. (2012). The science of neglect: The persistent absence of responsive care disrupts the developing brain (Working Paper 12). Retrieved from www.developing-child.harvard.edu

Mulligan, M. (2013) Understanding preterm infant behavior in the NICU. Emory University School of Medicine department of Pediatrics. An overview of Als' Hierarchy Hierarchy of Human Development. http://www.pediatrics.emory.edu/divisions/neonatology/dpc/nicubeh.html

Social and Emotional Development of Infants and Toddlers VHS Series (#816, #817, #825) **(2012).** Social and Emotional Development of Infants and Toddlers DVD Series (#8161, #8171, #8251)

INTERESTING LINKS

YouTube presentation of the Strange Situation: Use the key words *strange situation*

A YouTube video of the visual cliff experiment: Use key words *visual cliff*

A YouTube video of Alexander Thomas and Stella Chess talking about temperament: Use key words *Thomas and Chess*

Whole Child: www.pbs.org/wholechild/abc/index.html

This site has charts from PBS: The ABCs of Child Development, Developmental Milestones for Your Child's First Five Years, as well as articles on emotional health.

ZERO TO THREE Parent Pages: **zerotothree.org/**

ZERO TO THREE On this Web site click on "Parents." There are many interesting articles on emotional development under Social Emotional Development.

7

Social Development and Learning with Peers

LEARNING OUTCOMES

After reading this chapter, you will be able to:

- Explain why it is important for teachers and families to understand children's social development with peers
- Describe how children's unique temperaments and gender influence their peer relationships
- Describe cultural differences in how children may behave socially
- Explain how young children grow socially with peers in the context of responsive adult-child relationships
- Identify special needs that may occur in children's social relationships with peers
- Describe the qualities of programs that support children's peer relationships

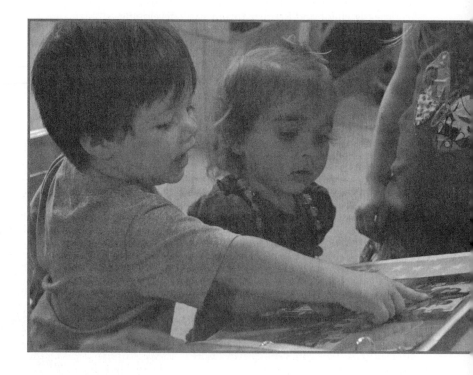

Sitting by herself on the floor of her child care center for the first time, a 7-month-old sees the room from a totally new perspective with other children near, and one is crying. She looks eagerly at the other infant to watch him making such a noise. Becoming fearful, she lifts up her arms, indicating that she wants to be picked up by a caring adult.

In her child care center, an 7-month-old pulls herself up to stand, holding tight to a bar fastened securely on the wall. She sees another child near and reaches out to pat him on the head. They smile at each other, but then one, with her awkward emerging motor skills, falls into the other and they both start crying.

An 18-month-old runs to her teacher to dump all kinds of little toys in the teacher's lap. Another toddler notices and soon is imitating the first toddler. Quickly, four toddlers join the others, running back and forth, following each other around the room. They squeal with delight as they move in and out of the group, communicating their joy with the toddler version of follow-the-leader.

The Uniqueness of Each Child

Capacities

As adults, we know that relationships are a source of joy. They are a fundamental element in the human experience. Relationships are important to young children, too. Infants and toddlers are capable of becoming impressive social partners with adults when they arrive in this world. Social interactions (the moment-to-moment initiations and responses) and positive social relationships (characterized by affection, desire to be with others, and reciprocal warm feelings for each other) are all part of early social development with adults. Whereas a primary focus of investigation has been the parent-child relationship and the teacher-child relationship, we are now "turning the lens" and focusing on peer interactions and relationships (Brownell & Kopp, 2007; McGaha, Cummings, Lippard, & Dallas, 2011; Rubin, Bukowski, & Laursen, 2008; Wittmer, 2008).

If you observe closely, you will also see just how many capacities infants and toddlers have to interact with peers. Over the infant and toddler years, they grow in their motivation and ability to play with other children. They learn to communicate with their peers in effective ways. As toddlers, they can become friends with other children and share moments of glee with them. As they grow from infancy to toddlerhood, they have the capacity to use positive social skills such as offering, playing beside, approaching, playing with, initiating play or contact, being friendly, forming friendships, comforting, helping, giving, showing a toy, hugging, showing empathy, and defending favorite adults and peers. Infants and toddlers also grow in their capacity to learn how to assert themselves and negotiate conflicts without being aggressive—a very difficult social task. During the infant and toddler

Carlos approaches Jenny with a light touch on the head.

socially competent

The ability to engage in social interactions that are mutually beneficial and that contribute to the physical and emotional good of the individual and others.

years children become increasingly **socially competent** with peers—engaging in social interactions that are mutually satisfying to both partners in a relationship. (See the Developmental Trends and Responsive Interactions chart at the end of this chapter for further information on the capacities of infants and toddlers and the development of social competence during infancy.)

Interaction among children is a fundamental experience during the first years of life. (Malaguzzi)

Recognizing the significance of quality peer experiences is important for four reasons. First, peer experiences contribute to infants' and toddlers' development. Piaget's (1954) theory emphasizes that young children construct knowledge about *how* to play with peers, cooperate, and negotiate conflicts. Vygosky's (1978) sociocultural theory highlights how children learn about their own and others' culture through peer interaction. Relationship-based theory (Emde, 1988; Hinde, 1988, 1992a, 1992b) emphasizes the importance of the quality of adult-child relationships on how children learn to be in healthy relationships and also stresses that children learn skills in peer relationships that they do not with adults.

Second, the percentage of mothers who are employed outside the home who have children younger than age 3 has increased; therefore, infants and toddlers are experiencing their peers more often in child development and education groups (U.S. Census Bureau, 2010). Experiences with peers occur daily for these children and are an integral part of their life.

Third, what parents and teachers do with infants and toddlers (and families) can make a difference in whether young children thrive socially. Research identifies the importance of positive parent-child and teacher-child relationships to ensure that young children become prosocial (Hastings, Utendale, & Sullivan, 2007) and learn to inhibit aggression (Tremblay, 2004; Tremblay & Nagin, 2005). Young children with challenging temperaments (irritable, difficult to sooth) are more likely to demonstrate externalizing behaviors (acting out, using aggression) when they are older when caregivers use harsh discipline, have higher rates of depression, or have lower rates of sensitivity when the children are infants and toddlers (Miner & Clarke-Stewart, 2008). There are ways that adults can interact with young children while being responsive to their temperament that help them thrive socially.

Fourth, there is continuity in social cognition from infancy to childhood. Paying attention to how infants and toddlers function socially is important so that adults can support children or intervene if the adults perceive that children may be demonstrating few social skills. Social skills and attitudes may look different for an infant than for an older child, but, for example, whether an infant looks to adults for comfort or help correlates with whether a preschool child can begin to think about how another person thinks or feels (theory of mind; Yamaguchi, Kuhlmeier, Wynn, & vanMarle, 2009). Adults, then, who are observant can support an infant's trust in adults so that the infant will begin to look to adults for emotional support, knowing that this will possibly result in a preschool child who can think about how peers and adults feel. Maternal depression is another factor to notice because "postpartum maternal depressive symptoms when the child is from 1 month to 3 years can greatly influence child outcomes" including social skills at ages 4.5 to 6 (Wu, Selig, Roberts, & Steele, 2011, p. 414). Because infant and toddler professionals know that there are long-term consequences of continuous maternal depression on children's social skills, they can provide prevention and intervention services for mothers. Helping infants and toddlers experience healthy relationships when they are young is vitally important for later social relationships.

Interacting and playing with other children facilitates development of language, self-concept, and sensorimotor thinking. (Bodrova & Leong)

We know that young children's capacities for satisfying interactions and relationships, peer play, **prosocial** behaviors, and negotiating conflicts are developed in the context of relationships with family members, teachers, other adults, and peers (Wittmer, 2008). We also know that young children are born with their own unique characteristics that are part of their temperaments, and that these attributes contribute to the nature and quality of their peer relationships.

prosocial
The skills and tendency that a child has to be kind, empathic, caring, helpful, thoughtful, considerate, compassionate, and supportive with others.

Attributes

Each infant and toddler expresses his uniqueness in social relationships. This individuality is a blend of a child's genetic characteristics and his experiences in his home, culture, and community. Attributes such as temperament and gender differences contribute to each child becoming an individual who knows how to relate to others in particular and special ways.

Temperament

The temperament of the child seems to influence play behaviors with peers. Temperament was highlighted in depth in Chapter 6, the chapter on emotional development and attachment. Here we emphasize three dimensions of temperament that are related to the identity of the child as it impacts social development (see Figure 7.1). Dimension 1 includes the ability of the infant and toddler to use focused attention, inhibit certain actions when necessary, and control and express intense emotions in a socially acceptable way. Dimension 2 describes the tone of children's emotions or mood, and dimension 3 describes children by their interest and ability to interact with others.

The first dimension, self-regulation of emotions, is a critically important child characteristic that predicts children's social competence—the ability to engage in mutually satisfying relationships with others (Fitzsimons & Finkel, 2010). Among preschoolers, highly regulated children usually (not always) demonstrate socially competent responses to emotionally intensive situations (Fabes et al., 1999). Socially competent children are also less likely to react negatively to difficult situations. Lack of self-regulation of emotions as demonstrated by negative emotional responses to peer situations contributes to observers and teachers rating children

FIGURE 7.1   Dimensions of temperament that affect social development

Dimension 1: Self-regulation
Dimension 2: Negative to positive emotions
Dimension 3: Shy to extroverted

Source: Rothbart and Bates (1998).

as less socially competent (Fabes et al., 1999). A young child's temperament, it seems, may affect the quality of social interactions if a child has a difficult time controlling his or her emotions. It is challenging for toddlers to always control their emotions, though, and adults cannot expect that they will. However, adults can support infants and toddlers to increasingly become self-regulated as they develop throughout the infant and toddler years. Recent research (Vallotton & Ayoub, 2010) concludes that girl toddlers' vocabulary predicts their ability to self-regulate, whereas toddler boys' vocabulary predicts improvement in their rate of change in self-regulation. Encouraging children to "use their words," supporting them in problem solving aloud, and providing a rich vocabulary for young children to imitate and learn make a difference in their use of self-regulation strategies.

> *The real issue may not be whether children are shy and anxious or overwhelmingly outgoing, but how they learn to regulate how they express who they are. (Shonkoff & Phillips)*

When the research on the second and third dimensions of temperament is examined, it is easy to see how self-regulation comes into play. For instance, the second dimension of temperament is mood; most children express a variety of moods in different contexts, but some children may be generally more negative or positive. If a toddler has a negative mood much of the time, especially if the toddler doesn't want others near her, then she may have fewer opportunities than other children to learn how to interact with other toddlers. This negative mood could occur for a variety of reasons, including biological conditions and a challenging environment.

Dimension 3, shy to **extroverted**, describes how children are more inhibited or more exuberant. The **exuberant** children (Degnan et al., 2011; Stifter, Putnam, & Jahromi, 2008)—the Tiggers of the world (Milne, 1926/1991)—are outgoing and demonstrative. Can't you just picture these enthused, happy children bouncing through a room? Their excitement is contagious and they are highly social, but they also can be overwhelming to other children. These vivacious children may actually be slightly more aggressive than others (Tarullo, Mliner, & Gunnar, 2011). Happy toddlers, no doubt, attract a group, are having fun, and are in the middle of everything. And when a child is in the middle of everything, the chances are higher that the child will bump into other children, take their toys, and boss them around. Again, self-regulation seems important. If these exuberant children control their emotions when appropriate and necessary, then they are more likely to be the children in the group who attract positive attention from peers (Rubin, 1998). However, once again, we must emphasize that we can't expect toddlers to control their emotions at all times—they are just learning how—and they need understanding adults to express their emotions verbally and to help them calm down when they become too exuberant or upset.

A contrasting temperament to exuberance is *inhibition* (Stifter et al., 2008). Some young children are very busy and often like to explore and play alone. These busy toddlers who sometimes play by themselves wouldn't be considered inhibited. **Inhibited** children are those who seem very shy, hesitant to interact with peers, anxious, and fearful of peers. They may also actively withdraw from other children (Rubin & Coplan, 2004). There is evidence that inhibition may have a biological component (Fox et al., 1995; Henderson, Marshall, Fox, & Rubin, 2004; Kagan, 1997). Toddlers with higher levels of social fearfulness had increases in the level of cortisol (a hormone that indicates stress) across the day

extroverted

A person who is active, outgoing, and focused on others.

exuberant

A person who is full of life, energetic, enthusiastic, and cheerful.

inhibited

A child who seems very shy, hesitant to interact with peers, and is anxious and fearful of peers.

in child care (Tarullo et al., 2011; Watamura, Donzella, Alwin, & Gunnar, 2003). There are, however, also environmental and relationship factors that contribute to whether or not a child continues to be inhibited, for example, harsh parenting or overprotective parenting contributes to a child's social withdrawal and inhibition (Bayer, Sanson, & Hemphill, 2006; Rubin, Coplan, & Bowker, 2009).

Parents and teachers need to begin early to support infants and toddlers who are inhibited with peers because inhibited toddlers are likely to be inhibited preschool children (Hay, Payne, & Chadwick, 2004). Young children who are inhibited (or withdrawn) need gentle support to enter the social world and learn language, social, and emotional skills to gain self-confidence in engaging in peer interactions. Do not ignore inhibited children or expect them to change quickly. They may not be interacting with other children because of the fear of rejection (Rubin & Coplan, 2004); when adults are critical or harsh with these children, they are more likely to continue to be withdrawn as they grow older (Rubin, Burgess, & Hastings, 2002). Furthermore, if adults are overprotective and do not encourage these children's peer interactions with kindness, these children may be more likely to continue to think that the world is a scary place. For instance, you can go with a hesitant child to a block area, engage the child with *one* other child at times rather than with the whole group, and go to the child to encourage him to go with you for a story with several other children.

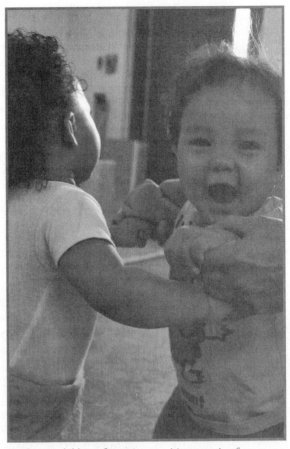

Exuberant children often attract positive attention from peers.

As children experience these peer relationships, adults can guide children with unique temperaments to try different ways of playing and interacting. New infant and toddler social skills develop through the assistance of helpful, but not intrusive, adults (Honig, 1994; Rubin et al., 2002; Vygotsky, 1978). As these infants and toddlers gain experience, they construct important ideas about how to master the task of interacting with a peer partner (DeVries & Zan, 1996). They have opportunities to imitate more **elaborate play schemes** and try them out within a safe environment (Bandura, 1977, 1989) (See Observation Invitation 7.1).

elaborate play schemes
The play of children that includes complex themes.

Gender Issues

Children's individuality in social development may also be influenced by gender. The behavior associated with gender may have biological roots, may be influenced by the environment, or may be influenced by a combination of both.

A question that is often asked is, "Do boys prefer to play with boys and girls with other girls?" If they do, is that a problem that should concern us? Moller and Serbin (1996) discovered that among almost 60 toddlers, primarily White, average age 35 months, only 21% of the males but 62% of the females engaged in **same-gender play**. Why do these toddlers seem to prefer **gender segregation**? Three theories that explain why young children might want to play with children of their own gender are presented in Figure 7.2. After carefully observing toddlers in their classrooms and collecting teachers' ratings of child gender behavior,

same-gender play
Patterns in which girls play with girls and boys play with boys.

gender segregation
The separation of boys and girls during play or other interactions.

FIGURE 7.2   **Three theories that explain children's desire to play with their own gender**

(1) **Cognitive Consonance Theory**
When children learn to identify their own gender as male or female, they highly value anything associated with their gender category.

(2) **Gender-Types Toy Preference Theory**
Children segregate according to their toy and activity preferences, and the activities chosen bring children into contact with other peers who also prefer that activity.

(3) **Behavior Compatibility Theory**
Gender segregation develops out of toddlers' attraction to peers who exhibit play styles that are compatible.

Source: Moller and Serbin (1996).

Moller and Serbin (1996) concluded that only one of the theories outlined in Figure 7.2 was supported: the compatible play style explanation. Children of the same sex with similar play styles preferred to play with each other.

As children develop, their interest in same-sex play increases. Fabes, Martin, and Hanish (2004) conclude from their research that by the time children enter preschool, they show a strong preference to spend time with same-gender peers, and this preference increases throughout the elementary years. This tendency occurs across cultures and may be a powerful influence on children learning gender-specific roles in their culture (Fabes et al., 2004).

Fabes and colleagues (Fabes et al., 2004; Fabes, Hanish, & Martin, 2003) summarized Maccoby's (1998) research as well as their own and concluded that preschool boys' play was frequently rougher and more active and involved more physical contact and taunting. Boys tended to play away from the teacher, engage in less structured play, follow peer direction, and engage in what could be considered math and science activities more than girls. Girls were more likely to emphasize cooperation and use forms of communication that promoted harmony. Girls played more often in the presence of a teacher and received more adult attention and direction from the teacher. They had more opportunities to regulate and control their behavior and emotions. Boys' and girls' different compatible play styles were fostering different behavioral norms and interaction styles, and these play styles were contributing to very different learning experiences for boys and girls in the preschool classroom.

You can observe toddlers during their play experiences to determine whether this type of gender segregation is occurring—and if so, whether the behaviors exhibited are of concern. You should be concerned with same-gender (and mixed-gender) play *if* the behaviors limit the potential of children for learning a variety of skills, if the children in a particular group become more aggressive when they are with one another, if a group frequently does not like to have an adult present, or if a child hardly ever wants to play with a child of the other sex: "Although it is important for children to develop a strong sense of self and incorporate what it means to be a girl or a boy, adults must help children see that neither girls nor boys should be limited by gender roles" (Chrisman & Couchenour, 2003, p. 116).

Observe to see if boys and girls are beginning to develop a stereotype that certain toys are only for boys and other toys only for girls. Zoe, a child described

These two boys play with each other frequently. What do you think they are learning from each other?

by Chrisman and Couchenour (2003) in their article "Developing Concepts of Gender Roles," was likely to deny boys a chance to play with her special toy because she mistakenly thought that only girls could play with that type of toy. If this happens, you could tell Zoe that both boys and girls like to play with the toy (e.g., dolls) and then give both boys and girls opportunities and encourage them to do so. Another strategy to encourage children to play with all types of toys is to display pictures of both boys and girls playing with many types of materials and toys (Derman-Sparks & the A.B.C. Task Force, 2003). Choose and read books that contradict gender stereotypes by showing girls and boys playing quietly with their toys *and* playing actively on the playground. However, finding children's books that show girls as the main character may be challenging. McCabe, Fairchild, Grauerholz, Pescosolido, and Tope (2011), in an examination of 21st-century children's books, found that "males are represented nearly twice as often in titles and 1.6 times as often as central characters" (p. 197).

Development and Learning Through Relationships

Letta reached out to touch the nose of her 9-month-old playmate, Carla. Carla, sitting quietly, let Letta softly stroke her nose and then reached out as if to offer a hug. Letta and Carla, ever so gently, touched noses, laughed, and then crawled away to play with some toys next to them.

Culture and Peer Relationships

Vygotsky (1978) noted that every behavior of a child occurred first on the social level in the child's culture and then on the individual level; first between people (**interpsychological**) and then inside the child (**intrapsychological**). Letta and Carla seemed to have experienced gentle touches, laughter, and reaching out to

interpsychological

The thinking that occurs between people, such as using language to communicate with others.

intrapsychological

The thinking that children do by themselves.

be with others on a social level in their culture (interpsychological) and now these behaviors are an integral part of who they are (intrapsychological), thus affecting their behavior in social situations with playmates.

> *It is principally through interacting with others that children find out what the culture is about and how it conceives their view of the world. (Bruner)*

Children's social interactions differ according to their cultural experiences. In Letta's and Carla's culture, adults value peer interaction at an early age. This belief influenced their parents, who are friends, to find a child care home where Letta and Carla could be together during the day. The parents and the family child care provider believe strongly that young children need early peer interactions to learn how to play together. Parents in their culture encourage children to "not be shy" and are concerned when infants and toddlers are socially inhibited.

Many families in Italy also believe in the value of early peer relationships. The authors of *Bambini* (Gandini & Edwards, 2001), a book describing Italy's Reggio Emilia approach to early childhood education, state that infant and toddler centers "are viewed as daily-life contexts with the potential to facilitate the growth and development of all children" (p. 25). Parents want early socialization experiences for their children, and they want teachers who will support young children's relationship development.

There may be families, however, in which shyness and social inhibition are *not* viewed as negative traits (Chen, French, & Schneider, 2006). These families may want their children to be socialized with family members rather than peers, especially during the infant-toddler years.

CULTURE CLOSE UP

Graciele, an Early Head Start teacher, was worried about two older toddlers who were in her multiage classroom of 8 children. One boy, Keelan, hardly ever wanted to be close to other toddlers and preferred to play by himself. He seemed embarrassed or shy when another toddler approached him. Yet, he was focused on his play and could engage with toys for long periods of time, even putting together a 25-piece puzzle by himself. The other child, Eiseo, was quite physical and when bumped by another child or when he wanted a toy that another child had he raised his fists in a threatening manner and sometimes pushed other children. If another child took Eiseo's toy, Eiseo would take the toy right back. Eiseo had started to grab Keelan's toys, push Keelan, and then run away with the toy. Keelan responded by looking sad, but then getting another toy. Graciele decided to talk with the boys' parents.

Keelan's parents reported that they want their children to be cooperative, helpful, and part of a peaceful family. They weren't concerned that Keelan played alone and didn't initiate play with other children. They wanted him to show self-control and not hurt anyone, even when another child hurt him. Eiseo's parents, one of whom had been a victim of bullying when young, reported that they did not want their child to be a victim of bullying. They wanted him to be assertive, independent, and self-reliant. Eiseo's parents were concerned that Eiseo was taking other children's toys; however, they were glad that Eiseo stood up for himself when another child took his toy. Graciele realized that the parents' views of child rearing reflected family cultural beliefs about individualism and collectivism. What would you do?

Social Development with Peers

Infants and toddlers go through many stages of social development and struggles as they learn how to be socially competent. You will observe, at times, that these very young children are interested in trying to learn how to be social with peers. At other times, the challenges of learning how to negotiate the "me" with the "other" is difficult, and conflicts between peers may seem to erupt often. An infant or toddler might reach out to comfort another child; 5 minutes later, she might bite that same friend, either out of sheer emotional exuberance for the joy of the moment or out of anger because her friend took her toy. However, as they grow from birth to age 3, young children learn an incredible amount about social interactions. Let's examine children's development of their motivation and capacity to be and play with other children.

The Developmental Trends chart at the end of this chapter presents a sequence of peer development. Let's take a closer look at many of the milestones highlighted in the chart by examining the development of four capacities of infants and toddlers. Infants and toddlers, over the first 3 years of life, become increasingly able to

- Communicate with peers
- Play with peers in increasingly complex ways
- Develop prosocial behaviors
- Manage negative feelings and conflict with peers

At the end of their first 3 years of life, children still have much to discover to maximize their potential in the social domain, but with adults who are knowledgeable of the abilities and motivation of infants and toddlers to learn, children gain a strong foundation of knowledge and skills from which to continue to build that potential.

Communication with Peers

How do infants and toddlers communicate with one another often when they lack the words to express their feelings, needs, and desires? Toddlers have a variety of communication skills that they use to initiate and maintain relationships with other children (Katz, 2004). They inform; direct; and use sounds, words, and laughter to keep other children involved in play with them. In a classic article Maya Pines (Pines, 1984) summarizes the research by Hubert Montagner, a French ethologist, on young children's communication strategies. Noted for his studies with insects, Montagner observed young children's behavior after a challenge from his colleagues in a university in Switzerland to apply his work to children's behavior. As he observed young children for 15 years, he captured their social behavior, particularly the **gestural language** and the individual nonverbal communication styles that affect children's social interactions with others: "Each child spoke a gestural language other children could understand clearly, even if adults could not necessarily decode it, and it affected how others treated the child" (Pines, 1984, p. 61).

gestural language
Movements of the body that communicate meaning.

Montagner discovered five major styles of nonverbal communication among children that begin as early as 9 to 12 months of age:

1. Actions that pacify others or produce attachment: Offering another child toys, lightly touching or caressing the other child, jumping in place, clapping one's hands, smiling, extending one's hand as if begging, taking the other child's chin in one hand, cocking one's head over one's shoulder, leaning sideways, rocking from left to right, or vocalizing in a nonthreatening way
2. Threatening actions that generally produce fear, flight, or tears in the target child: Loud vocalizations, frowning, showing clenched teeth, opening one's mouth wide, pointing one's index finger toward the other child, clenching one's fist, raising one's arm, leaning one's head forward, leaning one's whole trunk forward, or shadow boxing
3. Aggressive actions: Hitting with hands or feet, scratching, pinching, biting, pulling the other child's hair or clothes, shaking the other child, knocking the other child down, grabbing something that belongs to the other child, or throwing something at the other child
4. Gestures of fear and retreat: Widening one's eyes, blinking, protecting one's face with bent arms, moving one's head backward, moving one's trunk or one's whole body backward, running away, or crying after an encounter with another child
5. Actions that produce isolation: Thumb sucking, tugging at one's hair or ear, sucking on a toy or a blanket, standing or sitting somewhat apart from the other children, lying down, lying curled into the fetal position, or crying alone (Pines, 1984, p. 63)

The young children differed greatly in the combinations of gestures that they used with their peers. The secret to children's peer success (in fact, becoming a leader among peers) seems to be the children's use of as many of the pacifying gestures as possible, and defending themselves with threatening behaviors only when necessary. Children learn to "read" other children's behavior quickly, avoiding children who use frequent aggressive strategies. Our understanding of young children's remarkable ability to communicate nonverbally opens a window to a fresh view of infant and toddler peer communication.

The magical sequence: head tilted over one shoulder, a smile and outstretched hand. (Pines)

Conversations Between and Among Peers

What do infants and toddlers say to each other when they can communicate with words and how do they develop relationships as they talk with each other? Jane Katz (2004) and Elin Ødegaard (2006) have studied peer conversations among toddlers.

Katz (2004) emphasized the pragmatic skills of toddlers to initiate and maintain a relationship, and Ødegaard (2006) studied the mealtime conversations of nine Norwegian children ranging in age from 1 year to 3 years attending a preschool program. She found "two-year-olds trying to come to grips with the problems of life" (p. 83) as they talked about problems and expressed feelings such as anger, fear, loss, and desire. For example, one young child engaged his peers in a conversation about a scary event as he related a story about Santa Claus by saying, "Gloomy Santa Claus was there" (at the center of town). These young children also struggled with one another over who would control a story. Ødegaard reports that an almost 3-year-old Ane raised her fist in the air and shouted to another child, "Me talk." Soon the other child responded to Ane with stifled anger, "Ah, me talk." This conflict between the two children at mealtime continued into their play. The nature of these two children's relationship was apparent in both their words and their play.

Children express, develop, and adapt the meaning of their words and relationships as their conversations continue. Ødegaard (2006) emphasizes that conversations or narratives are co-constructed with the teacher and peers, often in a multiparty discussion. Through thoughtful questions and comments, a teacher often helps a child move from talking about the "here and now" (events and objects that are present) to the "there and then" (events and objects not present). Through reflection on children's words and conversations with their peers, the teacher can learn about children's cultures and the relationship experiences with the adults and peers in their lives. These peer conversations with or without adults contribute greatly to children's learning (Shatz, 2007).

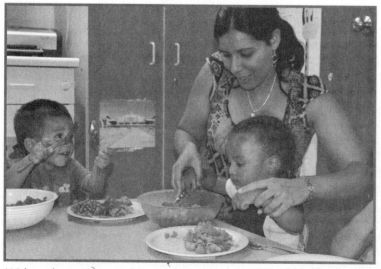

With teacher support, mealtime is a great time for peer conversations.

FIGURE 7.3   **Parten's stages of play**

"One of the most influential studies on children's social play was conducted by Parten (1932). Mildred Parten differentiated the social development of children into three levels. The first is non-social activity—unoccupied, onlooker behavior, and solitary play. The second is parallel play, which is a limited form of social participation. Children play side-by-side with similar materials, but do not talk about the play activity. The third is true social interaction including two forms of play: associative play and cooperative play. The difference between associative and cooperative play is that in associative play children engage in separate activities but interact with each other about the activity; whereas in cooperative play children act together towards a common goal such as a project or a make-believe theme." (This whole paragraph is a quote from p. 490)

Xu, Y. (2010). Children's social play sequence: Parten's classic theory revisted. *Early Child Development and Care, 180*(4), 489–498.

Parten, M.B. (1932). Social participation among pre-school children. *Journal of Abnormal and Social Psychology, 27,* 243–269.

Play with Peers

The second capacity of infants and toddlers is to learn to play with peers. As young children develop, they participate in more complex interactions. Researchers have tried to capture these developmental experiences by creating scales that identify the important characteristics of each stage of development. Parten (1932, 1933) identified stages of young children's play that included solitary play, parallel play, associate play, and cooperative play (see Figure 7.3 for a definition of each stage).

Howes expanded on Parten's work by developing a peer play scale in 1980 (See Figure 7.4). Howes's social sequence, as Parten's did, identified a stage of parallel play but added a stage of "parallel aware play" (a stage that captures the awareness that one child has for another when they play. The third stage, "simple social play," describes how young children take turns during play (as in run-chase games). When children work together on a common plan they are involved in "complementary and reciprocal play with mutual awareness". "Complementary

This video demonstrates Parten's categories of parallel play, associative play, and cooperative play.

FIGURE 7.4   **Howes's peer play scale**

I. 12–15 Months: Parallel Play
Parallel play (playing beside) often includes eye contact and/or exchanges of social behavior (A vocalizes, B smiles).

II. 15–20 Months: Parallel Play with Mutual Regard
Engagement in similar activities is accompanied with turn taking social exchanges (while digging in the sand-box, A smiles to B and B vocalizes back).

III. 20–24 Months: Simple Social Play
Social exchange is marked by each partner taking turns at reversing the actions of the other (run-chase game, rolling a ball back and forth).

IV. 24–30 Months: Complementary and Reciprocal Play with Mutual Awareness
Joint activity has a common plan and the pair's actions are integrated (conversation during joint building of a block structure shows that both intend it for trucks to drive underneath).

V. 30–36 Months: Complementary and Reciprocal Social Play
The social play activity shows differentiation of leader and follower roles (while jointly building a block structure, A directs building construction and B delivers blocks).

Source: Howes (1988).

and reciprocal social play" occurs when children clearly are both leaders and followers. Howes & Matheson (1992) observed 48 children from infancy through preschool using a revised Howes's scale. They found that "more than half the children engaged in complementary and reciprocal social play by 13–15 months and nearly all had achieved this type of play by 19–23 months. More than half the children engaged in cooperative social pretend play by 30–35 months" (p.964). This type of play involves children engaging in complementary roles (one child pretends to be the dog and the other a cat). These results tell us that care teachers can offer and expect different types of play, even at young ages.

Infants' and toddlers' ability to cooperate with each other on a task improves as they get older and is a remarkable achievement of toddlers (Brownell, Ramani, & Zerwas, 2006). In a research setting, Brownell and colleagues found that the majority of 27-month-old children could cooperate to activate a toy when two children had to pull handles that were strategically placed on opposite sides of the toy so that one child couldn't activate it. However, 1-year-olds (19 to 23 months olds) could not make the toy work by cooperating, even though the adults modeled how to cooperate and reminded the children about the goal of the task. We can wonder, though, and observe how infants and toddlers can cooperate if they know each other well in a program and if they are motivated to do a task such as fill a water table by cooperating to carry a bucket of water.

Vygotsky's work reminds us to observe, what young children can and cannot do when they are provided models (highest level of the zone of proximal development) and what they can do when they are playing independently (lowest level of the zone of proximal development).

Prosocial Development in Infants and Toddlers

Marissa, 2, runs to Minnie, 18 months, when she cries, patting her cheek as her own mother does to her. When Sam or Mark yells "Help," the other one runs to help move blocks or somehow resolve the crisis. Lenny, only 15 months old, lovingly tries to feed his teacher some of his applesauce. When Jo gets her finger stuck between some blocks and lets out a loud cry, Allison looks concerned, runs to pull on the teacher's leg, and looks back at Jo, as if to say, "Hurry—come help Jo."

We know that infants and toddlers are just learning how to be social—so there can be biting, hitting, grabbing, and pushing when they are together in groups. However, young children can be prosocial. Prosocial behavior includes giving, defending, offering, helping, and showing empathy through facial expressions, words, or gestures. Infants and toddlers hug, pat, look concerned, and often want to give their food to others. You can observe many prosocial moments if you know they exist and if you are watching for them and encouraging them.

In the early research of prosocial behavior in toddlers, Eckerman, Whatley, and Kutz (1975) found that within three age groups of children (10 to 12 months, 16 to 18 months, and 22 to 24 months), positive interactions with peers far outweighed negative ones. Howes (1988) concluded that toddlers interact in complementary and reciprocal ways and form stable friendships, and Roopnarine and Field (1983) observed that both infants and toddlers directed positive behaviors toward their peers more frequently than negative behaviors. Murphy (1936) studied sympathy and observed sympathetic behavior among 2-year-olds, including patting, hugging, kissing, picking up another child who fell, or pushing a swing when a child could not make it go. Howes and Farver (1987) studied children's responses to the distress of their peers. Toddlers from 16 to 33 months of age responded to a peer's distress 22% of the time. Of these times, 93% of the responses were prosocial in nature.

The important work of Zahn-Waxler, Radke-Yarrow, and King (1979) focused on the capacity of these very young children for compassion and various kinds of prosocial behaviors. In the researchers' observations in the homes of children between the ages of 10 months and 2 1/2 years, and after reading the records that parents faithfully kept for 9 months, the researchers noted many examples of infants showing empathy for the feelings of others. To their great surprise, as early as 1 year of age, some babies tried to comfort people who were crying or in pain. Infants used gentle touches, snuggles, and hugs to seemingly try to make an unhappy person feel better or, in a few cases, offered their own bottle or food to an exhausted dad or a sad mom. One baby even tried to defend his mother against a force much larger than himself. When the mother was having her throat swabbed at the doctor's office, her infant, not quite a year old, reached out and tried to knock the throat swab from the doctor's hand when his mother made a strangling noise.

As the children moved toward 18 months, Zahn-Waxler et al. (1979) discovered that some toddlers became more inventive at figuring out how to comfort another child. They gave toys and food to the crying child and urgently pulled an adult over to help the child in distress. Infants' and toddlers' prosocial acts, however, did not always comfort the other person because the offer from the young child mirrored their own needs rather than the needs of the other person. A sticky pacifier, chewed-up food, or an already used baby bottle may not be exactly what the adult or other child wants for consolation. However, these gifts represent a supreme sacrifice on the part of the toddler making such an offer and will ideally be appreciated as such by the receiving party. Figure 7.5 identifies ways that parents in Radkey-Yarrow's and Zahn-Waxler's study facilitated prosocial tendencies.

What does recent research tell us about prosocial attitudes and behavior among infants and toddlers? Warneken and Tomasello (2009) propose that children are intrinsically motivated to help others and that extrinsic rewards actually undermine these altruistic tendencies in 20-month-old infants (Warneken & Tomasello, 2008). Prosocial behaviors increase during the second year of life because of toddlers'

FIGURE 7.5   **Supporting and facilitating prosocial development**

Parents of toddlers who were most prosocial . . .

- Gave a clear, intense message that their child must not hurt others. A parent might say to the child, "Look what you did. You must never poke anyone's eyes" (said with feeling). The message was given to the child in a serious voice, but these parents did not slap or hurt their child in any way when the child hurt a peer.

- Helped their children see the connection between what they did and how it affected the other child. For instance, "You poked him. That hurt him" (said dramatically).

- Gave explanations for why the child should or should not behave in a particular way. Just saying "No" or "Stop" without giving any additional information did not help children be kind. Instead it taught them to stop any activity when confronted with another's distress.

- Taught their children what to do instead of biting, hitting, etc. A parent might say, "You can say 'Stop,' " or "Pat gently—it feels good when you pat gently."

- Were kind and loving toward their own children. They gave hugs and kisses, soothing words, band-aids, and tissues for gently wiping runny noses. The children modeled after their parents and used the same prosocial behaviors with their peers.

- Helped others when they saw that they were in distress. If the parent couldn't help—for example, if another child cried in the grocery store and that child's mom was already comforting her—then the parent talked to her own child about the event: "Yes, she's crying. She's feeling sad because she hurt herself on the cart. Her mom is making her feel better."

understanding of other children's and adults' emotions and perspectives (Nichols, Svetlova, & Brownell, 2009; Svetlova, Nichols, & Brownell, 2010). Empathic concern for another's distress also begins to emerge during the second year of life as toddlers begin to understand the difference between themselves and others (theory of mind) (Nichols et al., 2009; Quann & Wien, 2006).

Dunfield, Kuhlmeier, O'Connell, and Kelley (2011) describe prosocial behavior as having three specific types of responding—helping, comforting, and sharing. Warneken and Tomasello (2007) discovered that 14- to 18-month-olds helped a "helpless adult" by handing her objects when she couldn't reach them. Dunfield et al. (2011) found that 18- to 24-month-olds would share their food when an adult extended her hand as if to ask the child to share the food. Brownell, Svetlova, and Nichols (2009) in an article titled "To Share or Not to Share: When Do Toddlers Respond to Another's Needs?" (p. 117) found that 25-month-olds shared their food when a friendly experimenter vocalized her desire for the children to share.

Toddlers in programs can comfort each other as well. When Lonnie (26 months old) was sad, she grabbed her favorite stuffed bunny, sat on the floor, and hugged it tightly. Lukas and two other children saw that Lonnie was sad and sat beside her on the floor—reaching out to gently touch her. One toddler commented, "She sad," while another moved in closer and with a tilt of her head asked Lonnie, "What wrong—you OK?" The third toddler jumped up stating, "She like a sticker," as he ran off to get Lonnie a sticker to make her feel better. These children were growing in their ability to "think of the other" as they struggled to figure out what might make Lonnie feel better. After getting the sticker, Lonnie exclaimed, "All better now." These toddlers had found a way to comfort their friend in distress.

These prosocial strategies were modeled for them by their teachers, with themselves at times the recipient of such caring. The children were able to use the same loving strategies with their peers. It is gratifying to an adult who patiently and gently uses prosocial strategies with young children to see these types of peer-to-peer scenes that mirror the adult responses young children see and receive each day from their favorite adults.

There are strategies that you can use to enhance children's prosocial development—and in the process develop a community in an early care and education program where the small citizens begin to care about each other:

- *Provide continuity of care and groups.* Keeping groups of children together from infancy through toddlerhood promotes familiarity and friendships. Howes (1988), in her research on the social relationships of toddlers, found that peers who are familiar with each other are more likely to initiate play, be more positive, and engage in more complex interactions than children who are unfamiliar with each other. As discussed in the first chapter in this book, continuity of care (when one or more caregivers move to a different room *with* the children as they age from birth to 3) enables teachers and children to develop more trusting relationships, children are more positive with their peers in child care, children are less aggressive and negative at home, and children have increased cognitive and language skills (NICHD, 2001b).
- *Give children time together in an enriched environment.* If infants and toddlers can choose their activities, then they often choose to be near each other while learning how to help, comfort, and solve problems together.
- *Support positive social behaviors, comment on them, and cheer babies on to continue these caring behaviors.* Use specific approving words when an infant or toddler offers a toy or pats another child to comfort them. Using the words for positive social

behaviors, teachers may talk about sharing, caring, giving, helping, comforting, loving, and being generous. Infants and toddlers begin to learn these words and to take the perspective of others. As children begin to understand that positive behaviors are important to adults, those behaviors increase dramatically.

- *Young children need to feel what it is like to have an adult be prosocial with them.* Give them food and toys in a generous way and comfort them when they are distressed. Children need to feel that their emotional and physical needs are met before they can give love and show empathy for another's sadness. Just like a sponge needs to be filled with water before the water overflows, so do infants need to be filled up with love, before they overflow with love and kind attention to others. As babies experience warmth and kindness from adults, this behavior becomes a part of them that they can share with others.

- *In addition to having personal prosocial experiences, infants and toddlers need prosocial models.* Care teachers may provide positive models of prosocial behavior at many times during the day. Children see examples of adults being kind to each other and, more importantly, they feel the prosocial atmosphere of the room or child care home. Teachers can model giving to other teachers and to children in the classroom or child care home. Children might hear a care teacher say, "I'd like to share this with you," as she gives a book to another adult in the room.

- *Emphasize how being prosocial makes others feel.* Say things like, "Oh, Ian likes it when you pat him gently. Look, he's smiling." This type of comment helps babies begin to take the perspective of others.

Familiarity. In landmark research Stefani and Camaioni (1983) and Howes (1988, 1996) found that very young children find it easier to play with familiar peers. Stefani and Camaioni's work with 8- to 10-month-olds concluded that infants who are familiar with each other showed an increase in positive social interactions and a decrease in negative interactions. Time together (Galluzzo, Matheson, Moore, & Howes, 1990) with the same play partner enhances children's ability to play well together, probably as they learn the likes, dislikes, and play characteristics of the other child: "They [peers] are more likely to initiate play, direct positive affect to, and engage in complex interactions with familiar than with unfamiliar playmates" (Howes, 1988, cited in Shonkoff & Phillips, 2000, p. 167).

Because children who have time together and are familiar with each other play more easily together, programs should provide **group continuity of care**. A group of children who begin a program fairly close in time can be kept together as a group as they advance in age in the program. Group continuity of care provides the opportunity for familiarity to develop into friendships (van Hoogdalem, Singer, Wijngaards, & Heesbeen, 2012). The toddlers in Observation Invitation 7.2, who have known each other since they were infants, are happy and comfortable in each other's company.

group continuity of care

A group of children who stay together over time in an early development and education program.

Development of friendships. Is it possible for infants and toddlers to develop relationships? What is a friendship for infants and toddlers? Can they show how they might prefer to be with another infant or toddler and demonstrate more affection toward that other child? How do friendships develop? As Ross and Lollis (1989) note, friendships occur "when two people bring out qualities in one another that are neither exhibited nor elicited in their other relationships" (p. 1083). Toddlers demonstrate their friendships in a number of ways (see Figure 7.6). A 15-month-old's face lights up each time she sees her friend arrive in the child development and education center. An 18-month-old runs to the other side of the living room to greet a friend who has come to visit.

OBSERVATION INVITATION **7.2**

Describe what these two children are doing. What are they learning? What more would you like to know about these two children and how they play together?

FIGURE 7.6 **A relationship is a friendship when...**

> The relationship is considered a friendship when these conditions are met:
>
> 1. Toddlers have opportunities in their daily lives for regular play interactions with a particular partner.
> 2. Toddler partners are sufficiently well acquainted to have constructed scripted social interactions.
> 3. Companionship, intimacy, and affection can be inferred from these interactions.
>
> Behaviorally defined, friendships appear some time after children's first birthdays.
>
> *Source:* Howes (2000, p. 103).

Shin (2010), during observations of two toddlers (13 and 14 months old) concluded that, "In sum, infant friends displayed strong preference for each other as well as reciprocal affection and a high level of intensity and enjoyment. Infant friends express their joy and affection toward each other through their whole body reciprocally" (p. 297). The author of this observational study shared the following vignettes that demonstrate how friends greet each other and respond to the feelings of the other.

> Emily greeted Katie with hug and kisses. Emily comes to Katie, sitting on the floor, and sits down right in front of her. Emily faces Katie's face and says "hi." Katie also says "hi" to Emily and then both laugh. Emily gave Katie a big hug and held her tightly, calling her name repeatedly all afternoon. (Observation, p. 297)
>
> On the way back to classroom from the park, Katie starts fussing. Emily points to Katie who was sitting across from her in the cart and gently touches her body. Emily reaches into the backpack and takes out a tissue. Emily tries to help Katie wipe her running nose. (Observation, p. 297)

Toddlers who are friends may even grieve for each other if one child leaves a program or moves to another room (Whaley & Rubenstein, 1994).

Maria and Lisa had been together in the Boulder Journey School since they were babies. As toddlers they greeted each other, played together often, and obviously enjoyed each other very much. When Lisa's mother changed her work schedule, Lisa started attending the school on opposite days from Maria. Maria seemed to grieve for her friend. She would often go to the shelf with the "All About Me" books, choose Lisa's book, and lay on the floor looking at pictures of Lisa as a baby, of her first birthday, and as a toddler.

Of course, we also know that when very young children are together in groups, conflict will occur. Young children are learning to regulate their emotions, to gain an understanding of "mine" and "yours," to use language to express their needs, and to understand the meaning of "share" and "take turns." Infants and toddlers can make great progress in their journey toward managing negative emotions and conflict with peers with the support of understanding adults.

Conflicts in Peer Relationships

After watching this video, describe what young children learn during conflict.

Charissa toddled up to Ben, her favorite friend in the toddler room, and wrapped her arms around his head in a sweet, comforting way. Ben protested and tried to wriggle out of Charissa's head wrap. Later, Charissa clutched tightly to two toy telephones as Ben tried with all of his might to wrestle one from her grasp. Even later that day, Charissa handed Ben her special doll to hold and then quickly tried to take it back from him.

These scenes happen many times a day at home or in programs where there are two or more infants and toddlers. Older infants who are crawling and cruising and toddlers who are toddling sometimes give and sometimes take away. They often are very good at sharing their teachers, toys, food, and time. At other times, they have no intention of sharing anyone or anything. Words like "mine" and "no" ring out from toddlers. They cling to their special teacher and push other children away. They hang on for dear life to toys that just a moment ago they discarded in a corner. They are learning about social interactions, but they seem to be following the "Toddler Property Laws":

Toddler Property Laws

If I like it, it's mine.
If it's in my hand, it's mine.
If I can take it from you, it's mine.
If I had it a little while ago, it's mine.
If it's mine, it must never appear to be yours in any way.
If I'm doing or building something, all the pieces are mine.
If it looks just like mine, it is mine.
(Author unknown)

Conflict May Be Related to Social Competence

While infants and toddlers are learning to socialize, conflict happens and may actually be related to peer competence. Conflicts between peers include situations in which one person does something and another person objects. Indeed, conflict and aggression initially increase as children try to play together, peaking between ages 2 and 3 before they decline (Brownell & Carriger, 1990). In fact, research results indicate that socially competent children may be involved in more conflicts than their less socially competent peers. How can that be?

Conflict is different from mean-spirited aggression and may be related to social competence in two ways. The first involves the fact that socially competent children are not withdrawn or aggressive, but can be rather assertive in their play. They are full of confidence and often right in the middle of the play action, resulting in more opportunities for conflict with peers. Second, young children learn valuable skills during conflict with their peers. The negotiation and self-regulation skills necessary to prevent the conflict from escalating and interfering with play improve as these children gain experience in the art of disagreeing, resisting, or competing. Thus, involvement in conflict may actually play a positive role in peer development (Batya, Simoni, & Perrig-Chiello, 2008; Eckerman & Didow, 2001; Singer & Hannikainen, 2002).

The nature of young children's conflicts and care teacher strategies for supporting children's problem solving are shared in Chapter 14.

dominant

A person who is controlling or leading another person.

If you've observed toddlers and noticed that some toddlers seem more **dominant** than other toddlers, that they can take toys and the other children won't protest, or that they seem to be the leaders in play, you are noticing an interesting phenomenon. Hawley and Little (1999) noted that a prominent characteristic of dominant children was that they interact with the environment unhindered, while peers that are subordinate do not, at least while dominant peers are present. The researchers observed that toddlers who were physically stronger, more mature, more cognitively advanced, and more goal directed and who had more physical and social experience in a particular group setting seemed to be more dominant than other toddlers. They also observed that girls were dominant more often than boys. Among these children, who ranged in age from 1.4 to 3.2 years, the toddler's developmental maturity was the highest predictor of whether a toddler was or was not dominant (Hawley & Little, 1999).

It is fascinating that whether or not the toddler was dominant also was based on the toddler's play partner. A toddler might behave one way with one partner and another way with a different partner, depending on who was dominant in the group. These researchers' findings—that the behavior of a particular toddler changed based on his partner—were contrary to what was expected of these children. Prior to this, some researchers thought that toddlers acted the same way with all children and couldn't, at that age, adjust their behavior according to the behavior of a peer.

Dominant behavior has been observed in children as early as 19 months and may prevent aggression (Plusquellec, Francois, Boivin, Perusse, & Tremblay, 2007). As a teacher, you can help a toddler who is almost always dominant become an assertive *and* kind leader by using the strategies listed earlier in this chapter, in the section on prosocial development. You can also advocate for and aid a toddler who almost always is **subordinate** and can help the child become more self-confident in peer relationships. Look for these children's strengths and help them use them during play with dominant children.

subordinate

A person who is controlled by or led by another person.

Richness of Peer Development

The richness of peer development is brought to light with thoughtful documentation of the intricacies of peer interactions. When adults carefully observe the behaviors of infants and toddlers for child goals, strategies, and theories (Forman et al., 2003), then the adults' understanding of peer relationships blossoms. Capatides, Collins, and Bennett (1996) captured the nuances of toddler behavior in their observations of six toddlers (18 to 36 months old) one time a month for 6 months. The toddlers' social goal was to be with one another. The strategies they used were to move together. They established and maintained contact with one another through moving their bodies in space, coming together, leaving, holding a conversation with the body rather than with words, moving around the room together, and establishing contacts through physical movement and imitation. The young children's theory may have been "If I follow you, I can continue to be with you." Before playing with objects together, toddlers may need to move around the room together, experiencing and conversing kinesthetically. This social dance is so much more than parallel play. As children take turns being the leader and the followers, they demonstrate complementary and reciprocal interactions with mutual awareness and great enjoyment of one another.

The detailed description of children's moment-to-moment social behavior encourages an appreciation for the social competency of the toddler and an understanding of what leading and following mean to the advancement of toddler social relationships. We all learn from these types of observations. Rather than trying to keep toddlers from moving, wise parents and teachers will provide safe opportunities for toddlers to hold their kinesthetic conversations.

Another detailed observation revealed further capabilities of toddlers. When toddlers from ages 2½ to 3 were observed in a child development and education center, they were clearly capable of developing expectations for the behavior of other toddlers. The following vignette clearly demonstrates that some toddlers expect that a peer, Michael, will be hurtful in their play:

Michael, a 2-year-old in a child care center, picked up a small hammer that accompanied a xylophone. In the small room of approximately 12 toddlers, Michael started swinging the hammer back and forth as he moved quickly around the room. As other toddlers noticed, they scattered to get away from their swinging peer. Michael headed for the wooden lockers that held the toddlers' coats and sat down on the bottom of the locker between two toddlers who were using the lockers as sitting spots as well. As soon as he sat down, the other two toddlers took off, obviously running away from Michael.

At 2 years of age, Michael already had a reputation for aggression, and the other children had learned to stay out of his way. The peers' working model of relationships with Michael seemed to be "Move away fast or get hurt." Michael had learned one way to try to interact with peers. Perhaps this was his working model of relationships, his notion of how to be with others. Unfortunately, this working model won't help Michael make friends and have rewarding peer relationships. Without adult assistance, his negative peer reputation is likely to stay with him if he continues with this group of children, and he would likely behave the same way with a new set of peers. With adult assistance, he can learn social skills that will enhance his relationships with peers.

DaRos and Kovach (1998) highlighted an example of how documenting and reflecting on these documentations of peer interaction illuminate the goals of young children:

Jason, after clutching three plastic bottles filled with colored water, gives them to his peers; after a few minutes, he insists on collecting them. Of course, the toddlers who now possess these coveted, colorful bottles do not want to return them. Jason begins to cry as he reaches for a bottle and turns to his teacher for help. The teacher says to Jason, "That was nice of you to share the bottles with your friends; sharing makes your friends happy." (p. 27)

After documenting this example through written observation notes, DaRos and Kovach decided that Jason wasn't sharing—at least in the same way that adults share. Rather, he was distributing items to others for them to hold for a moment, but to give back to him when he wanted them.

Teachers and parents who observe this type of situation might come to the same conclusion through asking themselves a series of questions: What was Jason's goal? (Make a best guess.) What were the strategies he was using to achieve his goal? What theories did he have about how relationships work? His goal seemed to be to have his peers hold the bottles for a moment and then give them back. His strategies were to give or distribute the bottles among his peers and then let them know that it was time to give the bottles back to him. His theory about relationships may be that when you give others something, they should give it back if you still want it. This may have happened often in a give-and-take game with his parent who is more willing than a peer to give a toy back to him when he wants it.

These examples demonstrate how documenting the richness of peer interaction and then reflecting on these observations lead to adults "seeing" behaviors with new eyes. Infant and toddler development is fascinating when viewed through the lens of the child's perspective. Young children's behaviors that may have been seen through a negative filter are now wisely understood as progressive developmental steps toward the infant or toddler becoming socially competent.

Learning Through Relationships

The importance of parent-child relationships for children's emotional development was discussed in Chapter 6. Adult-child relationships also have an effect on infants' and toddlers' peer relationships. The quality of infants' and toddlers' emotional experiences with their primary caregivers (parents and care teachers) plays an important role. Infants and toddlers learn behaviors and have feelings in their first emotional relationships with the important adults in their lives. This, in turn, influences how the young child will behave in subsequent peer relationships. Infants and toddlers develop assumptions in their first relationships about how to interact with others and how others will treat them. Infants and toddlers then wisely apply the information they've gained from their first relationships to their subsequent peer relationships.

The children with secure, sensitive, warm, and encouraging relationships with parents seem more competent and more attractive as playmates both in the toddler years (NICHD, 2001a) and as preschoolers (LaFreniere & Sroufe, 1985; Park & Waters, 1989). Ziv, Oppenheim, and Sagi-Schwartz (2004) found that a group of children, average age 7.5 years, who were securely attached as infants expected their peers (those whose behavior was socially acceptable) to be emotionally and physically available to them. These young children have positive social expectations, know the rudiments of reciprocity in relationships, and have a sense of self-worth and self-efficacy (Rubin, Bukowski, & Parker, 1998). They feel safe to explore the environment and interact with peers, building on their experiences to become even more skilled at peer interactions (Rubin et al., 1998). They know that relationships with other adults and peers are rewarding and worth pursuing.

On the other hand, infants and toddlers who are angry and frustrated or experience negativism and rejection in their first adult-child relationships also carry these feelings and expectations to their toddler and preschool relationships (McElwain, Cox, Burchinal, & Macfie, 2003; Jacobvitz & Hazen, 1999). For example, when parents are aggressive toward their toddlers, the toddlers are more aggressive with peers (Brook, Zheng, Whiteman, & Brook, 2001).

It is important, however, to consider that in a relationship-based and bioecological model of human development, many factors could be influencing parent-child interactions. An infant's temperament or a toddler's fussiness, for example, may be challenging for a parent, or family members may be influenced by the stress of other relationships or challenges in their immediate environment or community. Family support can help parents become more sensitive, and this improves children's outcomes. When insecurely attached children at 15 months subsequently received high-sensitive mothering, they had better social, behavior, and language outcomes at age 3 (Belsky & Fearon, 2002).

STRATEGIES TO SUPPORT SOCIAL DEVELOPMENT AND LEARNING

Following is a summary of strategies that teachers and parents can use to enhance the social development of infants and toddlers:

1. Model kindness with infants and toddlers. They learn from adults whether to be calm, exuberant, friendly, and kind or whether they need to be on guard, angry, sad, and aggressive with others.
2. Observe the temperament of each child. Help each self-regulate his or her emotions with others. Individualize care based on a child's temperament.
   a. Realize that exuberant children may be slightly more aggressive than others just because they are often in the middle of an action.
   b. Help inhibited children by being understanding and supportive—do not attempt to over-control, scold, or be critical to get them to be involved with other children, as this undermines their social competence. Support their language and cognitive development and their interactions with peers.
3. Infants and toddlers learn social competence with peers in the company of "expert adults" who are helpful and not intrusive, and who help elaborate play schemes.
4. Help infants and toddlers get off to a good start in peer relationships. Help toddlers who are aggressive to feel loved and learn new behaviors.
5. Recognize and support prosocial behaviors.
6. Expect conflict as an important part of social development, and support children in learning how to resolve conflict with language and negotiation skills.
7. Infants and toddlers with disabilities may need adult encouragement and skills to play with children without disabilities, and vice versa.
8. Set up an environment that encourages peer interaction.
9. Include several peers in conversations. Comment on what other children are doing or saying.
10. Provide quality care.
11. Provide primary care.
12. Ensure continuity of peer groups.
13. Maintain appropriate ratios and group sizes.
14. Develop strong, positive adult-child relationships and sensitive, responsive care.

Children with Special Needs

Infants and toddlers with identified special needs often display delays in social interactions and the development of relationships. Parents and infant-toddler teachers can play a significant role in supporting and encouraging these children's social interactions with peers.

Trevor was the first child with a disability to attend the child care center. Trevor had cerebral palsy. At the age of 18 months he crawled, and he used sounds, but not words, to communicate.

Because of their own ideas about his disability, Trevor's care providers perceived him as fragile and in need of protection from everyone and everything in the environment. They kept him away from the other toddlers, strapped him into an infant seat at mealtimes, and held him on their laps during play times.

Trevor was very lonely in child care. The toddlers in the classroom did interesting things nonstop. They ran from one side of the room to the other, challenging each other with a look to join in or keep up. They copied each other's table banging and joyful sounds, making them louder with each imitation.

> *As Trevor watched the other children playing, moving, and singing, he became increasingly frustrated by the care providers' failure to move him along with the group. Sometimes he would join in the imitative play from a distance. He began to pounce on any opportunity when he was not physically constrained to crawl, and then walk, to where the other children were. His movements became faster and more purposeful. Trevor's moment-by-moment goal seemed to be to get close to the other children and do what they were doing. This interest in watching and imitating proved to be a powerful motivating force for him to try activities he'd refused before. (Wittmer & Petersen, 1992, pp. 55–56)*

As illustrated by the previous true example, infants and toddlers who have disabilities enjoy and learn from their peers without disabilities. Other research confirms this idea. In one study (Wittmer, 1991), approximately 70% of the total interactions of the observed toddlers with disabilities in an inclusive setting were with typical peers. In a study of six preschool children, friendships occurred between children with disabilities and those without. Similarity in play styles and the opportunities to engage in similar activities contributed to these friendships (Dietrich, 2005).

Adults can encourage social interactions between children with disabilities and children without disabilities. Research has shown that teachers play a crucial role in encouraging peer interactions among all children (Wittmer & Petersen, 1992). Teachers can do the following:

- Document how a child with disabilities likes to be touched or interact with peers so that the teacher can encourage those types of interactions.
- Place infants beside each other on the floor. Infants like to watch each other.
- Provide duplicates of toys to encourage children to play beside and with each other.
- Offer toys and activities that promote social interaction rather than isolated play. Some favorites among toddlers are a large bin full of balls (make sure they are not small enough for toddlers to put in their mouths and choke), water, sand, and coloring or painting on a huge piece of paper that everyone shares.
- Give children with disabilities toys that attract peers to their side, such as a new toy. Then support the child who has disabilities to show typical peers how to use the toy.
- Build on toddlers' inherent desires to imitate others by focusing the attention of the child with disabilities on the behavior of the other children. If other toddlers are patting a table, say "pat, pat, pat" as you show the child how to pat her hand on the table.
- Find a way for the child with disabilities to communicate with words, sign language, or a communication device and interpret the child's subtle cues to the other children. For example, say to the child without disabilities, "He said, 'Hi.' Say 'Hi' back," or, "She's really looking at the doll. Can you give her the doll?"
- Comment on how children are alike rather than different: "Look, Sarah likes shape boxes, just like you."
- Encourage toddlers to help by pulling another child in a wagon, turning on the faucet for a child with disabilities as the teacher holds her, or bringing toys to a child who has difficulty moving. Then point out how happy that makes the child being helped.

Your use of these strategies builds a harmonious environment where young children learn to see others for what they can do, not what they can't do.

Programs That Enhance Social Development and Learning

What will the child learn about relationships "out in the world"? If the infant or toddler attends a child development and education program, will the experiences be positive and enhance the growth of the child? Or will it tax all of the emotional and social efforts of the child to cope?

Quality Child Development and Education Programs

Research in the 1990s found that higher-quality child care and education programs result in more competent peer relationships (Howes, Hamilton, & Matheson, 1994; Howes, Matheson, & Hamilton, 1992; Howes, Phillips, & Whitebook,1992). More recent research (Deynoot-Schaub & Riksen-Walraven, 2006; NICHD, 2001a; Vandell et al., 2010) confirms that the higher the child care quality, the more positive the peer interactions.

As usual, we must look beyond the obvious to understand the effects of quality of child care on the social outcomes for children. For example, children with a difficult temperament as compared to other children were less involved with peers, but only when the quality of child care was lower (Deynoot-Schaub & Riksen-Walraven, 2006).

Continuity of Peer Groups

Howes (1988) noted that children who remain together with the same peers over the infant-toddler years in a child care and education home or center are more likely to maintain their friendships and increase their social skills. In a more recent article, de Groot Kim (2010) also concluded that moving children as a group in child care would be advantageous to both toddlers and parents. The author of the article, titled "There's Elly, It must be Tuesday: Discontinuity in Child Care Programs and Its Impact on the Development of Peer Relationships in Young Children," noted that Elly, who attended a child care center part time, took 6 months to develop a meaningful relationship with a peer. However, because children are moved to a new group based on their development or space available rather than as a group, Elly may soon have to start over to develop a new friend. The author noted that, "Importantly, the child care center's policies and practices for transitioning children in and out of classrooms seem to be at odds with current research on attachment, continuity, and the development of peer relationships" (p. 153).

Relationship with the Infant-Toddler Teacher

An infant or toddler teacher's relationship with a young child is strongly related to that child's competence with peers. This adult-child relationship can be classified as secure or insecure (see Chapter 6 for a detailed description of these concepts). In a secure attachment relationship, the teacher is sensitive and responsive to infant cues for food, attention, and play. The infant or toddler feels safe and confident and expects relationships to be emotionally satisfying. An infant or toddler with a secure attachment relationship is more competent with peers (Howes, Phillips, et al., 1992), and this secure attachment relationship predicts social competence at a later age. Howes et al. (1994) found that infants who had a secure attachment relationship with their teacher were more likely to participate in complex peer play and were more gregarious (sociable and expressive), less hostile, and less

DEVELOPMENTAL TRENDS AND RESPONSIVE INTERACTIONS

SOCIAL DEVELOPMENT AND LEARNING WITH PEERS

Capacities: To communicate with peers, be prosocial, play with peers, and manage negative emotions and conflict in peer interaction.

Development	Example
0–4 months (infant)	
• Infants like to look at each other (visual regard). • Infants prefer to look at faces, especially the edges and the eyes. • Infants may cry when they hear other babies cry (contagion).	After the teacher put Tamika by Sam on a blanket on the floor, Tamika stared intently at Sam.
4–8 months (infant)	
• Infants touch a peer, vocalize to each other, get excited, approach other babies, smile and laugh at each other. • Babies may treat other babies like objects—crawling over them, licking or sucking on them, or sitting on them. They are just learning the difference between people and objects. Infants may poke, push, or pat another baby to see what that other infant will do. They often look very surprised at the reaction they get.	Amna crawled over to Nadia who was lying on the floor. Touching Nadia's hair, Amna laughed out loud.
8–12 months (mobile infant)	
• Infants may show a peer an object, sit by each other, crawl after and around each other, play chase-and-retrieve games. • Babies smile and laugh at each other. • Babies make sounds to and with each other—may say first words with peers. • Peek-a-boo is a favorite game as babies explore separation: coming and going, in sight and out of sight. • Infants can learn to touch each other gently. • Because infants become more goal oriented at this age, they may push another baby's hand away from a toy or crawl over another baby to get a toy.	Shamaine peeked around the low toy shelf and saw Carla crawling toward her. Shamaine quickly turned around and crawled away with Carla close behind. Kai crawled over Bridger's legs to get a toy on the other side of Bridger.
12–18 months (mobile infant)	
• Imitation (motor) and interactive turns begin. Toddlers may copy each other—if one gives a toy to another child, the other may imitate. • Mobile infants begin to talk to each other. • Infants may show concern when other babies are distressed. • Mobile infants may take a toy from another child, say "no," push away the other child, clutch toy to self and say "mine." • Infants are little scientists at this age, experimenting to see how things work. This affects how they get along with peers. They are constantly doing things to other children to see what response they will get. • Biting may appear as infants bite others "to see what happens," to get the toy they want, to express frustration. Infants are on the cusp of communicating well; they may communicate through their mouths in the form of a bite.	Rashida banged her spoon on the table and soon two others tried it. They seemed to be physically following one another's lead (as in a conversation). First, Carmen tried pushing Toby away from her rocking horse. When that didn't work, she leaned over and took a bite out of his arm.

Teacher- or Parent-Child Interaction	Environment

0–4 months (infant)

• Hold two babies so they can look at each other. • Place a few babies on a blanket on the floor so that they can look at and touch each other.	• The arms of teachers provide the best environment. • Blankets on the floor—put two babies beside each other or so that their toes are touching.

4–8 months (infant)

• Move to music with a baby in each arm. • While holding one baby in your lap, point out and talk about what another baby is doing. • Place two babies on their tummies facing a mirror. • Instead of saying "Don't" or "Stop that" to exploring babies, say "Touch gently." Tell children what you want them to do—model it for them.	• Hang a safety mirror horizontally on the wall, so the bottom is touching the floor. • Cover an inner tube with soft cloth. Sit two babies in the inner tube so that their feet are touching.

8–12 months (mobile infant)

• Name parts of infants' bodies as two infants sit close to each other: Here is baby's eyes Here is baby's nose Touch the part that sees Touch the part that blows • Place a baby with one other baby (pairs), because more frequent, complex, and intense peer interaction occurs than when a child is with many peers. • Understand that infants are not being "naughty" when they push another child's hand away. Say "Jenny was holding that toy. Let's find you a different toy."	• While feeding, place high chairs so children can see each other. • Set up cozy corners in the room where babies can "disappear" (but adults can still see them). • Hang a long wide cloth (so babies won't get tangled in it) from the ceiling. Babies love to crawl around it. • Place containers with different sizes of blocks in them between two babies. Sit beside them as they begin to explore the materials. Talk about what each one is doing.

12–18 months (mobile infant)

• Show mobile infants how to roll down a small hill together. • Help mobile toddlers learn each other's names by singing greeting and good-bye songs with the children's names in them: "Here is Tanya, how are you?" and "Here is Henry, how are you?" as you point or touch each child who comes by you or is sitting in your lap. • Comment on prosocial behavior. Say "You gave him the doll. He likes that!" Babies may not understand your words, but they will be able to tell by your tone of voice that you are pleased with them. • They will enjoy looking at books together by forming an informal group (this means they move in and out of the group) around the legs, lap, and arms of a favorite parent or teacher.	• Provide a large cardboard box, open on each end. Encourage babies to crawl in and out of the box with each other. Windows on the side encourage babies to peek at each other through the windows. • Dolls, trucks, cars, and other play materials encourage interactions among peers. • They love sand and water and playing with different sizes of safe bottles and balls. When each has his own bin or tub of water or sand, play goes more smoothly. • Outside, large sandboxes or push toys encourage interactive play.

DEVELOPMENTAL TRENDS AND RESPONSIVE INTERACTIONS (Continued)

Development	Example
18–24 months (toddler)	

- Friendships can develop early. Friends are more likely to touch, lean on each other, and smile at each other than are children who are not friends.
- Toddlers imitate each other's sounds and words and talk to each other and begin to communicate with others across more space.
- Toddlers give or offer a toy or food to another toddler.
- Toddlers may get or pull an adult to help another child or will help another child by getting a tissue, for example.
- Toddlers can show kindness for other babies who are feeling distressed. A mobile infant or toddler, however, may assume that what will comfort him will also comfort the distressed child.
- Children take turns, for example, with a ball or jumping up. They may have toddler kinesthetic conversations as they follow a leader in moving around the room—moving in and out of the group, taking turns as leader and follower—as if in a conversation of listening and talking, learning valuable turn-taking skills.
- Pushing, shoving, grabbing, and hitting may occur as children struggle over "mine for as long as I want it" and "yours, but I want it, too." Toddlers may fight over small toys more than large, nonmovable objects.

Example: Paulie looked as if he was waiting by the door for Jamie to appear at the beginning of the day. When Jamie and his mom came in the door, Paulie toddled over and took Jamie's hand, a big smile on his face.

Tanya jumped (half fell) off a board several inches off the ground. Soon three toddlers were standing on the board and half jumping, half stepping off and on the board, enjoying the activity immensely.

| **24–36 months (toddler)** | |

- Toddler friendship is "proximity seeking," wanting to be close and to show affection, such as smiling, laughing, and hugging. Friends prefer each other as interaction partners. Friendships continue to develop and deepen.
- Toddlers exchange information and can imitate past actions of others.
- Toddlers may congregate and cluster together. When a teacher begins playing with an interesting activity with one child, children often come running from the corners of the room.
- Some toddlers are capable of inventing a variety of ways to help others who are hurt or sad. Some may have an impressive repertoire of altruistic behavior, and if one thing doesn't work, they will try another way.
- Peers work together toward a common goal, with one the leader and one the follower.
- Object, personal space, and verbal struggles can occur. Toddlers also engage in playful exchanges—rough and tumble, run and chase, and verbal games.
- Some children may gain a reputation with peers for aggressive or kind behavior.
- Children become more positive and less negative in their social play between 24 and 36 months.
- Dominance of one child over another can occur.

Example: Maria and Sally played on opposite sides of the small shelf of toys for 30 minutes, peeking over at each other every few minutes, and telling each other, "boat," "my boat," "hi," "want juice," "look at me," and saying each other's names over and over.

When a fire truck went by outside, several toddlers rushed to the window to look.

Josh and Mike pushed, pulled, rolled, and grunted as they worked hard to roll the huge pumpkin from inside to the playground where the toddlers and their teachers were going to cut it open and scoop out all of the seeds.

Teacher- or Parent-Child Interaction	Environment

18–24 months (toddler)

- When inside or outside, nurture toddlers as they come and go to "refuel" emotionally with a special teacher, encouraging several toddlers to sit together beside you or in your lap. Allow toddlers to touch each other gently.
- Encourage several toddlers to make animal sounds together and imitate each other as you show them the pictures in a book.
- Ask one child to help another child by getting a tissue, turning the faucet on, opening a door, and so on.
- Encourage kindness with one another. If one toddler cries, ask another what "we" could do to help.
- Encourage two peers to set a table together or sponge it off together after eating. Watch them imitate each other.
- Sing songs, encouraging toddlers to take turns with the actions.

- Inside and outside: Provide sand areas large enough for several toddlers and expect them to sit right in the middle of the area.
- Blankets on the floor or ground or over a table provide a spot for peers to play.
- Provide wagons: Pulling or pushing a friend in a wagon will result in squeals of delight.
- Provide balls and pull-toys that encourage interactive play.
- Places to jump safely encourage social exchanges.
- Provide musical toys, several of each kind, so children can make beautiful music together. Sometimes one will lead and another will follow, or vice versa.

24–36 months (toddler)

- Create situations where two toddlers need to work together—for example, to roll a pumpkin from one place to another or carry a bucket of "heavy" blocks from inside to outside.
- Put a Band-Aid on a doll's arm or leg and encourage toddlers to take care of the baby.
- Ask the toddlers, "How can we help Joey—he's sad—he's crying."
- Try to change the image of a child who is gaining a reputation for aggression. Keep the child close, show her how to touch gently, and comment on her helpful behavior. Give her an interesting toy that might interest other children to engage with her. Stay close and teach her how to play.

- Place hats and easy-to-put-on dress-up clothes in a cozy corner with a big mirror.
- Toddlers will enjoy each other as their friends change appearances under a floppy hat or wearing big shoes.
- Spaces on or under a short loft encourage peer interaction.
- Provide several types of dolls as well as safe feeding utensils, blankets, and small beds. Sit close and watch as toddlers pretend to care for their babies.
- Provide open-ended materials such as blocks, and activities that require cooperation such as painting with big brushes and water on outside walls or filling a big bucket with water from smaller containers.
- Large motor equipment such as climbers or rocking boats encourages toddlers to work together toward a common goal: everyone moving to the top of the climber or rocking the boat with everyone in it.

withdrawn at age 4. Secure, warm relationships with teachers help infants start on a path of positive feelings of self-worth, trust in others, and peer competence.

Another important facet of the quality of teacher strategies is how sensitive and responsive teachers are in their interactions with infants and toddlers. As noted in an NICHD (2001a) study of more than 500 children, summarizing the importance of a positive, responsive teacher for a child's development of social competence: "The most consistent finding for child care experience [for 24- to 36-month-old children] was that more sensitive and responsive behavior by caregivers was associated with less negative, more positive play with other children" (p. 1492).

Socialization Strategies of the Teacher

One aspect of an infant-toddler teacher's behavior includes the specific socialization strategies that you can use to promote peer development. You might use positive, peer-relationship-promoting strategies with toddlers that include physical or verbal help. Take a shy child's hand as you join a group of toddlers playing with blocks. Show a child how to "touch gently." If an infant starts pulling other children's hair, provide a doll with hair that the infant can play with. The strategies for supporting prosocial development for children with disabilities are useful for all children, with or without disabilities. These positive, peer-relationship-promoting strategies result in more complex play and fewer behavior problems.

If the teacher uses negative strategies—interrupting peer play without explanation, reprimanding or punishing peer contact, or separating children (Howes et al., 1994)—the children's social competence is affected. When educators use negative strategies, children participate in less complex peer play and teachers rate children as more difficult (Howes et al., 1994).

Summary

Infants and toddlers have the capacity to learn to enjoy peers, to play and communicate, to become prosocial, to become friends who enjoy each other's company, and to negotiate conflicts with peers. They become increasingly skilled during the first 3 years of life with parents and teachers who use sensitive, responsive strategies to promote these capacities and children's development.

- Children's attributes of temperament and gender influence peer relationships.

  - Children with an inhibited temperament will need support from parents and teachers to develop confidence and skills to play with peers.

- Exuberant children, the "Tiggers" of the world, may be engaged in more joyous as well as conflictual peer interactions.
- Toddlers' preference to play with children of the same sex may be explained by the "compatible play styles" theory.

- Culture plays a part in whether early peer interactions are valued by adults.
- Infants and toddlers, during the first 3 years of life, have the capacity to learn to

  - Communicate with peers
  - Increase their play skills
  - Develop prosocial behaviors and attitudes
  - Manage conflict and negative feelings with peers

- Children with special needs can gain social skills with typical peers.
- Adults can use many strategies to support peer development.

- Peer competence is associated with higher-quality care in programs, smaller group size, lower child-to-teacher ratios, the nature of the child's relationship with the teacher, and the specific strategies used.

Key Terms

dominant
elaborate play schemes
extroverted
exuberant
gender segregation

gestural language
group continuity of care
inhibited
interpsychological
intrapsychological

prosocial
same-gender play
socially competent
subordinate

Reflections and Resources for the Reader

REFLECTIONS

1. Jaheed and Michael often play with each other in the Early Head Start center-based program. They are becoming increasingly aggressive and try to play away from where teachers are in the room. What would you do if you were a care teacher in this room?
2. As a care teacher in a center or family child care home, how would you implement a program that emphasizes prosocial development?
3. How can you promote positive social interactions between children who do have special needs and those who do not? Why is this so important to the children, families, teachers, and program?
4. How does your culture influence how you interact with your peer group?

OBSERVATION AND APPLICATION OPPORTUNITIES

1. Use the Developmental Trends and Responsive Interactions chart at the end of this chapter and observe infants and toddlers in a center program. What social behaviors do you see at what age?
2. Observe an infant or toddler with a special need who attends a center or family program. What strategies does the teacher use to encourage peer interactions? What else could she do to promote positive peer interactions?

SUPPLEMENTAL ARTICLES AND BOOKS TO READ

Ashby, N., & Neilsen-Hewett, C. (2012). Approaches to conflict and conflict resolution in toddler relationships. *Journal of Early Childhood Research, 10* (2), 145–161.

Gloeckler, L., & Cassell, J. (2012). Teacher practices with toddlers during social problem solving opportunities. *Early Childhood Education Journal, 40*(4), 251–257.

Sloane, S., Baillargeon, R., & Premack, D. (2012). Do infants have a sense of fairness? *Psychological Science, 23*(2), 196–204.

Wittmer, D. S. (2012). The wonder and complexity of infant and toddler peer relationships. *Young Children, 67*(4), 16–25.

INTERESTING LINKS

http://www.educarer.com/current-article-relationships.htm
Educarer, Inc. Social Relationships of Infants in Daycare. Phyllis Porter highlights examples of how very young infants interact.

http://www.nncc.org
The National Network for Child Care NNCC provides access to articles on a variety of topics including children's social development.

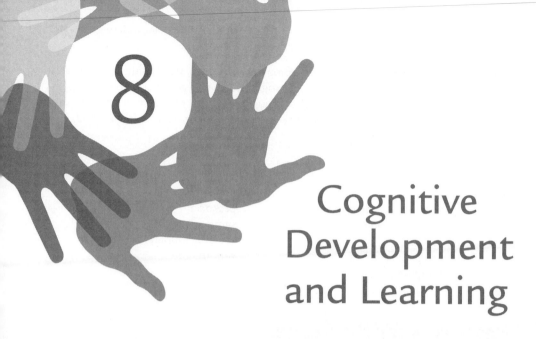

8

Cognitive Development and Learning

LEARNING OUTCOMES

After reading this chapter, you will be able to:

- Describe how infants and toddlers learn, including current theories, the role of regulation and attachment, approaches to learning, and the role of the senses.
- Explain how infants and toddlers develop cognitively within relationships, including cultural influences, the approaches to learning, the concepts they learn, and strategies to support learning.
- Identify the special needs that young children might have in their cognitive development.
- Describe the qualities of programs that have an effect on cognitive development.

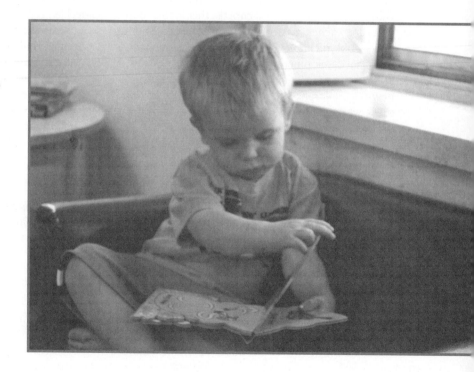

The newborn, hours after birth, quietly studies her mother's face.

The 1-year-old repeatedly empties little blocks from a plastic container and then drops them back in. Sometimes he concentrates on the blocks, looking at shapes or colors; sometimes he looks to his teacher for her approval.

Bryan, Sherod, and Mikey take the container of musical instruments off the shelf. Each 2-year-old reaches in and takes out a favorite rhythm instrument. Bryan starts to shake his bells. Mikey sings, "Twinkle, Twinkle, Little Star," a song they sometimes sing with their care teacher. Within moments the three are parading through the room, playing their instruments and singing.

The Uniqueness of Each Child

We no longer have an image of infants doing nothing but eating and sleeping. The word we most often hear used in describing newborns is "Amazing!" Thanks to research on early learning, we know that babies are born with knowledge gained in the womb and that they are actively working to build an understanding of their world in every waking moment.

This section describes the process of early learning: the various ways in which we understand infants and toddlers learn and what infants and toddlers are learning about their world.

Capacities

As part of the discussion of the capacities of the child, we highlight theories that give us information about those capacities, the emotional foundation for learning, and young children's approaches to learning.

Theories

There are many descriptions of how infants and toddlers learn. Each includes a central role for an invested, responsive adult; a safe and interesting environment; and the child as an active explorer trying to make meaning of his world. Here we describe three such theories: constructivist, core knowledge, and computational analysis.

The *constructivist theory* described in Chapter 3 asserts that children construct knowledge through their experiences in the world, including sensory experiences (Bruner, 1996a, 1996b; Piaget, 1954). They also learn, in part, through the scaffolding of information and experience provided by adults (Vygotsky, 1978). As children learn more about the world, they create basic changes in the things they are able to understand, going from the concrete to the theoretical.

The theory of *core knowledge* suggests that infants are born with basic cognitive systems that predispose them to be interested in and to learn about the things that are most important to survival. These include understanding the objects in the world, agents or the goal-directed actions of living things, number, and geometry or the ability to orient oneself in the environment (Spelke & Kinzler, 2007). As in constructivist theory, actual experiences in the world, such as being in relationship, change the child's perspectives, building knowledge that may support or modify the child's inherent understanding of the world.

The idea that learning is a *computational analysis* proposes that infants are figuring out language and the properties of objects by the patterns and frequencies with which they occur. A magnetic neuronal system is dedicated to learning the most cogent information (Meltzoff, Kuhl, Movellen & Sejnowski, 2009) .

Tyler digs in the sand industriously. As he finds rocks, he loads them into a toy dump truck, "drives" the truck across the sand table, and dumps them into another corner. "Build house," he says.
Mary also digs in the sand table. However, every movement in the room catches her attention. When a stranger enters the room, she stops her sand play and watches the stranger and her teacher.

The Emotional Foundation for Learning

For infants and toddlers, all learning happens within the context of relationships. There is an emotional foundation to cognitive development. First, the child's ability to learn depends on the ability to regulate emotions and the body, in order to attend to people, objects, or himself. As the adult calms the infant or teaches the toddler to calm himself, the child is capable of longer and longer alert times. Regulation is directly related to **executive functioning**—processes including inhibition, attention, working memory, and cognitive flexibility (Cartwright, 2012).

The second emotional foundation of learning is attachment. When an infant or toddler feels safe, she is able to explore the world. Even more than that, when the environment of the womb is safe, a very limited amount of stress hormones present during brain formation. These stress hormones (cortisol, adrenaline, and neopinepherine) can destroy parts of the developing brain. They are released when the mother and then the fetus are under serious, chronic stress. The parts of the brain involved with learning are particularly subject to damage prenatally and in the first years of life (National Scientific Council on the Developing Child, 2004).

Approaches to Learning

In addition to the emotional foundations for learning, infants and toddlers have specific tools for learning. These **approaches to learning** are built into the brain circuitry through a combination of genetic and environmental information. They are attention, curiosity, information gathering, problem solving, and persisting through small frustrations. They each come into action in the first years of life—and then we never stop using them.

The difficulty and effort, as Malaguzzi and Gandini (1993) point out, are part of the pleasure of learning for infants and toddlers:

> The pleasure of learning and knowing, and of understanding, is one of the most important and basic feelings that every child expects from the experiences he confronts alone, with other children or with adults. It is a crucial feeling which must be reinforced so that the pleasure survives even when reality may prove that learning, knowing and understanding involve difficulty and effort. (p. 174)

Attention.   Attention is the ability to focus on one interaction or experience without being easily distracted. Self-regulation helps the infant use "executive function and effortful contrrol" (Rothbart, Sheesa, Rueda, & Posner, 2011, p. 207). Attention is the first step in learning.

Curiosity.   Curiosity, or the desire to explore, is the balancing system to attachment. The child has a natural desire to explore and make meaning of the world. The adult best supports curiosity by providing physical and emotional safety and making safe, intriguing, and responsive play materials and experiences available.

Information gathering.   Infants appear to have several ways to gather information as explained earlier: core systems, sensorimotor, and the magnetic neuronal system. The fascinating thing is what information they are gathering. For years we've marveled at an infant achieving an understanding of object permanence or cause and effect. Yet

---

executive functioning
The ability to regulate, plan, sequence, organize, shift, and control one's own behavior.

Watch the **video** *Making a Discovery: The Water Table.* What discoveries is the child making as he plays?

approaches to learning
The attitudes and skills used in learning across all domains

Watch the first minute of this **video**. Observe the older toddler's approaches to learning, attention, and curiosity. What strategies is she using to learn about the properties of the unique toy?

from the moment they enter the world of their family, they are learning the sounds of their home language, how people behave around each other, and what rules their family and culture live by. Infants are collecting information about routines, physical properties, being in relationships, and their own bodies.

Memory.   Working memory describes the ability to take in new information while holding relevant, known information in mind. It seems that younger infants use several signals such as place, context, and other connections to "chunk" information in order to use it at a later time (Moher, Turek, & Feigenson, 2012), For example, 20-month-old infants were exposed to a novel, three-step sequence in one of three ways—watching, imitating, or learning—and tested for recall in 15 minutes. Then they were retested in 1, 2, and 3 days or 1, 2, and 3 months. The more in-depth the exposure to the task, the better the recall over time (Bauer, Güler, Starr & Pathman, 2011). Even very young babies appear to be showing the ability to remember actions from a week before.

 OBSERVATION INVITATION **8.1**

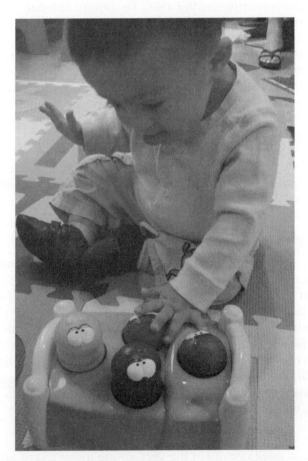

What kinds of information does this toy offer?
Make a list of things an infant or toddler could learn from this toy.

Problem solving.   Infants and toddlers are constantly solving problems. How do I roll over if my arm won't move? How do I use this spoon to eat? How do I get the toy I want, now? The world seems to provide many opportunities to try and think, maybe get help, and solve problems. Adults support problem solving by providing encouragement, helping just enough without solving the problem itself, and sometimes just by staying nearby and interested.

Some of the most frequent and natural problem-solving opportunities occur during social interactions. Toddlers are natually social, but they aren't equipped with all the social skills they need. Gloeckler and Cassell (2012) suggest seeing moments of conflict as opportunities to teach problem-solving skills: "You can tell Bahn you're hurt"; "Bahn, you can tell her she can have the car when you're done." Care Teachers, family child care providers, and home visitors can all support this intersocial problem solving.

Persisting through small frustrations.   In many ways persistence brings us back full circle to regulation. When a toy becomes too predictable, it is no longer fun. If a parent comes every time the infant makes a sound, calling the parent would require no effort. What engages learners best is a challenge whose solution is possible but not simple. In order to see such a challenge through to solution, the infant or toddler must be able to tolerate some frustration. The adult partner assists in this by helping the child stay focused and excited as well as able to pause and gather more information. In an intriguing twist, researchers wondered whether the child's competence affected the mother's investment and satisfaction in supporting her child. They looked at children at 6 and 18 months to measure their ability to complete physical and social tasks through some frustration. They also measured the mother's satisfaction and sense of competence as a parent. Competent infants had confident mothers. Less competent infants had less satisfied mothers. This might have been because the mothers had expectations that were too high or fewer skills to support their children's efforts. Either way, it suggests the possibility of a transactional nature to this approach to learning (Sparks, Hunter, Backman, Morgan & Ross, 2012).

Sensory Perceptions

To a great degree, a baby's ability to learn depends on her ability to perceive sensory information, then to process it, and make sense of and remember it. In fact, Piaget (1954) named the first, newborn stage of learning the *sensorimotor* period, describing the active perceptual work infants do to study faces, to remember smells, and to touch and taste everything they can bring to their lips.

Even in the womb, infants are taking in sensory information such as sounds and light. The synapses in the brain capture and transmit this sensory information—the muffled sound of their parents' voices, the specific taste of amniotic fluid, and the shifting pressures of their mother's moving body—so that they are born with surprisingly well-organized perceptual systems.

Seeing

The seriousness and intensity of the very young infant's gaze can be surprising. Watching the eyes of very young babies, it is easy to believe that they are intent on drinking in all the information the world has to offer and putting the information together to make sense.

Newborns are able to visually follow movement within a distance of 9 to 12 inches, although the focus is a little fuzzy. This provides the newborn with a wonderful care ability to look into his mother's eyes as she is feeding him from the breast or his teacher's eyes as she cuddles him with a bottle.

In the first months, the baby sees best out of the corner of his eye, using peripheral vision. He will be most interested in objects that offer high contrasts of light and dark and images that resemble the human face (Bower, 1977; Lamb, Bornstein, & Teti, 2002). By 3 months of age, infants are looking straight ahead and showing interest in their own hands. They enjoy the movement of mobiles twirling slowly above them as they practice using their two eyes together, learning to focus on an object and fuse the images entering each eye. If the eyes are not aligned—some people call them "crossed"—the baby will have "double vision" and will stop using one eye to clear up the image. If one or both eyes do not work properly, the connections between the eye and the brain may not develop. By 6 months of age, the infant's range of vision has stretched to focus on greater distances; by 9 months, he can see as well as an adult at both close range and distances (ZERO TO THREE, 2009). The sequence of visual development is illustrated in Figure 8.1.

FIGURE 8.1   Vision milestones

Age	Visual Ability
Birth to 2 months	Sees best at 9 to 12 inches Sees best out of the corner of the eye Loves to look at your face Likes objects with strong contrasts in light and dark Can follow slow movement Eyes are sometimes uncoordinated
2 to 6 months	Begins to recognize objects as one image Looks at own hands Uses vision to reach for objects May stare at anything interesting Looks in mirror Recognizes bottle
6 to 8 months	Sees all colors Sees as well as a teenager May touch self in mirror Turns head to see object Likes certain colors
9 to 12 months	Can see small objects such as cereal pieces Is developing depth perception Can follow fast movements
12 to 18 months	Can do simple shape puzzles Interested in pictures and books Recognizes own face in mirror
18 to 36 months	Can focus near and far Points and gestures for certain objects Scribbles, sometimes in imitation

Source: Milestones compiled from Morgan Stanley Children's Hospital of New York–Presbyterian. (n.d.). Age appropriate vision milestones. Retrieved from http://childrensnyp.org/

Edges and lines.   Although infants are highly interested in other human beings, they also spend quite a lot of time sorting out the pieces of the environment. Infants are surrounded by an endless number of colors, shapes, and noises. In order to learn, they must figure out which of these deserve their attention and which can be ignored. One of their first tasks is to organize the images they see and the sounds they hear into a recognizable and understandable order. Using their vision, very young infants study images with high contrasts between light and dark areas, and their eyes travel along the edges of objects as they learn where one object ends and one begins (Haith, 1980; Lamb et al., 2002).

Moving objects.   Babies combine their interest in edges and lines with an interest in movement to discern what comprises a single entity. They quickly learn that an object that appears to be one single entity—given its visual edges—should move in space in one piece. The movement may be an important part of figuring out what makes a single object. For example, the cover of a book may have a title on a banner (with edges of its own) and a picture of a teddy bear (with its own defining edges). However, when the book is lifted and carried, the edges of the whole book move together. Here, the movement helps define the object (Spelke, Breinlinger, Jacobson, & Phillips, 1993).

Babies understand the rules of movement in the physical world. In research situations, they show great surprise if an object moves in ways that are contrary to the laws of physics. If an object is moving in an arc toward a screen and then disappears behind the screen, the infant's eyes will move to the point on the other side of the screen where the object would appear if it continued in its arc. When the object appears at another point, babies look surprised. In experiments in which pieces of objects are placed so as to look like one object, babies are surprised if the parts move away from each other separately. Babies even show some knowledge of gravity. They are surprised when an object appears to stay in the air without support (Baillargeon, 1993).

Hearing

Infants are able to hear even before they are born. Newborns recognize sounds that are already familiar to them. Using particular patterns of sucking on specially designed pacifiers, newborn babies will suck harder and longer to hear voices similar to their mother's voice, which they hear in the last few months of gestation through the walls of the womb. Newborns demonstrate through their sucking that they prefer to listen to the language that they heard prenatally; they even prefer to hear familiar passages of stories that their mothers had repeatedly read aloud during the pregnancy (DeCasper & Spence, 1986; Mehler et al., 1988; Moon, Cooper, & Fifer, 1993).

Hearing milestones, as shown in Figure 8.2, are observed in relation to the baby's attention to language. From birth to 3 months, babies turn toward a sound. They pay attention to sounds in the environment, such as caregivers talking quietly to them. Between 3 and 6 months of age, infants understand a few words such as "bye-bye" or "no." They will babble and imitate sounds. Between 6 and 12 months, they begin to intentionally use simple words such as "mama" or "dada" (ZERO TO THREE, 2009).

Touch

The skin is the largest organ in the body and infants are very sensitive to touch. Infants use touch for comfort, for stimulation, to learn about the world; they suck on objects, feel them with their hands, and kick at them with their feet. Early studies

FIGURE 8.2   **Hearing milestones**

Age	Hearing Ability
Birth to 2 months	Can hear many sounds Prefers human speech Startles at loud sounds Can be soothed by soft sounds Turns head toward familiar voice
2 to 6 months	Looks toward new sounds Responds to different tones of voice Enjoys toys that make sounds May babble repeated sounds "ba-ba-ba" Frightened by loud noises
6 to 8 months	Is very interested in human voices Looks for the source of a sound Babbles Responds to own name Recognizes simple, common words
9 to 12 months	Shows interest in telephone Understands many words Looks at pictures as adult describes them Points to pictures when named Sometimes follows one-step directions
12 to 18 months	Enjoys playing with sounds Uses a few words, maybe a few words in a sentence Points to body parts when asked Follows directions without being shown
18 to 24 months	Understands yes/no questions Understands simple phrases Enjoys hearing stories Will understand your use of color words
24 to 36 months	Understands size words Understands action words

Source: Milestones compiled from Spectrum Health. (2009). Hearing milestones. Retrieved from https://www.spectrumhealth.org

of babies in institutions demonstrated that although babies may be fed adequate nutritional matter, if they are not held and touched they may actually die (Spitz, 1945). Lack of experience with being touched is identified as one of the factors that cause the brains of maltreated children to be underdeveloped (Perry, 1996).

Over decades of study, it has become clear that touch has many beneficial effects. A massage of moderate pressure can reduce heart rate, increase attention, help premature infants gain weight, lower cortisol and adrenalin, and increase oxytocin (Field, 2010). Touch is being utilized in some intensive care nurseries with premature infants. In a practice called *kangaroo care,* parents hold their premature infant in skin-to-skin contact on their chests for several hours a day. Studies show these babies regulate their heart rate and breathing sooner, sleep longer, grow faster, maintain their body temperature, and have brain activity

OBSERVATION INVITATION **8.2**

How does this picture make you feel?
Looking at it, can you imagine benefits of touch for the caregiver and the little girl?

that looks identical to the brain activity of contentment and the creation of synapses (Richardson, 1997). They score higher on developmental tests at 6 months (Feldman, Eidelman, Sirota, & Weller, 2002). Earlier studies showed that premature infants given gentle massage for 10 days, while still in the neonatal care intensive unit, increased their weight gain by nearly 50% over babies not receiving massage (Field & Brazelton, 1990). Mothers and fathers who are taught to give baby massages benefit as well. They are more sensitive to their baby's cues and at 3 months provide a better home environment (Feldman et al., 2002).

Smelling and Tasting

The sense of smell develops quickly in the newborn and seems to be used to help the baby recognize his mother. In a series of studies, 2-day-old babies could not differentiate a pad soaked with their mother's breast milk from a clean pad or one soaked with another mother's milk. By 5 days, babies show significantly more interest in the pad with their mother's milk than in the clean pad. On the sixth day of life, babies turned their heads to keep their faces near their mother's milk-soaked pad rather than that of another new mother (McFarlane, 1975). It is possible that smell has some role in the development of attachment in both the baby's and the adult's experience. Babies quickly learn the shampoo or cologne scents of their parents and are more easily comforted by blankets or stuffed animals that carry familiar smells (Mennella & Beauchamp, 2002). The combination of smell and other senses used together probably help us develop a more accurate understanding of the world around us, a sort of sensory redundancy (Schaal & Durand, 2012).

At birth, babies are able to taste sweet, sour, and bitter. They prefer sweet tastes and will bring their hands to their mouths when given something sweet in the first weeks of life. Some cultures—such as those in Egypt, Mexico, Jamaica, and India—give newborns sweet-tasting liquids to help them stay calm and sleep. Breast milk is also very sweet (Rochat, 2001). Although most babies do not taste salt until about 4 months, studies show that babies with a family history of hypertension are able to taste salt at 2 days—and they prefer it to other tastes (Zinner, McGarvey, Lipsitt, & Rosner, 2002). These studies suggest that salt sensitivity may be related to a predisposition to hypertension.

Babies show highly individual differences in their taste preferences. Some infants welcome the introduction of new foods at about 6 months of age; others demonstrate very clearly their preference for staying with the familiar. It is unclear if these differences are related to how babies taste differences, or whether it has more to do with their temperament and a desire to take risks versus keep everything pretty much the same.

Amodal Learning

Although we tend to separate the senses in trying to understand how they develop over time, babies use their senses in a coordinated way—or in a way that transcends the use of any one mode of taking in information. Babies are capable of this *amodal* or multimodal learning from birth (Bahrick, 1995; Lewkowicz & Lickliter, 1994). They are able to take in information through one sensory mode and translate it into usable information for another sense, even when the second sense had never been exposed to the object, proving that this is an innate coordinated skill, and not learned through experience. They are also able to combine information from two or more senses.

Meltzoff and Moore (1977) found evidence that infants can translate or transfer information from one sensory mode to another. They gave babies a rubber nipple to suck without letting the baby see the nipple. Some babies were given a smooth nipple; some were bumpy. After a few minutes of sucking, the baby was shown both the smooth and bumpy nipples. The babies consistently chose to look at the nipple that they had just felt in their mouth, as though recognizing it, although they had never seen it.

Babies also have expectations that their senses will provide them with coherent information. They want the information from their eyes to match the information from their ears. At 3 months, babies will look with interest at a video of their mother speaking while they hear her voice. However, they are distressed at the sight of their mother's face with someone else's voice coming from it or a picture of another woman with their mother's voice coming from it (Spelke & Owlsley, 1979). This coordinated use of senses has not been well studied, but it may be one of the most powerful tools babies use as they explore and master their environment.

Attributes

Following some heated exchanges over the issue of "natural superiority in math and science" of males at Harvard University, Dr. Elizabeth Spelke issued a paper that declared "mathematical and scientific reasoning develop from a set of biologically based cognitive capacities that males and females share" (Spelke, 2005, p. 956). At this point, early studies that seemed to suggest gender differences have largely been dismissed. There is such appreciation of the complexity of the learning process today that gender is only considered an as yet poorly understood factor in cognitive development.

Development and Learning Through Relationships

"Where's your nose?" asked Terri, showing great delight as Jeremy gleefully pointed to his nose. "Where're your eyes?" "Where's your mouth?" If she'd stopped to think about it, Terri would have imagined that teachers all over the world would be playfully asking these questions of 1-year-olds. But adults around the world have many different ways of helping babies learn.

Culture and Relationships

Piaget, from his observations of his own children as described in Chapter 3, helped us recognize how infants move from learning about the world primarily through sensorimotor experiences to the use of symbols as toddlers. Piaget believed that the processes of learning (reasoning, classification, logic, and memory) were general across all humanity (Rogoff, 2003). Cross-cultural studies, however, would argue that Vygotsky's sociocultural theory of learning provides a better basis for understanding the differences in cognitive development within different cultures.

Vygotsky (1978) suggests that cognitive skills develop not from a child individually interacting with materials in the environment, but through participation in sociocultural activities. People use cultural tools, such as literacy or mathematics, to think about tasks within their own culture. Thinking and learning occur within social relationships and cultural experience. Cognitive development describes the learning a person does to participate in his or her own culture. For example, an American mother may unintentionally teach the category of "animal" to her infant by always pointing out and naming the animals in pictures, but not the plants, tools, machines, or buildings. The infant learns to attend to this particular grouping of individual objects and sees them as a category. A mother in another culture might group horses and elephants with cars and trucks as part of the category of "things that take us places."

The questions asked by Terri, the teacher in the previous example, seem perfectly natural to most Americans. Our culture is filled with situations in which a person demonstrates competence by answering direct questions. Jeremy is actually learning to be a test taker in America. Some cultures respond very differently to direct questions. A study in North Africa found children unwilling to answer direct questions, because in their culture people do not ask questions to which they know the answers. This kind of question would be seen as a challenge or a trick (Irvine, 1978). In some cultures, although a 1-year-old might well know where her nose is, she would not be asked such a question because the role of children is to listen and obey adults, not to converse with them (Super & Harkness, 1997).

Our appreciation for children who quickly learn words and concepts might not be shared by Ugandan villagers who equate intelligence with words such as *slow, careful,* and *active* (Wober, 1972), or Navajo families who value reflection and planning (Ellis & Siegler, 1997). Kenyan parents might describe intelligence in terms of being trustworthy and participating in the family's life (Super & Harkness, 1997). Many cultures emphasize values of social responsibility over personal knowledge in describing intelligence.

CULTURE CLOSE UP

Ms. Katika ran a quiet home family care, offering a rich assortment of experiences. Her assistant Patty loved working there — except for one thing. For example, 2-year-old Rosie chose a tub of large pegs and a board to stick them into. Ms. Katika at first observed and then encouraged her. She gently but firmly kept Rosie there until all 10 pegs were in. Her East Indian belief included building a strong work ethic. Patty believed infants and toddlers should be free to explore. What do you believe and why?

The following descriptions of how children learn, how adults support learning, and what we expect children to learn should be considered more meaningful and accurate for children in the United States and Europe than as a general description of learning across cultures.

Tools of Learning

At 21 months, Sudie already loved books. She would stroll over to the book corner, browse through the shelves, and choose a book about dogs. She had favorite books about dogs but welcomed new ones. It fascinated her teacher that she could choose with such purpose.

Categorizing

Memory alone is not knowledge. If an infant or toddler stored every individual memory but had no way to organize the information, the world would be chaotic. The ability to recognize similarities and differences is a good one to use as an example of how infants understand the world in increasingly sophisticated and complex ways. Recognizing similarities is a precursor to the skill of *categorization:* sorting, matching, comparing, and contrasting. As infants have more experience with the world, between 3 and 5 months of age, they can create categories or representational groupings of objects. These categories are initially created to group objects with observable, physical similarities. For example, presented with a series of figures of cats, at first babies will look longer at "new" cats, figures they are seeing for the first time. Before long, new pictures of cats are no longer interesting. Babies begin to look less at new cats, even if they haven't seen that particular cat before, but perk up and pay attention when shown figures of other kinds of animals (Eimas & Quinn, 1994).

As children continue to interact with objects in the world, their ability to create categories becomes increasingly sophisticated as they include **invisible information** such as the function or purpose of an object. They understand that bottles, cups, and glasses are all for drinking. They group toys that *make noise when shaken* or toys that *roll when thrown*. These more subtle categories of invisible properties of objects go beyond what the child can see into a generalized mental representation called a *concept*.

> **invisible information**
> Properties of objects that can be known but not seen.

Fourteen-month-old toddlers demonstrated their increasingly complex conceptual understanding of being alive and how the world works. Researchers showed a toddler an activity such as pretending to give a toy dog a drink from a cup. The toddler was then given three toys to use in reenacting the activity: a cup, a bird, and an airplane. Toddlers would offer the cup to the bird but not to the airplane. Activities such as eating or sleeping were reenacted with the figures of animals; trucks and airplanes were chosen for activities such as using a key (Mandler & McDonough, 1996).

Symbolic Play

During the first 3 years of life, infants and toddlers have countless day-to-day experiences with language, with family photographs and picture books, with television, and with toy replicas of houses and cars and other real-life objects. They are constantly exposed to symbols of objects (or of feelings) being used by adults and older children as meaningfully as they use real objects. By the age of 3, most children have mastered the use of symbols themselves. They use language fluently and creatively. They follow stories told in pictures and they can incorporate models of household objects into their pretend play. It is our use of symbols that allows human beings to communicate, learn, and create.

Greenspan (1997) describes infants as initially being in a *behavior mode,* where being hugged by Mom or actually eating dinner are sources of contentment. As infants become toddlers and move into a *symbolic mode,* they can begin to feel satisfaction from the *knowledge* that "Mom loves me" or *knowing* that dinner is being prepared (Greenspan, 1997). As with every aspect of development, the key is in the relationship between the baby and the caregiver:

> The shift in modes therefore requires the long-term participation of someone who promotes interaction, who supports ever greater use of signals, who joins in the child's pretend play, who helps the child link the pleasures of relating to the skills of communicating symbolically. The sheer enjoyment of being listened to, the satisfaction of gaining attention through the use of images, motivates the first step in this epochal move. The child delights not only in getting what he wants or having his expectations confirmed, but in letting others know what they are. (Greenspan, 1997, p. 77)

Researchers have tracked how infants move from interest in looking at a picture, to understanding that a picture represents a real thing and, yet, is different from that thing. Five-month-olds were given time to study a doll. They were then shown pictures of that doll and of a new doll. As in other **habituation** studies described in this chapter, the babies demonstrated their familiarity with the real doll by losing interest in its picture. They treated the picture of the real doll exactly as they would have treated the doll itself; they looked longer at the new doll (DeLoache, Strauss, & Maynard, 1979). Nine-month-olds, presented with realistic picture books of objects, tried to touch and pick up the object, as though not recognizing that this was a *symbol* of the object. However, by 15 months, American infants with lots of experience with picture books would point to pictures and name the objects, demonstrating some idea of the representation (DeLoache, Pierroutsakos, & Troseth, 1997; DeLoache, Pierroutsakos, Troseth, Uttah, Rosengren, & Gottlieb, 1998).

Namy (2001) looked at how infants use a variety of types of symbols. At 12 and 18 months, infants were equally willing to accept words, gestures, pictures, or nonword sounds as the names of objects. After 18 months, the age at which toddlers generally show increased interest in language, they preferred to use words as names of objects.

Within a study of the development of social play, solitary pretend play, and social pretend play in toddlers, Howes, Unger, and Seidner (1989) describe a progression of increasingly complex use of symbolization. From about 12 to 15 months, toddlers will use auto-symbolic schemes in which they perform a pretend act aimed at themselves, such as pretending to drink from a cup (Howes et al., 1989). Toddlers love to pretend to sleep, smiling and looking at the teacher much of the time, while the teacher says, "Goodnight. Shhhh. Quiet everyone. Jacob's sleeping." Then Jacob jumps up laughing and the teacher says, "Jacob, you're up! Good morning!"—at which Jacob is likely to immediately repeat the routine, over and over (Gowen, 1995). It is easy to see how a responsive adult can support this play and this desire to learn in a young child.

> *The important thing is not so much that every child should be taught, as that every child should be given the wish to learn. (John Lubbock, 19th-century astronomer and mathematician)*

habituation
A simple form of learning in which an animal, after repeated exposure to a stimulus, stops responding.

decentered symbolic play
Play in which children, instead of performing an act themselves, move the action to a toy or object, performing the action on a symbolic level.

At around 15 to 20 months, in **decentered symbolic play**, the toddler directs the pretend action to a toy but with no intention assigned to the toy in the play (feeds the doll but doesn't say the doll is hungry). At 20 to 25 months, toddlers begin sequencing pretend actions such as waking the doll, feeding her, and bathing her, playing repetitions of familiar routines, such as preparing a meal, eating it, and cleaning up afterward using realistic replications of household objects (Westby, 1980). At 24 to 30 months, toddlers engage in internally directed symbolic play whereby they ascribe agency or intention to the toys (the doll is hungry) and then interact with the toy through a sequence of pretend actions. Over the next several months, the child is increasingly able to simply pretend—to use an object such as a block or a stick to be first a coffee cup and then a set of keys. Less familiar and frequent events may also appear within the stories of pretend play. At 30 to 36 months, in behavioral role-play, toddlers assign roles to their dolls and toys such as being the father or the dog, and the play incorporates the roles.

As they achieve greater use of language, the play becomes more filled with detail and the children have greater capacity to share their interests. Mastery of language and other symbols frees the child to think beyond the concrete experience of the moment (Gowen, 1995; Howes et al., 1989; Westby, 1980).

Learning Through Relationships

Sarah, as a young baby, tries to suck on her caregiver's cheek. The caregiver laughs warmly, makes eye contact with her, and says, "Sarah, you're sucking on my cheek! Are you ready for a bottle?" Following a series of experiences similar to this one, Sarah begins to understand that sucking works better with nipples and bottles and that looking, nuzzling, and smiling are good ways to connect with people.

Infants have enormous abilities to observe, learn about, and predict the behavior of the people around them. They develop mental representations, or understandings, of what they know, and when evidence convinces them that their beliefs are wrong, they change their beliefs to match the evidence. For example, the young infant just discussed may begin relating to others by sucking on the cheek or finger of any available adult. Through the warm interaction with her caregiver, she learns more effective ways of being with others.

Adults have endless opportunities to support early learning: "Our instinctive behaviors toward babies and babies' instinctive behaviors toward us combine to enable the babies to learn as much as they do" (Gopnik, Meltzoff, & Kuhl, 1999, p. 169). Some of the most effective strategies used are *modeling, imitation,* and *scaffolding.* Infants and toddlers are such active learners that adults rarely need to teach so much as they need to be available to support learning. Adults intuitively support cognitive development, helping toddlers understand how their world works.

modeling
The adult's demonstration of actions for the child.

imitation
The child's attempt to learn from the adult by repeating the action or sound that the adult performed.

In the second part of this video notice how many times the child imitates the adult. What is the child learning? Why do children imitate?

Modeling and Imitation

Literally from the first moments of life, babies are able to imitate the facial expressions of adults (Meltzoff & Moore, 1977). **Modeling** on the part of the adult and **imitation** on the part of the child may be the primary conduit for passing information from one generation to the next. By 14 months, toddlers can repeat the actions of peers and adults in different settings (Hanna & Meltzoff, 1993) and after a 1-week delay (Meltzoff, 2005). Toddlers imitate facial expressions, vocal intonations, body movements, and routines of their parents and teachers.

However, adults also imitate infants and toddlers. When adults repeat the expression, vocalization, or movement of a very young child, they are demonstrating to the child some understanding of the child's actions and experiences and a desire for connection and communication. Stern (2000) calls the adult's imitation of the baby **mirroring**. When adults do not directly imitate but match

mirroring
An adult's imitation of facial expressions made by the infant.

OBSERVATION INVITATION **8.3**

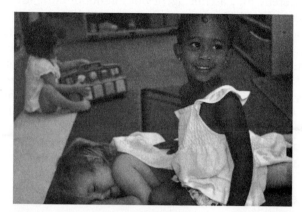

What bedtime experiences has this girl's family modeled for her?

attunement

An alignment of the internal states of an adult and baby through the adult's matching of the intensity, timing, and shape of the baby's behavior without actually imitating the behavior.

the emotional tone and vitality of a baby's expression, Stern calls it **attunement**. The adult's action of matching or imitating the infant or toddler increases the child's sense of being an active partner in reciprocal interactions. This often leads to the toddler making small changes or elaborations in the movements or sounds that make up the imitation, heightening the creative learning experience.

Scaffolding

scaffolding

The adult's continual adjustment of the level of her help in response to the child's level of performance, to help the child achieve what he could not do alone.

A second and equally important way that adults support early learning is identified by Vygotsky (1978) as **scaffolding**. As described in Chapter 3, Vygotsky saw the role of the teacher as one of recognizing not only the child's current developmental accomplishments but understanding the next steps in development, or the *zone of proximal development (ZPD)*. The adult then creates a scaffold that will support the child's movement from the current point in development to the next point of development. In the example of symbolic play described earlier, the teacher might scaffold Jacob's symbolic play of sleeping and waking by asking if he wants the teddy bear to sleep—and then supporting his movement into symbolic play with the teddy bear.

Adults scaffold learning by adding and elaborating language during conversations, by suggesting variations in the usual pattern of play, or by introducing new materials or new combinations of materials. The concept of scaffolding will be discussed further in Chapter 13.

Theory of Mind

theory of mind

The cognitive ability to understand others as intentional agents, having beliefs and desires of their own.

Along with their increasing capacities to think and talk and symbolize, toddlers are becoming aware of their own thinking and talking and symbolizing. The awareness and understanding that children discover about themselves and others, such as ideas, beliefs, thoughts, feelings, and desires is called **theory of mind**. Theory of mind describes the ideas an infant, toddler, or preschooler may have about how invisible forces such as feelings or thoughts affect their behavior or the behavior of other people.

This connection between activities of the mind and behavior is a major developmental step in understanding oneself and others. It begins with the understanding that "people act to fulfill their desires in light of their beliefs" (Astington & Barriault, 2001, p. 2). Therefore, the baby who is hungry but has learned not to cry out in a dangerous and chaotic home will "act to fulfill his desire" for food "in light of his belief" that it is dangerous to make noise. He will quietly suck on his hand until he falls asleep. The infant who has a loving, responsive caregiver, however, will cry out lustily in the belief that the adults in his life want to keep him safe, happy, and comfortable.

Theory of mind, say Astington and Barriault (2001), grows through ongoing exposure to "people talking about what they and others want, like, think, feel, and so on. Our understanding of one another, indeed all of our social interaction, is based on a theory of mind" (p. 2). They continue:

> There are two things we should make clear at the outset. First we think, know, want, and feel things; that is, we have beliefs, desires, intentions, and emotions, and we can ascribe beliefs, desires, intentions, and emotions (i.e., we can think about people's thoughts, wants, plans, and feelings). It is this latter aspect—thinking about thinking—that is the theory of the mind….Second, we do not expect children to be able to explain their theory of mind….We have to infer their theory from what they say and do in both naturalistic and experimental situations. (p. 2)

The infant or toddler, then, creates a picture of himself as a person with thoughts, ideas, feelings, knowledge, memories, and predictions about things that will happen. Within rich, complex, reciprocal relationships, the child also begins to learn that other people have equally multifaceted internal lives.

Concepts Infants and Toddlers Learn

> *Arman yelled "In!" as he pushed hard to make a large puzzle piece fit in the hole in the puzzle. He first tried a schema that had worked many times in the past: After tasting the piece, he placed it near the hole and pounded it with his fist. He then turned the piece one way and then another until it finally dropped in the hole. With a big sigh of contentment, he looked at his great accomplishment. Then he pulled out the piece and started all over again.*

This little moment of activity is filled with learning. Arman is using and learning language, practicing cause and effect in pushing the puzzle piece, working on spatial relationships between the puzzle piece and the hole, hypothesizing and trying strategies to make the piece fit, and demonstrating how his curiosity and his image of himself as a learner contribute to his ability to persist in the task even when it is hard. According to Piaget, the major discoveries of infancy are *object permanence, cause and effect, use of tools,* and *use of space* (Flavell, 1977). These are huge concepts but only part of what babies are learning through their moments with people and their interactions with the objects in the world. Infants are making Piaget's discoveries—and they are learning language and literacy, developing mental concepts and categories, and beginning to understand numbers. In the past several years, many states have taken on the task of articulating what infants and toddlers learn and how they are learning through early learning guidelines (see Box 8.1).

Object Permanence

An early discovery babies make is that people and things continue to exist whether or not you are with them and can see them—they are making discoveries about the permanence of objects and persons (Krøjgaard, 2005). Infants have numerous experiences with their parents and teachers coming and going, but always reappearing, helping babies develop an understanding of the permanence of the

Watch the first minute of this video. How does the young toddler demonstrate that he has object permanence? How is object permanence encouraged by the parent?

BOX 8.1

Early Learning Guidelines for Infants and Toddlers (ELG/ITs)

In 2002, the presidential initiative for early childhood, *Good Start, Grow Smart,* required the states to write early learning guidelines describing what preschoolers should know in language, literacy, and mathematics. Many states found these documents so beneficial that they chose to create guidelines articulating what infants and toddlers are learning as well.

ELG/ITs help parents and teachers understand what infants and toddlers should know and be able to do during specific age ranges. As adults understand and appreciate what infants and toddlers are learning, they can better support the children's natural curiosity, exploration, and discoveries. ELG/ITs are becoming a foundational element of professional development systems for state early childhood care and education.

existence of these people. The classic demonstration of object permanence involves hiding a toy under a cloth as the infant is watching. Very young babies behave as though the toy has disappeared and make no attempt to retrieve the toy. Somewhere around 8 months, however, the infant will lift the cloth with every expectation that the toy will be waiting (Uzgiris & Hunt, 1975).

Cause and Effect

Infants learn that people cause things to happen and that they can cause people to do things. Infants have numerous intrapersonal and interpersonal experiences with cause and effect. For example, an empty tummy makes a baby cry. The cry brings a caregiver with a loving cuddle and a warm bottle. Sucking the milk in the bottle causes the baby to feel comfortable and happy again. One event follows another in such a predictable way that the baby begins to have a sense of one event causing another to happen.

Toys also provide numerous opportunities for infants and toddlers to discover and practice cause and effect. Babies need toys that respond in a contingent manner to their actions. Toy pianos that play notes when a key is pushed or a pad is kicked, jack-in-the-box toys that pop up when a button is pushed or a lever flipped, balls that roll away when pushed, blocks that make sounds when squeaked all teach the baby about cause and effect—and give her a sense that she is someone who can make things happen! Many of the new electronic toys are not contingent—once turned on, they essentially provide a light and sound show to a passive baby. It might be entertaining, but infants and toddlers will not be learning about their own efficacy in the world from that kind of toy.

Use of Tools

Infants learn some things about the use of tools through their interactions with people. They watch people use tools and see that people can be used as tools. If you cry, someone will come and comfort and feed you. If you point, someone will reach the stacking rings for you. Toddlers learn to ask adults for help in tasks they find frustrating by pointing, looking from the person to the object and back again, and using sounds and language.

Toddlers use tools when they use forks and spoons to feed themselves, when they climb on a chair to reach a shelf, or when they use paintbrushes or markers to create pictures. They use tools when they use a wooden spoon to bang on a pot or use a push toy to help them take their first steps.

Use of Space

Babies learn that people have spatial relationships with each other and with the things in the world. People move through space in predictable ways, their bodies exist as a single entity, and they appear bigger when they are close and smaller when they are far away. Babies also have many opportunities to watch adults move objects around in space, put wallets in purses, cups in cupboards, and milk cartons in refrigerators. Babies bring this experience of watching adults to their own explorations of the world. The process of putting one thing into another can be endlessly fascinating to babies. Any collection of objects can become interesting when they are put into and dumped out of a bucket. Shape boxes that allow infants or toddlers to put a toy through a hole shaped like the toy will keep them trying over and over. For infants and toddlers, crawling, walking, and climbing are constant lessons in spatial relationships.

Language and Literacy

Language and literacy learning are such important aspects of development that they have their own chapter in this book, but in any list of what infants learn from and about others, it is essential to include language and literacy. As mentioned earlier, babies hear the sounds of language even before they are born. Infants quickly learn to use the sounds of language in turn-taking interactions with adults. They recognize and begin to understand words by listening to all of the exchanges around them—but best of all, by their parents and teachers responding personally to them in little one-on-one, face-to-face "conversations."

Numbers

Just as infants seem to understand some aspects of individual objects in the world, they may have an inherent—or very early—understanding of numbers. The National Council of Teachers of Mathematics (NCTM, 2000) includes references to infants in its standards for pre-K to grade 2. It points out that the foundation for mathematical learning is established in the earliest years, through ordinary experiences such as a parent counting crackers or cutting a sandwich into squares or triangles. Everyday life can provide infants and toddlers with many casual, offhand opportunities to understand the basics of mathematics.

Researchers find the study of early number understanding, such as counting, to be a controversial one. Wynn (1992) had 5-month-old babies look at a screen. She showed them a little toy Mickey Mouse and placed it behind the screen. If she removed the screen and two Mickeys appeared, the babies were surprised. If she showed the babies the hiding of two Mickeys, they were surprised if removal of the screen revealed only one Mickey Mouse doll. If the babies watched two Mickeys being hidden and saw one being removed, they would show surprise if two Mickeys were still revealed at the removal of the screen.

In other experiments, infants further demonstrated their understanding of numbers. Researchers showed a baby a ball and then put it in a box, out of sight. They added a second ball and told the baby, "Get the ball." Babies would reach into the box two times and retrieve both balls. They never reached in just once, never more than twice (Xu & Carey, 1996).

Could a lot of this just be memory? Some researchers think that infants are not really counting but are using perceived information such as overall size and surface area to understand differences in numbers (Feigenson, Carey, & Spelke, 2002). Nonetheless, infants do demonstrate a variety of early mathematical skills. Xu and Carey (1996) report that 6-month-olds

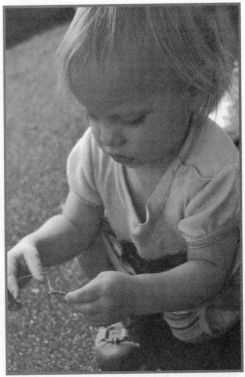

When young children play with objects, they are learning about space and mathematical concepts.

can discern one set of many items from another if they have a 2-to-1 ratio. Brannon (2002) finds that 11-month-old infants can tell the difference between visual displays of items that increase or decrease in number. See Chapter 13 for ideas for promoting children's understanding of numbers.

Children with Special Needs

Infants have enormous inborn capacities for learning, but there are also enormous challenges to their ability to learn. The foundations of learning can be threatened by developmental disabilities and environmental risks having wide variation in their effect on development.

Prenatal or postnatal insults to the central nervous system may cause delayed or impaired development in learning, social relationships, communication, or motor development. Some infants have biological risks from exposure to drugs, alcohol, or maternal stress hormones in utero. Sensory impairments may challenge a child's ability to perceive information from the world. Established conditions such as Down syndrome, cerebral palsy, autism, premature birth, or low birth weight may affect the child's ability to process or use the information in the environment (Guralnik, 2000; Shonkoff & Phillips, 2000).

Because the areas of development are so interrelated in infancy, very young children are particularly vulnerable to the effects of environmental difficulties such as exposure to violence, a parent's mental illness, poor nutrition, and low educational achievement in the home (Shonkoff & Phillips, 2000, p. 338). Large numbers of young children in our society are subject to abuse and neglect, are born to adolescents, or experience family disruption and/or foster care placement. Lead exposure through toys and foods from other countries may have harmful effects on infants, but in the United States, lead has been restricted from paint and gasoline for decades.

These children may be particularly well served by early intervention. Programs that deliver carefully designed interventions with well-defined goals can affect both parenting behavior and the developmental trajectories of a child whose life course is threatened by socioeconomic disadvantage, family disruption, or diagnosed disability. Programs that combine child-focused educational activities with explicit attention to parent-child interaction patterns and relationship building appear to have the greatest impacts (Shonkoff & Phillips, 2000, p. 379).

> *People's beliefs about their abilities have a profound effect on those abilities. Ability is not a fixed property; there is a huge variability in how you perform. People who have a sense of self-efficacy bounce back from failures; they approach things in terms of how to handle them rather than worrying about what can go wrong. (Albert Bandura)*

Care teachers are able to provide rich learning environments for each child by individualizing the way experiences are offered. Strong observation skills help the teacher understand how the child perceives and processes information. In addition to always attending to your own interactions and relationship with the child, here are some considerations for planning how to individualize learning activities for each infant or toddler:

Which materials best meet the needs and interests of each child?
How can I arrange the materials and equipment to encourage each child's participation?

How can the activity be more accessible to each child?

What can I do so children can come and go from the activity at their own pace?

(Mulligan, 1997)

A more detailed description of what infants and toddlers learn, and what adults can do to support that learning, can be found in the Developmental Trends and Responsive Interactions chart.

STRATEGIES TO SUPPORT COGNITIVE DEVELOPMENT AND LEARNING

Infants and toddlers will learn about themselves, about being in relationships with other people, and many of the basic concepts they need to understand the world. You can assist them with the following strategies:

1. Help infants maintain a quiet, alert state of attention by keeping them in comfortable positions, talking quietly, and looking at or manipulating things together.
2. Help toddlers keep focused and attentive by limiting distractions and interruptions. Express interest in their activities and try to observe and reflect on what you believe they are trying to accomplish.
3. Spark curiosity by offering materials in new ways, such as setting the dolls up in the book corner "reading" books, or the farm animals on a green cloth over blocks creating a gentle hill.
4. Spark curiosity by noticing things and suggesting, "Let's go see what that is!"
5. Support persistence through frustration by offering materials that are challenging enough to be interesting but not impossible, by offering a few choices, by expressing your interest and encouragement, and by sharing the joy children feel as they show you their accomplishments
6. Support sensorimotor learning by offering play and exploration experiences that provide a variety of sensory modes: sand, water, cornstarch, smelling bottles, and so forth.
7. Help children develop memories by keeping the routine and room arrangement predictable; keep toys where children know to find them. Talk with children about what they did earlier in the day or the day before.
8. Provide many opportunities to categorize, match, sort, compare, and contrast with toys and activities.
9. Encourage problem solving by not stepping in immediately when a problem occurs—for example, if a child can't reach the ball that has rolled behind the slide, ask, "What can we do?" and let the child try to figure it out.
10. Play games like peek-a-boo, read stories about mommies and daddies being gone and coming back, read books with pictures hidden under flaps to encourage the development of object permanence.
11. Provide toys that respond contingently to a child's actions, such as balls, busy boxes, or push lights to encourage the understanding of cause and effect.
12. Provide toys and materials such as stacking cups, rings on a post, little houses, or tunnels to crawl through to encourage understanding of use of space.
13. Provide markers, paint, water, replicas of household tools, play telephones, keys, and so forth, to promote understanding of use of tools.
14. Provide language, ideas, and materials in ways that make the child's play just a little more elaborate and complex, scaffolding the child's play to become richer or more symbolic.
15. Provide toys and language to introduce awareness of shapes, comparative sizes, amounts, numbers, and one-to-one correspondence. Talk about concepts of time such as today, now, later, before, and after.

Programs that Enhance Cognitive Development and Learning

Just as each adult, infant, and toddler brings his or her own skills and styles to learning, early childhood education and development programs have different approaches to supporting learning. Following is a description and discussion of several approaches, chosen for their diversity and not in an attempt to provide a comprehensive picture of methods and approaches to learning. Specific curricula are described in Chapter 12.

Child Care: Rich Environments and Responsive Relationships

High-quality child care actively promotes children's learning. The results of the NICHD study on child care demonstrated that child care quality matters (NICHD, 2002a, b).

High-quality care for young children is eloquently described by Carlina Rinaldi (2001) about Reggio Emilia:

> Our image is of a child who is competent, active, and critical; therefore a child who may be seen as a challenge and, sometimes, as troublesome....To us, the child is a producer of culture, values, and rights, competent in learning and competent in communicating....We have to try to organize a school, an infant-toddler center for this child. (p. 51)

DEVELOPMENTAL TRENDS AND RESPONSIVE INTERACTIONS

COGNITIVE DEVELOPMENT AND LEARNING

Infants and toddlers learn about themselves, others, and the world through their own unique capacities and attributes, by utilizing the cognitive tools of learning and basic concepts.

Development	Example
0–4 months (infant)	
• Infants follow a moving object visually. • Infants cry to bring an adult to comfort or feed them. • Infants will look around the room with interest. • Infants begin to reach for a toy. • Infants notice that their arms or legs made something happen and will repeat the movement. • Infants recognize familiar people and objects. • Infants begin to bring objects to mouth.	Megan lifted her head, resting on her arms as she lay on the blanket. With a serious expression on her face, she watched the teachers and children around her. Willie kicked the mobile hanging over him and made it wiggle. He stopped, looked at it, and then kicked some more, watching the mobile to see if anything might happen.
4–8 months (infant)	
• Infants like to examine toys. • Infants like to make toys do something—make a sound, put one inside another. • Infants imitate adult expressions and gestures. • Infants turn toward a sound to see where it came from. • Infants look for toys they dropped.	Angela is interested in everything. She watches her friends and then looks at the teacher and smiles. Roger reaches out to touch a dangling toy. When it swings, making a sound, he reaches out to do it again.

Programs for Infants and Toddlers at Risk

Early Head Start (EHS), a federally funded program for infants and toddlers in poverty and at risk for poor development, has adopted many of the aspects of quality identified by ZERO TO THREE and PITC (Program for Infant-Toddler Care) in its Head Start Program Performance Standards (HSPPS) for infants and toddlers. The HSPPS require EHS programs to promote the development of trust and security by having a limited number of consistent teachers over a long period of time in out-of-home settings. EHS also allows center, family child care, and home-based programs to promote children's cognitive development and school readiness. EHS has a holistic approach including services for health, nutrition, parent education, and economic stability.

Early Intervention

Early intervention services are available to infants and toddlers with disabilities through Part C of the Individuals with Disabilities Education Act (IDEA). As a field, early intervention has developed rapidly in the past 30 years or so. Most interventions are family centered and organized around the needs and interests of the child. Many infant-toddler services are offered in community child care. There is more on this topic in Chapter 14.

Teacher- or Parent-Child Interaction	Environment
0–4 months (infant)	
• Slowly move a small toy from one side to another while the infant follows it with his gaze. • Respond quickly to the baby's cries. • Provide quiet time for infants to look at what is happening around them. Talk about what they see. • React to infants' expressions with clear, even exaggerated facial expressions and language.	• Arrange the space so that infants can see some activity but still be protected. • Provide a few interesting things to look at—small toys on the floor during tummy time, dangling toys when infants are on their backs. • Provide nonbreakable mirrors.
4–8 months (infant)	
• Hold the infant in your arms as you walk around, looking at things and talking about them. • Sit nearby and talk to the baby about the toys she is looking at. • Call the baby by name from a short distance to reassure her you are nearby.	• Provide a variety of small toys to handle and examine. • Provide toys that make sounds when an infant moves them, fit inside each other, or dangle and move when touched. • Offer board books.

DEVELOPMENTAL TRENDS AND RESPONSIVE INTERACTIONS (Continued)

Development	Example
8–12 months (mobile infant)	
• Mobile infants like to take the pieces of a toy apart and put them back together.	Charlie loves to take each plastic animal out of the bucket and look at it. When the bucket is empty, he tosses it aside.
• Mobile infants like toys that do something when you touch them, pull them, bang them.	Aliya likes the push button and the swinging doors on the busy box but can't work all the mechanisms yet. Her teacher expresses surprise with Aliya when the doors pop open and every once in a while shows her how to work another of the knobs.
• Mobile infants begin very simple pretend play, such as lifting a cup to their mouth.	
• Mobile infants like to find small toys hidden under a cloth or cup.	
• Mobile infants like to pick up and examine a tiny item like a Cheerio.	
• Mobile infants point to objects, knowing you can also see them.	
12–18 months (mobile infant)	
• Mobile infants like to use their mobility to explore—crawling, walking, climbing, running.	Alexis and Dan are gleeful about being on two feet. They follow each other around, one daringly balancing his way up the sloping surface with the other right behind. Sometimes they both try to squeeze into the area under the slide.
• Mobile infants enjoy playing with sand, water, and dough with different kinds of tools.	
• Mobile infants are interested in spatial relationships in puzzles and pegboards.	
• Mobile infants use tools such as keys or telephones in their pretend play.	
• Mobile infants enjoy looking at books and naming objects, animals, or body parts.	Meredith loves to cuddle on her teacher's lap, pointing at pictures in books while her teacher names the animals or asks her to find a certain animal.
18–24 months (toddler)	
• Young toddlers enjoy the ease of their movement and like to use their hands to carry things around.	Lynn and Matt build little towers of blocks and then drive play trucks into them and knock them down.
• Young toddlers understand they can cause things to happen.	Before breakfast, Chris puts out his hands for the little song of thanks. When a child arrives and joins the table late, he reaches out for everyone to sing again.
• Young toddlers understand and remember the details of routines.	
• Young toddlers use objects as substitutes for other objects in their pretend play.	Fran takes out the box of 1-inch blocks and makes one pile of red blocks, one pile of blue blocks.
• Young toddlers enjoy increasingly challenging materials that suggest activities such as building, sorting, matching shapes.	
24–36 months (toddler)	
• Older toddlers begin to understand concepts such as color, size, shape, time, size, and weight.	Eric is feeling a little sad and carries a picture of his mommy around with him, saying, "After nap."
• Older toddlers are interested in the story and pictures in storybooks.	
• Older toddlers create new stories in pretend play or new structures in block building, becoming more imaginative and creative.	Sara takes charge of the dramatic play corner, handing out dolls and stuffed animals. She puts on a hat and says, "Mommy going shopping."
• Assign roles to toys and other children in pretend play; use chairs, blankets, and bookcases as substitutes for items in pretend play.	

Teacher- or Parent-Child Interaction	Environment

8–12 months (mobile infant)

- Help the infant focus on what is interesting to him, using your presence, your interest, and your enthusiasm to support his attention and exploration.
- Use your emotional expressions and words to show the mobile infant that you delight in his discoveries.
- Use words to describe the child's activity: "Look, you found a Cheerio. You're picking it up with your fingers."

- Provide toys like stacking cups, rings on a post, pop-beads, and tubs full of small, interesting objects such as toy animals.
- Provide child-size replicas of dishes or household tools.
- Provide toys that respond to children's actions—busy boxes, water-filled pads.
- Provide sensory materials such as water and sand with a variety of tools.
- Provide board books with photographs.

12–18 months (mobile infant)

- Allow mobile infants protected time and space to explore.
- Stay nearby to express interest, provide words, and make the activity more elaborate and complex.
- Help mobile infants express their interest in each other gently.
- Express enthusiasm for the things that interest mobile infants.

- Provide simple puzzles, pegboards, shape forms, wooden beads with thick strings.
- Provide small climbers, tunnels, interesting pathways.
- Provide toys that respond to winding and turning on and off.
- Provide simple props for pretend play.

18–24 months (toddler)

- Maintain predictable routines, reminding children of the order with questions like, "It's time to eat. What do we do?"
- Keep materials in orderly and predictable places.
- Provide scaffolding as toddlers think about their activities, with questions such as "What will you do next?" or "What will you buy at the store?"

- Have toys and materials arranged so that toddlers can make choices, reach them, and put them away (with reminders).
- Frequently review the materials you have available to ensure that you are keeping a balance between what is familiar and what is a little challenging.

24–36 months (toddler)

- Ask children how they might solve problems that occur and let them figure out answers.
- Support children working together with materials to share ideas.
- Use language that describes time (now, later, before nap, after lunch), weight (heavy, light), size (bigger, smaller).
- Count things during the day.

- Provide play opportunities that promote comparison of sizes, weights, colors, shapes, and quantities.
- Have books available in all areas of the program. Have several copies of old favorites and bring in new books.
- Allow children to combine materials from different areas in creative ways.
- Present new materials or new combinations of materials.

Summary

Infants and toddlers are active learners. They explore, pursue information, organize information, and use it in increasingly sophisticated ways when they have adults in their lives who help them understand the world. Learning in infancy is a complex endeavor.

- Learning in infancy is grounded in the tasks of emotional development. Self-regulation allows the infant to be alert and attentive. A secure attachment relationship provides a sense of safety that allows a child to explore.
- Curiosity about new things seems to be an inherent quality in young infants—but the ability to persist in learning tasks through some frustration, requires a supportive adult partner and an engaging environment.
- Young infants use their senses with great competence, long before they have motor control or language to learn about the world.
- The content of learning varies by culture, as cognitive development is not so much an objective set of knowledge as a way of learning what you need to know in your own culture.
- The tools of learning used by infants and toddlers include memory, sorting, categorizing, matching, comparing and contrasting, problem solving, and symbolic play.

- Adults help infants and toddlers learn through mutual modeling and imitation, and through scaffolding—providing just enough support for the child to move to the next level of understanding, which Vygotsky called the zone of proximal development.
- Mobile infants and toddlers begin to develop a theory of mind, an understanding that other people may have thoughts, feelings, and experiences that are different from their own.
- Infants and toddlers make cognitive discoveries about how the world works, such as object permanence, cause and effect, use of tools, and use of space. They learn concepts about how their culture organizes and communicates information, such as language, literacy, and numbers.
- Programs take different approaches to supporting learning. Early child care and education is often based on a developmental model supporting relationships and discovery. Programs for children at risk often include more direct services to the families as well. Programs for infants and toddlers with disabilities may take a more structured approach to learning.

Key Terms

approaches to learning
attunement
decentered symbolic play
executive functioning

habituation
imitation
invisible information
mirroring

modeling
scaffolding
theory of mind

Reflections and Resources for the Reader

REFLECTIONS

1. Read the quotation from Rinaldi on page 184. What is your image of the child?
2. If infants and toddlers need to be able to have an effect on toys, what qualities would you look for in toys and which would you avoid?
3. If an infant had all the interesting toys in the world, do you think the infant would learn without an interested, engaged, and helpful adult?

OBSERVATION AND APPLICATION OPPORTUNITIES

1. Visit an infant-toddler program. How does the teacher set up an engaging, responsive learning environment that facilitates cognitive development? What would you change?
2. How does the teacher use herself to support the learning? Does she seem to understand and anticipate that the infant or toddler is making new discoveries in his play?
3. What kinds of experiences might encourage a toddler's learning of object permanence, cause and effect, use of tools, or use of space?

SUPPLEMENTARY ARTICLES AND BOOKS TO READ

Dombro, A. L., Jablon, J. R., & Stetson, C. (2011). Powerful interactions: How to connect with children to extend their learning. *Young Children, 66*(1), 12–20.

Economic and Social Research Council (ESRC). (2011). Joking, pretending with toddlers gives them head start in life skills. *ScienceDaily*. Retrieved from www.science-daily.com/releases/2011/10/111027112508.htm

INTERESTING LINKS

Google the words *infant cognition laboratories*. A number of university programs that study infant learning will be listed—and are worth visiting.

developingchild.Harvard.edu
Center on the Developing Child This site includes publications and videos describing how children learn.

www.nytimes.com/2012/05/01/science/insights-in-human-knowledge-from-the-minds-of-babes.html
Insights from the youngest minds. A *New York Times* article profiling Elizabeth Spelke and the theory of core knowledge.

zerotothree.org/
ZERO TO THREE The section "School Readiness: Birth to 3" provides information and video clips on thinking skills as well as other areas of development.

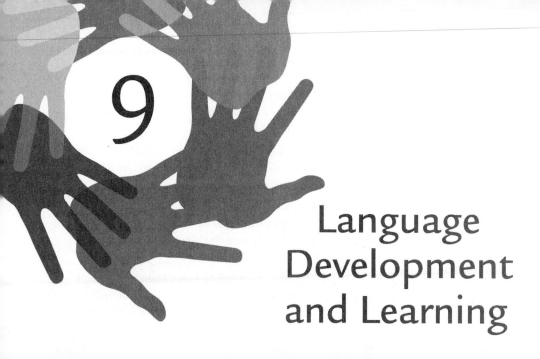

9

Language Development and Learning

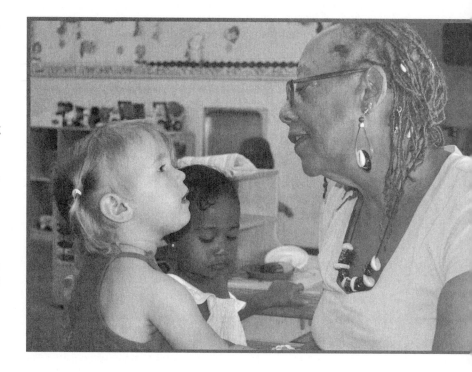

LEARNING OUTCOMES

After reading this chapter, you will be able to:

- Explain the influence of the unique characteristics of the child, including temperament and gender, on language development and learning in infancy
- Describe language development and learning through relationships, including the influence of culture, key research concerning children's acquisition of two or more languages, and strategies to promote language development
- Describe how special needs such as hearing impairment affect language development
- Describe characteristics of programs that enhance language development

Kareem danced around, half hopping and half jumping, as he chanted, "oo, me jump, me dance." His dad, who knew that Kareem was communicating his joy through sounds and words, chimed in too: "You're jumping, you're a jumper." Kareem danced and jumped higher and higher, around and around, saying, "Me jumping." This young boy and his wise father were engaged in a language dance, learning from each other as they took turns with the chant.

The Uniqueness of Each Child

In the opening vignette, when the father modeled the word *jumping*, the toddler immediately said, "Me jumping". Infants and toddlers engage in a remarkable process of learning to listen, talk, communicate their needs to others, make marks and scribbles on paper, and enjoy books—all aspects of language and literacy development. As relationship-based theory would predict, babies need adults as interactive partners as they make spectacular progress from producing soft *cooing* sounds (sustained production of single vowel sounds such as "ooo" and "aaa" that sound like a pigeon's coos) as newborns, to using single words by 1 year, and then progressing to fairly complex sentences by age 3.

Language is acquired through social interactions with others.

Language is used for communication with others and is affected by the quality of children's relationships, the social context, and the environment. Infants and toddlers desire human connection, and communication is a primary way for them to learn to socialize. The social experience is also how the child learns language—"it can be acquired only through social interaction with other human beings" (Tomasello, 1992; Vygotsky, 1978). It is through meaningful social interactions that babies, using their biological linguistic capacities, begin to understand that sounds form words, that words go together to form sentences, and that gestures and words communicate meaning.

As Bronfenbrenner (2004) would predict in his bioecological theory, the ecology or system of support for the infant or toddler contributes greatly to whether or not a child will learn language. Infants and toddlers are affected not only by their immediate social environment, but also by the systems of emotional and physical support available. For example, as discussed later in this chapter, the quality of the early childhood care and education program and the relationship between the family and program affect young children's language development. To study language development and relationships, however, it is important to know the definitions of common terms used.

Let's start with the basics. **Communication** is the giving of information through talk, signs, cues, gestures, or writing. An infant may communicate with eye gaze ("I'm interested in you"), arching the back ("Let me out of this situation"), sounds, or words. **Language,** as defined by Damasio and Damasio (1999), is "the ability to use words (or signs, if the language is one of the sign languages of the deaf) and to combine them in sentences so that concepts in our minds can be transmitted to other people. We also consider the converse: how we comprehend words spoken by others and turn them into concepts in our own mind" (p. 29). The word

communication

Giving information through talk, signs, cues, gestures, and writing.

language

The ability to use words or signs to communicate.

language can also be used to describe the particular way in which a group of people form words through sounds and convey messages to others.

Table 9.1 includes other typical terms used to describe various features of language development. Additional examples for these terms appear throughout the chapter.

TABLE 9.1   Language Terms and Definitions

Term	Definition	Example
Expressive language	Speaking or communicating to others through words, signs, or symbols	When Tonya speaks or writes, she is using expressive language. Matt used language well, both speaking and writing.
Morphemes	The smallest meaningful units of a word, whose combination creates a word (in sign languages, the equivalent of a morpheme is a visuomotor sign) (Damasio & Damasio, 1999)	"Run" is one morpheme and "running" is two morphemes. "Run" is a unit of meaning and the "ing" is a unit of meaning. The "ing" indicates that the action is happening now and changes the meaning of the word "run."
Phonemes	The individual sound units (such as "s," "n," "m") that when spoken in a particular order produce words	The word "run" is composed of the individual sound units of "r," "u," and "n."
Prosody	The vocal intonation that can modify the literal meaning of words and sentences (Damasio & Damasio, 1999); includes the tone, rhythm, tempo, and pace of language	A parent may use a higher tone and a slower rhythm when talking with her baby.
Pragmatics	The social features of language including how, where, and when language is used	These skills include taking turns in a conversation, following the cultural rules of conversation such as where it is appropriate to talk, and listening when someone is speaking. Pragmatics also includes the function of language, e.g. questioning, demanding, etc.
Receptive language	The act of attending, listening to, and comprehending language	Charlie listened carefully to his mother and then went and picked up his shoes that she asked him to find.
Semantics	The meanings that correspond to all words, parts of sentences, and all possible sentences	Alana's teacher responded to the semantics of her language rather than to the incorrect syntax.
Syntax	The rules governing the sequence of words and the relationships among parts of a sentence	In English we can say "How are you?" but it is not allowable (if a person wants to be understood) to say "Are how you?"
Lexicon	The collection of all words in a given language; may also refer to a specific person's lexicon of words that the person can understand and/or use	Tamara's personal lexicon included many words for animals.

Overview of Language Capacities

"Daddy, come here," a young child yells to her daddy, who has wandered from the grocery cart where the 2-year-old sits, "You getting losted." As children learn to speak, they create wonderfully unique and innovative words and sentences based on their understanding of the principles of language. One could ask many questions about young children's ability to learn to communicate. How do most children learn the complex rules of language and communication? Why and how do they construct words and sentences that they've never heard rather than just imitating? Why do most infants and toddlers progress in a fairly orderly fashion to learn language by making sounds, then words, then sentences, and then sequences of sentences to tell stories? How do most children learn so much in such a short time period?

The answer to these questions is that they are using their biological linguistic capacities in interaction with others to develop their language skills, as noted by Mei-Yu Lu (2000): "During the early years of language learning, children also create, test, and revise hypotheses regarding the use of language" (p. 3). Indeed, infants and toddlers are born with an amazing capacity to learn language to communicate with others: "They learn grammar and how to apply language across various contexts, audiences, and purposes" (Lu, 1998, p. 1).

The Capacity to Be Communicators

Infants are born with the capacity to be communicators. The Developmental Trends and Responsive Interactions chart at the end of this chapter lists capacities that infants and toddlers have. Refer to this chart often as you read the chapter. From birth, they can hear the differences in speech sounds, such as "m" and "n"; are motivated to listen to the sounds of language; strive to communicate through body movements and vocalizations; and thrive when listened to by caring adults. Throughout the first 3 years, infants and toddlers learn to make the sounds of the language spoken to them; combine sounds into words and then combine words into sentences; learn the syntax, pragmatics, and prosody of language; learn the meaning of an astonishing number of words; and communicate in a variety of ways—the furrowing of a brow, a loud screech, whining, pointing, talking, and shouting.

The language learning process in the first 3 years is remarkable. When infants and toddlers are learning to speak English, they learn to add morphemes such as "s" or "es" to words to make them plural and "ed" to words to indicate past tense. They create sentences that they have not ever heard before and learn to use words and sentences for different purposes—to request food, to demand attention, to inform, to express sadness or joy, and to tell an adult "no." Development is generally similar across children, and yet each child finds a unique way of attempting to learn the complex language or languages being used around and with them.

Interaction Between Brain Development and Language

Infants' brains are designed to learn a language. The capacity to learn a language or languages is a part of a child's biological makeup. As discussed in Chapter 5, when an adult names objects ("That's your cup"), describes what the adult is doing ("I'm changing your diaper"), sings songs, teaches a baby how to say "bye-bye," or talks about what the baby is doing ("You're playing"), the axon on a neuron in the brain sends an electrical signal and connects that neuron's dendrite

Observe in this video how the infant plays with language and demonstrates the joy of communication.

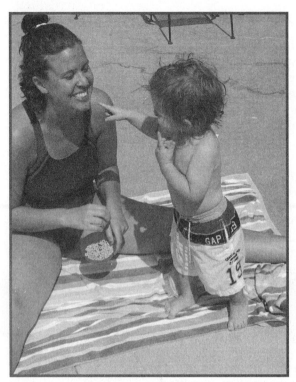

Early language experiences are essential for the development of young children's ability to play with words and ideas through gestures, verbal language, or sign language.

with another neuron's dendrite, creating another synapse. Synapses connect the neurons to enhance the child's ability to use language with ease for a variety of purposes, including thinking with language. However, infants and toddlers need responsive adults to learn a language well.

Researchers describe a synergy between early brain development and language experience that actually affects the capacity of a person to learn languages throughout life. When pleasant language experiences are repeated—a song is sung over and over, a book is read many times to a delighted 8-month-old, or a word is used in a variety of ways (e.g., "a *cup*, where's the *cup*, you've got a *cup*")—the connections or paths between neurons are made stronger and shape how easily the infant or toddler will continue to learn language. In the first year of life, as infants hear adults talking with them, a cluster of neurons begins to fire when a particular phoneme is heard. By 12 months, an auditory map has been created because of responsive language experiences with adults, with infants' brains already programmed to be able to distinguish the particular sounds in the language being spoken with them (Damasio & Damasio, 1999).

Early experiences with language are essential for the young child's development of these unique characteristics of human beings—the ability to share information, categorize knowledge, and play with words and ideas through verbal language. A baby needs to hear adults talking *with* her and have an opportunity to *respond* in order for the neurons and synapses in the brain that are related to language to develop. A toddler says "ttttt" while playing with a truck, the adult says "Yes, that's a truck," and the toddler responds "tuk." Placing an infant or toddler in front of a TV to hear a language doesn't work for language development because the child is not receiving the necessary auditory and visual feedback required to learn a language.

Attributes

Just as adult interaction and responsiveness affect the quality of language development, so does the gender of the child. Do girls gesture and talk earlier than boys? Do girls have larger vocabularies than boys do as infants and toddlers? One research study found that girls from 14 to 34 months were generally 3 months ahead of boys in their use of communication attempts that involved both gesture and speech, for example, saying "eat" and pointing at a cookie to indicate what they want to eat. Many researchers conclude that infant and toddler girls talk earlier and speak more than boys (Holdgrafer, 1991; Huttenlocher, Haight, Bryk, Seltzer, & Lyons, 1991; Van Hulle, Goldsmith, & Lemery, 2004). Research on the vocabulary development of 20-month-old children in three countries (Argentina, Italy, and the United States) found that among 252 children, girls had consistently larger vocabularies than boys (Bornstein & Cote, 2005). For both vocabulary and frequency of two-word combinations among toddlers, parents reported that language assessment scores across 10 countries were higher for girls than for boys (Eriksson et al., 2012). However, in Sweden, an egalitarian society, researchers who gathered parental language reports on 336 children ages 16 to 28 months did not find any significant gender differences in vocabulary, pragmatic skills, grammar skills, and the maximum length of utterance (Berglund & Eriksson, 2000).

Boys need parents and teachers to encourage language development. Karrass, Braungart-Rieker, Mullings, and Burke Lefeber (2002) found that boys at ages 4, 8, and 12 months needed higher levels of maternal verbal, visual, and physical encouragement of attention than girls in order to learn language. Another study by Vallotton and Ayoub (2011) found that language has a larger impact on boys' self-regulation than it does for girls. It seems important for adults to pay particular attention to whether boys are using gestures and speech and building a strong vocabulary, so that the adults can further support boys' language development.

Researchers suggest a variety of reasons for why girls talk earlier than boys. There may be biological differences, and these early differences then expand language opportunities for girls. Environment also plays an important part, however, in influencing differences in the rate of language development. Several researchers found that the social context including quality and quantity of adult talk with infants and toddlers affects young children's language development much more than characteristics such as gender (Hart & Risley, 1999; Hoff, 2006; Van Hulle et al., 2004).

You will want to focus on providing equal opportunities for boys and girls to engage in language interactions with responsive adults. Now let's examine some other differences that might occur in how young children develop and use language.

Development and Learning Through Relationships

In order to fully understand the language development of young children, we must view it through a family and cultural lens in a social context.

Culture and Language

Language is a major medium for transmitting culture across generations. Through language socialization, adults convey to children, from infancy onward, culturally valued beliefs, behaviors, and processes. (Katz & Snow)

Embedded within a language is a culture, and embedded within a culture is a language that communicates that culture's values, beliefs, style, and purpose for speaking. "**Communicative-linguistic parameters** such as the language used in the home, the communication patterns, and the values underlying those patterns affect every aspect of how we learn about ourselves and the world around us" (Barrera & Kramer, 1997). Language is a powerful medium, then, for infants and toddlers to learn about their own value within their culture and what is of value to learn. Children learn to understand their own culture through the language that is used by and that describes that culture.

communicative-linguistic parameters
Cultural factors that influence how children and adults use language and communicate with others.

In all cultures, language is one of the most powerful symbolic systems through which children learn to understand and interpret human behavior. (Harwood, Miller, & Irizarry)

Differences in When and How Language Is Used

When we observe children's language development through a cultural lens we can see that culture is revealed in the content of talk and in how language is used in social contexts. See Figure 9.1 for a list of the aspects of language that may differ based on family and cultural values.

Ritual and System Constraints

Ritual and system constraints are another reason why there may be differences in how young children use language and may be represented in how young children communicate to their teacher that they are hungry. The following scenario describes how Jamie, Cara, Mary, Tamika, and Carmen communicate their hunger differently to their teacher:

Jamie looks directly at her infant and toddler teacher as she demands "Eat," to tell her teacher very clearly that she is hungry and expects to be fed. Cara looks at the teacher with a longing look to tell her she is hungry. Mary moves in closely to the teacher, takes the teacher's face gently in her hands, and asks for milk by saying "milk" in a quiet voice, waiting up to 30 seconds for her favorite teacher to respond. Tamika waits until the teacher approaches her and asks her if she is hungry. Carmen starts to wail when she gets a hungry feeling in her tummy.

As we can see by the foregoing examples, language use among children and families may differ because of system constraints and ritual constraints (Goffman, 1976). "**System constraints** in conversation are such universal systems as the opening, the closing, the turn taking, and the rerun related to handling conversations in different languages and culture" (Pham, 1994, p. 5). In the previous example, Mary opens a "conversation" with her infant and toddler teacher by moving close to her and holding the teacher's face in her hands. She waits quietly for the teacher to respond before she takes her turn in the conversation.

system constraints

The opening, closing, turn taking, and rerun related to handling conversations in different languages and cultures.

FIGURE 9.1   Features of language that may differ based on family and cultural values

- When talk is appropriate.
- Who a child can speak to, and what are the appropriate ways of addressing people of different status or age.
- What is the acceptable volume or tone of voice for speech and when talk should be brief, discreet, or dispassionate.
- When the use of language can be unguarded or emotional, and how this varies by situation.
- Where you can talk and where is it important to be quiet.
- How much time you wait for someone to talk after you have stopped talking.
- How much eye contact you should give when you are talking to someone and the person is talking to you.
- How much personal space you allow between yourself and the listener when you are talking.
- What constitutes a "good" story and who can tell it.

Jamie, on the other hand, opens the conversation about her rumbling tummy by approaching the teacher and telling her, in no uncertain terms, that she wants to eat. "**Ritual constraints** are the conversationalist's strategies to regulate communication and protect feelings" (Pham, 1994, p. 5). Tamika may be regulating her communication and feelings by waiting until the teacher approaches her. Carmen uses a different style and openly, loudly, and with a great deal of feeling expresses her hunger to her understanding teacher. We can view ritual and system constraints as windows into different cultural and individual language styles rather than as limitations.

ritual constraints
The conversationalist's strategies to regulate communication and protect feelings.

Children as Conversational Partners in Different Cultures

Cultural differences exist in how children are viewed as conversational partners. The authors of *From Neurons to Neighborhoods* (Shonkoff & Phillips, 2000) summarize research by noting that "in some cultures, children are commonly spoken to directly as *participants* in conversation; in other cultures, children primarily *overhear* talk that is directed toward others" (p. 128, emphasis in original). When adults follow children's leads and adopt the topics and activities of interest to the child, they reflect the "Western [countries including the United States and Western Europe] notion that children—even from infancy—can be treated as conversational partners" (Pan, Imbens-Bailey, Winner, & Snow, 1996, p. 262). The preponderance of child-centered talk in many interactions reflects a Western model for interacting with children that has been referred to as **infant-directed speech**. In other words, many adults in Western cultures *adapt* their talk with children to a developmental level that is slightly above the child's level of talk, involving the very young child in conversations such as that in Box 9.1. In these interactions, the adult treats the child as a person who is capable of taking a conversational turn, learning how to wait for the other person to take a turn, taking her turn, and then waiting again for the other person to speak.

infant-directed speech
An adult (or older child) directing speech at infants or toddlers that is on or slightly above the young child's level of language use.

In some cultures, however, infants and toddlers learn language mostly by listening, or there is more of an emphasis on nonverbal communication. However, recent research (Shneidman & Goldin-Meadow, 2012) indicates that in the cultures where children *seem* to learn only from observing, rather than from speech specifically directed toward them, there may be certain ages at which children are spoken to more directly. In the Mayan culture, for example, researchers found that whereas infants do not hear much child-directed speech, children between the ages of 13 and 35 months do hear more adult speech directed toward them. These adults may believe that the child is learning language by being a conversational partner in a social situation, but at an older age than in Western societies.

As you work with children and families, it will be important for you to observe the particular patterns of communication of children and families, so that you can appreciate how, why, when, and where a child communicates to peers and adults.

Language Content and Culture

The content of adults' language with children may also differ by families and cultures. For example, families can differ in how they talk about past events with their children. One parent or family may engage a child in lengthy conversations: describing,

BOX 9.1

An Example of Infant-Directed Speech

Infant: Mommy.
Parent: I'm right here. Your mommy's right here.
Infant: Mommy.
Parent: Yes, I'm Mommy. Where's Daddy?
Infant: Aaaahhh.
Parent: Yes—he's over there.

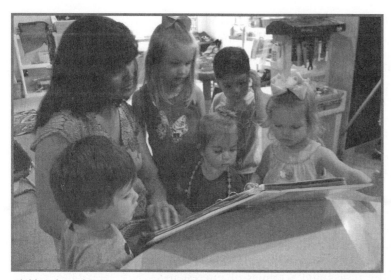

Children learn how to communicate by listening to stories, by listening to adults talk, and by interacting as conversational partners with adults and peers.

elaborating, reminiscing, and extending information about the past event. Other parents do not elaborate, but rather tell the more practical aspects of the past experience, prompting their child to remember, and asking many questions (Reese & Fivush, 1993). Reese and Fivush surmise that both of these styles may have their cultural value and purpose and prepare a child for styles of language use that prevail in their particular culture.

Bilingual and Bidialectical Children and Families

> *Bilingual language acquisition is the norm in many parts of the world and has fueled a prevailing belief that young children can effortlessly acquire two or more languages. (Petitto et al.)*

In addition to learning different styles of language, children may also be learning two or more languages—which prompts the question: Are infants and toddlers able to effortlessly learn two languages at the same time? Most infants and toddlers do have the brain capacity not only to hear the differences in the sounds and sequence of different languages, but also to learn the vocabulary of both languages and to speak two languages simultaneously. In fact, certain parts of the brain are dedicated to detect the different patterns in the languages that they hear; this allows the infant or toddler to learn multiple languages at the same time (Petitto et al., 2001). In an article, "The Roots of Bilingualism in Newborns," researchers Byers-Heinlein, Burns, and Werker (2010) asked if newborns were biologically prepared to learn two languages simultaneously. They are!!! Those newborns who heard their mothers speak one language (e.g., English) while they were still in the womb preferred to hear that language over another language (e.g., Tagalog—a language spoken in the Philippines). However, newborns whose mothers spoke both English and Tagalog while pregnant showed equal preference for the two languages they heard prenatally. This demonstrates the remarkable ability of humans to learn languages.

Yet, both parents and professionals are asking many important questions about the benefit or challenges inherent in children learning more than one language during their infant and toddler years. Addressing these questions is essential because the population of the United States is quickly becoming more culturally and ethnically diverse, and many families have the opportunity to raise their children to be bilingual. Does it harm or benefit infants and toddlers to learn more than one language during the infancy period?

● ● ● CULTURE CLOSE UP

A director of a program was surprised to hear that children who are learning two languages have a cognitive advantage over other children and that learning two languages is not harmful to their language development. He had been telling families that they should speak only one language, English, to their children so as to not confuse them; however, that was difficult for immigrant families that could not speak English well. He was concerned that he had actually caused harm to families because of his advice. He wanted to know all of the latest research and struggled with how to help the teachers and families in his program understand his profound change in how to think about bilingualism. He now wanted them to know all of the benefits of bilingualism and how to support children's learning of two or more languages starting at birth. Yet, he didn't want families who speak only one language to their children to begin to pressure young children to learn two languages. How would you present the research you are about to read to families and teachers?

Before delving into questions and concerns about young children learning two or more languages simultaneously, a few definitions are needed:

- *Simultaneous bilinguals* are children who acquire a second language before 3 years of age (Katz & Snow, 2000, p. 51).
- *Bilingual* children may be learning a verbal and sign language or two verbal languages.
- *Monolingual* children speak one language only.
- *Trilingual* children are learning three languages.
- *Bidialectical* children are learning two or more dialects. (A *dialect* is a particular version of a language, and although children who are bidialectical are learning basically the same language, such as English, they are learning two forms of that language.)

A Second Language: Harm or Benefit?

Parents and teachers have a number of questions and concerns about infants and toddlers learning two languages:

- Can infants and toddlers learn two languages simultaneously?
- Do children use words in both languages for the same object?
- Are language milestones achieved at the same time in each language?
- What about pragmatic skills?
- Do children learning two languages simultaneously have smaller vocabularies in each language?
- Are there cognitive, social, and emotional advantages for children who learn two or more languages early in their lives?

Let's examine these issues.

One concern that adults have is related to the timing of language achievement: Are language milestones achieved at the same time in each language when young children are simultaneously learning two languages? Are milestones reached at the same time in bilingual children as for monolingual children? Petitto and his colleagues (2001) conducted a unique study with exciting findings. They regularly videotaped, over a year, three children learning both **sign language** and French, and three other children learning both French and English. The researchers asked questions about whether children learning two languages would reach milestones such as first words at the same time in each language, and whether they would reach milestones, such as combining words, at the same age as monolingual children: "The results revealed that both groups achieved their early linguistic milestones in each of their languages at the same time (and similarly to monolinguals)" (p. 453).

Another question is whether, when children are learning two languages, they use words in both languages to label the same object. In the study of the three children learning sign language and French and the three children learning French and English, the researchers concluded that beginning when the children learned words or signs, they would use the appropriate word from each language (or the word from one language and the sign from the second language) when they were using that language (Petitto et al., 2001). This means that very young children used, for example, a word in each language for "ball"—rather than choosing just one word from one language and using that word exclusively. It seems that the infants and toddlers were truly learning the two languages "simultaneously."

Another question concerns pragmatic skills: Can infants and toddlers really learn to differentiate between their two languages and speak the appropriate language to the correct person, considering the language that the listener speaks and

sign language

A structured language using specific hand and arm movements to communicate with others.

understands? If infants and toddlers could use one language with one parent and another language with the other parent, then this would demonstrate that the children have learned the sociolinguistic rules concerning when and where to use each language (Nicoladis & Genesee, 1996). Amazingly, researchers (Genesee, Nicoladis, & Paradis, 1996) discovered that only 4% to 7% of the phrases and sentences that bilingual 2-year-olds used were mixed. Mixed utterances were ones that used words from two languages in the same sentence or phrase—for example, a child might say "doggy dodo," which is a mix of French and English words and means "doggy sleeping." Overall, the young children used English with the English-speaking parent and French with the French-speaking parent by 2 years of age. Another study discovered that children learning both French and English began to keep their two languages separate and speak the correct language with the correct person between the ages of 1 and 2 1/2 (Nicoladis & Genesee, 1996).

When young children do mix words from two languages that they are using, they may be modeling the adults in their environment. Many adults who know two or more languages may mix words in a sentence. Or, given that the primary purpose of learning language is to communicate with others, children may use all of their language knowledge to get their message across. This is an important concept and has implications for parent-child and teacher-child interactions. If parents and teachers want young children to learn to communicate, then they must respond much more to young children's desire to communicate and their message than to the exact use of certain words. Also, adults should not become upset when a very young child mixes the words from two languages. Children will learn each language as a distinct language if adults *model* each language separately. If children do continue to mix words from two languages, then it is probably because the children, just like many adults, mix two languages in order to communicate better with others.

Also, children may mix languages because they don't know the word in the second language, so they use a word that they do know (Nicoladis & Genesee, 1996), even if the person listening speaks a different language. Young children mix languages with people who they know can understand both languages and who won't get upset with them for mixing the two languages (DeHouwer, 1999). Again, the social context influences how a child uses the language skills that they know.

Finally, we address the issue of vocabulary. Specifically, parents and professionals are concerned about whether children who are learning two languages will have smaller vocabularies in each language than children learning only one language. One study showed that infants and toddlers learning two languages simultaneously do have smaller vocabularies in either language than monolinguals, but they have larger total vocabularies than monolingual age-mates (Pearson, Fernandez, & Oller, 1993). But, in research completed several years later, these same researchers (Pearson, Fernandez, Lewedeg, and Oller, 1997) concluded that because there is such a wide range of development for monolinguals, the vocabulary of the children who were learning two languages did not differ significantly from the vocabulary of monolinguals.

Does the amount of language input from adults in a particular language contribute to differences in children's vocabulary learning? Does it matter how much we, as adults, talk with infants or toddlers? Researchers have found that it matters significantly. After studying 25 simultaneous bilingual children from 8 to 30 months of age, researchers discovered that children who were talked with more learned more vocabulary from 12 to 24 months: "We have been able to show that the number of words learned in each language is, to a large extent, proportional to the amount of time spent with speakers of the language" (Pearson et al., 1997, p. 51). More recently, Garcia-Sierra et al. 2011 confirmed that early exposure makes a difference. Toddlers about 15 months old who were learning both English and Spanish spoke more English words if they were exposed to more English than Spanish from parents, relatives, and friends. However, these toddlers had a higher vocabulary in Spanish if they heard more Spanish at home than English.

There were exceptions. Some young children, it seems, may be better at learning, so they may need less language input from adults. Most children's language use, however, is related to how much adults talk with them and the quality of the relationship that the child has with the adult.

Infants may not learn a second language with just anyone. If the infant has a positive, loving relationship with an adult, then the child will be more likely to learn the language that the favorite adult speaks with the child. Also, infants and toddlers will learn more of a particular language if the adult uses active and responsive language teaching strategies: "The relative child-centeredness of the adult speakers of each language and the strategies adults employ to guide children's language choices are crucial for getting children to accept input in both languages" (Pearson et al., 1997, pp. 53–54).

The last question is, Are there cognitive, social, and emotional advantages for children who learn two or more languages early in their lives? The answer is that learning two languages is quite beneficial for infants' and toddlers' neural development and language processing; perceptual sensitivity (allows children to learn other languages more easily); and executive functioning, including ability to attend when there are distractions.

Let's take a closer look at the benefits to infants' and toddlers' (as well as adults') language processing of learning two languages. By 6 to 12 months, a baby's brain begins to focus on the languages she hears frequently. If a baby is exposed to one language (monolingual) during the first 6 months, then that baby will begin to lose the ability to hear differences in sounds in other languages; however, the baby's native language speech perception skills improve (Kuhl, Tsao, & Liu, 2003; Kuhl et al., 2008). There seems to be a "perceptual narrowing" (Pons, Lewkowicz, Soto-faraco, & Sebastián-Gallés, 2009) that occurs that interferes with infants hearing the subtle differences between sounds not spoken in the child's primary language. The infant's brain seems to make a neural committment (Kuhl et al., 2006) to learning the one language in monolingual families.

However, brains of infants exposed to two language spoken directly to them remain open to hearing the differences in sounds in other languages. The brain actually stays flexible to learning more languages. This language processing flexibility has been called the "perceptual wedge hypothesis" (Petitto et al., 2012).

Learning two languages seems also to improve perception. Weikum et al. (2007) found that bilingual infants who are 4 to 6 months old are able to watch silent videos of talking faces speaking English and French and even though the babies weren't exposed to English and French, they could distinguish when the speaker changed languages just by watching the speaker's mouth. Researchers could tell that the babies could distinguish the two languages because they looked longer at a speaker for a while when there was a change in languages.

Executive functioning also improves with bilingual children. Diane Poulin-Dubois, Agnes Blaye, Julie Coutya, and Ellen Bialystok (2010) found effects of bilingualism on 24-month-olds' ability to perform tasks without being distracted. Engel de Abreu (2012) discovered that bilingualism improves attention among low-income minority children as well.

So, what are some strategies that adults can use to support infants and toddlers while they learn two languages?

Strategies for Adults with Infants and Toddlers Learning a Second Language

From an infant's or toddler's perspective, it may be easier to learn two languages if one adult, such as the father, primarily speaks one language with the child and a second adult, such as the care teacher, speaks a second language with the child. This allows the child to consistently hear the differences in the sounds and words of the two languages. Although children may first confuse sounds and words in the two languages, they soon begin to keep the specific sounds, words, and sentence structure of each language separate and use the appropriate language with the right person who speaks that language with them. DeHouwer (1999) recommends that parents of children learning two or more languages can support their children's language development if they use the strategies identified in Figure 9.2.

Honoring the Home Language

Many educators believe that infants and toddlers who attend infant and toddler programs need at least one care teacher who speaks the child's native language in order to provide the child and family someone with whom they can communicate well. (Garcia, 1992; Sánchez & Thorp, 1998a, 1998b, 1998c). With so many languages spoken in the United States, however, administrators of programs may find it difficult to find teachers to speak the languages of the babies in their programs. But even if you don't know a child's home language, you can learn words and songs in that language to use frequently—especially words of endearment that help the infant or toddler feel safe and loved. Both the children and the families

FIGURE 9.2   Strategies for supporting children who are learning two languages

- Make sure that children hear both languages frequently and in a variety of circumstances.
- Create opportunities for your children to use the languages that they hear.
- Read books to and with your children in each of the languages that are important to their lives.
- Talk to all your children in the same way. For instance, don't use one language with the oldest child and another language with the younger. Language is tied to emotions, and if you address your children in different languages, some of your children may feel excluded, which in turn might adversely affect their behavior.
- Avoid abrupt changes in how you talk to your children, especially if they are under 6. For example, don't suddenly decide to speak French to them if you have only been using English.
- Be aware of doctors and teachers who tell you to stop speaking a particular language to your children.
- If you feel strongly about your children using one particular language with you, encourage them to use it in all of their communication with you.
- However, do not punish or criticize your children for using or not using a particular language. Instead, encourage them or offer them the appropriate words in the language you want them to speak.
- If a child is not learning either language well, ask a doctor for a hearing test in order to rule out medical problems.

Source: Based on DeHouwer (1999).

will benefit if you make an attempt to honor the child's home language. Whether the teacher is bilingual or speaks only English, for example, the parent should be encouraged to continue speaking the home language to the infant or toddler. Infants and toddlers deserve "linguistic continuity" (Sánchez & Thorp, 1998a, 1998b, 1998c). Programs that try to impose "English-only" rules on families may be doing great harm: "In fact, the abrupt end of the use of the home language by a child's parents may lead to great emotional and psychological difficulties both for the parents and for the child. After all, language is strongly linked to emotion, affect, and identity" (DeHouwer, 1999, p. 2). Also, if the parent doesn't have a great command of a language other than the home language, the language models as well as the emotional interactions may be limited for the child. Another language that is gaining in importance as a form of communication for all young children is sign language (Acredolo & Goodwyn, 2002).

Using Sign Language

Just as with a second verbal language, young children are capable of learning a sign symbol system to communicate. Infants can sign before they can speak because the fine motor development in their hands matures before the body parts needed to speak words, giving them a way to communicate prior to using words.

> *Dawson, at 1 year of age, could sign "more" and "down" because his parents modeled the sign "more" when he wanted more juice and the sign "down" when he wanted down from his high chair. Now Dawson, an 18-month-old, signs "more" and says the word as well. Learning sign language when he was younger helped him communicate with his parents and did not interfere with learning verbal language and won't as long as his parents use words with him as well as sign language.*

Parents and teachers are discovering that when 11-month-olds sign words like "more" and "drink," the adults can use this powerful tool to help them be responsive to the infants' needs. A baby who learns signs may be less frustrated, as he can communicate his needs (Grabmeier, 1999). Signing with an infant does not interfere with later verbal development; rather, it *contributes* to a child's language development (Goodwyn, Acredolo, & Brown, 2000; Grabmeier, 1999), and young children's first words are likely to be the ones they've learned to sign first (Grabmeier, 1999).

Summary of Bilingual Learning

The following statement provides an excellent summary to this section concerning children learning two languages:

> (1) A bilingual environment is most often a necessity, not a choice; (2) hearing two or more languages in childhood is not a cause of language disorder or language delay; (3) children's use of two languages within one sentence is not a sign of confusion; and (4) children do not just "pick up" a language; they need a strongly supportive and rich environment. (DeHouwer, 1999, p. 4)

In the next section, we consider the stages of language development and describe, in more detail, the strategies that adults can use to provide a strongly supportive and rich language environment.

Language Development in Relationships

What a remarkable journey we take with infants and toddlers who so seriously and competently listen to sounds, words, and sentences, figuring out the complex rules of language (Kuhl, 2007). Think about how you learned your first

In this video, a toddler who just turned 2 communicates with his grandfather. How many words is the child putting together in his utterances? Watch his eyes—he is telling a little joke—as he names the "juice" as "milk." How does his positive relationship with his grandfather influence the toddler's language development? How is the grandfather expanding and elaborating Kai's utterances?

language. You probably can't remember, because it happened so early in your life, and it now seems that the process was effortless. In reality, infants and toddlers are using a number of strategies to become a conversational partner with others, such as recognizing the voices of the special people in their lives, learning to predict when one word ends and another begins, or using words in the correct order to convey meaning. As we still do as adults, infants and toddlers learn to use nonverbal gestures and facial expressions to communicate their thoughts and feelings. Let's travel with infants and toddlers as they move through their language-learning journey.

Prior to Birth

Infants are practicing listening to sounds while still snug inside their mothers' wombs. More than 30 years ago, some ingenious researchers (DeCasper & Fifer, 1980) found that newborns can distinguish between their mother's voice and another female's voice, almost immediately after birth. The infants, at 3 days old, were asked to do something they could already do very well: to suck on a pacifier-like nipple. The nipple was connected through wires to a tape recorder. If a baby sucked on the nipple at a fast rate, for example, she could hear her mother's voice; if the baby sucked the nipple at a slower rate, she would hear a stranger's voice. The babies quickly learned which rate of sucking would produce their mother's voice and consistently produced the rate of sucking to generate that sound. How did the infants know how to do this incredible feat? Did they immediately learn their mother's voice after birth or were they eavesdropping prior to birth? To answer this question, researchers DeCasper and Spence (1986) tried a different variation on the first research study. They asked pregnant women to read a particular children's story (such as Dr. Seuss's *Cat in the Hat*) aloud each day for the final 6 weeks of pregnancy. After the infants were born, the researchers played recordings of the mother reading this same story or a previously unheard story. The newborns again used sucking patterns to demonstrate that they clearly preferred the sound of the story they heard in utero. Infants seem to be paying attention and discriminating between complex patterns of sounds even before birth.

Birth to 2 Months

"Infants are 'citizens of the world' at birth and early in life they can hear the differences between all the consonants and vowels used in any language" (de Boer & Kuhl, 2003). They can hear the differences in the sounds in words and are ready to begin to learn any language in the world (McDevitt & Ormrod, 2002). By 1 month of age, and probably earlier, infants prefer to hear talk that is directed toward them (higher pitch, sounds more articulated, simplified, repetitions in sounds and words) rather than adult-directed talk (Cooper & Aslin, 1990; Soderstrom, 2007).

Babies communicate in a variety of ways, one of which is to cry when they are in pain, hungry, or distressed. They yawn, scrunch up their face, turn away, look peaceful and calm, and communicate in myriad ways to the adult who pays attention to all of the verbal and nonverbal signals of the infant. Important caregivers in infants' lives begin to interpret the burps, quieting, and looking as forms of communication (see Box 9.2). By 2 months of age, infants begin to have different cries for hunger and pain, and an astute parent can hear these differences and respond accordingly, meeting the infants' needs and helping them begin to communicate successfully in different ways.

2 to 4 Months

From 2 to 4 months of age, infants engage in a *language dance* with their parents and other important adults in their lives. Josh, 3 months old, looks into his language partner's eyes. As he makes soft cooing sounds, his language partner patiently waits and then coos or sings or speaks softly to Josh. The partners, adult and infant, share the magic moment when a language connection is made and they are emotionally connected.

BOX 9.2

Babies' Nonverbal Communication

Mom to baby: "Oh, you're feeling tired. I can tell by those yawns. Oops, your tummy is growling. Are you telling me you're hungry?"

When adults treat infants' nonverbal behavior as forms of communication, babies begin to understand what it is like to be an interactive partner in a conversation.

Expressive language continues to progress. Babbling (repetition of consonant-vowel sounds, such as "ma" or "da") may begin toward the end of this age period and is enhanced when the infant's language dance partner imitates the infant's sounds. Infants are providing consistently different signals to express to their caregivers that they are hungry, distressed, or feeling pleasure.

4 to 8 Months

Seven-month-olds can remember Mozart music passages and can still recall these passages after 2 weeks of not hearing them (Saffran, Loman, & Robertson, 2000). Remarkably, they prefer to listen to passages that they've heard before and that are played in the same sequence. (What a wonderful

OBSERVATION INVITATION **9.1**

Language Development
Child's name: *Damika*
Parent's or professional's name: Sharon Nauen

What am I doing? What am I feeling?	What am I learning?
(2 months old) She said "ah" as she looked into my eyes.	I can make sounds and get a response.
(4 months old) I am making many sounds when I wake up in my crib. I'm feeling content.	To practice sounds and enjoy them.
(6 months old) I have started to babble "da" when I'm on my back on the floor. I'm happy.	I'm learning to put several sounds together to babble.
(8 months old) I babble to my mom and she babbles back.	I'm learning how to communicate to my mom.

What developmental milestone would you expect to happen next during the 8- to 12-month age period? Read the next section to find out.

way for the infants to demonstrate their long-term memory as well as their receptive skills!) Infants, during this age period, also begin to turn their heads toward a noise or someone speaking their name—again demonstrating their recognition of the sound of their own name. They also communicate in a variety of ways without using words.

Expressively, infants begin to demonstrate through their movements and facial expressions that they anticipate that their sounds and nonverbal communication (such as reaching up with their arms to be picked up) will get a reaction from an adult. They vocalize to get adults' valued attention. They are learning the social function of language before they learn words (Lu, 1998). As Katz and Snow (2000) note, "Children engage in conversation with adults and with each other before they have acquired their first conventional word" (p. 5).

In addition to communicating nonverbally, they also begin to babble. They are babbling monosyllables ("ba" "da") and toward the end of this age group are using reduplicative babbling ("bababa" "dadada"), repeating the consonant-vowel combinations. These first repeated babbling sounds are often interpreted by parents as infants calling them by name. The sounds for mother and father, in many cultures, are babbling sounds that the infant first makes, such as "pa-pa," "ma-ma," and "da-da." At 6 months, babies are biologically ready to speak any language that they hear frequently, as they can distinguish and make all sounds used in all languages (de Boer, & Kuhl, 2003). The quality and type of babbling, however, depends on both genetics and environment. Infants learning different languages will repeat sounds in their babbling that they hear when adults speak directly to them. For example, Lee, Davis, and Macneilage (2010) found that babbling patterns in infants learning Korean differed from those learning English. The vowel patterns of each group mimicked the vowel sounds that the infants heard when adults talked to them. Recent research has even demonstrated that the prosody of babbling differs based on the intent of the child at the moment. Esteve-Gilbert and Prieto (2012) found that babies learning Catalan used a wider pitch range when commicating requests and expressions of discontent than when communicating responses or statements. Thus, babbling differs based on the language the child is hearing and the child's intention when babbling.

8 to 12 Months

Infants have added listening abilities that contribute to learning a language well. Eight-month-olds show some ability to divide a continuous stream of speech sounds that they hear into individual words (Swingley, 2008). For example, they can begin to divide "Hereisthemilk" into "Here is the milk." Demonstrating their receptive skills, infants can perceive common sequences of sounds that form words. For example, they won't listen as well when sounds are embedded in nonsense words as when they are used within familiar words in English. By 1 year of age, infants are learning that certain sounds go together to form words in English, and that other sequences of sounds are not combined in English, based on the language patterns they are hearing from adults (Saffran, 2002). Infants are learning that certain sounds are likely to follow other sounds—such as in the word "baby," the "by" is more likely to follow the "ba" than are other sequences of sounds, and they are using both pitch and length of words to determine when a word begins and ends (Seidl, 2007).

In an interesting research study, Pruden, Hirsh-Pasek, Golinkoff, and Hennon (2006) found that the 10-month-olds they studied understood a new word after an adult named it five times, but they applied the new word to an interesting object, not a boring one, even though the adult looked at the boring object. The interesting object attracted their attention and they ignored the adult's eye gaze. At 12, 18, and 24 months, infants tune into the adult's social cue of looking at an object and understand that the label the adult uses is for that object. Brooks and Meltzoff (2005), however, studied whether 9-, 10-, and 11-month-old infants were more likely to turn and follow the gaze of an adult when the adult's eyes were open rather than closed. They found that the 10- and 11-month-olds who turned and followed adults with eyes open had higher language development scores at 18 months. It is important, then, during this age period for adults to watch where the infant is looking when they label or talk about an object.

All of this information about the capabilities of infants demonstrates how important it is to talk *with* babies during their first 8 months and definitely not wait until they say their first words to talk with them. If adults wait to talk with little babies, their language development may be compromised, because infants need to hear language and engage in the language dance with a responsive language partner during their first months of life. It is also important to be responsive and to talk about what interests the infant.

Additional receptive skills that appear around the child's first birthday include beginning to understand simple directions and the language in games. An adult or sibling might give a direction such as "Wave bye-bye" or "Give Mommy a kiss." Again, demonstrating the desire to be social, infants love it when adults play familiar games such as peek-a-boo, pat-a-cake, or "How big are you?"

Intentional communication increases as infants learn a repertoire of gestures (shaking head "no," holding hands up to be picked up, waving bye-bye), sounds, and first words to communicate their needs and desires. A responsive communication partner teaches an infant that gestures, sounds, and words get results, so that the infant does not need to cry to get his needs met. As described in the following example, when adults respond, infants enjoy communicating with a language partner:

> *Mika, 9 months old, sat in the bathtub with her mother on the floor beside the tub. Playing with the sound of her voice, Mika said "Da-da." Her mother said "Da-da" in a different tone. Mika said "Da-da" in a still different tone, putting emphasis on the second syllable. Her mother said "Da-da" in a higher tone. On they went, taking turns with different sounds bouncing off the wall of the bathroom, until many turns had been taken and "Da-da" had been exclaimed in as many melodies as possible.*

Mika was learning that communicating is fun, that language has prosodic features (pitch, tempo, pauses, and emphatic stress on parts of a word), that she could *initiate* a "conversation" (about "da-da"), and that she could *sustain* a conversation by continuing to take her turn. She was learning that she could be an important and effective conversational partner.

Babbling continues to develop with combined syllables such as "dada," "mama," "nana," and "tutu," but now the infant may be using these sounds to name the mother or father. These words are music to the ears of parents

OBSERVATION INVITATION **9.2**

**What could this infant be communicating
with her gestures?**
How would you be responsive to this infant?

who feel special when their infant repeats these sounds especially and primarily for them.

By the young age of 8 to 12 months, infants are beginning to lose the ability to make all of the sounds of all of the languages in the world, as they listen to and practice the sounds of the familiar language spoken to them in their immediate social interactions (Werker et al., 2007). For example, the English language distinguishes *R* from *L*, and the Japanese language does not (de Boer & Kuhl, 2003). Infants are now hearing the differences in sounds and words that are used in their own language, and losing the ability to hear all of the sounds of all of the languages in the world. So, Japanese children lose their ability to hear the differences in the sounds of *R* and *L* (de Boer & Kuhl, 2003; Kuhl, Williams, Lacerda, Sterens, & Lindblom, 1992): "However, if exposed to a second language at this remarkable time of learning, infants can keep the brain open to the sounds of foreign language" (de Boer & Kuhl, 2003). When 8- to 12-month-old children, who usually lose their ability to hear sounds in a foreign language at this age, were exposed to a second language through interacting with an adult for a total of 5 hours, they could distinguish the sounds of that language at 12 months. When infants looked at and heard a DVD or listened to a second language on a tape, though, they did *not* retain their ability to distinguish the sounds of the second language. It takes interacting with adults in a social context to "keep the brain open to sounds."

12 to 18 Months

Receptively, toddlers again demonstrate their beginning language sophistication by paying attention to different things when an adult uses a noun as opposed to an adjective (Waxman & Markow, 1995). They can follow simple directions, such as "Go get your coat" and can correctly point to their nose, eyes, hair, foot, tummy, and other body parts when a parent or teacher playfully asks "Where's your nose?" and "Where's your tummy?" Young toddlers between the ages of 13 and 18 months heard a word just nine times in 5 minutes and then were able to demonstrate that they understood what the word meant, even after a 24-hour delay (Woodward, Markman, & Fitzsimmons, 1994). For example, an infant hearing the word "ball" for the first time will go after the "ball" a day later when an adult uses the specific word (if "ball" has been used frequently during the previous day). Clearly, young toddlers can comprehend the meaning of words quickly during this age period.

Infants are likely to begin to point to objects and people with their tiny index finger by the time they are 12 months old, although some children begin earlier. In their attempt to *share attention*, infants may intentionally point at a person or object with a squeal of delight to direct another person's attention toward that object (Legerstee & Barillas, 2003). When an infant points, she is aware that objects are separate from her and that she can direct an adult's attention to some event or object—an observable and exciting step forward in cognitive language, motor, social, and emotional development. The infants are now sharing experiences with others as they "tune into others and get others to tune into them" (Legerstee & Barillas, 2003, p. 108). Also, infants point to gain information (Begus & Southgate, 2012). When caregivers tune in to the infant's pointing and respond with, for example, "You see a ball, don't you?" or "Ooh—a ball—I see it," infants enthusiastically continue to point and then progress over time to using words to focus *joint attention* on an object or person. You can still expect to see many gestures for a while, however, because in the 12- to 18-month age period, 85% of infants continue to use gestures as well as words to request and label objects and people (Acredolo & Goodwyn, 1985). Toddlers from 15 to 18 months will protest (shake their head "no,") request objects with an open and closed hand, request actions by pointing, take the hand of the adult, give an object, comment by pointing, and use gestures such has hugging and clapping (Crais, 2009).

The growth of a young toddler's vocabulary, though, is miraculous during this age period. Through *joint attention conversations* with adults, mobile infants learn that every action has a name and they can use these wonderful new words. When adults respond to mobile infants' pointing, they are moving children toward a language explosion.

This rapid word learning between 12 and 18 months is often referred to as a *language explosion* or *productive naming explosion* (Woodward et al., 1994), a very surprising increase in language development that demonstrates a toddler's desire to learn to label people, places, and things in a social context. Just as fireworks explode with a variety of colors and in many surprising directions, the language explosion delights adults who are in awe of the sudden increase and variety of words spoken by the toddler. The adult may wonder how these words can suddenly appear, but we know that the infant and growing toddler have been participating in a rich language dialogue since birth. Carey (1978)

FIGURE 9.3   **Language characteristics of a 16-month-old**

Lamar, at 16 months, was very busy learning language.

- "Sirt" (shirt) he exclaimed, while also pointing to a shirt his mom was holding.
- "Kitty," he said, as he looked at the kitty.
- "Buses teeth," as he pointed to his father who was brushing his teeth.
- "Mama, mama, porch," Lamar called out.
- Lamar joyfully practiced a new word: "Back, back, back," as he ran through the kitchen.
- The next day he said "juice" when his dad took the juice container out of the refrigerator.
- Other words that Lamar used over the next few days included "feet," "eye," "boke-boke" (broke) after breaking a plastic cup, "sut" (shut), and "pease" (please).

noted that at 18 months, toddlers were learning as many as nine new words a day. Phrases with two or more words are heard at the end of this age period, such as "more mik" (milk), "more juice," and "Mama, bush (brush) teeth." Figure 9.3 lists some words and phrases that a 16-month-old boy could use and that are characteristic of that age. Notice that Lamar says many words and is beginning to put two words together ("buses teeth").

Mobile infants continue to communicate in a variety of ways—using gestures, words, phrases, and simple sentences to reject, request, comment (Holdgrafer & Dunst, 1990), refuse, demand, and inform—and may, at times, be difficult to understand. For example, you will still hear toddlers *jargoning*—a sequence of sounds with intonation of an adult, such as "ba bad a da tu le?" with the rising intonation at the end to indicate a question. They may seem to be telling you a piece of very important information with a great deal of emphasis on different sounds, but it is difficult to understand what is being said. Parents and teachers often have to be mind readers in order to understand young toddlers who are intent on communicating something quite important, and who may get frustrated when adults don't understand them. Encouraging a young toddler to take your hand and show you can often help defuse the situation.

18 to 36 Months

While watching this **video**, identify gestures, facial expressions, and body movements (nonverbal communication) that communicate meaning. How does the adult expand the children's language in a responsive way?

Toddlers demonstrate that they can detect slight mispronunciations in words by looking at the objects when the researchers used the correct pronunciation (Bailey & Plunkett, 2002), such as "doll" instead of "dole" (for *doll*). They have accomplished what is called *fast mapping*, quickly attaching a name to an object. At 18 months, toddlers easily learn both gestures and words as names for objects, but by 24 months they interpret only words as names for objects, unless they are given additional practice with gestures. Their ability to use both words and gestures as symbols for an object becomes refined as they learn that, in most social situations, words are primarily used to name objects (Namy & Waxman, 1998). It is impressive that most toddlers become more focused on learning words rather than gestures, simply because they *observe* that people around them use mostly words rather than mostly gestures. Because of this ability to focus on learning words to name people, places, and objects rather than learning just gestures, toddlers are able to participate in their social group more effectively.

Listening to toddlers talk is a joy because they try so hard to communicate their excitement about all of the new things that they are learning. They want to tell their special adults what's bothering them, where to look, what to feed them, and how to dress them. They want to share what they've found with you and want you to share in the moment with them—to really be there emotionally and linguistically. As they develop autonomy, they demand, request, inform, and describe their world. Their language is a window—sometimes clear and sometimes foggy—into what they are thinking.

Toddlers enjoy listening to stories, singing songs, and doing finger-plays in informal groups.

From saying sounds to saying words to putting words together, infants and toddlers try to make sense of the language they are hearing. Toddlers make linguistic mistakes, but they are developmentally appropriate mistakes and tell us that toddlers are not just imitating what they hear, but are also applying some rules that they've discovered all by themselves. They may think that the word "dog" applies to all four-legged creatures, so the next cat, horse, or pig they see will enthusiastically be called "dog." This mistake of *overgeneralization* tells us that toddlers are listening to what we are saying and that their minds are very busy fast mapping the words to an object, animal, or person. They may also *undergeneralize* a word and not use it for all of the cases to which it applies. For example, to them, a cat is only a cat if it is a black cat. So, when they see a white cat, they think that it is named something else. After all, objects that they drink out of are strangely called cups, glasses, thermos, or bottles, so shouldn't there be different names for a black, white, spotted, gray, or furless cat? During this age period, as before, toddlers work very hard to figure out all of the names of things, the characteristics that differentiate them, and how to talk about them. We can help them by engaging them in conversations about all of the exciting things in their environment, such as their red shoes, the large refrigerator, cheddar cheese, and how a puppy is different from a kitty, as well as talking with them about their emotions—anger, sadness, worry, fear, and joy.

> *At 18 months, Carmen could say the words "up," "meow," "open," "down," "door," "diaper," "pretzel," and "neck." She also could use sentences such as, " go kitty," "go car," and " go Mommy"— open-pivot sentences, so labeled because different words pivot around one word, such as "go."*

Toddlers progress from saying mostly one-word and some two-word sentences at 18 months to multiword sentences at 36 months. As noted in the previous example, they begin to use *open-pivot* sentences. They also use *telegraphic speech*. Spoken sentences such as "Kitty eat food" are called telegraphic because, just as a telegram leaves out words for the sake of brevity, the toddler leaves out words and uses the essential parts of speech that communicate meaning. Soon, Carmen was saying "Dada, dada, I boke (broke) eggs," adding the "s" on words to indicate that they are plural. Next, she added "ing" to say "I jumping" rather than "I jump." Again, mistakes are made because of a toddler's active mind. Applying the "s" rule to indicate plurals, some exceptions in the English language such as "deer" may be called "deers" by the learning toddler (Brown, 1973). By 3 years of age, Carmen was saying wonderfully creative sentences, such as "People pee in the potty and puppies pee in the now (snow)," "Why you are crying?" or "It's too louder" (the music was playing at a high volume).

The language-learning journey continues for many years, but what incredible progress Carmen and other children make from birth to age 3. Adults can use a variety of strategies to support and enhance children's language development.

Strategies to Encourage Language Learning

The teacher's voice was warm and caring as she soothed Katrina after a fall. Katrina, 9 months old, crying intensely, stopped and looked up at the teacher. The teacher continued comforting Katrina with calm words. The teacher then stopped and waited expectantly for Katrina to take a turn in the conversation. Katrina started babbling, as if telling the teacher all about the nasty fall. This communication exchange seemed emotionally satisfying to both Katrina and the teacher, as Katrina stopped crying, gave a big sigh, and began babbling excitedly.

The teacher in this example is using responsive language. She is empathic and waits for Katrina to take a turn in the conversation. We have identified a dozen strategies like those represented in the scenario with Katrina that parents and teachers use to support children learning to express themselves, to hear and understand language, and to become competent communicators.

1. Build Relationships—Be an Empathic Language Partner

When a person cares about another person, he or she usually wants to communicate with that person. An infant or toddler will want to communicate with you when she feels safe and cared for in loving ways. Infants and toddlers communicate when it is pleasant to communicate, when the affect or feeling of the communication is warm and loving, and when they understand that their communication attempts will get a response.

2. Respond and Take Turns—Be an Interactive Language Partner

Through your interactions with the infant or toddler you are helping the child learn to use language to communicate. When a toddler asks for a drink and a parent or teacher responds, then the toddler learns that communication is an effective way to get his needs met. When an infant makes sounds or a toddler uses words, respond and then wait for the child to take a turn with sounds, words, or sentences. This **conversational dance** with each partner taking a turn helps the child learn the pragmatics of conversation—that people take turns exchanging ideas in a social context. These adult-child conversations build young children's vocabulary as well as their ability to take language turns—a skill that helps them become a *conversational* partner and a *capable communicator*. Try not to dominate the conversation with an infant or toddler (Girolametto, 2000) by taking more turns than the child or bombarding the child with language. Instead, focus on reciprocal and responsive interactions with equal give-and-take conversations.

Re-watch this video, seen earlier in this chapter. Which of the following 12 strategies covered in this text is the grandfather using to encourage the toddler's language development?

conversational dance

A conversation of sounds, words, or sentences, much like in a coordinated dance, in which partners take turns leading and following.

3. Respond to Nonverbal Communication

Can babies who can't talk try to tell you something? Yes, they can. A yawn can mean the baby is tired or bored, snuggling in to an adult's body tells you that the infant feels safe and relaxed, a toddler running to you tells you she wants to connect with you, and kicking feet say "I'm uncomfortable." When babies turn away, they may be communicating that they need a break from the interaction. When infants or toddlers use a strong communication cue, such as arching their back, it means "that hurts," or "stop what you are doing." When adults understand and respond to infants' and toddlers' nonverbal communication, they let children know that they are communication partners. With responsive adults, infants and toddlers are soon using sounds and words, while still maintaining many nonverbal ways to communicate.

4. Use Self-Talk and Parallel Talk

Self-talk is talk that adults use to describe what they are doing while with the infant or toddler. For example, a teacher who is diapering a baby might say, "I'm getting your diaper. Now I'm lifting your feet. I'm putting the diaper on. All done." **Parallel talk** occurs when an adult talks about what a child is doing. For example, while the child is playing or eating, the adult might say, "Mmm, you're eating your toast" while pointing to the toast. These strategies tie language to an act or object manipulation, making words come alive and have meaning for the child.

> **self-talk**
> Talk that an adult uses while with an infant or toddler to describe what the adult is doing.

> **parallel talk**
> Talk in which an adult describes to a child what the child is doing at the present time.

5. Talk Often with the Child, Using a Rich and Varied Vocabulary

Does it matter how much you talk with an infant or toddler, sing, and look at picture books together? Research shows that the number and quality of the conversations that adults have with infants and toddlers directly affects how they learn to talk (Hart & Risley, 1999; Honig & Brophy, 1996; Shonkoff & Phillips, 2000). The number of total words and different words that the parent uses with the child daily, the number of conversations, and the positive affirmations from the parent are all related to infants' and toddlers' language development (Hart & Risley, 1999).

Researchers have found astounding differences in how much parents talk with their children. Some infants and toddlers hear an average of 600 words an hour, whereas others hear as many as 2,100 words an hour. Some children hear 100 different words an hour, whereas others hear 500 different words an hour. These differences in the amount of language that children heard made a difference in their language development. By age 3, the children with talkative parents were talking more and with a richer vocabulary. They were averaging three times as many statements per hour and twice as many words per hour than the children of quieter parents: "The more time that parents spent talking with their child from day to day, the more rapidly the child's vocabulary was likely to be growing and the higher the child's score on an IQ test was likely to be at age 3" (Hart & Risley, 1999, p. 3).

Use language-rich routines and many interactions with infants and toddlers to build their vocabulary. Diapering, for example, is a perfect time for a parent or teacher to talk about "first" we get a clean diaper, "second" we take off your diaper, and so forth. Talking about hands, nose, ears, and toes enlightens the baby about body parts and makes diapering an easier job for you.

6. Use Joint Attention Strategies

Adults in Western cultures often point to the people or objects under discussion when talking with their young children, thereby directing their children's attention...and the mother of a young deaf child is most likely to sign to her child when she knows that the child can simultaneously see both her signs and the objects or events she is talking about. (Harris, 1992, reported in McDevitt & Ormrod, 2002, p. 240)

As noted, infants and toddlers learn best if the adult labels or talks about an object or person when the infant or toddler is focusing on it. Joint attention occurs when both the adult and the child are focusing on the same thing at the same time. Adults who point at the object of discussion or wait until the infant or toddler is looking at an object to talk about it ensure that the child will attach the language label to the correct object. This type of shared attention enhances language development (Adamson, Bakeman, & Deckner, 2004).

7. Use the Four Es Approach

Encourage children to communicate by listening, responding, and not correcting their language. *Expand* on both the semantics and the syntax of a child's words and conversational turns. *Elaborate* on (make more complex) and *extend* (lengthen) the sounds, words, and sentence—for example, by adding a different sound, a new word, or a slightly longer sentence. Imitating and then expanding on the language of the child models the next step in development. The child hears your expansion and is likely to begin to use the newly modeled language forms. An added benefit of using the four Es is that infants and toddlers feel *effective* and a language *equal*, promoting further use of language to communicate.

8. Use Semantically Responsive Talk

When adults took language turns with toddlers and stayed on the same topic, children were significantly more likely to reply than if the adult responded but changed the topic (Dunham & Dunham, 1996). Although a conversation made up of cooing sounds may seem as if it would be boring to an adult, the delight in an infant's eyes, the emotional connection, and the continuous development of the infant's language is reward enough to the caring adult. The adult's **semantic elaboration** supports the child's tendency to stay on the topic, as well. If a toddler is talking about the "airplane" and the listening adult responds semantically with information about the shape or color of the airplane, then the toddler is likely to stay on the topic and say something more about the airplane.

semantic elaboration

Conversations with children in which the adult stays on the same topic that the child is discussing but expands the meanings that the child is expressing.

9. Use Infant-Directed Speech

Janna, 13 months old, played quietly with a ball, rolling it and scrambling after it, only to roll it again across the carpet. When she tired of rolling the ball, she looked at her grandfather. Her grandfather sat on the floor beside her and said, "Ball, let's roll the ball." Janna smiled as she rolled the ball in Grandpa's direction. "Ball," she said quietly, imitating her grandpa's word.

Anne Fernald (1985) discovered that 4-month-olds prefer infant-directed speech. Most parents and grandparents use infant-directed speech and babies like Janna learn from it (McDevitt & Ormrod, 2002; Thiessen, Hill, & Saffran, 2005). As parents and teachers generally try to *simplify* language in order to maintain the infants' attention and teach them to use language, they use speech with a child that is significantly different from speech with an adult. For example, parents might stress a key word such as "jumping" in the phrase, "You are *jumping.*" Adults using infant-directed speech also point or direct the child's attention to the focus of the conversation—for example, pointing to a cup while saying "cup." Adults repeat words—for example, they might say to an infant or young toddler, "Look, a *bird.* The *bird* is flying." But, isn't the term *infant-directed speech* just another term for "baby talk"?

We've all heard that we shouldn't talk **baby talk** to an infant, but parents and teachers *do* use a special language when they interact with their infants because young children are more attentive when adults use it. Adults in most cultures use these practices, and in so doing, they are a communication partner and language model for infants and toddlers. Parents who use infant-directed speech are modeling bite-size pieces of language that infants and toddlers can digest and practice. Examples would include the following strategies:

baby talk
A special language that adults and older children use with younger children, in which the adult uses shorter sentences and decreased vocabulary.

1. Use responsive talk.
2. Use shorter sentences and decreased vocabulary.
3. Exaggerate the pitch and intonation of your voice.
4. Direct your communication at the infant or toddler.
5. Use longer pauses between words and utterances.
6. Frequently repeat words.
7. Don't be afraid to be redundant—for example, say, "A *bird*—a blue *bird,*" repeating the word *bird.*
8. Elongate the vowels in words ("Oooh, whaaaat is that?").
9. Use diminutive words ("blanky," "piggy," "doggy").
10. Use frequent paraphrasing or recasting of previous utterances (toddler says "We go" and parent recasts by saying "Yes, we're going").
11. Talk about what is immediately present.
12. Use frequent phrases and parts of sentences in isolation ("in the car").
13. Use questions and attempts to elicit speech.
14. Label words—nouns and actions—in context.

Many adults also simplify their speech pragmatically when speaking directly to an infant or toddler. For example, we use language for a variety of social goals: to inform, question, promise, request, refuse, play, and direct others (functions of language). Parents use fewer functions when infants are young and gradually increase the number and types of functions as the infant grows to become a preschooler and can better understand the intentions of language.

Newman and Hussain (2006), however, suggest that by 13 months, mobile infants may need more than infant-directed speech. They will need adults who responsively talk about past events, future events, feelings, and reasons for actions as well as adults who use sentences that are slightly above the child's level of language.

Infant-directed strategies, however, also build the affectionate relationship between parent and child. Although most adults stop using these strategies as infants become toddlers and preschoolers, some words are like emotional glue that binds an adult and child together across time and space. Some special words a parent and child will use forever when they are together. A mother of a 30-year-old might ask her grown child if she would like some "pasgetti" (spaghetti), reminding them both of the early years when the child could not say "spaghetti" and the close attachment between them. A grandmother's name may become "Ta-ta" forever, because those were the first sounds that the infant made when lying peacefully in the grandmother's lap.

10. Use Questions and Control Carefully

Adults often use questions to start a conversation with a child, to take a conversational turn, or to gain information. Some questions are **true questions** that are asked because the teacher doesn't know the answer. Other questions are asked to test children—for example, "What is that?" as they point to a toy on the floor. These questions are often referred to as **closed questions** because they usually have only one correct answer. There are thoughtful **open-ended questions** that have more than one acceptable answer, such as, "What song do you want to sing next?" **Choice questions**—for example, "Do you want juice or milk?"—are perfect questions for toddlers who are exerting their independence from adults.

Infants and toddlers enjoy and benefit from interactions with teachers who use a **conversation-eliciting style** characterized by conversational turns, maintenance of a mutually interesting topic, and infrequent use of directives. This style is in contrast to a **directive style,** which is characterized by frequent directives and monologues, infrequent questions, rapid topic changes by adults, and a low level of topic maintenance (Katz & Snow, 2000).

Use *behavior control* carefully. Behavior control refers to statements that are used by teachers to elicit group participation around a common activity or to manage safety concerns. Frequent prohibitions from adults (e.g., "stop that," "don't") result in less favorable child outcomes than when adults use more active listening strategies of repeating, paraphrasing, and extending infants' and toddlers' statements (Hart & Risley, 1992).

11. Listen with Your Eyes

A 3-year-old child's mother picked her up from child care and took her home immediately, so that the mother could prepare dinner. As the mother was pulling food out of the refrigerator, the little girl tried to tell her mommy about something that had happened during the day. The mother, focused on her task, commented, "Hmm, oh, that's nice." The little girl, obviously very frustrated with her mother's lack of response, said, "Mom, listen to me with your eyes."

Infants and toddlers—in fact, all human beings—love to be listened to with another person's full engagement and focus. The little girl described in the previous example wanted her mom to look at her and "listen with her eyes." Infants and toddlers thrive, learn to listen, and take language turns, when adults in their lives do the same with them. They learn that holding a conversation means taking turns with listening and talking, so they will look at you intently, waiting as patiently as they can for you to finish what you want to say. If a child or family member from a particular culture believes that it is disrespectful to "look into

true questions

Questions for which the asker does not know the answer.

closed questions

Questions that have one correct answer.

open-ended questions

Questions that allow for more than one correct answer.

choice questions

Questions that give the responder options.

conversation-eliciting style

Conversation that is characterized by conversational turns, maintenance of a mutually interesting topic, and infrequent use of directives.

directive style

Conversation that is characterized by frequent directives and monologues, rapid topic changes by adults, and a low level of topic maintenance.

your eyes" while talking, he may prefer for you to listen carefully with your ears and voice, acknowledging that you've heard.

12. Read, Sing, Use Finger-Plays and Social Games Like Peek-a-Boo

Playful activities are crucial to enjoyable language learning. Chapter 13 discusses these topics, including literacy development and experiences, in great detail.

Children with Special Needs

Individual infants and toddlers differ in how they develop and use language. Some children talk continuously and others are quieter; some talk to themselves as they are playing and others talk mostly with other people. As you observe infants and toddlers, you will also see differences in the ages at which babies begin to speak. Most developmental charts indicate that typically developing infants will say their first word around 12 months, some two-word sentences by 18 months, and *many* single words and two-word sentences by 2 years. However, some babies may say their first word as early as 8 months and some as late as 15 months. A child that we knew spoke 100 words at her first birthday (this is extremely rare), whereas other children that we've known were making many sounds but had no words at age 1. Whereas the average number of words that infants speak at 14 months is 10, the individual differences in development among children are quite significant. Knowing when to become concerned about a child's **language delay** (children not saying words and sentences when most other children do) may require discussing your observations with other professionals. Keep in mind that language delay at an early age may predict later language and reading challenges (Scarborough & Dobrich, 1990). Scarborough and Dobrich found that children who later had difficulty in reading in elementary school had shorter sentences and less sentence complexity at 2 1/2 years of age and difficulty understanding language and naming objects at age 3. It is very important, then, to identify language delay early in a child's life, so that the child and family receive support in developing language skills.

> **language delay**
>
> When children do not use words and sentences by the age that most other children do.

Differences may occur for a variety of reasons, including biological and environmental. One primary reason is that there are differences in how much children are exposed to language (Huttenlocher et al., 1991). Some children hear many words from adults and some do not. Usually, the more descriptive and kind words that infants and toddlers hear, the more words they will use. Use the strategies discussed on page 219 in this chapter.

Another reason for language delay may be hearing impairment. Children with hearing challenges may develop receptive and expressive language in a different way from other children. The pronunciation of sounds, as well as a child's vocabulary and syntax development, will all be affected by hearing challenges.

Hearing Impairment

Hearing loss is one of the most common abnormalities present at birth. Significant hearing loss is present in 1 to 3 per 1,000 newborn infants in the healthy nursery population and 2 to 4 per 100 in the intensive care nursery population. The average age of detection of significant hearing loss is 14 months. Unfortunately, by this time, infants have missed a wealth of language and learning experiences. Hearing screening by a pediatrician for babies between birth and 3 months is recommended and intervention must be in place before the baby is 6 months old for maximum benefit (AAP, 1999). Infants, who are diagnosed before 6 months of age are likely to develop better language skills than children diagnosed after 6 months of age (Yoshinaga-Itano, Sedey, Coulter, & Mehl, 1998).

It is often difficult for parents to read the sometimes subtle signs of hearing loss in their infant, especially if the hearing loss is mild. An infant who is hearing impaired may not turn her head toward a voice, smile in response to a person's voice, or look around when her own name is called (by 5 months of age). Older infants may babble, but the quality is different from typically developing children and babbling may diminish between 8 and 12 months, when the infant begins to practice just those sounds in the language that she is hearing. Infants and toddlers with hearing impairment may watch adults' gestures carefully and have a hard time following simple directions from words alone, without the additional information from the gestures. They may also be delayed in saying their first words and sentences. It is important that infants and toddlers with hearing impairment be exposed to a communication system early in their lives during the sensitive period for language development.

Not only does learning a communication system, such as sign language, enhance communication, but it also supports that child's developing cognitive abilities—thinking, problem solving, and categorizing. Mayberry, Lock, and Kazmi (2002) discovered that deaf adults who had experienced sign language as infants had higher levels of performance on English learned later in life than adults who had not experienced sign language in their first 4 years.

Programs That Enhance Language Development and Learning

As many infants and toddlers venture outside the home environment to participate in child care centers, family child care homes, or early intervention programs such as Early Head Start or programs for children with disabilities, they develop relationships that can enhance or discourage language development. A review of how these community programs influence infants' and toddlers' language development sheds light on specific factors that have positive effects.

Child Care: Relationships and Responsive Interactions

The results of the NICHD Early Child Care Research Network, (2000b) study, following 500 to 800 infants and toddlers in 10 sites in the United States including a variety of types of child care programs as well as those at home with a parent most of the time, found that the overall quality of child care and language stimulation in particular was related to children's language development at 15, 24, and 36 months. Also, the quality of the environment is correlated with the language outcomes for infants and toddlers, both receptive language and expressive communication skills (Burchinal, Roberts, Nabors, & Bryant, 1996).

Early Intervention Programs

Early intervention programs include programs for infants and toddlers at risk for learning challenges because of their socioeconomic status and programs for young children identified by assessment teams as having disabilities. The

FIGURE 9.4   **Effective strategies for improving language development in young children with disabilities**

1. Facilitating parent–infant language interactions during routines, such as bath time, feeding and eating, and trips to the grocery store
2. Accepting the child's communication bids by showing affection, attention, and verbal feedback
3. Using a facilitative (encouraging) versus a directive style (demanding)
4. Contingent responding through expansion of the child's sounds, words, and sentences
5. Using augmentative communication devices for children who cannot speak (picture symbols that the child uses or computer-like devices that speak for the child)

Source: From Prizant, Weatherby, and Roberts (1993).

parents of a child at risk or with a disability may receive home visits from a family support program or attend a family-centered child care center or intervention play group.

The communication enhancement strategies in Figure 9.4 acknowledge the strengths of each child, ensure the child's success, emphasize adult-child interactions as crucial for the language achievements of the child, and promote language development in the environments where the children use language.

STRATEGIES TO SUPPORT LANGUAGE DEVELOPMENT AND LEARNING

1. Recognize the capacities of infants and toddlers to understand language and communicate using gestures, facial expressions, sounds, and words.
2. Identify language delay early in a child's life so that the child and family receive support in developing language skills.
3. Follow DeHouwer's (1999) recommendations for parents of children learning two or more languages during the infant and toddler years.
4. Honor a child's home language by encouraging parents to continue using the language, employing native language speakers in the program, and using words and phrases from the child's home language during routines and interactions with the child.
5. Use the following dozen strategies to support children's language learning:
    a. Build relationships—be an empathic language partner.
    b. Respond and take turns—be an interactive language partner.
    c. Respond to nonverbal communication.
    d. Use self-talk and parallel talk.
    e. Talk often with the child using a rich and varied vocabulary.
    f. Use joint attention strategies.
    g. Use the four Es approach.
    h. Use semantically responsive talk.
    i. Use infant-directed speech.
    j. Use questions and control carefully.
    k. Listen with your eyes.
    l. Read, sing, and use finger-plays and social games like peek-a-boo.
6. The quality of the environment and teachers' use of responsive and sensitive language strategies are related to children's language development.
7. Use routine-based intervention strategies.

DEVELOPMENTAL TRENDS AND RESPONSIVE INTERACTIONS

LANGUAGE DEVELOPMENT AND LEARNING

Infants and toddlers develop the capacity to understand, express, and use language.

Development	Example
0–4 months (infant)	
• Infants may startle if they hear a loud sound. • Infants hear the differences in sounds. • Infants may stop crying when they hear a familiar adult's voice. • Infants prefer to hear talk that is directed toward them. • Infants listen when an adult talks or sings to them while looking at them. • Infants cry when they are in pain, are hungry, or are distressed. • By 2 months of age, babies have different cries for hunger and pain. • Infants "coo" (make soft vowel sounds). • Infants smile and laugh toward the end of this age period. • Infants will stare at interesting pictures in books.	Brenda held Jordon so they could gaze into each other's eyes. Jordon cooed softly and Brenda cooed back. Then she waited for Jordon to take another turn. Erica gave her father a big smile when he picked her up out of her crib.
4–8 months (infant)	
• Infants turn their head toward a noise or someone speaking their name. • Infants enjoy adults talking, singing, and laughing with them. • Babies vocalize with intention to get a response from the adult. • Babies make high-pitched squeals. • Infants practice their sounds when exploring and with favorite adults. • Infants begin to babble—at first with one consonant and then by combining two consonants. • Infants engage in turn-taking conversations with adults. • Babies will look at different pictures in a book and get excited at a favorite one or at the enthusiastic tone of an adult who is reading to them.	As Danielle, the infant teacher, was holding Donovan on her lap, she pointed to the pictures in the sturdy board book. "Look," she said, pointing to the picture, "a ball. There's your ball," as she pointed to a ball on the floor. Donovan looked at the picture, then at the ball on the floor, and back to the picture. "Tt" said Afi as he lay in his teacher's arms looking up at her. "Tada" exclaimed his teacher back to him. "Tt" repeated Afi as he took his turn in the conversation.
8–12 months (mobile infant)	
• Mobile infants are beginning to play social games such as peek-a-boo or "so big." • Infants enjoy listening to sound play (rhymes), songs, and finger-plays. • Babbling continues to develop with combined syllables such as "dada," "mama," "nana," and "tutu," but now the infant may be using these sounds specifically for mom or dad. • Infants will use sounds consistently for an object or person or animal. • If they hear another language *with* an adult through interactive conversational strategies, then infants can "keep the brain open to the sounds of a second language." • Infants may begin to use single words. • At the end of the age period, infants may begin to point to engage an adult. • They are using facial expressions and gestures such as shaking head or arms out to be picked up to communicate to adults or peers.	One of Dana's first words was "mama," which she said over and over again when she saw her mother. One of Trishanna's first words was "dada," which she excitedly said over and over again when she saw her father.

Teacher- or Parent-Child Interaction	Environment

0–4 months (infant)

- Use infant-directed speech.
- Hold and talk to babies. Engage in long eye gazes while having conversational dances. Respect the baby if he needs a break and turns his head away.
- Read books with rhythmic phrases and books with one picture on a page with 2- to 4-month-olds.
- Interpret babies' burps, cries, yawns, stretching, and sounds as forms of communication. Say, "Oh, you're telling me you're sleepy."
- Sing lullabies and other songs.
- Be an empathic language partner—comment on the baby's feelings.
- Use words and sounds to comfort babies.

- The best environment is in the arms of a caring adult who holds the baby and talks softly.
- Provide toys that make pleasant sounds. Gently hold the toy and share the sounds with the baby.
- Provide interesting materials to touch while you comment on the textures.
- Add mirrors low along a wall. Babies will look and possibly make sounds.

4–8 months (infant)

- Use infant-directed speech.
- Talk with babies often. Show them new objects and people and name them.
- Repeat the sounds that infants make and wait for the infant to make the sound again (turn taking).
- Use sign language for several familiar items such as "milk" or "dog."
- Sing songs and say finger-plays.
- Use words to describe children's feelings expressed through gestures, body postures, and sounds.
- Read simple books with one to two pictures on a page. Point to the pictures as you say the name of the picture.
- Read the same books over and over.
- Use joint attention strategies—point at a toy or picture in a book when you say the name or talk about it.

- Provide interesting toys and materials for babies to handle and explore.
- Provide cardboard books with handles so that babies can crawl to them and pick them up.
- Books with handles encourage babies to hang on to them.
- Make a peek-a-boo picture book by gluing a piece of cloth over each picture.
- Create a cozy book corner where teachers can be comfortable and read to babies.
- Provide sound boxes (safely sealed) with different objects in them that make different sounds when shaken.
- Add puppets to the environment. Use them at times to "talk" to the child. Put the puppet on the child's hand and wait to see what the child says or does.

8–12 months (mobile infant)

- Play familiar games such as peek-a-boo, pat-a-cake, or "how big are you?"
- Respond to infants' nonverbal communication with words.
- Look at and wait for infants to initiate sounds or words.
- Imitate the sounds and then expand, elaborate, and extend the baby's language.
- Model the next step in language development.
- Use self-talk and parallel talk.
- Talk often in a responsive way using a varied vocabulary. Don't bombard the child.
- Read books with enthusiasm—changing the tone of your voice with different characters.
- Talk about the pictures and the story as you read it. Engage babies in the story with your voice and gestures.
- Wait while looking at a picture for babies to initiate with sounds, pointing, or facial expressions.

- Create a cozy book corner where babies can easily reach and handle books.
- Create an "All About Me" book—small photo albums for each child with pictures of themselves, their family, their favorite toys, peers, teachers, and the family pets. Make them available to the children. Change the pictures as the child grows.
- Musical push toys encourage infants to handle them and make sounds.

DEVELOPMENTAL TRENDS AND RESPONSIVE INTERACTIONS (Continued)

Development	Example
12–18 months (mobile infant)	
• Mobile infants can follow simple directions such as "Come here" or "Go get your shoes" without you gesturing. • Mobile infants can play a social game without you demonstrating the action—for example, when you say "Wave bye-bye," they wave even though you don't show them how. • Mobile infants will point to engage adults and peers. • Rapid word learning—a language explosion—may occur with the children learning many new words. • Mobile infants will combine words toward the end of this age period. • Mobile infants will jabber (stringing many sounds together) using the intonation that adults use. • Mobile infants will use gestures and language to reject, request, comment, refuse, demand, and name objects and people. • Mobile infants use language to maintain an interaction or conversation with an adult or peer.	Janeika's teacher said, "Let's play pat-a-cake," and Janeika started clapping her hands together. Ross looked up expectantly at his teacher, jabbering many sounds together as if asking her a question.
18–24 months (toddler)	
• Toddlers can go get familiar toys from another room in the house when an adult asks them to and can follow directions such as "close the door." • Toddlers combine words to name things ("that cat"), to deny ("no bite"), and to reject ("no more"). • Toddlers are combining two to three words with meaning. • Toddlers use language for a variety of purposes, including asking "What that?" • Toddlers point to an increasing number of pictures in books when an adult talks about the picture.	"Hi, Kitty," "open door," and "hat on" were just a few of the two-word combinations Cheral used at 20 months of age. Tyra moved quickly over to the bookshelf, picked up a book with a bright cover, and rushed back to his teacher. After sitting comfortably in her lap, he opened the book and enthusiastically started pointing to the pictures as his teacher named them.
24–36 months (toddler)	
• Toddlers understand more complex directions and remember words to short songs and finger-plays. • Toddlers are using many two- to four-word sentences. • Toddlers can point to and name many body parts. • Toddlers add "ing" to words. • Toddlers begin using prepositions such as "on" and "in." • Toddlers add an "s" to words to indicate plurals. • Toddlers may begin to ask "Why?" • Toddlers will begin to tell you stories about what they did or what they saw. • Toward the end of this period, a toddler can use the pictures to tell you what is happening in a story.	Mindy started to add "ing" to words she had been saying for several months. She said, "I running" and "I eating" rather than "I run" and "I eat." "Look, he's playing," exclaimed Treat as he pointed to a picture in his favorite book.

Teacher- or Parent-Child Interaction	Environment

12–18 months (mobile infant)

- Stay on topic in a conversation with a mobile infant. See how many turns the child will take.
- Respond to the intonation of the child's jabbering. For example, if it seems as if the child is asking a question, answer what you think the child might be asking.
- Respond to mobile infants' pointing and other nonverbal communication with language.
- Use words that describe and compare sizes, shapes, and sounds.
- When a mobile infant uses words such as "I jump," model the next step in language development by saying "You're jumping," adding the "ing" to the word. Do this with both the content of the words and the structure of the words or sentences.
- Read books with longer stories, pausing as you go through the book to encourage mobile infants to talk about the pictures and the story.

- Introduce art materials such as play dough, clay, and paint.
- Add paper towel rolls for mobile infants to make sounds.
- Musical pull toys entice mobile infants to walk and pull objects behind them or push them.
- Sturdy music boxes encourage mobile infants to push buttons to "make music."
- Drums and other musical instruments can be made available.
- Add a sturdy CD player with a story from a parent taped on it.
- Use a tape recorder to tape mobile infants' voices and play it back to them.
- Provide bubble-making materials.
- Provide spaces for two or three children to encourage peer conversation.

18–24 months (toddler)

- Read books with longer stories, pausing as you go through the book to encourage toddlers to talk about the pictures and the story. Ask open-ended questions such as "How does the bear feel?"
- Wonder often with the child: "I wonder what will happen to the bear."
- Engage toddlers in conversation, trying to stay on the same topic as the child.
- Introduce new conversations about interesting objects and events.

- Set up an elaborate obstacle course and use words such as "in," "out," "over," "through," "around," "up," and "down" as the toddler goes through the course.
- Provide new books each week but keep children's favorites available.
- Provide a wider variety of art materials.
- Provide sensory materials.

24–36 months (toddler)

- Answer their "why" questions with patience and enthusiasm. This is how children learn and engage in social interactions.
- Listen with your eyes to the "stories" toddlers tell.
- Model saying words that are plurals, such as "dogs," "elephants," and so on.
- Use descriptive words such as "mozzarella cheese" rather than just "cheese," or "bluejay" rather than just "bird."
- Have long conversations with toddlers, following their lead.
- Read books to small informal groups or to individual children.

- Provide pictures for children to match.
- Puzzles of animals, people, vehicles, and food are important.
- Books with many pictures and short stories can be added to the environment.
- Dramatic play materials encourage conversation.

Summary

Infants and toddlers have the capacity to become proficient language learners in the first 3 years of life.

- Language is used for communication with others and is affected by the quality of the child's relationships, the social context, and the environment.
- Throughout the first 3 years, infants and toddlers learn to make the sounds of the language spoken to them; combine sounds into words and combine words into sentences; learn the syntax, pragmatics, and prosody of language; learn the meaning of an astonishing number of words; and communicate in a variety of ways—the furrowing of a brow, a loud screech, whining, pointing, talking, and shouting.
- Girls do seem to talk earlier and speak more than boys in the first 20 months of life. However, differences in language development between boys and girls do not

seem to last, and after age 20 months, fewer differences are found in the vocabularies of boys and girls.
- Hearing loss and prematurity are two factors that affect language development in young children.
- Cultural differences exist in how children are viewed as conversational partners.
- Young children do have the capacity to learn two languages simultaneously, and there are strategies to support infants and toddlers as they are learning.
- Young children progress through clear stages of language development.
- Adults can use 12 major strategies to support language development.
- When infant and toddler teachers are more responsive and sensitive, then the language development of the children increases.

Key Terms

baby talk
choice questions
closed questions
communication
communicative-linguistic
    parameters
conversational dance

conversation-eliciting style
directive style
infant-directed speech
language
language delay
open-ended questions
parallel talk

ritual constraints
self-talk
semantic elaboration
sign language
system constraints
true questions

Reflections and Resources for the Reader

REFLECTIONS

1. What are the key strategies that adults can use to support children as they learn two languages?

2. Identify the important features of a child care and education setting that support infants' and toddlers' language.

OBSERVATION AND APPLICATION OPPORTUNITIES

1. Jeff is 2 months old and his parents want him to learn to speak both English and Spanish. His dad speaks Spanish and English quite well and his mom speaks English. What advice would you give them?
2. Choose one stage of language development and expand on the concepts highlighted for that age group. What are the implications of the information for parents and teachers?
3. Choose one of the 12 strategies for promoting language development and give examples of a conversation between an adult and a child, with the adult using the strategy.
4. Observe infants or toddlers in a child development and education setting. Identify the skills that two children of different ages have in receptive and expressive language.

SUPPLEMENTARY ARTICLES AND BOOKS TO READ

Honig, A. S. (n.d.). Infants & toddlers: How to read to very young children. *Scholastic.* Retrieved from www.scholastic.com/teachers/article/infants-toddlers-how-read-very-young-children

Nemeth, K. (2012). *Many languages, building connections: Supporting infants and toddlers who are dual language learners.* Boston: Gryphon House.

Prieto, H. V. (2009). Rocking and rolling: Supporting infants, toddlers, and their families. One language, two languages, three languages. *Young Children, 64*(1), 52–53.

Suskind, D. L. (2012). Caregiver interventions to enrich early language. Retrieved from eclkc.ohs.acf.hhs.gov/hslc/tta-system/teaching/Broadcast%20Calls/fps-language-qa-7-2012.pdf

Vallotton, C., & Ayoub, C. (2011). Use your words: The role of language in the development of toddlers' self-regulation. *Early Childhood Research Quarterly, 26*(2), 169–181.

INTERESTING LINKS

www.deafness.about.com
About Deafness/Hard of Hearing This Web site provides excellent information on causes of hearing impairment. Also covered are topics such as medical issues, deaf culture, and sign language.

eclkc.ohs.acf.hhs.gov/
Head Start Early Childhood Learning & Knowledge Center (ECLKC). This site provides numerous excellent resources for infant/toddler educators.

www.pitc.org/
PITC provides many materials on language development.

www.zerotothree.org/
ZERO TO THREE: Early Language & Literacy This site offers articles, podcasts, handouts, and instructional materials.

10

Motor Development and Learning

LEARNING OUTCOMES

After reading this chapter, you will be able to:

- Describe how children develop reflexes and the unique ways in which attributes, such as gender and temperament, influence motor development

- Explain key issues in motor development, including the relationship between culture and motor development, types of movement, the link between perception and motor actions, and strategies to support motor development and learning

- Describe the special needs that young children may have in motor development

- Identify the key components of quality programs that support motor development and learning

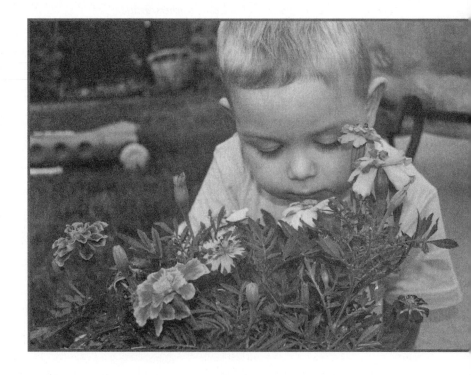

Joella flapped her arms and ran around the yard with glee. Every inch of her body spoke to her energy and excitement.

Michael froze in place, a serious, uncertain look on his face. His body was slightly hunched as he listened intently to the distant sound of a barking dog.

Raj squatted to study a bug moving across the play yard, a picture of concentration.

Helen, their teacher, watched them and thought, "I know so much about what they feel and think by watching their little bodies."

The Uniqueness of Each Child

In so many ways we think of infants and toddlers in terms of their motor development. We even name an entire stage of development after the toddling, balancing gait of the beginning walker. Our first thoughts of milestones, aside from smiling and sleeping through the night, tend to be motor milestones—rolling over, crawling, standing, and walking. It's not just the adults who think about motor development, either. Motor development occupies much of a baby's time and effort: moving her body to get where she wants to be, and reaching and holding to bring objects to look at and taste.

Capacities

Current theories of motor development propose that it is a complex, ongoing process of learning and not a simple process of maturation (Adolph, 2008). Throughout the first years of life, and even prenatally, infants and toddlers are constantly adjusting their movements to changes in height, weight, proportion, and posture. Whereas reflexes determine the earliest movements, the process of learning quickly takes over and becomes the driving force in motor development.

Infants are moving long before they are born. Using ultrasound, doctors have observed extension-like movements of the upper spine as early as 5 to 6 weeks of gestation, and movements of arms and legs by 8 to 9 weeks (Malina, 2004). The motor activity of the fetus is part of the developmental process, as the body and brain develop and store information about movement patterns. These movements help the fetus develop muscles and move through the birth canal.

Reflexes

Newborns are physically active, and reflexes that are an extension of prenatal movements drive much of their activity. Reflexes are the body's neurobehavioral reaction to events. Although reflexes have traditionally been understood to occur at the brainstem level, automatically keeping the infant alive, even reflexes are now understood to include regulatory processes between the adult and the infant and are imbued with culture (Liu &Tronick, 2011). Of the nearly 75 reflexes present in the newborn, the most well known support feeding, gazing, and grasping—as you can see in Figure 10.1.

The first reflexes used by an infant are referred to as **primitive reflexes**. The **rooting reflex** and **sucking reflex** help the newborn find the nipple and begin to eat, although babies also root and suck on their own hands to comfort themselves. When the baby feels a slight pressure against his cheek, he turns his head toward the pressure, "rooting" around for the nipple. When his lips come in contact with a surface, he begins sucking. Newborns are already practiced at sucking; it is reflexive and does not need to be learned. Newborns also have a reflex that

primitive reflexes

Immediate and involuntary reaction to a stimulus; in newborns they serve the purpose of survival until higher brain functions develop.

rooting reflex

A newborn's response, when stroked on the side of the face, to move her face in the direction being stroked, open her mouth, and search for a nipple.

sucking reflex

A newborn's response to suck when an object brushes across the lips.

FIGURE 10.1   **Primitive reflexes**

Tonic neck reflex

Grasp reflex

Step reflex

Crawl reflex

Moro reflex

Rooting

protects them from swallowing anything other than liquids. They have a tongue-thrust reflex that pushes everything out of the mouth. It's a good idea to wait to begin spoon feeding until this reflex disappears.

The **Moro reflex**, or startle reflex, is a physical response to a loud sound or the sense of falling. The baby throws back her head, extends her arms and legs, and then pulls them back in. The posture also seems to act as communication to parents and teachers that the baby is stressed and needs to be picked up and comforted. The **tonic neck reflex** moves the arms in response to the baby's head turning in supine (lying on his back) position. When the baby's head is turned to the right, his right arm will thrust out, his left will be raised straight up. If he turns his head to the left, the arms will adjust. This may help the baby keep one hand in front of his eyes. This reflex begins to disappear as the baby begins to bring his

Moro reflex

A newborn's startled response when experiencing a loud sound or the sense of falling.

tonic neck reflex

A newborn's response of maintaining an asymmetrical posture, with the head turned toward one arm extended upward and the other arm extended outward to the side.

hands together in the midline, where he can see them easily. The **palmar grasp reflex** causes the baby to close her fingers around something placed in the palm. She will grasp an adult's finger or hair, or a toy. Her feet will also curl when lightly brushed. When a baby is held upright, with her feet touching a solid surface, the **step reflex** makes the baby appear to be walking.

These primitive reflexes are very effective for the first few months and then begin to fade. As the primitive reflexes fade, another set of reflexes begins to emerge. **Postural reflexes** help the baby resist gravity and provide the basis for developing balance, posture, and voluntary movement. The postural reflexes become integrated into the central nervous system and function throughout life. These reflexes help a person turn his head or shift his weight to regain balance. They also help modulate the muscle tone so that a person may move his head without throwing his entire body into a reaction.

Even though reflexes are dominant for several months, the baby's interest in her parents and teachers, and in the play opportunities they provide, are important factors in early motor development. Being supported in various positions (tummy, back, snuggly, on the hip or shoulder) provides many opportunities to practice head and trunk control, using arms for support, and legs for kicking.

With a healthy brain and muscles, babies make remarkable progress in their ability to use their bodies to perceive sensory information and move toward or manipulate the source of the information. Within the first 3 years, babies make the journey from little controlled movement to running and jumping, and they advance from sucking on a hand to calm themselves to using buttons and zippers to get dressed.

Bodily Self-Awareness

Awareness of self is usually thought of in the emotional domain. That is the invisible, internal self. Researchers are now exploring how the very young child learns about his own body. In a series of fascinating studies, researchers are finding ways to "ask" children in what ways they are aware of their bodies: first, in relation to the sizes of openings and objects; second, as a group of parts that work together in many ways to make a whole. Brownell, Nichols, Svetlova, Zerwas, and Ramani (2010) performed a series of experiments on bodily self-awareness, or topography, with toddlers between 18 and 30 months.

Sticker task: The toddler and parent, an examiner (E) and the examiner's assistant (A) are together. The E says, "Look, I'm going to put a sticker on A there. See, I put a sticker there (touching or pointing). E gives child a sticker and says, "Now you put this sticker on you right there (no pointing) so it's just like A." The child's doing so demonstrates an ability to experience oneself internally but also as others see you.

Body size tasks:

- *Too small clothes.* E dresses a 12-inch doll in a dress, coat, and hat. Then E hands the child and identical item and says, "Here's your coat. Put it on." Actually trying to put the tiny clothing demonstates a lack of awareness of body size.
- *Door size.* With the parent on the other side of a styrofoam board, the toddler needed to choose between two doors to reach her. One was 12 inches by 12 inches and easy to crawl through. The other was about 3 inches wide and 3 feet tall—impossible for the toddler to pass. The choice of door size reflected the child's body size awareness.

palmar grasp reflex
A newborn's response to grasp and hold an object placed in the palm.

step reflex
Reflex that makes a baby appear to be walking when the baby is held upright with feet touching a solid surface.

postural reflexes
They help the infant resist gravity while managing posture, balance, and movement.

Some of the first discoveries of movement are learning about what pieces move! What is Rosie learning?

- *Replica toys.* The toddlers were first in a room with several toys their size (table and chairs, slide, and car to drive). The children then went to another room with toy-sized replicas of the first toys. If the child tried to sit on the tiny chair or put his foot in the car, it reflected a lack of awareness of body size.

Attributes

Attributes, motor abilities, and interests certainly vary within a wide range from person to person. To what extent are these differences related to gender and to what extent are they simply individual differences?

Gender

The bodies of men and women certainly differ. Men tend to be bigger and stronger, with bodies evolved to be hunters. Women are smaller, with bodies evolved to reproduce. But are these differences present in infants and toddlers? It is difficult to sort out whether the gender differences we see in motor development are a result of inherent differences, different environmental experiences and expectations, or simply stereotypes.

As with all other areas of development, we look increasingly at the effect of genes and hormones. Not that nature trumps nurture, but the neurodevelopmental role interacting with the physical and social environment is helping us understand just where gender might have more influence. Animal studies introduce male hormones to the womb of a pregnant mouse and produce female pups with more male sexualized behavior. Clearly, this is not an option with humans but some studies simply look at the different approaches of boys and girls to motor ability. Many look at a unique situation in which female fetuses are exposed to an unusually high level of testosterone in the womb because of a genetic disorder and the female child develops some more traditionally male physical and play-oriented behavior. Hines (2011) found that toddler boys and girls with high levels of testosterone (because of a genetic disorder) prefer toys that move in space such as balls. Both also demonstrate increased physical aggression, and more dominance in play. Benenson, Tenneyson, and Wrangham (2011) showed 6 to 9-month-old infants an adult male or an adult female cuddling or punching a balloon. Boys were far more likely to imitate the propulsive movement of the adult male punching the balloon than any other combination: "The typical boy differs little from the typical girl on activity level, but the most and least active children in a group are likely to be a boy and a girl, respectively" (Eaton, 2009).

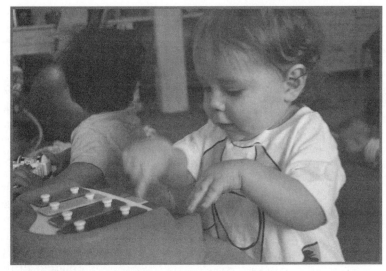

Terry is demonstrating how interrelated the areas of development can be. She is resisting gravity and balancing to stand. She has isolated a finger to strike the key. She is using language and imitation to sing a song and she is socially engaged with her audience.

Temperament

Temperament may affect motor development more directly than gender. The motivation of an active child to move, or the inhibition of a more fearful child, would certainly affect the competence a child achieves in motor skills. Hussey-Gardner describes some children as "motor driven," wanting to try everything and highly motivated to learn and practice motor skills. Others are described as "motor cautious," needing time to watch others before trying new activities (Hussey-Gardner, 2003).

Development and Learning Through Relationships

Infants and toddlers learn through their bodies and express themselves with their bodies. As they develop their relationships, they use their bodies to come close and connect to others or to move away.

Culture and Motor Development

As in nearly every aspect of child rearing, cultural beliefs and practices differ in approaches to motor development. Comparing cultural differences in opportunities for movement and the resultant differences in both the timing and the quality of mastering motor movements has led to a number of questions about the timing and progression of motor development. Are certain early experiences necessary

CULTURE CLOSE UP

A very friendly, enthusiastic Kenyan woman became a teacher in an infant room. Her English was competent and children and families loved her. Every day she found time to massage and exercise the legs of the young infants. She would hold them up as they "walked." The children seemed to enjoy the active play and many began walking at about 9 months. Parents were sort of pleased but not altogether. In some ways, the parents felt the teacher was pushing the children. In addition, the parents were not expecting their children to walk that early. Rather, the parents were expecting much longer periods of children's relative immobility when the parent could better control when and where the child went. The director knew he was looking at a clash of cultures, wasn't sure that one was more "right" than the other, and was not at all sure what was best for the children. How might you think it through? What might you do?

for motor development? Is the timeline of motor development genetically predetermined? Or do children develop the motor skills needed for living effectively in their own culture?

Adults provide different motor experiences for babies around the world. They vary from carrying the baby at all times to encouraging sitting, crawling, and walking. The developmental milestone timelines used in the United States may be relevant only for babies in our own culture.

Some cultures emphasize keeping babies in vertical postures and others in horizontal postures. Much of the cross-cultural research was done in the 1960s and 1970s. The Zinecanteco Indians of southeastern Mexico carry their babies in a *rebozo*, a sling across the mother's belly. The infants are quiet and alert but not very exploratory. However, they develop motor skills in the same order as children in the United States, even though their environment has been so different. The timeline of acquiring these skills is about a month later than children in the United States (Brazelton, 1972).

The Ache mothers of eastern Paraguay carry their babies all of the time. An Ache baby is in a sling on his mother's body 93% of the daylight hours and on her lap all night. Even at 1 year, their mothers will hold them 40% of the day. At 18 months, toddlers are taught to ride in baskets or piggyback on their father's back (Kaplan & Dove, 1987). Ache children begin walking about 9 months later than children in the United States.

The !Kung San, known as the Bushmen of the Kalahari Desert, have infants and toddlers with advanced motor skills compared to babies in Western countries. San mothers carry young infants positioned vertically in a sling. They invest time in promoting motor skills such as standing and walking and encourage babies to explore by 7 months. San children achieve motor skills earlier and better and concentrate harder than American toddlers (Konner, 1977).

Some cultural practices may seem at odds with promoting motor development (Thompson-Rangel, 1994). Adults who dress and feed older toddlers and even preschool-age children serve the cultural values of the Latino tradition. The Hopi and Navajo practice of keeping babies in cradleboards serves their traditional mother-infant relationships. When your cultural background differs from that of the families in your child care setting, it is important to remember that children from all cultural practices do achieve the same motor milestones eventually. Cultural practices and beliefs affect motor development, and cultural values need to be considered in the child development and education program's curriculum for motor development.

Motor Development Through Relationships

Notice in this video how the child can sit with stability and use his hands. Watch how the baby changes strategies to achieve his goal of putting the blocks into the container. Observe how the infant grasps and releases objects.

If simply the position and amount of time we carry our babies affect their motor development, then imagine the impact of the opportunities we provide for movement or the handling of objects, of our comfort with movement, and our attitudes toward safety and risk taking. Although teachers are not making a genetic contribution to a child's motor abilities, they are certainly having an influence at the environmental level.

Principles and Progression of Motor Development

Some common trends in motor development seem to be fairly constant across cultures or relationships. Development is

- **cephalocaudal**, muscle control moving from the head (cephalo) to the tail (caudal)
- **proximal-distal**, beginning with the midline (proximal or near) and progressing outward and downward (distal or distance)
- beginning with the large muscle groups and proceeding to the small muscle groups

Typical milestone charts are organized in ways that separate large and small muscle skills, but development is more interactive than that. For example, as a 3-month-old is gaining head and neck control, she will enjoy being on her tummy and looking around. As the control strengthens, she will be able to use a hand to hold something while she holds her head up. When she is able to sit with stability, not using her hands to balance, both hands are suddenly free to handle and play with objects. It is only after she has mastered stable sitting that she will develop the ability to pick things up, move them from hand to hand, put them into containers, and throw them. The Developmental Trends and Responsive Interactions chart at the end of this chapter lists the motor milestones.

> **cephalocaudal**
> Moving from head (cephalus) to tail (caudal).

> **proximal-distal**
> Moving in the direction from close (proximal) to distant (distal).

Movement

For infants and toddlers, motor skills are a way to achieve their goals in relationships (staying close to the care teacher) and in learning (figuring out how rings fit a stick). Most importantly, achieving new motor skills is a goal in itself. Infants and toddlers work tirelessly, attempting a new skill and practicing it over and over until they are proficient. However, they may go about their motor tasks in unique ways:

 Each child's development is truly unique. In this video, observe the differences in how two children learn to creep and crawl.

> I've always been impressed by the different paths babies take in their physical development on the way to walking. It's rare to see a behavior that starts out with such wide natural variation, yet becomes so uniform after only a few months. (Kutner, 1993)

▶▶▶ OBSERVATION INVITATION **10.2**

 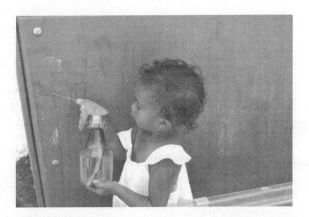

Sometimes a tool requires a whole new set of motor skills in order to be used as a tool. How are these art experiences also motor experiences?

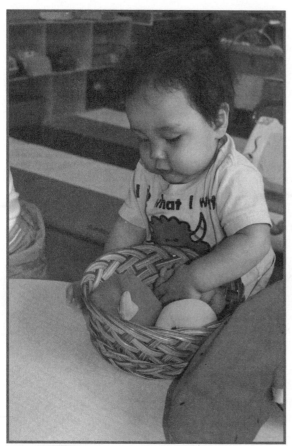

This young child's proprioceptive system is at work as he reaches into the basket and responds to the texture of the soft material.

Researchers who study the development of motor skills in babies see the progression of development as a dynamic system rather than a genetically preordained series of accomplishments. Adolph (2008), for example, sees motor development as a flexible response to new and challenging situations. Each new posture brings the baby into contact with new aspects of the world, new perceptual information. Being able to see and touch the bottom bookshelf presents the goal of emptying the shelf of its books. Being able to see and touch the cupboard door presents the goal of opening and closing it. Each new posture requires practice in reestablishing balance and control in pursuit of other interests (Adolph & Eppler, 2002).

This view of babies developing motor skills as solutions to problems posed by the interplay between perception and action is called the *dynamic systems approach* by researcher Esther Thelen. Rejecting the idea that motor development is purely maturational, Thelen describes it as an ongoing problem solving of the tension between a child's goals or desires and the constraints of his body's mechanics. The baby is constantly trying to reach or move and constantly correcting his efforts to adjust for his changing body weight, proportions, and postures (Thelen, 2000; Thelen & Smith, 1996). For example, the infant's head is large and heavy in comparison to the rest of the body. However, holding that head and neck upright helps the infant look around. As infants' trunk and limbs grow stronger, they are better able to support their head in an upright condition providing more opportunities for exploration. A more thorough description of motor progression is available at the end of the chapter in the section "Developmental Trends and Responsive Interactions."

As Lois Barclay Murphy (1994) describes so beautifully, the first steps are not the end of the locomotive adventure for the baby:

> As I sat on a bench at the side of the road in the zoo, watching the children brought by their mothers or fathers, I rarely saw a little boy walking quietly beside his parent. One was hopping, another was jumping. Others were leaping, or skipping, or loping, raising each foot higher than it needed to be lifted for ordinary walking. Some children waved their arms. Each one seemed to savor the feeling of the moment, wanting to discover the possibilities of locomotion. (p. 1)

vestibular system

Affects balance, muscle tone, equilibrium responses, the ability to use both sides of the body together, and coordination of the head, neck, and eye movements.

proprioceptive system

Gives the nervous system input on the position of muscles, joints, and tendons.

Vestibular and proprioceptive information speak directly to our motor systems. The **vestibular system** controls our body's sense of balance or equilibrium. The **proprioceptive system** controls information coming from muscles, tendons, joints, and the inner ear, and it detects the motion or position of the body or a limb by responding to sensations arising within the body. This sensory information is part of the motor system.

Several laboratory studies have attempted to determine exactly what sensory information infants use to plan the motor act of reaching. In one study, 6-month-old infants were presented with objects that gave off sounds under three conditions of illumination: in full vision, in the dark with the object glowing and making a sound, and in the dark with the location specified by sound alone. The babies used the same reaching motions with the same frequencies for objects in the light and for glowing objects in the dark. The reaches for the sound-emitting objects in the dark were faster, of shorter duration, and had more errors compared to the other conditions. These findings indicate that vision of the hand did not appear to affect infants' reaching in this situation, whereas vision of the target did (Clifton, Rochat, Robin, & Berthier, 1994).

A second study set up a more complex problem that required accommodating to somewhat challenging visual information, being able to predict an object's trajectory, and using the proprioceptive information of their own muscles to anticipate how and where to reach to capture the object. Infants were presented with a moving object under two lighting conditions to investigate the role of vision in early reaching. Infants were tested twice, at 5 and 7 ½ months of age, with a moving object in the light and the same object painted with luminescent paint in the dark. Infants successfully contacted the glowing object on about half of their attempts at both ages, although 7 ½-month-olds reached more often. Infants took into account the motion of the target object by aiming their reaches ahead of the object. These results suggest that proprioceptive feedback of their own arm and the sight of the target allow for successful reaching with limited visual information, even in relatively complex reaching tasks. The infants' success also demonstrates their ability to adapt their movements and reaching strategy to the speed and trajectory of the target object in order to reach predictively (Robin, Berthier, & Clifton, 1996).

When infants and toddlers are unable to integrate sensory information to use their bodies effectively in the environment, they may need particular supports. For example, a baby who cannot stand to be touched because she is hypersensitive may find it difficult to bond with a parent or teacher. She may be hungry but unable to tolerate a nipple in her mouth. The proprioceptive experience of being lifted and put down again can be overwhelming. All of the caregiving activities that are meant to soothe and comfort may feel like assaults. Adults caring for hypersensitive babies need to develop a firm and gentle touch. They need to use gentle pressure around the mouth to make feeding more comfortable. And they need to stay calm and limit the variations in position and handling used with the baby.

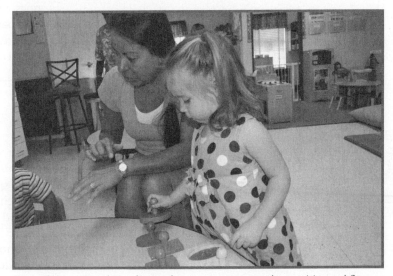

Aimee has mastered standing and can concentrate on the cognitive and fine motor tasks of doing this puzzle.

Affordances for Motor Development

An affordance is the way the environment is perceived as having possibilities for action. In order for infants and toddlers to engage in new small or large

STRATEGIES TO SUPPORT MOTOR DEVELOPMENT AND LEARNING

Infants and toddlers are highly motivated to use their bodies to move and to use tools. These skills do not develop automatically, though. Some strategies you can use to support motor development follow:

1. Provide opportunities for young babies to play on their tummies. Tummy time helps babies strengthen their trunk and neck control.
2. Limit the use of swings, infant seats, bouncers, or other furniture that restrains infants. When caring for several children at once, offer toys on the floor for tummy time, space for crawlers, or hanging toys for reaching from supine. Restraining babies makes them passive and discourages active exploration. Think of using their bodies as active, learning opportunities.
3. When young babies are playing on the floor on their backs, offering toys a little off to the side and above the head encourages reaching and turning, which develops into rolling over.
4. Create an environment that encourages movement at every stage of motor development. Think about how you can help babies develop an active lifestyle from the beginning, countering the possibility of childhood obesity.
5. Firm, washable cubes, pads, and inclines can be arranged to create interesting and challenging surfaces for crawling, creeping, walking, and climbing.
6. As mobile infants begin cruising, they need long, low, stable surfaces to hold. In homes, they use sofas and coffee tables. In centers, if they are using shelving units, be sure they are bolted to the wall.
7. Small stairs with platforms, climbing bars bolted to walls, and sturdy structures encourage toddlers to climb. If the stairs and platform provide access to a window or the climbing bars face a mirror allowing the toddlers to see themselves, there is even more motivation for climbing.
8. Use music for movement, not just as background sound. Infants love being held while you dance with them, swooping and spinning to the rhythm. Toddlers love singing and playing instruments while dancing or marching.
9. Spend as much time outdoors as the climate allows.
10. Be aware of the child's changing abilities to handle objects and offer materials that match these abilities. Young infants need lightweight rattles, older infants need small objects they can pick up with a **raking grasp** but large enough to prevent choking when they mouth them.
11. New walkers enjoy carrying objects in each hand. Older toddlers enjoy the precision of fitting rings on sticks, stacking cups, or fitting pegs in pegboards.
12. Use small chairs and tables for meals, allowing toddlers to sit and rise by themselves.

raking grasp

A young infant's use of open fingers to "rake" an object into the palm.

motor actions, the environment must offer opportunities or invitations. Using a popular evaluation tool, the *Affordances in the Home Environment for Motor Development*, researchers look at outside space, inside space, daily activities, fine and large motor toys, and child and family characteristics. Studies find that these affordances in infancy can predict motor and cognitive success later in life (Miquelote, Santos, Cacola, Montebelo & Gabbard, 2012). This same group, not surprisingly, found that families in higher socioeconomic brackets provided more affordances. Care teachers and families need to understand the impact of these opportunities and provide them during the first year of life. Thinking in terms of possibilities is an effective intervention.

Children with Special Needs

The progression of motor development consumes the interest of infants and toddlers as they practice the skills they have and undertake new ones. Healthy motor development is dependent on the brain, the central nervous system, the muscles, the bones, and the opportunities infants have for practice. However, motor development, often taken for granted, is vulnerable to a number of assaults.

Motor Concerns

Injury, prenatal substance exposure, poor nutrition, and disease can all affect motor development. Motor disorders may have a variety of symptoms, as described in Figure 10.2.

The most common motor disorder in infancy is **cerebral palsy (CP)**. Cerebral palsy is a nonprogressive disorder of the motor (muscle) control area of the developing brain: "The diagnosis is dependent upon two findings: evidence of nonprogressive damage to the developing brain and the presence of a resulting impairment of the motor (neuromuscular) control system of the body; the latter usually accompanied by a physiological impairment and functional disability" (UCP, 2009). Next to mental retardation, CP is the most common disorder of the developing brain; 70% of cerebral palsy occurs prenatally, 20% in the birthing process, and 10% in the first 2 years of life.

Cerebral palsy is a somewhat general term for a variety of conditions. Infants and toddlers with cerebral palsy may not be able to inhibit their primitive reflexes and so they continue to be subjected to reflexive reactions rather than developing voluntary actions. Because of central nervous system injury, infants may have **spastic cerebral palsy**, with muscles that constantly remain so tight that they proscribe voluntary action. This could affect the legs, one side of the body, or the whole body, depending on the location and severity of the injury to the brain (MOD, 2009a). **Athetoid cerebral palsy** affects the entire body with fluctuating muscle tone that may result in uncontrolled movements and difficulty speaking or eating. **Ataxic cerebral palsy** affects balance and coordination, creating an

cerebral palsy (CP)
A group of motor, postural, and physical disorders that result from a brain injury or abnormal brain development.

spastic cerebral palsy
Muscles are stiffly and permanently contracted; affects 70% to 80% of patients.

athetoid cerebral palsy
Characterized by uncontrolled, slow, writhing movements of the hands, feet, arms, or legs and, in some cases, the muscles of the face and tongue, causing grimacing or drooling.

ataxic cerebral palsy
A rare form of cerebral palsy that affects the sense of balance and depth perception.

FIGURE 10.2   **Warning signs of motor disorders**

- The child's limbs are stiff.
- The child's muscles seem floppy and loose.
- The child doesn't walk within expected parameters.
- The child walks on her toes.
- The child favors one hand or one side of his body.
- The child seems very clumsy.
- The child is constantly moving.
- The child has trouble grasping and manipulating objects.
- The child drools and has difficulty eating.
- The child's motor skills are regressing.

Source: From Baby Center (2008).

unsteady gait or difficulty with fine motor tasks (MOD, 2009a). Physical therapy can help children achieve the maximum possible control of their bodies within these conditions.

Effects of Motor Disorders

Motor disorders may affect more than movement. When a child is unable to participate in his part of the attachment relationship, the parent-child relationship may suffer. If the child is unable to smile at parents, to follow their movements visually, to reach out to be lifted, or to cuddle when held, the adults may be confused as to the child's feelings. Teachers and early interventionists are often most helpful by pointing out the ways the child signals his pleasure and comfort in being with familiar, well-loved people.

Emotional and cognitive development may proceed despite a motor disorder. Sometimes adults need to learn to read the unique cues of the child, whereas other times adaptations need to be made to materials in the environment. One of the side effects of a motor disorder is that the baby or toddler may be inaccurately assessed as having cognitive delays because so many developmental assessments rely on motor skills to demonstrate cognitive understanding. For example, we expect a baby to pull a cloth off a hidden object to demonstrate object permanence or to stack several blocks to demonstrate the ability to imitate. Children who lack the motor ability to perform these actions may be unable to show that they understand the concepts being assessed. Unfortunately, because of the limits of the testing situation, these children may have no way to demonstrate their knowledge.

Programs That Enhance Motor Development and Learning

Opportunities that invite movement, provide interesting materials to handle, and include attentive and engaged adult partners can be part of any program or experience for infants and toddlers. In this section, we discuss three programs with the potential to enhance motor development. Child development and education programs, serving more than 6 million infants and toddlers, have the potential to either support or impede motor development. Physical therapy and occupational therapy, professional services included in early intervention for children with disabilities, are briefly illustrated. Then, in a change of perspective, we examine a relatively new and still unstudied form of psychotherapy used with infants and toddlers: movement-based psychotherapy, a method of using the movement patterns of infants and toddlers as a way of understanding their experiences and increasing their empathy. Each of these approaches has the potential to significantly impact the quality of movement patterns of infants and toddlers.

Child Development and Education Programs

With more than half of America's infants and toddlers in out-of-home care, the program environment is influencing the quality of life of America's children. If teachers understand the process and pattern of early motor development, they can support it with minimal effort. Infants and toddlers need opportunities to move freely, balanced with holding, cuddling, and rocking. The strategies listed on page 236 provide many ideas for activities that support motor development. This section contains some broader guidelines.

Understanding a child's current developmental capacities allows you to provide developmentally appropriate activities. Very young babies, working on head control and functioning within the grasp reflex, need "tummy time"— time to play on a firm surface while practicing lifting their heads and shoulders off the ground. The surface should not have any coverings that could cause suffocation if the baby got caught up in them. On her back, she might enjoy turning her head slowly to visually track a toy the care teacher moves from one side to another. Throughout the first year of life, infants enjoy playing on the floor, rolling, sitting, and crawling—with an adult nearby talking to them and playing with them. Selections of small toys to hold or put into and take out of containers, pop-up boxes, and shape boards are available.

The important part of the environment, though, is a sense that physical activity is fun and encouraged. Oftentimes, teachers with too many babies to care for use a variety of swings, bouncy seats, and other equipment for containing babies. When this is the baby's experience hour after hour, he learns that he is not supposed to move and use his body to explore. He becomes passive and bored. Losing the ability to become interested in the world, he finds that nothing but being contained is comforting. Not only is the baby losing valuable opportunities for motor development and learning, he may be setting lifelong patterns of inactivity that lead to obesity and disease. In addition to the constraint, many of these pieces of equipment vibrate and play sounds at the same time. This can be simply too much stimulation for a baby. Any equipment used to restrain babies may have harmful effects, but next we describe one piece of equipment that is truly dangerous.

Baby Walkers

Child development and education programs often use baby seats, swings, and other equipment to provide a variety of postural and motor experiences for babies. All of these pieces of equipment should be used with discretion, but the mobile baby walker should not be in any program. A mobile baby walker is a piece of nursery equipment that holds a baby, who is too young to stand and walk, in a standing position. When the baby's feet touch the ground, small pressures of weight cause the walker to roll. The American Academy of Pediatrics (AAP, 2004) and the National Association for Children's Hospitals and Related Institutions have urged the Consumer Product Safety Commission to ban their manufacture and sale in the United States. The Canadian government has already banned the sale, advertisement, and importation of baby walkers.

Even following years of recalls and new standards, 3,600 children under age 5 were injured by baby walkers between 2004 and 2006 and five deaths resulted (Consumer Products Safety

BOX 10.1

Baby Walkers Are Dangerous!

Even when babies are supervised, they can be injured while using baby walkers. Documented injuries include the following:

- Rolling down stairs: Most common accident causing broken bones and head injuries
- Burns: Higher reach and mobility lead to burns from coffee cups, pots on stoves, radiators, fireplaces, and space heaters
- Drowning: Falls into pools, bathtubs, or toilets
- Poisoning: Higher reach for access to household chemicals
- Pinched fingers and toes: Caught between walker and furniture

Source: AAP (2004).

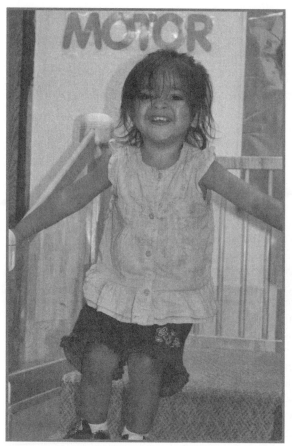

Aida is smiling with the challenge of walking down a ramp.

neuromuscular

The interrelationship between the central nervous system and the muscular system.

tonicity

The strength, tension, or health of a muscle.

low muscle tone

Hypotonia; muscles that are loose and floppy, limiting motor skills and postural support.

high muscle tone

Hypertonia; muscles that are tight and contracted, making movement constrained.

Commission, 2009). Most of these injuries happened when adults were watching but were unable to respond quickly enough (a mobile walker can move more than 3 feet in 1 second!). The American Academy of Pediatrics further urges parents not to leave their child in care anywhere that mobile baby walkers are utilized (see Box 10.1).

Although it seems as though the early experience of walking would be beneficial and enriching, a study of the effect of early experiences with walkers (Siegel & Burton, 1999) finds the opposite is true. The authors describe the use of walkers as early deprivation because walkers are designed in a way that deprives the baby of visual access to his own moving limbs. In a study of 109 infants from 6 to 15 months, the researchers found that babies with walker experience sat, crawled, and walked later than babies who didn't use walkers. The walker babies also scored lower on the Bayley Scales of Mental and Motor Development, a widely used assessment of cognitive, language, and motor development. The authors concluded that the risks far outweigh the benefits of walker use.

Physical and Occupational Therapy

Infants and toddlers identified with disabilities, or at risk for disabilities, may receive special therapies for their motor systems. Physical therapists tend to work with head and trunk control, the limbs, the large muscles, stability, balance, and locomotion. Occupational therapists work with the limbs and fingers, feeding and swallowing, adaptive and self-help skills. In fact, their work often overlaps. Both work with the **neuromuscular** system, composed of the central nervous system (brain and spine), as it learns and stores memories of movement patterns, and the muscles, changing **tonicity** or learning new motor patterns. Conditions such as Down syndrome often cause muscles to be weak and floppy—**low muscle tone**—making it difficult to achieve control of movement. Conditions such as cerebral palsy cause muscles to be too tight to move easily—**high muscle tone**—also limiting control. Neurological issues such as cerebral palsy or seizures may cause the primitive reflexes to remain in action, driving the body's movements. An additional group of infants and toddlers apt to receive occupational or physical therapy services are children with sensory impairments such as visual or hearing impairments. Given the strong connections between sensory perception and motor development, the benefits of motor intervention are obvious.

The most beneficial time to intervene in the neuromuscular or perceptual-motor domain is during the first 3 years of life. The central nervous system and muscles are still forming and able to learn patterns or sometimes find alternate neurological routes.

Approaches to intervention involve observation and assessment of the baby's movement patterns, muscle tone, and postures. They attend to the child's **mobility** (the ability to move his limbs), to control his **stability** (posture), to bear his own weight, and to manipulate objects. Many therapists also observe children's ability to tolerate and integrate sensory experiences in their environment. Treatment generally involves the therapist exercising or working the body and providing movement opportunities to stimulate the use of new neuronal patterns. Various sensory experiences such as with ice, brushing, vibration, or weight packs may be introduced to stimulate the muscles. Swinging, rocking, and swiveling experiences may be used to reach the proprioceptive and vestibular senses. Treatments are incorporated into the daily routines, activities, and even settings of children's lives in the hope of having the greatest generalization of skill development.

Movement Psychotherapy

This chapter has described the developmental progression of the motor system and suggested ways to support it. In a shift of perspective, we now describe a form of psychotherapy called *movement therapy*. The premise of this work is that the way we move our bodies is an expression of our experiences, our relationships, and our understanding of the world (Creighton, 2011; Loman, Cellini, Johnson, & Hallett, 2009). For infants and toddlers, in particular, whose lives are experienced in the sensorimotor realm, "nonverbal behaviors are expressions of self and have potential to be used for meaningful communication" (Tortora, 2004, p. 6). The movement psychotherapist is not trying to change the quality of movement so much as using the quality of movement as communication. The therapist "must always look through, behind, under, and over nonverbal behaviors, thinking, What might this child be trying to tell me through these actions?" (Tortora, 2004, p. 6).

The movement psychotherapist is observing the movement for its coherence, its ease, its rhythm, and the relationship between personal space and general space. A child who starts and stops actions, changing direction or intention, may have little experience with complete, satisfying circles of interaction. The freedom or lack of freedom shown by the child in moving through space, using the different areas of a room, may reflect his ability to safely relate outside of his own body. The ability to expand movement and contain it again may speak to the child's sense of safety in emotional expression.

The movement psychotherapist "tries on" the child's movement patterns, imitating them to see how they feel. Is there discomfort? Is there a feeling of constraint? No sense of control? The therapist then uses her ability to imitate the child's movements with variation to begin a nonverbal dialogue with the child. Tortora (2004) describes beginning her work with a child with autism by touching his outstretched toe with her own—creating their own nonverbal language. As their work progresses, she is able to support the child's discovery that he can maintain a sense of relationship with her, and with his mother, even as he is lost in the terror of a tantrum. Using their bodies, the therapist and the mother are able to communicate their emotional connection to the little boy as he finds his way back to some sense of control.

mobility
The ability to move freely, independently.

stability
The ability to maintain a posture.

pincer grasp
A child's more refined grasp of index finger and thumb to pick up an object.

DEVELOPMENTAL TRENDS AND RESPONSIVE INTERACTIONS

MOTOR DEVELOPMENT AND LEARNING

Infants and toddlers develop motor skills for locomotion, for using tools, and for coordinating perceptual information and motor actions.

Development	Example
0–4 months (infant)	
• Infants lift head when held at shoulder—hold head steady and erect.	Rosie held her head up and looked around at the other children as Sharon held her against her shoulder.
• On tummy, infants lift their head and shoulders off the ground and can hold a toy in hand.	Robert, on his tummy on a blanket, lifted his head to see himself in the mirror mounted at floor level on the wall.
• Infants turn head toward a familiar voice.	
• Infants hold body still to pay attention; wiggle and move to encourage continued interaction.	
• On back, infants thrust arms and legs in play.	
• Infants turn from side to back.	Jen held a rattle placed in her hand but seemed unaware it was there.
• Infants hold finger, light toy with reflexive grasp.	
• Infants suck on own fingers and hands, objects.	Filipe brought his fingers to his mouth and sucked on them, while looking intently at the toddlers.
• Infants move arms and legs.	
4–8 months (infant)	
• Infants turn from back to side, later roll from back to front.	Micky rolls from his back to his tummy to reach a toy, then rolls back over to play with it.
• Infants sit—first with support but steady alone by the end of this period.	
• Infants reach with one arm.	Erin, sitting steadily alone, loves using both hands to pick up objects and study them.
• Infants use raking grasp.	
• Infants crawl.	
• Infants shake, bang, hold, let go of objects.	
• Infants move objects from hand to hand.	
• Infants can hold their own bottle.	Freddy loves being held while he has his bottle, but he insists on holding it himself.
• Infants can bring objects to their mouth.	
8–12 months (mobile infant)	
• Mobile infants pull to stand.	Hershel crawls to his care teacher's side, then holds her leg as he pulls up to stand.
• Mobile infants cruise.	
• Mobile infants stand alone.	
• Mobile infants walk with help and then alone.	
• Mobile infants sit in a chair.	
• Mobile infants finger-feed.	
• Mobile infants use spoon, tippy cup.	Jem sits at the lunch table, alternating between using her spoon and her fingers to enjoy her meal.
• Mobile infants use pincer grasp.	
12–18 months (mobile infant)	
• Mobile infants stack and line up blocks.	Gary stood at the table, carefully using both hands to build a tower with colored blocks.
• Mobile infants can dress and undress self, arm into sleeve, foot into shoe.	
• Mobile infants can walk.	
• Mobile infants walk while carrying objects in each hand.	Michelle toddled across the room, with her teddy bear in one hand and her blanket in the other.
• Mobile infants climb stairs.	

Teacher- or Parent-Child Interaction	Environment

0–4 months (infant)

- Change the baby's position; sometimes on his back, sometimes on his tummy. Even when holding the baby, sometimes cradle him in your arms, sometimes hold him upright against your shoulder.
- When baby is on the floor, lie down face-to-face with him.
- When baby is on her back, reaching for toy a little beyond her head, support her trunk as she rolls over.

- A stiff blanket (to prevent the danger of suffocation) on the floor provides space for early movements.
- Small, interesting toys, pictures, and books to look at will encourage babies to lift their heads. A mirror bolted to the wall at floor level always provides something interesting to look at.
- As babies begin to reach, they enjoy stable bars that dangle toys for them to bat at or reach and grasp.

4–8 months (infant)

- Stay near the baby who is just beginning to sit alone.
- Know the progression of motor development; emotionally encourage and physically support new attempts.
- Believe in the lifelong health benefits of an active lifestyle.

- Provide safe places for rolling, sitting, and crawling. Protect babies from anything that might fall on them.
- Provide small, washable lightweight objects (too large for choking) for handling and tossing, and provide containers for objects.

8–12 months (mobile infant)

- Stay alert to when practicing walkers need a little help—and when to let them keep trying.
- Allow time for older infants to practice feeding themselves.

- Safe places to pull up to stand.
- Push and pull toys to help support practicing walkers.
- Busy boxes.
- Board books for turning pages, lifting flaps, and poking fingers through holes.

12–18 months (mobile infant)

- Imitate baby's growing variety of movements.
- Introduce songs with little dances and movements.
- Provide time and patience while a toddler practices putting on his own jacket.

- Stable, low-to-the-ground riding toys.
- Stable, low-to-the-ground rocking toys.
- Skill-based manipulatives such as stacking cups, rings on a stick.

DEVELOPMENTAL TRENDS AND RESPONSIVE INTERACTIONS (Continued)

Development	Example
18–24 months (toddler)	
• Toddlers point to objects to communicate. • Toddlers make marks on paper. • Toddlers pound, shape clay. • Toddlers run. • Toddlers sit on and get up from small chairs alone. • Toddlers are developing spatial confidence—exploring their body in space.	Mindy rolled the dough with her hands, then used tools to make designs. Joseph sat down at the table to eat, then took his dirty dishes to the tub.
24–36 months (toddler)	
• Toddlers thread beads, use scissors, paint with fingers or brushes, do simple puzzles. • Toddlers throw and kick a ball. • Toddlers stand on one foot. • Toddlers stand and walk on tiptoes. • Toddlers walk upstairs with one foot on each step. • Toddlers climb, slide, jump. • Toddlers eat with spoon and fork. • Toddlers can dress self. • Toddlers can pour milk from small pitcher.	Robert doesn't even have to think about his body as he runs to greet his dad at the end of the day. Peggy and Misha make a game out of imitating each other's tiptoe steps, postures, and gestures. Lawrence and Evelyn use the dress-up clothes for their game, struggling a little to pull on the pieces.

Teacher- or Parent-Child Interaction	Environment
18–24 months (toddler)	
• Provide materials that challenge toddlers' growing use of their fingers. • Stay present with toddlers as they try new skills and support them. • Provide opportunities for climbing, walking, running.	• Art materials with thick paintbrushes and markers, large surfaces for painting. • Smaller, skill-based manipulatives such as connecting beads and pegboards. • Lots of space for movement—dancing, balls, riding toys, climbing, slides.
24–36 months (toddler)	
• Be aware of the balance of time between active and quiet activities. • Watch for increasing accuracy in fine motor skills, as subtle issues may begin to be apparent. • Be available with encouragement and patience as toddlers increasingly feed, dress, and toilet themselves.	• Provide a variety of materials to practice fine motor skills: simple puzzles, shape boxes, threading beads, table blocks, clay, art materials. • Space, opportunity, and structures to encourage movement—outdoor time, obstacle courses, dancing, and riding toys.

Summary

The work of motor development is compelling for infants and toddlers and an ongoing source of interest and pleasure to the adults in their lives.

- Infants practice motor skills in the womb and use a repertoire of reflexes to guide their actions while they develop the strength for control and voluntary movement.
- Motor development generally follows the trends of cephalocaudal and proximal-distal direction and moves from large muscle to small muscle control.
- Different cultures approach motor development differently, and early experiences seem to affect the timeline and quality of development more than the progression of development.
- Motor skills are not mastered independently from other areas of development. Adult partners promote locomotion by providing opportunities for movement, keeping infants and toddlers safe, and encouraging and enjoying each new attempt. Infants and toddlers use increasing cognitive skills, as well, as they plan how to use their bodies to move around.
- Infants and toddlers progress from head and neck control, to trunk control, rolling, sitting, rocking, crawling, pulling to a stand, cruising, walking, and finally running, jumping, and climbing.
- These processes are echoed as infants and toddlers use their small muscles for handling objects and using tools—progressing from random movements of the hand to the face, to reaching, manipulating objects for exploration, and gradually using objects with purpose. The ability to plan and execute efficient motor actions is connected to the sensory information perceived by the body.
- Child development and education programs can encourage motor development by providing many opportunities for active play and the purposeful handling of objects. However, if programs use constraining equipment for infants and toddlers—such as bouncy seats, high chairs, and swings—they may hinder motor development.
- Child development and education programs *should never use baby walkers*.
- Physical and occupational therapy may be utilized for children when motor development is not proceeding in a typical course.

Key Terms

ataxic cerebral palsy
athetoid cerebral palsy
cephalocaudal
cerebral palsy (CP)
high muscle tone
low muscle tone
mobility
Moro reflex

neuromuscular
palmar grasp reflex
pincer grasp
Postural reflexes
primitive reflexes
proprioceptive system
proximal-distal
raking grasp

rooting reflex
spastic cerebral palsy
stability
step reflex
sucking reflex
tonicity
tonic neck reflex
vestibular system

Reflections and Resources for the Reader

REFLECTIONS

1. Does your image of an ideal infant or toddler include a child who is always active and on the move? Our inactive lifestyles are contributing to childhood obesity, but some of our child development and education programs are designed to keep children sitting quietly. How does your image of a healthy child affect how you would set up your space?
2. Are you naturally active? Would your personal preferences for activity or inactivity contribute to the kinds of motor activities you make available to the infants and toddlers in your care?

OBSERVATION AND APPLICATION OPPORTUNITIES

1. Observe an infant or toddler. How does she use her body to achieve some personal goal?
2. Notice how an infant or toddler handles objects. What sort of grasp does he use? Does he manage the objects well? Can he move them from hand to hand? Can he throw or release at will? Can he carry objects while moving around? Do different children use different ways of handling objects?
3. What materials would you offer infants and toddlers at different stages to support their increasingly effective grasps? Make a poster of the grasp and the materials that would support it. Share it in class.

SUPPLEMENTARY ARTICLES AND BOOKS TO READ

Pica, R. (2008–2011). Learning by leaps and bounds. A series of columns on movement from NAEYC's *Young Children*. Retrieved from www.naeyc.org/yc/columns/leapsandbounds

Petersen, S. H., & Wittmer, D. S. (2013). *Endless opportunities for infant and toddler curriculum: A relationship-based approach* (2nd ed.). Upper Saddle River, NJ: Pearson.

ZERO TO THREE. (2012). Jeepers creepers: Your baby is learning to crawl. Retrieved from www.zerotothree.org/child-development/early-development/crawling.html

INTERESTING LINKS

www.zerotothree.org/child-development/social-emotional-development/on-the-move-the-power-of-movement.html
This link discusses how movement activities are critical not just for children's physical development, but for their overall development.

www.psych.nyu.edu/adolph/index.php?page=publications
Motor researcher Karen Adolf makes dozens of publications available in PDF format.

11

Responsive Programs

Quality, Health, Safety, and Nutrition

LEARNING OUTCOMES

After reading this chapter, you will be able to:

- Identify the elements of quality in early development and education programs
- Describe the basic policies and procedures necessary to keep infants and toddlers in group care safe and healthy
- Explain the nutritional needs of infants and toddlers and how programs can meet those needs
- Demonstrate familiarity with tools used to evaluate quality in infant/ toddler programs and identify the policies, laws, and systems that support quality in child care programs

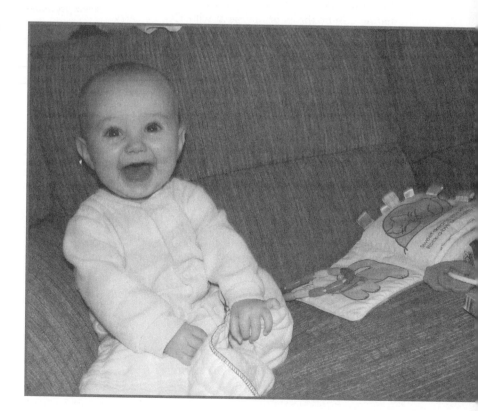

Sheila wanted to be responsive to each baby. But she could barely get through feeding and diapering. She was alone with six babies—and there was no way to do anything but run from one crying infant to another. She understood the importance of quality, but quality depended on more than her good intentions.

The issues of quality, availability, and funding of infant-toddler child care are inextricably intertwined. Given our current understanding of the effects of early relationships and environments on the development of the brain, or simply our own compassion for another human being's experience, we should ensure that the hours infants and toddlers spend in group care are filled with safe, loving, responsive, and enriching experiences. Almost 2 million children younger than age 1 are in non-maternal care at least part of the week (U.S. Census Bureau 2011). The quality of care that young children receive is directly related to their well-being, skill development, and subsequent adjustment (Ruzek et al., 2011).

Unfortunately, the high cost of providing quality care and ambivalent attitudes toward working mothers have left more than half the parents of infants and toddlers in America using child care that is of mediocre or poor quality. As mentioned in Chapter 1 of this textbook, a seminal study of more than 400 centers in the United States rated only 8% of infant classrooms as being of good or excellent quality (CQO Study Team, 1995). Studies of infant and toddler child care have helped clarify which elements are most important to ensuring quality. Low ratios, small group sizes, and well-trained teachers are necessary for the focused, warm, enriched relationships babies need for good development (NICHD, 2001b). These factors, of course, make for an expensive service. At the same time, many Americans believe that mothers should be at home raising their children and will not support public funding that ensures quality child care services for all children (Sylvester, 2001).

The essential measure of quality is the well-being of the children. Current questions for the field include why child care appears to be good for some children but not others. Instead of assuming that only the quality of the program matters, some researchers are wondering if by temperament and stress reactivity, group care is simply not a good idea for some young children (Phillips, Fox & Gunner, 2011).

What Is Quality . . . and Why Does It Matter?

In its simplest perspective, every description of quality includes these three items:

- The safety of the child
- Communication between the family and the teacher about the child
- A warm, responsive relationship between the teacher and the child (Kontos, Howes, Shinn, & Galinsky, 1995)

The definition of quality, however, is not that simple. Each of these items—safety, communication with families, and a warm relationship—has its own defining elements, established by research. Safety includes keeping the environment clean and free of hazards, preventing the spread of infection, and promoting healthy practices and good nutrition. Communication between families and care teachers begins with supporting the parent-child relationship and includes having clear policies that families are able to understand, respect for differing cultural beliefs and child-rearing practices, and ways to resolve conflicts that may arise. The quality of the relationship between the care teacher and the baby is affected by the teacher's own relationship history, training, knowledge, and skills, as well as the program's curriculum, variables such as ratios and group sizes, and individual characteristics of each baby such as the clarity of her cues or ability to be calmed.

Although it is true that all of these elements need to be considered in creating a high-quality program, in some ways it seems like a mix of apples, oranges, and bananas. Some are concrete and easily observable; others are subtle, subjective, and relationship based. Both are influenced by the societal attitudes and policies supporting or hindering the use of care and education programs. So, in order to really examine the elements of quality, we will separate them into structural (concrete) variables, process (affecting the interactions), and contextual variables.

Structural Variables of Quality

structural variables

Measurable aspects that affect quality in child care, including ratios, group sizes, caregiver training, and health and safety standards.

The **structural variables** of quality provide the foundation on which responsive relationships can be built. The variables include low child-to-teacher ratios; small group size; primary caregiving; continuity of care; and a well-educated, well-compensated, stable workforce. Comfortable, safe, healthy, and enriching environments are also important structural variables. Management structures within a program that support the smooth running of the program and support the efforts of teachers and families alike are also part of the underlying structure. In looking at this set of variables, it is clear that providing the foundation for high-quality infant-toddler care is an expensive endeavor. Therefore, adequate financing is also a structural variable. Let's explore some of these variables more deeply.

Ratios and Group Sizes

Caring well for only one baby can be a full-time job. In order for care teachers to provide the emotional connection and caregiving that promotes healthy development, one teacher cannot be responsible for more than a few babies. Very young children, in turn, are easily overwhelmed by the noise and activity of large groups of people; in order for them to focus and learn, they need to be in groups of limited size.

Benefits of low ratios include secure attachment relationships, more complex play with peers and objects, more proficient adaptive language, and fewer behavior problems such as aggression and anxiety (Howes & Smith, 1995). The NICHD Early Child Care Research Network (2000a) study of more than 1,000 children found that better ratios were also related to better communication skills in 12-month-olds and higher scores on the Bayley Mental Development Index (Burchinal, Roberts, Nabors, & Bryant 1996).

The funding challenges of child care make it difficult to keep group sizes small and ratios low, although the benefits have been known for a long time.

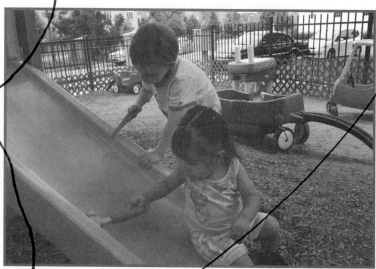

Benefits of low ratios include secure attachment relationships and more complex play with peers.

Ratio and group size tend to be determined by licensing regulations—and states vary in their legal requirements for child care programs, requiring from 3 to 12 infants per care teacher in regulated centers. The NICHD study of early child care found adult-to-child ratios ranging from 1:1 to 1:13 (Phillips & Adams, 2001).

Early Head Start defines the ratios and group size requirements in the Program Performance Standards, and several national organizations have weighed in with recommendations for best practices. Table 11.1 illustrates these recommendations with the ratio of teacher to children given followed by the recommended group size.

Primary Caregiving

Primary caregiving is the practice of assigning responsibility to one care teacher for each baby. This promotes consistent caregiving, allows the care teacher and the child to develop a predictable and always deepening relationship, and provides the family with one person to depend on for ongoing sharing of information. Primary caregiving does not mean exclusive caregiving. Generally, more than one care teacher is in a room with a group of infants or toddlers, and all care teachers strive to have warm, affectionate relationships with all of the babies.

The emphasis on primary caregiving comes from the ever-deepening understanding of the importance of caregiving relationships for healthy development. Emotionally available, attentive care teachers help infants and toddlers understand what is expected of them, what feels right in the world, as well as the patterns of social reciprocity, turn taking, and cooperation (Emde, Biringen, Clyman, & Oppenheim, 1991). Consistent relationships can promote interest in exploration, pleasure in play, and abilities to manage stressful and challenging situations (Emde, 1994; Zahn-Waxler & Radke-Yarrow, 1990).

A relationship with a primary teacher allows the intimacy and mutual knowledge for a relationship to grow in depth. It takes time to develop an attachment to a care teacher, and babies are less likely to form attachments if their teachers change frequently (Raikes, 1993). When infants and toddlers have to adjust to many new care teachers, they may not even try to know the new teacher but just try to re-create the character of the relationship with the last teacher (Howes & Hamilton, 1993). Having a focused relationship with one teacher over time, providing continuity of care, appears to be helpful for every aspect of a child's development.

Continuity of Care

Continuity of care extends the assignment of the primary teacher over a long period of time, preferably from the time of enrollment until the child is at

TABLE 11.1   **Recommended Ratios/Group Sizes**

Children's Age	Early Head Start (required)	American Academy of Pediatrics	NAEYC	ZERO TO THREE
Birth to 12 months	1:4 / 8	1:3 / 6	1:3 or 1:4 to 15 months / 6–8	1:3 / 6
13 to 30 months	1:4 / 8	1:4 / 8	1:3 or 1:4 for 16 to 28 months / 6–12	1:3 for 12 to 18 months / 9
30 to 35 months	1:4 / 8	1:5 / 10	1:4 to 1:6 for 28 to 36 months / 6–12	1:4 / 12

least 3 years of age. By allowing the caregiving relationship to exist over years, the child is able to experience the time and intimacy needed to learn about himself and form meaningful relationships. When care teachers change frequently, the baby may experience both the grief of losing a valued friend and the stress of having to learn a new person's expectations. When relationships are repeatedly disrupted early in life, an infant or toddler may stop investing the effort needed to new relationships, and life can become very distressing for the child.

A poignant case study of two toddlers transitioning into a preschool classroom in the same program demonstrates the depth of feeling in the established child-teacher relationship. Scott and Robbie transitioned into a preschool room from their infant-toddler room at about 2 ½ years. They were supported by visits with their toddler care teachers and everyone thought they would do well. Scott had entered the infant room at 2 months and had spent his whole life with his primary care teacher and the environment of the infant room. Robbie had spent only 10 months in the program, his third in 2 years. Robbie made the transition easily, although remaining somewhat watchful. Scott resisted the new rules and structure, cried, and took a long time developing a relationship with his new care teachers. Continuity of care had provided time for Scott to develop a deep attachment relationship that provided a sense of safety in the infant room. He mourned and resisted the loss of this attachment relationship, but it built a foundation for him to replicate secure relationships (Recchia, 2012).

Continuity of care between a child development and education provider and a baby may be achieved in several ways. The two most important elements involved in continuity of care approaches are

1. The day-to-day interactions between the primary teacher and the baby that give the baby a sense of predictability in her daily experiences
2. The deepening relationship and shared memories created through the enduring, year-after-year relationship between the primary teacher and the baby

Extended time together supports children's sense of history of themselves with the care teacher. It helps babies believe that people remain in their lives in caring, meaningful ways—that they can rely on and safely love other people. For families experiencing multiple challenges (e.g., unstable housing leading to multiple moves, unstable employment, or numerous adults or other individuals rotating in and out of the home), continuity in the caregiving environment is especially beneficial for the young child.

When continuity of care is provided by a primary care teacher, there are also many opportunities for the teacher and parents to develop a caring relationship. Care teachers may learn from parents how the infant or toddler expects to be handled and any cultural or personal care practices the family utilizes. The care teacher, in turn, may inform the family on the thinking behind some of the care practices in the program. Open, genuine communication between parents and teachers increases the continuity of the baby's experiences between home and child care.

Different structures for continuity of care include mixed age groups of infants and toddlers nurtured by primary teachers throughout their first 3 years, similar to the design of family child care. Another model is remaining with the same children in a close age group, and as the children grow older moving to a new, age-appropriate space with the same teacher, thus providing the teacher and child with the opportunity to maintain long-lasting bonds. As time progresses, teachers in this arrangement work with various age groups over several years. A third method is to maintain a close age group with the same care teacher but modify the environment as the children's abilities and interests change.

Although some care teachers may feel more competent with specific age groups and prefer to work, for example, only with young infants or only with 2-year-olds, the care teacher and baby will reap mutual benefits from a more long-term relationship spanning the duration of the child's enrollment. Care teachers can feel confident of their ability to really know a child, to be able to read each cues, and to know how to individually comfort and challenge each baby. The care teacher avoids the stress of constantly "learning" new babies.

Care Teacher Characteristics

Personal characteristics such as warmth, comfort with intimacy, a sense of humor, and enjoying children are important for infant and toddler care teachers. However, other factors such as general education level and specific training in child development (Burchinal, Howes, & Kontos, 2002), compensation and stability in the workplace, and the structure for ongoing supervision by the director consistently correlate to better child outcomes in studies of early care.

Care teachers with either a bachelor's degree or specialized training at the college level are more sensitive and less harsh with children, are warmer, more enthusiastic, and more developmentally appropriate in their communication (Whitebrook, Howes, & Phillips, 1998). Care teachers who are sensitive, use more stimulating materials, have more academic training and smaller group sizes have children with stronger academic skills (Flagler, 2010). In child care homes, caregivers who were better educated and had higher and more recent levels of training demonstrated more positive caregiving (Clarke-Stewart, Vandell, Burchinal, O'Brien, & McCartney, 2002). Care teachers with as little as two courses at the community college level are less authoritarian than those with no training at all (Arnett, 1989).

Care teachers with more education maintain cleaner, healthier environments and reduce the number of accidental injuries in their classrooms (Ulione, 1997). Their classrooms are likely to receive higher scores on global quality rating scales such as the Infant Toddler Environmental Rating Scale (ITERS). (ITERS and other rating scales are discussed later in this chapter.) However, most health and safety practices are best maintained when a program has established ongoing monitoring of its own practices (Ulione, 1997).

The stability of care teachers in their positions is also related to their education. Care teachers with more education are more likely to remain in the field (Whitebrook et al., 1998). Family home providers participating in initial training tend to seek out additional training and increase their commitment to their jobs (Galinsky, Howes, & Kontos, 1995). A study in Alabama found that preservice training reduced the turnover rate among child care employees, with 68% still employed in the field 1 year after graduation (Shirah, Hewitt, & McNair, 1993).

Of course, whereas education tends to improve both the performance and stability of the care teacher, the low wages and lack of benefits in most child care jobs make it difficult to recruit and retain people who have invested in their own education. In a review of the 2011 wage by occupation figures, no occupations earned less than child care workers. Gas station attendants, ushers, and laundry workers all earned slightly more than the average $19,000 per year of child care workers (Bureau of Labor Statistics, 2011). Family child care providers earned even less, averaging about $4.82 an hour in a 55-hour workweek (CCW, 2004). Benefits such as health insurance are rare, and wages are so low that workers often cannot afford to pay their share even when employers pay a portion of the

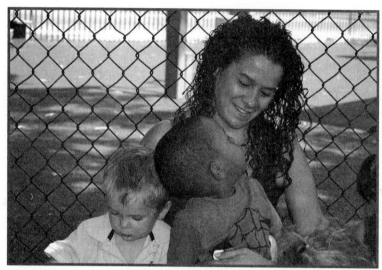

Nothing is more important than the ongoing relationship between the teacher and the children.

cost (CCW, 2004). The low wages result in a poorly trained workforce with a turnover rate of nearly 40%.

> *The most important predictor of the quality of care...is staff wages. (Lombardi)*

These structural variables—low ratios, small group sizes, primary caregiving, continuity of care, and well-trained and supported teachers—provide an environment that makes possible the kind of caring, responsive interactions by which we can ultimately judge the quality of a child's experience in child care. Without the foundation of these structural variables, process variables, discussed next, cannot possibly contribute to quality.

Process Variables of Quality

process variables

Actual experiences that occur in child care settings, including children's interactions with caregivers and peers and their participation in different activities.

The moment-by-moment experiences of children in child care must be observed to really understand quality from the child's perspective. These **process variables** include the interactions between children and teachers and among children, and the play, learning, and health activities in which the children participate (Vandell & Wolfe, 2001).

The process variables of greatest importance to infants and toddlers are responsive caregiving and planning, cultural and linguistic continuity, meeting the needs of the individual within the group context, and the physical environment. These topics are covered in depth in Chapter 12 as part of the discussion of the care teacher's role in a responsive, caring curriculum, and additionally in Chapters 13 and 14 as responsive teaching relates to promoting children's social, emotional, cognitive, language, and motor development. A brief summary of the definition of these items as related to the broader concept of quality follows.

Responsive teaching, of course, describes the process of understanding the child's experience and knowing how to respond appropriately. Lally (2001) writes of seven gifts that good child care and early education programs offer infants and toddlers. The gifts of nurturance, support, security, and predictability help children believe that they will be loved and cared for in the child care setting. The gifts of predictability, focus, encouragement, and expansion support the child's intellectual engagement and understanding of the world. These gifts provide a clear description of responsive teaching.

Cultural and Linguistic Continuity

Babies develop expectations of how they will be cared for in their first days of life. They become familiar with

CULTURE CLOSE UP

A group of highly educated and influential infant-toddler program directors and college faculty had the opportunity to visit Reggio Emilia infant programs in Italy. In the atelier, a specialized art room shared by all the children, were beautiful displays of recycled objects. These included well-worn sea stones, nuts and bolts, thumbtacks, corks, sharp scissors—all displayed in glass containers within the children's reach. Some teachers were outraged at the lack of safety: "This would never be allowed in the United States. These things are far too dangerous for 1-year-olds." The Italian teachers responded, "We believe in children's strengths. We have never had children swallow something dangerous or otherwise harm themselves. They learn how to use all kinds of materials." On the bus afterward, the U.S. teachers had a lively discussion about what they would want to do if licensing were not an issue.

the sound of their family's language, even in the womb. Care teachers, ideally, would be of the same culture and home language as the family. However, in today's diverse communities, it is unlikely that all children will have a care teacher from their native culture. Care teachers can, however, learn the words of affection from families and try to match the family's practices. They can include pictures, toys, or artifacts of a specific culture in their environment, and they must always speak of the child's culture with respect. In Chapter 12, we discuss specific strategies for developing relationships with families from diverse cultures.

Meeting the Needs of the Individual Within the Context of the Group

Care teachers need to find ways to respect the individual temperament, moods, preferences, and routines of each child in their care. This includes feeding on demand, being helped to fall asleep, and diapering or toileting as needed. Low ratios and small group sizes are critical factors in whether a care teacher will be able to attend sensitively to the individual and the group.

Physical Environment

The environment must be kept particularly clean, given the immature immune systems of infants and toddlers, and especially safe for young children who may mouth and swallow anything and are constantly developing new abilities in movement. The play spaces must offer interesting opportunities for exploration without being overwhelming with too many choices. Above all else, the environment must be set up and monitored to ensure the health and safety of the children in care.

An Emphasis on Health and Safety

Two resources are rich with up-to-the-moment information for infant and toddler health and safety. *Caring for Our Children: National Health and Safety Performance Standards: Guidelines for Out-of-Home Child Care Programs* (American Academy of Pediatrics, American Public Health Association, National Resource Center for Health and Safety in Child Care, 2011) is the most thorough, well-researched, and reviewed material available. The practices in this section come from that source and we highly recommend that every teacher use the original document (http://nrckids.org). The second is a new resource: The National Center on Health is newly funded by the Office of Head Start (eclkc.ohs.acf.hhs.gov/hslc/tta-system/health/center).

Keeping children safe and healthy in child care is a foundation of quality, but it is not enough, as expressed in the introduction to *Caring for Our Children*:

> Health involves more than the absence of illness and injury. To stay healthy, children depend on adults to make healthy choices for them and to teach them to make such choices for themselves over the course of a lifetime. (Chang & Aronson, 2002)

Health and safety practices in infant-toddler child care include a range of activities for the purpose of avoiding injury and infection and promoting health, including the following:

- Sanitizing and preventing the spread of disease
- Promoting safety and preventing injuries
- Adopting policies that promote and protect health

Sanitizing and Preventing the Spread of Disease

Babies are vulnerable. In the first weeks of life, they cannot even support their own heads when being held. They cannot take action to keep themselves dry, warm, fed, or safe—and they cannot, at the end of a day of care, tell us whether they were treated kindly. As parents, we are so aware of this vulnerability that we watch their breathing as they sleep, to reassure ourselves. And the most basic demand we make of nonparental care is that our babies will be healthy and safe.

This vulnerability is not simply our perception of babies. In the last 2 months of gestation, the mother's immune system creates enormous amounts of immunoglobulin, the protective agent against most infections, and sends it to the baby across the placenta. At birth, the newborn has a higher immunoglobulin count than his mother. However, also at birth, the baby stops receiving the immunoglobulin from his mother and the protection slowly decreases. The baby's immune system does not begin producing its own immunoglobulin until around 7 months, and by 2 years of age is still offering only about 80% of the average adult protection (Collier & Henderson, 2000). So babies are considerably more prone to infection, and less resilient in recovering from infection, than people at any other stage of human development.

When we understand the vulnerability to infection in the infant and toddler and then add the risks of repeated exposures to infection that are inherent in group care compared to being at home with one parent, it is clear that teachers have a responsibility to maintain a sanitary environment. See Box 11.1 for ways to find more information on health and safety practices for group care. For teachers of infants and toddlers, preventing the spread of disease depends on scrupulous attention to the following:

- Hand washing
- Diapering

BOX 11.1

Caring for Our Children: National Health and Safety Performance Standards: Guidelines for Out-of-Home Child Care Programs: Third Edition

Caring for Our Children was created by the American Academy of Pediatrics and the National Resource Center for Health and Safety in Child Care to provide the most current, evidence-based information on health and safety practices for group care. Standards describing best practices, scientific rationales, and comments address these areas:

- Staffing
- Program: Activities for healthy development
- Health promotion and protection in child care
- Nutrition and food service
- Facilities, supplies, equipment, and transportation

- Infectious diseases
- Children who are eligible for services under IDEA
- Administration
- Licensing and community action

Specific procedures for hand washing, diapering, cleaning and sanitizing, food handling, and every aspect of maintaining a safe and healthy environment are included.

The entire document is available online (http://nrckids.org), and updates are regularly posted as the current science provides new information for our decision making.

- Sanitizing toys, furniture, and bedding
- Excluding children who are ill

Hand washing

Hand washing is the primary defense against illness in child care. It is such a basic step in hygiene that it is amazing how often it is either not done when it should be or is done improperly, and thus ineffectively. Unwashed or improperly washed hands spread infection and may be the cause of diarrhea outbreaks among both children and staff. Centers that have implemented hand-washing training programs have decreased the incidence of diarrhea by 50%. Hand washing also reduces the spread of colds and respiratory infections and protects the children, as well as the teacher, from illness.

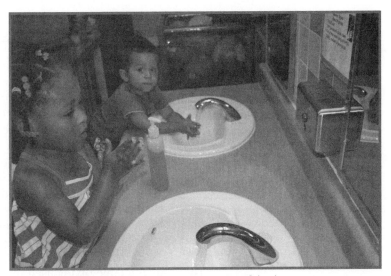

For these children, hand washing is a routine part of the day.

According to the National Health and Safety Performance Standards, all teachers, volunteers, and children should wash their hands when they arrive for the day or when they move from one care group to another. They should wash their hands before and after eating, handling food, feeding a child, giving medication, and playing in water that is used by more than one person. They should wash hands after diapering, using the toilet, or helping a child use the toilet; handling uncooked foods or animals; playing in sandboxes; cleaning; handling garbage; and handling bodily fluid from sneezing, wiping, and blowing noses, from mouths, or from sores (American Academy of Pediatrics et al, 2011).

Teachers should receive training in proper hand-washing procedures and be monitored for the accuracy of their use of the procedure and whether they are hand washing in every required situation. Programs should post proper hand-washing procedures above sinks. Specific procedures need to be in place describing how teachers will wash the hands of infants too young to do it themselves, or assist toddlers in washing their own hands.

Diapering

A second important area of hygiene in group care is diapering. The National Health and Safety Performance Standards caution that fecal contamination of objects or the hands of teachers or children can cause serious gastrointestinal diseases—so the first requirement concerning diapers is that they absorb liquid and hold solids tightly. Three kinds of diapers meet the standards for use in child care: disposable diapers with absorbent gelling material, one-piece reusable diapers with a cloth lining attached to a waterproof outer covering, or reusable cloth diapers worn with a front-closure waterproof cover. It is also important to use diapering procedures that prevent diaper dermatitis (irritation of skin that has been in contact with urine or feces).

Safe and healthy diapering procedures include changing diapers whenever it is obvious from the feel of the diaper through the clothing that it is wet or

Think about the health and safety procedures that the care teacher follows in this video. Is she following the infant/toddler licensing rules and regulations written by the state you live in?

BOX 11.2

Diluted Bleach Sanitizer

First clean the surface with detergent and rinse with water. Mix 1/4 cup of household liquid chlorine bleach in 1 gallon of water (or 1 tablespoon of bleach to 1 quart of water). Sprayed onto a cleaned surface, the sanitizer requires 2 minutes of surface contact to kill the usual infectious agents found in feces.

from the smell that indicates feces. Diapers should be checked with a visual inspection at least every 2 hours. Diapers should always be changed as soon as they are found to be wet or soiled. A specific area set aside for diaper changing will reduce the risk of contamination of other parts of the child care environment. Children's access to this area should be limited to the times when they are being changed. Diapers should not be changed in areas used for other purposes, especially not on any surface that is used for food preparation or mealtimes. If cloth diapers or training pants are used, they must never be carried through the child care area to place the fecal contents in the toilet. Soiled cloth diapers must be kept in a sealed plastic container and removed each night by the family or a commercial laundry service.

The changing table that is used must also be diligently sanitized using a solution such as the one described in Box 11.2. Changing tables must be made of a nonporous material, cleaned and sanitized after each use to remove visible soil, and followed by wetting with a sanitizing solution such as the diluted bleach solution. The sanitizer must be left on for the required contact time. Some sanitizers need to be wiped off afterward with water, but bleach does not as the chlorine evaporates, leaving only water on the surface (American Academy of Pediatrics et al, 2011; Standard 3.2.1)).

Sanitizing Toys, Furniture, and Bedding

In addition to careful diapering procedures and frequent hand washing, the National Health and Safety Performance Standards provide directions for the overall routine cleaning and sanitation of all aspects of the child care area. Infants and toddlers are likely to touch any surface they can reach, thereby both spreading infectious agents and coming in contact with contaminated surfaces anywhere in the environment. One precaution in the standards that is only for infant rooms is the requirement that people either cover their street shoes or replace them with slippers before walking on the infant room floor (American Academy of Pediatrics et al, 2011; Standard 3.3).

Infants and toddlers will sneeze and cough without covering their noses or mouths, they will mouth any toy or object, and they drool when they are teething. The potential for spreading disease is impressive. A routine for cleaning and sanitizing all surfaces should be established and implemented by all programs.

Excluding Children Who Are Ill

The National Health and Safety Performance Standards suggest that children who are ill be excluded from child care for a short period of time. Each state's licensing standards may have specific regulations regarding when children should be excluded from care, and health consultants or health advisory committees should also be consulted. However, the basic guidelines from the National Health and Safety Performance Standards include specific conditions for exclusion from the program. For instance, a child should be excluded if the illness prevents her from participating in the activities or the illness requires teachers to provide a higher level of care than they are able to do without compromising the other children. A child with any of the following conditions should be excluded from group care: fever; symptoms and signs of severe illness such as lethargy, uncontrolled coughing, persistent irritability or crying, difficulty breathing, wheezing, or other unusual signs; diarrhea; blood in stools; vomiting; persistent abdominal pain; mouth sores with drooling; rash with fever; purulent conjunctivitis (pink eye); pediculosis (head lice); scabies; tuberculosis; impetigo; strep throat; chickenpox; pertussis; mumps; hepatitis A virus; measles; rubella; respiratory tract illness; shingles; or herpes simplex.

Excluding children with mild infections has only a small effect on limiting the spread of infection because many viruses are spread before the child actually exhibits any symptoms of the disease. So programs should also consider the child's comfort and the needs of the staff when they create policies for excluding children who are ill (American Academy of Pediatrics et al, 2011).

Administering Medication

When children with mild illnesses or chronic conditions require medication, the child care program may be involved in medication administration. The National Health and Safety Performance Standards, the Head Start program performance standards, and most state licensing regulations require programs to have a written policy and procedures for medication administration. The best option is that medication be prescribed in ways that allow parents to administer it before or after the hours the child is in care. However, young children are prone to illnesses, and it is sometimes necessary for programs to take on the responsibility.

When programs must administer medications, the National Health and Safety Performance Standards have several standards concerning this issue, including Permissible Administration of Medication, Labeling and Storage of Medications, and Training of Teachers to Administer Medication. These standards limit the administration of medications to prescribed medications ordered by a health care provider with written permission of the parent or legal guardian and nonprescription (over-the-counter) medications recommended by a health care provider for a specific child or for a specific circumstance for all children, with written permission from the parent or legal guardian. So, a health care provider could write a standing order for the use of sunscreen or acetaminophen for use in specific circumstances (exposure to sun or fever higher than 101°. Parents must be notified of each application of any medication and each application should be logged.

Prescribed medications brought into the child care facility should be in their original containers, dated, labeled with the child's first and last names, the date the prescription was filled, the name of the health care provider who wrote the prescription, the expiration date, the instructions for administration, and the name and strength of the medication. Over-the-counter medications should be brought in their original container and labeled by the parent with the child's name and instructions from the health care provider. All medications should have child-resistant caps, be stored away from food, and be kept inaccessible to children.

A child care teacher who administers medication may be required by state licensing requirements to have specific medication administration certification.

Teachers are trained to check the match between the name on the medication and the child's name; to read and understand the directions in relation to dose, frequency, and circumstances such as in relation to meals; to administer the medication; to observe any side effects of the medications; and to document the administration of each dose (American Academy of Pediatrics et al, 2011; Standard 3.6).

Promoting Safety and Preventing Injuries

In addition to the vulnerability of very young children to disease, infants and toddlers are quite susceptible to injuries through accidents. They are just developing the ability to move around and do not automatically understand how to keep their balance, how to avoid falling over steep edges, or how to get themselves out of tight places they have somehow managed to squeeze into. Infants and toddlers who are so interested in the ideas of "in" and "out" apply those ideas to tiny objects that can choke them or to interesting openings in walls where adults plug in lamps and CD players. The world can be a dangerous place for the curious explorer who brings limited experience to his movements, or the consequences of his actions. It can be challenging to find a balance between keeping the child care area safe and still providing an environment that invites children to play, learn, and explore.

Accident Prevention

Care teachers who care for infants and toddlers are constantly scanning the environment for anything that may cause injury to their charges. A key to keeping the environment safe for infants and toddlers is to see the area through their eyes. Getting down on the floor and taking a child's eye view can alert the teacher to dangers she might not see from an adult height. Are tall shelves bolted to the wall so they can't fall down on a climbing child? Are outlets covered? Are more remote parts of the carpet vacuumed as frequently as the open spaces? Accident prevention requires an awareness of potential hazards, eliminating known hazards, knowing what to do in an emergency, and teaching children about safety (Watson & White, 2001).

With infants and toddlers, the teacher's vigilant observation of the children and the space is the most important factor in preventing accidents and injuries. Teachers arrange furniture to allow visual access to children at all times. Furniture is checked for stability, door edges are protected to prevent pinched fingers, electrical cords are not dangling or within reach of children, and outlets are covered. Infants and toddlers are never left unattended in high chairs, infant seats, or swings. Choking hazards such as small objects, broken parts of toys, curtain cords, balloons, popcorn, peanuts, hot dogs, grapes, gum, and hard candies are kept out of the environment.

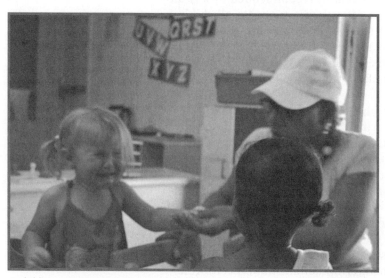

A child's-eye view can alert teachers to dangers and hazards in the environment.

Infant and toddler toys should be greater than 1¼ inches in diameter to avoid choking. Toys are chosen for their age-appropriateness, checking the labels for age recommendations. Toys should be nontoxic, wooden toys kept free of splinters, and cloth toys flame retardant.

All cleaning supplies and medications should be kept locked and out of the children's reach. Other potentially toxic substances include poisonous plants, small batteries, salves used in diapering, and even art materials. Colored inks used in magazines may contain lead.

Outdoor play must also be well supervised. Children should be dressed appropriately for whatever weather is present, with children kept well hydrated and safe from the sun. Playgrounds should be designed for infants and toddlers and provide surfaces that provide protection from the inevitable falls. You will read more about how to set up an interesting outdoor environment and how teachers can provide responsive outdoor care in Chapter 13.

Despite all precautions, accidents may still occur. Care teachers need to have current first aid and infant-toddler CPR training, fully stocked first aid kits kept handy, and written plans for reacting to emergencies. Programs should practice evacuation drills for fires, hurricanes, and tornados. Infant programs should have evacuation cribs to provide for quick transport of a group of infants.

Adopting Policies That Promote and Protect Health

All programs serving young children need health and safety policies that are written out, approved by a health consultant or health advisory committee, and understood by staff. Teachers should receive training on the policies and procedures and be monitored for their adherence to them. Hand washing, cleaning, sanitizing, diapering, and accident prevention are all areas that should be covered by those policies. Schedules that promote a balance between active and quiet play and rest times, good nutrition, and the constant presence of a responsive, caring adult all promote health.

Two additional areas are important to emphasize in a discussion of infant-toddler programs: safe sleep positioning and child abuse reporting.

In 1992, the American Academy of Pediatrics Task Force on Infant Positioning and SIDS (sudden infant death syndrome) made the strong recommendation that young infants be placed to sleep supine (on their backs) to reduce the risk of SIDS. Their public awareness effort became known as the "Back to Sleep" campaign. Between 1992 and 2001, the SIDS rate had been reduced by 53%. All child care programs should ensure safe sleeping positions as a policy. The most recent AAP (2013) policy statement on SIDS makes these recommendations:

1. Place infants on their backs to sleep.
2. Use a firm sleep surface.
3. Keep soft objects and loose bedding out of the crib.
4. Do not smoke during pregnancy.
5. Provide a separate nearby sleeping environment (recommended).
6. Offer a pacifier at naptime and bedtime.
7. Avoid overheating.

Child abuse and neglect are sensitive, emotionally charged issues for everyone. Parents fear for their child's safety when left in group care, with abuse sometimes being one of those worries. Teachers are often the first to recognize and identify signs of parental abuse and then have the difficult task of reporting the abuse or neglect to authorities. The National Child Care Information and Technical Assistance Center (NCCIC, 2009) defines child abuse as a "non-accidental injury or pattern of injuries to a child for which there is no 'reasonable' explanation." Abuse may include

- Non-accidental injury
- Neglect
- Sexual molestation
- Emotional abuse

Care teachers are required to report all suspected cases of abuse and neglect. It is important to have training in recognizing signs of possible abuse and characteristics of child abusers. It is also important to understand the legal mandate for reporting in your state, as well as the procedures for reporting suspected abuse or neglect. Programs should have policies in place to ensure that abuse never occurs within the program and should have a method for investigating any accusations of abuse that could be filed. Although this topic requires greater depth of training than can be given here, a short description of each of these issues will help in achieving some understanding. A care teacher's recognition of an indicator of abuse or neglect should be considered within the context of explanations given by the family, the medical history, and the ability of the child to participate in the activities said to cause the accident.

The indicators of abuse or neglect are as follows:

- Indicators of physical abuse: Any injury on an infant such as burns, fractures, bruises, welts, cuts, scrapes, head injuries, fear of adults, appearance of pain
- Indicators of emotional abuse: General unhappiness, reacting without emotion to unpleasant statements or actions, delayed emotional development, or for infants an appearance of freezing as though withdrawing completely from the present moment
- Indicators of sexual abuse: Difficulty in walking or sitting; torn, stained, or bloody underclothing; pain when urinating; bruises or bleeding in vaginal or anal areas, mouth, or throat, or vaginal infections; unwillingness to have clothing changed; being fearful of a particular person; or unusual interest in or knowledge of sexual matters
- Indicators of physical and emotional neglect: Infants or toddlers left in the care of other children, dressed inadequately for the weather, poor hygiene, not getting regular well-baby care, no weight gain, or always hungry

Characteristics of child abusers include these traits:

- Isolated, under stress, mental health issues
- Alcohol or drug influence
- Unfulfilled needs for nurturance and support
- Feeling that their failures are greater than their successes
- Lack of supports in marriage, extended family, or jobs
- Likely to feel that violence is an acceptable way of dealing with problems

Reporting suspected child abuse is one of the most difficult things care teachers may have to do, but it is not a choice. If you suspect abuse or neglect, you are legally required to report your suspicions to authorities. Each state has its own definition of what constitutes abuse or neglect. You are never required to have proof before reporting and must report an incident as soon as it is noticed. Part of your program's policy should include knowing which agency to call in your community. Many states will take an anonymous report over the phone, but it is useful to provide your contact information.

Care teachers may also need to consider how their program's discipline policy may be seen in light of issues of abuse and neglect. Corporal punishment may never be used in child care. Discipline must never interfere with a child's schedule of eating, sleeping, or toileting. However, a responsive care teacher will not use discipline with infants and toddlers. Her own good skills, an engaging but serene environment, and positive interactions with children will provide the guidance very young children need as they learn to control their own behavior. Chapter 14 presents specific strategies in regard to guidance for infants and toddlers.

The Importance of Good Nutrition

The nutrition infants and toddlers receive directly affects the ability of the brain to form and develop and may have a lifelong effect on the child's ability to learn, to cope with difficult circumstances, and to grow and have strong bones. Mothers who are severely malnourished in pregnancy produce babies with smaller head circumferences and smaller brain weight. The enormous spurts of growth in the last months of gestation and the first years of life require sufficient amounts of food and sufficient quantities of particular nutrients. Cell growth and division occur only during childhood. The nutrients available to each cell may determine which cell type becomes dominant within tissue, how large or small each cell becomes within each body part, and how efficiently each cell performs in the future (Roberts & Heyman, 2000).

Child care and education programs may play an important role in ensuring that infants and toddlers in care have adequate nutrition and establish healthy eating habits. By being knowledgeable about the foods babies need in order to grow and be healthy, helping them get used to a variety of healthy choices, and using proper food-handling techniques, programs can influence the patterns children set early in life. Care teachers must establish healthy eating habits, good sleep routines, a balance between active and quiet play, and some time outdoors every day to lay the foundation for good growth and development.

Nutritional Needs of Infants and Toddlers

Human breast milk is the best food for young human babies. The composition of the mother's milk changes as the baby grows, giving the baby exactly what she needs at the time. The protein is easily digested and the vitamins and minerals are almost entirely absorbed, compared to only 10% of iron and vitamins from formula. Certain fats found in breast milk, but not in formula, are used by the developing central nervous system and the photoreceptor rods in the retina (Lazarov & Evans, 2000; Meyers & Chawla, 2000). The American Academy of Pediatrics strongly endorses breast-feeding, in part because of the significant immunological benefits. More than 50 immune agents are transferred through breast milk, giving babies protection from otitis media (middle ear infections), fewer respiratory infections, and fewer gastric infections causing diarrhea (American Academy of Pediatrics, 2012). Breast-fed babies have a lower incidence of SIDS, allergies, childhood lymphoma, childhood-onset diabetes, and obesity (Lawrence, 1997). Infant and toddler programs can support mothers in their breast-feeding by encouraging them to visit their child during the day to breast-feed or to express milk to use in bottles. Infants weaned before 12 months of age should be fed iron-fortified formula.

Bottles of breast milk, formula, milk, or juice should never be propped for a baby to use without being held. The nurturing, social aspect of feeding is nearly as important as the nutrition for babies. Bottles should never be used as a way to help a baby fall asleep because the prolonged contact with the natural sugars in the liquids can cause tooth decay. Even very young babies should have their gums wiped with a moist cloth after feeding to remove any remaining liquid that could turn to plaque and cause tooth decay (American Academy of Pediatrics et al, 2011; Standard 4.3.1).

Certain micronutrients (vitamins and minerals) are essential for healthy growth and development. Iron, iodine, and zinc are all necessary for proper cell development. Babies are born with enough iron for the first 4 to 6 months; babies get iron from breast milk, iron-fortified formula, iron-fortified cereal, beans, vegetables, and meats. Iron is used by the body in the development of red blood cells and in brain tissue, including the network of neurotransmitters used for information processing (Beard, Connor, & Jones, 1997). Toddlers with iron deficiency have lower scores on both the mental and psychomotor indices of the Bayley Scales of Infant Development and are more wary, hesitant, easily tired, and less attentive, involved, and playful than children with adequate iron (Lozoff et al., 1998). Iron deficiency is often associated with poverty, but iron-fortified formulas or iron supplements can prevent anemia (Meyers & Chawla, 2000).

Micronutrients affect the child in utero and postnatally. Iodine deficiency has been associated with hypothyroidism and cognitive deficits (Huda, Grantham-McGregor, & Tomkins, 1999). Zinc deficiency occurs in children with malnutrition and poor diets and results in a variety of cognitive and behavioral problems (Golub, Keen, Gershwin, & Hendrickx, 1995). Zinc is available in oat cereals, meat and poultry, wheat germ, egg yolk, and cheddar cheese. Vitamin B_6 influences mother-infant interactions and behavior (McCullough et al., 1990).

Between 4 and 6 months, babies begin to supplement breast milk or formula with foods such as rice cereal or unsweetened applesauce—foods that are unlikely to trigger allergic reactions. Solid foods should be introduced one at a time, with a few days passing before introducing the next new food so that any reactions to the food can be easily identified. The introduction of these soft solid foods coincides with the baby's developing abilities to move the food in his mouth and swallow it.

From 6 months to the first birthday, babies continue to rely on breast milk or formula for most of their nutrition, but they are increasing the amount and variety of solid foods they are eating. At this time babies eat pureed cereals, fruits, vegetables, and meats. They learn to eat a wide variety of healthy foods, incorporating more solid foods as they have teeth for chewing. Foods that are likely to cause allergies or choking should not be introduced. Water is offered to quench thirst. Babies begin to finger-feed themselves toward the end of the first year and enjoy holding their own spoon while they are being fed. Important habits are being developed during this time. Babies should be fed when they express their hunger through crying, sucking on their fist, fussiness, or pointing to places where food is kept. They eat quickly when hungry and will begin to slow down and explore or socialize as the hunger abates. When the baby signals through a closed mouth or turning away that she is full, the care teacher should end the feeding. One of the lessons the baby is learning is to understand her own body's signals of hunger and fullness.

Babies cannot eat a great deal at a time, and they need food that is packed in healthy calories to ensure their growth and development. Babies need fat in their diet but they do not need salt or sugar to flavor their foods, and both salt and sugar should be kept to a minimum in their diets. High salt intake can lead to hypertension in adults, and it is not necessary to teach a baby to develop a desire for it. Sugar is linked to hyperactivity, diabetes, tooth decay, and other chronic diseases later in life (Meyers & Chawla, 2000).

Breast-fed babies may continue nursing after their first birthday if it is working well for the mother and the baby. However, formula-fed babies usually switch to cow's milk at about 1 year of age. Between 1 and 2 years, a toddler's daily nutritional needs include about 16 to 24 ounces of milk; 1/2 to 1 cup of fresh fruits and vegetables; 1 or 2 one-ounce servings of meat, poultry, fish, or eggs; about 200 to 500 calories of other good foods such as fortified cereal, breads, and legumes; and water for thirst. Between 2 and 3 years, toddlers need 16 to 24 ounces of milk; 3/4 to 1 1/4 cups

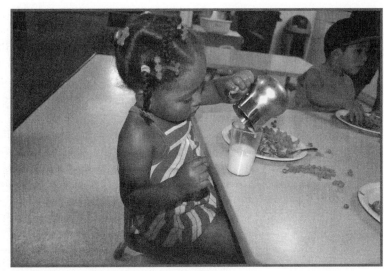

Serving themselves lunch can become an important part of the day. It takes a lot of skill and concentration.

of fresh fruits and vegetables; 1 to 3 servings of meats, poultry, fish, or eggs; about 400 to 800 calories of foods such as fortified cereal, breads, and legumes; and water for thirst (Roberts & Heyman, 2000). Care teachers must be sure to avoid serving foods that cause choking, such as hot dogs (whole or cut into rounds), raw carrot rounds or sticks, whole grapes, hard candy, or nuts. Other foods that present choking dangers include seeds, raw peas, popcorn, marshmallows, spoonfuls of peanut butter, and chunks of meat (American Academy Of Pediatrics, American Public Health Association, National Resource Center for Health and Safety in Child Care and Early Education. 2011. Caring for our children: National health and safety performance standards; Guidelines for early care and education programs. 3rd edition. Elk Grove Village, IL: American Academy of Pediatrics; Washington, DC: American Public Health Association. Also available at http://nrckids.org. APHA & AAP, 2011).

As toddlers are becoming skillful eaters with increasing appetites, teachers and parents can be teaching and encouraging healthy choices. Toddlers enjoy feeding themselves, having some choice in what they eat, eating when they are hungry, and being allowed to determine when they are through. Child care programs should not even have unhealthy salty or sugary foods available as possible choices. Children should see child care as a place where only healthy foods are available. As toddlers naturally use their mouths to explore during the second year of life, give them opportunities to explore a wide variety of foods. By age 2, children can have a repertoire of as many as 200 foods that they enjoy. Toddlers may want to eat the same food day after day for every meal and then suddenly get bored and refuse to touch those very foods at all. As long as children are getting a well-rounded diet that meets their nutritional needs, with ongoing opportunities to broaden their tastes, it is all right to allow them to make choices about what they eat at any one meal.

Child Development and Education Programs Supporting Safe and Healthy Nutrition

When providing foods for infants and toddlers in child care, the changing nutritional needs are only part of what teachers need to know. The National Health and Safety Performance Standards recognize the importance of the emotional

Watch the **video**, *Infant Feeding*, which you may recognize from Chapter 1. This time, focus on health and safety issues.

and social environment of snacks and meals, the safe handling of foods and the utensils used in meal preparation and eating, and the policies in place that ensure each infant or toddler has an individualized diet plan including how to respond to family preferences or allergic reactions to food.

The Social Environment of Feeding

It is almost impossible to separate the importance of nutrition from the importance of being held, touched, and talked to while being fed. In child care, as well as with parents, babies should always be held during bottle-feeding. Bottles should never be propped in a crib or carried around by the child. Care teachers should also feed infants on demand, and a consistent adult, preferably the primary teacher, being the one to feed the child as often as possible. The primary teacher develops the ongoing relationship with the baby that allows them to understand each other's cues and develop expectations about the rhythm and pattern of the feeding. The consistent adult partner will recognize signs of hunger before the child is so distressed that he is crying (American Academy of Pediatrics et al, 2011; Standard 4.5). As older infants begin to eat solid foods, they may at first be spoon-fed in the teacher's arms as part of the meal, which is still primarily bottle-feeding. However, as the child is able to sit, and the amount of solid food is increasing, the baby should be in a supported chair. The care teacher should be talking with the child and creating a pleasant tone for the feeding and always communicating a positive attitude toward the food, with words such as, "Oh yummy. These peas are soooo good. Green beans are so good for you! You really enjoy this, don't you?" Older toddlers will begin to have meals and snacks in small groups, the adult sitting with them, promoting the social aspects of mealtime such as passing foods to one another and having conversations.

Care teachers should never force children to eat or prevent them eating. Food may not be used as a punishment and should not be used as a reward (American Academy of Pediatrics et al, 2011; Standard 4.5).

Safe Handling of Food and Utensils

As in all areas of health and safety, the recommendations for the safe handling of food, eating areas, and utensils are thoroughly described in the National Health and Safety Performance Standards. Some of the most important points include having seating arrangements for infants and toddlers during meals in which they can sit comfortably, with tables coming between stomach and mid-chest levels, on seats that allow their feet to rest on a firm surface while eating. This provides the most comfort and increases the developing independence of the child. Seats that attach to the side of a table leaving little feet hanging in midair would not meet this recommendation (American Academy of Pediatrics, et al. (2011). APHA & AAP, 2002, Standard 4.028).

Utensils and eating surfaces must, of course, be kept clean and sanitized to prevent the spread of disease. Eating utensils should enable children to eat at their developmental level and should never have sharp edges that could cut the tissue inside a baby's mouth; plates and utensils must be free from chips; single-use materials such as paper plates or napkins must be discarded after one use; washable bibs, placemats, napkins, or tablecloths must be washed and sanitized after each use; imported dishware must be certified to be free from lead or other heavy metals; and all surfaces in contact with foods must be lead free. Table surfaces and even high chair trays appear to be much more likely to be contaminated by microorganisms than single-use or washed and sanitized dishes (American Academy of Pediatrics et al, 2011; Standard 4.5).

The food preparation areas must be kept separate from areas of the program used for eating, play, laundry, toileting, bathrooms, and any area where animals are permitted. Sinks used for food preparation may not be used for hand washing or any other purpose, and sinks used for hand washing and diapering may not be used for food preparation. Refrigeration must be able to keep foods at 40°F or lower, and freezers must maintain 0°F or lower at all times. No staff with symptoms of illness should handle food. Food that was unfinished on individual plates or family-style serving bowls should be discarded. The storage of foods, washing of dishes, and transporting of meals purchased from off-site food services should follow the regulations of the National Health and Safety Performance Standards and the Child and Adult Care Food Program of the U.S. Department of Agriculture (American Academy of Pediatrics et al, 2011; Standard 4.5).

Policies Supporting Safe and Healthy Food Services

In a role similar to that of a health consultant to a program, each child care program should have a nutritional consultant. This nutritionist can help determine how to meet individual requests from families (e.g., vegetarian, kosher), how to train and plan for food-related emergencies such as allergic reactions or choking, and how to be sure that feeding plans for individual children are meeting their nutritional needs. A program might develop policies regarding the consistent feeding by one adult for bottle-fed infants or limit the number of children per adult during a small group meal. Program policies can articulate the training and monitoring of staff for safe food-handling practices.

An additional role for a nutrition consultant may be to provide nutrition education for families or help teachers plan nutritional learning activities for toddlers. The consultant may help educate staff and parents about programs that can support their ability to provide healthy foods such as the Child and Adult Care Food Program (CACFP) described in Box 11.3.

Evaluating Quality in Child Care Programs

Given the aspects that contribute to quality already described in this chapter, it should be evident by now that assessing quality is anything but clear. When we walk into a child care program and find infants and toddlers quietly and intently engaged in their play and learning and looking to care teachers for a moment of emotional connection, the care teachers calm and interested in the children, we know we are looking at high quality. Understanding each child's experience is, of course, the most important way to assess quality, but it is very subjective. The evaluation tools available for infant-toddler programs use both structural and process variables as researchers develop increasingly sophisticated measures of quality.

There are several reasons to assess the quality of care. Researchers are continuously trying to determine which elements of quality have most impact on the developmental outcomes of young children. Policy makers use that information

BOX 11.3

The Child and Adult Care Food Program (CACFP)

CACFP is a federal program that provides healthy meals and snacks to children and adults receiving day care. It plays a vital role in improving the quality of day care and making it more affordable for many low-income families. CACFP reimburses participating centers and day care homes for their meal costs. It is administered at the federal level by the Food and Nutrition Service (FNS), an agency of the U.S. Department of Agriculture. The state education or health department administers CACFP in most states. Independent centers and homes and sponsoring organizations enter into agreements with their state agencies to operate the program.

In order to participate in CACFP, homes and centers must agree to meet the nutritional meal and snack requirements of the program. In turn, the program receives reimbursements for each snack and meal served.

Child Care Centers. Public or private nonprofit child care centers, Head Start programs, and some for-profit centers that are licensed or approved to provide day care may serve meals and snacks to infants and children through CACFP.

Family Day Care Homes. CACFP provides reimbursement for meals and snacks served to small groups of children receiving nonresidential day care in licensed or approved private homes. A family or group day care home must sign an agreement with a sponsoring organization to participate in CACFP. The sponsoring organization organizes training, conducts monitoring, and helps with planning menus and filling out reimbursement forms.

To learn more about CACFP, contact your state agency. If you have questions about any of USDA's nutrition assistance programs, check the information on the other pages of the USDA FNS Web site.

Source: Child and Adult Care Food Program, www.fns.usda.gov/cnd/Care/CACFP/aboutcacfp.htm.

to determine where to invest resources. Parents use quality indicators to help them choose the best care possible for their own child. Large public programs such as Early Head Start use program evaluation as a measure of accountability for the use of public funds. Programs can use measurement tools to assess their own quality and develop their own plans for improvement. Following are descriptions of some of the most frequently used measures.

Infant-Toddler Environmental Rating Scale (ITERS)

The ITERS–Revised (Harms, Cryer, & Clifford, 2006) is one of the most widely used measures of quality in the United States. It is part of a series of measures used for specific age groups or settings, including preschool, family child care, and school-age care. In its new revision, the ITERS–Revised consists of 39 items organized into seven subscales: space and furnishings, personal care routines, listening and talking, activities, interaction, program structure, and parents and staff. The observer has to notice materials or interactions taking place. Each item is measured on a 7-point scale ranging from inadequate to minimal to good to excellent. Each subset is scored and a global score is given. The information available from the measure can be helpful for a program working on improving quality.

The ITERS–Revised is often used in research as a reliable, valid measure. Many states have adopted its use as one factor to provide higher child care reimbursement rates to programs that offer higher quality. The ITERS–Revised and its related scales are sometimes criticized as overemphasizing the structural variables and not being sensitive to the subtleties of responsive caregiving.

Observational Record of the Caregiving Environment (ORCE)

The ORCE (NICHD, 1996) was developed on the theoretical basis of the overriding importance of the child's earliest experiences with teachers on his well-being and development. The focus of this tool is on the actual interaction between the teacher and the child. Four 44-minute-long observations are done over the course of 2 days. At the end of each 44-minute period, the teachers are rated on individual items, from 1 point = not at all characteristic to 4 points = highly characteristic. Higher scores describe a teacher who is sensitive, responsive, warm, positive, and cognitively stimulating, and neither detached nor hostile. This measure can be used across settings and ages, and across types of teachers.

Teacher Interaction Scale

The Teacher Interaction Scale (Arnett, 1989) was one of the earliest attempts to evaluate the teacher's sensitivity during interactions. Two observers, in two separate 45-minute observation periods, use the 26-item scale to develop three scores: sensitivity (warm, attentive, engaged), harshness (critical, punitive), and detached (low levels of interest, supervision, interaction).

The Head Start Program Monitoring Review Protocol

The Office of Head Start Monitoring Protocol (Head Start, 2013) is a complex system for reviewing Head Start and Early Head Start programs. A federal program officer and a team of reviewers spend several days reviewing every aspect of the program's services and management systems. The questions, checklists, and observational tools in the protocol all derive from the Head Start Program Performance Standards, the federal regulation that describes the requirements of virtually every aspect of a Head Start or Early Head Start program.

Policies, Laws, and Systems That Support Quality Programs

The Head Start Program Performance Standards (HSPPS) are a good example of how government uses regulations to influence quality. The HSPPS provide detailed descriptions of what is required of every aspect of the program; a system of technical assistance is available to help programs achieve the standards, and the programs are reviewed every 3 years against the full set of standards.

Whenever public funds are used for programs, some set of regulations provides the limits within which those funds may be used. The Head Start Bureau, the Child Care Bureau, state and city governments—all have policies and regulations ranging from minimum standards of safety to standards of quality. Public money and private institutions also provide a wide network of programs to support and encourage quality. Although this is not a comprehensive list, it will give students of child development an idea of the wider system in which they will be working.

Child Care Development Fund (CCDF)

The federal government provides funding for child care through the Child Care Bureau in the Administration for Children and Families (ACF) within the U.S. Department of Health and Human Services (HHS). The Child Care Development Fund (CCDF) provides each state with funds to subsidize the cost of child care for families that are in work or education programs as they transition from welfare assistance. A portion of each state's CCDF funds is to be used for increasing quality, and a specific portion has been earmarked for infants and toddlers. States use their infant-toddler earmarked funds to make infant-toddler–specific improvements in facilities, such as appropriate playgrounds or bathrooms. They support infant-toddler–specific training for teachers and infant-toddler specialists in the resource and referral networks. Some states use these funds to raise public awareness of the importance of the early years and the impact of good or poor quality child care on later development. CCDF is used to promote quality in child care, but there is not sufficient funding or authority to ensure quality care from the federal government. The overall quality of a child care system depends on the licensing regulations and initiatives of the individual state.

Licensing

Every state requires programs providing child care to be licensed. The actual licensing requirements and the range of settings that are exempt from licensing vary widely from state to state. At minimum, a state has basic safety requirements for a setting and age requirements for teachers. Many states have detailed regulations determining group sizes, ratios, training requirements for staff, health and safety practices, and even plans for learning activities. Most states have specific licensing requirements for programs serving infants and toddlers. However, even the most minimal requirements are not always enforced because of the many programs that may be exempt from licensing or may be operating illegally without a license. The licensing regulations for each state are available on the Internet, either on the state government Web site or on the Web site of the National Resource Center for Health and Safety in Child Care (nrckids.org/STATES/states.htm)

Each state has an office administrating the CCDF and child care licensing. These may not be the same offices, or even the same departments of state government. Nonetheless, each of these groups would like to be able to ensure safe and high-quality child care for every infant and toddler who requires out-of-home care. If it were possible, each state would set licensing requirements that ensure low ratios, small group sizes, highly trained staff, and strong health and safety policies at every program.

Unfortunately, high-quality child care is expensive, and states fear that by requiring high-quality child care and highly trained workers, they would reduce the availability of care—as private owners and nonprofit organizations would be unable to meet the cost of providing quality child care on the basis of the tuition they can collect. The states themselves are struggling with large deficits and are unable, or unwilling, to commit precious funds to supporting child care when their public schools and colleges are struggling for survival.

Unable to ensure high-quality child care by legislation, states and national organizations are trying a number of other strategies to promote and inspire quality. States are developing quality rating systems wherein they rate the quality of particular programs, either as a way of informing consumers or as the basis of providing differential subsidy reimbursements. National child care organizations offer accreditation to programs as a statement of recognized quality. We examine these two strategies next.

Quality Rating Systems and Tiered Reimbursement

Tiered quality systems are one way for states to inspire, recognize, and reward quality. A compendium of quality rating improvement systems was completed in 2010, assessing the QRIS from 26 states (Child Care Trends, 2010). In tiered reimbursements, states give higher subsidy payments to child care centers and homes that demonstrate quality beyond the requirements of licensing. These may include having a national accreditation or a variety of factors such as group size, ratios, teacher training, compensation, family involvement, and ratings on standardized tools. Some states have only two tiers, licensed and above. Other states have more complex systems, often symbolized by a rating of 1 to 4 stars. Quality rating systems, sometimes called star rating systems, may be tied to higher reimbursement rates, or they may be aimed primarily at getting consumers to demand higher quality. These systems are a sort of report card for programs. When they are most effectively used, programs are able to receive increased funds for better quality but are also able to receive technical assistance and support to help them make improvements (NAFCC, 2013).

> **tiered quality systems**
>
> Graduated sets of criteria developed to rate the quality of early childhood programs.

Accreditation

Many national early childhood organizations offer program accreditation as a way of promoting and recognizing high quality in child care. The two major national accreditation programs are from the National Association for the Education of Young Children (NAEYC, 2012) for centers, and the National Association for Family Child Care (NAFCC, 2009) for home and family programs. The NAEYC has more than 8,000 accredited child care programs around the country serving more than 700,000 children and families. In 2006, the organization introduced a revision of its accreditation process and criteria (NAEYC, 2006a, 2006b). Both NAEYC and NAFCC require an in-depth self-study by the program. The self-study report is validated by a team of trained visitors to the program (or individual to a home). The validated self-study is then submitted to a national commission; if the program is judged to be in compliance, it is granted accreditation for a limited number of years. In order to maintain accreditation, the program must submit yearly reports on progress and its responses to suggestions from the national organization. Accreditation carries considerable respect within the field of child development.

Summary

The potential of child care to have either positive or negative effects on infants and toddlers depends entirely on the quality of the program involved.

- For infants and toddlers to experience warm, nurturing, ongoing relationships, child care programs need
  - Low child-to-teacher ratios and small group sizes
  - Continuity of care—children staying with the same teacher over the course of years
  - Teachers who are warm, comfortable with intimacy, and enjoy children, as well as being well educated specifically in infant and toddler development, well compensated, and well supported in their work
  - Cultural and linguistic continuity with the home
  - Structure that meets the needs of the individual within the group
  - A comfortable, homelike environment with daily exposure to family-like routines as well as engaging learning experiences

- For infants and toddlers to be safe and healthy in child care, teachers must maintain good procedures for
  - Sanitizing and preventing the spread of disease
  - Hand washing
  - Excluding children who are ill
  - Administering medication
  - Promoting safety and preventing injuries and accidents
  - Meeting the nutritional needs of infants and toddlers
  - Providing safe handling of food
- Quality in child care programs may be assessed with a variety of tools that examine the environment and the interactions.
- Quality is supported by structures at the federal government and the state government and through national professional organizations offering accreditation.

Key Terms

process variables   structural variables   tiered quality systems

Reflections and Resources for the Reader

REFLECTIONS

1. If our greatest concern for quality, after the basics of health and safety, is the responsiveness of the teacher, why do we measure quality by the structural variables of group size and ratios?

2. Infant and toddler programs can be very busy places. What can a program do to ensure that care is always being taken with health, safety, and nutrition?

OBSERVATION AND APPLICATION OPPORTUNITIES

1. Visit an infant-toddler program and ask to review its health, safety, diapering, and food-handling policies. Do you see the policies as thorough enough to provide guidance to the staff? Is there a system for monitoring how the policies are implemented? Would you make any changes?

2. Contact a program in your community that has been accredited by the National Association for Family Child Care or the National Association for the Education of Young Children. Interview a staff member about the process of accreditation.

3. Contact a child care licensing agent in your community and interview him or her about the role of licensing in supporting quality.

SUPPLEMENTARY ARTICLES AND BOOKS TO READ

American Academy of Pediatrics. (2011). AAP updates recommendation on car seats. Retrieved from www.aap.org/advocacy/releases/carseat2011.htm

NAEYC for Families Toddler program health and safety checklist. Retrieved from families.naeyc.org/accredited-article/toddler-program-health-and-safety-checklist

Schumacher, R. (2010). Promote health and safety in infant/toddler child care. Retrieved from www.clasp.org/issues/in_focus?type=child_care_and_early_education&id=0237

INTERESTING LINKS

National Resource Center for Health and Safety in Child Care

nrc.kids.org

This Web site includes the full text of *Caring for Our Children: National Health and Safety Performance Standards for Out-of-Home Child Care* (3rd ed.). It also has links to each state's licensing standards.

Healthy Child Care America

www.healthychildcare.org

The Web site for Healthy Child Care America, a joint project of the Child Care Bureau and the Maternal and Child Health Bureau, is a great source of information on healthy practices in child care.

HealthyChildren.org

This Web site, supported by the American Academy of Pediatrics, includes up-to-date health and safety information and many brochures such as, *A parents' guide to safe sleep* and *A child care provider's guide to safe sleep.*

National Association for the Education of Young Children

naeyc.org/accreditation

The NAEYC Web site has information on many interesting topics, but this link takes you to the new accreditation criteria for programs, providing background information on the reasons for the criteria as well.

12

Creating a Relationship-Based Curriculum

LEARNING OUTCOMES

After reading this chapter, you should be able to:

- Describe the foundational elements of a responsive, relationship-based program

- Explain and evaluate the care teachers' roles in a relationship-based program

- Explain how to create a family and culturally sensitive program

- Describe how to plan in a responsive, relationship-based format

Hours in infancy have more power to shape us than months in middle age. The relative impact of time—time lost or time invested—is greatest early in life. Indeed, humanity was created in childhood. (Perry)

This chapter discusses a framework for designing and evaluating curricula for infants and toddlers. We analyze what curriculum means to children, care teachers, and families in an infant-toddler development and education center or a family child care home. The major elements of a child-centered, responsive, relationship-based curriculum for infants and toddlers are described.

This **video** describes key aspects of a developmentally appropriate program. What are the relationship and program features that characterize a quality infant/toddler program?

The curriculum roots are in Developmentally Appropriate Practice (age, individually, and culturally appropriate; National Association for the Education of Young Children, 2009) and Division for Early Childhood's (DEC's) Recommended Practice (Division for Early Childhood, 2013), both of which provide extensive guidelines for quality practice in early childhood programs.

The curriculum that we describe in this chapter and Chapter 13 has as its philosophical foundation a focus on the importance of relationships and planning strategies that are responsive to individual children's needs, interests, and strengths (in collaboration with families). The philosophy of a child-centered, responsive curriculum is inherent in many published curricula and approaches for infants and toddlers, such as the *Creative Curriculum for Infants, Toddlers, and Twos* (Teaching Strategies for Early Childhood, 2012), the HIGHSCOPE approach to caring for infants and toddlers in group settings (HIGHSCOPE, 2012), the Program for Infant/Toddler Caregivers (PITC, 2012), and the responsive approaches recommended by Gandini and Edwards (2001), Gonzalez-Mena and Eyer (2009), and Szanton (2001). A focus on relationships as the core of the curriculum is recommended by ZERO TO THREE in its book *Caring for Infants and Toddlers in Groups* (ZERO TO THREE, 2008)—a must-read for infant and toddler professionals working with young children in group settings.

The relationship-based approach discussed in this book fits well with most infant and toddler curricula and approaches and adds a planning process of *respect, reflect,* and *relate;* planning guides; and further detailed illumination of a relationship-based approach.

A responsive, relationship-based curriculum has as its primary focus the mental health of infants and toddlers. The curriculum is based on the perspective and needs of infants and toddlers and is focused on the responsive, caring, moment-to-moment and day-to-day experiences that lead to valuable, enduring relationships in each child's life—family-child, teacher-child, and peer-peer relationships. The moment-to-moment responsive interactions of the teachers with the children are the ingredients that together create nourishing relationships with them. Relationships are created over time, and they require a teacher's emotional commitment to each child's well-being as well as reciprocal emotional connections. In a program using a caring, responsive curriculum, the more

A relationship-based curriculum requires teachers' emotional commitment to the well-being of each child.

enduring relationships—between the children and their families, the care teachers and the children, and the care teachers and families—provide the foundation for children to love and learn and experience joy.

A relationship-based curriculum for infants and toddlers considers everything that happens to them from the moment they are carried or walk into the child development and education program until they leave to go home. Care teachers create the environment and then vary it as indicated by the changing developmental levels and interests of the infants and toddlers. The adult-child interactions are also responsive to the moment-to-moment, daily, and life needs of the children and families in the program. The care teacher is empathic with children's joy and pleasure and responds to children's unhappiness and distress with tender care (Weil, 1993). Teachers are kind, caring, considerate, and compassionate with young children's and their families' feelings, needs, and learning goals and know how to develop an enriched environment that supports important relationships in children's lives. The teachers use a philosophy of mind-mindedness (Meins, 1997, Meins, et al., 2003), which means that care teachers consider infants and toddlers to have a mind that can readily

TABLE 12.1   Important Components of a Curriculum

1. The Foundation—A Way of Thinking About Infants and Toddlers

What are the beliefs and assumptions about the nature of infants and toddlers?

What are the needs of infants and toddlers?

What is important for infants and toddlers to learn?

How do infants and toddlers develop and learn?

2. The Care Teachers' Roles in a Relationship-Based Program

What is the program's view of the nature of teacher-child interactions, the importance of teachers' emotional connections with the children, and the teachers' roles and responsibilities?

3. Relationships with Families and Culturally Sensitive Care

How does the program view partnerships with families?

How do program teachers respond to a child's and family's culture?

4. Responsive, Relationship-Based Planning

How do care teachers plan for each child and the group?

How do care individualize the curriculum for each child (including children with disabilities)?

5. Transitions and Routines—A Time for Relationships

What is the value placed on transitions, routines, rituals, and schedules?

6. Responsive and Relationship-Based Environments and Choosing Materials for "Day to Day the Relationship Way"

How is the environment developed, created, and adapted to individual children and groups?

7. Responsive Experiences and Opportunities

How are materials and experiences chosen and provided?

8. A Relationship-Based Approach to Guidance

What is the philosophy and what are the strategies used to guide infants and toddlers?

process information and express thoughts, feelings, and needs. Thus teachers are constantly trying to consider the perspectives and feelings of the children and families. Parents who have higher scores on mind-mindedness comment on what a child may be thinking. This behavior is related to a child's secure attachment (Meins et al., 2012).

The curriculum is truly "day to day the relationship way."

Table 12.1 describes the eight components of curriculum planning that are considered in Chapters 12, 13, and 14. Components 1 through 4 are discussed in this chapter and components 5 through 7 will be highlighted in Chapter 13. Component 8 is covered in Chapter 14.

Component 1: The Foundation—A Way of Thinking About Infants and Toddlers

Influencing factors for determining the foundation of the curriculum—a way of thinking about infants and toddlers—include care teachers' beliefs and assumptions about the nature of children, children's emotional and social needs, *what* is important for children to learn, and *how* children develop and learn. Let's begin with the beliefs and assumptions about the nature of children.

What Are the Beliefs and Assumptions About the Nature of Infants and Toddlers?

A framework for an infant-toddler program is based on certain principles and beliefs regarding the nature of infants and toddlers. There are two questions regarding the nature of babies: Do infants and toddlers have human rights and responsibilities? Are they capable learners?

Most adults think that young children have rights—the rights to be protected, to learn, to be loved and to love, and to be treated with respect. They have the right to belong and participate in their family, culture, and social life. The United Nations developed the Convention on the Rights of the Child in 1989:

> [The] Convention on the Rights of the Child is a universally agreed set of non-negotiable standards and obligations. It spells out the basic human rights that children everywhere—without discrimination—have: the right to survival; to develop to the fullest; to protection from harmful influences, abuse, and exploitation; and to participate fully in family, cultural, and social life. Every right spelled out in the Convention is inherent to the human dignity and harmonious development of every child. (UNICEF, 2009)

In addition to believing that children have rights, many adults also believe that infants and toddlers are capable learners—that they enter this world as active learners, discoverers, and problem solvers. When they are offered empathic care and an enriched environment, they quickly construct their knowledge in interaction with caring adults, family members, and peers. Jerome Bruner (1996a) emphasizes this point: "The child is *not* merely ignorant or an empty vessel, but somebody able to reason, to make sense, both on her own and through discourse with others" (p. 57, emphasis in original).

Adults' beliefs about the nature of children influence the attitudes that they have about their role in children's lives. If children are viewed as having rights and as being capable learners, then they are treated with respect for their "personhood" (Honig, 1993). In a relationship-based, responsive program, adults trust that very young children need and want to belong to a social group, that they strive to develop well and to be healthy, and that they would like to and can master their environment if given the opportunity and responsive care. Adults trust that meeting infants' and toddlers' basic needs for protection and nurturance will result in children who are more likely to be competent, caring, and courageous.

What Are the Needs of Infants and Toddlers?

As discussed in previous chapters, infants and toddlers need strong, positive, emotional connections with their families, teachers, and peers in order to thrive. Children have a neurobiological expectation for nurturance (Shonkoff & Phillips, 2000). This means that children are biologically programmed to expect to be protected and cared for in loving ways—and if they are, then they are more likely to develop optimally. As highlighted in Chapter 5, brain development occurs best when children receive tender care, when adults take the perspective of what it is like to be a baby and respond sensitively and perceptively to the children's needs. Babies need protection. They need to feel safe; they need adults whom they can count on to be emotionally and physically available to them. Ideally, there is one person who is "just crazy about him" (Bronfenbrenner, 1994), thinks he is precious, and knows him well—the funny way he wriggles his nose when he is hungry or the way he feels sad if the teacher looks sad.

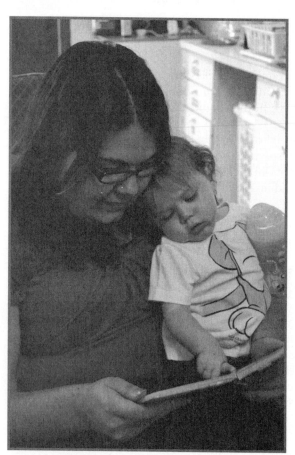

When an infant leans in and puts her head on the shoulder of the caregiver, we know she feels safe.

All infants and toddlers need affection, compassion, gentle holding, and kind touch. They need responsive, sensitive interactions and interesting things to do. Most of all, infants and toddlers need adults who are willing to invest emotionally in their well-being—to have a healthy relationship with them, develop a loving bond, and have an emotional commitment.

How can the basic needs of babies be met by parents and teachers? As Gonzalez-Mena and Eyer (2001) have said, "infants and toddlers need attention to their physical and psychological needs" (p. 6). They state that one of the most important needs of an infant is the pacing of care—a thoughtful, unhurried, finely attuned dialog between the infant and care teacher. Lally, Torres, and Phelps (1994) stress that settings for infants should offer "security, protection, and intimacy" to meet babies' needs.

We can see that infants and toddlers feel securely attached if the following happen:

- They can generally be comforted by the teacher and relax in the teacher's arms.
- They can engage in long, mutually satisfying gazes and conversations of sounds and words with the teacher.
- They show that they feel valued and loved by the teacher.
- They are generally happy to see the teacher.

- They can experience joy with the teacher.
- They (mobile infants and toddlers) move away from and explore the environment but hurry back if they sense danger or need a hug.
- They can focus and engage with toys, materials, and the environment. Toddlers still need the teacher for assistance, nurturing, scaffolding, and guidance.

Some care teachers may become concerned about becoming *too attached* to an infant or toddler in their care. Yet, as we learned in Chapter 6, children who are securely attached to the important, special people in their lives at home are more resilient, more trusting, and more likely to develop positive relationships with others. As we might expect, infants and toddlers in child care or early intervention programs who are securely attached to their care teachers are also more likely to be socially and emotionally competent (Howes, Phillips, & Whitebook, 1992) than children who experience insecure attachment with their teachers. Three criteria identify attachment figures other than the mother: (1) provision of physical and emotional care, (2) continuity or consistency in the child's life, and (3) emotional investment in the child (Shonkoff & Phillips, 2000):

> Securely attached children have a more balanced self-concept; more advanced memory processes; a more sophisticated grasp of emotion; a more positive understanding of friendship; and greater conscience development. (pp. 236–237)

Care teachers must acknowledge that even when young children spend a significant amount of time in child development and education programs, the parents are the most influential adults in their lives (NICHD, 2002b), and teachers should do everything possible to support children's primary relationships with their families: It is critical that infants and toddlers have a secure relationship with their parents. At the same time, teachers should not underestimate the importance of their own relationship with the child. Children cannot thrive in the absence of secure relationships with both parents and teachers. Relationships are one of the most significant needs of infants and toddlers, influencing healthy growth and psychological well-being. Each child who experiences healthy relationships carries within him the parallel hope for the universe.

What Is Important for Infants and Toddlers to Learn?

Children's motivation toward mastery, self-regulation and social commerce and their reliance on relationships with trusted teachers for support and guidance [are] seen as central to program planning. (Gandini & Edwards)

Gandini and Edwards (2001) emphasize that teachers should consider what children learn about themselves and what they learn about how to relate to others when creating the curriculum. These capacities described in detail in Chapters 6 through 10 are summarized in Table 12.2.

How is the child viewed—what needs, competencies, desires, are determined by the adult to need nurturing or to be squashed? (Szanton)

Szanton (2001) lists the following in answer to her question: readiness for change, flexibility with decisions, the ability to get along, competence with language,

TABLE 12.2 **Areas of Learning for Infants and Toddlers**

1. *Emotional Development*
   - Self-control (self-regulation) and expression of feelings: They develop the ability to modulate and control their own actions in age-appropriate ways—a sense of inner control. They learn to express feelings in socially acceptable ways.
   - A sense of self and identity as a person of worth who deserves to be treated well: They develop an identity as a unique person, a sense of worth, and expect others to treat them kindly.
   - Relatedness: They develop the ability and desire to engage with others based on the sense of being understood by and understanding others (this includes culture). They feel that they belong to a family, culture, and community. Children learn that relationships with others are satisfying and fun. They learn to feel secure and trust important adults to take care of them. Toddlers will show that they have the confidence and courage to go away from their special teachers and explore the room, but also know that they can come back to the protective arms of a teacher and "refuel emotionally" (Kaplan, 1978).

2. *Social Development*
   - Children begin to balance their own needs with those of others in a group.
   - As infants develop, they become generally affectionate, friendly, loving, and kind with others.
   - They are motivated to be with peers and develop in their ability to play with peers in cooperative ways.
   - During the second and third years of life, children are increasingly aware of the feelings of others, which leads to empathic responses to another in distress. They develop a sense of "I can care for others as well as myself."
   - As they grow, they become better able to handle conflict with others.

3. *Language Development*
   - Children have the wish and ability to exchange ideas, feelings, and concepts with others.
   - The desire to communicate is related to a sense of trust in others, and of pleasure in engaging with others, including adults.

4. *Cognitive Development*
   - Children are curious and sense that finding out about things is positive and leads to pleasure.
   - They are intentional—they wish and have the capacity to have an impact, and act upon that with persistence.
   - They sense that they are more likely than not to succeed at what they undertake, and that adults will be helpful.
   - They sense that they can contribute and make decisions and truly believe "I am a capable and competent person."
   - They become more proficient at using the tools of learning, and the concepts that they know increase each day.

5. *Motor Development*
   - Children become increasing able to use their large and small muscles to accomplish what they attempt to do.
   - They become more stable and can use their bodies effectively.

a belief that they can make a difference in their own lives and those around them, the ability to speak out, a use of words and logic instead of violence, a profound sense of the importance of equal opportunity and the dignity and rights of each individual, and the ability to be gifted parents. These are competencies that develop in children in a relationship-based program that emphasizes the attachment (emotional connections) between parents and children and between teachers and children.

OBSERVATION INVITATION **12.1**

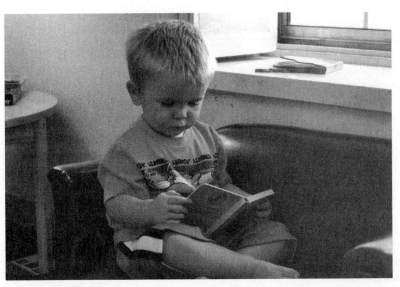

What is this child learning about adults, peers, and how the world works?

Lally (1995) discusses how care teachers must focus on helping infants and toddlers develop a sense of identity as a person of worth—what he calls a **working sense of self**:

> Preschoolers have formed a somewhat well-developed "working sense of self," with likes and dislikes, attitudes, and inclinations. [In contrast] infants and toddlers are in the process of forming this preliminary sense of self. Part of what infants and toddlers get from teachers are perceptions of how people act at various times in various situations (seen as how the infant should behave), how people act toward them and others (seen as how they and others should be treated), and how emotions are expressed (seen as how they should feel). The infant uses these impressions and often incorporates them into the self she becomes. (p. 59)

In addition to learning about themselves and others, infants and toddlers are learning about how the world works. What is grass, how does applesauce taste, where do caterpillars go when they crawl away, how many blocks can fit in a basket, what are the properties of water, and what a friend is are among the important things that babies learn about the world. There is so much for infants and toddlers to learn in the first 3 years of life, and there are so many exciting opportunities for nurturing adults to help these children to enjoy being in and learning about the world.

How Do Children Develop and Learn?

In addition to the question of *what* is important for infants and toddlers to learn, there is the question of *how* they develop and learn. We know that only when a child is secure in his relationship with the important adults in his life is there

working sense of self
The child's ongoing development of a sense of self.

As you watch and listen to this video, think about what children learn as they play. Think about emotional, social, cognitive, language, and motor development.

CULTURE CLOSE UP

Different family cultures have different beliefs about how children develop and learn and what is important to learn. Saliah wanted to create a toddler classroom that had many opportunities for children to explore by themselves, with peers, or with teachers, as she believed that children wanted to learn and could learn through experimentation with materials. She had seen a toddler spend a great deal of time at a low water table, closely supervised, but given time to pour water out of containers, watch water pour out of a sieve, and try to hold water in his hands. Saliah believed that because this child was closely attached to her, he could move away from her and feel safe exploring the environment. She believed that what the child chose to explore, play with, and investigate were the most important topics for the child to learn.

However, some parents wanted her to teach the toddlers their alphabet letters so that they would be ready for preschool. They had heard that there was testing in the preschools that asked children to name the letters, and they were nervous that their children weren't learning what they needed to learn in the toddler room so that they could be successful in the preschool room. Some parents also thought that there was too much play and not enough group lesson time.

What would you do to be culturally sensitive to the parents' needs and wishes while also providing a developmentally appropriate curriculum?

freedom to be independent in play with toys and peers (Honig, 1993). The way infants and toddlers develop and learn can be summarized as follows:

1. Learning is integrated.
2. Learning is developmental.
3. Children learn through play.

Let's start with integrated learning.

Learning Is Integrated

Marilee crawled across the carpet with great speed, making babbling noises to the cat. Her mother commented to her, "You are so fast!" Marilee picked up a colorful soft toy and turned it upside down, studying it carefully. She looked at her mother to see if she was still there sitting on the floor. Marilee smiled and crawled toward her mom.

As all children do in almost any experience, Marilee is developing in emotional, social, cognitive, language, and motor domains in one sequence of behavior. She develops emotionally and socially as she learns to trust her mother. She learns language as she practices babbling and hears her mother match words to her actions. As she studies the toy, her cognitive development is enhanced as she learns about how an object looks from another viewpoint. Her crawling is an important aspect of motor development. As she crawls toward her mother, she is establishing an emotional bond as well as improving her motor skills. Marilee is growing in all domains, not just sequentially, but simultaneously. Her learning is integrated with all developmental domains in use and affecting one another: "In infants and toddlers, all domains of development are interrelated. Each is a thread in the same cloth; pull one, and the others follow" (Parlakian, 2003, p. 4).

Adults divide children's development into the different domains to help them observe and learn about children, but children are including and applying all of their skills together to accomplish their goals. Development in one domain also affects development in another domain.

Learning Is Developmental

A child care and education program looks different for infants (0 to 8 months of age) than it does for mobile infants (8 to 18 months) or for toddlers (18 to 36 months). Children of these different ages have distinct needs and learning goals that develop as they grow (Mangione, Lally, & Signer, 1990), although we also know that they exhibit a broad range of individual differences. If we listen, infants and toddlers tell us what they are experiencing and how we can respond to these changing needs. Care teachers learn how to **dance the developmental ladder** (Honig, 2000).

The physical changes as children grow from infants to toddlers are easily seen. It is more difficult, however, to detect the changes in a child as he grows from a dependent baby to a more independent person—and the significance of this

dance the developmental ladder
How adults can respond to children's differing developmental levels in all domains.

development can be understood only by caring, observant adults who provide for both the group and the unique individuals within the group.

Infancy: 0 to 8 months.   Infants rely totally on parents and care teachers to meet their emotional and social needs; to provide nurturing, sensitive care, and calm and interesting environments; and to present opportunities for the infants to move and explore objects. Ideally, during the first 8 months of life, infants will become emotionally attached to their parent(s) as well as to primary teacher(s)—wanting to be with these special persons in their lives, receive comfort from them, and learn from them. The baby will turn to the sound of this person's voice, brighten when spoken to, and give a special smile just for the person(s) she is growing to love. The infant learns what to expect, how that person will treat her, and the tone of that person's voice. As early as several weeks of age, infants feel more comfortable when they are with their special person(s) and can become distressed when they are not. The most important thing that babies this age are learning is that they can trust adults to take care of them rather than having to defend and protect themselves most of the time. They need adults who can hold, rock, sing, and talk quietly to them, and who can play "follow the leader" by imitating the baby's eye-blinks, sounds, and facial movements and then waiting for the baby to take a turn.

The environment must be tailored for infants. Infants need safe places to be on the floor to practice their "tummy" moves. They need quiet, calm places to sleep and places to sit (without being knocked over), to bang objects on the floor or together in their hands. As they approach 8 months of age, many of the infants are ready to pull themselves up to a standing position. This requires that there be space for an adult on the floor; the infant can then inch himself up the trustworthy adult's body to look her in the eye or collapse safely in her arms.

Mobile infants: 8 to 18 months.   Mobile infants (8 to 18 months old) are on the move. They are often crawling, walking, and fitting their bodies into a variety of spaces. Infants who are on the move need nurturing adults who provide the emotional and social base from which they explore their world. They are often dashing back or fussing when an emotional connection to a caring teacher is needed. The most important thing that mobile infants learn in your care is that they can "make things happen" with both people and objects. This is what Cawlfield (1992) calls **Velcro time** with language, when mobile infants stick like Velcro to the teachers' responsive words, finger-plays, and book reading as their language bursts forth. The environment also changes as mobile infants develop.

Velcro time

How mobile infants stick like Velcro to the teachers' responsive words as their language bursts forth.

The environment requires open spaces and cozy corners to encourage both *interaction time* with teachers and peers and *alone time* to gather energy for the next adventure. For mobile infants, life is truly an adventure as they make exciting discoveries with toys and peers. Open-ended toys (with no correct product) encourage stacking, pulling, pushing, throwing, and filling. As mobile infants reach 18 months, they are ready for fat crayons, art materials, large beads and string, and more challenging motor activities. Mobile infants thrive in a room or family child care home that has space to explore, interesting materials to investigate, peers to imitate, and caring adults who admire their blossoming skills.

Toddlers: 18 to 36 months.   Toddlers need loving, understanding people in their lives who think they are very special with all of their new skills and antics. As stated by Lerner and Dombro (2000), "For babies, the world is a banquet to be gobbled up with eyes, ears, nose, mouth, and fingers" (p. 20). The light in a toddler's eyes when he discovers a bug, listens with his ears to the bathtub drain to hear where the water goes, or sees a kitten for the first time recharges an adult's sense of wonder and delight in learning about the world and in turn provides emotional energy for the child to continue learning. Experienced teachers even love when toddlers say "No," because they understand the emotional struggles of very young children who are so brave to stand up to a person more than twice their size. Living with toddlers requires that parents and teachers be ready for anything, as toddlers experiment with what happens when they poke a friend or when they continuously pull tissues out of a tissue box. It helps parents and teachers to remember that toddlers are learning with all of their senses and that their experimentation is their enthusiastic way of learning about their world.

Toddlers are little scientists who are inventing, taking apart, creating, and exploring on their way to figuring out the ways of the world. They have to touch to learn. They can't just look at an object—they have to investigate it. They can't just watch—they have to manipulate objects. They are problem solvers and it is the teachers' and parents' role to give them a physically and emotionally safe environment in which to explore and learn. It is also easier to be a teacher of toddlers when you understand that they are not purposely trying to frustrate you, but rather that they are experiencing important internal struggles on their way to becoming good decision makers and problem solvers.

Toddlers need materials to pound, squeeze, and cut (with safe scissors with rounded points). Puzzles with a variety of pieces and pictures are challenging and interesting for developing muscles that will soon try to write. Pasting, painting, and coloring are messy but fun for toddlers, as they love to "make their mark" on the world. Longer and more complicated stories and songs (but not too complicated) delight toddlers, and they love to move their hands and carry objects while walking and running.

▶▶▶ OBSERVATION INVITATION **12.2**

 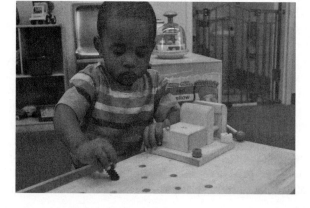

Why is play so important for young children?

For all of these ages—infancy, mobile infants, and toddlers—play is the way to learn.

Children Learn Through Play

Many theorists and researchers strongly believe, based on their observations and the results of research, that children learn through play and active exploration of their environment (Goncu & Gaskins, 2007; Hirsh-Pasek, Golinkoff, Berk, & Singer, 2009; Smith & Pellegrini, 2008). Bettelheim (1987) defines play as a child's activities characterized by freedom from all but personally imposed rules (which are changed at will). Play is an opportunity for pure enjoyment and is also important for many other reasons.

Why is play so important? Perry (2001) discusses why play is vital for the developing child: "We learn best when we are having fun" (p. 24). Play enhances "verbalization, vocabulary, language, comprehension, attention span, imaginativeness, concentration, impulse control, curiosity, more problem-solving strategies, cooperation, empathy, and group participation" (Smilansky & Shefatya, 1990, p. 220). Caruso (1988) states that "it is only through acting on the world using developmentally appropriate skills during exploratory play that infants build a meaningful understanding of the environment" (pp. 67–68). Howes and Phillipsen (1998) conclude from their research that complex play as a toddler predicts a child's prosocial behavior as a preschooler and less aggressive and less withdrawn behavior as a 9-year-old. It seems that as young children play, they learn many cognitive and social skills that result in social competence later in their childhood. As described in Box 12.1, from the view of the child, play is definitely the way to learn.

What will infants and toddlers do when they are playing? This will vary according to a child's developmental level. Generally, they are trying to figure out how the world works. Infants will mouth, bang, shake, and pound on toys to learn about them. They will watch other children with great interest. They vocalize and responsive caregivers respond. Mobile infants will imitate each other during play, turn objects around, put objects in and take them out of containers, and pull and push objects to see out how they work. They engage in games such as peek-a-boo with their favorite caregivers, who they trust will not really disappear. Toddlers will try many strategies to learn—change strategies, adapt strategies, try another strategy, go away from the problem, come back eons later (2 minutes or 2 days) and try again with toys, materials, and people. Older toddlers will begin to pretend as their understanding of symbols progresses (for example, using a toy telephone as if it were a real telephone), and, as we learned in Chapter 7 on social development, play becomes more reciprocal with peers. We can begin to appreciate how children work hard while playing when we see them move a large toy, position a block on top of a tower, or gain the attention of special adults and peers, not because they have to, but because they want to learn.

How to Encourage Play

Once we understand that toddlers learn by active involvement with people and by manipulating objects, it becomes clear that such activities as coloring books, worksheets, and models made of clay or other materials that children are expected to imitate are inappropriate. (Lally, Provence, Szanton, & Weissbourd)

BOX 12.1

Letter from a Toddler

For young children, play with others and by themselves is a way to learn. If toddlers could, they might describe what goes on in a good child care and education setting that encourages play in the following way:

Dear Teacher of Mine,

You looked a little tired and discouraged when the parents were coming to pick all of us up today. Then, when that one dad said, "Did they learn anything today or did they just play?" I thought you'd just about had it. I'm writing to cheer you up and tell you that I'm learning lots because you help us play.

Tonight at supper my big sister said that she learned "the nines table" in school today. I'm not sure what the "nines table" is but everyone seemed pleased and excited that she'd learned it.

I learned a lot today too. Unfortunately, I can't talk enough to describe what I learned about how the world works. I know that dumping out bins of toys, climbing, knocking over blocks, and squashing bananas on my feeding tray doesn't sound as mysterious as "the nines table," but I'm sure grateful that you know how important it all was.

Thank goodness you know I have to play to learn. For example, remember today how every time you'd kneel down and open up your arms, I'd run to you for a big hug? We were playing a game, of course, and we'd both laugh—but just the act of running was learning for me. Babies and toddlers learn through their big muscles, you know. When I ran into your arms, it not only made me feel loved and happy, it gave me a chance to practice the movements of using my arms and legs together. I'm brand new at that. Running strengthens those muscles too. It was fun. I wanted to do it over and over. I'm glad you had time to play so that I could learn. Thank you.

And I'm glad you noticed today how much fun I had tapping with the xylophone hammer, remember? I tapped the xylophone for a while, then the table, then the floor and lots of other objects. I discovered so many different sounds—metallic, strong, soft. Oh, by the way, sorry about Robby's head. It sure scared me when he cried so loud. Thanks for finding all those boxes and pans for me to tap. I am beginning to understand so much more about the world now because you realized I was learning, not "just playing."

I heard you say, "Tappers need things to tap!" You must believe that "dumpers need things to dump" too, because you filled up that coffee can with clothespins over and over and let me dump it out as much as I wanted to. You must have realized that I wasn't trying to make a mess when I dumped out all the tubs of toys yesterday. I need to dump things out. I'm so curious about how something can be full one minute and empty the next—and that I can make it happen. Dumping things out makes me feel big. After lots of play at dumping, I'll want to try filling. It's really the very first step toward being able to put things away neatly—when I'm older.

Thanks to your helping me play. I'm learning that it's good to be curious, it's good to explore and learn and understand. I get the feeling you think my play is pretty valuable. My play is all my own idea, you know. You must think that my ideas are pretty valuable, too. Hey, that must mean you value *me,* too. I'm important, and what I learn is important—even if it isn't "the nines table."

Please don't be discouraged. You helped me play today. You gave me gifts of learning and self-worth that nobody can ever take away.

See you tomorrow!

A Toddler in Child Care (author unknown)

Infants and toddlers learn by active involvement. To support infants' and toddlers' active involvement and play, first provide long play times where they can make choices with comforting and challenging materials, persist at activities, explore, and even have conflicts with peers that provide a foundation for future social relationships. This builds a child's confidence, sense of competence, and motivation to learn. When infants are kept in car seats, swings, walkers, and other containers and not allowed to move freely, they can feel trapped and become inactive and passive. Rather than all toddlers doing the same thing at the same time—such as everyone going first to the puzzle table, then a circle time, then an art activity, then back to a large group story time— they need time to explore alone, with peers, and with their favorite adults. When young children are not allowed to make choices during play we have seen them become passive and sad. From the outside looking in, it may even seem that these toddlers are quiet and "well behaved," but a closer look at their faces tells us that they are not engaged in the activities—and when toddlers (or adults) aren't engaged and interested, they are not learning. Infants and toddlers need to move their bodies, explore sensory materials, manipulate toys, and experience the consequences of their decisions in order to learn. The program in which children are provided a rich array of materials in a well-organized environment can, in fact, be noisy at times with the sounds of children learning through choice and initiation. Provide opportunities for children to explore materials on their own in their own way, with a favorite care teacher close by for emotional support.

Component 2: The Infant-Toddler Professional's Role—Creating a Relationship-Based Program

Developing a relationship-based program requires professionals who are special people who value emotional connections.

A Special Kind of Person

Because of the type of empathetic care—kind, concerned, and compassionate— that infants and toddlers need, the profession of teaching young children can be quite demanding emotionally and physically. It can also be very rewarding. It is satisfying for care teachers to experience emotional connections and relationships with the children and families, as they must if they are to meet the social and emotional needs of babies. As a professional working with infants, toddlers, and their families, you must be concerned and must invest yourself emotionally in the infants, toddlers, and families you will serve. At the same time, to do a good job, you must maintain an objective view of the needs of babies and families. Effective care teachers, then, facilitate children's learning about themselves, others, and the world while meeting their needs through responsive interactions and relationships.

> *Your work is not merely what you do, but how you are as you do it. (Pawl & Dombro)*

Teaching infants and toddlers is an important profession. Care are helping build the character and identities of children through responsive interactions and relationships. An infant-toddler care teacher is a person who nurtures, guides, and facilitates children's development in an emotional blanket of caring that warms the spirit of the child.

As you watch this video, think about Component 2: The Infant-Toddler Professional's role in creating a relationship-based program. What are the key features for children, teachers, and families of a relationship-based program?

BOX 12.2

The Top Eight Responsibilities of an Infant-Toddler Care Teacher

Whether in an education and development center or family child care home, the responsibilities of an infant-toddler teacher include the following eight components:

Component 1: Develop the foundation for a relationship-based program.

Component 2: Structure the program to emphasize the importance of relationships—provide primary care and continuity of care to the children. Take care of children's physical needs—keep children safe and healthy. Provide responsive and reciprocal interactions—give/take, engage/break, negotiate, and cooperate. Care for the spirit of the child—meet the emotional and social needs of children.

Component 3: Build caring, responsive relationships with families, diverse cultures, and the community.

Component 4: Use a responsive planning process—day to day the relationship way. Facilitate individual child development.

Component 5: Create a flexible schedule with responsive routines.

Component 6: Set up the environment for routines, nurturing, playing, learning, and relationships.

Component 7: Provide toys, materials, and opportunities that are individually, culturally, and age appropriate.

Component 8: Use a relationship-based approach to guidance that involves family members and other staff.

Box 12.2 highlights the roles of the infant-toddler professional in a program. Notice how these roles relate to the eight components of a curriculum. Teachers' relationships with other teachers, an encouraging administrative staff, and a supportive community are keys to teachers' successes with all of these roles. This topic receives in-depth coverage in Chapter 16. Let's begin here by discussing how teachers can develop a community of caring for infants, toddlers, and their families.

Creating a Relationship-Based Community

Communities are places where a group of people work and play together. Programs are communities where infants and toddlers and their care teachers often spend many hours together. Carter and Curtis (1998, p. 71) recommend that programs for young children and the staff, who spend many hours at work, resemble a home more than an institution to reduce staff's and children's stress and to develop a physical environment and structure to the day that "connects and nurtures people." The authors recommend the creation of an environment that includes interesting colors, a variety of textures and natural elements such as plants and rocks, cozy lighting, framed pictures of children and families, and inviting aromas.

Center programs are often housed in buildings that have separate rooms that look like classrooms. Because of this classroom arrangement, teachers and children are often isolated from each other. Greenman, Stonehouse, and Schweikert (2008) recommend using the term **homebases** rather than *classrooms* in center-based programs where "classrooms" are considered homes and there are common areas such as playgrounds where children and teachers from the different homes gather at times. Honig (2002b) recommends organizing children into **attachment groups**—small groups that emphasize continuity of care for children with their special teachers throughout their years in a center program. Whatever arrangement is chosen, babies need to feel safe and nurtured and have a sense of belonging.

homebases

"Classrooms" in a center-based program for infants and toddlers.

attachment groups

Small groups that stay with a special teacher throughout the infant and toddler years in a program.

Adult-Child Interactions and Relationships in a Relationship-Based Program

Care teachers Are Intentional

Infant and toddler teachers are deliberate in how they support children's development. Sometimes when a person who doesn't understand a responsive curriculum peeks into a child care and education home or center and sees babies playing or sitting on teachers' laps for a snuggle, the person may think that not much teacher planning occurs. Indeed, we know that teachers of young children carefully plan a responsive environment that meets the developmental needs of each child in the room. They also know how to *use the moment* to support children's development in emotional, social, language, cognitive, and motor development. They are purposeful in how they develop strong and positive relationships with families.

Care teachers Follow Children's Lead for What They Need

Adults follow children's leads for what they need in both moment-to-moment adult-child interactions and in weekly planning for changes in adult-child interactions and the environment. In the moment-to-moment responsive interactions, the professional or parent observes the child, reads the child's cues, tries to determine what the child is thinking, and then responds by continuing to observe or by responding to the child in a way that encourages further action on the part of the child. A 1-year-old, for example, may cover an adult's foot with a blanket, the adult wiggles his foot under the blanket, and then the infant laughs and pulls the blanket off the foot. The adult shares the delight of finding his own foot under the blanket. The infant covers the foot again as if to ask "Will the foot wiggle again?" It does! Again, the infant is delighted. This 1-year-old is not only sharing an emotionally gratifying moment with the adult, but he also is exploring cause-and-effect principles. He is learning how to learn and will likely explore different ways to make that foot move. At times, following children's lead may mean that the adult observes that the child is ready for the adult to initiate an opportunity for the child to use strategies to learn.

For example, after the adult offers a toy, rolls a ball to the child, or sits on the floor with a book, the adult then watches to see if the baby is interested in these opportunities. Does the baby begin to use strategies to pursue his own goal—starting to play with the toy, rolling the ball back to the adult, or showing delight in listening to the book? As Lerner and Dombro (2000) state so well, when the infant-toddler professional or parent sometimes leads and sometimes follows, the interactions feel like a satisfying dance to both the adult and the child:

> Learning and growing together is like dancing. Step by step, day by day, you and your child learn about each other and how your relationship works. Sometimes you lead, and sometimes you follow your child in the dance you create together. (p. 1)

Care teachers Are Responsive to Children's Emotional Needs

Because children's emotional development is the foundation for children to love and learn, teachers think about the well-being of the child from the child's perspective and ask, "What's it like to be an infant or toddler in this program?" and "What can I, as the adult, do to support this baby emotionally?" Teachers' interactions must care for the spirit—the emotional health and vitality—of the baby by demonstrating a profound respect for each child's emotional experiences. When you are a teacher in a center or family child care home for infants and toddlers, always ask the question, "How would it feel to be an infant or toddler in this setting?" and then respond to help babies feel loved, safe, and competent.

Figure 12.1 includes examples of responsive care and education practices that focus on supporting the emotional capacities of infants and toddlers through recognizing cues of communication and responding in ways that are satisfying to the infant or child. Teachers are not only responding to infants and toddlers, but also watching and learning from the children about what those children like and how those children think. Many of these concepts were introduced in earlier chapters in this book, but we discuss them now as they apply to teacher-child interactions and relationships in a program setting. Let's examine how these responsive teacher and parent strategies support emotional development, the foundation for learning.

FIGURE 12.1   **How adults can meet infants' and toddlers' emotional needs**

1. Protect children and keep them safe and healthy.
2. Develop strong, positive, secure relationships with children.
3. Be attuned (read, reflect, and respond) emotionally and physically to children's cues and communication attempts, reflect on their meaning, and respond as needed by child.
4. Interact by following a child's lead in a way that is satisfying to the child—take balanced turns (reciprocal interactions) and match the pace of interactions with the child.
5. Be approachable, accessible, and available to children, both emotionally and physically.
6. Maintain a pleasant and positive emotional tone throughout the day.
7. Respond to children's distress and intense emotional outbursts and other displays of displeasure calmly and in a way that comforts them and helps them regulate themselves physically and emotionally.
8. Notice, identify, encourage, and show admiration for strengths, interests, and new skills in each and every child in the group.
9. Appreciate development and differences—help children feel appreciated for their uniqueness.

Keep children safe and healthy.   The responsive care and education provider consistently protects children—keeps them safe and healthy.

Babies must feel protected and safe in order to love and learn. Sometimes we say the adult **holds and enfolds** the baby. Holding babies is, of course, a familiar idea. The concept of "enfolding" means to surround each child with a caring and supportive personal and physical environment. A care teacher can reflect whether she uses any of the following strategies during the day:

> **holds and enfolds**
>
> Holding a baby and surrounding that child with a caring and supportive personal and physical environment.

- Holds a crying infant
- Puts her arm around a toddler who is sitting near to her
- Responds helpfully to an infant or toddler who becomes upset when another parent comes into the room

Develop strong, positive relationships with children.   The responsive care and education care teacher is kind, affectionate, warm, empathic, caring, and compassionate with children. The care teacher helps each child feel safe, secure, lovable, loving, worthy of love, and cherished.

Babies must know that they can trust and count on the people who take care of them. Significant emotional connections and secure attachments are reflected in the happy eyes of infants and toddlers and their teachers. Babies demonstrate attachment by looking to special teachers when they are startled or afraid, by being comforted more easily by their special adults, and by looking happy to see their special teacher each day. Toddlers will show that they have the confidence to go away from their special teachers and explore the room, but also know that they can come back and be reassured of their teacher's attention. To support parent-child attachment, teachers can continually communicate with families about the children's day, while also asking and listening to parents concerning their children's interests, development, and unique personalities.

Babies need affection, kindness, and encouragement to flourish and to learn how to be affectionate and kind themselves. They need touch—people hugging, holding, and sitting near them—for healthy mental and social development. Infants and toddlers need adults who will hold them when they need to be held, are positive with them when they choose or need to be close, and are *always*

kind to them. Care teachers frequent smiles result in young children's affectionate responses (Zanolli, Saudargas, & Twardosz, 1997). Without affection, children learn to be on the defensive, to protect themselves, to be on guard, and
to generally distrust people. With affection, they learn that they are worthy of
being loved.

Care teachers show affection and warmth to children through smiles, gentle
touches, and mutual gazes. Honig (2002c) and Lally and colleagues (1994) emphasize that teachers need to be intimate with babies and have a relationship of genuine
caring and commitment to the child's well-being. Being intimate with a baby means
that there is a warm, friendly relationship that includes an emotional connection of
caring between an adult and child. *While adults in group care may not cherish each child,
each child needs to be cherished by at least one adult in the group and all adults need to be
warm and affectionate with all children.* A care teacher can ask herself whether she does
any of the following in a day:

- Uses frequent responsive, caring touch
- Uses kind words with children
- Shows affection for children
- Empathizes and shows compassion with children's feelings ("Ooh, that must
  hurt," or "I can tell you are feeling sad")

Be attuned to children's cues. The responsive care and education care
teacher is consistently attuned emotionally and physically to children's cues and
communication attempts, reflects on their meaning, responds *as needed by the
child,* and interprets children's cues and communication attempts.

Babies need care teachers who are attuned to their obvious and subtle communication signaling and who notice and understand the intentions and feelings
of the child. Being **attuned** means that a care teacher is sensitive to and understands what infants and toddlers are trying to communicate with facial expressions,
sounds, gestures, or words. For example, the care teacher might say "You want up"
in response to a child's upraised arms, or say "It seems like you are feeling sad" to
a baby with a sad expression on her face. When a caregiver is well attuned to a
baby, she will mirror the baby's experience in observable ways. A care teacher might
reflect on whether she does any of the following during the day:

> **attuned**
> To be sensitive to and understand
> what infants and toddlers are
> trying to communicate with facial
> expressions, sounds, gestures, or
> words.

- Shares a child's delight
- Asks children what they want or how they are feeling and helps them express
  feelings
- Focuses on what the baby is trying to communicate
- Actively listens with eyes and ears to the infant's or toddler's facial expressions,
  gestures, body movements, sounds, and words

Magda Gerber, an early infancy expert, would say to a baby, "I don't know
what you are trying to tell me, but I want to figure it out" (Mangione et al., 1990).
She believes that when an adult responds to a baby's communication attempts, the
baby gains a positive concept of self and others as communication partners. The
children will learn to use words to express their thoughts and emotions rather than
crying, yelling, or whining much of the time.

When adults cannot respond physically to a child, they can respond verbally.
For example, while the teacher is changing one baby's diaper, he might respond
in a reassuring voice to an infant who is crying, "I'm changing Jareem's diaper.
I'll be there soon." A teacher might reflect on his own responses to children's

communication and reflect on whether he uses any of the following strategies during the day:

- Looks for and reads both clear and subtle communication cues
- Uses words to identify feelings
- Responds *quickly* and *positively* to children's questions and other bids for attention

Follow the child's lead in your interactions. The responsive care and education provider interacts by following the child's lead in a way that is satisfying to the child, takes balanced turns (reciprocal interactions), and matches the pace of interactions with the child.

A reciprocal interaction is one in which there is a sense of give and take, of shared moments, and of joint attention. This important teacher skill not only promotes communication skills in young children but also meets their emotional need for "making things happen." If the infant coos, the teacher coos back. If the infant rolls the ball to the teacher, she rolls the ball back. The teacher may initiate the interaction by picking up a book and offering it to the toddler. The toddler then takes the book, sits down beside the teacher, and holds up the book to be read.

These are examples of balanced, reciprocal turn taking. Although not all interactions may be quite this even, taking balanced turns promotes a child's sense of confidence and skills as an interactive partner. Reciprocity helps a child feel some control over what happens to him or her—which is important if the child is to have motivation to learn. This sense of control and efficacy helps infants and toddlers become more engaged in an activity (Lussier, 1994) and tolerate small frustrations.

A care teacher might watch for moments like these to reflect on her abilities to follow the infant or toddler's lead and promote reciprocity:

- Being sensitive to a baby's cues in interaction
- Taking balanced turns in play, eating, and communicating
- Waiting to approach a young child without interrupting or disrupting his activity (noticing that Henry is concentrating on stacking blocks, so waiting a few minutes to change the toddler's diaper)
- Approaching children from within their visual range, rather than swooping them up from behind (leaning down or getting on the floor with the child and telling him what is happening next: "After you finish playing with your toy, I'm going to change your diaper.")
- Asking the child what he wants, how he is feeling, and/or what he would like to do next, either with gestures or verbally (rather than *assuming* that the child wants to be picked up, asking the child and then waiting for the child to respond with a look, a gesture, or words)

Be available, both emotionally and physically. The responsive care and education provider is consistently approachable, accessible, and available both emotionally and physically to children. Infants and toddlers develop a sense of security when an adult is emotionally and physically available to them. Reciprocal interactions are more likely to occur when a teacher is physically on the child's level; infants and toddlers learn to maintain focus and attention when emotionally available adults engage them in longer turn-taking exchanges through games such as peek-a-boo or through conversational interactions. If infants and toddlers approach an adult and are rejected (often because teachers mistakenly don't want the children to become *too* dependent on them or attached to them), infants and toddlers may actually become *more* dependent and clingy because they are not feeling safe and secure (Sears & Sears, 2001).

A care teacher might use these strategies to ensure her emotional and physical availability to children:

- Spend time with children by sitting on the floor with them—allow them to come close, to move away, and then come back to sit in or near her lap at their discretion
- Spend one-on-one time with each child each day
- Limit talking time with other adults so that infants and toddlers feel her emotional presence
- Sit on the infant or toddler's physical level to encourage eye contact and touch

Maintain a pleasant emotional tone.   The responsive care and education provider consistently maintains a pleasant and positive emotional tone throughout the day: "When adult voice tones are hurried, sharp, critical, or upset, babies pick up the emotional tone of any adult worry. They may cry, become distracted from play, and show tension in body and facial muscles. The calmer your voice tones, the more peaceful your classroom will be" (Honig, 2003b). Infants and toddlers pay considerable attention to the moods and emotions of the adults who care for them. Care teachers have an impact on each child in their program all of the time, not only when they are in direct interactions. The care teachers need to provide a sense of calm, comfort, and joy as they encourage the children to approach life with a sense of hope and optimism.

The care teacher creates a positive atmosphere in the room or family child care home when she uses these strategies:

- Finds ways to reduce her own stress
- Creates a peaceful environment by playing soft music and making the room beautiful
- Remains calm and reassuring throughout the routines of the day

Respond to children's distress in a calm, comforting way.   The responsive care and education provider consistently responds to children's distress and intense emotional outbursts and other displays of displeasure calmly and in a way that comforts children. The care teacher tries a variety of strategies to comfort children and helps infants and toddlers regulate and express a range of emotions in socially and culturally acceptable ways. The care teacher reduces stress and distress in the room or child care home.

Maintaining a sense of calm in an infant-toddler program may be a challenge when children express their feelings intensely. Teachers can encourage children to express feelings in appropriate ways. Even infants need to hear comments such as "You seem tired" or "You don't like it when I have to change your poopy diaper. I'll hurry so I can rock you and make you feel better." When parents and teachers encourage infants and toddlers to express feelings, there are fewer tantrums because they feel heard and acknowledged, and over time they learn to *use their words*. Dr. Honig often acknowledged the feelings of a friend's toddler, Dana, who could then say, "Me so mad and me so sad" when her mother said good-bye to her at her child care center (Honig, personal communication, January 6, 2005).

Care teachers might try these strategies for supporting self-regulation in moments of distress:

- Being willing to comfort a child to help her regulate her behavior
- Trying different strategies with individual children to calm and be calming

- Responding to initiations from a child for comfort (an infant may crawl over to you and want you to hold him for a minute; a toddler may want you to put a Band-Aid on a boo-boo)
- Responding to emotional outbursts and other displays of displeasure calmly and with a kind, understanding voice; trying to soothe the child, staying close rather than abandoning the child emotionally; saying things like (choose words appropriate to the age and experience of the child) "You seem angry," "You feel like stomping your feet," "You wanted the toy," "You can tell me what's wrong—I'd like to help you," or "Do you need a hug?"

Encourage the developing skills in every child.   The responsive care and education provider consistently notices, identifies, encourages, and admires the strength, interests, and new skills in each child in the group.

Young children gain a sense of self-worth when they are noticed in positive and caring ways. Young children thrive when adults share "joy and true delight" (Honig, 2002c) in their efforts and accomplishments. Say things like "You jumped up" or "You picked up the blue toy" rather than just giving praise, such as "Good" or "That's nice." Specific encouragement gives children more information than vague, general praise and encourages their sense of intentionality.

Care teachers might use these strategies to encourage and show admiration for the infants and toddlers in their care:

- Affirming the worth of each child by noticing and identifying the strengths of each child; saying things like "You are such a helpful person" or "You can make people smile"
- Being specific and avoiding phrases such as "good," "nice," "wonderful," and "cute" that have a different meaning to each person
- Showing admiration for new skills such as climbing, walking, jumping, talking, and helping
- Identifying at least five strengths of *each child* and talking about them often

Appreciate developmental differences.   The responsive care and education care teacher consistently appreciates children's developmental stages and differences and helps each child feel appreciated for his or her uniqueness.

Just as adults appreciate when others accept them for who they are, infants and toddlers develop a sense of identity as a unique person with special skills and attributes. A sound background in child development helps the care teacher accept children's behavior that is developmentally appropriate—including thumb sucking, spilling food (because the wrist movement isn't fully developed), falling into another toddler, or saying "No" as often as possible when they start to develop autonomy and want to do things by themselves.

Care teachers can demonstrate their understanding of child development and individual development by using these strategies:

- Showing approval for children attempting and mastering new skills without being critical or scolding
- Helping children enter play if they need the support
- Staying with children in new situations until they feel comfortable
- Checking in frequently with quiet children and providing active children with opportunities to use their energy
- Helping children negotiate challenges when they need help
- Accepting developmental stages (sucking thumb, needing blanket, trying to use spoon but spilling)

Care Teachers Imitate the Child in an Interaction

When an adult imitates a child, the child, in turn, is stimulated to imitate the adult by increasing his output in the task at hand. (Forman & Kuschner)

Imitating children not only helps the adult tune into their developmental level, but also stimulates children to continue their play and discoveries. An infant will bat at a musical toy and it will make a jingly sound. The adult bats at the toy and looks at the infant. The infant is likely to bat the toy again and may bat it in a different way. She will be discovering that the different ways to bat the toy result in different sounds. She is exploring cause and effect and is more motivated to continue because of a partner in the exploration. Providing a model for the children to imitate is another effective teacher strategy.

Care Teachers Scaffold Learning in All Domains of Development

Teachers and other adults, as well as peers, can support children's learning through *scaffolding* (as discussed in Chapter 3, under Vygotsky's theory). Just as a scaffold holds a painter to keep the painter from falling, a teacher figuratively holds the infant or toddler while the child learns. Rather than painting *for* the painter, the scaffold helps make it possible for the *painter* to paint—to figure out *how* best to paint. Scaffolding a young child's learning in all developmental domains is similar. For example, if a toddler is challenged while trying to put together a three-piece puzzle, the teacher could do one of several things to scaffold the child's goal of mastering the puzzle. Toddlers often have a theory that pushing hard on the pieces will make them "work" in the puzzle. Rather than tell the toddler that pushing doesn't work, it is important to provide teacher support while the toddler experiments. The teacher could hold the frame of the puzzle so the toddler could "push" the pieces in to see how they fit. The teacher could suggest that they take out one piece of puzzle at a time and look carefully at each piece. This helps the toddler see the colors or pictures on the puzzle pieces and then the toddler can more easily put the pieces back in the puzzle frame in the right places. If the toddler is getting frustrated, a teacher might suggest that the toddler turn the piece slightly so that it will fit, thus helping the child *learn a strategy* for how to put puzzles together.

Or, to scaffold for the future, a teacher might add several two-piece puzzles to the environment or three-piece puzzles with handles on each piece to support the toddler when he experiments with strategies for putting a puzzle together. The teacher is providing a supportive personal and physical environment to help the child experiment and learn *different* strategies to achieve his goals. Although completion of a task provides satisfaction to the child, the most important goal is not that the toddler completes the puzzle, but rather that the toddler learns different *strategies* for how to put a puzzle together.

The secret to scaffolding is to support children's thinking about *how* to use a tool for learning—initiating to a peer, learning how to express emotions, building, dumping, filling, or asking—and to take the next step in development. Another aspect of scaffolding is to provide the materials to support children's learning. When a teacher observes that a toddler is trying to learn how to jump off a short platform, she can provide a mat on the floor. An environmental prop often is just the thing to encourage a tentative child to try something new.

One of the most important ways to scaffold young children is to develop an emotional climate for exploration. Show an interest in what a child is trying to learn. Your smiles and attention will encourage him to continue his "work."

Listening demonstrates that you value what the child has to say. Holding the hand of a child learning to jump or a toddler learning to climb (when they want you to) scaffolds a next step in development. Do not worry that you will make the child dependent on you—a child who is motivated to learn won't always want your hand. For now, your hand provides the emotional and physical support the child needs to have the courage to try.

Component 3: Relationships with Families and Culturally Sensitive Care

Considerations for families and culture were covered in Chapter 2. Here we discuss specific strategies that care teachers and other infant and toddler professionals can use to create relationships with families in the context of a child development and education program.

Strategies for Developing Relationships with Families

Care teachers relationships with families and the community weave a network of support for infants and toddlers that provides for their well-being. Positive relationships and interactions with families begin at the first telephone call or visit of the family to the child care center. An intake form is usually completed with a program director or family child care provider and parent together. Not only is crucial information collected from the family that supports the child's development, but budding relationships are formed that provide a firm foundation for all future interactions with the family. Information is exchanged—teachers provide information about the program and parents provide information on how to best meet the child's needs. Table 12.3 highlights some strategies for developing a family-centered program: one that recognizes and respects the child's need for a strong, positive relationship with his family and that provides as much consistency as possible for the child across the two settings.

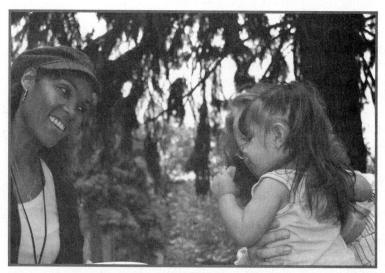

One way that teachers and administrators build strong, positive relationships with families is to support the child's transition to the parent at the end of the day.

Strategies for Developing Relationships with Families from Diverse Cultures

Each family has a culture. As *culture* pertains to child-rearing practices, it is a set of beliefs about how children should be viewed and the role that parents and teachers should play in a child's life (Copple, 2003). Teachers will have their own cultures as well. Child care providers, Early Head Start teachers, or family child care home providers may agree or disagree with parents about how to care for a child. Areas of agreement or difference may include when children should start feeding themselves, when and how children should learn to use the toilet,

TABLE 12.3   Characteristics of a Family-Centered Program

1. *Support the relationship between each child and his family.*
   - Display photographs of each child's family around the room and place them where children can easily see them. They may be laminated and held to the wall with Velcro, so that an infant or toddler can take the picture of his family and carry it around. Or, the children's family photos could be displayed on a large poster board with a piece of fabric over each picture, so that mobile infants and toddlers can play peek-a-boo with their own and others' family pictures.
   - Be sure books or photograph albums with pictures of the children and their families are available to the children.
   - Ask family members to make tape recordings, telling a story or singing a song.

2. *Make family members feel welcome in the program through your own welcoming attitude and through a friendly classroom environment.*
   - Institute an open-door policy for families. They can be with their children at all times of the day and for as long as they like, visiting and interacting with the children.
   - Have a family-friendly bulletin board that describes opportunities for families to visit and volunteer and that includes notices and announcements.
   - Provide a private area for family members who want to give their child a bottle or breast-feed their babies or spend some moments alone with their children.
   - Have a "family information" space (filing box or cabinet, for example) with information on resources, discipline, reading to children, and so on that parents can add to it or help themselves to articles, pamphlets, and brochures that build family-child relationships.

3. *Involve families in the program. Whereas certain strategies will fit one type of program more than another, as well as one type of family more than another, the important factor is creating a feeling of partnership between the program and the child's family.*
   - Survey families concerning the different ways that they would like to be involved.
   - Include families in policy decisions by inviting families to serve on a board of directors or policy council for the program.
   - Plan social events, with family input, that include the whole family.
   - Invite parents into the program to take pictures of children or record language samples that can then, for example, be made into a display of children's interests and learning.
   - Develop a sense of community by including parents in the planning and writing of a monthly newsletter that includes interesting information about the program, monthly events, children, and families.
   - Involve parents in fund-raising activities.
   - Provide opportunities for family members to help at home by making homemade toys (sock puppets, "feely boxes," beanbags, lotto games) for the program.
   - Provide opportunities and information about resources for family support—for example, learning a second language, divorce support groups, teenage parenting, and learning about Medicaid and Medicare.

4. *Develop a system for daily exchange of information between families and child care staff.*
   - Create a friendly place inside the room or family child care home where information concerning a child's needs for the day can be written by a family member and shared with the teacher.
   - Create a friendly place inside the room or family child care home where information about each child's day is kept so that families can easily pick up the information and talk to teachers about how the day went.
   - Create a friendly "Conversation Corner" somewhere in the center or family child care home so that teachers and families can have a private place to talk.

5. *Be sure families have ample opportunity to continually express preferences, beliefs, values, and concerns regarding the practices of the child care and education center (e.g., routines, feeding, holding, naps, play, holidays, and language). Be sure the teachers are responsive to families' requests.*
   - Develop a process for communicating with parents who speak a different language from the teachers. If necessary, obtain a translator to assist in communication with children and/or families.
   - On a regular basis, ask parents to share information indicating their own and their child's needs, interests, developmental history, and any other relevant information that will help make the program more responsive to the child's individual needs.

what types of food children should eat and when, to what degree children should be kept clean, or whether a baby should be placed on the floor (or on a blanket or mat). These varying convictions about children's behavior are supported by conscious or unconscious beliefs about the meaning of what happens, for example, when babies start feeding themselves (Barrera, Corso, & Macpherson, 2003; Gonzalez-Mena, 2008). For *many* families, the child's ability to feed himself means that he is no longer as dependent on the parent. For *some* families, this is a good thing and means that the child is on the road to independence, a valued trait in those families. Other families might believe that children need to be dependent longer in order to develop strong family bonds, so it is not a positive thing if a child is feeding himself with his hands or a spoon at 1 year of age. For some families, food should not be wasted, so the parents feel strongly that they must spoon-feed their 1-year-olds rather than let them pick up food from a high chair tray and, more than likely, drop some precious food on the floor as well as smear it all over their faces. How can early care and education teachers be responsive to parents' wishes and cultures?

With healthy dialog, teachers and families can negotiate an agreed-upon practice in the child care and education program. And, as always, a *relationship of mutual respect*—of asking and listening—can be developed between parents and teachers in regard to the most important issues about child rearing. Gonzalez-Mena (2001) states wisely that "no matter what culture a person comes from, a goal should be to develop a person-to-person relationship. Treating people with respect solves many cross-cultural problems" (p. 16).

Whereas the items in Table 12.4 are important, it is the *relationships* between teachers and families that are most important. Developing healthy relationships with families involves listening *to* them and dialoging *with* them on key issues of potential conflict. Gonzalez-Mena (2001) recommends that teachers dialog with families rather than trying to convince them that the teacher is right. Arguing involves trying to win somebody over to your side through persuasion, she says, whereas in dialoging everyone tries to understand the other's perspective. She summarizes the difference between arguments versus dialoging as follows:

- The object of an argument is to win; the object of a dialog is to gather information.
- The arguer tells; the dialoger asks.
- The arguer tries to persuade; the dialoger tries to learn.
- The arguer tries to convince; the dialoger tries to discover.
- The arguer sees two opposing views and considers the valid or better one; the dialoger is willing to understand multiple viewpoints. (2001, p. 4)

When teachers and parents take time to dialog, then issues about feeding, schedules, whether the child should wear pull-ups or pants while learning to use the toilet, and what the infant or toddler could be learning become opportunities to build relationships. These relationships are built on trust that the other will listen, try to understand, and problem solve to find the best solution at that moment in time.

Teachers must be able to self-reflect about their own cultural values and how those are represented in their behavior. Something as simple as whether a teacher sits on the floor with a child illustrates that teacher's cultural values regarding the role of children.

TABLE 12.4   **Providing Culturally Responsive Care**

Families
- Always take time to talk to families about their beliefs about child rearing.
- Include questions about routines (separation, feeding, diapering, sleeping) and time for the teacher and family to dialog about routines when the child enters the program and again frequently throughout the year.
- Invite families to share a day in play at your education and development center or family child care home.
- Invite families to help redecorate the room; discuss the important aspects of a diversity-rich and stereotype-free environment.

Language
- Use important words from the infants' and toddlers' home languages whenever possible.
- Ask the families for words of endearment in the home language and use them with children.

Eating and Feeding
- Encourage families to let you know what their children like to eat.
- Encourage families to let you know how and when their children like to eat.

Toys
- Ask families what the child's favorite toy is and try to provide it.
- Select toys and dolls that represent different cultures (and not just the cultures represented in the classroom).

Books
- Select books that demonstrate a variety of cultures in positive roles.
- Select books that show women and men in a variety of roles.

Songs
- Ask families to share their favorite cultural songs, CDs, and other music.
- Ask a family member to come in and sing with the infants and toddlers as they play.
- Play and sing a variety of music from a variety of cultures including your own.

Posters, Pictures, and Wall Hangings
- Display pictures of children's families (including pets), laminated and adhered to the wall with Velcro, at the child's level. Allow a child to pull off a picture and carry it around.
- Provide small pillows with a picture of the family tucked inside a pocket. Let infants and toddlers carry them around.
- Display posters of a variety of cultures.
- Display quilts, cloths, paintings, and wall hangings from a variety of cultures (always ask your licensure person what is safe).

Dramatic Play
- Include clothing, shoes, and accessories from a variety of cultures.
- For toddlers, include clothing, hats, shoes, tools, and other items from different types of jobs and roles in the community.

The very act of sitting down on the same level with the crawling baby or toddling child is symbolic of a more equal relationship between the adult and child. It levels the playing field. Whether an adult is sitting with feet spread apart and rolling a ball back and forth with a toddler or watching what the child is playing with and talking about it with her, that adult is giving the message, "You are as important as I am. Your interests are my interests." (Szanton)

To become more culturally self-aware teachers can

1. Engage in conversations with other teachers and families about cultural issues
2. Read books such as *Skilled Dialogs* by Barrera et al. (2003)
3. Engage in discussions with professionals and parents from diverse cultures to learn their points of view on child rearing and education issues
4. Attend conferences or sessions at conferences about diversity
5. Keep a private journal of thoughts about cultural issues and reflect on beliefs and bias

Providing culturally responsive care is a skill that teachers can learn. Table 12.4 provides some ideas for how to honor children's and families' cultures in a child care and education program.

Component 4: Responsive, Relationship-Based Planning

Curriculum planning is a continuous circle of energy that flows from the children through perceptive teachers and returns to the children with the power to motivate, recharge, and inspire them. (Wittmer)

At the heart of a responsive curriculum is the ability of the teacher to astutely observe children, perceptively document their learning, and use the information for planning supportive environments and interactions with children. In a responsive, relationship-based curriculum, the moment-to-moment, day-to-day, and weekly needs and interests of the *children and their families* guide teachers' planning process. The teacher does not start planning the curriculum with a list of activities, but rather starts planning for the day or week by *observing* what the children are doing and learning in all developmental domains. (See the Developmental Trends and Responsive Interactions charts at the end of Chapters 6 through 10.)

We believe infant care should be based on relationship planning—not lesson planning—and should emphasize child-directed learning over adult-directed learning. Rather than detailing specific lessons for caregivers to conduct with infants, the PITC approach shows caregivers ways of helping infants learn the lessons that every infant comes into the world eager to learn. (Lally)

The teacher observes, documents her observations, and uses the information to plan interactions and changes in the environment and experiences provided for the child that support the child's learning. For example, the teacher observes and documents that Hiawanda is starting to walk. She also considers that starting to walk influences Hiawanda's development in the social, emotional, and cognitive domains because he will be seeing and experiencing the world in new ways. Based on her *respect* for Hiawanda's internal motivation to walk, her *reflections* on how his efforts influence his development in all domains, the teacher *relates* (communicates, shares feelings, observes with interest) to the child. She responds by frequently sitting on the floor to provide a secure base for Hiawanda's walking adventures. She also responds by examining the environment to ensure that he has space to take his first steps. The teacher has thought about changes in the environment and her responsive interactions based on her observations of Hiawanda's goals that he is setting for himself. She has used the 3 R approach to curriculum planning—respect, reflect, and relate. Box 12.3 defines these terms.

The process begins with *respect*. At the beginning of the chapter, we discussed the concept of respect for the personhood of infants and toddlers. As Emde (2001) puts it: "Each child is valued as a child, not just for what adults want the child to become" (p. viii). Children will pursue their goals in an emotionally supportive and physically interesting environment. A child who is figuring out how to stack blocks will often work on it for a long period of time. A child who is learning to walk will practice until she "gets it right" (p. xi). No one has to say, "Now it is time to practice your walking—start walking." A teacher who *respects* the internal motivation of young children to work at goals that they set for themselves and their ability to "figure things out" will then be intentional about *reflecting* on the children's goals and feelings and what the child is learning, how the child is learning it, and what the child is "telling" you he needs. Reflecting includes both observing and thinking about what you are observing. It also is a *self-reflective* process because you consider how you (the adult) are feeling and what you are thinking. Often, reflection takes place in a split second when you have to respond to a screaming baby, but it may also take place over time as you ponder the meaning of observations and interactions with the child. *Relating* includes the actions that you take after you respect and reflect. Relating includes being responsive by continuing to observe with interest, interacting, communicating, sharing feelings, or changing the physical environment for and with the child with a focus on healthy relationships—again, both in the moment and over time.

We have provided individual and group planning forms that teachers can use to plan a curriculum that is responsive to children's individual and group needs and interests. See Appendix D for full-page ready-to-use planning forms. The individual planning forms are completed by the teacher(s) responsible for planning for a few specific children. If the primary group system is used, then each teacher is responsible for completing guides on a small number of children each week. Infant and toddler professionals who conduct home visits in a family support or early intervention program could complete these forms with the family. Teachers should try to complete two individual guides a week to document the child's feelings, discoveries, and explorations.

There are two versions of individual planning forms. Version 1 (Box 12.4) and Version 2 (Box 12.5) allow for documenting children's interests with

BOX 12.3

What Care Teachers Can Do to Be Responsive

Respect: Value what the child is trying to do and how the child feels. Admire the child's feelings, goals, and how the child is learning.

Reflect: Observe, think, and feel. How is the child showing you how he or she feels? What are the child's goals? What is the child learning? How is the child trying to learn it? What does the child need?

Relate: Be responsive by observing with interest, interacting, communicating, sharing feelings, or changing the physical environment.

BOX 12.4

Individual Child Planning Guide: Version 1

Child's Name: <u>Sophie</u>

Plans for Week of (Date): <u>March 9–13, 2012</u>

Person(s) Completing the Guide: <u>Matt and Carla</u>

Respect: Child's Emotions, Effort, Goals, Learning, and Relationships

Write an observation or use a photograph or other documentation here—date all notes: 3/9/12

| Respect and Reflect | Relate |

What am I doing?
- I am kissing my favorite doll, wrapping her in a blanket, and tucking her in the doll bed.

How am I feeling?
- I am feeling safe to focus on taking care of the doll.

What am I learning?
Emotional
- I am gaining self-confidence in my ability to make things happen. I am learning how to focus (self-regulation) and manage my emotions (emotional regulation). I am learning how to nurture others.

Social

Cognitive
- I am learning about spatial concepts.
- I am learning about cause and effect (I can do something that will have an effect).
- I am pretending and engaging in symbolic play.

Language
- I am learning how to communicate that I like something or someone (with a kiss).

Motor
- I am learning to control my body so that I can wrap the doll in the blanket and place her carefully in the doll bed. I am gaining both fine-motor and large-motor skills as I play.

What will you do to support my development and learning?
(These are examples. A team of teachers would choose which ones to focus on during the week.)
Responsive Interactions
- We will use language to describe what you are doing.
- We will continue to model how to be gentle, caring, and prosocial.

Environment, Toys, Materials, and Experiences
- We will bring in toys that provide opportunities for you to explore cause/effect and spatial concepts.
- We will place different dolls, different sizes of blankets, baby bottles, and other baby toys in the dramatic play area to support your ability to nurture.
- We will talk with your family to learn more about how you nurture others at home and how you engage in symbolic play.
- We will think about providing more experiences for the children to participate in dramatic/symbolic play, document children's experience, and then plan additional opportunities.

BOX 12.5

Individual Child Planning Guide: Version 2

Child's Name: <u>Sheila</u>

Plans for Week of (Date): <u>March 9–13, 2012</u>

Person(s) Completing the Guide: <u>Chloe</u>

Respect: Child's Emotions, Effort, Goals, Learning, and Relationships

Write an observation or use a photograph or other documentation here—date all notes:

3/9/12: Sheila is on the floor and she is lying on her back shaking a ring toy up and down. She has a smile on her face. She is making sounds such as "ba," "ma." She rolled over and crawled crablike across the floor.

3/10/12: When Dad came to pick her up today she was sitting in Chloe's lap. She squealed loudly and smiled when she saw her dad.

Reflect

What am I doing?

- I have started to crawl. I put my hands forward, bunch up, and crawl crablike across the floor. I squeal with a big smile on my face when I see my dad at the end of the day. I hold the plastic ring toys when I am on my back and make them jingle loudly—shaking them quickly up and down. I am starting to make sounds like "ba," "ma."

How am I feeling?

- I seem to feel very happy when my dad comes. I enjoy making noise with the ring toys.

What am I learning?

- I am learning that Dad will respond happily when I squeal in delight when I see him and that I can make things happen (jingly ring toy). I'm also learning that I can make the jingly noise (cause and effect) when I shake the ring toy and that toys can make noises. I'm learning to communicate by babbling.

Relate

What will you do to support my development and learning?
Responsive Interactions

- I will ask her father what you like to do at home.
- The teachers will babble back to you and then wait for you to take a turn.
- Martha will be your primary care teacher. She will try to be the one to feed you and rock you to sleep.

Environment, Toys, Materials, and Experiences

- I will bring in some different ring toys for you to shake.
- We'll add other cause-and-effect toys to several of the cozy corners.
- We'll make sure that there is a clear space to crawl.

photos or anecdotal records. Both guides ask you to think about what the child is doing as well as what the child may be feeling (inference) and also what the child is learning (concepts and developmental milestones). Under the Respect and Reflect sections, Version 1 asks teachers to write what the child is learning in each developmental domain, whereas Version 2 asks teachers to write a response that integrates learning. For a brief list of possible concepts that the child might be exploring, see Table 12.5. Teachers and parents can add more to the list as they observe children. They could also use an observation system such as the OUNCE (Meisels, Dombro, Marsden, Weston, & Jewkes, 2003) to describe behaviors, knowledge, and developmental steps (such as beginning to use two words together or beginning to crawl). They could use additional observation systems to describe the goals, strategies, and theories of each child. Teachers in center programs or family child care homes can ask the family members to share information about what they have observed at home.

On the individual planning guides, the teachers and/or parents use the observation to plan for the changes that could be made in regard to responsive interactions (teacher-child, parent-child, peer-peer, and teacher-family), including routines and a responsive environment (environmental arrangement, equipment, materials, and experiences offered to children) to support the child's learning in all domains of development. We have discussed responsive interactions, but routines, environment, and experiences will be described in Chapter 13. After reading Chapter 13 and seeing several models of individual planning guides, you will be ready to complete the Relate section of the individual planning guide.

Many of these changes are implemented immediately, in the moment-to-moment interactions with the infant or toddler, and some may be implemented over time. The Developmental Trends and Responsive Interactions charts found at the end of Chapters 6 through 10 provide many ideas for responsive interactions and changes in the environment. Figure 12.1 earlier in this chapter also has ideas regarding responsive adult-child interactions.

There are two forms for group planning as well. The form shown in Box 12.6 is to be used at the end of a week to plan special opportunities for the following week. When teachers develop the group plan together, they bring the individual planning guides and share information so that all of the teachers can contribute to the recommended changes in interactions and the environment. As you plan, you build on the concepts and developmental steps, interests, and strengths of the children in the group.

The second group planning form (Box 12.7) provides space for teachers in center or home programs to reflect on routines of the day and develop a community of caring and should be completed at least once a month. The group planning guides could also be used by home visitors to plan with families to make routines, such as bath time, more successful for everyone involved.

TABLE 12.5　"I'm Exploring and Learning..."

Emotional/ Attachment	Social/Peers	Cognitive	Language/Literacy	Motor
Whether I am worthy of love	What peers will do	How to solve problems	How to communicate my needs with gestures	How to move
Who will protect me and keep me safe	How I can play with others	What will happen when I'm curious	How to talk	How to control my body
How to get my needs met	Who will play with me	How I can use tools to do what I want them to do	How to understand what another is saying	How to crawl
Who I can trust to take good care of me	Who will treat me kindly and who will hurt me	How to dump objects out of a container or fill a container	How to get others to understand what I am communicating	How to "pull to stand"
How others feel about me	How I can get another person's attention	The properties of objects and materials	How to take language turns with another person	How to walk
How to get adults to pay attention to me and be with me	How I can comfort or help a peer	Cause and effect: How I can make things happen	Who will respond to my sounds, words, and language	How to jump
How to express my feelings	How to protect myself and my things	Cause and effect: What causes what	How to ask questions	How to balance
How others express feelings	How to handle conflict	How to fit objects into a space (spatial relationships)	How words fit together to make a sentence	How to move objects around
How to express myself without falling apart (self-regulation)	How to make a peer laugh	Strategies to accomplish my goals	How to add endings to words to express meaning	How to climb
How to wait	How to make a peer go away	Time	How to hold books	How to get down
How to separate from my loved ones	How to share space	Putting objects in sequence based on height, etc.	What pictures in books tell me	How to crawl or walk up stairs
How I should react to strangers	How to share the special adults in my life	How to sort objects	How to open and close books	How to wiggle my body into spaces

BOX 12.6

Individually Responsive Group Planning Guide

Name of Group: Robin

Week of: March 16–20, 2012

Person(s) Completing This Guide: Matt, Carla, Chloe

Respect and Reflect

(Use information from the individual planning guides.) The children in my group are...

Exploring cause and effect
Gaining self-confidence as they learn new things and make things happen
Trusting adults to respond to them and have fun with them
Learning to express themselves through squealing and words

Relate: Plans for the Week to Meet Children's Interests and Needs

Songs/Finger-Plays
Continue singing songs with children in a responsive way.
Sit on the floor and start singing several children's favorite songs.
Bring in pictures or real objects to accompany the songs.
Sing the bubble song while playing with bubbles.

Stories/Books
Build on Sophie's interest in cause and effect.
Sit on the floor and invite children to listen to a story several times a day.
Respond when a child wants a story read.

Responsive Interactions
Be sure to follow children's lead in interactions.
Be sure to comment on children's feelings.
Respond to children's language:
  Respond to Sheila's babbling by babbling back and saying words to her.
  Use new words with Sophie and other children.

Environment, Toys, Materials, and Opportunities
To build on Sophie's interest in cause and effect add flashlights to the cozy corner to provide opportunities for children to explore turning them on.
In the middle of the week add colored cellophane.
Make sure there is room for Sheila to crawl.
Add a cause-and-effect toy (a waterwheel) to the water table. Add "tubs for two" with water to encourage social interactions. During the middle of the week add bubbles to the water table and "tubs for two" for opportunities for them to learn more about bubbles.
Develop an obstacle course outside.
Add different sizes of balls to the active area with baskets of various sizes.
Add more ring toys to provide opportunities for cause-and-effect play.

Experiences with Families
Exchange information with families about how their children explore cause and effect and make things happen at home and in the program.
Ask families for ideas about what toys, materials, experiences their children might like during the day in the program.

Special Experiences
Silvio's dad will visit on Tuesday and will play his flute.

BOX 12.7

Group Planning for Routines

Name of Group: <u>Robins</u>

Week of: <u>March 16–20, 2012</u>

Persons Completing This Form: <u>Matt, Carla, Chloe</u>

Developing a caring community: Think about what is happening and what could happen to develop a relationship-based program for children, families, and care teachers

Routine	What is going well for the children and care teachers	What could we do to improve the experience for children, families, and the care teachers
Greeting time or good-bye time	A teacher is greeting each parent and getting information on how the child's night was.	Place the forms for parents to write on about their child's night or any special information closer to the door. Provide a comfortable adult chair by the door.
Feeding infants and toddler eating times	The toddlers are enjoying the songs that we are singing when they are seated and are waiting for the food.	To make the atmosphere more pleasant we could provide placemats and some flowers on the table for the toddlers.
Infant sleep and toddler nap time	The toddlers are falling asleep easily after we read stories to those who want a story read to them.	To make the transition from lunch to nap time easier, we will give each toddler a special hug before going to sleep.
Diapering	We are talking to them and they are talking to us.	No change.
Toileting	The older toddlers are beginning to use the toilet. There is no pressure, but when one starts to sit on the toilet several others do as well.	Remember to encourage them but not to ever force them. We want to emphasize that they are learning how rather than that we are training them how.
Play times	Most of the toddlers are engaged in play most of the morning.	Continue to plan based on what we are observing are their interests and needs.
Outdoor times	We created some shade so that the toddlers can sit in the shade while outside.	Ask families to help build a sandbox with a lid.
Transitions	Singing the "cleanup" song has helped establish a routine for cleanup.	Put pictures of several items on the shelf so that they can match the object to the picture
Other routines		

Summary

The emotional development of infants and toddlers creates a foundation for the child to learn and love. Care teachers responsive strategies promote children's sense of well-being; meet infants' and toddlers' emotional needs for affection, love, and encouragement; and help them learn. Scaffolding is an adult strategy that can be used to promote emotional, social, language, cognitive, and motor development. Care teachers observe and document children's learning and use the information for planning to develop a responsive curriculum.

- A curriculum for infants and toddlers is responsive to individual children's needs, interests, and strengths (in collaboration with families) and focuses on the development of children's healthy relationships. A curriculum is everything that children experience from the beginning to the end of the day—they are constantly learning.
- There are eight components to a curriculum, with components 1 through 4 discussed in this chapter. The eight components are
  1. The foundation
  2. The care teachers roles
  3. Relationships with families and culturally sensitive care
  4. Responsive, relationship-based planning
  5. Transitions and routines
  6. Responsive and relationship-based environments
  7. Responsive experiences and opportunities
  8. A relationship-based approach to guidance
- The teachers' beliefs about the nature and needs of infants and toddlers, what is important for them to learn, and how they best learn form the philosophical foundation for a curriculum. Play is an important way that infants and toddlers learn.
- One of the most important roles of the teacher is to create a relationship-based community to ensure that babies feel safe, nurtured, and experience a sense of belonging. Teachers are intentional in how they scaffold children's emotional, social, language, cognitive, and motor development and follow children's lead for what they need. Nine dimensions of adult-child interactions promote children's emotional development, the foundation for all learning.
- When teachers develop strong, positive relationships with families from a variety of cultures, they weave a network of support for the well-being of infants and toddlers. To create respectful relationships, teachers and parents must take time to dialog.
- In a responsive, relationship-based curriculum the moment-to-moment, day-to-day, and weekly needs and interests of the children and their families guide the planning process. A responsive planning process that includes *respect, reflect,* and *relate* will ensure that the curriculum is truly "day to day the relationship way."

Key Terms

attachment groups
attuned
dance the developmental ladder

holds and enfolds
homebases

Velcro time
working sense of self

Reflections and Resources for the Reader

REFLECTIONS

1. What are the key components to planning a curriculum for infants and toddlers? Which are most important?
2. What do you think are the most important goals for infants and toddlers?
3. What does it mean to respect an infant or toddler?
4. What are the nine responsive strategies that care teachers. can use to promote infants' and toddlers' emotional development—a foundation for learning? Why are these strategies important for children, families, and care teachers?

OBSERVATION AND APPLICATION OPPORTUNITIES

1. Use the items in Tables 12.3 and 12.4 to observe an infant and toddler program and to interview the care teachers to determine how they develop responsive relationships with families in general and also families from diverse cultures. Write a summary of your observations and interviews and make recommendations for improvement.
2. Analyze the following: Abria is 28 months old. Abria's parents want the care teachers to feed her with a spoon and do not want her to play with her food at lunchtime. In the program that Abria attends, the toddlers sit together at a table and feed *themselves* with a spoon, even though it is often messy. Sometimes they get tired and pick up food with their fingers. The care teachers in the program think that it is important for children to learn to feed themselves. How would you dialog to discuss this issue with the family?

SUPPLEMENTARY ARTICLES AND BOOKS TO READ

Daniel, J. (2009). Intentionally thoughtful family engagement in early childhood education. *Young Children, 64* (5), 10–14.

Dombro, A. L., Jablon, J., & Stetson, C. (2011). *Powerful interactions: How to connect with children to extend their learning.* Washington, DC: NAEYC.

Gillespie, L. G., & Hunter, A. (2011). Rocking and rolling. Creating healthy attachments to the babies in your care. *Young Children, 66* (5), 62–63.

McGaha, C. G., Cummings, R., Lippard, B., & Dallas, K. (2011). Relationship building: Infants, toddlers, and 2-year-olds. *Early Childhood Research and Practice, 13*(1). Retrieved from ecrp.uiuc. edu/v13n1/mcgaha. html.

INTERESTING LINKS

Center for the Study of Social Policy

http://www.cssp.org/about
This Web site, focused on strengthening families, provides many publications on the topic.

PITC

www.pitc.org/cs/pitclib/view/pitc_res/182
This site includes video clips from PITC's video—*The next step: Including the infant in the curriculum.*

UNICEF

www.unicef.org/crc/
This Web site includes a link to the Convention on the Rights of the Child. Available on this link is the full text of this international human rights treaty, which articulates a new world vision committed to protecting children's rights.

13

Routines, Environments, and Opportunities

Day to Day the Relationship Way

LEARNING OUTCOMES

After reading this chapter, you will be able to:

- Explain how to provide responsive transitions and routines
- Create a responsive, relationship-based environment including how to
  - Create quality learning spaces and places
  - Choose equipment, toys, and materials
- Explain how to provide a variety of learning opportunities
- Describe various curriculum approaches

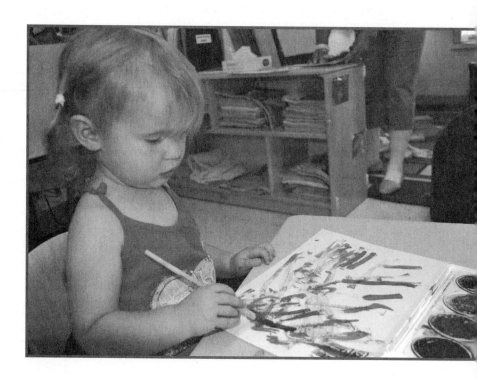

In this chapter, you will learn how to establish responsive routines and create an enriched environment in a responsive curriculum. You will also learn how to provide opportunities for very young children to develop within the context of relationships, and you will see examples of the *respect, reflect,* and *relate* (3 R) planning process. At the end of the chapter, we describe other infant and toddler curriculum approaches to use in group settings. But first, see Box 13.1, where you can peek into an infant and toddler classroom that focuses on responsive interactions and relationships. The infants and toddlers in the program described here are having profound experiences that will influence how they view themselves, relationships, and the world. Considered alone, each experience may not seem important, but when they are combined, they are transformed into who a child is and will become. How do we

BOX 13.1

A Responsive Classroom

Every infant in Angie Hicks's classroom shares the attention of a teacher with just one or two other children. Designated teachers have primary responsibility for three or four children. These teachers spend the bulk of their day with their children and monitor their basic needs. On the day of our visit, this arrangement is evident in the children's behavior. When one of the teachers goes to get a bottle, Samantha's eyes trail after her, then start to tear up. The other teacher, seeing Samantha's concern, says comfortingly, "Are you getting sad because Jeannie is leaving?"

The large infant rooms are very calm. Soft music plays for the children who are awake. Two additional rooms contain cribs as well as a quiet area where mothers can breast-feed. Teachers rock children to sleep in their arms and often sing lullabies before placing the babies in a crib.

The room is well organized and well labeled so teachers do not have to spend time searching for supplies. Personal belongings, including diapers and pacifiers, are all kept in labeled locations. Food allergies and sunscreen requirements are posted in large letters on the wall. The providers are fastidious about health precautions, maintaining clean facilities, washing their hands between feedings and diaper changes, and using rubber gloves while wiping children's noses. The room has a voice-activated speakerphone that picks up in the active part of the classroom, so that no teacher has to lift a telephone receiver. Parents frequently call to check on their children.

Most important, the infant teachers have worked consistently with babies for many years. As Director Burroughs says, "The teachers in this room prefer to work with very young children and have not experienced the burnout" so common in the infant care profession. Their devotion to the children is apparent. One teacher lovingly hugs a child who had just awakened, then rubs his back, allowing him to transition slowly into the activities of the day. Conversations are filled with encouraging and caring comments. "Keep crawling—you are almost there!" "Thank you for handing that to me!" Teachers convey their excitement to parents, proudly reporting on the children's activities.

The teachers follow the children's lead. When one child carries a book to one of the teachers, the gift prompts a group reading session. When an infant pushes back on the pillows supporting him and begins to cry, a teacher takes the cue to move him onto his back, where he becomes immediately content. Another teacher asks a toddler, "What are you trying to tell me, Jenny? Do you want me to blow the bubbles?" Jenny gives an enthusiastic "Bubba ba ba." The teacher helps Jenny blow the bubbles herself, then encourages other children to come join the activity.

Since toddlers learn to communicate verbally, most of the conversation in the toddler room develops out of the children's ideas. Astar holds out a plastic ice cream cone and says, "Daddy." The teacher responds, "Does Daddy buy ice cream?" When Astar then picks up a milkshake cup, she asks, "Is that a milkshake you are making? Let's all go and get some ice cream." In the house area, the toddlers play ice cream scenarios. After a while, a boy excitedly announces that he has made a cake. The teacher and the children start to sing "Happy Birthday."

Source: Kinch and Schweinhart (2004).

give these young children the experiences they deserve—day to day the relationship way? One of the most important experiences for infants and toddlers is how they transition into a program and the routines that they experience each day. As you will remember, this is component 5 of a curriculum, as described in Chapter 12.

Component 5: Transitions and Routines—A Time for Relationships

Transitions and routines are important opportunities for strengthening a child's relationships and learning with teachers, families, and peers. *Transitions* are times of change that occur in a child's life, such as when an infant or toddler enters an education and development center or family child care home or when an infant changes rooms in a center as he grows and has new needs (hopefully with a favorite care teacher moving "up" with him). Daily transitions occur when a child or group moves from one experience to another—for example, from indoor play to outdoor play. *Routines* are regularly occurring events that the child experiences during a day, such as diapering time, feeding time, or moving from play into nap time.

Transition of Entering a New Child Care and Education Program

One of the more difficult times for babies may be when they enter a program or child care home for the first time. Care teachers and parents can work closely to support the child during this time of separation and adjustment to a new environment, new adults, and new experiences. Notice how difficult it is for Tim in the following example reported by Pawl and St. John (1998):

> Tim stood just inside the entrance to the big playroom. He was sturdy for two and a half years, but short. The noise was jarring, and he looked around for the woman his mother talked to when they came in. She had said to his mother, "He'll be fine—I'll get him started," and she had taken his hand. But now, just as fast, she was gone. It scared him as much as the other time. This was not a good place to be. He wanted his mother, and he wanted to go home. A boy running past bumped him hard and Tim nearly fell, but he caught himself and made his way to the corner of the room. He still couldn't see that big person or the other one—just lots and lots of small kids. He sat down and fingered some colored blocks on the floor. A big boy came and grabbed one and stepped on Tim's hand. Tim yelped and cried and looked around. He held his hurt hand in the other, and the tears ran down his cheeks. No one saw. (p. 12)

What could have made it easier for Tim, his mother, and the teacher? Remembering how hard it is for us to separate from a loved one helps us take the perspective of the child and parent. The parent may feel anxious and/or guilty, as if she were giving up a part of herself. T. Berry Brazelton, pediatrician and child development expert, noted that some parents may express their feelings openly, others seem distant as they prepare themselves to separate from their baby, and others seem angry as they attempt to maintain control but really feel out of control (Griffin, 1998). Babies like Tim can be confused and sad.

Transitions During the Day

At the beginning of the day, parents and teachers could use *ciao* time—a word that means both "hello" and "good-bye" in Italian—instead of *dropping off*. The morning is "good-bye" time from the infants' and toddlers' perspectives, as the babies say good-bye to their parents. However, it is also "hello" time, as the infant or toddler and the parents say hello to the child's teacher. Thus, it is both good-bye and hello if we think about this transition time from the child's perspective.

An infant's or toddler's good-bye to the parent and hello to the teacher" time must be handled with care, as it is an emotional exchange of the child between the parent and teacher. Although a baby is held emotionally through time and space by the physically absent parent, an infant or toddler will not be able to think about how the parent still loves her after the parent disappears (according to the child's perspective). The child has to *transition her trust* from the parent to the teacher—not an easy task unless the relationships with both are positive.

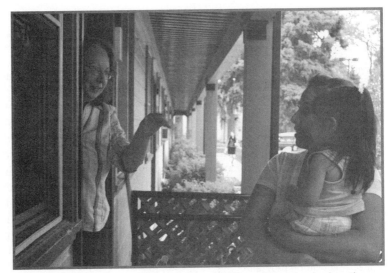

Ciao time is an emotional exchange of the child from the teacher back to the family.

A routine provides child, parent, and the care teacher predictability—a sense of expectancy—about ciao time, leading to smoother transitions for all.

As an infant, Kia's mom made sure she was comfortable in the child care home and sang her one song before saying good-bye. The teacher always greeted Mom and Kia and asked how the baby's night had been and if there were any special needs for the day. As a mobile infant, the teacher did the same thing, only now she greeted Kia with a special hug. Kia's mom sang one song and read one story and then said good-bye with hugs and kisses, telling Kia that she would be back after Kia's nap in the afternoon. The teacher made sure she was near and ready to pick up Kia, hold her, or read a story to help Kia settle in for the day. In the toddler room, the teacher sat at a table near the door with interesting things like play dough, books, or new toys. When a child came in the door with a parent, the teacher could be right there asking the parent about special needs and greeting Kia with a smile. Kia took off her shoes and put on her special slippers for the day. This routine helped her make the transition into the center and she was able to say good-bye to her mother with a big hug and a kiss.

These transition times at the beginning of the day are repeated at the end of the day in a similar way to smooth the child's transition from program to home.

Transitions during the day are important times for building teacher-child relationships. Inform children before individual and group transitions occur and give them time. For example, to an infant who needs to have a diaper change, says things like, "It is time to change your diaper...." *before* you pick up the child. Help them finish a task before toddling toward the diaper table. Snatching mobile infants and toddlers from their play for diaper changes can result in child defensiveness and anger. Remember, when you transition to another part of the room or out of the room, it is also a change for the children. To help children feel more secure, you can tell infants and toddlers when you are leaving to change another child's diaper or fix food, *and when you will be back.* Transitions from one room to another in a center are difficult for infants and toddlers unless there is continuity of care. This concept was discussed in Chapter 11.

How is responsive care demonstrated in this **video?** Notice how individual children are feeling. What do care teachers do to help toddlers feel safe as they transition to nap and as they nap? What more could the care teachers do to create a calm, relaxing personal and physical environment?

This **video,** demonstrates older toddlers' and young preschool children's transitions to a child care and early education program at the beginning of the day. How does the care teacher help the child and parent feel safe and comfortable? How might "families good-byes" be expressed in different cultures?

Responsive Routines

"Family routines are patterned interactions that occur with predictable regularity in the course of everyday living" (Kubicek, 2003, p. 4). Caregiving routines are important opportunities for strengthening teacher-child relationships and child learning and include diapering and toileting, feeding and eating, and sleeping times. Infants and toddlers learn to expect that they will be fed when they are hungry and helped to sleep when they are tired. From a baby's perspective, a routine is a time for physical and *emotional* needs to be met. Routines are incredibly intimate and emotional times when infants and toddlers gain a sense of self-worth, learn about the kindness of others, and develop relationships with those who meet their needs in responsive, kind ways. With responsive routines, babies become self-regulated (a sense of inner control) rather than, for example, out of control because they are crying frantically for food. They learn whether adults are trustworthy. Their brains become organized as they experience the patterns of routines (Butterfield, 2002).

Routines are times for teaching the important lessons in life—how to feel about oneself and others. They are social, emotional, cognitive, language, and motor experiences that provide teachable moments for the child and care teacher. Talking softly to infants and toddlers who are eating, naming pictures on the wall for babies being diapered, and patting the backs of toddlers transitioning to nap time while singing their favorite lullabies are only a few ways that teachable moments become moments of relationship building. As always in a family-centered program, teachers and parents constantly coordinate routines; they share information each day and they negotiate differences in how routines are achieved so that babies experience as few changes between home and program as possible (Griffin, 1998).

For infants, routines are individualized and responsive to their needs. Babies know they are hungry or overwhelmed and usually let you know. The teacher reads the cues of the child concerning an empty or full tummy, a need for interactions, or a diaper change. These interactions form the core of relationship building between the infant and teacher—and begin the formation of the infant's identity as someone who can trust others and who feels lovable. For mobile infants, routines are times for shared relationships as they participate in conversations (cooing, babbling, and first words) with teachers during diapering, eating, and rocking time for sleep. Infants and toddlers are included in the diaper-changing process. When a teacher says, "It is time to take your diaper off. I'm putting on a clean diaper" the routine is completed *with* the child, not *to* the child. Toddlers share routine times with teachers and peers as, over time, diapering time turns into toilet time, feeding turns into eating with peers at small tables, and helping infants fall asleep becomes supporting toddlers as they transition to nap time. Teachers can use Table 13.1 to determine how responsive their routines are for the infants and toddlers in their program.

Routines happen continuously in a program and there is a danger that they will become routinized (monotonous). Teachers may wonder why they

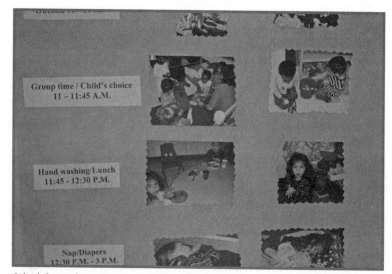

Schedules and routines are negotiated with parents to ensure that they are responsive to children's needs.

TABLE 13.1   **Responsive Routines**

1. Responsive Daily Routines

- Provide a daily routine that follows each infant's need for feeding and sleep.
- Implement a flexible routine (eating, sleeping, inside-outside) that the toddlers learn to predict.
- Use routines as opportunities for emotional interaction and learning.
- Provide primary caregiving.

2. Responsive Routines for Infant Feeding and Toddler Eating

- Provide a private place for parents to feed an infant, if parent desires.
- Respect the mother's wish to breast-feed or not.
- Ask families about their cultural and family preferences for the child's eating habits, needs, and food preferences.
- Sit with toddlers for eating rather than hovering above.
- Respond to young children's requests and comments while feeding and eating with the children—name foods; use words that describe the color, shape, size, texture, and taste of foods; and talk about pleasant events while feeding and eating with the children.
- Hold infants gently for bottle-feeding. Babies need to be held for feeding to ensure safety and to meet babies' emotional needs. Talk softly, hum, sing, or remain quiet according to the infant's needs.
- Speak in a soft, kind, friendly, gentle, encouraging, and positive way to the children during feeding and eating activities.
- Respond when infants or toddlers indicate that they are hungry or want more food, and respect children when they indicate that they are satisfied or want to stop eating.
- Use plates and place mats instead of napkins or paper plates to serve toddlers.
- Provide opportunities for toddlers to begin to serve themselves, pour milk out of a small pitcher, and clean the table with a sponge.
- Provide a system for giving daily information to families concerning how, when, what, and with whom the child ate.
- Provide a system for documenting families' wishes on issues related to weaning from the breast or bottle.

3. Responsive Routines for Diapering and Toilet Learning

- Provide pictures of family members or other interesting pictures on the wall at the baby's eye level in the diapering area.
- Make diapering a special time for adults to talk, sing, and be with infants.
- Use encouraging and positive words and self-talk such as "first," "next," and comforting words.

- Coordinate toilet learning with the parents to provide continuity from home to program.
- Help toddlers and talk gently to them when they use the toilet.
- Never force toddlers to use or stay on the toilet.

4. Responsive Routines for Sleeping

- Provide long, luxurious holding times for infants and toddlers.
- Gently rock or pat babies who need help to get to sleep, watch and listen for infants to signal when they want to be picked up from a crib, and respond positively and quickly when they signal that they want out of crib or bed.
- Provide each toddler with a cot that is labeled, both with her or his first name and a special symbol or picture. Label sheets, pillows, and blankets in the same way.
- Plan and implement a transition time from play to sleep with a predictable sequence for toddlers. To build positive relationships, read stories, talk gently, and/or pat a child gently to sleep according to the child's needs. Toddlers may pick a special book or have their own stuffed toy or blanket if needed.
- Allow toddlers to sleep as long as they need. Plan a quiet activity for toddlers who wake up.
- Help toddlers transition from nap to wake time.
- Prepare the nap area for toddlers before lunch, so that if a toddler is tired or falls asleep during lunch the teacher can help the child transition to nap time.

5. Responsive Greeting and Good-Bye Times

- Greet each infant, toddler, and parent warmly in the morning. Help children transition from home to the program at the beginning of the day. Give family members a chance to communicate needs, priorities, and concerns.
- Greet each family member warmly when the family picks up the baby. Help children transition from the program to parent at the end of the child's day. Talk about the daily record with the family. Give each infant and toddler a special good-bye.

CULTURE CLOSE UP

Mia, the infant/toddler coach who visited infant/toddler rooms in child care centers to support teachers, was clearly upset. She called her mentor when she observed that an almost 3-year-old was being treated like a baby by being lifted up on a changing table (rather than climb up a set of safety stairs), fed with a spoon and not allowed to touch his food, and talked to in "baby talk." Encouraged by her mentor to ask the teacher, Shaleen, respectful questions about her practices, Mia found that Shaleen was being responsive to the child's parents' wishes, although questioning whether it was the right thing to do for the child. However, Shaleen had learned and was trying to understand that in the child's family, interdependence rather than independence was encouraged. Shaleen was being responsive to the parents so as not to confuse the child with different practices at home and at the center because the family had just recently arrived in the United States. What are your thoughts on Mia's, Shaleen's, the child's, and the family's experiences?

are wiping noses, cleaning bottoms, and feeding toddlers. They may wonder what routines have to do with teaching. When we recognize that these times represent opportunities for learning and emotional connections, then we will treat them for what they are—perhaps the most important part of the day.

Component 6: Creating Responsive, Relationship-Based Environments

Another role of the infant-toddler professional is to set up a relationship-based, responsive environment with equipment, materials, and opportunities that support children's development. Torelli and Durrett (2007) describe many elements of a quality environment that infants, toddlers, and their care teachers would enjoy:

A developmentally-designed environment supports children's individual and social development. It encourages explorations, focused play, and cooperation. It provides choices for children and supports self-directed learning. A developmentally designed environment also supports the teacher-child relationship. It minimizes management and custodial activities, allowing teachers more time for interactions, observation, and facilitation of children's development.

A Quality Environment for Centers and Child Care Homes

Other elements of a responsive environment include the following:

- innovations that are responsive to children's and adults' sensory needs, and "our need to gather, be comforted, rest, and explore" (Carter & Curtis, 1998, p. 75)
- spaces that encourage play
- aspects that support children's development of trust and security, their ability to make choices, and their sense of mastery.

Greenman (1988) discusses how developing a learning environment begins with recognizing what babies need to *do* and determining how to maximize their opportunities to have the appropriate experiences. He asks, "What do babies do for a living?" He answers:

Most simply, it is to make sense of the world of people and things and to develop their capacities to the fullest. Babies are explorers and scientists; they test and discover their own properties, the properties of objects and people, and the relationships between the elements of the world. (p. 99)

And, of course, we can't forget babies' needs for environments that promote relationships—both adult-child and peer relationships. With all of these purposes in mind, teachers can set up an environment that is a home away from home. See Figures 13.1 and 13.2 for examples of floor plans for an infant room and a toddler room. For babies to feel both safe and motivated to learn, a quality environment needs the elements found in Table 13.2. Environments need cozy spaces and special places for infants and toddlers to delight in their surroundings.

FIGURE 13.1 **Floor plan for an infant and mobile infant room (2 months to 18 months)**

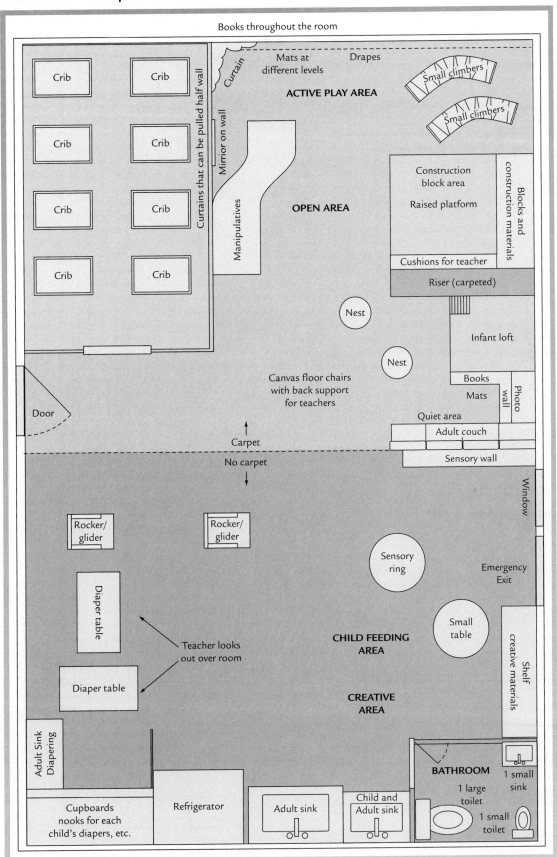

FIGURE 13.2 **Floor plan for a toddler room (18 months to 3 years)**

TABLE 13.2   Environment observation guide

1. **Environments for children are clean, safe, properly lighted, ventilated, and provide appropriate temperature regulation.**
   - The environment is free of materials or conditions that endanger children's health and is constantly monitored by the teachers for hazards.
   - The environment is clutter free.

2. **Environments contain design elements that reduce stimulation, create a sense of calm, and enable children to focus on each other, their teachers, and the materials they are exploring.**
   - The environment is bright, cheerful, and beautiful.
   - The environment is not overstimulating with paint that is too bright or wallpaper that has too many figures on it.
   - The environment has soft items—small couches and pillows, and a variety of textures.
   - The environment offers spaces for teacher-child interactions.
   - There are spaces for one child or several children to be alone (but can still be seen by the teacher).

3. **The environment has furniture and equipment that is child size.**
   - The environment includes short toddler chairs so that toddlers' feet can touch the floor when they are sitting.
   - The environment includes short tables so that toddlers can sit in toddler chairs and easily eat or play.
   - The environment has short and sturdy shelves so that babies will not knock them over but can reach toys easily.

4. **The environment has comfortable spaces that are inviting to children.**
   - Spaces are clearly divided by low shelves or cloth hung from ceiling.
   - The environment is divided into clear areas for play and children can delineate.
   - The environment feels organized—not cluttered.
   - The environment contains features that encourage children to interact and develop relationships with each other.
   - There are spaces at different levels, for example, platforms, lofts, and mats.

5. **Teachers provide indoor and outdoor environments that provide a rich variety of activity choices, materials, and toys that respond to children's varying levels of development.**
   - Materials and toys are attractively displayed on shelves (not dumped into a toy box).
   - Materials can be used in a variety of spaces in the environment.
   - Materials and toys are in good shape, working, and are not broken or dirty.
   - Materials and toys can be used by children who are at different developmental levels.
   - Materials and toys encourage active exploration and play.
   - Materials and toys are changed according to children's interests, while the majority of the toys remain to provide stability and consistency for the infant or toddler.

6. **Environments support adults in interacting, supervising, and observing children.**
   - There are "camping" type chairs that allow teachers to sit on the floor with their backs supported.
   - There are pillows and bolsters that allow teachers to lean comfortably against a wall while sitting on the floor.
   - There are rocking chairs that allow teachers to sit comfortably and rock babies to sleep.

> What are the learning opportunities for children offered by the environment and the adults in this setting? What is the value for the child and care teacher when the infant/toddler is encouraged to make choices?

Cozy Spaces and Special Places

Learning spaces are well-defined places with materials that support relationships and learning. Integrated learning in all domains (emotional, social, language, cognitive, and motor) occurs in all areas of the room. As care teachers set up these corners, nooks, cozy spaces, and special places, they can think about all of the opportunities for children to laugh and learn. All of the equipment and materials are not available at one time, but instead the care teachers alternate materials based on the interests and developmental levels of the children. As a teacher sets up these areas, she can think about each child in her group and how that child might use these materials. Remember, play is the way for children to learn—and they will play, explore, experiment, eat, and rest if enticing spaces are created (Sawyers & Rogers, 2003). The care teacher is physically and emotionally available to promote children's emotional well-being, their feelings of safety, enduring relationships with adults and peers, and learning in all of the developmental domains.

Spaces invite, entice, and engage children. Table 13.3 describes a variety of spaces that could be created in an infant and toddler room in a center and

TABLE 13.3   Creating Cozy Spaces

A quiet space
- A space away from active play
- A space with
  - a mat or layers of mats with a low mirror on the wall beside it
  - family photograph books, dolls and blankets, soft toys, quiet toys, puppets, and books
  - a nest (*Kaplan Early Learning Company Catalog*, 2013); or create one with an inner tube with a blanket over it
  - boxes large enough for child to crawl in and out

A nest provides a special place to nurture infants and toddlers.

Special Places for Nurturing Children
- A comfortable space away from active play for teachers to sit on the floor (with back support) and hold a child
- A loft
- An adult-size couch
- A mat on the floor against the wall with pillows with washable covers
- A rocking chair/glider

Spaces for Delighting the Senses
- Short tables for toddlers for play dough and other creative materials
- A space with
  - small tubs, other containers, or water tables with water for infants and toddlers (always monitor children very carefully with water—children have drowned in an inch of water in a container)
  - containers or tables for sand and other natural materials
  - a light table (see Reggio materials)

Sand delights children of all ages.

- wading pools filled with different textured balls or other safe materials
- a space to use feeling and sound boxes and bubbles with various sizes of wands
- a sticky wall (Isbell & Isbell, 2003, p. 67)

A Space to Use Materials to Create
- A space without carpet for painting on paper on the floor
- A space to use nontoxic paint; thick crayons; clay; play dough; large pieces of paper to tear, draw, and paint on; brushes; short easels
- A table for toddlers to use materials to create

A table for toddlers to create with crayons.

A Space for Peek-a-boo and Other Social Games
- A space made with a cloth hanging from ceiling with a mirror on the wall
- Boxes of various sizes with holes cut out of the sides—add cloth over the holes for variation and "peek-a-boo" games
- Lofts with a Plexiglas panel in the floor so babies that are up can look down and babies that are down can look up and enjoy one another

A Space for Active Play
- Floor space so that children can move freely with
  - balls of all sizes
  - couches to walk around and climb up on
  - ramps and short climbers to climb
  - rocking boats
  - tunnels to crawl through
  - mats at different levels for climbing
  - objects that can be moved such as child-size shopping carts, doll strollers, and riding toys
  - a bar fastened to the wall on various levels so that children can pull to stand
  - large empty appliance boxes with windows cut out of them and/or the end off of them so that children can crawl through the box

Mats at different levels provide a place for mobile infants and toddlers to climb.

A Space for Toys and Other Manipulatives
- Short shelves and space in front of shelves to play on the floor with
  - a child-size table and chairs for mobile infants and toddlers
  - toys that move, make noise, and change shape
  - toddler nesting blocks, ring towers, large beads, cause-and-effect and "take apart" toys, blocks, shape sorters
  - wooden animals, little houses, multiethnic play people, trucks and cars
  - small balls, blocks of various sizes, large pegs, large beads for stringing, puppets, puzzles, dolls, toy telephones
  - tubes of varying lengths and sizes

A puzzle with a handle on each piece is perfect for infants.

A Space to Build and Construct
- A platform for building
- Blocks of all sizes, shapes, and textures
- Wooden animals, little houses, play people, trucks and cars

(Continued)

TABLE 13.3   Continued

A Space for Dramatic Play With

- mirrors, low pegs to hang clothing, scarves, purses, safe kitchen utensils, hats, pots and pans, containers of various sizes, dress-up clothes
- multiethnic dolls, doll blankets, baby bottles, baby bed
- puppets of varying sizes and shapes
- child-size tables, stoves, sinks, refrigerators, pots and pans, dishes (for mobile infants and toddlers)

A Space for Reading to Children

- A special place that is designed for older infants, mobile infants, and toddlers to choose books from an attractive, easily reached display and "read" or be read to in comfort
- Also place books around the room (any space is a great space for reading to a child)

Feeding and Eating Spaces With

- comfortable floor chairs for adults to feed infants sitting in infant seats
- gliders for feeding bottles to infants
- child-size chairs and tables for toddlers to eat
- a refrigerator
- a sink at children's level for mobile infants and toddlers
- an adult-size sink

Sleeping, Diapering, and Toileting Spaces

- Sleeping
  - cribs for infants
  - cots for mobile infants and toddlers
- Diapering
  - a diaper table with storage space
  - sturdy stairs with sides for toddlers to climb to diaper table
  - an adult-size sink
- Toileting
  - child-size toilets for toddlers who are learning to use the toilet
  - a child-size sink

Toddlers pretend with a child-size stove and sink.

This attractive book holder shows the covers of the books.

adapted for a family child care home. Provide the equipment, toys, and opportunities based on children's individual interests and developmental level.

No space is marginal, no corner is unimportant, and each space needs to be alive, flexible, and open to change. (Malaguzzi)

How the space is organized, the equipment, and the materials all provide opportunities for relating and learning. As Greenman (1988) states, "Teachers are sure to think about how to creatively use each corner in the room to entice and tempt babies to explore." Teachers also provide special opportunities for learning in each of the cozy corners.

Component 7: Responsive Opportunities

Don't think in terms of activities; think in terms of each child's and the group's interests and levels of development. Think of providing opportunities for learning from which children choose—and then *respecting, reflecting,* and *relating* to children as they experience these opportunities. As noted by Maria Montessori:

> It is not the quality of the object that holds a child's interest, but the opportunity it affords the child for action. (Torrence & Chattin-McNichols)

Planning Opportunities

Care teachers can buy many books full of activities for children—some include activities that are responsive and that provide a rich array of opportunities to entice infants and toddlers to explore, problem solve, and discover. Some, however, are much too structured for infants and toddlers and require enforced group time, which is not appropriate for children so young. The questions in Figure 13.3 will guide you as you think about whether the *opportunity* is appropriate for the children in your group.

Following is an example of how a care teacher used the guidelines to decide whether an experience was appropriate for the children in her group:

> Mara, a teacher in a room for children 18 months to 3 years old, had several children in her room who loved to play with balls. She read about an experience that she might provide in her room in a book, Infant and Toddler Experiences by Hast and Hollyfield (1999, p. 133). The experience entailed bringing balls of different textures, sizes, and qualities into the room as well as baskets or containers to put the balls in. The activity recommended that she fill the room with all of the balls and let the toddlers discover them. After thinking about the questions in Figure 13.3 she thought that she would try it. She decided, however, that instead of filling the room, she would place the balls and containers in the active area so that the children would not be overstimulated. For Tommy, who couldn't walk yet, she would place a small basket and small balls near him to explore with other children.

FIGURE 13.3 **Choosing materials and opportunities**

1. Does it meet one or more children's needs and strengths?
2. Does it provide for a variety of developmental levels (infants, mobile infants, toddlers)?
3. Is it safe? Durable? Washable? Nontoxic?
4. Does it support learning in a variety of developmental domains (motor, communication, thinking, social, emotional, and cultural)?
5. Does it spark the interest of a child or a number of children?
6. Does it support a child doing a number of different things with the toy or material (for example, with a ball a child may chew on it, bounce it, roll it, put it in a container, etc.)? A toy may lend itself to one response (such as a puzzle); however, a child could explore the toy in a variety of ways.
7. Does it support non-gender-biased, multicultural thinking, and nonviolent-prosocial behavior?
8. Can I use the materials or the activities by offering them as opportunities for children rather than a forced activity?
9. Can the material or experience be adapted for children with special needs?

FIGURE 13.4   **Opportunities for infants and toddlers**

Quiet and calm opportunities
Nurturing opportunities
Social opportunities
Prosocial opportunities
Opportunities for social experiences for and with children with disabilities
Language opportunities
Cognitive opportunities
Delighting-the-senses opportunities
Creative opportunities
Writing and drawing opportunities
Music, song, and creative movement opportunities
Numeracy, space, and shape opportunities
Opportunities for active play and motor development
Outdoor opportunities

Let's explore some wonderful opportunities (see Figure 13.4) for children that could be provided in the cozy corners. Not all of these experiences are available at one time and the environment, materials, and opportunities change in response to children's needs and interests. Care teachers may *plan* for opportunities to occur in specific cozy places, such as the ball experiences described previously in the active area or literacy experiences in the corner where books are available. Opportunities for creative activities with crayons or paints will likely take place in the creative arts cozy corner. However, we want to emphasize that most of the following opportunities can take place in *all* of the cozy spaces described in Table 13.3—for example, opportunities for nurturing; social, prosocial, language, cognitive, and motor development; delighting the senses, music, and learning about literacy and numeracy happen in *all* of the cozy corners. If care teachers are *reflective* of the possibilities for learning in all of the areas, they will *respect* infants' and toddlers' choice of equipment, toys, materials, and cozy corners and will *relate* to children based on the opportunities for learning inherent in all of children's experiences (Petersen & Wittmer, 2013).

Quiet and Calm Opportunities

Quiet spaces create opportunities for children to calm themselves, suck their thumbs, gather their energies, and rest either by themselves or with another peer, the care teacher or a parent. These spaces have softness in them—quiet, visually pleasing toys, and pillows for mobile infants and toddlers. A large inner tube with a blanket that covers the inner tube creates a nest inside which an infant or two can be placed or where a toddler can relax. Boxes with pillows in them for mobile infants and toddlers provide a place to hide away from the group, slow down, and unwind.

Nurturing Opportunities

Opportunities for children to experience nurturing can also happen in many spaces and at many times throughout the day. Nurturing children is one of the most important roles of the infant or toddler teacher—for example, when a toddler falls and cries and an adult finds a Band-Aid (the magic cure). Examine a room. Are there places for care teachers or parents to nurture their children? Quiet spaces may double as nurturing places, but rooms will also need rocking chairs, a stuffed chair, or a comfortable corner for two or three. A soft blanket to wrap an infant or a small quilt to cover a toddler adds a sense of comfort to a nurturing space.

1. Create areas where the adult and children can be cozy together and the teacher can hold and comfort children.
2. Create comfortable areas where the adult can sit with his back supported—then infants and toddlers can sit close, lean on the adult, or plop on a lap.
3. Create spaces where the teacher can see eye-to-eye with children.
4. Provide a firm mattress on the floor in front of a safety mirror hung low on the wall, so that infants, toddlers, and teachers can enjoy looking in the mirror, patting the images they see, singing songs to their reflections, and making faces at the faces looking back at them.
5. Provide pictures of families that teachers laminate so that the children can carry them around.
6. Provide peek-a-boo pictures of children and family members on a board with a piece of cloth over each one so children can lift up the cloth and see the picture.

Social Opportunities

As discussed in Chapter 7, infants and toddlers show great interest in peers very early in their lives. Care teachers can support children's early interactions and developing friendships by

- Supporting infants' interest in each other by laying or sitting children near each other. For example, place infants close enough so they can touch each other.
- Providing long periods of play during which infants and toddlers can imitate, approach, follow, and try to engage other children.
- Sharing the strategies that infants and toddlers use to engage others. Continually document through pictures or video how young children enjoy each other. Share the information with parents. Encourage parents to share their pictures and examples of their child's interest in other children. See Box 13.2 for an example of how a care teacher might plan for a child based on a photograph of a social interaction.
- Setting up cozy areas for several children—for example, a box for one or two or more, a small couch, and a nook under the loft.
- Providing two or more of each favorite toy or similar toys so that children can enjoy them together. Sometimes the best "friendships" develop for toddlers when each has her own materials but can easily see and interact with one other child (parallel and reciprocal play).
- Using large motor equipment that promotes social play, such as a climber or a rocking boat. Conflict between peers occurs less often with large pieces of equipment than with small toys (although those are necessary as well).
- Providing places for infants and toddlers to have alone time to promote emotional and social development. Private spaces, such as a box on its side that one mobile infant or toddler can fit into, allow for emotional refueling. Too much togetherness, and no opportunity for alone time, *for some babies* can contribute to their feelings of stress.

BOX 13.2

Day to Day the Relationship Way
Individual Child Planning Guide

Child's Name: Brogan

Plans for Week of (Date): Sept. 7–11, 2012

Person(s) Completing the Guide: Denmon

Respect: Child's Emotions, Effort, Goals, Learning, and Relationships

Write an observation or use a picture or other documentation here—date all notes:

Respect and Reflect	Relate

9/7/12

What am I doing?
I was crawling through the tunnel and now I am peering out…
seeing what the world looks like on this side of the tunnel.

How am I feeling?
I am enjoying playing and moving my muscles.

What am I learning?
Emotional
• I am learning how to focus (self-regulation).
Social
I'm learning how to lead a friend through the tunnel.
Cognitive
• I am learning about spatial concepts like "in" and "out" and "through."
• I am learning about cause and effect (I can do something that will have an effect).
Language
• My teacher said to me: "Look, you crawled through the tunnel."
Motor
• I am learning to use my large muscles and maintaining balance.

What will you do to support my development and learning?

Responsive Interactions
We will continue to provide a long play time during the day to provide an opportunity for peer play and self-mastery.

Environment, Toys, Materials, and Experiences
We will bring in more challenging cause-and-effect toys to enjoy with friends.
We will continue to provide more objects and play equipment for you and your friends to explore spatial concepts such as "through," "over," and "under."
We will document the children's understanding and exploration of spatial concepts.

Language Opportunities

Care teachers of infants and toddlers play a significant role in facilitating infants' and toddlers' language development. Each interaction and experience that the child has with teachers and peers provides opportunities for children's language development. Review the 12 strategies for language learning in Chapter 9 and use them often throughout the day. As a child climbs on the climber, you can use parallel talk and say, "You are climbing up. Now you are climbing down." When you are responding to an infant's or toddler's sounds or words, you can use semantically responsive talk and you can elaborate and expand the child's language. When a child climbs into your lap, you can ask him how he is feeling today. An astute teacher doesn't bombard children with comments and questions but rather uses responsive talk and turn-taking strategies at all times so that infants and toddlers experience the joy of communicating.

Miller (1999) describes materials that teachers can add to the environment to encourage language development and communication between children. Large, empty gift-wrap tubes provide opportunities for children to experiment with how their voices sound different when they talk through the tube. Mobile infants and toddlers will use pretend phones to "talk" to Mommy or Grandma. Picture cards of favorite people, animals, toys, and babies that teachers laminate and place in a box provide opportunities for children to name the pictures. Miller suggests putting a different object in a hinged box each day to provide an opportunity for naming and conversing about the "surprise" object.

Cognitive Opportunities

Cognitive activities occur every day in every way. With cognitive development, the environment, toys, and materials facilitate children's development of the learning sparkle. The materials in the environment and the adult-child interactions will facilitate each child's sense of wonder, joy, interest, and discovery in all areas of the room. It is this sense of wonder that leads to learning and the love of learning.

Provide toys that adapt to changes in the child's development. For example, a stacking toy can usually be chewed and examined and passed from hand to hand by an infant. It can also be stacked, at first incorrectly and then correctly (after much experimentation) by a toddler. The toy hasn't changed, but the way that the child plays with the toy has changed. This toy is adaptable and can be used by children who are at different developmental stages in their ability to play with this toy and by the same child as he develops. Adults also provide opportunities for children to develop the foundations for learning discussed in Chapter 8 through the materials that they provide and their responsive interactions.

Infants and toddlers gain confidence in their ability to initiate, be intentional, persist at tasks, and problem solve when they are given opportunities to discover what they can do with toys and materials. This may include tasting, sucking, banging together, tapping, moving, dumping, building, and tasting again. To help them gain confidence and the desire to problem solve give them many opportunities to succeed by providing materials that interest them and that are at or slightly above their developmental level.

Infants and toddlers often gravitate toward different and interesting materials, such as using crayons with corrugated cardboard—two materials that often aren't used together. The cardboard provides a challenge that sparks the child's problem

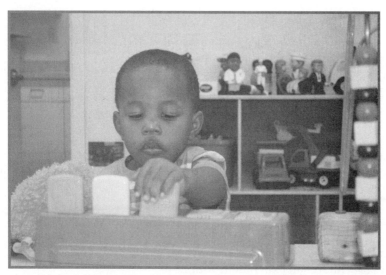

Long periods of exploration time are important for infants and toddlers to investigate toys and materials and have time to be intentional and problem solve.

solving and initiation. Mobile infants and toddlers like surprises. Provide a container with a hole in the bottom or a slotted spoon in the water table, a solid block in with the stacking rings, or a toy that doesn't make music with a small basket of musical toys. Toddlers enjoy and are surprised by contact paper with the sticky side up. Tape it to a wall or the floor. Place toys, feathers, and other material nearby so that toddlers can experiment with placing and removing items on the paper. These materials create disequilibrium—a concept discussed in Chapter 3.

Also, create and share the "wow" moments with infants and toddlers. Create and look for the moments when an infant seems puzzled by a wobbly toy or when a mobile infant has the look of surprise when she discovers how balls sound different from blocks as they are dumped from a basket. Share those wow moments with your own surprised looks to build an emotional feeling of excitement about learning. When care teachers support children's learning dispositions, they support children's desire and confidence to learn and build positive relationships with the children.

Delighting-the-Senses Experiences

Infants and toddlers are using all of their senses—hearing, seeing, feeling, tasting, and smelling—in all areas of the room. When children delight their senses, they are learning about object permanence, cause and effect, and attributes of objects and materials. With a responsive care teacher and peers, infants' and toddlers'

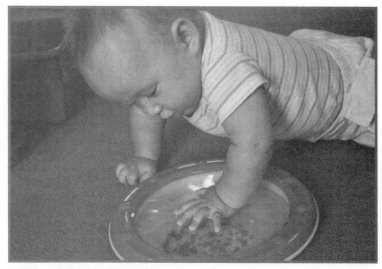

Provide materials of different textures for infants and toddlers to explore.

language development grows by leaps and bounds. As they play with sand and water, they are also developing their small motor skills.

Sand provides a delightful sensory experience. Sand in a short sand/water table indoors and outdoors encourages mobile infants and toddlers to feel the texture, pour sand through their fingers, and experiment with filling and emptying cups and other containers. Waterwheels, funnels, sifters, containers of different sizes, and plastic animals encourage toddlers to experiment. Create a sandbox beach (Cryer, Harms, & Bourland, 1988) inside for toddlers, with a small swimming pool full of sand, safe low beach chairs, large plastic sunglasses, beach towels, and magazines.

BOX 13.3

Sink Play

When it is too cold for water play outside, we invite the children to immerse themselves in water at the sinks [standing, with only diapers on, in front of low sinks filled partially with water and toys]. I always find it interesting to observe the different ways children play even while standing right next to each other. Kevin and Trent stood side by side, each engrossed in his own task. Trent concentrated intently on filling the large bucket and carefully pouring it out again into the sink. He poured water on a single washcloth and then would hold it up and watch the water drip steadily down into the sink.

Kevin was interested in filling many small containers with water and then pouring them into each other. He also used a bottle with a squeeze-lid to spray the water into the containers. He used the bottle to "feed" his baby doll and also to wash the baby's hair. He experimented by filling a container to the top, pushing his hands and arms into the container, and watching the water pour out.

The children were using many words to describe what they were doing: "pour," "top," "wash baby," "water," "my baby," "mine." Not only do the children enjoy playing in the water, it also seems to soothe them, and they learn many things about their world. They also learn about such concepts as cause and effect, size, shape, and quantity. And, they get to share a pleasurable experience with their classmates and learn from each other.

Source: Vernon, in *Focus on Infants & Toddlers*, *15*(1), p. 5 © 2003 ACEI.

Provide water in a variety of containers for mobile infants and toddlers (always watch carefully to prevent drowning). (In Box 13.3, Vernon [2003] provides a wonderful example of how toddlers enjoyed water in her program.) Provide small basins of water for mobile infants and water tables for toddlers. Add different materials each day or week to encourage exploration. Refill the containers of water often to reduce the spread of infection. Water tables have drains on the bottom for ease of emptying. Squeeze bottles and paintbrushes encourage toddlers to use water outdoors to "paint" a fence.

Provide infants with materials of different textures to touch. Feelie bags (cloth or paper bags) with different objects in them delight mobile infants and toddlers as they cautiously put their hands in the bags.

Think about how to offer opportunities for children to explore with their other senses in addition to touch. Listening boxes can be made by placing different items in each box (be sure to tape them up well). Stop and have the children listen when there is a new noise. Use "loud," "soft," "noisy," and "quiet" and other descriptive words to enhance language development while exploring sound. Provide visually pleasing materials such as bottles (again, taped closed very carefully) with oil and food coloring combined in them.

Creative Opportunities

Serena was excited. She hurried over to the paints and large pieces of paper that the teacher had placed carefully on the low table. Serena's teacher helped her put her smock over her head and then adjust it, Serena grasped a wide-handled paintbrush in a hammer grip, dipped the brush part into the short-side containers of paint, lifted the brush, and watched as the beautiful yellow paint dripped off the end. As she started to move the pretty paintbrush toward her mouth to taste it, the teacher said, "Here, put the paint on this paper," and helped guide Serena's hand toward the paper on the table. Serena was fascinated by the yellow mark that appeared.

Infants and toddlers love to create—make messes, invent new sounds, make a toy move in a surprising way, or put two or more items together in an innovative manner. When watching young children, adults can see the joy and wonder expressed when toddlers make marks on paper with crayons or when they glue two pieces of wood together. When young children are making messes, dumping, mushing, exploring, discovering, inventing, collecting, imagining, observing, and playing with materials, they are creating.

Being a creative person begins in infancy. An infant reaches out to touch his parent's face, the parent's eyes open wide in delight, and the infant has created an emotional connection. The infant squeezes a toy and creates a funny, squeaky noise. She plays with her mouth and creates new sounds. He bats at a musical toy and creates a beautiful tune. A mobile infant, who is just beginning to walk, creates a stir as adults marvel at this new development. Toddlers throw toys into a box and create crashing noises. They place one block beside another and begin to create a row. One day they stack a block on top of another and create a tower. A toddler will accidently stick his finger into the neck of an empty soda bottle and create a new toy that waves around when he moves his finger. Turning the pages of a cardboard book creates a new scene to enjoy. Colorful marks made with crayons and nontoxic paints are masterpieces to a toddler budding artist. Groups of toddlers with colorful scarves create a kaleidoscope of colors. As infants and toddlers create in this way they learn that they can *produce, build, generate new ideas,* and *construct*—all aspects of being a creative person. They also develop a healthy sense of mastery; a positive self-concept; and a feeling of being effective, capable, and competent.

Honig (2003a) notes that "working with art materials gives sensory joy to toddlers as they knead play dough or watch in awe as cornstarch goop stretches in their fingers" (p. 22). Creative, sensory, open-ended materials engage children and often reduce stress. Open-ended materials are those that allow the child to use them in a variety of ways. Care teachers make the materials available and young children experiment *rather than try to make a product.* The *process* of feeling, pouring, dumping, lifting, examining, turning over, and testing is what is important for very young children—not the end product.

Offer play dough and clay, then stand back and watch the wonderful exploration and investigation that occurs. As they delight their senses, children are learning about the composition of materials, how to shape and reshape them, number, quantity, and mass. All of these activities provide perfect opportunities for care teachers to support the language development of infants and toddlers. Toddlers are also learning social skills as they negotiate space and share the materials.

Create a cozy corner where children play with play dough on the floor or on a short table. Place separate piles of play dough on the table or provide one large ball of play dough in the middle of the table. If the materials are available for lengthy periods of time and almost every day, infants and toddlers will relax as they trust that the materials will be available and have time to test their theories about how the material works.

One of Kyanne's first pictures (shown here) demonstrates how young children enjoy painting. Nontoxic paint that is especially made for young children and purchased through catalogs or in a teacher supply store can be offered to toddlers with large pieces of paper on a table or on the floor. Toddlers can use their hands or large paintbrushes with the paint to test their theories on how to make a mark on a page. Short easels for toddlers spark their creativity with crayons and

paint. Smocks (aprons) can be purchased to cover toddlers' clothing if parents or the children are concerned
about getting paint on their clothes. Toddlers can learn to
go get their smocks before they begin to paint but often
need help from a care teachers or peer to get them on
correctly.

Ditto sheets to color or requiring toddlers to create
products such as egg carton caterpillars are not appropriate tasks for mobile infants and toddlers because
they stifle creativity. Toddlers are *making something
happen* rather than *making something.* Be open to all of
the possibilities for what children do with the materials. Materials should always be offered as a *choice,* and
children should not ever be forced to touch or play
with them. Let them wash their hands as soon as they
would like, to build enjoyment in the experience of
being creative.

Writing and Drawing Opportunities

Infants and toddlers make their mark on the world
through drawing with nontoxic crayons, magnetic
boards with an attached large pen, and markers (without the lids, which are a choking hazard). Mobile infants
like Dawson (as shown in Box 13.4) grasp the big pen
with an overhand grasp, using the large muscles in his
arm to make big circles on the paper. Infants will bang
or jab their crayon on the paper, but soon they will
make straight lines. Vertical lines usually appear before
horizontal lines. Dawson has had quite a bit of experi-

Display children's open-ended art on the wall.

ence using crayons and other writing materials, so he is already making circles
with his pen on his magnetic board.

Provide comfortable small chairs, such as Dawson is using, or create a cozy
corner with a small table where mobile infants and toddlers can use nontoxic
crayons and large pieces of blank paper. Opportunities to use crayons on sand-
paper and other unusual materials, chalk outside, and finger painting spark a
mobile infant's or toddler's interest in writing and drawing.

Opportunities with Blocks

Blocks may be small or large, plastic or wooden, of various sizes and shapes.
Hirsch (1996) has identified six stages of block development: carrying, stacking
and placing in rows, bridging, building enclosures, creating patterns, and representational play. An infant will mouth the blocks, a mobile infant will carry
them around and begin to explore their properties, and a toddler will begin to
stack them one on top of the other. Soon rows of blocks will appear, and then
varying forms of bridges. You may see a toddler creating an enclosure with blocks
on all sides to contain a zoo full of wooden animals. Patterns may appear—for
example, a toddler may use four blocks of the same size to support a large unit
block. Toward the end of the toddler period, children may begin to use the blocks

BOX 13.4

Day to Day the Relationship Way
Individual Child Planning Guide

Child's Name: <u>Dawson</u>

Plans for Week of (Date): <u>Sept. 7–11, 2012</u>

Person(s) Completing the Guide: <u>Torren and Nicole</u>

Respect: Child's Emotions, Effort, Goals, Learning, and Relationships

Write an observation or use a picture or other documentation here—date all notes:

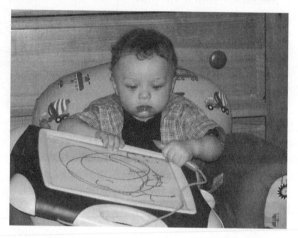

Respect and Reflect	Relate
9/7/12 **What am I doing?** I am making large circles on a magnetic board. I am holding the large attached pen with my left hand and holding the board with my right. This is called holding and operating. I am using an overhand grasp, which is typical for my age and allows me to use the large muscles in my arm to draw. **How am I feeling?** I am feeling very focused. I am intent on what I am doing. **What am I learning?** I am learning how to use the large muscles in my arms and the small muscles in my hands to write and to create. I am learning to focus and attend when I want to accomplish something. I am learning, "I can do it," and I am learning about cause and effect.	**What will you do to support my development and learning?** **Responsive Interactions** We will talk with your parents about how much you enjoyed this experience and we will ask them what you like to do at home. We will use words to describe what you are doing (parallel talk). **Environment, Toys, Materials, and Experiences** We will provide other creative experiences such as play dough, finger paints, and crayons as well as other "cause and effect" toys.

as symbols for another object, such as a firefighter's hose, and may begin to pretend—for example, to be a firefighter.

Blocks provide opportunities for learning at all ages and provide opportunities to support development in all domains. As infants and toddlers manipulate the blocks and then play with them in a purposeful way, they are developing self-regulation. Playing with blocks is often a social experience and provides opportunities for children to learn to play together and resolve conflicts. Creativity blossoms as toddlers build with blocks. Toddlers will also knock down a block tower that they have built to *create* a noise and to *create* a mess. Knocking down blocks, as well as building with them, is about learning about the properties of materials. They are also using many of the problem-solving strategies, as described in this example cited by Reindle (2004):

> Tyrone, 2, discovered that the teacher had built a bridge out of three blocks and had placed it on a short table next to the block area. He pushed a little car he found under the bridge and soon it came tumbling down. He picked up the blocks and stacked them one on top of the other, because that was the schema that he used to build. After realizing, on his own, that his blocks did not have a space under them, he moved two blocks so that they were apart by a few inches. He then took the other block and placed it across the two base blocks to make a bridge. Tyrone had figured it out. (p. 3)

When an older toddler pretends to build a house, a fence around a pretend playground, or a birthday cake, he is building a foundation for literacy development (Stroud, 1995). Stroud identifies ways that block play supports success in literacy development:

1. Children learn about representation and symbols as they pretend with blocks and block structures. When children begin to reproduce and name their buildings, for example, block building becomes representational and serves as an introduction to symbolization: "The blocks themselves become symbols for other objects, just as printed letters and words are symbols for objects and ideas" (p. 9).
2. Visual discrimination—a skill necessary for distinguishing similar letter and word formations during the reading process—is enhanced by block play. Children are continually looking at, comparing, and matching blocks of varying shapes and sizes. Cleanup provides another opportunity to sort and return blocks to a labeled position on storage shelves.
3. Fine-motor strength and coordination used for writing are developed with blocks. Writing skills needed to manipulate crayons and pencils are developed through grasping, carrying, and stacking blocks.
4. Oral language develops as young children label the toys as "blocks," describe them, and talk about them with others.

Stroud also recommends adding books and writing materials to the block area to encourage literacy experiences.

Children's receptive and expressive language develops as adults and peers name the blocks, describe their attributes, and talk about spatial concepts. An adult says, "You put the red block on the blue block" and then waits for the infant or toddler to respond with a sound, a gesture, an action, or words. The adult listens for these language expressions and responds by observing, imitating, expanding, elaborating, or extending the child's language.

Block areas invite young children to have fun as they learn many spatial concepts.

Motor capacities develop as babies handle the blocks with their hands (small motor), pick up blocks and carry them around (large motor), and explore how they feel and listen to how they sound when they fall (sensory development).

When infants and toddlers play with blocks of all sizes and shapes, have a cozy corner where they are displayed and easy for babies to reach, room for floor play with the blocks, and responsive care teachers then the possibilities for learning in all of the developmental domains is endless. Place blocks on a low shelf with each shelf clearly labeled. As children "clean up" after play time, they learn to classify as they replace the blocks on the shelves in their designated places.

Music, Song, and Creative Movement Opportunities

Sarah, just a year old, laughed as her teacher played pat-a-cake with her. As her teacher began singing the song, Sarah clapped her hands together repeatedly with delight. After the song ended, Sarah's teacher pointed to Sarah's hands with delight and said, "You clapped your hands." Sarah looked joyfully at the teacher as if to say, "Do it again."

While diapering Jamika, her teacher sings, "You have ten little *fingers,* and ten little *toes,* two little *arms,* and one little *nose.*" As her teacher touches her fingers, her toes, her arms, and her nose, Jamika wriggles in delight at hearing this familiar tune. Soon Jamika will start chiming in with her teacher as she sings this song.

Care teachers can sing songs throughout the day. A good-morning song helps infants and toddlers transition from home to child care. A good-bye song signals that a parent is here to pick up his child. Songs sung throughout the day comfort children or help them transition from one activity to another, such as from indoor play to outdoor play. As Jamika waits for her mom and dad at the end of the day, one teacher sings to Jamika, modeling how to clap and tap: "Two little hands go clap, clap, clap. Two little feet go tap, tap, tap." Soon, several toddlers are sitting with the teacher. Jamika watches her friends intently as they clap and tap in all different and unique ways. These familiar activities are opportunities for young children to enjoy music and learn concepts in fun, responsive, sensitive ways. Care teachers don't have to have the best singing voices in the world to sing to infants and toddlers. Babies love to hear songs and it doesn't matter to them how a teacher sings them—children love the warm feelings that are conveyed (Honig, 1995; Ilari & Johnson-Green, 2002). There are many benefits to children of singing, listening to music, making rhythms, and moving their bodies. These experiences

- Provide opportunities for pure joy
- Provide opportunities to move, practice crawling, pull to stand, jump, run, experience rhythms, and feel comfortable with their bodies in space
- Increase self-awareness and worth

- Provide opportunities for children to learn concepts such as "up" and "down"
- Provide opportunities for children to interact and learn prosocial behavior
- Help children make transitions and make routines and learning times fun
- Provide opportunities for children to learn words and longer sentences in their own and other languages
- Encourage children to listen and follow directions
- Encourage creativity and problem solving
- Provide opportunities for representational and symbolic play—for example, when toddlers sing "Twinkle, Twinkle, Little Star" they use their hands to represent stars
- Music can comfort and soothe children and help them fall asleep

Literacy Opportunities

Literacy experiences are among the most important that a care teacher can provide to young children. What is literacy? How does it develop? What is the relationship between talking, social experiences, and learning to read and write? McLane and McNamee (1991) define literacy as "the notion that writing and reading are ways of making, interpreting, and communicating meaning" (p. 1).

Becoming literate is about learning to read and write—and *becoming* begins in infancy when an infant hears the sounds of language and begins to make sounds herself.

> Many people believe that children learn to read and write in kindergarten or first grade; however, the foundation for literacy skills is laid years before children enter school. Emergent literacy, much like any other cognitive skill, begins at birth. During the early years, children develop competency in language and literacy not through a set curriculum, but through interactions and experiences with the adults around them. (Im, Osborn, Sánchez, & Thorp, 2007, p. 9)

Language is a strong bridge that connects to later reading and writing because infants and toddlers learn how to communicate—the ultimate purpose of reading and writing. Play is a necessary bridge—playing with sounds and words, and making marks on a page. Learning about symbols is also a connecting bridge to literacy as toddlers learn that a picture or an object (a plastic apple) can represent something real that is seen and touched. This leads to a later understanding that squiggly lines called letters have meaning. Experiences with water, sand, toys, animals, and people are essential bridges because the child can bring a wealth of understanding to written concepts and when they are older, they can write stories based on their many rich understandings. And certainly, one of the most important bridges to becoming literate is the love of books—a foundational bridge that provides a link to later reading and writing. Positive relationships with special adults and peers are the supports that strengthen the bridges to literacy.

Learning to Love Books

Ezra, 26 months old, snuggles against his teacher's arm as she reads a book to him and two other toddlers who are sitting together on the floor. He likes turning the brightly colored pages with the pictures of familiar toys, and he especially likes to hear his teacher's animated voice as she reads the story aloud. Ezra loves books and often finds books in the room and runs to his teacher holding out the book for her to read.

When does this interest in books start and why do most babies love books? Most young infants adore looking at visually interesting images found in books.

They tune into the reader's voice and learn about the rhythms, tones, and sounds of language. Nursery rhymes and poetry can soothe a baby with their reassuringly rhythmic sounds. Books with one word and picture on a page spark a baby's interest as the adult "reads" the pictures. Cloth and soft vinyl books allow infants to grasp, chew, suck, and crinkle books as they learn through all their senses. Sitting in a care teacher lap is the perfect way for an infant to see the pictures and enjoy a fun, colorful book.

Mobile infants love to look at books as they sit, walk, and toddle around. For mobile infants, books are playthings that can be touched and turned, and they reveal a world of surprises with every flip of the page. Because mobile infants are absorbing language and learning new words every day, they're beginning to relate the pictures in books to objects in real life. A book about toys or animals is a great choice for this age group. Choose short books with simple stories. Books made of heavy cardboard allow mobile infants to use newly developed motor skills to turn pages.

Toddlers love stories about familiar animals, objects, and people. Pictures with a few printed words on every page can keep a busy toddler's attention as she points to the pictures and asks, "What's that?" Interactive pop-up books, with their hidden surprises, trigger grins of delight from curious toddlers.

Allow toddlers to choose from books displayed on shelves with the cover showing—rather than thrown in a box, where they're hard to identify. Even toddlers are beginning to learn how books work: that you start at the front and read from top to bottom, that the story is usually about the picture, and that some of those strange squiggles sound the same each time an adult reads them.

Here are some ways you can help infants and toddlers have fun with and learn to love books:

- *Create cozy "reading" corners.* Schickedanz (2003) talks about creating a book nook for infants and toddlers. Equip these corners and nooks with a small, soft-covered mattress, a cloth-covered inner tube, and for toddlers a short couch just their size. Make sure that the corner is comfortable for teachers to lie on their backs while holding up a book with a baby by their side, who is looking up as well. Or, create a place where teachers can sit with their backs supported by the wall or pillows (no pillows for infants for safety reasons). Mobile infants and toddlers will enjoy looking at books together.
- *Place books around the room.* That way, they greet and tempt a child at every turn. Be creative. Putting a book about bears right next to a stuffed bear makes that book hard to resist!
- *Read throughout the day.* Infants can look and listen when teachers hold them in their comfortable laps. Toddlers like one-on-one time with a teacher as well, but also enjoy clustering together around a favorite teacher on a couch, in a cozy corner, or wherever books are in the room. Take your cues from the children and read whenever they ask you. Instead of having a structured reading time for toddlers, teachers can entice them to listen to a story by sitting down where toddlers can join together. Don't be surprised if other toddlers come running to hear the story as well. Let them come and go—they will soon learn to sit for a whole story. When toddlers are forced to sit in groups to listen to a story, they often become disinterested quickly and their love of books can be jeopardized. Toddlers learn to love books when they are shared with an adult who makes them feel safe, loved, excited, soothed, or important, depending on the child's need at the time.

- *Choose books carefully.* Cloth and heavy cardboard books (sometimes called board books) are sturdy and can be transported, carted, stashed, put in containers, and "read" by curious infants and energetic toddlers. Choose books with rhythmical language, touch-and-smell books, and books with clear pictures (ZERO TO THREE, 2012). Select books with pictures of children and families from a variety of cultures and books that show both boys and girls in a variety of activities.

- *Read responsively.* Use interactive storybook reading strategies (Whitehurst et al., 1999). Notice which pictures children seem to enjoy, point to them, name them, and when possible, point out the real objects they represent. Interact with children as you read the story and encourage their engagement. Encourage infants to make sounds and toddlers to discuss their experiences as you read a story. Answer their questions. Avoid pestering children with too many one-right-answer questions such as "What's this?" and "Who's that?" Have fun reading, use lots of feeling, exaggerate sounds, and wait for infants and toddlers to respond with their own sounds, words, and gestures.

- *Exchange information with families through home visits, book bags to borrow, and information about the importance of reading as well as how to read to infants and toddlers.* The ZERO TO THREE Web site (www.zerotothree.org) and the National Center for Family Literacy (NCFL) Web site (www.famlit.org) provide tip sheets, activities, and research related to supporting families. Ask families what books their infants and toddlers like at home and what secrets they have for sparking their children's interest in books.

- *Provide a literacy-rich environment.* Books and printed words should be found in all parts of an infant or toddler room. Make photograph albums of family members, friends, and pets available with the name of the pet, for example, written at the bottom of the page. Add their names and photos to their cubbies. Rather than quiz children, comment with excitement when a child is looking at a word.

Math, Space, and Shape Opportunities

All of the materials in an infant-toddler room or home offer opportunities for learning about numerals (the symbols that represent numbers, such as the numeral 2) and numbers (the concept of amount—there are two blocks) as well as other math concepts. As an infant holds one block in one hand and another block in another and looks back and forth from one to the other, he is learning about numbers—that he now has more blocks than he did before when he was holding one block. "More" becomes evident as the infant feels what two are like compared to one.

Care teachers and parents can nurture infants' and toddlers' understanding of mathematical concepts (Geist, 2003). An adult's role is to set up a rich menu of math *opportunities* for young children and to support their interest and exploration through math interactions. Teachers and parents can promote children's ability to process information—how to think. To support mathematical understanding, toddlers are not given worksheets and they are not drilled in their numbers and shapes by adults. Rather, possibilities for learning about math concepts in a play environment are found everywhere that children go in their home, center room, or family child care home and in many interactions that occur daily with teachers. Adults who are knowledgeable about mathematical concepts and see the possibilities for supporting mathematical understanding every day in relaxed and informal ways take advantage of playful moments and the environment to help young children learn. Here each concept is defined and a list of materials and interactions that promote mathematical understanding are described. Understand though, that most materials and interactions have the possibility of promoting many concepts—for example, a finger-play with a toddler (such as "Round and round the garden, like a teddy bear, one step, two steps, tickle you under there") uses concepts of shape (round and round the garden) and counting (one step, two steps), as well as builds relationships. (Use your finger to trace a circle around and around the palm of a young child's hand. Walk your fingers up the baby's arm as you say "one step, two steps" and then *if the baby is enjoying the finger-play* gently tickle the baby under the arm. Wait at least 5 seconds to see if the baby puts out her hand for another turn. If so, repeat the finger-play. If not, try again another time.)

Opportunities for Learning About Counting

Infants and toddlers learn to count in myriad ways if the adults in their lives are aware of the many daily opportunities for counting. *Model* counting during play as you point to and count children, toys, and books. For toddlers, start counting "1" and then point to the next item and wait to see if the toddler counts the next item. If not, continue modeling in a warm tone of voice. Routines provide opportunities as adults count children's fingers and toes in playful and responsive ways. Snack time provides many opportunities for counting pieces of food, cups, plates, and silverware. Once adults are aware that it is important that they model counting for children, then they will see many opportunities during the day to count. As always, count when the infant or toddler seems receptive and the counting doesn't interfere with a goal that the child is attempting to achieve, such as carefully stacking blocks.

Opportunities for Learning About One-to-One Correspondence

One-to-one correspondence occurs as babies begin to understand that there is a number for each item that is counted. Provide an environment that contains a variety of objects that work together in a one-to-one relationship: cars and garages, containers with lids, and dolls with beds. Provide opportunities for toddlers to put the plates on the table for a snack or meal—one for each child in the group or one for each member of the family. You can say, "One plate for Daddy, one plate for Mommy, and one plate for you," as you point to the plates.

Opportunities for Learning How to Classify

Infants and toddlers are also learning concepts about classifying people and objects. Classification is a concept that describes a child's actions of comparing similarities and differences, sorting by various attributes, putting objects into different categories, and arranging objects by various characteristics. Infants, for example, begin to categorize which adults are friendly and which aren't. Mobile infants figure out which items make a noise when shaken or which items roll. Use responsive planning and provide the child with objects that make noise and objects that don't to encourage further discoveries. Table 13.4 includes a number of opportunities that teachers can provide to encourage infants' and toddlers' exploration of classification, spatial relationships and shapes, quantity, patterning, and seriation.

TABLE 13.4   Learning Opportunities: Sorting, Numeracy, Space, and Shape

Opportunities to Learn About Classification (Sorting)

- Compare objects—point out similarities and differences in color, shape, and size.
- Provide an environment that includes a variety of manipulatives (parquetry blocks, unit cubes), collections (pebbles, plastic animals), dramatic play props (variety of clothing, dishes, dolls), and art materials (fabric samples, tongue depressors) in different colors, shapes, and sizes to offer classifying and sorting experiences throughout the day.
- Provide opportunities for children to assemble collections (walk to the park to collect pinecones or fallen leaves) and talk about why the children sort, classify, and order objects in a certain way.
- Use language and point out similarities and differences in, for example, toys and blocks, as toddlers put them on the shelf during cleanup time.
- Compare collections one-to-one to determine "more," "less," and "same as."
- Provide opportunities for toddlers to sort objects according to two characteristics at the same time (big red, small red, big yellow, small yellow). Understand, though that this is challenging for toddlers.

Opportunities to Learn About Spatial Relationships and Shapes

- Provide opportunities for mobile infants and toddlers to explore spatial relations (next to, above, below, inside, outside) during the day. You can say as you point, "Sarah is sitting *next to* Amanda." "Oh, you're putting the block *in* the basket." "Put the puzzles on the shelf *above* the blocks."
- Provide opportunities for children to build complex 2-dimensional and 3-dimensional shapes by putting simple shapes together (pattern blocks, tangrams, unit blocks).

Opportunities to Learn About Quantity

- Provide different sizes of containers during water and sand play.
- Provide opportunities for mobile infants and toddlers to experiment with full and empty.

Opportunities to Learn About Patterning

- Provide opportunities for children to notice patterns (visual pattern in bricks in the sidewalk, auditory pattern in the melodies of music, repetitive language of predictable stories, physical patterns in exercise).

Opportunities to Learn About Seriation (Ordering by One or More Dimensions)

- Provide materials for toddlers to explore seriating (various sized cups in water table to sort by size, paint-chip samples to seriate by color hue, fabric squares to sort by texture from softest to least soft).
- Use terms such as *short, tall, high, low, wide, thin* to compare objects.

Opportunities for Active Play and Motor Development

Large Motor and Active Play

Provide spaces for infants and toddlers where they can use their large muscles to crawl, pull to stand, stand alone, walk, climb, toddle, and run. They will need space away from the quiet, nurturing, and creative areas. The equipment in this indoor area usually includes mats stacked to create different levels, a rocking boat, a short climber, a large tube to climb through, or a few steps to a loft area. These large pieces of equipment promote social as well as motor development (Honig, 2001). For small spaces, these pieces of equipment can be shared with other homerooms in centers and teachers can alternate these exciting opportunities.

At various times, depending on the interests and needs of the children, balls of various sizes and shapes, large containers and boxes, push and pull toys, small "grocery" carts, riding toys, wagons, and blankets with toys on them for pulling can be introduced. Miller (1999) describes large-muscle motor opportunities; for example, place large boxes with the ends cut out end to end and cover them with blankets to create box tunnels. Punch a hole in the ends of shoeboxes and tie them together, end to end, to make a little train. Leave a string about 10 inches long on one end so that the child can pull the train. Children will place various toys from around the room into the boxes to give them a little ride. These open-ended materials (no one correct way to use them) provide numerous opportunities for infants and toddlers to problem solve, exploring their multiple uses (Segatti, Brown-DuPaul, & Keyes, 2003).

Small Motor and Manipulative Opportunities

Provide spaces for infants and toddlers where they can use their large muscles to crawl, pull to stand, stand alone, walk, climb, toddle, and run. They will need space away from the quiet, nurturing, and creative areas. The equipment in this indoor area usually includes mats stacked to create different levels, a rocking boat, a short climber, a large tube to climb through, or a few steps to a loft area. These large pieces of equipment promote social as well as motor development (Honig, 2001). For small spaces, these pieces of equipment can be shared with other homerooms in centers and care teachers can alternate these exciting opportunities.

Outdoor Opportunities

Joshua looked with anticipation at his teacher when she announced, "Time to go outside." This was the time of day that Joshua seemed to like best. When the door to the outside opened, Joshua was the first to toddle outside. He put his face to the sun and then scurried to the sandbox to bury his hands deep into the cool sand. It was all his teacher could do to keep up with him as she carried a big box of sand toys to the area.

Outdoor time brings opportunities for infants and toddlers to poke and dig in the sand and dirt, push and pull wagons, touch everything in sight, and feel the soft breezes on their faces. They savor the scent of flowering trees, learn new outside vocabulary, and gain a sparkle in their eyes from invigorating and challenging physical experiences such as walking in sand and climbing over safe obstacles.

Outdoor time also brings challenges for teachers as they strive to provide interesting and exciting experiences for infants and toddlers, allow them to explore with all of their senses, and yet provide a sense of security and safety that infants and toddlers need so much, indoors or outdoors (see Table 13.5).

Infant and toddler professionals can challenge themselves to think about the potential for children's learning in all of the equipment, materials, and experiences available in a center, a family child care home, or a family's home environment. Children choose from these opportunities and learn from each experience that they have in a carefully planned environment and in teacher and peer interactions that happen moment to moment and day to day the relationship way.

We have described the experiences that can be offered as opportunities for learning. Teachers are very intentional about setting up an environment that engages infants and toddlers and they choose from the opportunities. Almost any opportunity that they choose offers possibilities for children to learn in all domains of development.

TABLE 13.5 Security and Safety Issues for Outdoor Time

Age	Activities (Delighting the Senses)	Security and Safety Issues
Young Infants (Birth to 8 Months)		
During this age period infants will begin to turn over, then roll, and crawl. Grasping improves and soon everything in sight, including grass and bugs, may go to the mouth.	Place babies on a soft blanket to allow them to practice their physical skills. Bring each baby's grasping and biting toys outside. Small plastic swimming pools in the shade (without water in them) provide a separate and safe place for young infants. Continue activities like "reading" picture books, repeating sounds, and providing responsive toys.	Young infants need to know that their special teacher is near and nurturing. Infants need particular care when outdoors to protect them from the sun and extreme temperatures.
Mobile Infants (8 to 18 Months)		
Crawling, toddling, and running are skills that may emerge during this period. Walking backward and climbing up and down a low set of stairs are challenging tasks for this age. Small motor skills improve greatly during this period. Many very small and large items go straight to the mouth. Infants like being near each other, exchanging looks, touches, and sometimes even toys. Older infants in this stage may learn to say "Mine" and clutch items closely.	Provide equipment that is safe for cruising infants to pull themselves up on and walk around. Gather push-and-pull toys such as small trikes and wagons for the walking crowd. Balls and stacking toys are great outdoors as well as inside. Fill small plastic pools with balls or safe manipulatives. Large boxes with doors and windows cut out are the perfect places for mobile infants to play peek-a-boo and crawl-in-and-out. Small individual tubs of water are perfect for this age, but need one-on-one attention for safety reasons. Language develops as teachers comment on walking, jumping, climbing, in, out, up, down, over, and around.	Children tire easily and need a lap to sink into to regroup and gain energy for the next physical tasks. "Watching them like a hawk" has special meaning at this age to prevent unwanted and unknown objects from finding their way to the mouth. Provide shady spots for all sun-sensitive infants. Watch water play, even in very small containers, because infants and toddlers have drowned in pails or small pools of water. Provide nutritious safe snacks and plenty of fluids.
Toddlers (18 to 36 Months)		
This age delights in practicing all of their physical skills. They will challenge themselves to climb and jump higher and farther. Imitating an adult or a peer occurs frequently. Toddlers may become frustrated easily because they want to do more than their physical skills allow. Some toddlers may begin to "pretend" to be firefighters or other characters that they have experienced live or on TV. They want to be with peers and will play beside or with others. Toddlers alternate between wanting to "do it myself" and wanting adults to help them. They need special teachers who understand how they struggle between wanting to be grown up, but still need loving, nurturing, and holding (on their terms, of course).	Sand and water are favorites. Provide sand areas large enough for several toddlers and expect them to sit right in the middle of the area. Bring *many* sand toys for pouring, digging, and poking safely. Pulling or pushing a "friend" in a wagon will result in squeals of delight from both. Expect conflicts over toys, just as indoors. Paintbrushes and water go together for an outdoor art experience. Set up other art materials such as crayons, paints, and a variety of paper on the ground or a low table. Dolls, trucks, cars, and other play materials encourage interactions among peers. Blankets on the ground or over a card table for puzzles, stories, and manipulatives provide a spot for a quiet break from large motor activities. Provide a nurturing place with soft blankets and pillows for a toddler to "refuel" emotionally with a special teacher.	Remember, toddlers need time to experiment, problem solve, and explore materials alone and with peers. When they tire they will need to be near an adult whom they trust and like. Try to accumulate many toys for toddlers outdoors. Otherwise, they will become bored with the few toys available. Provide nutritious, safe snacks and plenty of fluids. Survey the playground for sharp objects and broken equipment before allowing children outside each day.

Curriculum Approaches

We have shared information on seven components of planning a responsive, relationship-based curriculum. Many of these components are shared by the curricula and programs available to purchase, although some emphasize the importance of relationships more than others. With any of the following that we describe here, however, a care teacher's emphasis on the importance of relationships and responsive interactions and planning can complement the materials available. Let's start by discussing a program that has lead the way in promoting a relationship-based approach to curriculum planning.

The Program for Infant/Toddler Care (PITC)

We begin by describing the *Program for Infant/Toddler Care* (PITC), a comprehensive training program for infant-toddler teachers, because this program has greatly informed the authors of this book. The goal of PITC is to help teachers recognize the crucial importance of giving tender, loving care and assisting in the infants' intellectual development through an attentive reading of each child's cues. The PITC videos, DVDs, guides, and manuals are designed to help child care administrators and teachers become sensitive to infants' cues, connect with the children's families and cultures, and develop responsive, relationship-based care. The training materials provide the foundation for teachers to study the children in their care, reflect on and record information about the children's interests and skills, and search for ways to set the stage for the child's next learning encounters.

As a relationship-based approach, PITC particularly emphasizes the importance of primary caregiving, continuity of caregiving, small group sizes, low ratios, and responsiveness as foundations of child care settings in which infants and toddlers are able to learn and thrive. PITC holds an image of the child as an active learner who will make important discoveries about the world through her own exploration, if supported by a responsive adult in an engaging environment. Videos and training materials for PITC are available from www.pitc.org.

HighScope

HighScope is an approach to preschool and infant and toddler education that highlights key experiences to frame early learning and development. The book *Tender Care and Early Learning: Supporting Infants and Toddlers in Child Care Settings (Post, 2011)* describes these key experiences. These include sense of self, social relations, creative representation, movement and music, communication and language, exploring objects, early quantity and number, space, and time. The environment is organized to promote child initiation and choice among a variety of interesting materials. Teachers assess children for key experiences using the *Child Observation Record* (COR) for infants and toddlers and then use the information for planning changes in the environment and experiences for children.

The Creative Curriculum for Infants, Toddlers & Twos

The Creative Curriculum for Infants, Toddlers & Twos provides extensive information for planning a responsive curriculum (Teaching Strategies for Early Childhood, 2012, www.teachingstrategies.com). Table 13.6 describes the main components

TABLE 13.6   Five components of *The Creative Curriculum for Infants, Toddlers & Twos* curriculum

1. Knowing infants, toddlers, and twos
   Describes development and the unique characteristics of children

2. Creating a responsive environment
   Describes how to set up an environment that is responsive to individual children

3. What children are learning
   Describes relationships, interactions, materials, and experiences that are building blocks of learning

4. Caring and teaching
   Describes the diverse roles of teachers including how to use ongoing assessment

5. Partnering with families
   Describes how to partner with families in a respectful and responsive way

Sources: Berke, Rudick, & Dodge (2007); Dodge, Rudick, Berke, & Dombro (2006).

of this well-known curriculum. Also see www.teachingstrategies.com for information on the philosophy, goals, strategies, assessment tools, and resources available.

Reggio Emilia

According to researchers, "For the last three decades, certain Italian regions and localities have been sites of extraordinary efforts by educators and public officials, working together with parents and other citizens, to build high-quality public systems of care and education to serve families with young children" (Gandini & Edwards, 2001, p. 1). The fundamental points of the Reggio philosophy can be summarized as follows:

> One of the fundamental points of the Reggio philosophy is an image of a child who experiences the world, who feels a part of the world right from birth; who is full of curiosities, full of desire to live; a child who is full of desire and ability to communicate from the start of his or her life; a child who is fully able to create maps for his or her personal, social, cognitive, affective, and symbolic orientation. Because of all this, a young child reacts with a competent system of abilities, learning strategies, and ways of organizing relationships. (Rinaldi, 2001, pp. 50–51)

Bambini: The Italian Approach to Infant-Toddler Care by Gandini and Edwards (2001) describes the Reggio Emilia approach in detail. The Italian approach to early childhood education grows from a well-articulated image of the child. The image of the infant and toddler as highly capable of making discoveries and constructing knowledge is, of course, congruent with research findings on early learning. This image drives the organization of the infant-toddler centers in Reggio Emilia.

Respect for very young children's ability to construct knowledge from their relationships and their environment is central to the organization of the early childhood programs and the environments, relationships, and experiences they offer in supporting learning. The key tool used by teachers is purposeful observation and documentation of the children's activities. This documentation process is not simply recording activities or accomplishments—it is a method of coming to thoughtful, reflective understanding of the children's activities and thinking, and it is the basis of the teacher's planning for introducing new activities or materials into the center. The documentation process consists of forming a question or hypothesis; observing, recording, and collecting artifacts; organizing observations and artifacts; analyzing and interpreting the observations and artifacts, which leads to building theories; possibly reframing the original questions; and then planning and responding from one's understandings of the children's knowledge and interests (Gandini & Goldhaber, 2001).

Summary

- Responsive routines that provide stability, consistency, and opportunities for learning for infants and toddlers are a key component of a relationship-based program.
- An environment set up with cozy spaces and places and the opportunities provided within this environment entice children to choose, play, develop, relate to others, be nurtured, and learn.

- Every experience offers an opportunity for children to develop their capacities in the emotional, social, cognitive, language, and motor domains.
- A variety of infant and toddler curricula are available to purchase and each offers unique possibilities for child development.

Reflections and Resources for the Reader

REFLECTIONS

1. How do responsive environments support infants' and toddlers' relationships with adults and peers?
2. How would you interact with a toddler during diaper time to help him or her feel safe and enjoy the time with you?

OBSERVATION AND APPLICATION OPPORTUNITIES

1. Use the environment guide (Table 13.2) at the beginning of this chapter to observe an infant or toddler environment. What components does the environment include? What do you think needs to be added or changed in the environment?
2. Observe an infant or toddler program. What literacy and math opportunities do you see provided for children (interactions, environment, materials, and experiences)? Are children able to choose among these literacy and math opportunities?

3. Choose one curriculum described at the end of this chapter and report to other students on the eight components of a curriculum described at the beginning of Chapter 12.

SUPPLEMENTARY ARTICLES AND BOOKS TO READ

Greenberg, J. (2012). More are gone, empty, full: Math talk every day in every way. *Young Children, 67*(3), 62–64.

Guyton, G. (2011). Using toys to support infant-toddler learning and development. *Young Children.* Retrieved from www.naeyc.org/files/yc/file/201109/Using%20 Toys_Guyton_Online_0911.pdf

Petersen, S., & Wittmer, D.S. (2012). Relationship-based infant care: Responsive, on demand, and predictable. *Young Children, 63*(3), 40–42.

ZERO TO THREE. (2012). Choosing books for babies. Retrieved from main.zerotothree.org/site/ PageServer?pagename=ter_key_language_bookselection

INTERESTING LINKS

Better Brains for Babies

www.fcs.uga.edu/ext/bbb
This site provides research-based information about brain development and numerous resources to support young children's development.

National Child Care Information Exchange.

nccic.org
The NCCIC has several Web pages of helpful information about literacy development.

PITC Demonstration Programs: Virtual Tours!
www.pitc.org/
To get ideas for an infant and toddler environment, take a virtual tour through five California community college children's centers that are implementing the PITC approach to infant-toddler care.

14

Respect, Reflect, and Relate

The 3 R Approach to Guidance

LEARNING OUTCOMES

After reading this chapter, you will be able to:

- Explain the difference between the terms *discipline* and *guidance*
- Describe the meaning of *respect, reflect,* and *relate* in a relationship-based approach to guidance and explain in detail 10 strategies to use in a relationship-based approach
- Describe why relationship realignments are a necessary part of the teacher/child relationships
- Describe strategies and programs that are effective with children who exhibit challenging behavior and experience mental health issues

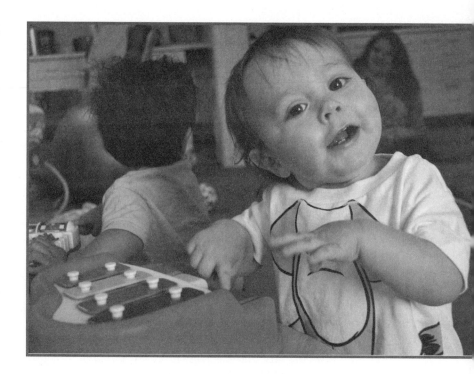

At the beginning of this chapter, we discuss the eighth component of planning a curriculum: a relationship-based approach to guiding infants' and toddlers' behavior while meeting their emotional needs. In planning the guidance component, we use the 3 R approach (respecting, reflecting, and relating)—a way of thinking about children's development, the reasons for their behavior, and how adults can respond in ways that build children's social and emotional skills and relationships with family, care teachers and peers. The 3 R approach to guidance builds on the relationship-based model presented in Chapter 1. This model reminds us to consider how the individual child's attributes, capacities, and uniqueness as well as the child's family, culture, and ecology affect the quality of the child's relationships, which then influence a child's development and behavior.

We will apply the 3 R approach to developmental issues—topics such as separation anxiety, biting, tantrums, and toilet learning. These are everyday challenges that care teachers family specialists, and early interventionists experience with children at home and in programs. Adults who have increased knowledge of what the child is experiencing during these times of emotional change, and sometimes turbulence, are more likely to use empathic responses that promote children's capacities.

Unfortunately, sometimes children who are experiencing problems in their lives engage in challenging behaviors to get their needs met. In the last part of the chapter, we discuss ideas for understanding and helping children who are angry, aggressive, sad, or anxious or who have experienced **traumatic events**. Let's begin with a discussion of the difference between guidance and discipline and why we use the word *guidance* in this chapter.

> **traumatic events**
>
> Events that are upsetting, distressful, and emotionally or physically painful.

The Difference Between Guidance and Discipline

Jose takes off his diaper during playtime. William starts playing with his food. Lynn bites peers who get too near to her when she is tired. Laura grabs toys from other children when she wants them. Before the teacher can stop them, Deanna and John quickly jump up on a chair in order to see better, but the chair topples over and they tumble to the floor.

What do these examples have in common? They are *opportunities* for adults to *socialize* children to the ways of a culture, to *guide* them to try different strategies of relating and getting their needs met, and to *teach* them in order for them to be successful in a world that requires social and emotional competence.

The term **discipline** has traditionally been used to mean adult control, restraint, and authority as well as child obedience—but another meaning of the term discipline is *to teach* infants and toddlers new behavior. Because of the confusion between the two meanings of the term *discipline*, we will use the term **guidance** to indicate a developmental, relationship-based, problem-solving approach to supporting young children's social and emotional competence.

> **discipline**
>
> 1: *(n)* Adult control, restraint, and authority. 2: *(v)* To teach.

> **guidance**
>
> The act of helping and assisting.

A guide shows the way and supports those she guides on the journey. A guide encourages, models, and structures a journey so that everyone can be successful. *Guiding* means that infants and toddlers are supported as they learn an enormous amount of information in such a short period of time—how to use a spoon or why they shouldn't take off their own diaper in the middle of the room in the socialized

Made social; able to live in one's
society, culture, or group.

middle of the day. They learn the important guidelines for their culture, such as when it is acceptable to laugh and how to help another person in distress. They can also learn how to get what they need without using aggression. *Guidance* implies the use of a positive philosophy and strategies for supporting children as they become **socialized** in the cultures in which they live. Guidance includes assistance, facilitation, and setting limits. It is ongoing throughout the day and doesn't occur just when children "misbehave." In fact, it describes a way for care teachers and parents to help children become capable and caring human beings who can guide their own behavior.

Component 8: A Relationship-Based Approach to Guidance

Respect

Respect for infants and toddlers includes respect for their emotional needs, respect for individual differences and strengths, and respect for the power of development.

Respect for Children's Emotional Needs and Their Goals

When developing an approach to guiding young children's behavior, we begin with an understanding that infants and toddlers need protection, secure and caring relationships, responsive interactions, and a sense of self-worth. The importance of adults meeting these needs has been discussed in previous chapters, and we mention those needs here to remind you that they are the foundation for how we think about guidance as well as how children learn in all domains of development.

Infants and toddlers need to *feel* that you really care about them. If they are securely attached and feel a positive emotional connection to you, they are more likely to be cooperative with you. They need to know that you care enough to stop them if they are hurting themselves or others. They trust that they can bury their head in your shoulder when they are sad. They know that you will comfort them when they are hurt. They know that you are emotionally present when they are struggling to learn to walk or climb or talk, empathizing with them. They know that you are there to protect them when they run into your arms when a stranger comes into the room. They trust that you will respond with affection so that they can see their own self-worth in your eyes and voice. They feel as if you are there *for them*.

Respect for Individual Differences in Children

Respect for infants and toddlers also entails appreciation for what children bring to a relationship in terms of capacities, attributes, and individual styles of interacting and learning. When we recognize that each child is unique, we will reflect on how their temperament, personality, needs, and strengths influence what and how we are guiding them. We will *individualize* our guidance strategies for each child's unique personality.

Tune into children's illness, temperament, energy levels, fatigue, and **sensory challenges.** This concept has been emphasized throughout this book, and the following example demonstrates how a care teacher is accepting of Tim sucking his thumb, knowing that he uses it to self-regulate before he courageously crawls into the midst of play:

sensory challenges

Difficulty with any of the senses—touch, vision, hearing, taste, or smell.

Tim sat on the floor sucking his thumb contently while watching all of the action in his child care home. Martha, his teacher, watched Tim and reflected on how Tim liked to observe before crawling into the midst of the other infants playing on the floor. She admired his ability to regulate and calm himself by sucking his thumb. Martha smiled at Tim, Tim smiled back, and he began to crawl toward another baby.

Tim has found a unique way to ready himself for peer play by jumping into the fray *only* after he is ready, and sucking his thumb helps him self-regulate and gain strength and confidence. Martha's respect for Tim's style of playing allows him to develop at his pace and in his own way.

An infant's or toddler's temperament influences how that child will react to the differences in quality of care. Among 66 toddlers between 24 and 35 months observed in child care, children with reactive temperaments were more socially integrated when the quality of the environment and teacher-child interactions was higher (Phillips et al., 2012). Reactive toddlers were quite responsive to the sensitivity, intrusiveness, and detachment of the care teacher and the quality of the environment. Other researchers (Deynoot-Schaub & Riksen-Walraven, 2006) found that among 70 children age 15 months, "children with a relatively difficult temperament were less involved in contacts with contacts initiated by peers although only in cases of lower quality childcare" (p. 709). Although infants or toddlers with reactive and more negative temperaments may be challenging for care teachers, their knowledge and awareness of a child's temperament will help them meet the children's needs for responsive sensitivity and social involvement.

Perceptive adults also focus on children's strengths and what they *can* do rather than what they *can't* do. Build on what the child can do and think of each child in terms of his or her competencies. Avoid labeling a child as, for example, an "aggressive child," which defines the very essence of who this child is. For example, Sal is a helper, builder, or a climber rather than a biter. He happens to be biting right now, but biting doesn't define his character. When care teachers think of the strengths of each child, they are building the identity and spirit of the child. Thinking about strengths also provides a road map for strategies that will help the child focus on what he can do rather than what he can't do.

Gonzalez-Mena (2006, 2008) emphasizes that we need to show respect for cultural differences in children's families, and that recognizing these differences will influence the strategies we use. Some children require more personal space around them whereas others require less; some children smile to be friendly whereas others smile only when they are happy. Some children may have learned that they convey respect by looking downward rather than into an adult's eyes. If we recognize these differences in ourselves and others, we can value them rather than misinterpret them.

Have you experienced an infant or toddler who doesn't respond to your attention? Vallotton (2009) observed student caregivers interacting individually with infants between 4 and 19 months who were being taught "baby signing." The caregivers interacted more with babies who responded to the caregivers' initiations and attempts at communication with gestures or signs. It is paramount that adults who interact with children are aware of how an infant's responsiveness, language, temperament, and behavior influence them. We may need to be more responsive to infants and toddlers who are not engaging others.

Respect for the Power of Development

We understand that children are developing their emotional and social skills, that it takes time to learn new skills and ways of being. During some periods of their life, for example, when they are first separating from their parents or when they are using to learn the toilet, life is even more challenging for them. Each stage of development may require different adult strategies. What do we need to understand about child development in relation to guidance strategies?

An infant cries when he sees someone new, and a mobile infant sucks her thumb when she gets tired. A young child just learning to use a spoon will get tired and start picking up food with his hands. A toddler suddenly starts saying "No" to everything and has to have his bib tied just the right way to be happy.

As discussed in previous chapters, as infants and toddlers mature in all domains of development—emotional, social, cognitive, language, and motor—they go through different stages. These stages of achievement can also be times of disquiet and disequilibrium for both infants or toddlers *and* their parents and care teachers (e.g., when an infant begins to experience stranger anxiety). If teachers don't understand the forces of development, they may have unrealistic expectations that contribute to demanding too much of children (such as expecting a toddler to eat without spilling food). When this happens, infants and toddlers become very frustrated or feel increasingly *incompetent*. Conversely, if a teacher does not notice a certain behavior, such as a 9-month-old patting his hands together, the teacher may not provide interesting, developmentally appropriate interactions such as playing pat-a-cake. Care teachers can use the Developmental Trends and Responsive Interactions charts at the end of Chapters 6 through 10 and in the appendices in this book to observe the development of the child, gain realistic expectations, and provide experiences that are responsive to child development.

If an infant or toddler has a developmental delay or disability in one area of development, a second area of development may be affected as well. You will remember from previous chapters that a *developmental delay* is a lag or difference in development that is caused by a variety of genetic or environmental factors. Several researchers have discovered that when young children, especially toddlers, are experiencing language delay, they are more likely to also be experiencing social and emotional delays (Irwin, Carter, & Briggs-Gowan, 2002). Care teachers and parents must give infants and toddlers with language delay extra support to help them learn to communicate their needs in socially appropriate ways. Watch for these types of connections between delays in other domains of development.

Respect for Self

Know yourself. What has your culture taught you about how children should behave? How does this influence the way you guide young children? Think about what makes you angry, sad, frustrated, and anxious when you are with children. The more you know yourself and why you respond as you do, the more you will use reflective practice.

Reflect

Reflection includes thinking about what an experience is like for a child, observing what children are communicating through their behavior, and deciding what you would like the child to do instead. The following reflection strategies pave the way for relating in a way that meets children's emotional needs and teaches them a new behavior.

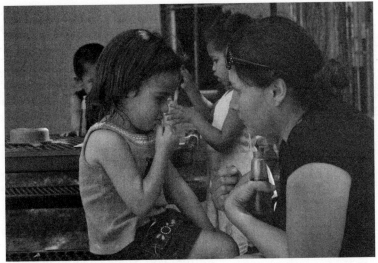

Respect for children includes taking time to figure out what emotions they are experiencing.

1. Ask: "What is the child experiencing? What is the child's perspective on the situation?"

Tasha cries every morning when her mother says good-bye and Richard has a hard time transitioning from lunch to nap time. What is each child experiencing? It may be difficult to think about what they are experiencing rather than what we, as adults, are experiencing with them. When we understand what the experience is like from the child's perspective, then we are much more likely to empathize and offer support in ways that are helpful to the child. Tasha may really miss her mother, and Richard may be afraid to be alone on his cot when he can't see his favorite care teacher.

Take the example of Serena, cited by Van De Zande and the Santa Cruz Toddler Care Center Staff (1995). Although her thought processes are not this sophisticated, she is experimenting with what happens when she spits in various places and at different times with different people:

"How interesting," Serena seems to think. "Mommy gets mad if I spit on the table! ... Was that just at breakfast or also at lunch? ... What about dinner? ... Just yesterday, or also today? ... It seems okay to spit in the bathtub.... She made me spit out a bug ... what if I spit on these papers on her desk?" (p. 15)

After thinking *with* Serena and taking her perspective, an understanding adult will give Serena more information about where and when it is okay to spit rather than punish her without explanation.

2. Ask: "What, when, where, how, and with whom does the behavior occur?"

Observe frequently to try to understand when, where, and with whom a child may be behaving in a certain way. For example, after observing that Peter, a toddler, seemed upset on Mondays, the care teacher realized that when he came into the toddler room on those days, he needed several hours to readjust to the room, his peers, and his teachers after a weekend with his mom, who was experiencing stress in her life. Tara, the teacher, tried to make him feel welcome by having him stay by her side as she checked the classroom pets. Soon, Peter was off playing and checking back with her occasionally when he needed a hug. The information that the care teacher gathered was a guide to the strategies she chose.

3. Ask: "What is the child communicating that he wants or needs? What is the purpose of the child's behavior? What is the meaning of the child's behavior?"

Young children communicate their needs in a variety of ways. Infants yawn or turn away when they need a break from an interaction. When they are extremely upset, they may arch their back or kick their feet. Mobile infants may crawl away or cling to you to tell you they are upset or afraid. They may

TABLE 14.1   **Observation of Julie**

Date	What Happens Before	The Child's Behavior	What Happens After	Possible Purposes of the Behavior
12/1	Tasha took Julie's crayon out of Julie's hand.	Julie hit Tasha with an open hand on Tasha's side.	Tasha cried and dropped the crayon. Julie picked it up and started using it.	To get her crayon back
12/5	Dale stepped on Julie's block structure.	Julie hit at Dale's leg when Dale went by her.	Dale left the area and Julie continued playing.	To get Dale to leave her alone

throw a toy down on the floor to tell you that they are frustrated. Toddlers fall into a heap crying when they are trying to tell you that they intensely want something or are trying to assert their independence and separateness from you. Some children may try to distract you with cute faces and antics to avoid having to do something they don't want to do, and some children may hit other children to either get what they want or to tell you, "I'm not feeling safe and I have to protect myself." Some children may even want you to leave them alone—they have learned that adults aren't to be trusted. Children can't usually tell us verbally, but they tell us with their behavior what it is they need or want. We can often decide what they need or the purpose of their behavior by using the observation system depicted in Table 14.1.

4. Ask: "What do I want the child to do?"

What do the family and care teachers and peers want the child to do *instead* of the behavior the child is using to communicate her needs? Will the new behavior help the child meet her needs? Once you have determined what it is that you want the child to do, then you can begin to support the child to learn new ways to meet her needs. In the example in Table 14.1, the parents and care teachers decided that they wanted Julie to learn to say "Stop" to other children when they try to take something away from her or interfere with her play.

Relate

Respecting and *reflecting* may give adults insight that needs no further response on their part to support the child. However, they will often *relate* (use strategies) to help children learn and express their individual personalities and develop positive and healthy relationships. Box 14.1 summarizes the relate strategies that are described in detail in this section.

For each of the three general ways to relate that are listed in Box 14.1, there are specific guidance strategies that can be used to meet children's emotional needs and support them as they become competent and caring individuals. These strategies create children who have internal guides to behavior and who can uniquely contribute to the well-being of themselves and others through engaging in positive relationships. Let's start with building relationships.

(1) Relate: Support Children's Healthy Relationships with All of the Important People in Their Lives

In other chapters, we have emphasized the importance of teachers supporting the family-child relationships as the key ongoing foundation in a child's life. We

BOX 14.1

A Summary of Relate Strategies

1. Support Children's Healthy *Relationships* with All of the Important People in Their Lives:
   - Support the child's relationship with his or her family.
   - Constantly communicate with families and other staff to learn about their culture, wishes, and guidance practices.
   - Use a problem-solving approach with families.
   - Build a strong, positive relationship with each child—a truly caring relationship.
   - Use primary care and continuity of care systems to promote ongoing, secure teacher-child and peer relationships.

2. Focus on Adult-Child *Responsive Interaction* Strategies That Promote Children's Capacities:
   - Empathize with the child's goals, struggles, and feelings.
   - Build emotional vocabulary—acknowledge and help children express strong feelings.
   - Patiently guide children toward controlling their own impulses and behavior.
   - Recognize behavior as communication, and teach children to communicate.
   - Explain and teach the child what to do. Make clear, positive statements to children.
   - Provide limits that keep the child safe, others safe, and materials safe.
   - Help children take the perspective of others through other-oriented guidance.
   - Help children learn how to problem solve and handle conflicts.
   - Give children choices that you can live with.
   - Create routines to provide security for mobile infants and toddlers.
   - Gradually build toddlers' ability to wait or to handle disappointment.
   - Use time-in rather than time-out.

3. Create and Change the Environment:
   - Create an environment that contributes to children's engagement and relationships—cozy corners, private spaces, spaces for two, and interesting things to do.
   - Change the environment as needed to ensure positive behavior and help children be successful.

also know that the quality of other relationships that the child might observe or experience affects the relationships that the child has, for example, with teachers or peers. In their studies of aggression in toddlers, Brook, Zheng, Whiteman, & Brook (2001) found that there were associations with parenting style and marital relations. When the relationship between the mother and father was strained, toddlers were more likely to exhibit aggressive behavior with their peers. This is a good example of how important it is to consider the ecological and relationship factors that influence a very young child's behavior. Let's think about how a care teacher might support the parent-child relationship.

- **Support the child's relationship with his or her family.**

Karin seemed happy all day at the care center, but when her father came to the door each evening, she fell apart.

In this example, how can teachers use a relationship-based approach as a framework to think about solutions to this challenge for Karin? The teacher wonders how to handle it so that her relationship with Karin *and* Karin's relationship with her father are both strengthened. It is tempting to think that Karin likes her care teacher better than her father, but this could be a mistake. Brazelton (1992) talks about how children can "hold it together" emotionally during the day, but that they can literally "fall apart" as the day ends and transitions occur. The care teacher can acknowledge how hard the end of a day is for both Dad and Karin and do what she can to support them both. She decides to ask Dad if he could call ahead when he left work and then the teacher could prepare Karin that Dad was coming and help her get ready to go. This strategy of respecting the importance of *all the relationships in Karin's life* influences how the teacher promotes and supports parent-child relationships as well as the teacher's relationship with Karin. Also, if an infant or toddler is unhappy, aggressive, or fearful, the care teacher can reflect on how to build a better relationship with the child using all of the strategies for building emotional development that we have been discussing so far. The care teacher can also partner with everyone who has a relationship with the child—including parents, siblings, grandparents, and other teachers.

- Constantly communicate with families and other staff to learn about their culture, wishes, and guidance practices.
- Use a problem-solving approach with families.

Bromwich (1997) recommends a six-step problem-solving approach that teachers, home visitors, and other infant-toddler professionals can use when talking with families about guidance issues:

1. *Listen Empathetically to the Parent* (pp. 114–115). Try to see things from her perspective, and try to understand her perceptions of her child and of herself in the context of the family. Listen carefully and convey that what she says, does, and feels is important to you. Comment on the parent's feelings—for example, to a parent who is concerned about her child screaming, say, "It must have felt pretty frustrating to have him continue screaming after you picked him up and tried to cuddle him." However, be careful about not encouraging the parent to talk about issues and feelings before she indicates that she wants to talk about them. Try not to become involved in highly personal matters for which you do not have the knowledge and skills to help the parent. Discuss with other staff when to refer the family to a therapist or human services agency.

2. *Observe* (pp. 114–115). Help the parent become a sensitive observer in order to read his infant's or toddler's cues and respond to them. Observe with the parent to call the parent's attention to the details of behavior that reveal important developmental changes in the child, no matter how small. Observing *with* the parent means that parent and staff share with each other what they have observed.

3. *Ask* (pp. 118–119). Ask the parent to share what she knows about her child that you do not know, recognizing that the parent knows the child best. Build on the parent's strengths by asking her to describe her successful handling of the child in one situation. For example, ask a mother how she calms her child so successfully when he is fussy on weekends. These ideas can be applied to other times when the parent is having difficulty with her baby when she fusses and also when you are trying to calm the baby. Ask parents specific questions as a first step in the cooperative problem-solving process, such as, "What situations seem to happen right before the child has a tantrum?" or "When did the behavior start?"

4. *Comment Positively* (pp. 116–117). Comment positively on what you see the parent is doing that seems to work with her child. Be specific—for example, "Your baby really lights up when she sees you smiling at her."

5. *Discuss* (pp. 117–118). Discussion usually includes sharing information on typical development. For example, you might say to a parent who is concerned because her child drops things off her high chair, "Many children in this age range drop things from the high chair to experiment with what happens to them and to play." Focus on the observations of the child's current behavior and relate the discussion to those observations. The developmental information may help the parent respond more effectively or anticipate the next stage in development.

6. *Experiment* (p. 122). Problem solve with the parent to determine a variety of ways to interact with the child. With the baby who was fussy, the parent may notice that the baby is calmer when wrapped snugly in a blanket. You may have noticed that the baby is calmer when the room is quieter. One solution will not work forever and some may not work at all. If you talk with the parent about experimenting, then you don't set up the parent for failure. This encourages both you and the parent to try new things and share information about how the solutions worked. If they don't work, then you can begin the six-step process over again—all in the spirit of collaboration.

   • Build a strong, positive relationship with each child—a truly caring relationship.
   • Use primary care and continuity of care systems to promote ongoing, secure teacher-child and peer relationships.

These recommendations for strengthening the relationship between the professional and child have been discussed in previous chapters, but are important reminders to professionals to recognize the power of these relationships for the child.

(2) Relate: Focus on Adult-Child Responsive Interaction Strategies That Promote Children's Capacities

All of the strategies discussed in Chapter 12 on how to support infants' and toddlers' emotional and social development—such as "noticing and encouraging strengths and positive behavior," "showing affection," and being responsive (Ekas, Braungart-Rieker, Lickenbrock, Zentall, & Maxwell, 2011)—provide the foundation upon which guidance interaction strategies are based. Now would be a good time to review those strategies, as they are critical to remember as the underpinnings to building children's capacities. Approaches that you can use to guide children are discussed here, but they are not likely to be effective if you are not using the basic strategies. Following are the 12 additional strategies that teachers and parents can use to guide adult-child interactions with mobile infants and toddlers.

• **Empathize with the child's goals, struggles, and feelings.**

Eight-month-old Marku seemed tired and crabby all day. He cried easily and wouldn't sit by himself on the floor. He wanted to be in the teacher's lap and sobbed whenever she had to put him down to help another child.

What is Marku feeling? We don't know for sure, but we can tell that he is not happy. The teacher said to Marku over and over, "I can tell you are unhappy today. What can I do to make you feel better?" Although Marku couldn't understand all of the teacher's words, he could feel that she really cared and empathized with him. She didn't think he was spoiled or "just trying to get attention." Instead, she trusted that Marku had special emotional needs today and that there was a reason, which she didn't understand yet, for why he was clingy. She knew that today was a "care for the spirit of Marku" day, that her special care would help him learn to trust her, and that their positive relationship would provide a foundation for Marku to feel safe to both express and regulate his emotions.

Always start by trying to state what you think the child may be feeling, trying to communicate to you, or trying to achieve. This will help you "tune in" to the child and take the child's perspective in the situation. Then ask, "What can I do to help?"

Honig (personal communication, January 6, 2005) recommends saying, "You wish..." to the child to help yourself tune into the child's feelings and acknowledge that you are listening to the messages that the child is communicating to you. For example, you could say, "I know you wish you could have that toy. Tina Marie has it now."

- **Build emotional vocabulary—acknowledge and help children express strong feelings.**

This strategy is similar to the first one, but focuses on helping children describe their own emotions. For infants, teachers describe the emotions that they think the child *might* be feeling. Teachers are making their best guess as they read the child's facial expressions and body movements. For mobile infants, teachers frequently use emotion words to describe the child's feelings and encourage the child to say a word—for example, "You can tell me you feel *sad*." Teachers continue describing a broader range of feelings for toddlers—for example, "You look disappointed"—and continue encouraging the child to express his feelings in a variety of situations.

▶▶▶ OBSERVATION INVITATION **14.1**

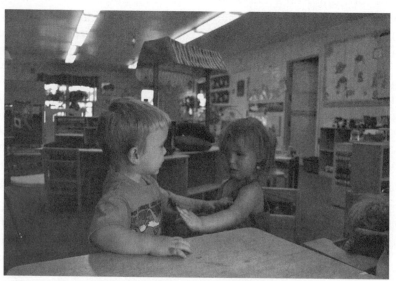

What are these children's gestures communicating?
What could you say that would help these children express their feelings with words?

- **Patiently guide children toward controlling their own impulses and behavior.**

Nate stood at the sand table, gleefully throwing sand on the floor and then listening to the sounds he could make. Cara, the teacher, got down on his level and said, "Sand stays in the sand table. Let's see if we can make noises with the shovel in the table," recognizing his interest in cause and effect and making different sounds.

Because of the care teacher's patience, Nate is learning that he can control his own behavior as he starts making noises with his shovel in the table.

- **Recognize behavior as communication, and teach children to communicate.**

The toddler who runs over and kicks another toddler's blocks is possibly communicating that he wants to play but doesn't know how to do so. He needs help learning new strategies of communication for entering play with another child, because his present strategy certainly isn't working very well!

In Chapter 9, sign language was discussed as a useful means of communicating with infants and toddlers. Parents and teachers are reporting that when they use a few signs, such as those for *milk* or *more,* then infants and toddlers learn these signs from the modeling of the adult, begin to use them around 9 months of age, and are less frustrated because they can communicate their needs. Michigan State University (n.d.) provides a demonstration of many signs an older infant or toddler might learn.

"Use your words" is a phrase that is often repeated by teachers of toddlers as they try to teach children to use words rather than aggression to obtain a prized toy from another child or protect themselves or a toy that another toddler covets (de Hann & Singer, 2003). Saying "use your words" is helpful only if the mobile infant or toddler knows the words to use. It is more helpful in the beginning to tell the mobile infants or toddlers the *specific* words that can be used, such as "please" (often said as "peas") when they want a toy, or "no" or "later" when they don't want someone to take a toy from them. When words are modeled by adults, then mobile infants and toddlers soon begin to use them—a step toward becoming a communicator in social situations.

Building children's emotion vocabulary and vocabulary in general is important for the development of their ability to control and express emotions. Vallotton and Ayoub (2011) collected data on toddlers who were 13, 24, and 36 months and found that children's language skills, particularly their vocabulary, influenced girls' self-regulation and the rate of change in boys' self-regulation.

- **Explain and teach the child what to do. Make clear, positive statements to children.**

Give short reasons and explanations to help young children begin to internalize the rules and their reasons. To help infants and toddlers begin to understand why they should touch a breakable item very gently, give simple explanations such as "Touch gently, it is fragile."

To Verina who just bit Sarah, say, "No biting; that hurt Sarah. Look, she's crying. You can say 'No' to Sarah instead."

Make positive statements about what to do—for example, instead of saying "Don't run," say "Please walk." When a care teacher says "Don't run," a young child may just hear the word "run."

> When Mario, 28 months old, picked up an interesting piece of dirt and started putting it in his mouth for a taste, he said aloud to himself, "I put it in my mouth. I shouldn't do it. It dirty."

The words that he heard from his care teachers and parents now became an internal guide to behavior. At the moment and more likely in the future, he will not need someone telling him not to put strange things in his mouth. When infants and toddlers hear the reason for doing or not doing a certain behavior, then that reason becomes a part of them. They will then have self-control rather than always needing external control from adults.

- **Provide limits that keep the child safe, others safe, and materials safe.**

> Dina climbed up on the chair and looked at the teacher to see what she would do. The teacher helped Dina down, held her in her arms, and said, "I will keep you safe. I don't want you to climb on the chair because you could get hurt." After several days of this, Dina seemed more relaxed and could concentrate on playing in a more focused way.

Follow through when a child hurts himself, another child, or materials.

> Andrew, 18 months old, pushed Julie hard on his way to get the box of blocks. The teacher took him gently in her arms and said firmly, "You pushed Julie. That hurt Julie. I want to keep everyone in the room safe. You can go around her like this ... ," taking his hand and showing him the way.

- **Help children take the perspective of others through other-oriented guidance.**

> Joshua stepped over Jerry as he toddled fast to the new blocks. The teacher walked over to Joshua, bent down to Joshua's level, and helped him look back at Jerry, who was crying. "Look, he's crying. You stepped on him. That hurt his hand. Let's go help Jerry," as the teacher gently took Joshua's hand and led him over to Jerry.

other-oriented guidance

Guidance that helps children take the perspective of others.

justification

Use of reason.

resolution

Trying to bring the conflict to a solution agreeable to all.

mitigation

Trying to lessen the conflict.

When care teachers use **other-oriented guidance**, they steer children to begin to think about how others feel. Guiding mobile infants and toddlers to look at the face of another child, interpreting the feeling of the other child, and then thinking aloud about how to help a child who is hurt, for example, starts a child on the challenging and often bumpy road of taking other people's perspective.

- **Help children learn how to problem solve and handle conflicts.**

Thirty-month-old children of mothers who used **justification** (use of reason), **resolution** (trying to bring the conflict to a solution agreeable to all), and **mitigation** (trying to lessen the conflict) during conflict with their children had higher levels of social and emotional development at 36 months of age (Laible & Thompson, 2002). Conflict is inevitable; for example, a toddler might decide that he doesn't want to get dressed or put on a coat. When care teachers and parents talk with toddlers and negotiate solutions, toddlers learn important lessons about the give and take of making decisions (Laible & Thompson, 2002).

Infants and toddlers benefit from participating in conflicts with peers (Batya, Simoni, & Perrig-Chiello, 2008; Gloeckler & Cassell, 2012; Singer & Hannikainen, 2002) if care teachers and other adults help them learn how to negotiate, develop emotion regulation and self-regulation, learn problem-solving skills, and most importantly learn that others have perspectives that are different than their view of the world (theory of mind). Instead of using directions, distractions, warnings, and threats, care teachers can ask open-ended questions, invite children to participate in dialogue, offer choices, and help them make decisions. Toddlers and twos can learn to problem solve (Gloeckler & Cassell, 2012). When a teacher asks, "What could we do to help Amy?" or "What could you do if you want the toy?" then toddlers *begin* to understand the nature of problem solving. They will need continuous help to think of possible answers, but if teachers keep asking and modeling answers, then toddlers become great problem solvers as they grow.

- **Give children choices that you can live with.**

    Give more choices to mobile infants and toddlers with each passing month. Carmen, the toddler care teacher knows that Lulu's diaper needs to be changed, but Lulu is very busy putting blocks in and out of a can. The teacher approaches Lulu, bends down to her level, and asks, "I see you need to have your diaper changed." Lulu loudly says, "No!" "I can see that you are enjoying your blocks," replies Carmen, "I'll be back in a few minutes to change your diaper." After a few minutes, Carmen approaches Lulu again. "It is time to have your diaper changed; would you like to walk or would you like me to carry you?" Lulu holds her hands up to be carried.

- **Create routines to provide security for mobile infants and toddlers.**

    A routine becomes a habit and provides emotional security to the child. Children can predict what will happen when routines are consistent. Details of how to proceed do not have to be explained each day. Use a cleanup song when it is time to put away toys: "It's cleanup time. It's cleanup time. It's time to put our toys away." Use routines for saying good-bye and a routine for going outside. Sing songs if you have to wait for lunch to arrive. Use a routine for moving from lunch to nap time, so toddlers know that when they are done eating, they can get their "blankie" or "lovie" and a care teacher will read to them on their cots.

- **Gradually build toddlers' ability to wait or to handle disappointment.**

    > Toddlers who don't learn gradually about disappointment lose their resilience through lack of practice in give-and-take with other people's needs. They can become self-centered, demanding, and difficult to like or to be with (Lieberman, 1993, p. 52).

    As infants become toddlers, they can *gradually* learn about waiting for the food to be warm enough to eat or to go outside, for example. Children are more likely to learn patience and to take the perspective of others if adults talk in a soothing voice to children while they are waiting. Disappointment may occur when children can't go outside because of the weather or because a favorite care teacher is absent for a day. Thinking about how you feel when you are disappointed will remind you of how important it is for adults to explain what is happening, acknowledge toddlers' disappointed feelings, and demonstrate coping strategies for how to handle frustration and sadness.

- **Use time-in rather than time-out.**

    Time-out is a strategy that has often been used by parents and teachers to punish children by placing them in a time-out chair, a cubby, or a place alone away from

time-out
A brief period during which a child is removed from the action or situation when the adult thinks that there is a "discipline" problem.

everyone else after the child has "misbehaved." Schreiber (1999) discusses the issue of time-outs for toddlers and asks, "Is our goal punishment or education?" When care teachers use time-out, it is often in a punitive way; the teacher angrily places the child in a separate place and tells the child to stay there until he can "learn not to bite." The child usually focuses on protecting himself in a time-out situation rather than focusing on what happened, why it happened, how he and the other child feel, and what else he could have done instead. **Time-in** is a strategy that involves a parent or care teacher spending time with a child who, for example, bit another child—calming the child and teaching the child what to do instead of biting. If a cozy area of the room with soft toys and pillows is always available as a "cozy corner," toddlers, when upset, may go there by themselves to calm themselves or they may ask or pull a care teacher to come with them to the cozy corner.

> **time-in**
>
> Time that children spend with an adult care teacher after the child feels challenged emotionally and socially.

(3) Relate: Create and Change the Environment

The mobile infants in the child care home began to crawl up the stairs, so Melissa put a baby gate across the bottom of the stairs. The toddlers were continually running at full speed through the room until the teachers placed a small climber in the center. Instead of blaming the children for the challenges, the teacher examined what she could do to change the environment to be more developmentally appropriate.

Create an environment that contributes to children's engagement, self-regulation, and relationships—cozy corners, spaces for two, and interesting things to do. If the environment includes caring people and interesting equipment, toys, and

OBSERVATION INVITATION **14.2**

What about this environment helps this child self-regulate, engage with the materials, and practice nurturing another?

materials with which the child can be successful, then children are more likely to be engaged. If an environment is attractive and calm, then children are more likely to be able to self-regulate.

Change the environment as needed to ensure positive behavior and help children be successful. Always ask, "How can I change the environment to help this child be successful?" For example, if an infant seems to have difficulty falling asleep, try creating a more private space in the room so that you can rock the infant to sleep without distractions. A small change in the environment can make a big difference for a child.

Relationship Realignments

Separation Anxiety

> For months, Karin's dad had been dropping off his 10-month-old daughter at the same family child care home without seeing so much as a tear from her. But lately, after the usual good-bye hugs and kisses, Karin has started wailing, clinging fast to Dad's leg. Martha, Karin's special teacher, was surprised by this sudden change in behavior and tried to distract the baby with a favorite toy. As the crying continued, however, she and Karin's dad wondered, "What are we doing wrong?" With new knowledge comes the fear of being abandoned, unloved, or physically damaged. (Lieberman)

A young baby may cry when a parent leaves, but at about 7 months of age infants may actively show **separation anxiety,** searching for their loved one, scowling, crying, pushing away others who offer comfort, and having difficulty saying good-bye. Knowing that a person exists when out of sight (person permanence) contributes a cognitive understanding to the infant's growing awareness of "out of sight, but not out of mind." Often infants don't want their favorite care teacher to disappear, even behind the bathroom door. Separation anxiety can occur for several months, but the length of this stage varies in children. There are children who by 18 months feel very comfortable saying good-bye to parents, but there are also children who have difficulty with separation all of their life. Care teachers can hold an infant, allow her to stay as close as she wants, talk to her in nurturing tones, and appreciate the emotional struggle that the infant is experiencing.

When children enter an early care and education program between 1 and 2 years of age, they may take several weeks to several months to adjust to the new situation. The first several days may go smoothly, but as the toddler begins to realize that the new setting is where he is going to be each day, he may begin to protest more. Other children are frightened from the beginning of this new separation from parents and they protest vehemently, yet they don't have the language skills to express themselves clearly. Children of this age have a difficult time cognitively understanding where the parent is going and when he or she will return. Many children this age seem very sad after their parents leave and in the midst of their play, they may turn to the door with a hopeful "Mommy?" when they hear someone enter, only to get sad all over again when it isn't their loved one returning. When adults understand that cognitive development affects social and emotional development, and vice versa, they can

separation anxiety

A child's fear and worry about being separated from favorite adults.

help young children during this scary time by being emotionally and physically available and commenting on the child's (even a young baby's) feelings—for example, by saying, "I know you thought that was Mommy. Mommy will be here after your nap."

A child can also experience separation anxiety as she leaves the program at the end of the day—crying and fussing at having to make another transition. Care teachers can support children and parents in as many ways as possible to ease the transition from program to home with the parent. Teachers can make sure the child is ready to transition with a clean diaper and a full tummy, or if the parent wants to feed the child, the teacher supports the parent-child relationship by timing the feedings (while still being responsive to the child) so that the parent can experience bonding time with the child. If a child fusses at leaving his favorite care teacher it is important that teachers help build the parent-child relationship through interpreting the feelings of the child. Care teachers can say to the parent, "She is happy to see you; she just wasn't ready to have her coat put on" or "She just seems tired today— I think she needs some cuddle time with her dad."

Toddler Resistance

Care teachers and parents of toddlers often feel as if they are on an emotional roller coaster with their children, who are sometimes pushing for independence and at other times want to be taken care of as if they were still infants. Toddlers are learning how to be autonomous, or self-directing. They often attempt to gain control but become frustrated at their lack of control. A toddler can feel mixed up, sometimes wanting to be a grownup and the next minute feeling scared, lonely, or just out of energy and wanting to sit in your lap. Toddler care teachers often experience the full range of emotions that toddlers feel in the course of a day—from pure delight and contagious giggles to overwhelming frustration.

Toddlers can get frightened when a parent or care teacher doesn't stop them from doing something dangerous; they can feel that there is no one there to hold, help, restrain, or contain them (Lieberman, 1993). They say "No" to tell you that they are a person who can express feelings and to test the safe limits and boundaries of the world. It helps care teachers and parents if they appreciate that developmental changes can occur rapidly between 18 months and 3 years of age. It is the care teacher of this age group who masterfully gives toddlers opportunities to be self-directing while providing the boundaries for behavior that keep children feeling safe and emotionally secure.

Tantrums

tantrums

Times of distress when children literally seem to fall apart emotionally.

Mobile infants and toddlers may have what adults call **tantrums**—times of distress when they literally seem to fall apart. Some children cry loudly, scream, whine, flail, fall to the floor, stomp their feet, or become stiff or floppy. A care teacher may not have put a bib on a child in quite the right way or the teacher may have denied a child a second banana. It is difficult to predict when a young child might have a tantrum. They are very taxing and challenging to both the child and the care teachers. Let's now take a look at Keri, who has started having tantrums, to see how many of the guidance strategies discussed in this chapter can be applied to a real-life situation, one that care teachers often face in their work with children ages 15 months to 3 years:

Keri, 2 years old, is in a family child care home for 3 days a week. She eats her banana with great delight. After swallowing the last [delicious crumb, and with banana still dribbling out of her mouth], she gestures to her care provider that she would like another one, only to hear, "I'm sorry, Keri, just one banana today. It sometimes gives you a tummy-ache if you eat two bananas." Keri scowls, jumps up from her chair, stomps her feet, and puts her hands on her hips. As her teacher approaches, Keri suddenly falls to the floor in a heap, crying as loudly as she can.

As toddlers begin to assert themselves, strong emotions and resistance—**negativism**—can occur out of the blue. As Lieberman (1993) explains,

> When toddlers are unable to speak about urgent matters, they must resort to crying or screaming. This happens even with adults. The voice is the carrier of emotion, and when speech fails us, we need to cry out in whatever form we can to convey our meaning. Often, what passes for negativism is really the toddler's desperate effort to make herself understood. (p. 38)

What is Keri feeling, and what is she trying to say? Is she more likely to have a tantrum on certain days or times of the day? What are Keri's language skills? Very young children are starting to use words and voice intonation to express strong feelings—but their language skills are still developing, so they often fall back on using tears and tantrums. Recording the observations of Keri can result in strategies that meet her needs. The strategies that adults use in these situations can either set up negative communication patterns between adults and children or support children emotionally as they learn new ways of expressing strong feelings.

Accentuate the Child's Strengths

Instead of thinking of Keri as the little girl who has tantrums, think of Keri's strengths and what she loves to do. She is enthusiastic about everything that she does and she loves it when she can make a choice. Keri's teachers decided to build on this enthusiasm and Keri's desire to make choices by offering her more choices throughout the day—for example, asking her if she would like a blue bib or a white bib as they move toward the table, or if she wants to have her diaper changed before or after a favorite puzzle.

Use Responsive Interactions: In the Moment

Will responding to children's tantrums encourage their negative behavior and spoil them—or can we, as adults, respond to tantrums in a way that helps children learn to use words to communicate their feelings? When deciding how to react, think of outbursts as part of a developmental stage most toddlers go through. Your job is to teach children new ways to express strong emotions, not to discourage these feelings by ignoring them. Your support through this difficult stage will help children learn to communicate more maturely. Following are some ways in which you can encourage this process:

1. Validate children's feelings. Even though you won't give Keri another banana, you can let her know you understand why she's upset. By saying in a soothing voice, "Keri, you seem very frustrated. I realize you want another banana," you're sending the message that she's been heard and that it's okay to have strong feelings.
2. Build children's emotional vocabulary. Children can learn, from you, the words to express how they feel. So, when you comment on a child's emotions,

negativism
Attitude of refusing, or resisting.

model words she can use. You might say, with feeling, "Keri, you seem sad. You're crying. You can tell me, 'I'm sad.' "

3. Share children's books about emotions. As you read together, discuss what the characters are feeling, and make connections to events in the child's life. You might read *Miss Spider's Tea Party* by David Kirk and then say, "Keri, Miss Spider was sad because she thought nobody would come to her party. You were sad the other day because you wanted two bananas. Let's see what she did when she was sad." Use books as springboards to discussions about emotions and different ways people handle them.

4. Observe facial expressions, gestures, and body movements to learn when a toddler might be getting ready to tantrum. Catching the toddler *before* she tantrums is one of the keys to preventing tantrums and helping her learn new ways to express disappointment, frustration, and anger.

5. Encourage problem solving by offering choices. Providing options helps toddlers discover new solutions to old problems. For example, giving Keri a choice of more juice or more milk (instead of another banana) will help her feel as if she has some power in the situation. It will give her a sense of control over herself and her environment, while letting her know that a loving adult is watching out for her well-being.

6. Model ways to express strong feelings. To let Keri know she isn't the only person who has feelings, share how you feel with her. You might say, with the appropriate expression, "Keri, it makes me worried to see you upset. I feel upset, too, when you scream at me."

Discussing feelings is neither *giving in to children* nor *giving them everything they want* (common adult fears). Rather, when you show children how to communicate through words and gestures, you're helping them take the next developmental step toward becoming good communicators and problem solvers while providing them safe and healthy boundaries in which to build relationships and learn.

Build Relationships: Beyond the Moment

Whereas many toddlers tantrum because they are overwhelmed in the moment, events that happened at home or in the child care and education program may have affected Keri. Care teachers and parents should aim to have a strong, positive relationship so that there can be an open discussion about whether there has been any change in Keri's life that may be affecting her emotionally, such as sudden changes in who is taking care of her at home.

Create and Change the Environment in Responsive Ways

If adults find themselves saying "No," "Stop that," "You can't do that," or constantly removing children from dangerous situations, then the environment *definitely* needs to be improved so that children, peers, and adults are safe and engaged in many fulfilling and interesting activities together. When there is a "No" environment, toddlers will feel quite frustrated and confused concerning what they can and cannot do. The environment can be changed to be more interesting, less stimulating, or more supportive of the child's emotional and social development.

Children Who Bite

One of the biggest challenges in group programs is children biting each other and the teacher. So let's explore the topic of why children bite and the strategies that adults can use to deal with the problem.

Jaheed's mother is coming to the door of the child care center to pick up Jaheed and take him home. About an hour ago, Jaheed bit Aaron. Jaheed didn't break the skin, but Aaron cried for a long time after Jaheed bit him. What are you going to say to Jaheed's mother? What are you going to say to Aaron's mother?

Before babies have teeth, they gum, mouth, and suck on any object they can get into their mouths. Babies are encouraged to "bite" their food and try new oral delights. It is no wonder that as they become more physically active and enter the stage of "true experimentations" between 12 and 18 months, people become one of the new objects that must be tested and tried to see how they taste.

Biting, then, provides babies with comfort (as they suck their fists, fingers, and food) and opportunities to learn (as they discover what is soft, hard, chewy, tasty, or yucky). Yet, biting, which is so enjoyable and so necessary, can get the toddler into trouble when it extends into the world of adults, children, and animals.

Children may bite other people for various reasons. It will help you handle a biting child if you think about the many possible reasons toddlers bite others. You can then try the solutions based on the particular reason a particular child is biting people. Table 14.2 presents the reasons children bite, as well as possible solutions.

TABLE 14.2   Why Children Bite: Relationship-Based Solutions

Why Children Bite Others (Reflect)	Program Solutions (Respond)
A. "Holding On and Letting Go"	
As children's muscles mature, toddlers experiment with two simultaneous ways of handing experiences: *holding on* and *letting go*. Toddlers are learning to both hold on and let go of (1) parents and other adults, (2) toys, (3) bowel movements, etc. Thus, they are also learning to hang on/let go with their mouths. Often young children are not fully in *control* of their walking, running, handling small objects, bowel movements, urine, or speech. Sometimes the skin of the other child can "just happen" to get between the child's teeth.	Help ease infant or toddler separations (letting go) from their parents. If the baby cries when the parent leaves, then say to the baby, "You're feeling very sad that Mommy/Daddy has to leave. It's hard to say good-bye. Mommy/Daddy will come back after lunch/nap" (some concrete event). Give toys to baby for hanging on/letting go, such as blocks to put into containers. Don't pressure toilet training. Wait until the child shows that he or she can "let go" in other areas of life. Study your environment carefully to ensure opportunities for infants and toddlers to practice blossoming motor skills.
B. Autonomy	
Toddlers are developing autonomy: doing things for themselves, making *choices*, needing to *control*, making demands of adults and the environment, wanting power, moving out and away from adults. Biting can be an expression of a toddler's separation from the adult; infants and toddlers are no longer one with adults if they can bite the adult. Infants and toddlers are showing control of the other person and the situation when they bite. Biting gives children power over others. Toddlers may be allowed to get "out of control" by loving adults who are hesitant to set limits for them.	Toddlers must be helped to achieve a balance between their need for control and their need for loving, firm limits to be placed on their often uncontrollable urges. Because there are so many situations in which adults must control toddlers, allow and provide as many situations as possible when they can *choose* and have *power:* "the red marker or the blue marker," "the Cheerios or the Rice Krispies," whether to have "milk or no milk" on their cereal. Set up the environment so that infants and toddlers can have long stretches of time to explore and learn in a relaxed manner.

(Continued)

TABLE 14.2 **Continued**

Why Children Bite Others (Reflect)	Program Solutions (Respond)
C. Exploration	
Biting is a part of sensorimotor exploration. Toys, food, and people must be touched, smelled, and, of course, tasted if the toddler is to learn. Babies are sensuous creatures who learn through their senses and their motor actions on things and around things.	Provide a variety of sensorimotor experiences. Infants and toddlers should experience closely supervised play with water, paints, play dough, and sand. Infants and toddlers can crawl and tumble over a variety of hard, soft, rough, and smooth surfaces. A colorful array of toys that can be mouthed and easily washed should be available.
D. Teething	
Teething can cause an infant's or toddler's mouth to hurt. Babies often need something or someone to gnaw on to comfort them.	Provide infants and toddlers with teething toys, frozen bagels, and chewy foods that disintegrate in the mouth and will not cause choking. Older toddlers can be *encouraged* to bite on apples and firm teething toys. Clean frozen cloths provide cooling relief for teething toddlers (and for the child who has been bitten).
E. Peer Interaction	
Infants and toddlers are just beginning to learn how to engage peers in positive ways. Infants usually do not understand they are hurting others when they bite them (older toddlers may). Infants and toddlers do not know how to approach their peers in acceptable ways. They often express their interest by biting, pulling hair, pushing, etc.	Children need lots of social experiences in order to learn how to interact with others. Take their hand as they reach out to others roughly and say, "Touch gently—that makes her feel happy." Acknowledge their interest in other children by saying, "I know you like Darin—you can give him a toy." Provide enough age-appropriate materials and equipment so children can play beside each other (parallel play). Notice positive peer interaction such as one child hugging another, giving a toy to another, and smiling to another.
F. Cause and Effect	
Infants and toddlers truly investigate cause-and-effect relationships beginning at approximately 12 months. It is as if they are saying, "What will happen if I bite Susie? What reaction will I get?" Biting gets a reaction—usually a very strong one! The baby often receives a loud scream from the other baby, and a yell of protest from an adult.	Provide extensive time for play. Provide toys that "do something" when the child acts on the toy. For example, when a button is pushed, a figure pops up, or when a knob is turned, music plays. Sand, dirt, water, paints, blocks, and crayons allow for creative, open-ended experiences that offer many opportunities for the child to make something happen. Help them notice the positive reaction they get when they pat, hug, or give a toy to another child.
G. Imitation	
Babies learn by imitating others, and biting is one behavior that is often learned from other young persons. After 15 months, babies can observe a behavior (such as biting), store it in their memory, and perform the act	Model loving, nurturing, sharing, polite, positive behavior for young children to imitate. Develop a repertoire of responses for handling children's negative behavior: redirecting to a positive activity,

TABLE 14.2   Continued

Why Children Bite Others (Reflect)	Program Solutions (Respond)
later when conditions are right (this is called *deferred imitation*). Research has shown that children who are physically punished are much more likely than their peers to be aggressive with both adults and peers—especially younger, smaller peers. They learn that hitting and biting others is an acceptable way of handling their anger if they see adults responding in that way.	acknowledging their feelings (e.g., "You are feeling angry at Sarah—she took your toy and that made you feel angry"). Teach the child alternative positive behavior. Positive techniques do work! Children comply more readily and they learn positive ways of interacting with others.

H. Attention

The young child may bite to get attention from others; it is true that negative attention seems to be better to many toddlers than no attention at all. Everyone hates to be ignored, and children younger than age 3 are no exception. Some children may actually be receiving more negative attention from teachers and peers than positive attention, thus continuing the cycle of negative behavior.	Saturate the biter with positive, warm, nurturing attention. This can be difficult for infant-toddler professionals, especially when they are feeling exceedingly frustrated with the little biter. Remember, however, that when children's positive, busy, curious, helpful, productive behaviors are noticed and rewarded, the children are much more likely to continue those behaviors and behave that way more often. Break into that negative cycle of child behavior with adult positive comments and hugs for desirable infant-toddler behavior.

I. Frustration

Young children may bite others due to feelings of anger and frustration because of unmet needs or because of harsh discipline techniques. A child who cries or whose more positive bids for attention go unheard, or a child who is hit, slapped, yelled at, or bitten by adults may become an angry, biting child. Too many children, too high adult-to-child ratios, or not enough space can lead to frustrated, biting children.	Help young children develop their own repertoire of behaviors for handling frustrations and angry feelings. Help children learn to say "Not now!" to another child who grabs a toy. Teach children to say "I feel angry (sad, happy, etc.)" to adults and peers. This is not "smarting-off" to adults—it is a healthy sharing of feelings. If infant-toddler professionals or parents are using punitive techniques, they need opportunities to *learn* about the effects of positive versus hostile discipline techniques. Children who have been severely punished will need time to develop trust in adults who use positive strategies. The environment for the young children may need to be changed before biting will be decreased. Smaller numbers of children can make a big difference in a classroom.

J. Anxiety

Young children may be experiencing generalized anxiety about events happening to them or around them (such as parents' divorcing or fighting, the loss of or separation from loved ones, etc.). Anxiety may lead to biting others to relieve tension (just as adults smoke cigarettes, chew gum, or bat a ball around).	Work with parents to determine the source of anxiety. Provide calming activities such as water or sand play. Allow children to suck a thumb and/or hold transitional objects (such as blankets or stuffed animals). Provide time for one-on-one with a special adult. Pat backs and sing songs at nap time to quiet toddlers into sleep. Use infant massage strategies to calm a child. Play soothing lullabies. Stay close to nurture children and explain and help them through transition times.

When an infant or toddler bites another person, show the biter with your voice and facial expression that you are very concerned. Speak in a serious voice with the child. Look directly into the child's eyes. Hold the child gently by the shoulders if necessary. For example, you might say, "You bit Candace" (state the behavior). "She doesn't like it. She's crying" (pointing out how the bite's behavior affected the other child). "You can bite this cloth" (food, biting toy, etc.), or "You can tell Candace how you feel" (what the child can do instead). Use words appropriate to the child's developmental level and try to restore the relationship between the two children. With toddlers and twos, an adult can ask the victim to tell the biter what would make him feel better.

Help the victim of the biter. Keep ice packs on hand to place on the bite. If the skin is broken, wash it well with soap and water. If possible, bring the biter along to assist the victim (however, the victim may appropriately want the biter to stay far away). Call the parent of the child who received the bite. If the skin is broken, then the parent must take the child to a doctor.

Often the biter is as frightened about what happened as the victim. If punishment for the biter is too harsh, the young biter nurses her own hurt rather than concentrating on and helping the victim of the bite. If you punish or yell at the child or put her in time-out, she will try to protect herself, think only of herself, and will not be open to learning about alternatives to biting others.

If one child's biting continues after several days of repeating these techniques, meet with the family and other care teachers to determine what might be causing the child to bite and plan together to provide consistency across home and the child education program. The infant or toddler deserves our best planning, caring, and teaching. Implement a more intense program of time-in and emotional connection with an adult. An adult stays near the child, meets the child's emotional needs, shows the child affection and encouragement, catches her *before* she bites, teaches her alternative behaviors, and teaches her how to be gentle or use sign language or words to express her needs.

Keep in mind the following points:

- When adults hit or bite children for biting others, the child learns that biting is OK if you are bigger and stronger than the other person. The child will be *more* likely to bite peers (especially smaller ones).
- Observe when the biting and attempts to bite occur. Keep records. The biting may occur before lunch or when the child is crowded by others.
- Explore with the parents what the reasons for biting may be. Try a solution based on the possible reasons. Work with the parents of the biter so that the guidance techniques used at home and at the center are consistent.
- Have a staff meeting. Review all the reasons that toddlers bite and all the techniques that can be used. Individualize strategies for each child and then work together to provide *consistency* for that child. Staff can help one another be consistent in the use of the techniques.
- *Before parents and family members become upset* about a biting problem, hold a parent meeting or send a newsletter home to let parents know what techniques they and the staff can use. Parents need to know *why* toddlers bite, that it is a *common* problem whenever toddlers are brought together in a group, and that the name of the biter will not be revealed. Tell parents that the staff will do *everything* possible to ensure the safety of the children.

If a solution works, give yourself a big pat on the back. If a solution does not work, provide the time-in approach. If the child continues biting, bites viciously, or bites and then smiles, seek professional help. Too many parents are asked to take their child out of a center for biting. This solves the problem for the program but not for the child or the family. In collaboration with the parent, you can seek support for the child from professionals in the local early intervention team in your school district (see Chapter 15). These professionals will provide an assessment and ongoing support if needed to parents and care teachers. Children can learn that infant-toddler teachers are there to help them learn new positive ways of interacting with peers and adults.

Toilet Learning

Here's what children do in order to use a toilet. Children must (1) feel the urge to eliminate; (2) understand the urge is a signal to eliminate—"Hey, I gotta go, NOW!"; (3) suppress the immediate urge; (4) get to the toilet (quickly!); (5) pull clothing out of the way; (6) situate and balance on the potty; and (7) relax urinary or sphincter muscles to eliminate. (Stephens, 1999, p. 78)

And, those are just the *physical* skills necessary for toddlers to be successful using a toilet. There are also emotional issues. As mentioned in our discussion of toddler resistance, toddlers do want to be grown up—but they often want to grow up on their own timetable.

Most child development specialists who have written about toilet learning recommend waiting until the child shows signs of readiness (see Box 14.2). They use the term *toilet learning* rather than *toilet training* to indicate that children are learning on their own terms, rather than adults training them on the adult's timetable. Learning to use the toilet is a "step up to independence" (Stephens, 1999). It is an opportunity for the toddler to express his autonomy. If forced, he will express his autonomy by resisting the adult. We want the child to feel as if it is his idea, not ours, for him to use the toilet and it is his accomplishment, not ours, when he does.

Brazelton and Sparrow (2004) have written a book outlining Brazelton's method for helping toddlers learn to use the toilet. They recommend a relaxed method of taking the child to the toilet and letting him sit on it with his clothes on. If there is no resistance, then take the child to the toilet without a diaper on. Always let the child get up and leave if he wants to. At some point you

BOX 14.2

Readiness for Toilet Learning

Parents

- are willing to collaborate with teachers to provide consistency for the child.
- are willing to be encouraging and not punitive with the child.
- respect the child's timetable (e.g., a child may start the process and then stop for a period of time).
- agree that the child is ready to learn.

Teachers

- have an adult-to-child ratio that is conducive to a teacher being available to the child learning to use the toilet.
- have a trusting relationship with the child.

The child

- has an interest in imitating adults when they use the toilet.
- can communicate his or her needs with sign language, gestures, or words to adults.
- is not in a resistant stage of development.
- is willing to sit on the toilet with and without diapers.
- can pull pants off and on fairly easily.
- has sphincter (anal) muscles that are sufficiently developed to hold on and let go of a bowel movement.
- has a dry diaper for longer periods of time indicating that the child's bladder is maturing.

CULTURE CLOSE UP

Toilet learning can be a frustrating time for parents if they would like to complete the process quickly to eliminate the costly expense of diapers and not have to clean up the sometimes "big messes" that toddlers can make in their diaper. In some cultures, parents may "train" children early (in the first 2 years of life) by learning to read the signs that a child gives when he is going to urinate or defecate and then placing the child on the toilet or a potty chair. The parent may ask you to do the same in the program. This can be challenging in a program where a teacher often has at least three infants to take care of, and even more if the teacher works with toddlers. How would you use the dialog methods recommended in Chapter 12 for listening to parents and negotiating strategies with them?

will "catch" the child's urine or stool, and the child will begin to get the idea of how to use the toilet. If the child resists or the process does not seem to be working, wait at least a month before trying again. Be encouraging but be careful not to praise too loudly or too much. The child is doing this for himself, not just for you. To provide consistency for the child at home and in a program, it is best if the parents and teachers meet to discuss the toilet learning process.

Toddlers may touch their own genitals while they are learning to use the toilet, and infants may during diapering. This is typical behavior and should not be punished. If you ignore this normal behavior, their curiosity will be satisfied.

When they share their observations of the child, parents and care teachers can usually agree on methods and a cooperative plan of action—especially if a relationship of mutual trust has been established.

The goal is that toddlers end up with a sense of pride in using the toilet—a very grown-up thing to do—rather than a sense of shame due to failure or anger because he is being forced against his will. And finally, as Stephens (1999) cautions: "Anticipate accidents by asking parents to provide at least three pairs of extra LABELED underwear, pant/shorts, and an extra pair of shoes. When accidents occur, don't spank, threaten, ridicule, tease, or otherwise punish a child. Reassure them that every boy and girl has accidents when learning to use the toilet" (p. 80).

Challenging Behavior and Mental Health Issues

Managing challenging behaviors in infants and toddlers are just that—a challenge! Infant and toddler teachers and parents have listed children's behaviors that are challenging to them: sadness; flat affect; distress or crying frequently; continuously hurting others (biting, pushing, grabbing, hitting); hurting self; *frequently having tantrums and falling apart*; not sleeping; excess clinginess; noncompliant, defensive, angry, anxious, or fearful behavior; and a general lack of response to guidance strategies. Note that these behaviors *more seriously affect and disrupt infants' and toddlers' sense of well-being, long-term behavior, and sense of self-worth.* They represent a more serious challenge for the child, family members, teachers, and peers and are beyond typical development issues that respond to socialization and guidance strategies. These expressions of a child's need engender intense feelings on the part of everyone involved and are often difficult to understand. Challenging behaviors can leave adults feeling powerless as they try to problem solve to help the child toward well-being and away from distress.

In this section, we again emphasize that behavior is a way for young children to communicate their joys, needs, and frustrations. If we can "read" the behavior, then we have a key for unlocking the meaning of the behavior for the child. The child is clearly telling us that he or she needs help.

When adults talk about challenging behavior, they usually mean that the child is challenging them—typical guidance strategies just aren't working. However, the *child* is feeling challenged, too. Infant mental health specialists have helped care teachers and parents understand that infants and toddlers can and do have strong feelings in response to their experiences in life and that it is important to intervene early.

What do children with behavioral challenges have in common? Often they are communicating their distress through their behavior rather than using language. They may be ill, tired, or overwhelmed by stimulation. A child who "doesn't listen" may not be hearing well. A child who falls apart frequently and with intensity when there is too much stimulation may be sensitive to noise. A child may be delayed in language development, which then affects how well she can communicate her needs. Children may not be able to tell you with their words, but they are telling you with their behavior that something doesn't feel right.

A child who is feeling challenged may feel overprotected or underprotected. If adults are watching every move and constantly warning the child of dangers, then the child may feel as if the world is a scary place. The child then feels afraid to venture out and explore the environment. This child may feel *overprotected*. Alternatively, if an adult is not setting limits for the toddler—such as "hitting hurts" or "jumping off high furniture is not safe"—a toddler may feel as if he has too much power and thus will not feel safe. This toddler may do "daring" things as if to say "Doesn't someone care enough to stop me?" In these cases, children may feel *underprotected*. Let's examine some emotions that infants and toddlers may express, what they mean, and what care teachers can do to support the child and family.

Anxious, Fearful, Vigilant

A child who is anxious, fearful, or vigilant (on guard) may have multiple or specific fears; become agitated easily; or display uncontrollable crying or screaming, facial tics, and tension. The child may be easily upset, not explore, cling to an adult, or run and hide when something fearful happens. Children who are anxious may seem to be constantly watchful of others and the environment. Anxiety is increased by helplessness and lack of knowledge, which makes babies very prone to it (Lieberman, 1993, p. 124).

The child may have had overwhelming, frightening experiences or be experiencing sensory overload—too much stimulation for this particular child's temperament and ability to process information through several senses at once.

You can help these children by doing the following:

- Offer challenges gradually.
- Speak in a calm voice.
- Keep your promises to read a book or to help the child.
- Do not *send* the child over to a new situation. *Go* with her and draw her in. Stay with her until her mood has changed.
- Say often, "This is a safe place. I will keep you safe."
- Provide a primary caregiver model where at least one caregiver "moves up" to the next classroom with the child.

Work closely with families. Researchers Crockenberg, Leerkes, and Lekka (2007) studied how families' marital relationships influence infant behavior. They found that aggressive marital conflicts predicted infant withdrawal at 6 months. The results of this study demonstrate how important it is for early educators to think about children's behavior within the context of the family from a bioecological perspective and provide as many family-friendly policies and opportunities as possible. When talking directly with families, use the 6-step problem-solving approach discussed earlier and the 10-point problem-solving guide at the end of this chapter.

Angry and Defiant

Infants and toddlers can feel angry. Infants may cry loudly and their faces may scrunch up and turn red as they express their rage. An angry mobile infant may throw things such as toys or scratch another child who gets too near, and an angry toddler may even throw chairs. A very upset toddler screams many angry words—words that you didn't know a young child could say. A defiant toddler might destroy materials or toys, throw things, and threaten others.

What might contribute to this behavior? Perhaps this child is easily overstimulated and has difficulty with self-regulation. Perhaps an adult in the child's life doesn't understand development, and so scolds or punishes typical behavior. This child may have difficulty trusting others because she hasn't experienced predictable, kind, understanding, or responsive relationships. A child who is angry may have experienced a traumatic event or events. If you look closely, you may actually see a fearful child who is lashing out to protect himself—before someone hurts him.

An angry child can make the adults around her angry, too. It is hard to stay calm in the face of so much feeling from a child so young. Your anger, though, is not helpful to the child. The child may be trying hard to trigger your anger, because that is what the child expects from adults. When we understand the intention of the child, we then can respond with the message (through words or actions) that "I'm not going to respond to you the way you have come to expect." Instead, value the feelings of the child. Help identify the child's feelings by saying, "You are very angry!" in a tone that tells the child you understand. You may need to repeat this several times. Tell the child what he can do instead of hurting others or destroying property. Say, "You can stomp when you are angry" and then show him how. Figure out what the child is trying to communicate and what the child needs; help the child learn appropriate ways to get those needs met. Adapt your solutions to the needs of the individual child. Some possible responses may include the following:

- Take time to be emotionally available—be a respite in the storm. Sit on the floor near the child. Hold and comfort the child as often as possible. Give the child one-on-one time each day.
- Be firm about not expressing anger through aggression. Say (depending on what the child can understand), "Hitting hurts and we need to keep everyone safe. You can tell me, 'I'm angry.'"
- Help the child feel safe.
- Be responsive so the child feels he can "make something happen" in socially acceptable ways.
- Give choices—for example, say, "Do you want juice or milk?"

- Provide a quiet area (cozy corner) in the room where the child can go when he is angry. Do not force him to stay in that area, but rather encourage him to use it when he is angry.
- Provide places for boisterous play such as climbing and running.
- Provide a calm environment with places for cuddling, comforting, and caring.

Meet together with the family in a supportive way. The family members may be experiencing stress that they do not want to share. Parents and care teachers must know that "toddlerhood represents a critical period when behavioral and emotional problems of potentially clinical significance emerge (Baillargeon et al., 2007, p. 12). The children who exhibit extreme oppositional and defiant behavior, and the children's families and teachers should receive extensive support from an infant mental health professional (Baillargeon, Sward, Keenan, & Cao, 2011).

Children Who Behave Aggressively

Aggression is defined as behavior that harms others either directly through physical damage or indirectly through manipulation of peer relationships. An adult in an infant or toddler room may experience children who bite, scratch, hit, kick, spit, or pull hair. A toddler may call another child names or purposely ignore another child. Children may be reacting to another's aggression or being proactive and initiating aggression (Crick, Ostrov, & Kawabata, 2007). Observe these children so that you can understand what they are communicating to you through their behavior. They may be communicating that they don't want other children to be near them or that they need to feel powerful. A toddler may have learned that she gets her needs met (attention, noticed, out of an activity) when she is aggressive or she is experimenting with new behaviors that she observed other toddlers use.

Aggressive children may feel "out of control" and frightened because there are no clear or consistent rules or boundaries and they are not learning to regulate their behavior. Children who have delayed language development may not be able to communicate their needs, so they resort to physical aggression. Your observation and discussions with family members will help you determine what the child is trying to communicate.

In a longitudinal study of 10,658 Canadian children, one-sixth of the children demonstrated a consistent pattern of high levels of aggression from toddlerhood to preadolescence. These children were primarily boys from low-income families whose parents used "hostile/ineffective parenting strategies" (Cote, Vaillancourt, LeBlanc, Nagin, & Tremblay, 2006, p. 71). On the other hand, parental sensitivity was related to a decrease in angry, acting out behavior (Mesman et al., 2009). This research supports the importance of listening to and supporting families. If parents are using hostile/ineffective parenting strategies, provide them opportunities for home visits, parent-to-parent stress reduction classes, and guidance classes.

You can help these children by doing the following:

- Work hard to develop the child's trust in you and a positive relationship. Greet the child warmly each day and provide one-on-one teacher-child cozy, comforting time.
- Make 10 times more positive remarks than negative ones: Notice, notice, notice positive behavior.

- Keep teaching prosocial behavior. Help the child get his needs met in more positive ways.
- Talk to the child about his character in a positive way. Say, "You are the *kind of child* who helps others."
- Give the toddler a toy or stuffed animal and say, "This is your toy, and you can hold it all day if you'd like—you don't have to share it. The other toys are for all of the children to share and use."
- If the toddler hits you, hold the toddler's hand and say, "I don't like to be hit. It hurts. You can tell me, 'I'm mad.' "
- Help the child take the perspective of the other child. Say, "No biting, that hurt him—look, he's crying."
- Say, "I know you are angry, but I do not want you to kick him."
- Reduce stimuli, create a calm and safe environment, provide cozy corners and a private place for the child (can be an open box), so the child can be alone when needed (this is not a time-out spot).
- Create an interesting environment with cause-and-effect toys so the child can feel more powerful.
- Reduce spaces for running in a classroom, but provide places for large motor activities.

Baillargeon, et al. (2007) reminds us that the toddler years are critical for supporting children's use of prosocial rather than aggressive behaviors.

Posttraumatic Stress Disorder

posttraumatic stress disorder

Anxiety and fear caused by experiencing a traumatic event.

Unfortunately, some infants and toddlers experience extremely unpleasant events such as a car accident, hospitalization, abuse, or witnessing domestic abuse or even murder. **Posttraumatic stress disorder** can occur after an infant or toddler experiences a traumatic event. Gaensbauer (2004), a professor of psychiatry who helps children who experience trauma in their lives, reports that young children usually relive the trauma through their actions rather than verbally. He reports that a child placed in foster care at 4 months of age had been severely traumatized by a mother with mental illness. She would undress him and wrap him in cold towels. At 9 months of age, when he was reunited with his mother for a supervised visit, she started to undress him. At that moment the infant started to scream and the visit was stopped. He seemed to have a memory of the trauma from when he was 4 months old.

A person, object, or event may trigger memories of the painful, disturbing, or upsetting experience. These memories of the experience may cause fear, anxiety, withdrawal, aggression, crying, or shock. The infant or toddler may become still with vacant eyes or hyperactive with frantic looks. A toddler who experienced cockroaches in his diaper while suffering neglect in his home became frenzied when he felt a prickly or crawling sensation on his skin (Lieberman, 1993). It may seem as if the toddler is having a tantrum, but he is expressing fear. A mobile infant may cling to a blanket or piece of clothing that reminds her of her deceased mother. A child may begin to panic when she sees a pair of scissors because this is what her mother used to protect herself during a domestic violence incident. An open hand raised to help a toddler may cause a child to "freeze" or panic because of parental abuse with an open hand. These children may want to overcontrol their environment and people *or* may withdraw in order to keep themselves safe. *The overwhelming feeling that a child (or an adult) seems to experience during the traumatic event is one of helplessness, inability to control the situation, and feelings of not being safe or protected.* Adapt your strategies to the individual child's temperament and experience. The purpose of your strategies is to assure the child that you will keep him safe. You can do the following:

- Talk with a mental health specialist for support and strategies that meet this particular child's need.
- Observe and document the child's behavior.
- Help the child learn strategies when lost in a flood of anxiety—for instance, go to the teacher or a safe place at home or in classroom.
- Always tell when you are going out of the room—and say "I'm back" when you return.
- Help the child feel competent with toys and materials at her developmental level.
- Acknowledge the child's feelings—say, "It looks as if you are feeling afraid. I'm here, I'll keep you safe." Say, "This is a safe place."
- Use contingently responsive strategies—for instance, when a child pops up out of a box, say, "Oh, there you are." The child may replay the scene over and over to feel as if he is "making something happen."
- Provide a primary caregiver, continuity of care, and a consistent routine.
- Provide a cozy corner or "safe place" with boundaries and comforting toys (could be a box).
- Simplify things for the child—provide her own bin of water for water-play instead of a bin for two, so the child doesn't have to share for a while.
- Provide water—it *may* be soothing to a child.
- Take obnoxiously loud toys out of the environment.

Work with a mental health specialist as you support the family. If the child has been removed from his home, you may be working with the foster parent(s). Help families understand, and learn *from* families how the child is expressing his or her reaction to trauma. Problem solve *with* the family on how to comfort the child. And, of course, if you suspect abuse, you must report it.

What Philosophy Will You Use?

A responsive care, relationship-based model that includes a family- and culture-centered approach works very well for helping us think about how to help a child who is challenged and challenges parents, teachers, and peers. Ask: "What strategies promote healthy relationships and are responsive to the child's needs? What strategies make the child feel safe, secure, and able to express emotions in a healthy way? What helps him regulate his own behavior, problem solve, and want to be prosocial? How can you win the heart of a child with challenging behavior?"

Are the important adults in the child's life working together to improve *all* of the child's relationships? If the child is to be helped, it isn't enough to improve only the relationship between the teacher and the child, although that can certainly help the child emotionally. The child's relationship with his or her parents, siblings, or grandparents must also be improved for long-term results. There is no place for blaming the child (as in "He's mean")—but rather, it is the responsibility of adults to positively support the child and work toward the child's mental health and well-being.

Following is a 10-point process for helping children with challenging behavior. The key people in the child's life *work together* to answer the following questions that then lead to a relationship-based approach with the child. Only after all of the key people reflect on the questions can appropriate strategies be developed that truly meet the child's needs.

1. Ask: "Who is this child? Who has positive relationships with this child? What are his strengths? Who likes what about this child?"

   It is important to see the "whole" child with strengths, interests, and needs rather than defining the child only by the challenging behavior.

2. Clearly define the behavior that is challenging the child, the teacher, or family members.

   Before deciding on strategies, the behavior must be clearly defined. Write down the behavior (he bites other children), not an attribute of the child (the child is aggressive). What is the challenge for the child? For example, "The child bites peers." How often does it occur? How long has it occurred? Who does it happen with? Where does it happen? Is it developmentally appropriate?

3. Why is the behavior a challenge?

   Why is the behavior a challenge for the child, the parent, the teacher, and peers? How are the parents and teachers feeling about it? (Angry, sad, rejected, proud, frustrated?) How is it affecting the child and others? Who is it a problem for? What's the meaning for the family and teachers? What are the cultural issues?

4. Why do the family and teacher think the child does the behavior?

   Brainstorm several possibilities. Always rule out any medical problems first. Then observe the child. Observe for temperament, developmental level, delay, disability, coping style, sensory needs, imitation, anxiety, fear, anger, stress, hypersensitivity, sleep deprivation, grief, depression, need for positive attention, recent loss or transitions, trauma, or abuse. Think about how the child is keeping himself safe. Has he learned to avoid adults to protect himself or has he learned to "make himself heard" and use more intense ways of getting the attention of the adult in order to be protected (Crittenden, 1995)?

5. What's the purpose of the behavior? What is the child trying to communicate?

   The behavior is working for the child and helping her cope. What does the child gain from the behavior? (If the child hits, the child gets a toy away from a peer.) After observing, complete the following chart:

Date	What Happens Before	The Challenging Behavior	What Happens After	Possible Purposes of the Behavior

6. What is the child feeling and experiencing? What's the emotional need being expressed by the child? How is the child feeling challenged? Look at behavior from the child's perspective.

7. What are the child's short-term and long-range social and emotional needs?

8. What do the family, teachers, and peers want the child to be able to feel and do instead of the challenging behavior? Is it developmentally appropriate? Will it help the child meet his needs? Does the child possess the skills to meet the need in a more appropriate way?

9. Think about the strategies you've tried: What's worked, what hasn't? How did they work? How did these make the child feel? How did they make the adult feel? Were the strategies consistent with achieving the goal(s) for the child? Were they consistent with your beliefs about what infants and toddlers need and how they learn?

10. What support do the adults and peers need to help this child? Who can help the child, the family, peers, and the teachers? Whoever has a strong, positive relationship with the child should be the key ones to help. What are some strategies that meet children's needs; help children achieve their goals; guide children to use more positive behavior; and are developmentally, individually, and culturally appropriate?

Summary

This chapter completed our discussion of the components of a curriculum by examining component 8 (a relationship-based approach to guidance). In planning the guidance component, we applied the 3 R approach: *respect, reflect,* and *relate.* If your guidance strategies include respect for child differences and development; reflection on why, when, and where a behavior occurs and what you want to teach the child; and relating through responsive interactions, building the child's relationships, and considering how the environment affects children—then you are on your way to using guidance well.

- The 3 R approach to guiding infants' and toddlers' behavior includes respecting, reflecting, and relating to meet their emotional needs. When adults guide young children, they are teaching them in order for them to be successful in a world that requires social and emotional competence.

- Respect for infants and toddlers includes valuing their emotional needs, individual differences and strengths, and the power of development. Care teachers must also respect themselves and know how their culture and past experiences affect their beliefs about how children should behave and become socialized.

- When adults reflect, they think about what an experience is like for a child, observe what the children are communicating through their behavior, and decide what they would like the child to learn to do instead.

- When adults relate with infants and toddlers, they support children's healthy relationships with all of the important people in their lives, focus on adult-child responsive interactions that promote children's capacities and development, and create a supportive environment.

- Separation anxiety, toddler resistance, challenges with learning to use the toilet, tantrums, and biting peers and adults are behaviors that are sure to happen with infants and toddlers. When adults understand that young children experience times of emotional turmoil as they develop and learn new behaviors, they can be more understanding and supportive.

- Some infants and toddlers may feel anxious, fearful, and vigilant; angry and defiant; aggressive; or may experience posttraumatic stress disorder. Use a relationship-based philosophy to collaborate with all of the adults in a child's life to support the child's emotional and social development when the child is feeling challenged.

Key Terms

discipline
guidance
justification
mitigation
negativism

other-oriented guidance
posttraumatic stress disorder
resolution
sensory challenges
separation anxiety

socialized
tantrums
time-in
time-out
traumatic events

Reflections and Resources for the Reader

REFLECTIONS

1. Elaborate on the 3 R approach (respect, reflect, and relate) for thinking about guidance. What would you add to each step of the process?
2. What is the child experiencing when he or she is having a tantrum? How do you or other adults you know usually handle toddler tantrums? What would you do to support a child who is having a tantrum and help the child learn new ways to express emotions?
3. Trishanna is 20 months old, in a family child care setting, and feels very angry much of the time. She bites her peers, kicks furniture, and resists any efforts on the part of the care teacher to comfort her when she is distressed. What would you do if you were the provider?

OBSERVATION AND APPLICATION OPPORTUNITIES

1. Observe an early development and education program. How do the adults guide young children's behavior? Are the strategies supporting the infants' and toddlers' social and emotional development and helping them learn new appropriate behaviors?

2. Choose one of the challenging behaviors discussed in this chapter and read more about children who may be experiencing anxiety, fear, anger, or posttraumatic stress disorder.
3. Choose one of the developmental issues discussed in this chapter. Develop a guidebook for parents on strategies that they can use when their children are experiencing separation anxiety, biting, tantrums, or learning to use the toilet. Help them understand the issue from the child's perspective.

SUPPLEMENTARY ARTICLES AND BOOKS TO READ

Elliot, E., & Gonzalez-Mena, J. (2011). Babies' self-regulation: Taking a broad perspective. *Young Children, 66*(1), 20–25.

Marion, M. (2011). *Guidance of young children* (8th ed.). Upper Saddle River, NJ: Pearson.

Vallotton, C., & Ayoub, C. (2011). Use your words: The role of language in the development of toddlers' self-regulation. *Early Childhood Research Quarterly, 26*(2), 169–181.

Whittaker, J. E. V., & Harden, B. J. (2010). Beyond ABCs and 123s: Enhancing teacher-child relationship quality to promote children's behavioral development. *NHSA Dialog, 13*(3), 185–191.

INTERESTING LINKS

Center on the Social and Emotional Foundations for Early Learning

www.vanderbilt.edu/csefel/
This national center focuses on strengthening the capacity of child care and Head Start programs to improve the social and emotional outcomes of young children.

Child Trauma Academy

www.childtrauma.org
This site offers educational materials and articles concerning child trauma, including sections for caregivers and interdisciplinary teams.

Technical Assistance Center on Social Emotional Intervention

www.challengingbehavior.org
The center promotes the use of evidence-based practice to meet the needs of young children who have, or are at risk for, challenging behavior.

The Clearinghouse on Early Education and Parenting

ceep.crc.uiuc.edu/poptopics/biting.html
CEEP provides an article on biting and other resources on biting for parents and teachers.

15

Including Infants and Toddlers with Disabilities in Child Development and Education Programs

LEARNING OUTCOMES

After reading this chapter, you will be able to:

- Describe infant and toddler disabling conditions
- Explain Part C of the Early Intervention System including family-centered practice
- Discuss teachers' attitudes and strategies that are beneficial to the inclusion of children with special needs in programs

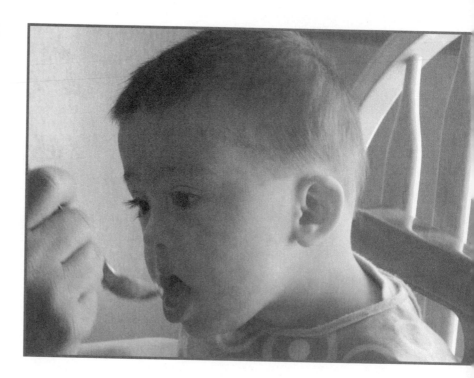

Diane stopped in the doorway of the toddler room in the child development and education center as she entered to pick up her daughter Lucy at the end of the day. She couldn't stop the tears that were welling up. Pat, Lucy's teacher, rushed over to her, concerned. "I'm OK," Diane said. "It's just that for a moment, when I looked around the room, I didn't know which one was Lucy. They're all busy and playing. I've never seen her just blend in before."

Moments like this are possible for Diane because community-based child care programs are increasingly likely to include children with special needs. According to the 2010 report on the settings where infants and toddlers are receiving early intervention services, the huge majority are in the child's home with the parents present. Up to about 20% of children from birth through 2 years are served in community settings. Out of almost 35,000 served outside the home, only several hundred were enrolled in settings only for children with disabilities (U.S. Department of Education, 2011). At this point, many teachers have served many infants and toddlers with disabilities—and served them well.

Throughout this book, we have included information on infants and toddlers with disabilities because most of their needs will be met through the same knowledge and strategies used with typically developing children. We include that information to illustrate our own commitment to the full inclusion of children with disabilities in child development and education programs. However, there is further, specific information teachers need about children with disabilities.

This chapter provides a description of more common types of disabling conditions and challenges to development found in infants and toddlers. The early intervention system is described, particularly in regard to supports available to child development and education programs. Finally, although in most cases the aspects of high-quality infant-toddler care that have been described earlier in this book will translate into high-quality care for all children, we will discuss some specific strategies teachers can use to help infants and toddlers with disabilities successfully participate in experiences and develop friendships with other children.

What Disabilities Do We See in Infants and Toddlers?

Before naming a list of disabling conditions, it is worth pointing out that terms such as *disability* or *special needs* are so general they are almost meaningless. Yet, for any individual, these words can be fraught with meaning. In addition, the diagnosis of a disability does not fully describe a particular child. The disability is only one aspect of the child. There is no meaningful way, for example, to describe "infants with Down syndrome." Any one infant with Down syndrome is born into a particular family with its unique resources and stressors, as well as its own understanding and meaning of the disability. The child may be born relatively healthy or with complicating health issues. The child has his own personality and temperament and quickly establishes his own history, a sense of who he is, and his own expectations of the world. He may be an only child, a new child among siblings, or live within an extended family. The surrounding culture may contribute particular beliefs about Down syndrome, a wealth or lack of supporting resources, and a welcoming or rejecting attitude.

CULTURE CLOSE UP

In 1982, an immigrant Hmong family gave birth to a little girl in California. Early on, she developed a seizure disorder. When she was 4, she suffered a grand mal seizure that left her without language or the ability to move. Her father declared, "The spirit captured her and she fell down," describing his belief that a powerful spirit was now living inside her. Was this child being gifted as a shaman or was her brain being destroyed by seizures? Anne Faddiman reported their story in a book subtitled *A Clash of Cultures.* This was a fascinating story of the American medical culture and the Hmong spiritual culture both trying to help this child—and getting tragically in each other's way. Is illness or disability physical or spiritual? What happens when an early childhood learning and development program and a family have very different beliefs? Ms. Lee died in 2012 at the age of 30, in her mother's home, surrounded by family.

person-first language

Use of language describing people with disabilities by never using the disability as the descriptor and pointing out that this is a person first.

genetic syndromes

Abnormalities caused by information within the genetic material.

Thus, because no child can be described fully by the name of his disability, we use **person-first language**: We say "a person with a disability" or "a child with a disability" or "a child with Down syndrome," *not* "a disabled child" or a "Down's child." The child is a person *first* with all of the differing individual characteristics, strengths, needs, interests, and desires that all children have. The disability is a part of who that child is, but only a part.

Groups of Disabilities

Nonetheless, we do classify disabling conditions. The disabilities most often identified in infancy tend to be relatively significant, including genetic syndromes, sensory disorders, and central nervous system disorders. These conditions tend to have serious impacts on a child's ability to take information from the world, to process and understand that information, and to control the movement of the child's own body. Causes may include circumstances around the gestation and birth such as intrauterine substance exposure, prematurity, low birth weight, or toxic stress (Fattal-Valevski, Leitner, Kutai, Tal-Posener, Tomer, & Lieberman, 1999; National Scientific Council on the Developing Child, 2010; and Watemberg, Silver, Harel, & Lerman-Sagie, 2002). They may be established conditions such as Down syndrome, cerebral palsy, or seizures (Besag, 2002). Language and communication impairments are often secondary disabilities caused by the primary condition, because producing speech requires considerable muscle control, and learning language requires both sensory and processing abilities (Parkinson, 2002).

It is impossible to name each potential disability and explain its effects. There are thousands of genetic syndromes alone. Nonetheless, young teachers frequently request some overview that would help them understand the kinds of disabling conditions that may present themselves. In this section, we describe some disabling conditions that would fit under the category "established biological risk," some of their potential effects on development, and some interventions that support development for children with these conditions. Remember, children with each of these conditions have been successfully included in child development and education programs.

Chromosomal Abnormalities and Genetic Syndromes

As described in Chapter 5, the gene is the basic component of inherited information, carrying traits from parent to child. The gene reproduces at each cell division and produces exact copies of its DNA and proteins. Normally, each cell in the body, except the egg and sperm, has 23 matching pairs, or 46 chromosomes. Each gene is located on a specific spot of the DNA of a particular chromosome. (See Box 15.1.)

Genetic syndromes occur when the genes are damaged in cell division or when sets of genes from the mother and/or father carry defective information that prevents the gene from expressing itself. *Chromosomal abnormalities* occur when there are too many or too few chromosomes, or when a chromosome has

BOX 15.1

Turning Genes On and Off

In recent years, scientists have been studying how environmental occurrences or exposures cause genes to express themselves or not (turn on or off). This process is called *epigenetics.* In September 2012, a study involving 442 scientists from 32 labs released an amazing discovery.

About 10 feet of DNA are coiled into every cell in our bodies. For years scientists were studying what appeared to be the active sections of the strands of DNA that direct how each cell will grow. Lengths of proteins between these informational DNA sections were considered "junk DNA." This huge project, called "Encode," has discovered that the junk DNA gathers around a particular cell and turns it on and off—like a light switch. One scientist described the Human Genome Project (HGP) as a satellite picture of DNA whereas this new information is a street map.

It's no longer called "junk" either. It is now called the "dark matter" (Kolata, 2012).

missing pieces, extra pieces, or pieces attached to another chromosome (Human Genome Project, 2011).

Chromosomal abnormalities are often identified prenatally, at birth, or soon after birth. Some common chromosomal and genetic abnormalities include the following:

- *Down syndrome:* Caused by an extra, or third, 21st chromosome. Because of the cause of the syndrome, it is also known as *trisomy 21.* This occurs most often when the 21st chromosome duplicates in either the egg or the sperm as a pair, rather than as a single chromosome. Down syndrome has a number of visible characteristics such as an upward slant to the eyes, a small mouth and facial features, small stature, a flattened back of the head, and small hands with a single crease across the palm. Children with Down syndrome may have congenital heart defects, poor muscle tone that can delay motor development, and varying degrees of mental retardation. Although children with Down syndrome eventually develop speech, they often begin communication successfully by using sign language (National Down Syndrome Society [NDSS], 2005).

  Supporting development: Given low muscle tone, infants and toddlers with Down syndrome may need support in sitting and in being engaged to stay near the other children. Physical therapists may recommend experiences to develop muscle tone. During the first year of life, they will benefit from using sign language or other communication systems as they have much to communicate but are likely to be delayed in language. Teachers use play as a way to help these infants and toddlers focus and maintain their attention (Kumin, 1998).

- *Fragile X syndrome:* Caused by a partially broken area (fragile) on the X chromosome. Because girls have two X chromosomes and boys have only one, the damage usually has more impact on boys. Children with fragile X syndrome are likely to have mild to severe mental retardation, although they may also have normal intelligence. They may have a large head with noticeably large forehead, nose, jaws, and ears. Some children with fragile X syndrome have attention problems and some have autistic-like tendencies (National Fragile X Foundation [NFXF], 2008).

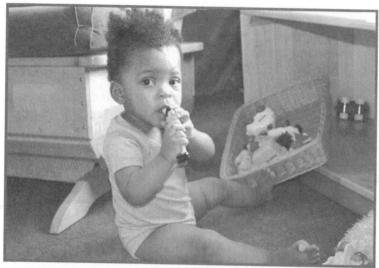

Many syndromes show no symptoms in the first months of life.

Supporting development: Children with fragile X syndrome have traditionally been identified at or later than the age 3, but amniocentesis and newborn screening are providing early identification (Cassels, 2008). Infant-toddler teachers may need to help overcome feeding difficulties and promote social interest and language and motor imitation.

- *Cystic fibrosis:* A disorder in which genes lack the enzymes to break down and absorb fats, causing malnutrition. Thick secretions cause chronic lung damage; teachers may be involved in performing exercises to help the infant or toddler clear his lungs (Cystic Fibrosis Foundation [CFF], 2009). Cystic fibrosis is the most common, inherited, deadly disease of Caucasians in the United States.

Supporting development: Teachers may learn to position the infant or toddler with cystic fibrosis and tap the chest and back in ways that help loosen the mucus so that it may be coughed out (Lewis, 2007).

- *Sickle cell anemia:* An abnormality in which some red blood cells are crescent or sickle shaped. The red blood cells carry hemoglobin to the cells throughout the body delivering oxygen. The sickle cells live for half the time of a healthy cell and greatly reduce the total number of red cells in the body. Sickle cell occurs primarily in African Americans, causes fevers and great pain in joints and the abdomen, and is incurable (National Heart, Lung, and Blood Institute, 2012).

Supporting development: Infants and toddlers with sickle cell anemia must have an individualized health care plan that informs teachers what symptoms are of concern and steps to be taken from notifying parents to initiating transport to an emergency medical facility.

- *Rett syndrome:* Usually characterized by typical development for the first 6 to 18 months of life, followed by a rapid loss of cognitive, language, motor, and self-help skills. The progressive loss of skills quickly deteriorates to severe or profound mental retardation; obsessive, repetitive movements such as hand wringing; and often the development of seizures. Rett syndrome occurs almost exclusively in girls (International Rett Syndrome Research Foundation [IRSF], 2009).

Supporting development: Teachers may spend additional time with feeding or even use nasogastric or gastrointestinal feeding tubes, if allowed by the state. Each child is different but skill development is limited and regression is common, so teachers need to be prepared to maintain a high intensity of caregiving (Kantor, 2006).

Sensory Impairments

sensory impairments

Problems affecting hearing, vision, or other senses.

Sensory impairments describe the categories of problems that can occur with receiving or processing information through the senses. Sensory impairments can occur prenatally or as a result of illness or injury, ranging in severity from mild to total. Hearing impairment, for example, may range from a mild loss of ability to hear to complete deafness. Visual impairment also includes a range from easily correctable issues to complete blindness. Tactile defensiveness, or hypersensitivity to touch, is a less well-known disorder. It involves a child's difficulty in receiving information from his body and results in poor motor planning and poor body awareness (Coleman, 1999). Sensory processing disorders may make it difficult for a young child to manage loud noises, certain textures, eating, and changes in routine.

Supporting development: Teachers will work with early intervention teams and families to meet the needs of infants and toddlers with sensory impairments. Teachers may change the environment, adding a darkened space with light-oriented activities for infants and toddlers with visual impairments. Teachers will carefully provide tactile-rich and language-rich experiences. They may learn and use sign language with all of the children, if there is a child with a hearing impairment. Teachers may learn to do exercises with tactile defensive children to help them become more comfortable with touch.

Metabolic Disorders

Metabolic disorders result from inherited deficiencies of particular enzymes. The enzymes are not available to break down materials such as amino acids, which then build up and cause damage to the brain. Some metabolic disorders can be diagnosed and treated, such as phenylketonuria (PKU). Others, such as Tay-Sachs, cannot be treated and are fatal.

PKU is a condition in which children cannot break down the enzyme phenylalanine, which is present in almost all foods. Without treatment, phenylalanine builds up in the bloodstream and causes brain damage and mental retardation. PKU is a genetic disease. Newborns are now tested at all U.S. hospitals, and it is recommended that babies tested within the first 24 hours be retested at 2 weeks (NIH, 2000).

Tay-Sachs is also an inherited metabolic disorder, caused by the absence of a vital enzyme called hexosaminidase A (Hex-A). Without Hex-A, a fatty substance (or *lipid*) called GM2 ganglioside accumulates abnormally in cells, especially in the nerve cells of the brain. There is progressive damage to the cells and children do not live past early childhood. People of European Jewish descent are most likely to be carriers of the defective gene (National Tay-Sachs & Allied Diseases Association [NTSADA], 2009).

Supporting development: Because this is a severe medical condition usually resulting in death in the first 4 years of life, program staff must carefully consider how they will provide emotional support to the teachers, parents, the child, and the child's peers.

Central Nervous System Disorders

The brain and the spinal cord make up the central nervous system. They receive information from the body through a network of nerves. The brain and spinal cord can be malformed in the womb because of exposure to toxic substances, poor nutrition, maternal infections, or poor migration of cells. Neural cells may also be damaged during the birth process if the baby is deprived of oxygen. The nervous system may not develop well after birth if the child is in a chaotic or barren environment, if nutrition is poor, or if the child is exposed to environmental toxins such as lead. The central nervous system may also be damaged by high fevers, disease, and injury.

central nervous system disorders

Damage to the brain, spine, or the nerve network that affects learning, sensory, or motor abilities.

Some commonly seen **central nervous system disorders** include the following:

- *Cerebral palsy:* A disorder of motor and postural control from nonprogressive damage to the brain. The type and severity of the disorder depend on the area of the brain that is affected and the degree of damage. Cerebral palsy ranges from a mild motor impairment to almost no voluntary control of movement. Intelligence is not necessarily affected by the damage, but seizures often occur with cerebral palsy (UCP, 2013). This condition was described in Chapter 10.

    Supporting development: Children with cerebral palsy are included in group care very successfully, with the support of the family and the early intervention team. Teachers will have to learn the individual child's strengths and needs for support. Supports may include physical positioning, feeding, individual learning capacities, and alternate communication systems.

- *Spina bifida:* A birth defect that occurs because the neural tube did not close entirely while forming prenatally. The effect of spina bifida depends on which vertebra are exposed and can range from almost no effect to complete paralysis below the spinal opening and severe mental retardation. Some 70% of the cases of spina bifida could be prevented with adequate intake of folic acid during pregnancy (Spinal Bifida Association, 2012).

    Supporting development: Most children with spina bifida have normal intelligence and should be responsive learners and relationship partners. They are likely to have significant problems with mobility and bladder and bowel problems. Special services concentrate on these issues.

- *Attentional disorders:* Hyper-reactivity, hypersensitivity, hyposensitivity, and attention deficit disorder—a group of disorders probably caused by small abnormalities in the brain. Symptoms include difficulty in maintaining focus and attention, being easily distracted, difficulty controlling impulses, and being overly sensitive and reactive to sensory information (Coleman, 1999).

    Supporting development: Maintaining attention is a basic developmental task of infancy. Care teachers support development by helping infants regulate their reactions to the events around them. Limiting distractions is helpful, although sometimes difficult in group care.

- *Shaken baby syndrome:* A set of symptoms found when a baby has been violently shaken. Symptoms include bleeding in the brain and the retinas of the eyes. It can result in cognitive and motor damage and often results in death (National Center on Shaken Baby Syndrome [NCSBS], 2009). If the child survives the shaking, he may develop these symptoms over time: lethargy, vomiting, poor sucking or swallowing, lack of smiling, unequal pupil size, and an inability to focus visually or to lift his head (KidsHealth, 2008).

    Supporting development: The care teacher may be the one to recognize the symptoms of this head trauma. Every program must have a plan in place for how to report suspected child abuse.

Congenital Infections

Congenital infections are diseases that affect the baby prenatally. As briefly described in Chapter 5, maternal infections do cross the placenta and can cause harm to the fetus. The most commonly seen infections, grouped under the acronym STORCH or TORCH-S, are syphilis, toxoplasmosis, other infections (such as HIV or hepatitis B), rubella, cytomegela virus, and herpes. These infections, when transmitted in the womb or at birth, can cause mental retardation, growth retardation, sensory impairments, and even death (MedlinePlus, 2012).

Disorders Secondary to Exposure to Toxic Substances

Toxins that the mother actively inhales or ingests, such as tobacco, illegal drugs, and alcohol, as well as toxins to which the mother is passively exposed, such as cleaning solvents, lead, pollutants and pesticides, are all able to cross the placenta and harm the developing nervous system of the fetus. Damage to the nervous system can cause cognitive impairments and diminished growth. The range of effects depends to some extent on the timing and dosage of exposure. These conditions are described more fully in Chapter 5.

Chronic Illness

Chronic illnesses requiring some use of medication or medical technology are increasingly common in child development and education settings. Asthma and allergies are very common chronic conditions. Hemophilia is less common but is often reported by caregivers in workshops on disabilities (Coleman, 1999).

- *Asthma:* A chronic respiratory disorder causing wheezing, coughing, and difficulty breathing. Ten to 12% of American children have asthma and the numbers are rising, although no one is sure why. It is usually attributed to the increase of pollution and allergens in the air, particularly because the greatest increase is in African-American boys living in poverty (Medicinenet.com, 2012). Care teachers sometimes administer medication for asthma with a machine called a nebulizer.
- *Allergies:* Sensitivity to normally harmless substances. Allergic reactions may include rashes, irritability, vomiting, swelling, difficulty in breathing, or even shock. Individualized health care plans include instructions for how to respond to known allergic reactions.
- *Hemophilia:* An X-linked disorder caused by a lack of proteins needed for blood clotting. Children may spontaneously bleed or be unable to stop bleeding from minor cuts.

   Supporting developments: Care teachers must have plans in place describing how to recognize and respond to symptoms. These conditions are episodic and may be emergencies; nonetheless, on a day-to-day basis teachers should be using their well-developed skills of responsive caregiving, individualized planning, and relationship building.

Conditions of Risk for Poor Development

In addition to the disorders already listed, *pervasive developmental disorders* (PDD) comprise another group of developmental disorders, including autism, Rett's disorder, childhood disintegrative disorder, and pervasive developmental disorder, that are characterized by impairment in social interaction and communication skills, extreme reactions to change, and obsessive and repetitive behaviors. PDD can have moderate

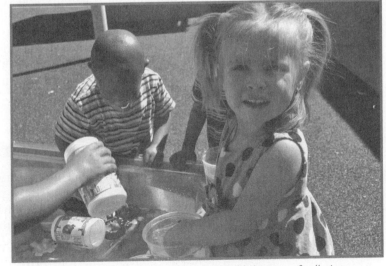

Conditions such as asthma are on the rise, probably because of pollution.

to severe effects on a child's ability to function. The NICHCY (2003) Web site includes detailed information on these disorders.

Autism has become a national and growing concern. In 2007, the U.S. Centers for Disease Control and Prevention reported that autism is on the rise with a prevalence rate of 1 in every 150 American children and 1 in 94 boys. In 2012 the rate was 1 in 88 births and 1 in 54 boys (Center for Disease Control). The Autism Society of America Web Site (www.autism.society.org/) contains valuable information for parents and professionals on the definition of autism, the prevalence, causes, research, and intervention strategies. It is important that parents and teachers of infants and toddlers know that early diagnosis (ideally within the first 2 years) is critical for better child outcomes. Ozonoff et al. (2008) found that autism can be diagnosed earlier than others have thought. Atypical object exploration (spinning, rotating, and repetitive behaviors) at 12 months of age was associated with a diagnosis of autism at 3 years of age.

The Autism Society's home page on "About Autism" states the following: "Autism is treatable. Children do not 'outgrow' autism, but studies show that early diagnosis and intervention lead to significantly improved outcomes."

Here are some signs to look for in the children in your life:

- Lack of or delay in spoken language
- Repetitive use of language and/or motor mannerisms (e.g., hand-flapping, twirling objects)
- Little or no eye contact
- No response to own name
- Lack of interest in peer relationships
- Lack of spontaneous or make-believe play
- Persistent fixation on parts of objects

A Reminder

Above all, it is important to remember that with children with special needs, there is a little person with whom the teacher has all the necessary skills and compassion to develop a meaningful and loving relationship. This child is part of a family that is quickly learning a great deal of new information, dealing with a shock, perhaps becoming new parents, and very possibly worrying about how they will be welcomed anywhere. Early childhood programs can serve infants and toddlers with disabilities well. A program can provide wonderful opportunities for learning and relationships and can be welcoming and reassuring to the family. If the early childhood program conveys a message that "we are a program, a community, and a society that has room for all children," it will always be deeply appreciated by families.

Early Intervention: Part C of IDEA

Although child development and education programs play an important role in the lives of families, they do not have the primary responsibility for providing therapeutic services to infants and toddlers with disabilities. Since 1986, the federal law providing special education services in the United States has also provided for early intervention services for infants and toddlers. It was reauthorized in 2005 and the regulations were released in 2011. The Individuals with Disabilities Education Act (IDEA) requires all states to provide special education services to children between 3 and 21 years of age. The Program for Infants and Toddlers with Disabilities (Part C of IDEA, PL 105-17) was designed to

- Enhance the development of infants and toddlers with disabilities
- Reduce the educational costs by minimizing the need for special education through early intervention
- Minimize the likelihood of institutionalization and maximize independent living
- Enhance the capacity of families to meet their child's needs (NECTAC, 2012)

The Program for Infants and Toddlers with Disabilities is a grant program from the federal government to the states to help them provide early intervention services for infants and toddlers through age 2 and their families. The state has to meet a set of 16 components, as shown in Box 15.2 and must ensure that it will meet the needs of every eligible child and family.

Eligibility

Part C requires each state to determine its own criteria for eligibility. States are required to provide services to children who have conditions of established risk, "a diagnosed physical or mental condition which has a high probability of resulting in developmental delay." This includes many of the conditions described previously, including "chromosomal abnormalities, genetic or congenital disorders;

BOX 15.2

Required Components of a State's Part C (IDEA) System

1. A rigorous definition of developmental delay
2. Appropriate early intervention services based on scientifically based research, to the extent practicable, available to all infants and toddlers with disabilities and their families, including Indian and homeless infants and toddlers
3. Timely and comprehensive multidisciplinary evaluation of needs of children and family-directed identification of the needs of each family
4. Individualized family service plan and service coordination
5. Comprehensive child find and referral system
6. Public awareness program
7. Central directory of services, resources, and research and demonstration projects
8. Comprehensive system of personnel development
9. Policies and procedures for personnel standards
10. Single line of authority in a lead agency designated by the governor
11. Policy pertaining to contracting for services
12. Procedure for timely reimbursement of funds
13. Procedural safeguards
14. System for compiling data on the early intervention system
15. State interagency coordinating council
16. Policies and procedures to ensure that to the maximum extent appropriate, early intervention services are provided in natural environments except when early intervention cannot be achieved satisfactorily in a natural environment

Source: NECTAC (2012).

Certain disorders make a child automatically eligible for Part C because we know they can delay development.

severe sensory impairments, including hearing and vision; inborn errors of metabolism; disorders reflecting disturbance of the nervous system; congenital infections; disorders secondary to exposure of toxic substances, including fetal alcohol syndrome; and severe attachment disorders." Many states add to this list biological conditions that increase the likelihood of, but do not necessarily result in, developmental delays. These would include low birth weight, intraventricular hemorrhage at birth, chronic lung disease, and failure to thrive. Some states also choose to provide services to children who are considered to be at environmental risk for development because of factors such as parental substance abuse, parental mental illness, and child abuse or neglect.

Individualized Family Service Plan (IFSP)

If a child is eligible for services under Part C, the child receives a thorough developmental evaluation from two or more professionals, and the family and the early intervention team develop an *individualized family service plan* (IFSP) that determines the goals for development and the services and supports needed to achieve them. See Figure 15.1 for a sample page of an IFSP. Ideally, each IFSP looks quite different from any other and takes into consideration the priorities, strengths, and needs of each family and child. If a program is providing child development

FIGURE 15.1   **Sample individualized family service plan (IFSP)**

Early Intervention Action Plan

What we see now:

Sierra is very active and able to raise her head when on her tummy and to turn over at will.

Our strategies to get there:

- *Continue using supported sitting positions.*
- *Increase exercise through play that will increase muscle tone and trunk control.*

How we will know we are there:

Sierra will be able to sit independently during mealtimes and to play.

What we want to see for baby/family:

Sierra is starting to eat more solid foods, so her mom wants her to be able to sit up.

Services and supports we will use:

- *Jen, our OT, will continue weekly visits and provide drawings of current exercises.*
- *Mom and Dad will work with Sierra in the evenings.*
- *Shirley, her care teacher, will include exercise in diaper changing and play times.*

Comments:

We want to encourage Sierra's becoming stronger in her trunk and neck—but not to push her if she's not ready.

and education services, the director or teacher should be included as a member of the intervention team; she can provide valuable information about how the child manages his interactions with other children and can offer her own expertise on typical development. As summarized by O'Brien (1997):

> Unlike many educational documents... the IFSP presents developmental information in a way that encourages parents' understanding and contribution....The IFSP contains a narrative description of the child's current level of performance in each of the major developmental domains, and both family members and professionals can offer descriptions to be included here. (p. 57)

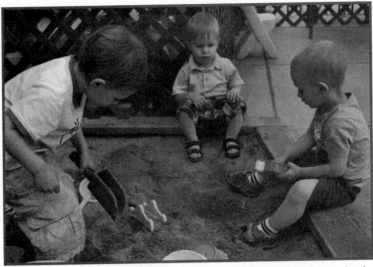

Most children with disabilities fit in well in family child care and infant and toddler classrooms.

Early Intervention Services

Under Part C, infants and toddlers with disabilities may receive services from early childhood special educators, speech-language pathologists, physical therapists, occupational therapists, or psychologists. A service coordinator manages the variety of services and often coordinates many sources of funding. Part C requires states to "have policies and procedures in place to ensure that to the maximum extent appropriate, early intervention services are provided in natural environments."

The steps in the intervention process are as follows:

1. Family contacts Part C provider with concerns.
2. Multidisciplinary assessment of child's development is made.
3. Eligibility is established.
4. Service coordinator is assigned.
5. Individualized family service plan (IFSP) is developed.
6. Services are delivered.
7. Evaluation and plan are reviewed at 6-month intervals.

In many states, the early intervention services are offered within the child development and education program, or, at the very least, with ongoing consultation to the staff. Early interventionists may provide advice on how to physically position a child to maximize his ability to control and use his body, they may offer strategies for adapting toys and materials, they may have tips to make feeding more efficient and satisfying, and they may offer a variety of communication alternatives to help adults understand the cues and signals of the infant or toddler with disabilities. The families of the children receive support as well from the early interventionist and the teacher—family and early interventionist(s) work as a team. O'Brien (1997) describes how the child's skills and abilities may be discussed:

> Even the way developmental domains are described on IFSPs is different from the way most educators have been taught to talk about them, because the labels used need to be focused on the types of skills and abilities cared about by families.

Rather than cognitive development, an IFSP label might read as *thinking* and *problem solving*. Similarly, gross motor development could be listed as *muscles and movement;* fine motor development as *reaching and playing;* communication as *talking, listening, and understanding;* social and behavioral development as *getting along with others;* and adaptive or functional skills as *daily living*. When presented in these terms, the discussion about the child's development can be shared equally between parents and professionals. (p. 57)

States have different rules limiting the medical procedures that can be performed by anyone other than a nurse. These rules are outlined in each state's Nurse Practice Act. The program's health consultant should be involved in planning care for a child who requires a feeding tube, nebulizer treatments, or any other actions that might be construed as practicing medicine.

The requirement for offering services in natural settings was designed to take full advantage of the benefits to the child with disabilities that are inherent in an inclusive environment. The natural interest of any infant or toddler in her peers provides motivation for children with disabilities to actively work to join their friends in their very compelling activities. The play and exploration of typically developing children can be highly engaging for the child with disabilities and can provide models of a variety of ways to play. All children benefit when they learn to create friendships with children with differing skills.

BOX 15.3

Screening Tools

The Ages & Stages Questionnaire is filled out by parents every several months. Teachers then code the results to track children's development. The pamphlets utilize parent observations while helping inform parents of the predicted course of development. They can be used with children from 2 months to 5 1/2 years (see www.brookespublishing.com/ for more information and samples).

Ages & Stages Questionnaires®, third edition (ASQ-3) Squires, J. & Bricker, D. (2009) A parent-completed, child-monitoring system Baltimore: Brookes.

The Denver Developmental Screen is used by professionals or trained paraprofessionals to track development. A few items in each developmental domain are scored at each observation to see if the child's development is within the normal range. It can be used from birth to 6 years and is known as the Denver II.

The Denver Developmental Materials (www.denverii.com)

Making Referrals

Children may come to your program already identified by Part C and receiving services, or your program may have some developmental concerns about a child you are already serving. It is important for every infant and toddler development and education program to understand how to access the Part C program in its community and how to talk to families about making a referral. If the family is concerned about the child's development, Part C must provide a timely, multidisciplinary evaluation to determine whether the child is eligible for services.

There are many ways to assess child development. Many programs routinely review development with a brief assessment called a *screening*. Screening tools (see Box 15.3) are usually composed of a few items describing typical development in each domain. Teachers may set up situations in which to observe whether a child is performing the task or may answer the items from ongoing observations. Some screening tools ask families to use their experience with the child to report on development. Screening tools are not diagnostic but can help identify areas of potential concern. All child development and education programs could use screening tools periodically as part of their continuous system of observing and recording development. When each child's development is part of the ongoing conversation between families and the program, concerns can be addressed quickly and with mutual understanding.

If a program and family are sufficiently concerned about a child's development in one or more areas, the family may request an evaluation from the Part C program in the community. The results from regular screening in the child development and education program can provide useful information to the early intervention team. Besides the tools presented in Box 15.3, ongoing assessments such as the Ounce (Meisels, Dombro, Marsden, Weston, & Jewkes, 2003) may also be used to document children's development. An example of the Ounce Scale and how it is used was presented in Chapter 12.

Child Development and Education as a Natural Environment

Even now, in the 21st century, despite laws such as the Americans with Disabilities Act (ADA) designed to prevent discrimination, some teachers, directors, and home family providers routinely turn away any child identified as having a disability (see Box 15.4). In studies and workshops on this topic, teachers frequently voice concerns about not having the knowledge to care for children with disabilities, about children with disabilities requiring one-on-one care, and about the discomfort other children and families may feel (Kontos, 1988). Family care providers are concerned that the child with disabilities will require so much attention that they will have to serve fewer children and thus reduce their income (Buell, Gamel-McCormick, & Hallam, 1999). Although that may be true for an infant with multiple disabilities—for example, on a respirator and gastrostomy tube, with visual and hearing impairment—that description would match only a very few of the thousands of infants and toddlers identified each year with disabilities.

Teachers and families who have experienced inclusive services describe them as having many benefits. Teachers with positive experiences in serving infants and toddlers with disabilities enjoy their jobs more and have more positive attitudes toward serving other children with disabilities (Soodak & Erwin, 2000). When they were given opportunities to prepare themselves, learn additional strategies, and establish the supports they felt they needed, teachers were positive about supporting a child's membership in their community (Cross, Traub, Hutter-Pishagi, & Shelton, 2004). Those teachers who approached the challenge with confidence believed that inclusion promotes gains in socialization among all children (Diamond, 2001).

BOX 15.4

Child Care and the Americans with Disabilities Act (ADA)

1. The ADA applies to privately run and publicly run child care centers and the program's interactions with children, parents, guardians, and potential customers as well as in their employment practices. Child care centers run by religious organizations may be exempt.
2. The ADA has these specific requirements for child care centers:

- Centers cannot exclude children with disabilities from their programs unless their presence would pose a *direct threat* to the health or safety of others or require a *fundamental alteration* of the program.
- Centers have to make *reasonable modifications* to their policies and practices to integrate children, parents, and guardians with disabilities into their programs unless doing so would constitute a *fundamental alteration.*
- Centers must provide appropriate auxiliary aids and services needed for *effective communication* with children or adults with disabilities, when doing so would not constitute an *undue burden.*
- Centers must generally make their facilities accessible to persons with disabilities. Existing facilities are subject to the *readily achievable* standard for barrier removal, whereas newly constructed facilities and any altered portions of existing facilities must be *fully accessible.*

Source: U.S. Department of Justice (1997).

Teacher Attitudes and Strategies

Maintain a Positive Attitude

Nothing is more important for the successful inclusion of an infant or toddler with disabilities than the attitudes of the adults involved. Teachers should reflect on their own feelings about disabilities and discuss any concerns they might have about serving a child with disabilities—concerns, for example, about possibly harming the child through lack of knowledge or skills or being unable to manage the regular ratios when the group has a child perceived to have high needs. Program directors or early intervention team members may be helpful in participating in this conversation.

Ask for Information Sharing

Teachers need adequate information in order to serve every child. Teachers should have the opportunity to form their questions and have them answered by the family, health professionals, or early intervention providers. Families should also feel free to ask questions regarding the program's ability to provide any specific services or adaptations needed by their child. If Part C is serving the child, the service coordinator can be helpful in facilitating what might be an uncomfortable conversation. Inclusion is most successful when care teachers and parents have frequent opportunities to exchange information, when they are open to each other's suggestions and ideas, and when they value each other's contributions to the children and the success of the experience (Cross et al., 2004).

Document Children's Competence

Documentation can be useful in helping care teachers maintain positive attitudes toward children with disabilities. Documentation of infants and toddlers with disabilities can reflect images of active, productive, and social experiences back to the child, as well as help keep positive images of the child in the care teacher's mind. Although it is easy to see how this sort of chart (see Table 15.1) would be appropriate for any child, it can be particularly helpful in keeping the child's strengths, rather than needs and disabilities, in the teacher's mind. The chart shown in Table 15.1 describes the interests and abilities of an 18-month-old girl with Down syndrome.

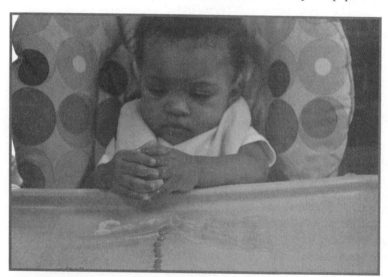

This child is feeling the sponge used for painting, tentatively but with interest. She explores new tactile experiences very slowly.

Adapt Materials and Activities

The large list of disabling conditions described at the beginning of this chapter demonstrated that disabilities might have all sorts of functional effects. Some children have normal or high intelligence but are unable to control their

TABLE 15.1   **Sarah's Favorite Things to Do!**

Toys	Meals	Outdoors
Sarah loves hugging and carrying her doll, being just like her own mommy. Sarah can put the rings on the stick and the shapes in the box—and she likes to practice that a lot!	Sarah is a good friend at the table. She drinks from a cup and feeds herself "finger food" snacks. She smiles and laughs and is interested in her friends. Sarah signs to Miss Rose to tell her what she wants at mealtimes.	Sarah stays close to Miss Rose outdoors. She likes pulling the "horsie" riding toy around the playground as much as riding it. Sarah loves playing in sand and water.

Friends	Grown-ups	Nap Time
Sarah looks for Ona and Peter when she gets to school. She likes to be near friends and to give hugs.	Sarah loves her mommy, daddy, and grandmas. She especially likes to be with Miss Rose during the day. Sometimes Sarah likes grown-ups to help her when she gets frustrated with a toy or a puzzle.	Sarah gets tired at school and sleeps heavily at nap time. She likes to listen to stories, quiet music, and have her back rubbed as she falls asleep. Cuddling in the rocking chair is a big treat!

bodies. Some move well but have difficulty processing and understanding information. Some have difficulty focusing attention. Some have difficulty in social relationships. Some have poor sensory abilities. Obviously, different strategies serve different children.

Without question, there is no easier age group for full inclusion than infants and toddlers. Infant and toddler services are already highly individualized. In fact, early childhood educators are constantly making unconscious little adjustments to particular needs: Riley needs protected space to play, Freddie won't eat foods of a certain texture, Rachel needs lots of warning before a transition, and Li needs moments of quiet connection and cuddling throughout the day. Care teachers make these adjustments without thinking about them. High-quality programs have low ratios and small groups. The typically developing infants and toddlers haven't lived long enough to greet their peers with disabilities with any preconceived biases. Still, a number of considerations and strategies ensure that inclusion results in a successful, meaningful experience for everyone involved:

> One of the roles of teachers in inclusive child care settings is to serve as *inclusion facilitators*. Facilitating inclusion simply means making sure that children with special needs are incorporated into all of the ongoing activities of the classroom, including daily living activities as well as play activities. An emphasis on facilitating inclusion ensures that children who have disabilities are not set apart from the other children, such as by eating separately because they need individual care, being kept indoors when the other children are on the playground, or being entertained by one teacher while other children are involved in group activities.
>
> *(O'Brien, 1997, p. 35)*

TABLE 15.2   **Principles of Adapting Toys and Materials**

Stability	Usefulness of Information	Achieving Goals Through Play
Increases baby's control of objects, ability to explore and learn	Provides information through senses and use of body most effective for the baby	Naturally engages baby to attempt goals such as bringing hands together at midline, isolating fingers, or making sounds
• Use Velcro or tape to hold items to table. • Large handles make an item easier to pick up or move. • A weighted bottom makes the item less likely to tip over. • Use thicker materials (e.g., board books rather than paper).	• Simplify materials by offering fewer pieces. • Use sharp contrasts for child with visual impairment. • Take out sound-makers for children who are sensitive to too much stimulation.	• Offer toys that require both hands to hold them. • Blow bubbles to pop when hands are clapped together. • Poke at bubbles with one finger. • Offer toys that require an isolated finger such as a little piano or telephone.

As shown in Table 15.2, adapting toys and materials for infants and toddlers with special needs is a three-step process: (1) understand what the children are learning and how they learn, (2) provide materials that contain the information in a relevant form, and (3) ensure that the materials are stable. One of the first considerations in planning learning activities for infants or toddlers with disabilities is to understand which concepts and skills are currently emerging for them and which kinds of toys and materials they find interesting. For example, infants who are just beginning to learn that they can hold on to an object and move it enjoy rattles that are light, fist size, and make noise. Infants who are beginning to explore spatial relationships enjoy putting objects into containers and dumping them out again. Infants and toddlers with disabilities are making the same cognitive discoveries as typically developing infants, although possibly not on the same timeline or through the same sources of information. Provide materials that are responsive to the actions they are capable of producing. Infants and toddlers with disabilities do well when the materials they use are stable enough to stay in one place and not be easily knocked over or roll away. The information must be available to them in ways that make sense—for example, simplify the information in stacking cups by offering fewer at a time or use a light table as the playing surface for a child with visual impairment.

View the part of the video that emphasizes the importance of inclusion for children with special needs. What strategies are care teachers using to include and support children with special needs?

Arrange the Environment

As older infants become mobile, it might become necessary for the teacher to move the young child with physical impairments to be able to stay close to her friends. Supportive seating that allows the toddler to sit at the snack table with everyone else is more conducive to participation than a seat with its own tray. Children with visual impairments, in particular, need the furniture and pathways in the environment to remain unchanged so that they are able to learn how to get from one area to another on their own.

Use Group Affection Activities

In so many ways, we encourage infants and toddlers to be kind to each other. We remind them to be gentle in their touch and give them the general advice to "Be nice." We can be specific in our directions to children as to how they can be most helpful to a child with a disability. It might be "Take her hand," or it might be "Just wait—he'll get it." Teachers can reinforce the toddler with special needs, using positive descriptive words, when he stays close to the other children and observes or imitates their social play: "You really like watching Andre with those trucks. Andre has a good time playing cars and trucks." A further step would be to help the typically developing child invite the child with special needs into the activity: "Andre, would you please give this truck to Jack?" (Lowenthal, 1995, p. 22).

Meet Therapeutic Goals

Infants and toddlers with disabilities should have an early intervention team working with them and an IFSP defining their therapeutic goals. Teachers can promote the mastery of these goals through well-chosen play activities, whereby the toys and materials inherently suggest the therapeutic actions. Children with nervous system and motor disorders are often working on goals such as using both hands at midline, loosening their fists to use their fingers, using fingers in isolation, and using increasingly sophisticated grasps. Play activities that promote these goals would include offering toys large enough to require both hands be used together, toy pianos, tape players, and other single-button-activated toys. Small toys (but not so small as to be a choking hazard) and foods such as bits of bananas or cereal pieces all encourage grasps. One of the best materials for promoting these actions is bubbles. Smashing bubbles with both hands clapping is a great way to bring the hands to midline. Poking bubbles promotes the use of isolated fingers.

Teachers may use a variety of positioning techniques to support children with motor issues to maximize their use of their bodies. Therapists may show teachers how to use simple material such as rolled-up towels to support positions or may provide standing boards or special chairs. Children with severe motor issues may be introduced to toys that run on switches, devices that direct battery-operated toys through the use of whatever part of the body has most control. Switches may be operated through touch, sound, head position, sucking, or blowing. The early intervention team should provide these materials to child development and education programs.

Many therapeutic goals for infants and toddlers require only the same materials and teacher interactions as those for typically developing children. Care teachers create environments that encourage focus, attention, and exploration. They expand play and language. They provide an emotional tone of calm interest to support learning and joyful celebration to support accomplishment. They respond to vocalizations from infants as though they were words spoken with meaning. They promote kindness and empathy toward other children. These actions all support the achievement of therapeutic goals by infants and toddlers with disabilities.

Summary

Infant and toddler care teachers today routinely serve children with disabilities in their community settings. High-quality practices serve children with disabilities well, but it is helpful for teachers to know some additional things:

- Although there are thousands of potentially disabling conditions, no condition or diagnosis defines a child. Early childhood educators need to learn about each child, her likes and dislikes, her personality, her routines and expectations, and the effects of the disabling condition. No one needs to know about all disabilities and their effects; a care teacher simply needs to know how to understand one baby at a time, how to read her cues, and how to develop a relationship with that one child.
- The Program for Infants and Toddlers with Disabilities (Part C of the Individuals with Disabilities Education Act) provides early intervention services including service coordination, physical therapy, occupational therapy, speech therapy, and educational services.
- Early intervention teams serving infants and toddlers with disabilities should be able to support the child in child development and education. Care teachers may have a copy of the individualized family service plan (IFSP), which describes the developmental goals and strategies to help the child achieve the goals. The early interventionists may provide special equipment needed to support the child. Early intervention services may actually be provided within the child development and education setting.
- Care teachers use many strategies to adapt materials and activities for their successful use by the infants and toddlers with disabilities. Toys need to be stable, match the child's current interests, and provide contingent responses to the child's actions. Care teachers need to promote the close physical proximity of infants and toddlers with disabilities to typically developing children as well as the social and emotional connections among children.
- Well-trained infant-toddler educators have the ability to serve all children well because the elements of quality are the same for all children. It is the willingness of the care teacher to include a child with disabilities that is the greatest indicator for success.

Key Terms

central nervous system disorders   genetic syndromes   person-first language
sensory impairments

Reflections and Resources for the Reader

REFLECTIONS

1. Our own life experiences, or lack of experiences, around people with disabilities may influence our comfort with inclusive services. Reflect on your experiences and how they influence your feelings about serving infants and toddlers with disabilities in a child development and education program.

2. If you were designing an inclusive infant-toddler environment, would you do anything differently from what you would do only for children without disabilities?

OBSERVATION AND APPLICATION OPPORTUNITIES

1. Contact the Part C coordinator in your community and see if you could talk to parents of an infant or toddler with a disability about their child's disability, their use of a child development and education program, and their early intervention experiences.
2. Observe an inclusive infant-toddler program. What works well? What would you change?
3. If you were preparing a parent handbook for an infant-toddler program, what would you include to let families know that you serve all children? Have a parent review the handbook and give you feedback on the relevance and completeness of the document.

SUPPLEMENTARY ARTICLES AND BOOKS TO READ

Brekken, L. (2011). Early Head Start and early intervention. Partnerships that make a difference for young children with disabilities and their families. *ZERO TO THREE JOURNAL, 31*(4), 32–38.

Cook, R., Klein, M., Chen, D., & Tessier, A. (2012). *Adapting early childhood curricula for children with special needs* (8th ed.). Columbus, OH: Pearson.

Gebhard, B., & Oser, C. (2012). Putting the pieces together for infants and toddlers. Comprehensive, coordinated systems. ZERO TO THREE. Retrieved from www.zerotothree.org/public-policy/policy-toolkit/systemssinglesmarch5.pdf

Hebbeler, K., Greer, M., & Hutton, B. (2011). From then to now: The evolution of Part C. *ZERO TO THREE JOURNAL, 31*(4), 4–10.

McWilliam, R. A. (2011). The top 10 mistakes in early intervention in natural environments—and the solutions. *ZERO TO THREE JOURNAL, 31*(4), 11–16.

INTERESTING LINKS

The Arc of the United States

www.theARC.org/
The Arc of the United States makes many helpful documents available at this Web site. For instance, *All Kids Count: Child Care and the Americans with Disabilities Act* (ADA) is a resource manual published by the Arc that can be downloaded from this site.

Child Care Plus

www.ccplus.org/
Child Care Plus (the Center on Inclusion in Early Childhood) publishes a wonderful newsletter for teachers—and the site has interesting and practical articles on adapting materials, environments, and activities for children with special needs.

Council for Exceptional Children

www.cec.sped.org/
Here you will find the Individuals with Disabilities Education Act (IDEA) reauthorization bill of 2004.

YouTube

www.youtube.com
Use the key words "sticky mittens" to see a toddler using velcroed mittens to play.

16

The Infant-Toddler Professional

Identity, Relationships, and Resources

LEARNING OUTCOMES

After reading this chapter, you will be able to:

- Describe what it means to be an infant and toddler professional
- Explain key aspects of an infant and toddler professional's experience
- Describe key components of professional development and write your visions, values, and philosophy
- Describe a program organizational structure that is relationship based, including key components of conflict resolution and a mentor-mentee relationship
- Write an advocacy statement for the importance of quality infant and toddler programs

The Infant and Toddler Profession

We end the book by coming full circle in our quest for quality experiences for infants and toddlers. We began the book by discussing how important the infant and toddler years are as a foundation for the development of children's capacities to learn and love. We have endeavored for you to *always* consider the experience of infants and toddlers—from their perspective. In many chapters we have detailed *respect for the child*: what the individual child brings to a relationship; the uniqueness of each child; and how active, curious, and motivated a child is to learn. We have emphasized the importance of *responsive and loving relationships* in the home and in a program for the child's sense of well-being and his or her future as a capable and caring human being. We have stressed that we cannot underestimate the importance of *quality early experiences* for infants and toddlers and their families.

All of this information leads us to the importance of the infant and toddler **professional** who creates the opportunities for infants and toddlers and their families to thrive (ZERO TO THREE, 2012). As defined in Chapter 1, infant and toddler professionals are teachers or administrators in child development and education centers, family child care providers, and early intervention specialists. This chapter is about the importance of developing an identity as an infant and toddler professional; becoming reflective; creating and nurturing relationships for professional development; and advocating for yourself, children, families, programs, and your community to move the profession forward.

> **professional**
>
> A person who is qualified, skilled, or trained.

This chapter encourages infant and toddler professionals to make choices about their own professional path. Professionals are decision makers; they take an active part in determining the quality of their work and the quality of the program where they work.

Greenman and Stonehouse (1996) define *professionalism* as "the ability to accept responsibility and to commit to a standard of performance that sets an example and earns the respect of others" (p. 302). But how do we know that there is an infant and toddler profession?

Professional Identity

> *When Jeffrey, an infant teacher at Wee Care Child Care, walked out into the sunshine on the first day of the National Early Childhood Conference, he felt like a professional for the first time. After attending several sessions, he realized that he really did have some specialized knowledge about how to work with infants and their families. He felt good about his chosen profession.*

> Listen to Sue Bredekamp speak in the clips on Advice for Those Entering Early Childhood Education: Part 1 and Part 2. As you listen, think about the important characteristics of an infant/toddler professional.

Carter and Curtis (2012) describe the early childhood (birth to 8 years) profession as follows:

> Over the past thirty years, the early childhood profession has come of age. Early childhood caregivers and teachers have now become a full-fledged workforce with standards, a code of ethics, a shared language, definitions of core competencies and best practices, and a huge selection of conferences and resources. An ever-expanding body of research-based knowledge includes professional development and accreditation systems. (p. 16)

Katz (1995) identified eight attributes of a profession:

1. The well-being of a society is served.
2. Enough emotional distance is maintained from those served that the professional can exercise clear judgment.

3. There are agreed-upon principles and ethics.
4. A specialized knowledge base is present and maintained.
5. Prolonged and specialized training is required.
6. There are clear standards of practice.
7. Work is performed with some autonomy on the part of the client (i.e., professionals are not supervised every moment of the day).
8. There is an altruistic mission or vision.

With respect to the last attribute, a profession sees itself as altruistic—that is, doing work that is essential to society. Professionals identify their goals with the good of humanity. This altruism can mean working longer hours on occasion and inhibits professionals from slipping into customer/sales language.

The infant and toddler profession has all of the attributes listed and we will discuss them in this chapter. Several of the criteria relate to a profession having a specialized knowledge base. This specialized knowledge base is reflected in the **professional standards of practice** developed for a profession.

professional standards of practice
Knowledge, skills, and dispositions needed by the professional.

Professional Standards

Standards ensure that infants and toddlers will experience high-quality interactions and environments and set high expectations for the preparation and performance of early childhood professions—the knowledge, skills, and disposition that all professionals should possess.

Let's examine the standards for professionals who work with children from birth to age 8 developed by national organizations, and then we will explore the specific standards set for infant and toddler professionals.

Standards Set by Professional Organizations

The National Association for the Education of Young Children (NAEYC, 2011) has written standards that are intended for early childhood professionals who are being prepared at the associate, baccalaureate, and graduate levels to work with children from birth to age 8. Early childhood professional standards include the values of the profession as well as a vision for the preparation of early childhood professionals. As you can see in Table 16.1, the NAEYC standards identify the knowledge, skills, and dispositions (attitudes and values) that research has identified as crucial for professionals to have to perform their work with young children well. The NAEYC standards are taught in an approved college or university that is recognized by NAEYC as an accredited institution.

The Council for Exceptional Children (CEC, 2009) has also developed standards for professionals working with children with disabilities from birth to age 8. These standards represent the knowledge, skills, and dispositions that all beginning early

This family child care provider knows how to develop a relationship-based program.

TABLE 16.1 NAEYC Standards Summary

Standard 1: Promoting Child Development and Learning

1a: Knowing and understanding young children's characteristics and needs

1b: Knowing and understanding the multiple influences on early development and learning

1c: Using developmental knowledge to create healthy, respectful, supportive, and challenging learning environments

Standard 2: Building Family and Community Relationships

2a: Knowing about and understanding diverse family and community characteristics

2b: Supporting and engaging families and communities through respectful, reciprocal relationships

2c: Involving families and communities in young children's development and learning

Standard 3: Observing, Documenting, and Assessing to Support Young Children and Families

3a: Understanding the goals, benefits, and uses of assessment

3b: Knowing about and using observation, documentation, and other appropriate assessment tools and approaches

3c: Understanding and practicing responsible assessment to promote positive outcomes for each child

3d: Knowing about assessment partnerships with families and with professional colleagues

Standard 4: Using Developmentally Effective Approaches

4a: Understanding positive relationships and supportive interactions as the foundation of their work with children

4b: Knowing and understanding effective strategies and tools for early education

4c: Using a broad repertoire of developmentally appropriate teaching/learning approaches

4d: Reflecting on own practice to promote positive outcomes for each child

Standard 5: Using Content Knowledge to Build Meaningful Curriculum

5a: Understanding content knowledge and resources in academic disciplines.

5b: Knowing and using the central concepts, inquiry tools, and structures of content areas or academic disciplines

5c: Using own knowledge, appropriate early learning standards, and other resources to design, implement, and evaluate developmentally meaningful and challenging curriculum for each child

Standard 6: Becoming a Professional

6a: Identifying and involving oneself with the early childhood field

6b: Knowing about and upholding ethical standards and other early childhood professional guidelines

6c: Engaging in continuous, collaborative learning to inform practice

6d: Integrating knowledgeable, reflective, and critical perspectives on early education

6e: Engaging in informed advocacy for young children and the early childhood profession

Source: NAEYC (2009). Pages 11–16. Used with permission from NAEYC. Excerpted from NAEYC, "NAEYC Standards for Early Childhood Professional Preparation," Position statement, (Washington, DC: NAEYC, 2009). Copyright © 2009 NAEYC. Reprinted with permission. Full text of this position statement is available at http://www.naeyc.org/files/naeyc/files/2009%20Professional%20Prep%20stdsRevised%204_12.pdf

childhood *special education* teachers should have and include standards related to the development and characteristics of learners, individual learning differences, instructional strategies, learning environments and social interactions, language, instructional planning, assessment, and professional and ethical practice. The CEC Web site (www.cec.sped.org/) contains detailed information concerning the standards.

NAEYC and CEC have collaborated in writing the standards for each organization to ensure that *all* early childhood professionals are prepared to work with children with a range of abilities and disabilities. There are also specific established standards for infant and toddler professionals.

Specific Standards for Infant and Toddler Professionals

One example of standards specific to the infant and toddler professional is the Child Development Associate (CDA). The CDA credential is a nationally recognized credential awarded to early childhood teachers and caregivers who demonstrate competencies related to nurturing children's physical, social, emotional, and intellectual growth in a child development framework. Only the Council for Professional Recognition in Washington, D.C., can award a CDA credential. There are four types of CDA credentials:

- Center-Based Preschool
- Center-Based Infant/Toddler
- Family Child Care
- Home Visitor

The CDA Competency Standards are the core of the CDA program. Composed of Goals and Functional Areas, they are statements of the skills needed to be a competent teacher and the basis upon which teachers are assessed. The Competency Goals establish the framework for caregiver behavior, and the 13 Functional Areas describe the major tasks or functions caregivers must complete in order to carry out the Competency Goals. The goal areas and functional areas are the same for each type of credential, but the content varies with each credential. The Competency Goals are as follows:

Goal I: To establish and maintain a safe, healthy learning environment
Goal II: To advance physical and intellectual competence
Goal III: To support social and emotional development and to provide positive guidance
Goal IV: To establish positive and productive relationships with families
Goal V: To ensure a well-run purposeful program responsive to participant needs
Goal VI: To maintain a commitment to professionalism

If a professional does not have a degree in early childhood education or early intervention, then earning a CDA credential is important. See web site www.cdacouncil.org for more information on the requirements of earning the CDA credential, including why it is important to do so.

A state may require a specific infant and toddler credential as well. New York, for example, provides the New York State Infant Toddler Care and Education credential to formally recognize a professional's specialized knowledge of infant and toddler care and development. This credential is one of the options required of child care providers to be head of a group in a center program.

All of these standards have similar content and define the knowledge base of the infant and toddler profession and, by doing so, advance the recognition of the profession as legitimate and important. These standards are based on research that provides evidence for particular professional knowledge, skills, and dispositions that result in optimal infant and toddler development and educational experiences. The standards represent key concepts supported by research evidence that are now a part of best practice recommendations (Lally, 2003). These include the importance of

- Continuity of relationships among parents, teachers, and children
- Attachment to primary caregivers

- Reading infants' cues
- The need for attention to individual children's sensitivities and temperamental characteristics in group care
- The interrelatedness of developmental domains
- The role of day-to-day encounters in shaping the child's development of self

It is important for professionals to know the standards of their profession because they represent the knowledge base for that profession. Infant and toddler professionals can be proud that there is specialized knowledge they should have in order to provide optimal care and education experiences for babies.

The Professional's Experience

What's Different About Being an Infant and Toddler Professional?

The primary difference between infant and toddler professionals and professionals who work with older children centers on the intensity and intimacy of relationships. *First, there is the relationship with the infant or toddler.* There is a physical and emotional intensity about working with infants and toddlers (Honig, 2013; Recchia & Loizou, 2002). Keenan (1997, 1998), in her journey to become an infant and toddler professional, noted that in this work professionals provide more intimate contact and physical support with infants and toddlers than they do when working with older children.

The physical nature of the work requires an infant and toddler professional to be involved in the most intimate routines with the infant and toddler—diapering, toileting, feeding, wiping noses, and drying tears. The emotional nature of the work requires that professionals and infants and toddlers develop an attachment to each other—an emotional connection. Although other professions do not recommend establishing an emotional relationship with the client, it *is* professional for infant and toddler professionals to have an emotional connection with each child, because that is what infants and toddlers need to thrive. Infants and toddlers need that emotional bond to the professional because (as has been emphasized through this textbook) it is through relationships that babies develop their sense of self-worth, their basic ability to trust others, their concept of how adults and people in general will treat them, and how effective they can be in relationships and in mastering their environment. Infant and toddler professionals must be emotionally available each day with each child in order to ensure that infants and toddlers thrive. In addition to making emotional connections, infant and toddler professionals create an environment in which everyone, including the professionals, can *live* together, not just *learn* together.

An infant and toddler professional knows how important it is to spend time with children individually or in very small informal groups.

Greenman, Stonehouse, and Schweikert (2008) highlight the importance of infant and toddler professionals in center or family child care and education programs creating a homelike environment. They emphasize that because children and adults live together often for many hours during the day, we need to consider that child care settings should be great places to live.

The second relationship that can be different for professionals of infants and toddlers is with families. Infant and toddler professionals, because of the emotional nature of the work, can sometimes have conflicting ideas with parents about what is best for the children. It can be challenging for families to share the care with professionals without becoming jealous or resentful, especially—which is important for the child—if the professional develops a close relationship with the infant or toddler. It can be challenging for the professional not to become competitive with the family over who knows what is best for the child. More so than professionals who work with older children, infant and toddler professionals must have *very* close relationships with families—constantly sharing information, delicately negotiating conflicts, and enthusiastically supporting the parent-child relationship.

The third relationship that is different for infant and toddler professionals is with other staff:

> Team collaboration takes on a particular significance in infant child care due to the physical and emotional demands of caring for such young children, the need for lower ratios of adults to children, and the inability of the children being cared for to speak for themselves.
>
> *(Recchia & Loizou, 2002, p. 134)*

Infant and toddler professionals must work as a team in center care and education programs and trust each other completely. When an infant or toddler needs to have a diaper changed in a center program, the teacher who is diapering trusts that the other teachers are automatically emotionally and physically available to the other children. So much of the communication is nonverbal. Professionals must work closely together, often in a small space, and respect each other's style of interacting with the children. Goals for the children must be made explicit. Tasks must be divided fairly. We discuss how to develop a caring community and use effective communication and conflict resolution strategies later in the chapter.

Infant and Toddler Professionals Must Know Themselves Well

Infant and toddler professionals must have self-awareness—"personal integration and inner security" (Cartwright, 1999, p. 4). This means that professionals will not impose their personal needs onto their relationships with children, nor do they project intentions onto an infant or toddler, such as thinking that an infant is crying *just* to aggravate them or that a toddler is saying "No" *just* to annoy them. Honig (1986) emphasizes how caregivers can do some internal personal history searching to make them more responsive professionals:

> One interesting way for caregivers to feel more comfortable about floor games and creative games with babies is to do some internal personal history searching. Inside each of us are old record players. Some records play positive praises and comforting comments from our past. Some of our old personal records carry warning, shaming, prohibitions about being a silly child, a naughty child, a bad baby. A caregiver needs to leave on the nurturant positive record players that can support and encourage safe explorations and expressions of curiosity and delight.

She or he may have to work hard to turn off punitive and disapproving records playing from the past. Such hard work will pay off as the caregiver becomes a person who is freer to enjoy toddlers with their "messiness" and with their delightful whimsies. (p. 209)

Infant and toddler professionals must reflect on how they handle separation and grieving. Professionals may have their heart broken because they must say good-bye to a child who has been with them since he was an infant and now is ready to transition to a preschool or kindergarten classroom. But infant and toddler professionals are willing to have their heart broken when a child transitions into a classroom for older children because they have been willing to invest in a strong, positive relationship with a child for 3 years. They know that the emotional connections developed because of *continuity of care* and *primary care* are absolutely vital for young children's optimal emotional and social development. If professionals have not done the work of reflecting on how they handle close relationships and good-byes, then the professionals may protect their own feelings rather than implement practices that they know are necessary for infants' and toddlers' well-being:

> Knowing ourselves involves exploring our strengths and vulnerabilities. We need to wonder about, and try to understand the meaning of, our reactions ("I got angry so quickly. Why is that?"), our frustrations ("I really get aggravated with judgmental staff members."), and the parts of our job that bring us joy ("I love it when families graduate from the program."). This exploration can sometimes be difficult or uncomfortable.
>
> *(Parlakian & Seibel, 2001, p. 6)*

Parlakian and Seibel (2001) note that when we, as infant and toddler professionals, are self-reflective, we can "better manage our emotional responses, better recognize our limitations, and better leverage our skills and strengths" (p. 6). A reflective professional also develops vision, values, and a philosophy of practice.

Professional Development: Visions, Values, and Philosophy

> If we are going to have infant care, then why not create places where babies love to go and we love to have them go? Instead of setting our sights so low, why not create places where our children will be amazed, enlivened, and overjoyed each day? Why stop at "Do no harm?"
>
> *(Lally, 2003, p. 34)*

Becoming the professional you want to be requires courage, commitment, and caring. Your values and vision will guide you to make important difficult decisions regarding your practice. Part of being a reflective, theory-based professional is to reflect on your vision for children and families, professional philosophy, ethical values, and professional plan (your vision for yourself).

What if care teachers in a center are being bounced around from classroom to classroom each day with no regard for the relationship that you know is critical for infants' development? Because care teachers have knowledge of and a value for the importance of relationships, including primary and continuity of care, they problem solve with others to try to make the situation better for infants and toddlers. Your values and vision are a guide to your behavior in this situation and others. How do you develop a vision?

Your Vision

Imagine the child care of our dreams, not just child care that's good enough. (Whitebook)

To develop a vision, reflect and discuss with others the following questions:

- What is the primary purpose of your work?
- What do you wish for infants and toddlers?
- What do you wish for families of infants and toddlers?
- What do you wish for programs for infants and toddlers?
- What do you wish for your community, nation, and world to support infants' and toddlers' optimal development?

A vision is different from a mission statement, as noted by Carter and Curtis (2010) and others:

> A mission statement is about purpose, but it is seldom about a dream. Typically, a mission statement tries to address a problem with a statement of services. A vision, on the other hand, goes beyond how things are to describe how we would like them to be. In the words of Susan Gross (1987), a vision is "what the world or society or an environment or community would like if that purpose were realized." (p. 20–21).

To develop your vision, ask, "What kind of life and experiences do I want for children and families?" Carter and Curtis (1998) tell us that "Your vision plays the same role in your program as your breath plays in your body—distributing the life force of oxygen throughout your system, exploring where things are tense and need some attention, and providing a rhythm for your muscles to do their collaborative work" (p. 10). Another way for infant and toddler professionals to clarify their vision and values is to develop a philosophy statement.

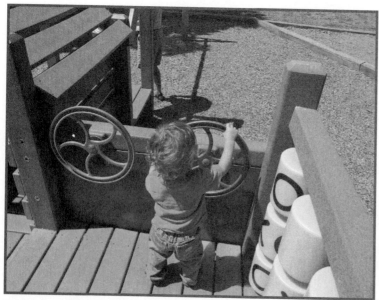

What is your vision for the type of community you want for infants and toddlers?

A Professional Philosophy Statement

A professional's philosophy statement includes what you believe about the rights of children, goals for children, what children need, how they learn best, the definition of *quality*, and why it matters for children and families. It includes what you believe about the role and responsibilities of the infant and toddler professional with children and families, your attitudes about inclusion of children with diverse needs and abilities, the critical aspects of an environment, and what type of curriculum and assessment process you think is important to provide. Developing a philosophy is a process rather than a product. It is ongoing and professionals should rewrite it often in their careers as they grow in knowledge and experience. Professionals can use their philosophy statement to reflect on their values and stay true to their principles as they progress in the profession.

Developing and Using a Code of Ethics

> *Ethics is how we treat children, families, colleagues, and community members—the people we work with, work for, and come to work to serve. (Israel)*

NAEYC and CEC have developed codes of ethical conduct for early childhood professionals. A code of ethics states the values of the profession and the guidelines for responsible behavior. See Box 16.1 for definitions of *code of ethics, values,* and *core values.*

NAEYC's (2005) Code of Ethics is divided into sections:

> Section I identifies the ethical responsibilities to children.
> Section II identifies the ethical responsibilities to families.
> Section III identifies the ethical responsibilities to colleagues.
> Section IV identifies the ethical responsibilities to community and society.

BOX 16.1

Ethics Terminology

code of ethics: Defines the core values of the field and gives guidance for what professionals should do in situations in which they encounter conflicting obligations or responsibilities in their work.

values: Qualities or principles that individuals believe to be desirable or worthwhile and that they prize for themselves, for others, and for the world in which they live.

core values: Commitments held by a profession that are consciously and knowingly embraced by its practitioners because they make a contribution to society. There is a difference between personal values and core values of a profession.

Infant and toddler professionals are encouraged to become familiar with this Code of Ethics and apply it to their work with children, families, colleagues, and the community and society.

The Division for Early Childhood (DEC) of the CEC has developed a Code of Ethics for professionals working with children with disabilities (DEC, 2009). The code provides principles and guidelines for practice including professional practice, professional development and preparation, responsive family practices, and ethical and evidence-based practices. For example, the principle Professional Practice states that "We shall demonstrate in our behavior and language respect and appreciation for the unique value and human potential of each child."

Both the NAEYC and DEC Codes of Ethics provide guidelines for your vision, your values, and your personal philosophy. Infant and toddler professionals work in organizations, though. How can organizations support infant and toddler professional development?

Organizational Structure, Programs, and Policies

Infant and toddler professionals (except for family child care home providers) usually work within an organizational structure in a program. Carter and Curtis (1998) note that "while a growing emphasis has been placed on staff qualifications and training, little attention has been given to the working conditions and resources caregivers and teachers need to do their jobs well" (p. 19). When a structure is in place, it can either support or undermine the professional's development.

The Organization of a Program: Are You Treated Like a Professional?

Bittel (reported in Shoemaker, 2000) discusses how supervisors can treat their employees as professionals:

1. Realize that professional employees want to be recognized as members of a profession.
2. Ensure that credit and recognition from top management and parents are given to employees for outstanding work and unusual accomplishments.
3. Give proper dignity to the title of each position held by each employee.
4. Adopt liberal policies with respect to time off for personal reasons.
5. Encourage knowledgeable workers to take part in the activities of their professional societies. (p. 202)

Decker and Decker (2001) note that in early childhood programs, "the most important role of the administrator is to enable conditions that lead to enriching professional life for staff" (p. 122). As you consider employment in a particular program, you may want to reflect on the organizational structure, policies, and procedures of the program. Ask for an organizational chart to determine where you fit in the organizational structure. Some center programs may have a board of directors that has authority over the program director, who then is responsible for office staff, maintenance staff, and head teachers in a center. Other organizations may have different structures.

As a potential employee, you will want to consider the policy and procedures manual developed by the program. This manual should contain the goals or specific purposes of the program and how the program will achieve these goals. Policies are written as comprehensive statements of decisions, principles, or courses of action to achieve the goals. Policies directly answer the question "What is to be done, and by whom?" For example, there may be a statement that one of the care teacher's responsibilities is to supervise teaching assistants who work in the same classroom as the teacher. Job descriptions are critical to your understanding of the role and responsibilities of a particular position in a program.

The organizational structure, policies, and procedures will inform you of the type of program to which you are applying, including the goals, procedures for achieving those goals, and who is responsible for accomplishing the goals. You also may want to consider if the program emphasizes shared decision making.

Shared Decision Making

shared decision making

Meaningful, collaborative decision making.

Shared decision making is a concept discussed by Jorde-Bloom (2000) to emphasize the importance of the participation of professionals in decisions that are made in the program where they work. Meaningful participation by all of the professionals who work together in a program enhances the trust and commitment to the organization. In a program that emphasizes shared decision making, a professional would be involved in a variety of decisions.

The infant and toddler professional could

1. decide on the content for new staff orientation and contribute ideas for the type of training they receive
2. collaborate with the administration to select materials, set the daily schedule, and create a curriculum

3. contribute to the development of strategies to inform and involve the community, including fund-raising activities

4. establish policies for working with families in a responsive way

5. contribute to a monthly newsletter to families with information on child development and quality practices

6. contribute to the agenda, goals, and content of staff meetings

Shared decision making may take place in some or most of the ways described. Usually there is a continuum of the professional's level of participation in these decisions. When there is shared decision making in an infant-toddler program, then there is likely to be improved employee morale, job satisfaction, and commitment to the organization (Jorde-Bloom, 1995). As you look for employment, you may want to consider whether shared decision making is emphasized in the organization to which you are applying.

As an administrator in infant and toddler organizations, you will want to emphasize the following:

1. Strong leadership that encourages creativity and success

2. Empowerment of teachers to make some decisions on their own

3. The opportunity for professional growth and career advancement

4. Membership and participation in professional organizations

5. The feeling of support and collaboration among staff

6. Real opportunities to work with peers to gather information, share ideas, and get support

All professionals deserve a quality work environment, as described by Eggbeer, Mann, and Gilkerson (2003):

> All individuals working with babies and toddlers deserve a work environment that values and supports their curiosity, their attempts to understand the meaning of behavior, their efforts to observe closely and to try new things, and their striving to be a more responsive partner to the children in their care and to the parents of these children. (p. 39)

A supportive program structure and shared decision making can support professional development. Of course, in a bioecological model (Bronfenbrenner, 2004), we know that funding, public policies, and the value our country places on infants, toddlers, and their families affect the work environment.

Developing Relationships and Community Within the Program for Professional Development

Relationships with other staff in a program or in your professional organization are among the most important aspects of your work, contributing to your positive or negative feelings about the work situation and your career as an infant and toddler professional (Klinkner, Riley, & Roach, 2005) Whether your relationships with other professionals are productive or destructive will also affect the children and families with whom you work. When everyone on a staff is working together and there is a sense of community in the workplace, then positive feelings filter down to the staff's relationships with children and families. In this section, we explore a variety of ways that relationships can support professional development.

Developing a Professional Relationship-Based Community

The skills needed to create a supportive and inspiring workplace include *respect, reflect,* and *relate*—concepts that we can apply to professionals' relationships with each other as well as their relationships with children. Carter and Curtis (1998) state that professionals need to discover who they can be *together:* "To build a group culture and a sense of community, we need to know who we are and why we are here, and to begin to discover who we can be together" (p. 85). This process starts with respect.

Respect

Respect for your teammates includes recognizing their humanity—their need for feeling as if they are contributing and valued members of the team. It is recognizing that the need for emotional connections is just as strong for adults as it is for children. And, it is respecting that each person has strengths and can contribute in different ways.

Zoglio (1997) asks the following questions, which we think capture part of what it means to respect others on your team:

1. At meetings, do you listen well to others?
2. When you disagree with others, how often do you differ with the idea, not the person, encouraging members to share even unusual ideas or minority opinions?
3. How often do you recognize special talents of your colleagues by asking them for input on particular projects?
4. If other members miss a meeting, how often do you let them know that they were missed, perhaps expressing disappointment because you would have liked their input on something?
5. How often do you personally compliment team members when they offer ideas, facilitate decision making, or put aside personal interests for the good of the group?*

Besides respecting the strengths of others, you can also reflect on your emotional and recognition needs as a team member and how you are contributing to the program.

Reflect

To become a relationship-based team member, you can ask yourself: "What are my communication skills and how do I handle conflict?" When you are communicating with others, do you express yourself clearly? Do you listen with your eyes by looking at the speaker? Do you let others finish their sentences before you respond? What are your **responding habits**?

responding habits

Typical ways of reacting to other professionals.

Zoglio (1997) suggests questions that can help you reflect on your responding habits. We have added the examples after each question to be relevant to the infant and toddler profession.

1. Do you demonstrate that you are listening by reflecting the feeling of the speaker? *("So, you are feeling upset with the parent who yelled at you.")*
2. Do you check your understanding of what others say by paraphrasing the content? *("Your main concern is finding time to talk with Visha's parent?")*

*Source: From *Teams At Work: 7 Keys to Success* by Suzanne Zoglio, PhD. Used with permission.

3. Do you try to expand your understanding of what was said by asking related questions? *("Are you saying that Visha's mom was upset with you because she thought you didn't talk with her enough?")*

4. Do you begin your response with agreement first and objections second? *("I agree with you about the importance of having a special conference with each parent each month. I'm concerned about how we will find time to do that.")*

5. When disagreeing, do you state under what conditions you agree? *("I could go along with that idea if we can do it within the workday and not have to come out again at night.")*

6. When disagreeing, do you show respect for the individual's thinking, sharing, and taking a risk? *("That's a creative idea; let's talk to the coordinator about discussing it at the next staff meeting.")**

Despite reflecting on and using great communication skills, conflicts happen! When people work closely together in an environment where decisions with teammates often have to be made quickly and where you *live* together every day for long periods of time, then there are going to be differences of opinion, disagreements about practice, and diversity in how people relate to each other. How you and your teammates resolve conflicts will make or break your experience in the workplace. **Conflict resolution skills** are among the most important that you can learn. Zoglio (1997) identifies steps to a win-win conflict management strategy:

> **conflict resolution skills**
> Skills for deciding solutions to disagreements.

1. Prepare powerfully.
   - Identify your position/interest. Ask, "What do I want? Why do I want it?"
   - Speculate on the other party's stated position and underlying interests. Ask, "What do they want? Why do they want it?"

2. Approach positively.
   - Acknowledge that you have thought about the other party's needs: "I've thought about what's important to you. You'd like _____. Is that pretty close?"
   - State your win-win intent: "I really want to find a solution that will satisfy both of us."
   - Seek commitment to a win-win (collaborative) process.

3. Clarify both points of view.
   - Check any areas of agreement: "Let's review where we agree. We both want _____. Right?"
   - Clarify areas of disagreement: "Let's review where we differ. You would like _____, and I would like _____. Right?"

4. Create alternatives.
   - Agree not to evaluate solutions, but to generate possibilities.
   - Brainstorm alternatives together.

5. Select a solution and agree on implementation.*

These strategies work if the conflict is not about the health, safety, or emotional well-being of infants and toddlers and also if the conflict is not about philosophy, beliefs, or ethics. When the conflicts are about these matters—for example, whether or not to pick up crying toddlers—then there has to be a discussion of why you think as you do, drawing upon research and what you know about the importance

*Source: From *Teams At Work: 7 Keys to Success* by Suzanne Zoglio, PhD. Used with permission.
*Source: From *Teams At Work: 7 Keys to Success* by Suzanne Zoglio, PhD. Used with permission.

of a child learning to trust others and develop self-regulation, the foundation for emotional health and learning. Being an ethical professional entails supporting your point of view with scientific evidence and standing by your principles of "do no harm" and "meet the emotional and social needs of children." You may need to ask a third person to help you and the other staff member sort out the reasons why a certain practice is critical to the health and well-being of children and families. Having an attitude of "let's find out" what information is available can lead to collaborative learning as a way to solve conflict.

Respond with Relationships in Mind

Respond to others by developing and committing to agreements. Agreements that are created in a collaborative way before disagreements occur make explicit basic values for how professionals will treat each other. Here are some areas for staff agreements, and approaches to criticism when those agreements are broken, as proposed by Carter (1992):

1. We will each have an attitude of flexibility and cooperation in our work here, thinking of the needs of others and the group as a whole, along with our own needs.
2. We will each carry a full share of the workload, which includes some extra hours outside our work schedule (i.e., parent-teacher conferences, meetings, planning and preparation of activities, record keeping, progress reports).
3. We will each communicate directly and honestly with each other. We will be respectful and honorable in our interactions.
4. When problems or difficulties related to our work arise, we will address them rather than ignore or avoid them.
5. We will all be informed of significant problems that affect the center. These will be communicated in person as soon as possible and in writing as necessary.
6. We understand that it is appropriate to seek help from the director on sensitive or difficult issues.
7. When necessary, we will use a criticism/self-criticism discussion process to identify attitudes and behaviors that are negatively affecting our agreements. (pp. 78–79)

Agreements are necessary for those times when the core values for how professionals treat each other are violated. However, responding to others in a caring and compassionate way that supports positive relationships can usually prevent troubles and lead to mutually satisfying solutions to problems.

The terms *respect, reflect,* and *relate* can be used to remind professionals of the important steps in developing a community of caring. By making a commitment to your own and others' sense of well-being in the workplace, you are modeling your focus on the importance of healthy relationships for families and children and making it possible to do relationship-based work with them. Let's examine more closely how to ensure your professional growth and that of others in your caring community by using a **reflective practice model** of professional development that includes reflective supervision and/or **mentoring**.

reflective practice model
Thoughtful consideration of your own beliefs and performance.

mentoring
Guiding another professional.

A Reflective Practice Model

A reflective practice model has two major characteristics. One is that professionals engage in reflecting on their professional practice and constructing their knowledge through active engagement in the problems of practice. The second is that there are relationships with other professionals that enhance and support the professionals' self-reflection. In regard to the first characteristic, professionals are encouraged to "reflect and construct knowledge for themselves in an active and participatory manner" (Friedman, 2004, p. 65). In a reflective practice model of professional development, professionals are encouraged to experience and solve real problems with an "emphasis on *how* classroom strategies were implemented and *why* teachers engaged in certain practices" (p. 65, emphasis in original). In regard to the second characteristic, a relationship is established between a professional and another who is good at helping others grow professionally. A relationship is established that renews each partner in it.

Both reflective supervision and mentoring are relationships for learning. These relationships involve regular meetings and strategies for supporting a person's professional development. Think about reflective supervision and mentoring both from the perspective of the one receiving supervision and mentoring *and* as one who is in the role of being a reflective supervisor or mentor. It is likely that the infant and toddler professional will be in both roles at some point in his or her career.

In both reflective supervision and the mentoring process, the golden rule is revisited:

This teacher benefits from reflective supervision and mentoring to help her improve her practice. She knows that sensitive responding to infants' and toddlers' needs is part of being a professional.

> *Treat adults as you want them to treat children. (Carter & Curtis, 1998, p. 123)*
> *Do unto others as you would have others do unto others. (Pawl & St. John, 1998)*

Both rules emphasize the idea that if we want professionals to treat children and families in thoughtful ways that build on the children's and families' ability to make decisions and problem solve, then we need to treat professionals in the same way in the mentoring process.

Reflective Supervision

Carly was looking forward to her weekly meeting with her reflective supervisor. Mia actually listened to her and empowered her to think through problems. Carly couldn't wait to tell Mia about her problem with Sheila, a new toddler in her class who was biting Cal, the smallest child in her group.

Reflective supervision entails regular meetings during which the two parties discuss what they are feeling and thinking with a supportive and thoughtful partner (Eggbeer, Mann, & Seibel, 2007; Heller & Gilkerson, 2009; Parlakian & Seibel, 2001; Schafer, 2010).

ZERO TO THREE describes three necessary ingredients for reflective supervision to work—regularity, collaboration, and reflection (Parliakan, 2001). Fenichel (1992) also emphasizes that each member of the relationship shares power, that there are mutual expectations for the relationship, and that there is open communication. Reflective supervision requires trust in one another, confidentiality, and trust in the ability of the supervisee to solve her own problems. The reflective supervisor provides the time and space for thoughtful reflection. The reflective supervisor engages in active listening (rephrasing the meaning of what the other says and does) and thoughtful questioning.

> *ZERO TO THREE describes supervision as an ongoing relationship, characterized by continuity and predictability, where power is shared, and where the supervisee has the opportunity to continually conceptualize what he/she is observing, feeling, and doing. In their words, supervision is a relationship for learning. (Gilkerson)*

Mentoring and Being Mentored

protégé

The person being mentored; a mentee.

Mentors, as defined by Bellm, Whitebook, and Hnatiuk (1997), are guides and role models who help whomever they are mentoring—their **protégés**, or **mentees**—to develop their *own* professional goals. They are capable of developing a supportive relationship with their protégés that is based on trust and confidentiality.

Responsibilities of the Mentor

mentee

A person being mentored; a protégé.

What are the responsibilities of mentors? As proposed by Bellm and colleagues (1997), mentors

- Share information
- Link their mentees to appropriate resources
- Share teaching strategies and information
- Guide and give ideas
- Assist the mentee—for example, in setting up the classroom
- Observe and discuss what was observed
- Promote self-observation and analysis
- Encourage reflection and model professionalism

Technology is enhancing the ability of mentors to provide opportunities for both new and experienced teachers to improve their practice. As Betty Walters from the Alaska Statewide Mentor Project stated, "Day-to-day interaction with other mentors and staff through email, on the telephone, and via Skype has been an enormous support for me as a first-year mentor" (Morehouse, 2008, n.p.).

Responsibilities of the Mentee

Protégés also have responsibilities as they participate in the relationship for learning. According to Bellm and colleagues (1997), protégés think about what they want to learn, are willing to examine their own practices, and engage in problem solving for change and improvement.

supervisor

One who manages, directs, and evaluates another in the workplace.

The mentoring relationship is built on trust, confidentiality, and commitment (Chu, 2014). Mentors are not in a position to evaluate the mentee's job performance—that responsibility is for a **supervisor**. For trust to develop, the protégé and the mentor must be able to discuss difficult issues and the challenges that the protégé is experiencing without fear of reprisal or judgment. The only exception, of course, is if the mentor suspects that the mentee is neglecting or abusing children. It must be made clear at the beginning of the relationship that the mentor is ethically and legally required to report suspected child abuse.

Parlakian and Seibel (2001) recommend that the following questions be used to create a more positive reflective supervision and mentoring relationship. If you are the one being supervised, then you could suggest that you would like to complete the questionnaire to help your mentor get to know you.

1. How did you become interested in infant-family issues?
2. When did you start the program? What positions have you held with this program?
3. Where did you work before?
4. What is your educational background?
5. How long have you been in your current position?
6. What are the best things about your job? What are the things you like the least about your job?
7. What do you find really motivating about working here?
8. What would you change about your job if you could? The organization?
9. What are your long-term goals? What would you like to be doing 5 years from now?
10. What do you think you are learning on the job right now? What are you struggling with at the moment?
11. What skills or abilities would you like to develop? (p. 19)

Becoming an Advocate

Never doubt that a small group of committed citizens can change the world. Indeed, it is the only thing that ever has. (Margaret Mead)

The role of being an advocate for children, families, programs, communities, and yourself is the last characteristic of an infant and toddler professional that we will discuss. An **advocate** is an enthusiastic supporter of a cause. We hope that you will become an advocate for the importance of the early years and relationship-based practice. As Margaret Mead stated, a small group of committed citizens can change the world. You have learned information in this book that will guide your advocacy efforts.

advocate
An enthusiastic supporter and promoter of a cause.

Early learning begets later learning and early success breeds later success. (Heckerman)

We know that the research on brain development concludes that what happens during the first months and years matters a lot (National Scientific Council on the Developing Child, 2010a, 2010b). We recognize the importance of relationships and responsive adult-child interactions for the optimal development of children's capacities in emotional, social, cognitive, language, and motor domains. We know how important it is to support families in their efforts to raise their children, and we know the effect of quality programs on children's development and sense of well-being. We know the importance of individualizing for children's unique strengths and interests, of children choosing among opportunities in an environment that the teacher intentionally provides, and of responsive planning. We know the power of the infant and toddler profession to make change in practice become more relationship based by developing standards for professional development, developing a vision, using the code of ethics, embracing reflective professional development practices, and advocating for the profession. We know that we need to advocate at the local, state, and national levels because social policies affect the quality of life for children, families, and infant and toddler professionals.

We know these things and now we must share this information with others. The authors of the book *From Neurons to Neighborhoods* (Shonkoff & Phillips, 2000) ask us to rethink the meaning of "both shared responsibility for children and strategic investment in their future" (p. 414).

In the first chapter we said our goal is that you gain an appreciation for how vitally important the prenatal period and the first 3 years of life are for children and the future adults they will become. Our hope is that you will become knowledgeable about and gain a passion for promoting the well-being, competence, and quality of life for infants and toddlers and their families.

We hope that we have accomplished our goal.

Summary

We end the book by coming full circle in our quest for quality experiences for infants and toddlers. The infant and toddler professionals are the ones who ensure that quality will be created and will continue. The following points are covered in this chapter:

- Professionals commit to a standard of performance that earns the respect of others.
- The infant and toddler profession meets the criteria determined to be necessary in order to be a profession.
- Early childhood professional standards include the values of the profession as well as a vision for the preparation of early childhood professionals.
- It is important for professionals to know the standards of their profession because they represent the knowledge base for that profession.
- The primary difference between infant and toddler professionals and professionals who work with older children centers on the intensity and intimacy of relationships.

- Part of being a reflective, theory-based professional is to reflect on your vision for children and families, professional philosophy, ethical values, and professional plan (your vision for yourself).
- The organizational structure of a program can support or undermine the professional.
- The professional will want to participate in shared decision making.
- A reflective practice model includes reflective supervision and mentoring.
- Advocacy is an important part of what it means to be a professional.
- Our goal in this book was for you to recognize the importance of relationships and responsive adult-child interactions for the optimal development of infants' and toddlers' capacities in emotional, social, cognitive, language, and motor domains.

Key Terms

advocate
conflict resolution skills
mentee
mentoring

professional
professional standards of practice
protégé
reflective practice model

responding habits
shared decision making
supervisor

Reflections and Resources for the Reader

REFLECTIONS

1. What are the key attributes of the infant and toddler profession?
2. Describe the knowledge, skills, and dispositions that an infant and toddler professional must have to work with children who have a range of abilities and disabilities.
3. What are the unique challenges of the infant and toddler professional?

OBSERVATION AND APPLICATION OPPORTUNITIES

1. Design a vision statement for an infant and toddler program.
2. A teammate is using practices that you think are harmful to the children (such as not comforting an infant who is crying). What are your ethical responsibilities to the children, families, colleagues, and the community and society? How would you communicate your concerns to your teammate?
3. Write a letter to a legislator on the importance of the infant and toddler years.

SUPPLEMENTARY ARTICLES AND BOOKS TO READ

Bloom, P. J., Hentchel, A., & Bella, J. (2010). *A great place to work: Creating a healthy organizational climate.* The Director's Toolbox series. Lake Forest, IL: New Horizons. Available from NAEYC.

Duncan, S. (2010). Intentional and embedded professional development. Four steps to success. *Exchange.* Retrieved from www.ecementor.org/articles-on-teaching/Intentional_Embedded_Professional_Development.pdf

Hanover Research Council. (2008). *The exemplary staff development model.* Washington, DC: Author.

Lutton, A. (Ed.). (2012). *Advancing the early childhood profession: NAEYC standards and guidelines for professional development.* Washington, DC: NAEYC.

Shahmoon-Shanok, R. (2009). What is reflective supervision? In S. Heller & L. Gilkerson (Eds.), *A practical guide to reflective supervision* (pp. 7–20). Washington DC: ZERO TO THREE.

Sullivan, D. R. (2009). Lifting as you climb. *LEADERSHIP EXCHANGE.* Retrieved from www.ecementor.org/articles-on-teaching/Lifting_as_you_Climb.pdf

INTERESTING LINKS

Child Care Information Exchange

www.ccie.com/
This site promotes the exchange of ideas among leaders in early childhood programs worldwide through its magazine, books, training products and seminars, and international conference.

Early Head Start National Resource Center

www.ehsnrc.org/
This Web site, developed by ZERO TO THREE for Early Head Start, is a storehouse of early childhood expertise. It promotes the sharing of information, including recent conferences and webinars.

Families and Work Institute

www.familiesandwork.org/
The institute is a nonprofit center providing data on the changing workforce, family, and community. It offers some of the most comprehensive research on the U.S. workforce available.

The National Center for Research on Early Childhood Education

www.ncrece.org
This Web site supports research, disseminates research findings, and provides leadership to improve the quality of early childhood education.

Appendices

Appendix A

Portraits of Development

Portraits of Infants and Toddlers

Acknowledgments to Florida State University Center for Prevention & Early Intervention Policy, www.cpeip.fus.edu, for their formatting suggestions for this material.

	Development	Example
	0–4 Months	
Emotions/ Attachment	• Infants are taking in a lot of information about the world. • Infants can get overwhelmed and begin to yawn, look away, or fuss. • Infants begin to calm themselves by sucking on their hands or listening to an adult talk quietly to them. • Infants gaze into their teacher's eyes as she feeds them. • Infants turn their heads toward a familiar voice. • Infants relax and allow themselves to be comforted by familiar people. • Infants cry when they are hungry, tired, or uncomfortable.	Carlos followed Karen with his eyes wherever she went in the room. When she came close to him, he looked at her as though he wanted her to join him. Accepting his invitation to play, she sat with him on the floor. As he began to tire and fuss, she swaddled him in a blanket, held him close, and spoke softly to him.
Learning with Peers	• Infants like to look at each other (visual regard). • Infants prefer to look at faces, especially the edges and the eyes. • Infants may cry when they hear other babies cry (contagion).	After the teacher put Tamika by Sam on a blanket on the floor, Tamika stared intently at Sam.
Cognitive	• Infants follow a moving object visually. • Infants cry to bring an adult to comfort or feed them. • Infants will look around the room with interest. • Infants begin to reach for a toy. • Infants notice that their arms or legs made something happen and will repeat the movement. • Infants recognize familiar people and objects. • Infants begin to bring objects to mouth.	Megan lifted her head, resting on her arms as she lay on the blanket. With a serious expression on her face, she watched the teachers and children around her. Willie kicked the mobile hanging over him and made it wiggle. He stopped, looked at it, and then kicked some more, watching the mobile to see if anything might happen.
Language	• Infants may startle if they hear a loud sound. • Infants hear the differences in sounds. • Infants may stop crying when they hear a familiar adult's voice. • Infants prefer to hear talk that is directed toward them. • Infants listen when an adult talks or sings to them while looking at them. • Infants cry when they are in pain, are hungry, or are distressed. • By 2 months of age, babies have different cries for hunger and pain. • Infants "coo" (make soft vowel sounds). • Infants smile and laugh toward the end of this age period. • Infants will stare at interesting pictures in books.	Brenda held Jordon so they could gaze into each other's eyes. Jordon cooed softly and Brenda cooed back. Then she waited for Jordon to take another turn. Erica gave her father a big smile when he picked her up out of her crib.

Teacher- or Parent-Child Interaction	Environment
0–4 Months	

• Keep young babies close to you, in your arms, in a snuggly, or on a blanket nearby.	• Being close to a familiar teacher is best.
• Recognize the signals that indicate a baby wants to be with you—intent gazing, reaching, a happy look—and respond with quiet, verbal and nonverbal turn taking.	• A serene, quiet space with gentle lighting limits the information an infant needs to take in.
	• Avoid playing background music all day.
• Recognize the signals that indicate a baby needs a break—yawning, drooling, looking away—and sit back quietly and wait while the baby regroups.	• Limit the number of objects, sounds, color, and movements around a young infant.
	• The teacher is the most interesting thing for a baby to watch, but other babies, mirrors, and toys within the baby's visual range of focus are also interesting.
• Comfort babies whenever they cry.	

• Hold two babies so they can look at each other.	• The arms of teachers provide the best environment.
• Place a few babies on a blanket on the floor so that they can look at and touch each other.	• Blankets on the floor—put two babies beside each other so their toes are touching.

• Slowly move a small toy from one side to another while the infant follows it with his gaze.	• Arrange the space so that infants can see some activity but still be protected.
• Respond quickly to the baby's cries.	• Provide a few interesting things to look at—small toys on the floor during tummy time, dangling toys when infants are on their backs.
• Provide quiet time for babies to look at what is happening around them. Talk about what they see.	
• React to infants' expressions with clear, even exaggerated facial expressions and language.	• Provide nonbreakable mirrors.

• Use infant-directed speech.	• The best environment is in the arms of a caring adult who holds the baby and talks softly.
• Hold and talk to babies.	
• Engage in long eye gazes while having conversational dances. Respect the baby if he needs a break and turns his head away.	• Provide toys that make pleasant sounds. Gently hold the toy and share the sounds with the baby.
• Read books with rhythmic phrases and books with one picture on a page with 2- to 4-month-olds.	• Provide interesting materials to touch while you comment on the textures.
• Interpret babies' burps, cries, yawns, stretching, and sounds as forms of communication. Say, "Oh, you're telling me you're sleepy."	• Add mirrors low along a wall. Babies will look and possibly make sounds.
• Be an empathic language partner—comment on the baby's feelings.	
• Use words and sounds to comfort babies.	

	Development	Example
	0–4 Months	

| Motor | • Infants lift head when held at shoulder—hold head steady and erect.
• On tummy, infants lift their head and shoulders off the ground and can hold a toy in hand.
• Infants turn head toward a familiar voice.
• Infants hold body still to pay attention, wiggle and move to encourage continued interaction.
• On back, infants thrust arms and legs in play.
• Infants turn from side to back.
• Infants hold finger, light toy with reflexive grasp.
• Infants suck on own fingers and hands and on objects.
• Infants move arms and legs. | Rosie held her head up and looked around at the other children as Sharon held her against her shoulder.
Robert, on his tummy on a blanket, lifted his head to see himself in the mirror mounted at floor level on the wall.
Jen held a rattle placed in her hand but seemed unaware it was there.
Filipe brought his fingers to his mouth and sucked on them, while looking intently at the toddlers. |

| | **4–8 Months** | |

Emotions/ Attachment	• Infants like to look at their hands and feet. • Infants wave their arms and kick in excitement when they see a familiar person. • Infants will smile at a teacher expecting her to smile back. • Infants use their faces and bodies to express many feelings: everything from frowning and crying to laughing out loud. • Infants express their feelings more clearly to familiar people and are more reserved with strangers.	Deborah loves being carried in her teacher's arms as they move around the room "talking" about the things they see. Her eyes are wide and bright, she smiles, and she makes cooing sounds as though taking her turn in the conversation. When a visitor enters the room, Deborah gets very quiet and serious and holds tightly to her teacher's shoulder as she looks at the visitor.
Learning with Peers	• Infants touch a peer, vocalize to each other, get excited, approach other babies, smile and laugh at each other. • Babies may treat other babies like objects—crawling over them, licking or sucking on them, or sitting on them. They are just learning the difference between people and objects. Infants may poke, push, or pat another baby to see what that other infant will do. They often look very surprised at the reaction they get.	Anna crawled over to Nadia who was lying on the floor. Touching Nadia's hair, Anna laughed out loud.
Cognitive	• Infants like to examine toys. • Infants like to make toys do something—make a sound, put one inside another. • Infants imitate adult expressions and gestures. • Infants turn toward a sound to see where it came from. • Infants look for toys they dropped.	Angela is interested in everything. She watches her friends and then looks at the teacher and smiles. Roger reaches out to touch a dangling toy. When it swings, making a sound, he reaches out to do it again.

Teacher- or Parent-Child Interaction	Environment

0–4 Months

• Change the baby's position: sometimes on his back, sometimes on his tummy. Even when holding the baby, sometimes cradle him in your arms, sometimes hold him upright against your shoulder. • When baby is on the floor, lie down face-to-face with him. • When baby is on her back, reaching for a toy a little beyond her head, support her trunk as she rolls over.	• A stiff blanket (to prevent the danger of suffocation) on the floor provides space for early movements. • Small, interesting toys, pictures, and books to look at will encourage babies to lift their heads. A mirror bolted to the wall at floor level always provides something interesting to look at. • As babies begin to reach, they enjoy stable bars that dangle toys for them to bat at or reach and grasp.

4–8 Months

• Provide opportunities for babies to look in mirrors as they play. • Mirror the emotional expressions of the infant and add appropriate words: "I'm so excited to see you today!" • Respond to babies in a way that helps them be calm and active; if babies are crying, soothe them.	• Mount unbreakable mirrors on walls. • Provide floor time where babies play with their feet while on their backs and move around on the ground. • Books and posters of photographs of real faces with different emotional expressions are very interesting to infants.
• Move to music with a baby in each arm. • While holding one baby in your lap, point out and talk about what another baby is doing. • Place two babies on their tummies facing a mirror. • Instead of saying "Don't" or "Stop that" to exploring babies, say "Touch gently." Tell children what you want them to do—model it for them.	• Hang a safety mirror horizontally on the wall, so the bottom is touching the floor. • Cover an inner tube with soft cloth. Sit two babies in the inner tube so that their feet are touching.
• Hold the infant in your arms as you walk around, looking at things and talking about them. • Sit nearby and talk to the baby about the toys she is looking at. • Call the baby by name from a short distance to reassure her you are nearby.	• Provide a variety of small toys to handle and examine. • Provide toys that make sounds when a baby moves them, fit inside each other, or dangle and move when touched. • Offer board books.

Development		Example

4–8 Months

| Language | • Infants turn their head toward a noise or someone speaking their name.
 • Infants enjoy adults talking, singing, and laughing with them.
 • Babies vocalize with intention to get a response from the adult.
 • Babies make high-pitched squeals.
 • Infants practice their sounds when exploring and with favorite adults.
 • Infants begin to babble—at first with one consonant and then by combining two consonants.
 • Infants engage in turn-taking conversations with adults.
 • Babies will look at different pictures in a book and get excited at a favorite one or at the enthusiastic tone of an adult who is reading to them. | As Danielle, the infant teacher, was holding Donovan on her lap, she pointed to the pictures in the sturdy board book. "Look," she said, pointing to the picture, "a ball. There's your ball," as she pointed to a ball on the floor. Donovan looked at the picture, then at the ball on the floor, and back to the picture.

 "Tt" said Afi as he lay in his teacher's arms looking up at her. "Tada" exclaimed his teacher back to him. "Tt" repeated Afi as he took his turn in the conversation. |
| Motor | • Infants turn from back to side, later roll from back to front.
 • Infants sit—first with support but steady alone by the end of this period.
 • Infants reach with one arm.
 • Infants use raking grasp.
 • Infants crawl.
 • Infants shake, bang, hold, let go of objects.
 • Infants move objects from hand to hand.
 • Infants can hold their own bottle.
 • Infants can bring objects to their mouth. | Micky rolls from his back to his tummy to reach a toy, then rolls back over to play with it.

 Erin, sitting steadily alone, loves using both hands to pick up objects and study them.

 Freddy loves being held while he has his bottle, but he insists on holding it himself. |

8–12 Months

| Emotions/ Attachment | • Mobile infants may be fearful with strangers.
 • Mobile infants will call upon familiar adults to help them when they are upset.
 • Mobile infants will look at a familiar adult to determine whether a situation is safe or dangerous.
 • Mobile infants will cling to a familiar adult when they are in a strange situation.
 • Mobile infants will find humor in silly games and adults making big facial expressions. | Jamie is enjoying his new ability to quickly crawl anywhere he wants to go. He loves the little climber that lets him look out the window. But when the ramp feels a little shaky, he likes to look back at his teacher, Fred—just making sure he's still safe. |

Teacher- or Parent-Child Interaction	Environment

4–8 Months

• Use infant-directed speech. • Talk with babies often. Show them new objects and people and name them. • Repeat the sounds that infants make and wait for the infant to make the sound again (turn taking). • Use sign language for several familiar items such as "milk" or "dog." • Sing songs and say finger-plays. • Use words to describe children's feelings expressed through gestures, body postures, and sounds. • Read simple books with one to two pictures on a page. Point to the pictures as you say the name of the picture. • Read the same books over and over. • Use joint attention strategies—point at a toy or picture in a book when you say the name or talk about it.	• Provide interesting toys and materials for babies to handle and explore. • Provide cardboard books with handles so that babies can crawl to them and pick them up. • Books with handles encourage babies to hang on to them. • Make a peek-a-boo picture book by gluing a piece of cloth over each picture. • Create a cozy book corner where teachers can be comfortable and read to babies. • Provide sound boxes (safely sealed) with different objects in them that make different sounds when shaken. • Add puppets to the environment. Use them at times to "talk" to the child. Put the puppet on the child's hand and wait to see what the child says or does.
• Stay near the baby who is just beginning to sit alone. • Know the progression of motor development; emotionally encourage and physically support new attempts. • Believe in the lifelong health benefits of an active lifestyle.	• Provide safe places for rolling, sitting, and crawling. Protect babies from anything that might fall on them. • Provide small, washable lightweight objects (too large for choking) for handling and tossing, and provide containers for objects.

8–12 Months

• Encourage mobile infants to move off and explore by reassuring them that you are watching and keeping them safe. • Understand that mobile infants may become afraid of new situations that wouldn't have been frightening a few months ago. Be comforting and reassuring.	• Play peek-a-boo. • Read stories about mothers and fathers who go away and come back. • Read books with flaps to lift to find things. • Keep room arrangements and routines predictable.

Development	Example
8–12 Months	

Learning with Peers
- Infants may show a peer an object, sit by each other, crawl after and around each other, play chase-and-retrieve games.
- Babies smile and laugh at each other.
- Babies make sounds to and with each other—may say first words with peers.
- Peek-a-boo is a favorite game as babies explore separation: coming and going, in sight and out of sight.
- Infants can learn to touch each other gently.
- Because infants become more goal oriented at this age, they may push another baby's hand away from a toy or crawl over another baby to get a toy.

Shamaine peeked around the low toy shelf and saw Carla crawling toward her. Shamaine quickly turned around and crawled away with Carla close behind.

Cognitive
- Mobile infants like to take the pieces of a toy apart and put them back together.
- Mobile infants like toys that do something when you touch them, pull them, bang them.
- Mobile infants begin very simple pretend play, such as lifting a cup to their mouth.
- Mobile infants like to find small toys hidden under a cloth or cup.
- Mobile infants like to pick up and examine a tiny item like a Cheerio.
- Mobile infants point to objects, knowing you can also see them.

Charlie loves to take each plastic animal out of the bucket and look at it. When the bucket is empty, he tosses it aside.

Aliya likes the push button and the swinging doors on the busy box but can't work all the mechanisms yet. Her teacher expresses surprise with Aliya when the doors pop open, and everyone once in a while shows her how to work another of the knobs.

Language
- Mobile infants are beginning to play social games such as peek-a-boo or "so big."
- Infants enjoy listening to sound play (rhymes), songs, and finger-plays.
- Babbling continues to develop with combined syllables such as "dada," "mama," and "tutu," but now the infant may be using these sounds specifically for mom or dad.
- Infants will use sounds consistently for an object or person or animal.
- If they hear another language with an adult through interactive conversational strategies, then infants can "keep the brain open to the sounds of a second language."
- Infants may begin to use single words.
- At the end of the age period, infants may begin to point to engage an adult.
- They are using facial expressions and gestures such as shaking head or stretching arms out to be picked up to communicate to adults or peers.

One of Dana's first words was "mama," which she said over and over again when she saw her mother.

One of Trishanna's first words was "mama," which she excitedly said over and over again when she saw her mother.

Teacher- or Parent-Child Interaction	Environment
8–12 Months	

- Name parts of infants' bodies as two infants sit close to each other:

  Here is baby's eyes
  Here is baby's nose
  Touch the part that sees
  Touch the part that blows

- Place a baby with one other baby (pairs), because more frequent, complex, and intense peer interaction occurs than when a child is with many peers.
- Understand that infants are not being "naughty" when they push another child's hand away. Say "Jenny was holding that toy. Let's find you a different toy."

- While feeding, place high chairs so children can see each other.
- Set up cozy corners in the room where babies can "disappear" (but adults can still see them).
- Hang a long wide cloth (so babies won't get tangled in it) from the ceiling. Babies love to crawl around it.
- Place containers with different sizes of blocks in them between two babies. Sit beside them as they begin to explore the materials. Talk about what each one is doing.

- Help the baby focus on what is interesting to him, using your presence, your interest, and your enthusiasm to support his attention and exploration.
- Use your emotional expressions and words to show the mobile infant that you delight in his discoveries.
- Use words to describe the child's activity: "Look, you found a Cheerio. You're picking it up with your fingers."

- Provide toys like stacking cups, rings on a post, pop-beads, and tubs full of small, interesting objects such as toy animals.
- Provide child-size replicas of dishes or household tools.
- Provide toys that respond to children's actions—busy boxes, water-filled pads.
- Provide sensory materials such as water and sand with a variety of tools.
- Provide board books with photos.

- Play familiar games such as peek-a-boo, pat-a-cake, or "how big are you?"
- Respond to infants' nonverbal communication with words.
- Look at and wait for infants to initiate sounds or words.
- Imitate the sounds and then expand, elaborate, and extend the baby's language.
- Model the next step in language development.
- Use self-talk and parallel talk.
- Talk often in a responsive way using a varied vocabulary. Don't bombard the child.
- Read books with enthusiasm, changing the tone of your voice with different characters.
- Talk about the pictures and the story as you read it. Engage babies in the story with your voice and gestures.
- Wait while looking at a picture for babies to communicate sounds, point, or use facial expressions.

- Create a cozy book corner where babies can easily reach and handle books.
- Create an "All About Me" book—small photo albums for each child with pictures of themselves, their family, their favorite toys, peers, teachers, and the family pets. Make them available to the children. Change the pictures as the child grows.
- Musical push toys encourage infants to handle them and make sounds.

Development	Example
8–12 Months	

Motor
- Mobile infants pull to stand.
- Mobile infants cruise.
- Mobile infants stand alone.
- Mobile infants walk with help and then alone.
- Mobile infants sit in a chair.
- Mobile infants finger-feed.
- Mobile infants use spoon, tippy cup.
- Mobile infants use pincer grasp.

Hershel crawls to his teacher's side, then holds her leg as he pulls up to stand.

Jem sits at the lunch table, alternating between using her spoon and her fingers to enjoy her meal.

| **12–18 Months** | |

Emotions/ Attachment
- Mobile infants will imitate the actions of familiar adults, such as using the phone or caring for a baby doll.
- Mobile infants will seek adult attention by pulling on their leg or taking their hand.
- Mobile infants will use a favorite blanket or stuffed animal to help calm themselves.
- Mobile infants will protest loudly when their parents leave them.
- Mobile infants will relax and be comforted by cuddling with a familiar adult.
- Mobile infants will let their likes and dislikes be clearly known.

Amelia carries her teddy bear around all morning. Sometimes she copies her teacher Sophia's actions, patting its back or "feeding it a bottle." When she gets tired, she rubs teddy against her ear and sucks her thumb.

Learning with Peers
- Imitation (motor) and interactive turns begin. Toddlers may copy each other—if one gives a toy to another child, the other may imitate.
- Mobile infants begin to talk to each other.
- Infants may show concern when other babies are distressed.
- Mobile infants may take a toy away from another child, say "No," push away another child, clutch toy to self and say "Mine."
- Infants are little scientists at this age, experimenting to see how things work. This affects how they get along with peers. They are constantly doing things to other children to see what response they will get.
- Biting may appear as infants bite others "to see what happens," to get the toy they want, to express frustration. Infants are on the cusp of communicating well; they may communicate through their mouths in the form of a bite.

Rashinda banged her spoon on the table; soon two others tried it. They seemed to be physically following each other's lead (as in a conversation).

First, Carmen tried pushing Toby away from her rocking horse. When that didn't work, she leaned over and took a bite out of his arm.

Teacher- or Parent-Child Interaction	Environment

8–12 Months

- Stay alert when practicing walkers need a little help—and know when to let them keep trying.
- Allow time for older infants to practice feeding themselves.

- Safe places to pull up to stand.
- Push and pull toys to help support practicing walkers.
- Busy boxes.
- Board books for turning pages, lifting flaps, and poking fingers through holes.

12–18 Months

- Demonstrate your interest in babies' activities.
- Show your pride in babies' accomplishments.
- Let babies use you as a secure base from which to explore the world.
- Let babies know you understand their feelings and respond with respect.
- These are still very young children who needs lots of cuddling and holding.

- Provide child-size copies of tools adults use: telephones, dishes, keys, etc.
- Post photographs of the infants with their family on the wall.
- Laminate photos of the infants with their family for carrying around.
- Make photo albums of the children at your program and talk about the pictures.
- Have adult chairs and quiet, comfortable spaces for holding children.

- Show mobile infants how to roll down a small hill together.
- Help mobile toddlers learn each other's names by singing greeting and good-bye songs with the children's names in them: "Here is Tanya, how are you?" and "Here is Henry, how are you?" as you point to or touch each child who comes by you or is sitting in your lap.
- Comment on prosocial behavior. Say "You gave him the doll. He likes that!" Babies may not understand your words, but they will be able to tell by your tone of voice that you are pleased with them.
- They will enjoy looking at books together by forming an informal group (this means they move in and out of the group) around the legs, lap, and arms of a favorite parent or teacher.

- Provide a large cardboard box, open on each end. Encourage babies to crawl in and out of the box with each other. Windows on the side encourage babies to peek at each other through the windows.
- Dolls, trucks, cars, and other play materials encourage interactions among peers.
- They love sand and water and playing with different sizes of safe bottles and balls. When each has his own bin or tub of water or sand, play goes more smoothly.
- Outside, large sandboxes or push toys encourage interactive play.

Development	Example
12–18 Months	

Cognitive

- Mobile infants like to use their mobility to explore—crawling, walking, climbing, running.
- Mobile infants enjoy playing with sand, water, and play dough with different kinds of tools.
- Mobile infants are interested in spatial relationships in puzzles and pegboards.
- Mobile infants use tools such as keys or telephones in their pretend play.
- Mobile infants enjoy looking at books and naming objects, animals, or body parts.

Alexis and Dan are gleeful about being on two feet. They follow each other around, one daringly balancing his way up the sloping surface with the other right behind. Sometimes they both try to squeeze into the area under the slide.

Meredith loves to cuddle on her teacher's lap, pointing at pictures in books while her teacher names the animals, or asks her to find a certain animal.

Language

- Mobile infants can follow simple directions such as "Come here" or "Go get your shoes" without you gesturing.
- Mobile infants play a social game without you demonstrating the action.
- Mobile infants will point to engage adults and peers.
- Rapid word learning—a language explosion—may occur with the children learning many new words.
- Mobile infants will combine words toward the end of this age period.
- Mobile infants will jabber (stringing many sounds together) using adultlike intonation.
- Mobile infants will use gestures and language to reject, request, comment, refuse, demand, and name objects and people.
- Mobile infants use language to maintain an interaction or conversation with an adult or peer.

Janeika's teacher said, "Let's play pat-a-cake," and Janeika started clapping her hands together.

Ross looked up expectantly at his teacher, jabbering many sounds together as if asking her a question.

Motor

- Mobile infants stack and line up blocks.
- Mobile infants can dress and undress self, arm into sleeve, foot into shoe.
- Mobile infants can walk.
- Mobile infants walk while carrying objects in each hand.
- Mobile infants climb stairs.

Gary stood at the table, carefully using both hands to build a tower with colored blocks.

Michelle toddled across the room, with her teddy bear in one hand and her blanket in the other.

18–24 Months	

Emotions/ Attachment

- Toddlers begin to control some impulses, saying, "no, no, no" as they begin to throw blocks.
- Toddlers may stop their actions when told to by a teacher.
- Toddlers may not want to stop playing when their parent comes to pick them up.
- Toddlers may cry when they are unable to master what they are trying to do.
- Toddlers know their own names and may use "me" and "mine."

Frankie climbs up onto the table, looking his disapproving teacher right in the eye and says "no, no, no."

Teacher- or Parent-Child Interaction	Environment
12–18 Months	
<ul><li>Allow mobile infants protected time and space to explore.</li><li>Stay nearby to express interest, provide words, and make the activity more elaborate and complex.</li><li>Help mobile infants express their interest in each other gently.</li><li>Express enthusiasm for the things that interest mobile infants.</li></ul>	<ul><li>Provide simple puzzles, pegboards, shape forms, wooden beads with thick strings.</li><li>Provide small climbers, tunnels, interesting pathways.</li><li>Provide toys that respond to winding, turning on and off.</li><li>Provide simple props for pretend play.</li></ul>
<ul><li>Stay on topic in a conversation with a mobile infant. See how many turns the child will take.</li><li>Respond to the intonation of the child's jabbering. For example, if it seems as if the child is asking a question, answer what you think the child might be asking.</li><li>Respond to mobile infants' pointing and other nonverbal communication with language.</li><li>Use words that describe and compare sizes, shapes, and sounds.</li><li>When a mobile infant uses words such as "I jump," model the next step in language development by saying "You're jumping," adding the "ing" to the word.</li><li>Read longer stories, pausing to encourage mobile infants to talk about pictures and story.</li></ul>	<ul><li>Introduce art materials such as play dough, clay, and paint.</li><li>Add paper towel rolls for mobile infants to walk and pull objects behind them or push them.</li><li>Sturdy music boxes encourage mobile infants to push buttons to "make music."</li><li>Drums and other musical instruments can be made available.</li><li>Add a sturdy CD player with a story from a parent recorded to play on it.</li><li>Use a tape recorder to tape mobile infants' voices and play it back to them.</li><li>Provide bubble making materials.</li><li>Provide spaces for two or three children to encourage peer conversation.</li></ul>
<ul><li>Imitate baby's growing variety of movements.</li><li>Introduce songs with little dances and movements.</li><li>Provide time and patience while a toddler practices putting on his own jacket.</li></ul>	<ul><li>Stable, low-to-the-ground riding toys.</li><li>Stable, low-to-the-ground rocking toys.</li><li>Skill-based manipulatives such as stacking cups, rings on a stick.</li></ul>
18–24 Months	
<ul><li>Keep your sense of humor. Understand that sometimes toddlers can stop themselves from doing things, but sometimes they cannot.</li><li>Respect the strong feelings of toddlers. Taking turns and sharing come later—now "me" and "mine" are an important part of developing a strong sense of self.</li></ul>	<ul><li>Provide spaces that allow children to explore without ever being out of sight.</li><li>Have enough copies of the same toy for several children to each have one without sharing or taking turns.</li><li>Let children bring comfort items like blankets or stuffed animals to your program. Provide a quiet place where they can comfort themselves.</li></ul>

Development	Example
18–24 Months	

	Development	Example
Learning with Peers	• Friendships can develop early. Friends are more likely to touch, lean on one another, and smile at each other than are children who are not friends. • Toddlers imitate each other's sounds and words and talk to each other and begin to communicate with others across more space. • Toddlers give or offer a toy or food to another toddler. • Toddlers may get an adult or pull an adult to help another child or will help another child by getting a tissue, for example. • Toddlers can show kindness to other babies who are feeling distressed. A mobile infant or toddler, however, may assume that what will comfort him will also comfort the distressed child. • Children take turns (e.g., with a ball, or jumping up). They may have toddler kinesthetic conversations as they follow a leader in moving around the room—moving in and out of the group, taking turns as leader and follower—as if in a conversation of listening and talking, learning valuable turn-taking skills. • Pushing, shoving, grabbing, and hitting may occur as children struggle over "mine for as long as I want it" and "yours, but I want it, too." Toddlers may fight over small toys more than large, unmovable objects.	Paulie looked as if he was waiting by the door for Jamie to appear at the beginning of the day. When Jamie and his mom came in the door, Paulie toddled over and took Jamie's hand, a big smile on his face. Tanya jumped (half fell) off a board several inches off the ground. Soon three toddlers were standing on the board and half jumping, half stepping off and on the board, enjoying the activity immensely.
Cognitive	• Young toddlers enjoy the ease of their movement and like to use their hands to carry things around. • Young toddlers understand they can cause things to happen. • Young toddlers understand and remember the details of routines. • Young toddlers use objects as substitutes for other objects in their pretend play. • Young toddlers enjoy increasingly challenging materials that suggest activities such as building, sorting, matching shapes.	Before breakfast, Chris puts out his hands for the little song of thanks. When a child arrives and joins the table late, he reaches out for everyone to sing again. Lynn and Matt build little towers of blocks and then drive play trucks into them and knock them down. Fran takes out the box of 1-inch blocks and makes one pile of red blocks, one pile of blue blocks.
Language	• Toddlers can go get familiar toys from another room in the house when an adult asks them to and can follow directions such as "close the door." • Toddlers combine words to name things ("that cat"), to deny ("no bite"), and to reject ("no more"). • Toddlers are combining two to three words together with meaning. • Toddlers use language for a variety of purposes, including asking, "What that?" • Toddlers point to an increasing number of pictures in books when an adult talks about the picture.	"Hi, Kitty," "open door," and "hat on" were just a few of the two-word combinations Cheral used at 20 months of age. Tyra moved quickly over to the bookshelf, picked up a book with a bright cover, and rushed back to his teacher. After sitting comfortably in her lap, he opened the book and enthusiastically started pointing to the pictures as his teacher named them.

Teacher- or Parent-Child Interaction	Environment
18–24 Months	

- When inside or outside, nurture toddlers as they come and go to "refuel" emotionally with a special teacher, encouraging several toddlers to sit together beside you or in your lap. Allow toddlers to touch each other gently.
- Encourage several toddlers to make animal sounds together and imitate each other as you show them the pictures in a book.
- Ask one child to help another child by getting a tissue, turning the faucet on, opening a door, etc.
- Encourage kindness with one another. If one toddler cries, ask another what "we" could do to help.
- Encourage two peers to set a table together or sponge it off together after eating. Watch them imitate each other.
- Sing songs, encouraging toddlers to take turns with the actions.

Environment column:
- Inside and outside: Provide sand areas large enough for several toddlers and expect them to sit right in the middle of the area.
- Blankets on the floor or ground or over a table provide a spot for peers to play.
- Provide wagons: Pulling or pushing a friend in a wagon will result in squeals of delight.
- Provide balls and pull-toys that encourage interactive play.
- Places to jump safely encourage social exchanges.
- Provide musical toys, several of each kind, so children can make beautiful music together. Sometimes one will lead and another will follow, or vice versa.

- Maintain predictable routines, reminding children of the order with questions like, "It's time to eat. What do we do?"
- Keep materials in orderly and predictable places.
- Provide scaffolding as toddlers think about their activities, with questions such as "What will you do next?" or "What will you buy at the store?"

Environment:
- Have toys and materials arranged so that toddlers can make choices, reach them, and put them away (with reminders).
- Frequently review the materials you have available to ensure that you are keeping a balance between what is familiar and what is a little challenging.

- Read books with longer stories, pausing as you go through the book to encourage toddlers to talk about the pictures and the story. Ask open-ended questions such as "How does the bear feel?"
- Wonder often with the child: "I wonder what will happen to the bear."
- Engage toddlers in conversation, trying to stay on the same topic as the child.
- Introduce new conversations about interesting objects and events.

Environment:
- Set up an elaborate obstacle course and use words such as "in," "out," "over," "through," "around," "up," and "down" as the toddler goes through the course.
- Provide new books each week but keep children's favorites available.
- Provide a wider variety of art materials.
- Provide sensory materials.

Development	Example
18–24 Months	
Motor	
• Toddlers point to objects to communicate. • Toddlers make marks on paper. • Toddlers pound, shape clay. • Toddlers run. • Toddlers sit on and get up from small chairs alone. • Toddlers are developing spatial confidence—explore their body in space.	Mindy rolled the dough with her hands, then used tools to make designs. Joseph sat down at the table to eat, then took his dirty dishes to the tub.
24–36 Months	
Emotions/ Attachment	
• Toddlers can sometimes be independent, but they like to know the teacher is close by. • Toddlers like to study pictures of themselves, their friends, and their families. • Toddlers listen to your words and the tone of your voice when you talk about them. They want you to be interested and proud of them. • Toddlers need clear and consistent limits. They will forget rules, or test rules, but feel secure when you remind them and help them to follow the rules. • Toddlers may use words to express their feelings, or they may hit or bite. • Toddlers care about the feelings of others and will comfort someone who is sad or hurt.	Kiki carried her baby doll over to the photos of her own family on the wall. She crooned to her baby while looking at her own mother's face.
Learning with Peers	
• Toddler friendship is "proximity seeking," wanting to be close and to show affection, such as smiling, laughing, and hugging. Friendships continue to develop and deepen. • They exchange information and can imitate past action of others. • Toddlers may congregate and cluster together. When a teacher begins an interesting activity with one child, children often come running from the corners of the room. • Some toddlers are capable of inventing a variety of ways to help others who are hurt or sad. • Peers work together toward a common goal, with one the leader and one the follower. • Object, personal space, and verbal struggles can occur. Toddlers also engage in playful exchanges—rough and tumble, run and chase, and verbal games. • Some children may gain a reputation with peers for aggressive or kind behavior. • Children become more positive and less negative in their social play between 24 and 36 months. • Dominance of one child over another can occur.	Maria and Sally played on opposite sides of the small shelf of toys for 30 minutes, peeking over at each other every few minutes, and telling each other, "boat" "my boat," "hi," "want juice," "look at me," and saying each other's names over and over. When a fire truck went by outside, several toddlers rushed to the window to look. Josh and Mike pushed, pulled, rolled, and grunted as they worked hard to roll the huge pumpkin from inside to the playground where the toddlers and their teachers were going to cut it open and scoop out all of the seeds.

Teacher- or Parent-Child Interaction	Environment
18–24 Months	
• Provide materials that challenge toddlers' growing use of their fingers. • Stay present with toddlers as they try new skills and support them. • Provide opportunities for climbing, walking, running.	• Art materials with thick paint brushes and markers, large surfaces for painting. • Smaller, skill-based manipulates such as connecting beads and pegboards. • Lots of space for movement—dancing, riding toys, climbing, slides.
24–36 Months	
• Establish clear and consistent rules. Be prepared to remind the toddlers frequently of how to follow the rules: "We don't bite. Biting hurts." • Give toddlers enough of your time and attention so that they feel understood. • Echo the enthusiasm toddlers can bring to their play. • Notice and comment on the interactions that toddlers are watching and thinking about.	• Provide many photographs of the children with their family: on the walls, in little books, and laminated to carry around. • Provide protected spaces for quiet play. • Maintain predictable routines and room arrangement. • Provide books that tell simple stories of coming and going, of families, and of friendship. • Sing songs about feelings such as "When you're happy and you know it" and "When you're sad, angry..."
• Create situations in which two toddlers need to work together—for example, to roll a pumpkin from one place to another or carry a bucket of "heavy" blocks from inside to outside. • Put a Band-Aid on a doll's arm or leg and encourage toddlers to take care of the baby. • Ask the toddlers, "How can we help Joey? He's sad; he's crying." • Try to change the image of a child who is gaining a reputation for aggression. Keep the child close, show her how to touch gently, and comment on her helpful behavior. Give her an interesting toy that might interest other children to engage with her. Stay close and teach her how to play.	• Place hats and easy-to-put-on dress-up clothes in a cozy corner with a big mirror. • Spaces on or under a short loft encourage peer interaction. • Provide several types of dolls as well as safe feeding utensils, blankets, and small beds. Sit close and watch as toddlers pretend to care for their babies. • Provide open-ended materials such as blocks, and activities that require cooperation such as painting with big brushes and water on outside walls or filling a big bucket with water from smaller containers. • Large motor equipment such as climbers or rocking boats encourage toddlers to work together toward a common goal: everyone moving to the top of the climber or rocking the boat with everyone in it.

Development	Example
24–36 Months	

	Development	Example
Cognitive	• Older toddlers begin to understand concepts such as color, size, shape, time, and weight. • Older toddlers are interested in the story and pictures in storybooks. • Older toddlers create new stories in pretend play or new structures in block building, becoming more imaginative and creative. • Assign roles to toys and other children in pretend play; use chairs, blankets, and bookcases as substitutes for items in pretend play.	Erick is feeling a little sad and carries a picture of his mommy around with him, saying, "After nap." Sara takes charge of the dramatic play corner, handing out dolls and stuffed animals. She puts on a hat and says, "Mommy going shopping."
Language	• Toddlers understand more complex directions and remember words to short songs and finger-plays. • Toddlers use many 2- to 4-word sentences. • Toddlers can point to and name body parts. • Toddlers add "ing" to words. • Toddlers begin using prepositions such as "on" and "in." • Toddlers add an "s" to words to indicate plurals. • Toddlers may begin to ask "Why?" • Toddlers will begin to tell you stories about what they did or what they saw. • Toward the end of this period, a toddler can use the pictures to tell you what is happening in a story.	Mindy started to add "ing" to words she had been saying for several months. She said, "I running" and "I eating" rather than "I run" and "I eat." "Look, he's playing," exclaimed Treat as he pointed to a picture in his favorite book.
Motor	• Toddlers thread beads, use scissors, paint with fingers or brushes, and do simple puzzles. • Toddlers throw and kick a ball. • Toddlers stand on one foot. • Toddlers stand and walk on tiptoes. • Toddlers climb stairs with one foot on each step. • Toddlers climb, slide, and jump. • Toddlers eat with spoon and fork. • Toddlers can dress self. • Toddlers can pour milk from small pitcher.	Robert doesn't even have to think about his body as he runs to greet his dad at the end of the day. Peggy and Misha make a game out of imitating each other's tiptoe steps, postures, and gestures. Lawrence and Evelyn use the dress-up clothes for their game, struggling a little to pull on the pieces.

Teacher- or Parent-Child Interaction	Environment
24–36 Months	

• Ask children how they might solve problems that occur and let them figure out answers. • Support children working together with materials to share ideas. • Use language that describes time "now, later, before nap, after lunch"), weight ("heavy, light"), size ("bigger, smaller"). • Count things during the day.	• Provide play opportunities that promote comparison of sizes, weights, colors, shapes, and quantities. • Have books available in all areas of the program. Have several copies of old favorites and bring in new books. • Allow children to combine materials from different areas in creative ways. • Present new material or new combinations of materials.
• Answer their "why" questions with patience and enthusiasm. • Listen with your eyes to the "stories" toddlers tell. • Model saying words that are plurals, such as "dogs," "elephants," and so on. • Use descriptive words such as "mozzarella cheese" rather than just "cheese," or "bluejay" rather than just the word "bird." • Have long conversations with toddlers, following their lead. • Read books to small informal groups or to individual children.	• Provide pictures for children to match. • Puzzles of animals, people, vehicles, and food are important. • Books with many pictures and short stories can be added to the environment. • Dramatic play materials encourage conversation.
• Be aware of the balance of time between active and quiet activities. • Watch for increasing accuracy in fine motor skills, as subtle issues may begin to be apparent. • Be available with encouragement and patience as toddlers increasingly feed, dress, and toilet themselves.	• Provide a variety of materials to practice fine motor skills: simple puzzles, shape boxes, threading beads, table blocks, clay, art materials. • Space, opportunity, and structures to encourage movement—outdoor time, obstacle courses, dancing, and riding toys.

Appendix B

Portraits of Development–Spanish

Retratos de Bebés y Niños Pequenos

	Desarrollo	Ejemplo
	0 a 4 meses (bebé)	
Los sentimientos/ Las ataduras	• Los bebés absorben una gran cantidad de información acerca del mundo. • Los bebés pueden sentirse abrumados y comenzar a bostezar, mirar hacia otro lado o molestarse. • Los bebés comienzan a calmarse chupándose las manos o escuchando a un adulto que les hable suavemente. • Los bebés miran fijamente a los ojos de su maestra mientras les da de comer. • Los bebés voltean la cabeza hacia voces conocidas. • Los bebés se calman y se consuelan con personas conocidas. • Los bebés lloran cuando tienen hambre o están cansados o incómodos.	Carlos seguía a Karen con los ojos por donde quiera que fuera por el salón. Cuando ella se le acercó, la miró como si quisiera que ella se quedara con él. Karen aceptó la invitación a jugar y se sentó con él en el piso. En cuanto comenzó a cansarse y a ponerse molesto, Karen lo envolvió en una manta, lo abrazó estrechamente y le habló con voz suave.
El aprender entre los pares	• A los bebés les gusta mirarse mutuamente (mirada visual). • Los bebés prefieren mirar caras, especialmente los bordes y los ojos. • Puede que los bebés lloren cuando oyen llorar a otros bebés (contagio).	Después de que la profesora puso a Tamika y a Sam sobre una manta en el piso, Tamika se quedó mirando fijamente a Sam.
La Cognición	• Los bebés siguen visualmente un objeto en movimiento. • Los bebés lloran para atraer la atención del adulto a fin de que los consuele o les dé de comer. • Los bebés miran a su alrededor por el salón con interés. • Los bebés comienzan a intentar alcanzar juguetes. • Los bebés notan que sus brazos y piernas han causado algo y repiten el movimiento. • Los bebés reconocen personas y objetos. • Los bebés comienzan a llevarse objetos a la boca.	Megan levantó la cabeza, apoyándose en los brazos mientras estaba recostada sobre la manta. Con una expresión seria miró a la maestra y a los niños a su alrededor. Willy comenzó a patear el móvil que colgaba encima y logró que se meneara. Luego paró, lo miró y volvió a patearlo mirándolo para ver si pasaba algo.

Interacciones entre Maestro o Padre/Madre–Niño	Ambiente
0 a 4 meses (bebé)	

• Mantenga a los bebés pequeños cerca, en brazos, en un saco de bebé, o sobre una manta.	• Estar cerca de una maestra conocida es lo mejor.
• Reconozca las señales de por qué el bebé quiere estar con usted—mirada fija, tenderle los brazos, mirada feliz—y respóndale hablándole suavemente, alternando la comunicación verbal y no verbal.	• Un espacio sereno y tranquilo con luces bajas, limita la información que el bebé necesita absorber.
	• Evite tener música de fondo todo el día.
	• Limite el número de objetos, sonidos, colores y movimientos alrededor de un bebé pequeño.
• Reconozca las señales que indican que el bebé necesita un descanso—bostezar, babear, mirar hacia otro lado—y apártese en silencio esperando a que el bebé se recupere.	• La maestra es lo más interesante que el bebé tiene para mirar, pero para otros bebés, los espejos y juguetes que se encuentran en su campo visual, también son interesantes.
• Consuele a los bebés cuando lloren.	
• Sostenga a dos bebés para que puedan mirarse mutuamente.	• Los brazos de la maestras ofrecen el mejor ambiente.
• Ponga varios bebés sobre una manta en el piso para que puedan mirarse y tocarse entre sí.	• Ponga a dos bebés sobre unas mantas en el piso—uno junto a otro, de manera que los dos se estén tocando con los dedos de los pies.
• Mueva lentamente un juguete pequeño de lado a lado mientras el bebé lo sigue con la mirada.	• Organice el espacio de manera que los bebés puedan ver actividad sin dejar de estar protegidos.
• Responda rápidamente al llanto del niño.	• Suministre unos cuantos objetos interesantes para mirar—juguetes pequeños en el piso, cuando están boca abajo; juguetes colgantes cuando los bebés están boca arriba
• Déles tiempo a los bebés para que estén tranquilos mirando lo que pasa a su alrededor. Hable acerca de lo que ven.	
• Reaccione ante las expresiones de los bebés con expresiones y lenguaje claro y hasta exagerado.	• Ponga espejos irrompibles a disposición de los bebés.

	Desarrollo	Ejemplo
	0 a 4 meses (bebé)	
El Lenguaje	• Los bebés se pueden asustar si oyen un ruido fuerte. • Los bebés captan las diferencias entre los sonidos. • Los bebés pueden dejar de llorar cuando oyen la voz de un adulto conocido. • Los bebés prefieren oír hablar cuando se les habla a ellos de forma directa. • Los bebés escuchan cuando un adulto les habla o les canta mientras los mira. • Los bebés lloran cuando sienten dolor, tienen hambre o están afligidos. • A los 2 meses de edad, los bebés tienen llantos específicos de hambre y dolor. • Los bebés "arrullan" (producen sonidos vocálicos suaves). • Hacia el final de este período, los bebés sonríen y se ríen. • Los bebés miran fijamente imágenes interesantes en libros.	Brenda sostenía a Jordán de manera que pudieran mirarse a los ojos. Jordán arrulló suavemente y Brenda le arrulló también. Luego, ella esperó a que Jordán lo volviera a hacer. Érica le sonrió de oreja a oreja a su padre cuando él la levantó de la cuna.
El desarrollo musculoso	• Los bebés levantan la cabeza cuando los llevan en brazos contra el hombro; sostienen la cabeza firme y erguida. • Boca abajo, los bebés levantan la cabeza y los hombros y pueden sostener un juguete en la mano. • Los bebés giran la cabeza hacia una voz conocida. • Los bebés se quedan quietos para prestar atención; se contonean y se mueven para inducir la continuación de la interacción. • De espaldas, los bebés estiran los brazos y las piernas a manera de juego. • Estando de lado, los bebés se dan vuelta para quedar de espaldas. • Los bebés sujetan un dedo o un juguete liviano con agarre reflejo. • Los bebés se chupan los dedos, las manos y otros objetos. • Los bebés mueven los brazos y las piernas.	Rosie mantuvo la cabeza erguida y miró a su alrededor a los otros niños mientras Sharon la llevaba contra el hombro. Robert, boca abajo sobre una manta, levantó la cabeza para mirarse al espejo montado a nivel del suelo en la pared. Jen tenía un sonajero en la mano, pero no parecía darse cuenta de que lo tenía. Filipe se llevó los dedos a la boca y se los chupó mientras miraba atentamente a los niños pequeños.

Interacciones entre Maestro o Padre/Madre–Niño	Ambiente
0 a 4 meses (bebé)	

• Use lenguaje dirigido al bebé. • Tenga a los bebés en brazos y hábleles suavemente. Mírelos largamente a los ojos mientras baila conversando. Respete al bebé si necesita un descanso y aparta la cabeza. • Lea libros con frases rítmicas y con una sola imagen en una página, con 2 imágenes a los de 4 meses de edad. • Interprete los eructos, llantos, bostezos, estiramientos y sonidos de los bebés como formas de comunicación. Diga "Ah, me estás diciendo que tienes sueño". • Cante canciones de cuna y otras canciones. • Sea un compañero de lenguaje que se identifique y comente los sentimientos del bebé. • Diga palabras y produzca sonidos para consolar a los bebés.	• El mejor ambiente son los brazos de un adulto afectuoso que tenga al bebé en brazos y le hable suavemente. • Suministre juguetes que produzcan sonidos agradables. Sostenga con cuidado el juguete e intercambie sonidos con el bebé. • Suministre materiales interesantes para tocar mientras comenta las texturas. • Coloque espejos bajos a lo largo de una pared. Los bebés se miran y es posible que produzcan sonidos.
• Cambie la posición del bebé; a veces de espaldas, otras boca abajo. Cuando lleve en brazos al bebé, acúnelo en sus brazos o sosténgalo erguido contra el hombro. • Cuando el bebé está en el piso, acuéstese cara a cara junto a él. • Cuando la bebé está de espaldas y trata de alcanzar un juguete un poco más allá de su cabeza, sosténgale el tronco mientras rueda.	• Una manta rígida (contra el riesgo de asfixia) en el suelo da espacio para los primeros movimientos. • Los juguetes pequeños e interesantes, las imágenes, y los libros para mirar cuando quieran animan a los bebés a levantar la cabeza. Un espejo atornillado a la pared a nivel del suelo siempre ofrece algo interesante que mirar. • A medida que comienzan a estirarse para alcanzar, a los bebés les gustan las barras estables con juguetes colgantes que puedan batear, alcanzar y agarrar.

Desarrollo	Ejemplo
4 a 8 meses (bebé)	

Los sentimientos/ Las ataduras

- A los bebés les gusta mirarse las manos y los pies.
- Los bebés agitan los brazos y patalean emocionados cuando ven a una persona conocida.
- Los bebés le sonríen a la maestra esperando que ella les sonría también.
- Con la cara y el cuerpo, los bebés expresan muchos sentimientos: desde fruncir el ceño y llorar hasta reírse a carcajadas.
- Los bebés expresan sus sentimientos claramente ante personas conocidas, y son más reservados con los desconocidos

A Deborah le encanta que la maestra la lleve en brazos mientras va por el salón "hablándole" de lo que ven. Tiene los ojos bien abiertos y brillantes, sonríe y hace ruiditos de arrullo cuando le corresponde hablar en la conversación. Cuando un visitante entra en el salón, Deborah se queda muy callada y seria, y se sujeta firmemente al hombro de la maestra mirando al visitante.

El aprender entre los pares

- Los bebés tocan a otros bebés, se dirigen vocalizaciones, se entusiasman, se acercan a otros bebés, sonríen y se ríen unos de otros.
- Los bebés pueden tratar a otros bebés como si fueran objetos - pasándoles por encima al gatear, lamiéndolos, chupándolos, sentándose encima. Están simplemente aprendiendo la diferencia entre personas y objetos. Los bebés pueden pinchar con el dedo, empujar, dar palmaditas a otros bebés, para ver lo que el otro bebé va a hacer. A menudo se sorprenden con la reacción que logran.reacción que logran.

Ana le pasó por encima gateando a Nadia que estaba acostada en el piso. Tocándole el pelo a Nadia. Ana se rió a carcajadas.

La Cognición

- A los bebés les gusta examinar los juguetes.
- A los bebés les gusta hacer que los juguetes hagan algo—sonar, encajarse uno dentro de otro.
- Los bebés imitan las expresiones y los gestos de los adultos.
- Los bebés se vuelven hacia los sonidos para ver de dónde vienen.
- Los bebés buscan juguetes que han dejado caer.

Ángela se interesa en todo. Mira a sus amigos y luego mira a la maestra y sonríe.

Roger se estira para tocar un juguete colgante. Cuando se balancea y suena, Roger se estira para hacerlo de nuevo.

El Lenguaje

- Los bebés giran la cabeza hacia un ruido, o una persona que dice su nombre.
- A los bebés les gusta que los adultos hablen, canten y se rían con ellos.
- Los bebés vocalizan con la intención de obtener una respuesta del adulto.
- Los bebés dan chillidos agudos.
- Los bebés practican sus sonidos cuando exploran y cuando están con adultos conocidos.
- Los bebés comienzan a balbucear; al principio una consonante y luego combinaciones de dos consonantes.
- Los bebés participan en conversaciones turnándose con los adultos.
- Los bebés miran distintas imágenes de un libro y se emocionan cuando ven una que les gusta o cuando les gusta el tono entusiasta del adulto que lee.

Mientras sostenía a Donovan en su regazo, Daniela, la maestra del bebé, señalaba con el dedo las imágenes del libro de tapas de cartón. "Mira," dijo señalando la imagen, "una pelota." Luego dijo "Ahí está tu pelota" y señaló hacia una pelota en el piso. Donovan miró la imagen, luego la pelota en el piso y finalmente volvió a mirar la imagen.

"Tt" dijo Afi cuando estaba en brazos de su maestra mirándola. "Tada" le dijo la maestra. "Tt" repitió Afi cuando le tocó hablar en la conversación.

Interacciones entre Maestro o Padre/Madre–Niño	Ambiente
4 a 8 meses (bebé)	

• Déles a los bebés oportunidades para que se miren al espejo mientras juegan. • Refleje las expresiones emocionales del bebé y agregue palabras apropiadas: "Estoy tan contenta de verte hoy." • Responda a los bebés de una manera que les ayude a calmarse y mantenerse activos. Si el bebé llora, cálmelo.	• Monte espejos irrompibles en las paredes. • Deje que los bebés pasen un rato en el piso mientras están boca arriba, jugando con sus pies y moviéndose por el piso. • Los libros y los álbumes de fotografías con caras reales mostrando diferentes expresiones emocionales son muy interesantes para los bebés.
• Muévase al ritmo de la música con un bebé en cada brazo. • Con un bebé sobre el regazo, apunte y hable sobre lo que el otro bebé está haciendo. • Ponga a dos bebés boca bajo frente a un espejo. • En vez de decirles "No" y "Deja de hacer eso" a los bebés que están explorando, dígales, "Tócalo con cuidado." Dígales a los niños lo que usted quiere que hagan...muéstreselo.	• Cuelgue un espejo seguro en la pared de manera horizontal, para que la parte de abajo esté tocando el piso. • Cubra la cámara de aire de la rueda de un auto con un paño suave. Siente a dos bebés en la cámara para que se toquen con los pies.
• Lleve en brazos al bebé, mientras camina por el salón mirando cosas y hablando acerca de ellas. • Siéntese cerca y háblele al bebé sobre los juguetes que está mirando. • Llame al bebé por su nombre a poca distancia para asegurarle que está cerca.	• Suministre una variedad de juguetes pequeños para que los manipule y los examine. • Suministre juguetes que suenan cuando se mueven, se encajan unos dentro de otros o se cuelgan y mueven cuando se tocan. • Ofrezca libros de tapas de cartón.
• Use lenguaje dirigido al bebé. • Hable a menudo con los bebés. Muéstreles objetos y personas nuevos y nómbrelos. • Repita los sonidos que los bebés producen y espere a que repitan el sonido (turnarse). • Refiérase a varios artículos conocidos, tales como "leche" o "perro," con lenguaje de señas. • Cante canciones y haga juegos de dedos. • Describa con palabras los sentimientos de los niños expresados a través de gestos, posturas corporales y sonidos. • Léale libros sencillos con una o dos imágenes por página. Señale con el dedo las imágenes mientras dice el nombre de la imagen. • Léale los mismos libros una y otra vez. • Aplique estrategias de atención conjunta—señale con el dedo un juguete o una imagen de un libro diciendo el nombre o hablando al respecto.	• Suministre juguetes y materiales interesantes para que los bebés los manipulen y examinen. • Suministre libros de cartón con asas para que pueden gatear hasta ellos y tomarlos. • Los libros con asas animan a los bebés a llevarlos. • Haga un libro de imágenes *de te veo, no te veo* pegando un pedazo de tela sobre cada imagen. • Forme un rincón de lectura acogedor donde las maestras puedan estar cómodas y leer a los bebés. • Suministre cajas de sonido (bien selladas) con distintos objetos adentro que produzcan distintos sonidos al sacudirlas. • Incorpore títeres al ambiente. Úselos a veces para "hablar" con el niño. Coloque los títeres en la mano del niño y espere a ver lo que el niño dice o hace.

Desarrollo	Ejemplo

4 a 8 meses (bebé)

| El desarrollo musculoso | <ul><li>Los bebés de espaldas se ponen de lado y luego se vuelven a poner de espaldas.</li><li>Al final de este período, los bebés se sientan; primero con apoyo pero luego estables y solos.</li><li>Los bebés se estiran para alcanzar objetos con el brazo.</li><li>Los bebés agarran rastrillando.</li><li>Los bebés gatean.</li><li>Los bebés sacuden, golpean, sujetan y sueltan objetos.</li><li>Los bebés se pasan objetos de una mano a otra.</li><li>Los bebés pueden sostener su biberón.</li><li>Los bebés se pueden llevar objetos a la boca.</li></ul> | Estando de espaldas, Micky rueda para quedar boca abajo y alcanzar un juguete, luego vuelve a rodar para jugar con el juguete.

A Erin, sentada sola establemente, le gusta recoger objetos con las dos manos y examinarlos.

A Freddy le gusta que lo tomen en brazos mientras toma su biberón, aunque insiste en sujetarlo solo. |

8 a 12 meses (bebé móvil)

| Los sentimientos/ Las ataduras | <ul><li>Los bebés móviles pueden tenerle miedo a los desconocidos.</li><li>Los bebés móviles pueden llamar a los adultos conocidos para que los ayuden cuando están enojados.</li><li>Los bebés móviles miran al adulto conocido para determinar si una situación es peligrosa o no.</li><li>Los bebés móviles se aferran al adulto cuando están en una situación desconocida.</li><li>A los bebés móviles les parecen divertidos los juegos tontos y las expresiones faciales exageradas que ponen los adultos.</li></ul> | Jaime está disfrutando de su nueva habilidad, que es ir gateando rápidamente a donde quiera ir. Le encanta el pequeño trepador que le permite mirar por la ventana. Pero cuando siente que la rampa es un poco inestable, se vuelve a mirar a Federico, su maestro, para asegurarse de que no hay peligro. |
| El aprender entre los pares | <ul><li>Los bebés pueden mostrar a otros bebés un objeto, sentarse juntos, perseguirse gateando y jugar a perseguir y recoger objetos.</li><li>Los bebés se sonríen y se ríen entre sí.</li><li>Los bebés se dirigen sonidos—y es posible que sus primeras palabras se las digan entre sí.</li><li>Uno de los juegos preferidos de los bebés es el *te veo, no te veo* mientras exploran la separación: irse y volver, aparecer y desaparecer.</li><li>Los bebés pueden aprender a tocarse uno al otro con cuidado.</li><li>Como a esta edad los bebés actúan en gran medida en función de sus objetivos, pueden apartar la mano de un bebé que esté tocando un juguete, o gatearle por encima para alcanzar un juguete.</li></ul> | Shamaine miró la estantería baja de juguetes y vio que Carla venía gateando hacia ella. Shamaine se dio la vuelta rápidamente y se alejó gateando con Carla siguiéndola de cerca.

Kai pasó gateando por encima de las piernas de Bridger para alcanzar un juguete que estaba al otro lado de Bridger. |

Interacciones entre Maestro o Padre/Madre–Niño	Ambiente

4 a 8 meses (bebé)

• Quédese cerca del bebé que recién comienza a sentarse solo. • Conozca el avance del desarrollo motor; anime emocionalmente y apoye físicamente al bebé en sus nuevos intentos. • Crea en los beneficios a largo plazo para la salud de un estilo de vida activo.	• Deles lugares seguros para rodar, sentarse y gatear. Proteja a los bebés de cualquier cosa que pueda caerles encima. • Deles objetos livianos pequeños y lavables (grandes para evitar que se asfixien) para que los manipulen y los lancen, y deles recipientes para los objetos.

4 a 12 meses (bebé)

• Anime a los bebés móviles a moverse y explorar asegurándoles que usted los está mirando y cuidando. • Entienda que los bebés móviles pueden asustarse ante situaciones nuevas que quizás no los habrían asustado hace unos meses. Consuélelos y tranquilícelos.	• Juegue al *te veo, no te veo*. • Léales cuentos sobre madres y padres que se van y vuelven. • Léales libros con solapas que se pueden levantar para encontrar cosas. • Mantenga una previsibilidad de hábitos y rutinas del salón.
• Nombre partes del cuerpo del bebé mientras dos bebés están sentados juntos: Estos son los ojos del bebé Esta es la nariz del bebé Toca la parte con que ves Tócate la parte que te suenas • Ponga un bebé con otro (en parejas) porque las interacciones más frecuentes, complejas e intensas entre niños se producen cuando un niño está con varios compañeros. • Comprenda que los bebés no son "malos" cuando le apartan la mano al otro. Diga "Jenny tenía ese juguete. Vamos a buscarte otro."	• Mientras están comiendo, coloque las sillas altas de manera que los niños se puedan ver unos a los otros. • Disponga de rincones agradables en el salón donde los bebés puedan "desaparecer" (pero pudiendo aún ser vistos por adultos). • Cuelgue del techo un paño largo y ancho (para que los bebés no se enreden en él). A los bebés les encanta gatear alrededor. • Ponga contenedores con bloques de diferentes tamaños entre dos bebés. Quédese sentada junto a ellos mientras comienzan a explorar los materiales. Hable acerca de lo que está haciendo cada uno.

Desarrollo	Ejemplo
8 a 12 meses (bebé móvil)	

La Cognición

- A los bebés móviles les gusta desarmar los juguetes y luego volver a armarlos.
- A los bebés móviles les gustan los juguetes que hacen algo cuando se tocan, se jalan o se golpean.
- Los bebés móviles comienzan juegos imaginarios muy simples, tales como llevarse un vaso a la boca.
- A los bebés móviles les gusta encontrar juguetes pequeños debajo de un paño o de un vaso.
- A los bebés móviles les gusta levantar y examinar objetos pequeños tales como un Cheerio.
- Los bebés móviles muestran objetos con el dedo sabiendo que usted también puede verlos.

A Carlos le encanta sacar cada uno de los animales de plástico del balde y mirarlo. Cuando el balde queda vacío, lo lanza a un lado.

A Aliya le gusta el botón que se aprieta y las puertas oscilantes de la caja mecánica, pero todavía no puede hacer funcionar todos los mecanismos. Su maestra expresa sorpresa a Aliya cuando las puertas se abren y, de vez en cuando, le enseña cómo funciona otra de las perillas.

El Lenguaje

- Los bebés móviles comienzan a participar en juegos sociales tales como el *te veo, no te veo* o el *"así de grande."*
- A los bebés les gusta escuchar juegos de sonidos (rimas), canciones y juegos de dedos.
- El balbuceo continúa desarrollándose con sílabas com–binadas tales como "dada," "mama," "nana" y "tutu" y a esta altura el bebé puede usar estos sonidos específicamente para referirse a su mamá o su papá.
- Los bebés repiten sonidos consistentemente para referirse a un objeto, una persona o un animal.
- Si oyen otro lenguaje *con* un adulto a través de estrategias conversacionales interactivas, los bebés pueden "tener una actitud abierta hacia los sonidos de un lenguaje extranjero."
- Los bebés pueden comenzar a decir palabras aisladas.
- Al final de este período, los bebés pueden comenzar a señalar con el dedo para atraer la atención de un adulto.
- Los bebés emplean expresiones faciales y gestos tales como agitar la cabeza o los brazos para que los tomen en brazos, y así comunicarse con los adultos o con sus compañeros.

Una de las primeras palabras de Dana fue "mamá," y la repetía una y otra vez cuando veía a su madre.

Una de las primera palabras de Trishanna fue "mamá," y la repetía con entusiasmo una y otra vez cuando veía a su madre.

El desarrollo musculoso

- Los bebés móviles jalan de algo para ponerse de pie.
- Los bebés móviles se pasean.
- Los bebés móviles se quedan de pie solos.
- Los bebés móviles caminan con ayuda al principio y después solos.
- Los bebés móviles se sientan en una silla.
- Los bebés móviles comen con los dedos.
- Los bebés móviles pueden usar una cuchara y un vaso hermético.
- Los bebés móviles agarran atenazando.

Hershel gatea hasta su maestra, luego se agarra de su pierna y jala para ponerse de pie.

Jem se sienta a la mesa del almuerzo, y alterna la cuchara y los dedos para disfrutar de la comida.

Interacciones entre Maestro o Padre/Madre–Niño	Ambiente
8 a 12 meses (bebé móvil)	

- Con su presencia, su interés y su entusiasmo, ayude al bebé a concentrarse en lo que le interesa para apoyarlo en su atención y exploración.
- Con sus expresiones y palabras afectivas, demuéstrele al bebé móvil que usted disfruta de sus descubrimientos.
- Con palabras, describa la actividad del niño: "Mira, encontraste un Cheerio. Lo estás recogiendo con los dedos."

- Suministre juguetes tales como vasos para apilar, anillos en poste, piezas que se interconectan y cubos llenos de objetos pequeños interesantes, tales como animales de juguete.
- Suministre réplicas tamaño infantil de platos o herramientas domésticas.
- Suministre juguetes que reaccionen—cajas mecánicas, almohadillas llenas de agua.
- Suministre materiales sensoriales, como agua y arena con una variedad de herramientas.
- Suministre libros de tapas de cartón con fotos.

- Organice juegos conocidos tales como te veo—no te veo, palmitas—palmitas o "*¿cómo eres de grande?*"
- Responda con palabras a la comunicación no verbal de los bebés.
- Observe y espere a que los bebés inicien sonidos o palabras.
- Imite los sonidos y luego expanda, detalle y amplíe el lenguaje del bebé.
- Modele el siguiente paso en el desarrollo del lenguaje.
- Emplee hablarse a sí mismo y hablar en paralelo.
- Hable a menudo de manera receptiva con un vocabulario variado. No bombardee al niño con palabras.
- Lea los libros con entusiasmo—cambiando el tono de su voz con los distintos personajes.
- Hable sobre las imágenes y el cuento a medida que lee. Involucre a los bebés con la voz y los gestos.
- Mientras miran una imagen, espere a que el bebé produzca sonidos, señale con el dedo o haga expresiones faciales.

- Cree un rincón de lectura acogedor en que los bebés puedan alcanzar fácilmente los libros y manipularlos.
- Haga un libro "Todo sobre mí"—álbumes pequeños de fotos para cada niño con imágenes de ellos, su familia, sus juguetes preferidos, sus compañeros, sus maestras y los animales domésticos de la familia. Déjelos al alcance de los niños. Cambie las imágenes a medida que el niño crece.
- Los juguetes musicales para empujar animan a los bebés a manipularlos y producir sonidos.

- Esté atenta para saber cuándo ayudar al bebé que comienza a caminar y cuándo dejar que lo siga intentando.
- Dé tiempo para que los bebés mayores practiquen comer solos.

- Lugares seguros para ponerse de pie apoyándose en algo.
- Juguetes para empujar y jalar para que los que comienzan a caminar puedan jalar y empujar.
- Cajas mecánicas.
- Libros de cartón para pasar las páginas, levantar las solapas y meter los dedos a través de los agujeros.

	Desarrollo	Ejemplo
	8 a 18 meses (bebé móvil)	
Los sentimientos / Las ataduras	• Los bebés móviles imitan las acciones de los adultos conocidos, tales como hablar por teléfono o llevar en brazos a una muñeca bebé. • Los bebés móviles intentan atraer la atención del adulto jalándole la pierna o tomándole la mano. • Los bebés móviles se calman con su manta o su animal de peluche favorito. • Los bebés móviles protestan ruidosamente cuando sus padres los dejan. • Los bebés móviles se relajan y se consuelan acurrucándose con un adulto conocido. • Los bebés móviles hacen saber claramente lo que les gusta y lo que no les gusta.	Amelia carga toda la mañana su osito de peluche por todos los lados. A veces copia las acciones de Sofía, su maestra, dándole al osito palmaditas en la espalda o alimentándole con biberón. Cuando se cansa, se frota el osito contra la oreja y se chupa el pulgar.
El aprender entre los pares	• Comienzan los turnos imitativos (motores) e interactivos. Los niños pequeños pueden imitarse unos a otros—si un bebé le da un juguete a otro, el otro puede imitarlo. • Los bebés móviles comienzan a hablarse unos a otros. • Los bebés pueden demostrar preocupación cuando otros bebés están afligidos. • Los bebés móviles pueden quitarle el juguete a otro bebé, decirle "no," empujarlo, agarrar firmemente el juguete y decir "mío." • A esta edad, los bebés son pequeños científicos que experimentan para ver cómo funcionan las cosas. Esto afecta la relación que tienen con sus compañeros, pues están constantemente haciéndoles cosas para ver cómo reaccionan. • Morder puede aparecer cuando los bebés muerden a otros "para ver lo que pasa," para obtener el juguete que quieren, para expresar su frustración. Los bebés están al borde de comunicarse bien; pueden comunicarse por la boca en forma de mordedura.	Rashida golpeó la mesa con la cuchara; poco después, otros dos comenzaron a hacerlo. Parecían estar siguiendo el ejemplo físicamente (como si estuvieran conversando). Primero, Carmen intentó alejar a Toby del caballito de balancín. Cuando eso no dio resultado, se inclinó hacia él y lo mordió en el brazo.
La Cognición	• A los bebés móviles les gusta poner en práctica su movilidad para explorar gateando, caminando, trepando, corriendo, etc. • Los bebés móviles disfrutan jugando en la arena, el agua, con plastilina y varios tipos de herramientas. • A los bebés móviles les interesan las relaciones espaciales de rompecabezas y tableros con agujeros. • Los bebés móviles utilizan herramientas tales como llaves o teléfonos en sus juegos imaginarios. • Los bebés móviles disfrutan al mirar libros y nombrar objetos, animales o partes del cuerpo.	Alexis y Dan están contentísimos de estar de pie. Se siguen mutuamente por todas partes, uno subiendo atrevidamente por un plano inclinado, con el otro inmediatamente detrás. A veces los dos intentan meterse debajo del tobogán. A Meredith le encanta acurrucarse en el regazo de su maestra y mostrar con el dedo imágenes en libros mientras la maestra nombra los animales o le pide que encuentre uno en particular.

Interacciones entre Maestro o Padre/Madre–Niño	Ambiente
12 a 18 meses (bebé móvil)	

• Muestre interés en las actividades del bebé.	• Disponga de objetos de mayores en tamaño infantil: teléfonos, platos, llaves, etc.
• Muestre su orgullo por los logros del bebé.	• Ponga fotografías de bebés con su familia en la pared.
• Deje que los bebés la utilicen como una base firme, para explorar el mundo.	• Lamine las fotos del bebé con su familia para que las lleve consigo.
• Deje que los bebés sepan que usted entiende lo que sienten y responda respetuosamente.	• Haga álbumes de fotos de los niños del programa y hable acerca de las fotos.
• Estos niños son todavía muy pequeños, y necesitan que se les acurruque y abrace mucho.	• Disponga de sillas de adulto y espacios tranquilos y cómodos para tener a los niños en brazos.
• Muéstreles a los niños pequeños móviles cómo rodar juntos por una pequeña pendiente.	• Suministre una caja de cartón grande abierta por los dos lados. Anímelos a entrar y salir de la caja gateando juntos. Ventanas a los lados de la caja estimulan a los bebés para que se miren entre ellos por la ventana.
• Ayude a los niños pequeños móviles a que aprendan los nombres de los demás, cantando canciones de saludo y despedida incluyendo los nombres de los niños: "Esta es Tania, ¿cómo estás?" y "Este es Enrique, ¿cómo estás?" y apuntando o tocando a cada niño que pasa junto a usted o al que está sentado en su regazo.	• Muñecas, camiones, autos y otros materiales de juego, promueven las interacciones entre compañeros.
• Comente el comportamiento social activo. Diga "Le diste la muñeca. Eso le gusta." Puede que los bebés no entiendan sus palabras, pero son capaces de darse cuenta por el tono de voz que usted está contenta con ellos.	• A los bebés les encanta la arena y el agua y jugar con botellas y pelotas seguras de diferentes tamaños. Cuando cada uno tiene su propio contenedor o cubo con agua o arena, el juego se desarrolla sin altibajos.
• A los bebés les gusta mirar libros juntos, creando grupos informales (esto significa que entrar y salir del grupo) alrededor de las piernas, el regazo y los brazos del padre, la madre o la maestra que más les gusta.	• Al aire libre, grandes cajas de arena o juguetes para empujar, estimulan el juego interactivo. Tendencias de Desarrollo e Interacciones Receptivas.
• Déle a los bebés móviles tiempo y espacio protegido para explorar.	• Suministre rompecabezas simples, tableros con agujeros, formas, cuentas de madera con cordones gruesos.
• Quédese cerca para expresar interés, sugerir palabras y hacer que la actividad sea más elaborada y compleja.	• Suministre trepadores pequeños, túneles y trayectos interesantes.
• Ayude a los bebés móviles a que expresen su interés en otros bebés cuidadosamente.	• Suministre juguetes que funcionen al darle cuerda, o que se enciendan y apaguen.
• Exprese entusiasmo por lo que les interesa a los bebés móviles.	• Suministre artículos simples para el juego imaginario.

	Desarrollo	Ejemplo
18 a 24 meses (niños pequeños)		
El Lenguaje	• Los bebés móviles pueden seguir instrucciones sencillas tales como "Ven aquí" o "Trae tus zapatos" sin que haya que hacer gestos. • Los bebés móviles pueden jugar socialmente sin que haya que demostrar la acción. Por ejemplo, cuando usted dice "Dile adiós" ellos mueven las manos aunque usted no les muestre cómo hacerlo. • Los bebés móviles señalan con el dedo para llamar la atención de los adultos y de sus compañeros. • Se puede producir un aprendizaje rápido de palabras—una explosión de lenguaje—en los niños que están aprendiendo muchas palabras nuevas. • Hacia el final de este período, los bebés móviles combinan palabras. • Los bebés móviles farfullan (hilando muchos sonidos) con la misma entonación que los adultos. • Los bebés móviles hacen gestos y se valen de palabras para rechazar, pedir, comentar, negarse, exigir y nombrar objetos y personas. • Los bebés móviles se valen del lenguaje para mantener una interacción o conversación con un adulto o uno de sus compañeros.	La maestra de Janina le dijo "Juguemos a dar palmitas, palmitas," y Janina comenzó a aplaudir. Ross miró a su maestra con expectación, farfullando muchos sonidos juntos como si le hiciera una pregunta.
El desarrollo musculoso	• Los bebés móviles apilan y alinean bloques. • Los bebés móviles pueden vestirse y desvestirse solos, meter el brazo en una manga y el pie dentro de un zapato. • Los bebés móviles pueden caminar. • Los bebés móviles caminan con objetos en las manos. • Los bebés móviles suben escaleras.	Gary se paró frente a la mesa y construyó cuidadosamente con las dos manos una torre con bloques de colores. Michelle caminó por la habitación con su osito de peluche en una mano y su manta en la otra.
18 a 24 meses (niños pequeños)		
Los sentimientos / Las ataduras	• Los niños pequeños comienzan a controlar ciertos impulsos diciendo "no, no, no" a medida que comienzan a lanzar bloques. • Los niños pequeños pueden dejar lo que están haciendo cuando la maestra se lo dice. • Los niños pequeños pueden no querer dejar de jugar cuando su padre o su madre viene a buscarlos. • Los niños pequeños pueden llorar cuando no consiguen hacer algo que están intentando. • Los niños pequeños saben su propio nombre y puede que usen el "mi" y "mío."	Francisco se sube a la mesa mientras mira directamente a los ojos de la maestra que desaprueba lo que él hace, y dice "no, no, no."

Interacciones entre Maestro o Padre/Madre–Niño	Ambiente

12 a 18 meses (bebé móvil)

- Mantenga el tema en una conversación con un bebé móvil. Vea cuántas veces hablará el niño.
- Responda a la entonación del parloteo del niño. Por ejemplo, si parece que el niño hace una pregunta, responda a lo que usted cree que el niño puede estar preguntando.
- Responda con palabras a las señales hechas con los dedos y otros medios de comunicación no verbal de los bebés móviles.
- Describa y compare con palabras tamaños, formas y sonidos.
- Cuando un bebé móvil dice palabras tales como "Yo salto," modele el próximo paso en el desarrollo del lenguaje diciendo "Tú estás saltando," añadiendo "ando o iendo" a la palabra. Haga esto tanto con el contenido de las palabras como con la estructura de las palabras u oraciones.
- Léale libros con cuentos más largos, haga pausas a medida que avanza por el libro para animar a los bebés móviles a hablar sobre las imágenes y el cuento.

- Introduzca materiales de arte tales como plastilina, arcilla y pintura.
- Déle rollos de toallas de papel a los bebés móviles para que produzcan sonidos.
- Los juguetes musicales para jalar animan a los bebés móviles a caminar y jalarlos o empujarlos.
- Las cajas de música resistentes animan a los bebés móviles a apretar botones para "hacer música."
- Se pueden poner a disposición tambores y otros instrumentos musicales.
- Incorpore un reproductor de CD resistente con un cuento que haya grabado el padre o la madre.
- Grabe las voces de los bebés móviles con una grabadora y haga que las escuchen.
- Suministre materiales para hacer burbujas.
- Facilite espacios para animar a dos o tres niños a conversar con sus compañeros.

- Imite la cada vez mayor variedad de movimientos del bebé.
- Introduzca canciones con pequeños bailes y movimientos.
- Dé tiempo y tenga paciencia mientras el niño pequeño practica ponerse solo la chaqueta.

- Juguetes para montar estables y no muy altos.
- Juguetes mecedores estables y no muy altos.
- Juegos de manipulación basados en habilidades, tales como apilar vasos o ensartar aros en un palo.

18 a 24 meses (niños pequeños)

- Mantenga su sentido del humor. Entienda que los niños pequeños pueden dejar de hacer ciertas cosas a veces, pero no siempre.
- Respete los sentimientos fuertes de los niños pequeños. El turnarse y compartir viene después; ahora "mí" y "mío" son una etapa importante del desarrollo de un sólido sentido de identidad.

- Disponga espacios que permita que los niños exploren, pero siempre sin perderlos de vista.
- Tenga suficientes juguetes iguales para que varios niños puedan tener el suyo, sin tener que compartir o turnarse.
- Deje que los niños traigan al programa artículos que los calmen, tales como mantas o animales de peluche. Asígneles un lugar tranquilo donde puedan consolarse solos.

Desarrollo	Ejemplo
12 a 24 meses (bebé móvil)	

El aprender entre los pares

- Las amistades pueden desarrollarse a muy temprana edad. Los amigos son más propensos a tocarse, apoyarse y sonreírse entre sí, que otros niños que no son amigos.
- Los niños pequeños imitan mutuamente los sonidos y las palabras que dicen y se hablan y comienzan a comunicarse con los demás a mayores distancias.
- Los niños pequeños dan u ofrecen un juguete o comida a otros niños pequeños
- Los niños pequeños pueden llamar a un adulto y jalar al adulto para que ayude a otro niño, o pueden ayudar a otro niño llevándole un pañuelito de papel, por ejemplo.
- Los niños pequeños demuestran bondad hacia otros bebés que se sienten afligidos. Sin embargo, el bebé o niño pequeño móvil puede suponer que lo que lo consuela a él, también consuela al afligido
- Los niños pueden turnarse, por ejemplo, con una pelota o para saltar. Pueden tener conversaciones cinéticas de niño pequeño mientras siguen a un líder por el salón—entrando y saliendo del grupo, turnándose para ser líder y seguidor—como si estuvieran en una conversación, en la cual escuchan y hablan, aprendiendo la importante habilidad de cómo turnarse.
- Empujar, dar empujones, agarrar y golpear pueden ocurrir a medida que los niños luchan con la idea de "mío durante todo el tiempo que yo quiera" y "tuyo, pero yo también lo quiero." Los niños pequeños puede que se peleen más por juguetes pequeños, que por objetos grandes que no se mueven.

Paulie parecía estar esperando en la puerta a que apareciera Jamie al principio de la jornada. Cuando Jaime y su mamá llegaron, Paulie se dirigió hacia ellos y le tomó la mano a Jaime con una gran sonrisa en la cara.

Tania saltó (medio se cayó) de una tabla situada a varias pulgadas del suelo. Pronto tres niños pequeños estaban parados sobre la tabla, y casi saltando, casi bajando de la tabla y disfrutando inmensamente de la actividad.

La Cognición

- Los niños pequeños de corta edad disfrutan de su facilidad de movimiento y les gusta llevar cosas en las manos.
- Los niños pequeños entienden que pueden hacer que ocurran cosas.
- Los niños pequeños entienden y recuerdan los detalles de las rutinas.
- Los niños pequeños sustituyen unos objetos por otros en su juego imaginario.
- Los niños pequeños disfrutan cada vez más de los materiales problemáticos que sugieren actividades tales como construir y hacer corresponder formas.

- Mantenga rutinas predecibles recordándole a los niños el orden de las etapas con preguntas tales como "Es hora de comer. ¿Qué hacemos?"
- Tenga los materiales en lugares predecibles y ordenados.
- Con preguntas tales como "¿Qué vas a hacer ahora? ¿Qué vas a comprar en la tienda? Apoye a los niños pequeños cuando piensen en sus actividades.

Interacciones entre Maestro o Padre/Madre–Niño	Ambiente
18 a 24 meses (niños pequeños)	

• Ya esté adentro o afuera, atienda a los niños pequeños cuando entran a "reponerse" emocionalmente con su maestra especial animando a varios niños pequeños a sentarse junto a usted o en su regazo. Permita que los niños pequeños se toquen mutuamente con cuidado. • Anime a que varios niños pequeños hagan sonidos de animales y se imiten entre sí mientras les muestra las imágenes de un libro. • Pídale a un niño que ayude a otro, trayendo un pañuelito de papel, abriendo la llave del agua, abriendo la puerta, etc. • Estimule la bondad mutua. Si un niño pequeño llora, pregúntele a otro lo que "podríamos" hacer para ayudarlo. • Anime a dos niños pequeños a que pongan la mesa o la limpien después de comer. Mire como se imitan. • Cante canciones, animando a los niños pequeños a que se turnen con las acciones.	• Adentro y afuera: Ponga a su disposición áreas con arena que sean suficientemente grandes para varios niños pequeños, es de esperar que se sienten justo en el medio del área. • Las mantas sobre el piso, el suelo o una mesa son un centro para que los niños pequeños jueguen. • Suministre vagones: Empujar o jalar a un amigo en un vagón dará como resultado chillidos de deleite. • Suministre pelotas y juguetes para jalar que estimulen el juego interactivo. • Lugares para saltar sin peligro estimulan los intercambios sociales. • Suministre juguetes musicales, varios de cada clase, para que los niños puedan tocar juntos una música bella. A veces uno dirigirá y el otro le seguirá, o viceversa.
• Mantenga rutinas predecibles recordándole a los niños el orden de las etapas con preguntas tales como "Es hora de comer. ¿Qué hacemos?" • Tenga los materiales en lugares predecibles y ordenados. • Con preguntas tales como "¿Qué vas a hacer ahora? ¿Qué vas a comprar en la tienda? Apoye a los niños pequeños cuando piensen en sus actividades.	• Tenga los juguetes y los materiales organizados de manera que los niños pequeños puedan escogerlos, alcanzarlos y guardarlos (con recordatorios). • Revise frecuentemente los materiales a su disposición para asegurarse de que mantiene un equilibrio entre lo que es conocido y lo que es un poco difícil.

	Desarrollo	Ejemplo
El Lenguaje	• Los niños pequeños pueden ir a buscar juguetes conocidos en otra habitación de la casa cuando un adulto se los pide, y pueden seguir instrucciones tales como "cierra la puerta." • Los niños pequeños combinan palabras para nombrar cosas ("ese gato"), para negar ("no muerde") y para rechazar ("no más"). • Los niños pequeños combinan dos o tres palabras con significado. • Los niños pequeños se valen del lenguaje para varios propósitos, tales como preguntar "¿Qué eso?" • Los niños pequeños señalan una cantidad de imágenes cada vez mayor en los libros cuando un adulto les habla sobre la imagen.	"Hola Kitty," "puerta abierta" y "sombrero puesto" fueron sólo algunas de las combinaciones de dos palabras que Cheral dijo a los 20 meses de edad. Tyra corrió rápidamente hasta el librero, tomó un libro con tapa brillante y regresó de prisa hasta su maestra. Después de sentarse cómodamente en su regazo, abrió el libro y comenzó a señalar con entusiasmo las imágenes mientras su maestra las nombraba.
El desarrollo musculoso	• Los niños pequeños señalan objetos con el dedo para comunicarse. • Los niños pequeños hacen marcas en un papel. • Los niños pequeños trabajan y dan forma a la plastilina. • Los niños pequeños corren. • Los niños pequeños se sientan y se levantan solos de sillas pequeñas. • Los niños pequeños están desarrollando su confianza espacial; explorando su cuerpo en el espacio.	Mindy estiró la plastilina con las manos y luego hizo figuras con las herramientas. Joseph se sentó a la mesa para comer, luego llevó los platos sucios al fregadero.

24 a 36 meses (niños pequeños)

Los sentimientos / Las ataduras	• Los niños pequeños a veces pueden ser independientes, pero les gusta saber que la maestra está cerca. • A los niños pequeños les gusta mirar fotos de sí mismos, sus amigos y su familia. • Los niños pequeños oyen sus palabras y el tono de su voz cuando usted habla acerca de ellos. Quieren que usted se interese en ellos y se enorgullezca de sus logros. • Los niños pequeños necesitan límites claros y consistentes. Olvidarán o pondrán a prueba las reglas, pero se sentirán a gusto cuando usted les recuerda las reglas y les ayuda a obedecerlas. • Los niños pequeños pueden utilizar palabras para expresar sus sentimientos, o pueden dar golpes o morder. • Los niños pequeños se ocupan de los sentimientos de los demás, y consuelan a quien esté triste o le llevan una curita a quien se haya lastimado.	Kiki llevó su bebé a ver las fotos de su propia familia en la pared, y la arrullaba mientras miraba la cara de su propia madre.

Interacciones entre Maestro o Padre/Madre–Niño	Ambiente

18 a 24 meses (niños pequeños)

- Léale libros con cuentos más largos, haga pausas a medida que avanza por el libro para animar a los niños pequeños a hablar sobre las imágenes y la historia. Haga preguntas abiertas tales como "¿Cómo se siente el oso?"
- Pregúntese a menudo con el niño: "Me pregunto qué va a pasar con el oso."
- Haga que los niños pequeños conversen intentando mantenerse en el mismo tema que el niño.
- Introduzca nuevas conversaciones sobre objetos y eventos.

- Disponga una pista de obstáculos complicada y use palabras tales como "adentro," "afuera," "por arriba," "a través," "alrededor," "arriba" y "abajo" mientras el niño pequeño recorre la pista.
- Suministre libros nuevos todas las semanas, pero mantenga cerca los libros preferidos de los niños.
- Suministre una mayor variedad de materiales de arte.
- Déle materiales que estimulen los sentidos.

- Ponga a disposición de los niños materiales pequeños que los induzcan a poner en práctica su creciente capacidad de manipulación de objetos con los dedos.
- Quédese con los niños pequeños y apóyelos mientras intentan poner en práctica capacidades recientemente desarrolladas.
- Deles oportunidades de trepar, caminar y correr.

- Materiales de arte tales como brochas gordas, marcadores y superficies grandes para pintar.
- Artículos pequeños, tales como cuentas que se interconectan y tableros para clavijas, para practicar actividades de manipulación.
- Mucho espacio para el movimiento: bailes, juguetes para montar, estructuras para trepar, toboganes.

18 a 36 meses (niños pequeños)

- Establezca reglas claras y consistentes. Esté preparada para recordar a los niños pequeños con frecuencia, la manera de obedecer las reglas: "No se muerde; morder duele."
- Dedique a los niños pequeños suficiente tiempo y atención para que se sientan comprendidos.
- Haga eco al entusiasmo que los niños pequeños pueden darle a su propio juego.
- Note y comente las interacciones que los niños pequeños están mirando y en las que están pensando.

- Tenga muchas fotografías de niños con sus familias en las paredes, en libros pequeños, y laminadas para que las lleven consigo.
- Disponga espacios protegidos para el juego tranquilo.
- Mantenga rutinas y disposiciones de salón previsibles.
- Tenga libros con cuentos simples sobre ir y venir, familias y amistad.
- Canten canciones sobre sentimientos tales como "Cuando estás contento y lo sabes" y "Cuando estás triste y enojado..."

	Desarrollo	Ejemplo
	24 a 36 meses (niños pequeños)	

El aprender entre los pares

- La amistad de los niños pequeños es "búsqueda de proximidad," deseo de estar cerca y mostrar cariño como sonreír, reírse y abrazarse. Los amigos se prefieren mutuamente como compañeros de interacción. Las amistades continúan desarrollándose y se profundizan.
- Los niños pequeños intercambian información y pueden imitar las acciones pasadas de los demás.
- Los niños pequeños pueden congregarse y amontonarse. Cuando una maestra comienza a hacer una actividad interesante con un niño, por lo general los otros llegan corriendo de todas partes del salón.
- Algunos niños pequeños son capaces de idear maneras diferentes de ayudar a otros cuando se han lastimado o están tristes. Algunos pueden tener un impresionante repertorio de comportamientos altruistas, y si algo no funciona, intentan hacer otra cosa.
- Los compañeros colaboran hacia metas comunes, haciendo uno de líder y otro de seguidor.
- Pueden producirse peleas por objetos, espacio personal y palabras. Los niños pequeños también se dedican a intercambios juguetones, tal como empujar y caerse bruscamente, correr y perseguirse, y realizar juegos verbales.
- Algunos niños pueden ganarse cierta reputación entre sus compañeros por comportamiento agresivo o bondadoso.
- Los niños se vuelven más positivos y menos negativos en su juego social entre los 24 y los 36 meses de edad.
- Puede haber dominación de un niño sobre otro.

Ejemplo:

María y Sally jugaron durante 30 minutos en extremos opuestos de la pequeña estantería de juguetes, mirándose mutuamente cada varios minutos y diciéndose "barco," "mi barco," "hola," "quiero jugo," "mírame" y llamándose por su nombre una y otra vez.

Cuando pasó un camión de bomberos afuera, varios niños pequeños se acercaron corriendo para mirar por la ventana.

José y Miguel empujaron, jalaron, rodaron y resoplaron haciendo rodar una gran calabaza desde dentro hasta el patio de juegos, donde los niños pequeños y sus maestras iban a abrirla y sacarle las semillas.

La Cognición

- Los niños pequeños de más edad comienzan a entender conceptos tales como el color, el tamaño, la forma, el tiempo y el peso.
- Los niños pequeños de más edad se interesan en las historias y en las imágenes de libros de cuentos.
- Los niños pequeños mayores crean nuevos cuentos en el juego imaginario o nuevas estructuras en la construcción de bloques y se vuelven más imaginativos y creativos.
- Asigne papeles a los juguetes y a otros niños en el juego imaginario; utilice sillas, mantas y estanterías como sustitutos en el juego imaginario.

Ejemplo:

Eric se siente un poco triste y lleva una foto de su mamá diciendo, "después de siesta."

Sara se encarga de la esquina de juego dramático entregando muñecas y animales de peluche. Se pone un sombrero y dice "la mamá va a comprar."

Interacciones entre Maestro o Padre/Madre–Niño	Ambiente

24 a 36 meses (niños pequeños)

• Organice situaciones en que dos niños pequeños deban trabajar juntos—como por ejemplo, hacer rodar una calabaza de un lugar a otro, o traer de afuera un balde con bloques "pesados."	• Coloque sombreros y ropa que sea fácil de poner, en un rincón acogedor y con un espejo grande.
• Póngale una curita a una muñeca en el brazo o en la pierna y anime a los niños pequeños a que cuiden al bebé.	• Los niños pequeños disfrutarán de una mutua compañía cuando los amigos cambian de aspecto poniéndose un sombrero de ala ancha o unos zapatos grandes.
• Pregunte a los niños pequeños "¿cómo podemos ayudar a José? Está triste, está llorando."	• Los espacios que quedan encima o debajo de un ático bajo estimulan la interacción entre los niños pequeños.
• Intente cambiar la imagen de la niña que se está ganando una reputación de agresividad. Téngala cerca, muéstrele cómo tocar con cuidado y comente su comportamiento servicial. Déle un juguete interesante que pueda inducir a otros niños a jugar con ella. Manténgase cerca y enséñele a jugar.	• Suministre varios tipos de muñecas, así como cubiertos de mesa no peligrosos, mantas y camas pequeñas. Siéntese cerca y mire como los niños pequeños juegan a cuidar a sus bebés.
	• Suministre materiales sin propósito específico, como bloques, y actividades que requieran cooperación, tales como pintar con agua un muro exterior utilizando una brocha gorda, o llenar de agua un balde grande con envases pequeños.
	• Un equipo de motor grande, como los trepadores o los barcos de balancín, animan a los niños pequeños a colaborar para alcanzar una meta común: todos se van a la parte de arriba del trepador, o balancean el barco con todos dentro.
• Pregúntele a los niños cómo podrían resolver problemas que se presentan y luego deje que los resuelvan solos.	• Facilite oportunidades de juego que promuevan la comparación de tamaños, pesos, colores, formas y cantidades.
• Apoye a los niños que trabajan juntos con materiales para que compartan ideas.	• Ponga por todas partes libros para los niños. Tenga varias copias de libros favoritos antiguos, y traiga libros nuevos.
• Hable con un lenguaje que describa el tiempo ("ahora," "más tarde," "antes de la siesta," "después de almuerzo"), peso ("pesado," "ligero"), tamaño ("grande," "pequeño").	• Permita que los niños combinen materiales de diferentes áreas de maneras creativas.
• Cuente cosas durante el día.	• Presente nuevos materiales o nuevas combinaciones de materiales.

	Desarrollo	Ejemplo
	24 a 36 meses (niños pequeños)	
El Lenguaje	• Los niños pequeños comprenden instrucciones complejas y recuerdan palabras de canciones cortas y juegos de dedos. • Los niños pequeños se valen de muchas oraciones de dos a cuatro palabras. • Los niños pequeños pueden señalar con el dedo y nombrar muchas partes del cuerpo. • Los niños pequeños añaden "ando o iendo" a las palabras. • Los niños pequeños comienzan a usar preposiciones tales como "sobre" y "dentro." • Los niños pequeños añaden una "s" a las palabras para indicar plurales. • Los niños pequeños podrían empezar a preguntar "¿Por qué?" • Los niños pequeños comienzan a contar historias sobre lo que hicieron o lo que vieron. • Hacia el final de este período, el niño pequeño puede usar las imágenes para contar lo que ocurre en un cuento.	Mindy comenzó a añadir "ando o iendo" a las palabras que había estado diciendo durante meses. Dijo "Yo corriendo" y "Yo comiendo" en vez de "Yo corro" y "Yo como." "Mira, está jugando," exclamó Treat mientras señalaba con el dedo una imagen en su libro preferido.
El desarrollo musculoso	• Los niños pequeños ensartan cuentas, usan las tijeras, pintan con los dedos o con pinceles, arman rompecabezas sencillos. • Los niños pequeños lanzan y patean una pelota. • Los niños pequeños se paran en un solo pie. • Los niños pequeños se paran y caminan en puntillas. • Los niños pequeños suben escaleras poniendo un pie en cada escalón. • Los niños pequeños trepan, se deslizan y saltan. • Los niños pequeños comen con cuchara y tenedor. • Los niños pequeños se pueden vestir solos. • Los niños pequeños pueden verter leche de una jarra pequeña.	Robert ni siquiera tiene que pensar en su cuerpo cuando corre para saludar a su papá al final del día. Peggy y Misha inventan un juego imitándose mutuamente los pasos en puntillas, posturas y gestos. Forcejeando un poco, Lawrence y Evelyn juegan con la ropa para disfrazarse.

Interacciones entre Maestro o Padre/Madre–Niño	Ambiente
24 a 36 meses (niños pequeños)	

- Responda sus preguntas de "por qué" con paciencia y entusiasmo. Así es como los niños aprenden y desarrollan interacciones sociales.
- Escuche con sus ojos las "historias" que los niños pequeños cuentan.
- Modele decir palabras plurales, tales como "perros," "elefantes," etc.
- Use palabras descriptivas tales como "queso mozarella" en vez de sólo "queso" o "urraca de América" en vez de sólo "pájaro."
- Tenga conversaciones largas con los niños pequeños, siguiendo lo que dicen.
- Lea libros a grupos informales pequeños o a niños por separado.

- Déle imágenes para que los niños las hagan corresponder.
- Los rompecabezas de animales, personas, vehículos y alimentos son importantes.
- Se pueden agregar al ambiente libros con muchas imágenes y cuentos cortos.
- Los materiales para el juego dramático estimulan la conversación.

- Esté consciente del equilibrio necesario entre el tiempo dedicado a actividades enérgicas y a actividades tranquilas.
- Esté atento al aumento de precisión de las capacidades motrices ligeras, pues pueden comenzar a manifestarse sutiles problemas.
- Esté a disposición de los niños pequeños animándolos y teniéndoles paciencia conforme comen, se visten y van al baño solos con más frecuencia.

- Ponga a su disposición una variedad de materiales para practicar capacidades motrices ligeras: rompecabezas simples, cajas de formas, cuentas para hacer collares, bloques de mesa, arcilla, materiales de arte.
- Espacio, oportunidad y estructuras para fomentar el movimiento: períodos de tiempo al aire libre, carreras de obstáculos, bailes y juguetes para montar.

Appendix C

Developmental Trends and Responsive Interactions—Spanish

Tendencias de Desarrollo e Interacciones Receptivas (Capítulo 6)

Tanto los bebés como los niños pequeños desarrollan un sólido sentido de identidad a través del aumento de la autorregulación, el aprendizaje de la expresión emocional efectiva y el desarrollo de relaciones de cariño.

Desarrollo	Ejemplo
0 a 4 meses (bebé)	
• Los bebés absorben una gran cantidad de información acerca del mundo. • Los bebés pueden sentirse abrumados y comenzar a bostezar, mirar hacia otro lado o molestarse. • Los bebés comienzan a calmarse chupándose las manos o escuchando a un adulto que les hable suavemente. • Los bebés miran fijamente a los ojos de su maestra mientras les da de comer. • Los bebés voltean la cabeza hacia voces conocidas. • Los bebés se calman y se consuelan con personas conocidas. • Los bebés lloran cuando tienen hambre o están cansados o incómodos	Carlos seguía a Karen con los ojos por donde quiera que fuera por el salón. Cuando ella se le acercó, la miró como si quisiera que ella se quedara con él. Karen aceptó la invitación a jugar y se sentó con él en el piso. En cuanto comenzó a cansarse y a ponerse molesto, Karen lo envolvió en una manta, lo abrazó estrechamente y le habló con voz suave.
4 a 8 meses (bebé)	
• A los bebés les gusta mirarse las manos y los pies. • Los bebés agitan los brazos y patalean emocionados cuando ven a una persona conocida. • Los bebés le sonríen a la maestra esperando que ella les sonría también. • Con la cara y el cuerpo, los bebés expresan muchos sentimientos: desde fruncir el ceño y llorar hasta reírse a carcajadas. • Los bebés expresan sus sentimientos claramente ante personas conocidas, y son más reservados con los desconocidos.	A Deborah le encanta que la maestra la lleve en brazos mientras va por el salón "hablándole" de lo que ven. Tiene los ojos bien abiertos y brillantes, sonríe y hace ruiditos de arrullo cuando le corresponde hablar en la conversación. Cuando un visitante entra en el salón, Deborah se queda muy callada y seria, y se sujeta firmemente al hombro de la maestra mirando al visitante.
8 a 12 meses (bebé móvil)	
• Los bebés móviles pueden tenerle miedo a los desconocidos. • Los bebés móviles pueden llamar a los adultos conocidos para que los ayuden cuando están enojados. • Los bebés móviles miran al adulto conocido para determinar si una situación es peligrosa o no. • Los bebés móviles se aferran al adulto cuando están en una situación desconocida. • A los bebés m5óviles les parecen divertidos los juegos tontos y las expresiones faciales exageradas que ponen los adultos.	Jaime está disfrutando de su nueva habilidad, que es ir gateando rápidamente a donde quiera ir. Le encanta el pequeño trepador que le permite mirar por la ventana. Pero cuando siente que la rampa es un poco inestable, se vuelve a mirar a Federico, su maestro, para asegurarse de que no hay peligro.

Interacciones entre Maestro o Padre/Madre–Niño	Ambiente

0 a 4 meses (bebé)

- Mantenga a los bebés pequeños cerca, en brazos, en un saco de bebé, o sobre una manta.
- Reconozca las señales de por qué el bebé quiere estar con usted—mirada fija, tenderle los brazos, mirada feliz—y respóndale hablándole suavemente, alternando la comunicación verbal y no verbal.
- Reconozca las señales que indican que el bebé necesita un descanso—bostezar, babear, mirar hacia otro lado—y apártese en silencio esperando a que el bebé se recupere.
- Consuele a los bebés cuando lloren.

- Estar cerca de una maestra conocida es lo mejor.
- Un espacio sereno y tranquilo con luces bajas, limita la información que el bebé necesita absorber.
- Evite tener música de fondo todo el día.
- Limite el número de objetos, sonidos, colores y movimientos alrededor de un bebé pequeño.
- La maestra es lo más interesante que el bebé tiene para mirar, pero para otros bebés, los espejos y juguetes que se encuentran en su campo visual, también son interesantes.

4 a 8 meses (bebé)

- Déles a los bebés oportunidades para que se miren al espejo mientras juegan.
- Refleje las expresiones emocionales del bebé y agregue palabras apropiadas: "Estoy tan contenta de verte hoy."
- Responda a los bebés de una manera que les ayude a calmarse y mantenerse activos. Si el bebé llora, cálmelo.

- Monte espejos irrompibles en las paredes.
- Deje que los bebés pasen un rato en el piso mientras están boca arriba, jugando con sus pies y moviéndose por el piso.
- Los libros y los álbumes de fotografías con caras reales mostrando diferentes expresiones emocionales son muy interesantes para los bebés.

8 a 12 meses (bebé móvil)

- Anime a los bebés móviles a moverse y explorar asegurándoles que usted los está mirando y cuidando.
- Entienda que los bebés móviles pueden asustarse ante situaciones nuevas que quizás no los habrían asustado hace unos meses. Consuélelos y tranquilícelos.

- Juegue al te veo, no te veo.
- Léales cuentos sobre madres y padres que se van y vuelven.
- Léales libros con solapas que se pueden levantar para encontrar cosas.
- Mantenga una previsibilidad de hábitos y rutinas del salón.

Desarrollo	Ejemplo

12 a 18 meses (bebé móvil)

- Los bebés móviles imitan las acciones de los adultos conocidos, tales como hablar por teléfono o llevar en brazos a una muñeca bebé.
- Los bebés móviles intentan atraer la atención del adulto jalándole la pierna o tomándole la mano.
- Los bebés móviles se calman con su manta o su animal de peluche favorito.
- Los bebés móviles protestan ruidosamente cuando sus padres los dejan.
- Los bebés móviles se relajan y se consuelan acurrucándose con un adulto conocido.
- Los bebés móviles hacen saber claramente lo que les gusta y lo que no les gusta.

Amelia carga toda la mañana su osito de peluche por todos los lados. A veces copia las acciones de Sofía, su maestra, dándole al osito palmaditas en la espalda o alimentándole con biberón. Cuando se cansa, se frota el osito contra la oreja y se chupa el pulgar.

18 a 24 meses (niños pequeños)

- Los niños pequeños comienzan a controlar ciertos impulsos diciendo "no, no, no" a medida que comienzan a lanzar bloques.
- Los niños pequeños pueden dejar lo que están haciendo cuando la maestra se lo dice.
- Los niños pequeños pueden no querer dejar de jugar cuando su padre o su madre viene a buscarlos.
- Los niños pequeños pueden llorar cuando no consiguen hacer algo que están intentando.
- Los niños pequeños saben su propio nombre y puede que usen el "mi" y "mío."

Francisco se sube a la mesa mientras mira directamente a los ojos de la maestra que desaprueba lo que él hace, y dice "no, no, no."

24 a 36 meses (niños pequeños)

- Los niños pequeños a veces pueden ser independientes, pero les gusta saber que la maestra está cerca.
- A los niños pequeños les gusta mirar fotos de sí mismos, sus amigos y su familia.
- Los niños pequeños oyen sus palabras y el tono de su voz cuando usted habla acerca de ellos. Quieren que usted se interese en ellos y se enorgullezca de sus logros.
- Los niños pequeños necesitan límites claros y consistentes. Olvidarán o pondrán a prueba las reglas, pero se sentirán a gusto cuando usted les recuerda las reglas y les ayuda a obedecerlas.
- Los niños pequeños pueden utilizar palabras para expresar sus sentimientos, o pueden dar golpes o morder.
- Los niños pequeños se ocupan de los sentimientos de los demás, y consuelan a quien esté triste o le llevan una curita a quien se haya lastimado.

Kiki llevó su bebé a ver las fotos de su propia familia en la pared, y la arrullaba mientras miraba la cara de su propia madre.

Interacciones entre Maestro o Padre/Madre–Niño	Ambiente

12 a 18 meses (bebé móvil)

• Muestre interés en las actividades del bebé. • Muestre su orgullo por los logros del bebé. • Deje que los bebés la utilicen como una base firme, para explorar el mundo. • Deje que los bebés sepan que usted entiende lo que sienten y responda respetuosamente. • Estos niños son todavía muy pequeños, y necesitan que se les acurruque y abrace mucho.	• Disponga de objetos de mayores en tamaño infantil: teléfonos, platos, llaves, etc. • Ponga fotografías de bebés con su familia en la pared. • Lamine las fotos del bebé con su familia para que las lleve consigo. • Haga álbumes de fotos de los niños del programa y hable acerca de las fotos. • Disponga de sillas de adulto y espacios tranquilos y cómodos para tener a los niños en brazos.

18 a 24 meses (niños pequeños)

• Mantenga su sentido del humor. Entienda que los niños pequeños pueden dejar de hacer ciertas cosas a veces, pero no siempre. • Respete los sentimientos fuertes de los niños pequeños. El turnarse y compartir viene después; ahora "mí" y "mío" son una etapa importante del desarrollo de un sólido sentido de identidad.	• Disponga espacios que permita que los niños exploren, pero siempre sin perderlos de vista. • Tenga suficientes juguetes iguales para que varios niños puedan tener el suyo, sin tener que compartir o turnarse. • Deje que los niños traigan al programa artículos que los calmen, tales como mantas o animales de peluche. Asígneles un lugar tranquilo donde puedan consolarse solos.

24 a 36 meses (niños pequeños)

• Establezca reglas claras y consistentes. Esté preparada para recordar a los niños pequeños con frecuencia, la manera de obedecer las reglas: "No se muerde; morder duele." • Dedique a los niños pequeños suficiente tiempo y atención para que se sientan comprendidos. • Haga eco al entusiasmo que los niños pequeños pueden darle a su propio juego. • Note y comente las interacciones que los niños pequeños están mirando y en las que están pensando.	• Tenga muchas fotografías de niños con sus familias en las paredes, en libros pequeños, y laminadas para que las lleven consigo. • Disponga espacios protegidos para el juego tranquilo. • Mantenga rutinas y disposiciones de salón previsibles. • Tenga libros con cuentos simples sobre ir y venir, familias y amistad. • Canten canciones sobre sentimientos tales como "Cuando estás contento y lo sabes" y "Cuando estás triste y enojado…"

Tendencias de Desarrollo e Interacciones Receptivas (Capítulo 7)

Habilidades: Comunicarse con sus compañeros, ser socialmente activo, jugar con sus compañeros, y controlar emociones negativas y conflictos durante interacciones con los compañeros.

Desarrollo	Ejemplo
0 a 4 meses (bebé)	
• A los bebés les gusta mirarse mutuamente (mirada visual).	Después de que la profesora puso a Tamika y a Sam sobre una manta en el piso, Tamika se quedó mirando fijamente a Sam.
• Los bebés prefieren mirar caras, especialmente los bordes y los ojos.	
• Puede que los bebés lloren cuando oyen llorar a otros bebés (contagio).	
4 a 8 meses (bebé)	
• Los bebés tocan a otros bebés, se dirigen vocalizaciones, se entusiasman, se acercan a otros bebés, sonríen y se ríen unos de otros.	Amna le pasó por encima gateando a Nadia que estaba acostada en el piso. Tocándole el pelo a Nadia, Amna se rió a carcajadas.
• Los bebés pueden tratar a otros bebés como si fueran objetos—pasándoles por encima al gatear, lamiéndolos, chupándolos, sentándose encima. Están simplemente aprendiendo la diferencia entre personas y objetos. Los bebés pueden pinchar con el dedo, empujar, dar palmaditas a otros bebés, para ver lo que el otro bebé va a hacer. A menudo se sorprenden con la reacción que logran.	
8 a 12 meses (bebé móvil)	
• Los bebés pueden mostrar a otros bebés un objeto, sentarse juntos, perseguirse gateando y jugar a perseguir y recoger objetos.	Shamaine miró la estantería baja de juguetes y vio que Carla venía gateando hacia ella. Shamaine se dio la vuelta rápidamente y se alejó gateando con Carla siguiéndola de cerca.
• Los bebés se sonríen y se ríen entre sí.	Kai pasó gateando por encima de las piernas de Bridger para alcanzar un juguete que estaba al otro lado de Bridger.
• Los bebés se dirigen sonidos—y es posible que sus primeras palabras se las digan entre sí.	
• Uno de los juegos preferidos de los bebés es el *te veo, no te veo* mientras exploran la separación: irse y volver, aparecer y desaparecer.	
• Los bebés pueden aprender a tocarse uno al otro con cuidado.	
• Como a esta edad los bebés actúan en gran medida en función de sus objetivos, pueden apartar la mano de un bebé que esté tocando un juguete, o gatearle por encima para alcanzar un juguete.	

Interacciones entre Maestro o Padre/Madre–Niño	Ambiente

0 a 4 meses (bebé)

- Sostenga a dos bebés para que puedan mirarse mutuamente.
- Ponga varios bebés sobre una manta en el piso para que puedan mirarse y tocarse entre sí.

- Los brazos de la maestras ofrecen el mejor ambiente.
- Ponga a dos bebés sobre unas mantas en el piso—uno junto a otro, de manera que los dos se estén tocando con los dedos de los pies.

4 a 8 meses (bebé)

- Muévase al ritmo de la música con un bebé en cada brazo.
- Con un bebé sobre el regazo, apunte y hable sobre lo que el otro bebé está haciendo.
- Ponga a dos bebés boca bajo frente a un espejo.
- En vez de decirles "No" y "Deja de hacer eso" a los bebés que están explorando, dígales, "Tócalo con cuidado." Dígales a los niños lo que usted quiere que hagan... muéstreselo.

- Cuelgue un espejo seguro en la pared de manera horizontal, para que la parte de abajo esté tocando el piso.
- Cubra la cámara de aire de la rueda de un auto con un paño suave. Siente a dos bebés en la cámara para que se toquen con los pies.

8 a 12 meses (bebé móvil)

- Nombre partes del cuerpo del bebé mientras dos bebés están sentados juntos:

  Estos son los ojos del bebé
  Esta es la nariz del bebé
  Toca la parte con que ves
  Tócate la parte que te suenas

- Ponga un bebé con otro (en parejas) porque las interacciones más frecuentes, complejas e intensas entre niños se producen cuando un niño está con varios compañeros.
- Comprenda que los bebés no son "malos" cuando le apartan la mano al otro. Diga "Jenny tenía ese juguete. Vamos a buscarte otro."

- Mientras están comiendo, coloque las sillas altas de manera que los niños se puedan ver unos a los otros.
- Disponga de rincones agradables en el salón donde los bebés puedan "desaparecer" (pero pudiendo aún ser vistos por adultos).
- Cuelgue del techo un paño largo y ancho (para que los bebés no se enreden en él). A los bebés les encanta gatear alrededor.
- Ponga contenedores con bloques de diferentes tamaños entre dos bebés. Quédese sentada junto a ellos mientras comienzan a explorar los materiales. Hable acerca de lo que está haciendo cada uno.

Desarrollo	Ejemplo

12 a 18 meses (bebé móvil)

- Comienzan los turnos imitativos (motores) e interactivos. Los niños pequeños pueden imitarse unos a otros—si un bebé le da un juguete a otro, el otro puede imitarlo.

- Los bebés móviles comienzan a hablarse unos a otros.

- Los bebés pueden demostrar preocupación cuando otros bebés están afligidos.

- Los bebés móviles pueden quitarle el juguete a otro bebé, decirle "no," empujarlo, agarrar firmemente el juguete y decir "mío."

- A esta edad, los bebés son pequeños científicos que experimentan para ver cómo funcionan las cosas. Esto afecta la relación que tienen con sus compañeros, pues están constantemente haciéndoles cosas para ver cómo reaccionan.

- Morder puede aparecer cuando los bebés muerden a otros "para ver lo que pasa," para obtener el juguete que quieren, para expresar su frustración. Los bebés están al borde de comunicarse bien; pueden comunicarse por la boca en forma de mordedura.

Rashida golpeó la mesa con la cuchara; poco después, otros dos comenzaron a hacerlo. Parecían estar siguiendo el ejemplo físicamente (como si estuvieran conversando).

Primero, Carmen intentó alejar a Toby del caballito de balancín.

Cuando eso no dio resultado, se inclinó hacia él y lo mordió en el brazo.

18 a 24 meses (niños pequeños)

- Las amistades pueden desarrollarse a muy temprana edad. Los amigos son más propensos a tocarse, apoyarse y sonreírse entre sí, que otros niños que no son amigos.

- Los niños pequeños imitan mutuamente los sonidos y las palabras que dicen y se hablan y comienzan a comunicarse con los demás a mayores distancias.

- Los niños pequeños dan u ofrecen un juguete o comida a otros niños pequeños.

- Los niños pequeños pueden llamar a un adulto y jalar al adulto para que ayude a otro niño, o pueden ayudar a otro niño llevándole un pañuelito de papel, por ejemplo.

- Los niños pequeños demuestran bondad hacia otros bebés que se sienten afligidos. Sin embargo, el bebé o niño pequeño móvil puede suponer que lo que lo consuela a él, también consuela al afligido.

- Los niños pueden turnarse, por ejemplo, con una pelota o para saltar. Pueden tener conversaciones cinéticas de niño pequeño mientras siguen a un líder por el salón—entrando y saliendo del grupo, turnándose para ser líder y seguidor—como si estuvieran en una conversación, en la cual escuchan y hablan, aprendiendo la importante habilidad de cómo turnarse.

- Empujar, dar empujones, agarrar y golpear pueden ocurrir a medida que los niños luchan con la idea de "mío durante todo el tiempo que yo quiera" y "tuyo, pero yo también lo quiero." Los niños pequeños puede que se peleen más por juguetes pequeños, que por objetos grandes que no se mueven.

Paulie parecía estar esperando en la puerta a que apareciera Jamie al principio de la jornada. Cuando Jaime y su mamá llegaron, Paulie se dirigió hacia ellos y le tomó la mano a Jaime con una gran sonrisa en la cara.

Tania saltó (medio se cayó) de una tabla situada a varias pulgadas del suelo. Pronto tres niños pequeños estaban parados sobre la tabla, y casi saltando, casi bajando de la tabla y disfrutando inmensamente de la actividad.

Interacción entre Maestra-Niño, o Padre/Madre–Niño	Ambiente

12 a 18 meses (bebé móvil)

- Muéstreles a los niños pequeños móviles cómo rodar juntos por una pequeña pendiente.
- Ayude a los niños pequeños móviles a que aprendan los nombres de los demás, cantando canciones de saludo y despedida incluyendo los nombres de los niños: "Esta es Tania, ¿cómo estás?" y "Este es Enrique, ¿cómo estás?" y apuntando o tocando a cada niño que pasa junto a usted o al que está sentado en su regazo.
- Comente el comportamiento social activo. Diga "Le diste la muñeca. Eso le gusta." Puede que los bebés no entiendan sus palabras, pero son capaces de darse cuenta por el tono de voz que usted está contenta con ellos.
- A los bebés les gusta mirar libros juntos, creando grupos informales (esto significa que entrar y salir del grupo) alrededor de las piernas, el regazo y los brazos del padre, la madre o la maestra que más les gusta.

- Suministre una caja de cartón grande abierta por los dos lados. Anímelos a entrar y salir de la caja gateando juntos. Ventanas a los lados de la caja estimulan a los bebés para que se miren entre ellos por la ventana.
- Muñecas, camiones, autos y otros materiales de juego, promueven las interacciones entre compañeros.
- A los bebés les encanta la arena y el agua y jugar con botellas y pelotas seguras de diferentes tamaños. Cuando cada uno tiene su propio contenedor o cubo con agua o arena, el juego se desarrolla sin altibajos.
- Al aire libre, grandes cajas de arena o juguetes para empujar, estimulan el juego interactivo.

18 a 24 meses (niños pequeños)

- Ya esté adentro o afuera, atienda a los niños pequeños cuando entran a "reponerse" emocionalmente con su maestra especial animando a varios niños pequeños a sentarse junto a usted o en su regazo. Permita que los niños pequeños se toquen mutuamente con cuidado.
- Anime a que varios niños pequeños hagan sonidos de animales y se imiten entre sí mientras les muestra las imágenes de un libro.
- Pídale a un niño que ayude a otro, trayendo un pañuelito de papel, abriendo la llave del agua, abriendo la puerta, etc.
- Estimule la bondad mutua. Si un niño pequeño llora, pregúntele a otro lo que "podríamos" hacer para ayudarlo.
- Anime a dos niños pequeños a que pongan la mesa o la limpien después de comer. Mire como se imitan.
- Cante canciones, animando a los niños pequeños a que se turnen con las acciones.

- Adentro y afuera: Ponga a su disposición áreas con arena que sean suficientemente grandes para varios niños pequeños, es de esperar que se sienten justo en el medio del área.
- Las mantas sobre el piso, el suelo o una mesa son un centro para que los niños pequeños jueguen.
- Suministre vagones: Empujar o jalar a un amigo en un vagón dará como resultado chillidos de deleite.
- Suministre pelotas y juguetes para jalar que estimulen el juego interactivo.
- Lugares para saltar sin peligro estimulan los intercambios sociales.
- Suministre juguetes musicales, varios de cada clase, para que los niños puedan tocar juntos una música bella. A veces uno dirigirá y el otro le seguirá, o viceversa.

Desarrollo	Ejemplo

24 a 36 meses (niños pequeños)

- La amistad de los niños pequeños es "búsqueda de proximidad," deseo de estar cerca y mostrar cariño como sonreír, reírse y abrazarse. Los amigos se prefieren mutuamente como compañeros de interacción. Las amistades continúan desarrollándose y se profundizan.

- Los niños pequeños intercambian información y pueden imitar las acciones pasadas de los demás.

- Los niños pequeños pueden congregarse y amontonarse. Cuando una maestra comienza a hacer una actividad interesante con un niño, por lo general los otros llegan corriendo de todas partes del salón.

- Algunos niños pequeños son capaces de idear maneras diferentes de ayudar a otros cuando se han lastimado o están tristes. Algunos pueden tener un impresionante repertorio de comportamientos altruistas, y si algo no funciona, intentan hacer otra cosa.

- Los compañeros colaboran hacia metas comunes, haciendo uno de líder y otro de seguidor.

- Pueden producirse peleas por objetos, espacio personal y palabras. Los niños pequeños también se dedican a intercambios juguetones, tal como empujar y caerse bruscamente, correr y perseguirse, y realizar juegos verbales.

- Algunos niños pueden ganarse cierta reputación entre sus compañeros por comportamiento agresivo o bondadoso.

- Los niños se vuelven más positivos y menos negativos en su juego social entre los 24 y los 36 meses de edad.

- Puede haber dominación de un niño sobre otro.

María y Sally jugaron durante 30 minutos en extremos opuestos de la pequeña estantería de juguetes, mirándose mutuamente cada varios minutos y diciéndose "barco," "mi barco," "hola," "quiero jugo," "mírame" y llamándose por su nombre una y otra vez.

Cuando pasó un camión de bomberos afuera, varios niños pequeños se acercaron corriendo para mirar por la ventana.

José y Miguel empujaron, jalaron, rodaron y resoplaron haciendo rodar una gran calabaza desde dentro hasta el patio de juegos, donde los niños pequeños y sus maestras iban a abrirla y sacarle las semillas.

Interacción entre Maestra–Niño, o Padre/Madre–Niño	Ambiente

24 a 36 meses (niños pequeños)

- Organice situaciones en que dos niños pequeños deban trabajar juntos—como por ejemplo, hacer rodar una calabaza de un lugar a otro, o traer de afuera un balde con bloques "pesados."
- Póngale una curita a una muñeca en el brazo o en la pierna y anime a los niños pequeños a que cuiden al bebé.
- Pregunte a los niños pequeños "¿cómo podemos ayudar a José? Está triste, está llorando."
- Intente cambiar la imagen de la niña que se está ganando una reputación de agresividad. Téngala cerca, muéstrele cómo tocar con cuidado y comente su comportamiento servicial. Déle un juguete interesante que pueda inducir a otros niños a jugar con ella. Manténgase cerca y enséñele a jugar.

- Coloque sombreros y ropa que sea fácil de poner, en un rincón acogedor y con un espejo grande.
- Los niños pequeños disfrutarán de una mutua compañía cuando los amigos cambian de aspecto poniéndose un sombrero de ala ancha o unos zapatos grandes.
- Los espacios que quedan encima o debajo de un ático bajo estimulan la interacción entre los niños pequeños.
- Suministre varios tipos de muñecas, así como cubiertos de mesa no peligrosos, mantas y camas pequeñas. Siéntese cerca y mire como los niños pequeños juegan a cuidar a sus bebés.
- Suministre materiales sin propósito específico, como bloques, y actividades que requieran cooperación, tales como pintar con agua un muro exterior utilizando una brocha gorda, o llenar de agua un balde grande con envases pequeños.
- Un equipo de motor grande, como los trepadores o los barcos de balancín, animan a los niños pequeños a colaborar para alcanzar una meta común: todos se van a la parte de arriba del trepador, o balancean el barco con todos dentro.

Tendencias de Desarrollo e Interacciones Receptivas (Capítulo 8)

Los bebés y los niños pequeños se conocen a sí mismos, a los demás y al mundo, a través de sus propias capacidades y atributos, utilizando instrumentos cognitivos de aprendizaje y conceptos básicos.

Desarrollo	Ejemplo
0 a 4 meses (bebé)	
• Los bebés siguen visualmente un objeto en movimiento. • Los bebés lloran para atraer la atención del adulto a fin de que los consuele o les dé de comer. • Los bebés miran a su alrededor por el salón con interés. • Los bebés comienzan a intentar alcanzar juguetes. • Los bebés notan que sus brazos y piernas han causado algo y repiten el movimiento. • Los bebés reconocen personas y objetos. • Los bebés comienzan a llevarse objetos a la boca.	Megan levantó la cabeza, apoyándose en los brazos mientras estaba recostada sobre la manta. Con una expresión seria miró a la maestra y a los niños a su alrededor. Willy comenzó a patear el móvil que colgaba encima y logró que se meneara. Luego paró, lo miró y volvió a patearlo mirándolo para ver si pasaba algo.
4 a 8 meses (bebé)	
• A los bebés les gusta examinar los juguetes. • A los bebés les gusta hacer que los juguetes hagan algo—sonar, encajarse uno dentro de otro. • Los bebés imitan las expresiones y los gestos de los adultos. • Los bebés se vuelven hacia los sonidos para ver de dónde vienen. • Los bebés buscan juguetes que han dejado caer.	Ángela se interesa en todo. Mira a sus amigos y luego mira a la maestra y sonríe. Roger se estira para tocar un juguete colgante. Cuando se balancea y suena, Roger se estira para hacerlo de nuevo.
8 a 12 meses (bebé móvil)	
• A los bebés móviles les gusta desarmar los juguetes y luego volver a armarlos. • A los bebés móviles les gustan los juguetes que hacen algo cuando se tocan, se jalan o se golpean. • Los bebés móviles comienzan juegos imaginarios muy simples, tales como llevarse un vaso a la boca. • A los bebés móviles les gusta encontrar juguetes pequeños debajo de un paño o de un vaso. • A los bebés móviles les gusta levantar y examinar objetos pequeños tales como un Cheerio. • Los bebés móviles muestran objetos con el dedo sabiendo que usted también puede verlos.	A Carlos le encanta sacar cada uno de los animales de plástico del balde y mirarlo. Cuando el balde queda vacío, lo lanza a un lado. A Aliya le gusta el botón que se aprieta y las puertas oscilantes de la caja mecánica, pero todavía no puede hacer funcionar todos los mecanismos. Su maestra expresa sorpresa a Aliya cuando las puertas se abren y, de vez en cuando, le enseña cómo funciona otra de las perillas.

Interacción entre Maestra-Niño, o Padre/Madre–Niño	Ambiente

0 a 4 meses (bebé)

- Mueva lentamente un juguete pequeño de lado a lado mientras el bebé lo sigue con la mirada.
- Responda rápidamente al llanto del niño.
- Déles tiempo a los bebés para que estén tranquilos mirando lo que pasa a su alrededor. Hable acerca de lo que ven.
- Reaccione ante las expresiones de los bebés con expresiones y lenguaje claro y hasta exagerado.

- Organice el espacio de manera que los bebés puedan ver actividad sin dejar de estar protegidos.
- Suministre unos cuantos objetos interesantes para mirar—juguetes pequeños en el piso, cuando están boca abajo; juguetes colgantes cuando los bebés están boca arriba.
- Ponga espejos irrompibles a disposición de los bebés.

4 a 8 meses (bebé)

- Lleve en brazos al bebé, mientras camina por el salón mirando cosas y hablando acerca de ellas.
- Siéntese cerca y háblele al bebé sobre los juguetes que está mirando.
- Llame al bebé por su nombre a poca distancia para asegurarle que está cerca.

- Suministre una variedad de juguetes pequeños para que los manipule y los examine.
- Suministre juguetes que suenan cuando se mueven, se encajan unos dentro de otros o se cuelgan y mueven cuando se tocan.
- Ofrezca libros de tapas de cartón.

8 a 12 meses (bebé móvil)

- Con su presencia, su interés y su entusiasmo, ayude al bebé a concentrarse en lo que le interesa para apoyarlo en su atención y exploración.
- Con sus expresiones y palabras afectivas, demuéstrele al bebé móvil que usted disfruta de sus descubrimientos.
- Con palabras, describa la actividad del niño: "Mira, encontraste un Cheerio. Lo estás recogiendo con los dedos."

- Suministre juguetes tales como vasos para apilar, anillos en poste, piezas que se interconectan y cubos llenos de objetos pequeños interesantes, tales como animales de juguete.
- Suministre réplicas tamaño infantil de platos o herramientas domésticas.
- Suministre juguetes que reaccionen—cajas mecánicas, almohadillas llenas de agua.
- Suministre materiales sensoriales, como agua y arena con una variedad de herramientas.
- Suministre libros de tapas de cartón con fotos.

Desarrollo	Ejemplo
12 a 18 meses (bebé móvil)	
• A los bebés móviles les gusta poner en práctica su movilidad para explorar gateando, caminando, trepando, corriendo, etc. • Los bebés móviles disfrutan jugando en la arena, el agua, con plastilina y varios tipos de herramientas. • A los bebés móviles les interesan las relaciones espaciales de rompecabezas y tableros con agujeros. • Los bebés móviles utilizan herramientas tales como llaves o teléfonos en sus juegos imaginarios. • Los bebés móviles disfrutan al mirar libros y nombrar objetos, animales o partes del cuerpo.	Alexis y Dan están contentísimos de estar de pie. Se siguen mutuamente por todas partes, uno subiendo atrevidamente por un plano inclinado, con el otro inmediatamente detrás. A veces los dos intentan meterse debajo del tobogán. A Meredith le encanta acurrucarse en el regazo de su maestra y mostrar con el dedo imágenes en libros mientras la maestra nombra los animales o le pide que encuentre uno en particular.
18 a 24 meses (niños pequeños)	
• Los niños pequeños de corta edad disfrutan de su facilidad de movimiento y les gusta llevar cosas en las manos. • Los niños pequeños entienden que pueden hacer que ocurran cosas. • Los niños pequeños entienden y recuerdan los detalles de las rutinas. • Los niños pequeños sustituyen unos objetos por otros en su juego imaginario. • Los niños pequeños disfrutan cada vez más de los materiales problemáticos que sugieren actividades tales como construir y hacer corresponder formas.	Antes del desayuno, Chris tiende las manos para la cancioncita de gracias. Cuando un niño llega más tarde y se sienta a la mesa, Chris tiende las manos para que todos canten nuevamente. Lynn y Matt construyen pequeñas torres de bloques y luego las chocan con camiones de juguete para derribarlas. Fran saca de la caja bloques de una pulgada y hace una pila de bloques rojos y una pila de bloques azules.
24 a 36 meses (niños pequeños)	
• Los niños pequeños de más edad comienzan a entender conceptos tales como el color, el tamaño, la forma, el tiempo y el peso. • Los niños pequeños de más edad se interesan en las historias y en las imágenes de libros de cuentos. • Los niños pequeños mayores crean nuevos cuentos en el juego imaginario o nuevas estructuras en la construcción de bloques y se vuelven más imaginativos y creativos. • Asigne papeles a los juguetes y a otros niños en el juego imaginario; utilice sillas, mantas y estanterías como sustitutos en el juego imaginario.	Eric se siente un poco triste y lleva una foto de su mamá diciendo, "después de siesta." Sara se encarga de la esquina de juego dramático entregando muñecas y animales de peluche. Se pone un sombrero y dice "la mamá va a comprar."

Interacción entre Maestra-Niño, o Padre/Madre-Niño	Ambiente

12 a 18 meses (bebé móvil)

- Déle a los bebés móviles tiempo y espacio protegido para explorar.
- Quédese cerca para expresar interés, sugerir palabras y hacer que la actividad sea más elaborada y compleja.
- Ayude a los bebés móviles a que expresen su interés en otros bebés cuidadosamente.
- Exprese entusiasmo por lo que les interesa a los bebés móviles.

- Suministre rompecabezas simples, tableros con agujeros, formas, cuentas de madera con cordones gruesos.
- Suministre trepadores pequeños, túneles y trayectos interesantes.
- Suministre juguetes que funcionen al darle cuerda, o que se enciendan y apaguen.
- Suministre artículos simples para el juego imaginario.

18 a 24 meses (niños pequeños)

- Mantenga rutinas predecibles recordándole a los niños el orden de las etapas con preguntas tales como "Es hora de comer. ¿Qué hacemos?"
- Tenga los materiales en lugares predecibles y ordenados.
- Con preguntas tales como "¿Qué vas a hacer ahora? ¿Qué vas a comprar en la tienda? apoye a los niños pequeños cuando piensen en sus actividades.

- Tenga los juguetes y los materiales organizados de manera que los niños pequeños puedan escogerlos, alcanzarlos y guardarlos (con recordatorios).
- Revise frecuentemente los materiales a su disposición para asegurarse de que mantiene un equilibrio entre lo que es conocido y lo que es un poco difícil.

24 a 36 meses (niños pequeños)

- Pregúntele a los niños cómo podrían resolver problemas que se presentan y luego deje que los resuelvan solos.
- Apoye a los niños que trabajan juntos con materiales para que compartan ideas.
- Hable con un lenguaje que describa el tiempo ("ahora," "más tarde," "antes de la siesta," "después de almuerzo"), peso ("pesado," "ligero"), tamaño ("grande," "pequeño").
- Cuente cosas durante el día.

- Facilite oportunidades de juego que promuevan la comparación de tamaños, pesos, colores, formas y cantidades.
- Ponga por todas partes libros para los niños. Tenga varias copias de libros favoritos antiguos, y traiga libros nuevos.
- Permita que los niños combinen materiales de diferentes áreas de maneras creativas.
- Presente nuevos materiales o nuevas combinaciones de materiales.

Tendencias de Desarrollo e Interacciones Receptivas (Capítulo 9)

Los bebés y los niños pequeños desarrollan la capacidad de entender, expresar y decir palabras.

Desarrollo	Ejemplo
0 a 4 meses (bebé)	
• Los bebés se pueden asustar si oyen un ruido fuerte. • Los bebés captan las diferencias entre los sonidos. • Los bebés pueden dejar de llorar cuando oyen la voz de un adulto conocido. • Los bebés prefieren oír hablar cuando se les habla a ellos de forma directa. • Los bebés escuchan cuando un adulto les habla o les canta mientras los mira. • Los bebés lloran cuando sienten dolor, tienen hambre o están afligidos. • A los 2 meses de edad, los bebés tienen llantos específicos de hambre y dolor. • Los bebés "arrullan" (producen sonidos vocálicos suaves). • Hacia el final de este período, los bebés sonríen y se ríen. • Los bebés miran fijamente imágenes interesantes en libros.	Brenda sostenía a Jordán de manera que pudieran mirarse a los ojos. Jordán arrulló suavemente y Brenda le arrulló también. Luego, ella esperó a que Jordán lo volviera a hacer. Érica le sonrió de oreja a oreja a su padre cuando él la levantó de la cuna.
4 a 8 meses (bebé)	
• Los bebés giran la cabeza hacia un ruido, o una persona que dice su nombre. • A los bebés les gusta que los adultos hablen, canten y se rían con ellos. • Los bebés vocalizan con la intención de obtener una respuesta del adulto. • Los bebés dan chillidos agudos. • Los bebés practican sus sonidos cuando exploran y cuando están con adultos conocidos. • Los bebés comienzan a balbucear; al principio una consonante y luego combinaciones de dos consonantes. • Los bebés participan en conversaciones turnándose con los adultos. • Los bebés miran distintas imágenes de un libro y se emocionan cuando ven una que les gusta o cuando les gusta el tono entusiasta del adulto que lee.	Mientras sostenía a Donovan en su regazo, Daniela, la maestra del bebé, señalaba con el dedo las imágenes del libro de tapas de cartón. "Mira," dijo señalando la imagen, "una pelota." Luego dijo "Ahí está tu pelota" y señaló hacia una pelota en el piso. Donovan miró la imagen, luego la pelota en el piso y finalmente volvió a mirar la imagen. "Tt" dijo Afi cuando estaba en brazos de su maestra mirándola. "Tada" le dijo la maestra. "Tt" repitió Afi cuando le tocó hablar en la conversación.

Interacción entre Maestra-Niño, o Padre/Madre–Niño	Ambiente

0 a 4 meses (bebé)

- Use lenguaje dirigido al bebé.
- Tenga a los bebés en brazos y hábleles suavemente. Mírelos largamente a los ojos mientras baila conversando. Respete al bebé si necesita un descanso y aparta la cabeza.
- Lea libros con frases rítmicas y con una sola imagen en una página, con 2 imágenes a los de 4 meses de edad.
- Interprete los eructos, llantos, bostezos, estiramientos y sonidos de los bebés como formas de comunicación. Diga "Ah, me estás diciendo que tienes sueño."
- Cante canciones de cuna y otras canciones.
- Sea un compañero de lenguaje que se identifique y comente los sentimientos del bebé.
- Diga palabras y produzca sonidos para consolar a los bebés.

- El mejor ambiente son los brazos de un adulto afectuoso que tenga al bebé en brazos y le hable suavemente.
- Suministre juguetes que produzcan sonidos agradables. Sostenga con cuidado el juguete e intercambie sonidos con el bebé.
- Suministre materiales interesantes para tocar mientras comenta las texturas.
- Coloque espejos bajos a lo largo de una pared. Los bebés se miran y es posible que produzcan sonidos.

4 a 8 meses (bebé)

- Use lenguaje dirigido al bebé.
- Hable a menudo con los bebés. Muéstreles objetos y personas nuevos y nómbrelos.
- Repita los sonidos que los bebés producen y espere a que repitan el sonido (turnarse).
- Refiérase a varios artículos conocidos, tales como "leche" o "perro," con lenguaje de señas.
- Cante canciones y haga juegos de dedos.
- Describa con palabras los sentimientos de los niños expresados a través de gestos, posturas corporales y sonidos.
- Léale libros sencillos con una o dos imágenes por página. Señale con el dedo las imágenes mientras dice el nombre de la imagen.
- Léale los mismos libros una y otra vez.
- Aplique estrategias de atención conjunta—señale con el dedo un juguete o una imagen de un libro diciendo el nombre o hablando al respecto.

- Suministre juguetes y materiales interesantes para que los bebés los manipulen y examinen.
- Suministre libros de cartón con asas para que pueden gatear hasta ellos y tomarlos.
- Los libros con asas animan a los bebés a llevarlos.
- Haga un libro de imágenes de te veo, no te veo pegando un pedazo de tela sobre cada imagen.
- Forme un rincón de lectura acogedor donde las maestras puedan estar cómodas y leer a los bebés.
- Suministre cajas de sonido (bien selladas) con distintos objetos adentro que produzcan distintos sonidos al sacudirlas.
- Incorpore títeres al ambiente. Úselos a veces para "hablar" con el niño. Coloque los títeres en la mano del niño y espere a ver lo que el niño dice o hace.

Desarrollo	Ejemplo

8 a 12 meses (bebé móvil)

- Los bebés móviles comienzan a participar en juegos sociales tales como el *te veo, no te veo* o el *"así de grande."*
- A los bebés les gusta escuchar juegos de sonidos (rimas), canciones y juegos de dedos.
- El balbuceo continúa desarrollándose con sílabas combinadas tales como "dada," "mama," "nana" y "tutu" y a esta altura el bebé puede usar estos sonidos específicamente para referirse a su mamá o su papá.
- Los bebés repiten sonidos consistentemente para referirse a un objeto, una persona o un animal.
- Si oyen otro lenguaje *con* un adulto a través de estrategias conversacionales interactivas, los bebés pueden "tener una actitud abierta hacia los sonidos de un lenguaje extranjero."
- Los bebés pueden comenzar a decir palabras aisladas.
- Al final de este período, los bebés pueden comenzar a señalar con el dedo para atraer la atención de un adulto.
- Los bebés emplean expresiones faciales y gestos tales como agitar la cabeza o los brazos para que los tomen en brazos, y así comunicarse con los adultos o con sus compañeros.

Ejemplo:

Una de las primeras palabras de Dana fue "mamá," y la repetía una y otra vez cuando veía a su madre.

Una de las primera palabras de Trishanna fue "mamá," y la repetía con entusiasmo una y otra vez cuando veía a su madre.

12 a 18 meses (bebé móvil)

- Los bebés móviles pueden seguir instrucciones sencillas tales como "Ven aquí" o "Trae tus zapatos" sin que haya que hacer gestos.
- Los bebés móviles pueden jugar socialmente sin que haya que demostrar la acción. Por ejemplo, cuando usted dice "Dile adiós" ellos mueven las manos aunque usted no les muestre cómo hacerlo.
- Los bebés móviles señalan con el dedo para llamar la atención de los adultos y de sus compañeros.
- Se puede producir un aprendizaje rápido de palabras—una explosión de lenguaje—en los niños que están aprendiendo muchas palabras nuevas.
- Hacia el final de este período, los bebés móviles combinan palabras.
- Los bebés móviles farfullan (hilando muchos sonidos) con la misma entonación que los adultos.
- Los bebés móviles hacen gestos y se valen de palabras para rechazar, pedir, comentar, negarse, exigir y nombrar objetos y personas.
- Los bebés móviles se valen del lenguaje para mantener una interacción o conversación con un adulto o uno de sus compañeros.

Ejemplo:

La maestra de Janina le dijo "Juguemos a dar palmitas, palmitas," y Janina comenzó a aplaudir.

Ross miró a su maestra con expectación, farfullando muchos sonidos juntos como si le hiciera una pregunta.

Interacción entre Maestra-Niño, o Padre/Madre–Niño	Ambiente

8 a 12 meses (bebé móvil)

- Organice juegos conocidos tales como te veo—no te veo, palmitas—palmitas o "¿cómo eres de grande?"
- Responda con palabras a la comunicación no verbal de los bebés.
- Observe y espere a que los bebés inicien sonidos o palabras.
- Imite los sonidos y luego expanda, detalle y amplíe el lenguaje del bebé.
- Modele el siguiente paso en el desarrollo del lenguaje.
- Emplee hablarse a sí mismo y hablar en paralelo.
- Hable a menudo de manera receptiva con un vocabulario variado. No bombardee al niño con palabras.
- Lea los libros con entusiasmo—cambiando el tono de su voz con los distintos personajes.
- Hable sobre las imágenes y el cuento a medida que lee. Involucre a los bebés con la voz y los gestos.
- Mientras miran una imagen, espere a que el bebé produzca sonidos, señale con el dedo o haga expresiones faciales.

- Cree un rincón de lectura acogedor en que los bebés puedan alcanzar fácilmente los libros y manipularlos.
- Haga un libro "Todo sobre mí"—álbumes pequeños de fotos para cada niño con imágenes de ellos, su familia, sus juguetes preferidos, sus compañeros, sus maestras y los animales domésticos de la familia. Déjelos al alcance de los niños. Cambie las imágenes a medida que el niño crece.
- Los juguetes musicales para empujar animan a los bebés a manipularlos y producir sonidos.

12 a 18 meses (bebé móvil)

- Mantenga el tema en una conversación con un bebé móvil. Vea cuántas veces hablará el niño.
- Responda a la entonación del parloteo del niño. Por ejemplo, si parece que el niño hace una pregunta, responda a lo que usted cree que el niño puede estar preguntando.
- Responda con palabras a las señales hechas con los dedos y otros medios de comunicación no verbal de los bebés móviles.
- Describa y compare con palabras tamaños, formas y sonidos.
- Cuando un bebé móvil dice palabras tales como "Yo salto," modele el próximo paso en el desarrollo del lenguaje diciendo "Tú estás saltando," añadiendo "ando o iendo" a la palabra. Haga esto tanto con el contenido de las palabras como con la estructura de las palabras u oraciones.
- Léale libros con cuentos más largos, haga pausas a medida que avanza por el libro para animar a los bebés móviles a hablar sobre las imágenes y el cuento.

- Introduzca materiales de arte tales como plastilina, arcilla y pintura.
- Déle rollos de toallas de papel a los bebés móviles para que produzcan sonidos.
- Los juguetes musicales para jalar animan a los bebés móviles a caminar y jalarlos o empujarlos.
- Las cajas de música resistentes animan a los bebés móviles a apretar botones para "hacer música."
- Se pueden poner a disposición tambores y otros instrumentos musicales.
- Incorpore un reproductor de CD resistente con un cuento que haya grabado el padre o la madre.
- Grabe las voces de los bebés móviles con una grabadora y haga que las escuchen.
- Suministre materiales para hacer burbujas.
- Facilite espacios para animar a dos o tres niños a conversar con sus compañeros.

Desarrollo	Ejemplo

18 a 24 meses (niño pequeño)

- Los niños pequeños pueden ir a buscar juguetes conocidos en otra habitación de la casa cuando un adulto se los pide, y pueden seguir instrucciones tales como "cierra la puerta."

- Los niños pequeños combinan palabras para nombrar cosas ("ese gato"), para negar ("no muerde") y para rechazar ("no más").

- Los niños pequeños combinan dos o tres palabras con significado.

- Los niños pequeños se valen del lenguaje para varios propósitos, tales como preguntar "¿Qué eso?"

- Los niños pequeños señalan una cantidad de imágenes cada vez mayor en los libros cuando un adulto les habla sobre la imagen.

"Hola Kitty," "puerta abierta" y "sombrero puesto" fueron sólo algunas de las combinaciones de dos palabras que Cheral dijo a los 20 meses de edad.

Tyra corrió rápidamente hasta el librero, tomó un libro con tapa brillante y regresó de prisa hasta su maestra. Después de sentarse cómodamente en su regazo, abrió el libro y comenzó a señalar con entusiasmo las imágenes mientras su maestra las nombraba.

24 a 36 meses (niño pequeño)

- Los niños pequeños comprenden instrucciones complejas y recuerdan palabras de canciones cortas y juegos de dedos.

- Los niños pequeños se valen de muchas oraciones de dos a cuatro palabras.

- Los niños pequeños pueden señalar con el dedo y nombrar muchas partes del cuerpo.

- Los niños pequeños añaden "ando o iendo" a las palabras.

- Los niños pequeños comienzan a usar preposiciones tales como "sobre" y "dentro."

- Los niños pequeños añaden una "s" a las palabras para indicar plurales.

- Los niños pequeños podrían empezar a preguntar "¿Por qué?"

- Los niños pequeños comienzan a contar historias sobre lo que hicieron o lo que vieron.

- Hacia el final de este período, el niño pequeño puede usar las imágenes para contar lo que ocurre en un cuento.

Mindy comenzó a añadir "ando o iendo" a las palabras que había estado diciendo durante meses. Dijo "Yo corriendo" y "Yo comiendo" en vez de "Yo corro" y "Yo como."

"Mira, está jugando," exclamó Treat mientras señalaba con el dedo una imagen en su libro preferido.

Interacción entre Maestra-Niño, o Padre/Madre–Niño	Ambiente

18 a 24 meses (niño pequeño)

- Léale libros con cuentos más largos, haga pausas a medida que avanza por el libro para animar a los niños pequeños a hablar sobre las imágenes y la historia. Haga preguntas abiertas tales como "¿Cómo se siente el oso?"
- Pregúntese a menudo con el niño: "Me pregunto qué va a pasar con el oso."
- Haga que los niños pequeños conversen intentando mantenerse en el mismo tema que el niño.
- Introduzca nuevas conversaciones sobre objetos y acontecimientos interesantes.

- Disponga una pista de obstáculos complicada y use palabras tales como "adentro," "afuera," "por arriba," "a través," "alrededor," "arriba" y "abajo" mientras el niño pequeño recorre la pista.
- Suministre libros nuevos todas las semanas, pero mantenga cerca los libros preferidos de los niños.
- Suministre una mayor variedad de materiales de arte.
- Déle materiales que estimulen los sentidos.

24 a 36 meses (niño pequeño)

- Responda sus preguntas de "por qué" con paciencia y entusiasmo. Así es como los niños aprenden y desarrollan interacciones sociales.
- Escuche con sus ojos las "historias" que los niños pequeños cuentan.
- Modele decir palabras plurales, tales como "perros," "elefantes," etc.
- Use palabras descriptivas tales como "queso mozarella" en vez de sólo "queso" o "urraca de América" en vez de sólo "pájaro."
- Tenga conversaciones largas con los niños pequeños, siguiendo lo que dicen.
- Lea libros a grupos informales pequeños o a niños por separado.

- Déle imágenes para que los niños las hagan corresponder.
- Los rompecabezas de animales, personas, vehículos y alimentos son importantes.
- Se pueden agregar al ambiente libros con muchas imágenes y cuentos cortos.
- Los materiales para el juego dramático estimulan la conversación.

Tendencias de desarrollo e interacciones receptivas (Capítulo 10)

Los bebés y los niños pequeños desarrollan capacidades motrices para la locomoción, el uso de herramientas y la coordinación de información perceptiva con acciones motrices.

Desarrollo	Ejemplo
0 a 4 meses (bebé)	

- Los bebés levantan la cabeza cuando los llevan en brazos contra el hombro; sostienen la cabeza firme y erguida.
- Boca abajo, los bebés levantan la cabeza y los hombros y pueden sostener un juguete en la mano.
- Los bebés giran la cabeza hacia una voz conocida.
- Los bebés se quedan quietos para prestar atención; se contonean y se mueven para inducir la continuación de la interacción.
- De espaldas, los bebés estiran los brazos y las piernas a manera de juego.
- Estando de lado, los bebés se dan vuelta para quedar de espaldas.
- Los bebés sujetan un dedo o un juguete liviano con agarre reflejo.
- Los bebés se chupan los dedos, las manos y otros objetos.
- Los bebés mueven los brazos y las piernas.

Rosie mantuvo la cabeza erguida y miró a su alrededor a los otros niños mientras Sharon la llevaba contra el hombro.

Robert, boca abajo sobre una manta, levantó la cabeza para mirarse al espejo montado a nivel del suelo en la pared.

Jen tenía un sonajero en la mano, pero no parecía darse cuenta de que lo tenía.

Filipe se llevó los dedos a la boca y se los chupó mientras miraba atentamente a los niños pequeños.

4 a 8 meses (bebé)

- Los bebés de espaldas se ponen de lado y luego se vuelven a poner de espaldas.
- Al final de este período, los bebés se sientan; primero con apoyo pero luego estables y solos.
- Los bebés se estiran para alcanzar objetos con el brazo.
- Los bebés agarran rastrillando.
- Los bebés gatean.
- Los bebés sacuden, golpean, sujetan y sueltan objetos.
- Los bebés se pasan objetos de una mano a otra.
- Los bebés pueden sostener su biberón.
- Los bebés se pueden llevar objetos a la boca.

Estando de espaldas, Micky rueda para quedar boca abajo y alcanzar un juguete, luego vuelve a rodar para jugar con el juguete.

A Erin, sentada sola establemente, le gusta recoger objetos con las dos manos y examinarlos.

A Freddy le gusta que lo tomen en brazos mientras toma su biberón, aunque insiste en sujetarlo solo.

8 a 12 meses (bebé móvil)

- Los bebés móviles jalan de algo para ponerse de pie.
- Los bebés móviles se pasean.
- Los bebés móviles se quedan de pie solos.
- Los bebés móviles caminan con ayuda al principio y después solos.
- Los bebés móviles se sientan en una silla.
- Los bebés móviles comen con los dedos.
- Los bebés móviles pueden usar una cuchara y un vaso hermético.
- Los bebés móviles agarran atenazando.

Hershel gatea hasta su maestra, luego se agarra de su pierna y jala para ponerse de pie.

Jem se sienta a la mesa del almuerzo, y alterna la cuchara y los dedos para disfrutar de la comida.

Interacción entre Maestra-Niño, o Padre/Madre–Niño	Ambiente

0 a 4 meses (bebé)

- Cambie la posición del bebé; a veces de espaldas, otras boca abajo. Cuando lleve en brazos al bebé, acúnelo en sus brazos o sosténgalo erguido contra el hombro.
- Cuando el bebé está en el piso, acuéstese cara a cara junto a él.
- Cuando la bebé está de espaldas y trata de alcanzar un juguete un poco más allá de su cabeza, sosténgale el tronco mientras rueda.

- Una manta rígida (contra el riesgo de asfixia) en el suelo da espacio para los primeros movimientos.
- Los juguetes pequeños e interesantes, las imágenes, y los libros para mirar cuando quieran animan a los bebés a levantar la cabeza. Un espejo atornillado a la pared a nivel del suelo siempre ofrece algo interesante que mirar.
- A medida que comienzan a estirarse para alcanzar, a los bebés les gustan las barras estables con juguetes colgantes que puedan batear, alcanzar y agarrar.

4 a 8 meses (bebé)

- Quédese cerca del bebé que recién comienza a sentarse solo.
- Conozca el avance del desarrollo motor; anime emocionalmente y apoye físicamente al bebé en sus nuevos intentos.
- Crea en los beneficios a largo plazo para la salud de un estilo de vida activo.

- Deles lugares seguros para rodar, sentarse y gatear. Proteja a los bebés de cualquier cosa que pueda caerles encima.
- Deles objetos livianos pequeños y lavables (grandes para evitar que se asfixien) para que los manipulen y los lancen, y deles recipientes para los objetos.

8 a 12 meses (bebé móvil)

- Esté atenta para saber cuándo ayudar al bebé que comienza a caminar y cuándo dejar que lo siga intentando.
- Dé tiempo para que los bebés mayores practiquen comer solos.

- Lugares seguros para ponerse de pie apoyándose en algo.
- Juguetes para empujar y jalar para que los que comienzan a caminar puedan jalar y empujar.
- Cajas mecánicas.
- Libros de cartón para pasar las páginas, levantar las solapas y meter los dedos a través de los agujeros.

Desarrollo	Ejemplo

12 a 18 meses (bebé móvil)

• Los bebés móviles apilan y alinean bloques. • Los bebés móviles pueden vestirse y desvestirse solos, meter el brazo en una manga y el pie dentro de un zapato. • Los bebés móviles pueden caminar. • Los bebés móviles caminan con objetos en las manos. • Los bebés móviles suben escaleras.	Gary se paró frente a la mesa y construyó cuidadosamente con las dos manos una torre con bloques de colores. Michelle caminó por la habitación con su osito de peluche en una mano y su manta en la otra.

18 a 24 meses (niño pequeño)

• Los niños pequeños señalan objetos con el dedo para comunicarse. • Los niños pequeños hacen marcas en un papel. • Los niños pequeños trabajan y dan forma a la plastilina. • Los niños pequeños corren. • Los niños pequeños se sientan y se levantan solos de sillas pequeñas. • Los niños pequeños están desarrollando su confianza espacial; explorando su cuerpo en el espacio.	Mindy estiró la plastilina con las manos y luego hizo figuras con las herramientas. Joseph se sentó a la mesa para comer, luego llevó los platos sucios al fregadero.

24 a 36 meses (niño pequeño)

• Los niños pequeños ensartan cuentas, usan las tijeras, pintan con los dedos o con pinceles, arman rompecabezas sencillos. • Los niños pequeños lanzan y patean una pelota. • Los niños pequeños se paran en un solo pie. • Los niños pequeños se paran y caminan en puntillas. • Los niños pequeños suben escaleras poniendo un pie en cada escalón. • Los niños pequeños trepan, se deslizan y saltan. • Los niños pequeños comen con cuchara y tenedor. • Los niños pequeños se pueden vestir solos. • Los niños pequeños pueden verter leche de una jarra pequeña.	Robert ni siquiera tiene que pensar en su cuerpo cuando corre para saludar a su papá al final del día. Peggy y Misha inventan un juego imitándose mutuamente los pasos en puntillas, posturas y gestos. Forcejeando un poco, Lawrence y Evelyn juegan con la ropa para disfrazarse.

Interacciones entre el niño y la maestra, el padre o la madre	Ambiente

12 a 18 meses (bebé móvil)

• Imite la cada vez mayor variedad de movimientos del bebé. • Introduzca canciones con pequeños bailes y movimientos. • Dé tiempo y tenga paciencia mientras el niño pequeño practica ponerse solo la chaqueta.	• Juguetes para montar estables y no muy altos. • Juguetes mecedores estables y no muy altos. • Juegos de manipulación basados en habilidades, tales como apilar vasos o ensartar aros en un palo.

18 a 24 meses (niño pequeño)

• Ponga a disposición de los niños materiales pequeños que los induzcan a poner en práctica su creciente capacidad de manipulación de objetos con los dedos. • Quédese con los niños pequeños y apóyelos mientras intentan poner en práctica capacidades recientemente desarrolladas. • Deles oportunidades de trepar, caminar y correr.	• Materi.ales de arte tales como brochas gordas, marcadores y superficies grandes para pintar. • Articulos pequeños, tales como cuentas que se interconectan y tableros para clavijas, para practicar actividades de manipulación. • Mucho espacio para el movimiento: bailes, juguetes para montar, estructuras para trepar, toboganes.

24 a 36 meses (niño pequeño)

• Esté consciente del equilibrio necesario entre el tiempo dedicado a actividades enérgicas y a actividades tranquilas. • Esté atento al aumento de precisión de las capacidades motrices ligeras, pues pueden comenzar a manifestarse sutiles problemas. • Esté a disposición de los niños pequeños animándolos y teniéndoles paciencia conforme comen, se visten y van al baño solos con más frecuencia.	• Ponga a su disposición una variedad de materiales para practicar capacidades motrices ligeras: rompecabezas simples, cajas de formas, cuentas para hacer collares, bloques de mesa, arcilla, materiales de arte. • Espacio, oportunidad y estructuras para fomentar el movimiento: períodos de tiempo al aire libre, carreras de obstáculos, bailes y juguetes para montar.

Appendix D

Planning Guides

Directions for Using the Planning Guides

Individual Child Planning Guides

1. **Choose which Individual Child Planning Guide you would like to use.** Version 1 divides the *Reflect* section into developmental domains, whereas Version 2 provides a space under the *Reflect* section for you to write a sentence or two about the child's development that integrates the domains.
2. **Choose the child or children to observe during the week.** In a center program, care teachers decide which children each care teacher will observe during the week. In a center using a primary caregiving system, each teacher will complete a guide on her primary group children. In a family child care home, the teacher can choose several children to observe during a particular week. For a home visiting program, the home visitor completes the guide with the family.
3. **Complete the *Respect* section.** For both versions, each care teacher writes an anecdotal record; uses a photograph (or series of photographs) of the child involved with the teacher, peers, equipment, toys, materials, and experiences; or uses other documentation (e.g., an example of the child's scribbling). You can attach these to the page.
4. **Complete the *Reflect* section.** This section is completed by you, with other care teachers, and/or with family members. When completing the section ***What am I doing?,*** objectively describe the behavior represented under the ***Respect*** section. You could use the Chart of Concepts and the Developmental Trends and Responsive Interaction Charts found in Chapters 6 through 10 to help you complete ***What am I learning?.*** For Version 1, describe what concepts the child is exploring and/or describe development. For Version 2, describe what concepts the child is exploring and what the child may be thinking.
5. **Complete the *Relate* section.** This section is completed by you, with other teachers, and/or with family members. In both versions, decide what interactions and changes in the environment are responsive to the concepts the child is exploring and the development observed.
6. **Create a portfolio for each child and include the Individual Child Planning Guides.** Use them to reflect on changes in the child's interests and the child's developmental progress over time. Give the portfolios to the family of the child when the child changes rooms or when the child leaves the program.

Group Planning Guides

1. **Complete the Individually Responsive Group Planning Guide with other care teachers and/or with family members.** Each care teacher in a center-based program brings her completed Individual Child Planning Guides to a team meeting. The team discusses the information from the individual guides and then completes the group guide by summarizing the concepts and developmental efforts of the individual children observed that week. You could use resource books that provide ideas about interactions, equipment, and experiences and then choose ***opportunities*** that are responsive to the individual children and the group. Provide the opportunities during the following week.
2. **Complete the Group Planning for Routines Guide each month.**

Individual Child Planning Guide: Version 1

Child's Name: _____   Plans for Week of (Date): _____

Person Completing the Guide: _____

Respect: Child's Emotions, Effort, Goals, Learning, and Relationships

Write an observation or use a picture or other documentation here—date all notes:

Respect and Reflect	Relate
What am I doing?	**What will you do to support my development and learning?** **Responsive Interactions**
How am I feeling?	
What am I learning? • *Emotional*	**Environment, Toys, Materials, and Experiences**
• *Social*	
• *Cognitive*	
• *Language*	
• *Motor*	

Permission is granted by the publisher to reproduce this form for evaluation and record keeping. From Donna S. Wittmer and Sandra H. Petersen, *Infant and Toddler Development and Responsive Program Planning: A Relationship-Based Approach* (3rd ed.). Copyright © 2013 by Pearson Education, Inc. All rights reserved.

Individual Child Planning Guide: Version 2

Child's Name: _____   Plans for Week of (Date): _____

Person(s) Completing the Guide: _____

_____

_____

_____

Respect: Child's Emotions, Effort, Goals, Learning, and Relationships

Write an observation or use a picture or other documentation here—date all notes:

_____

Reflect

What am I doing?

How am I feeling?

What am I learning?

Relate

What will you do to support my development and learning?
Responsive Interactions

Environment, Toys, Materials, and Experiences

Permission is granted by the publisher to reproduce this form for evaluation and record-keeping, From Donna S. Wittmer and Sandra H. Petersen, *Infant and Toddler Development and Responsive Program Planning: A Relationship-Based Approach* (3rd ed.). Copyright © 2013 by Pearson Education, Inc. All rights reserved.

Individually Responsive Group Planning Guide

Name of Group: _____

Week of: _____

Person(s) Completing This Guide: _____

Respect and Reflect

(Use information from the individual planning guides.)

Relate: Plans for the Week to Meet Children's Interests and Needs

Songs/Finger-Plays

Stories/Books

Responsive Interactions

Environment, Toys, Materials, and Opportunities

Experiences with Families

Special Experiences

Permission is granted by the publisher to reproduce this form for evaluation and record-keeping, From Donna S. Wittmer and Sandra H. Petersen, *Infant and Toddler Development and Responsive Program Planning: A Relationship-Based Approach* (3rd ed.). Copyright © 2013 by Pearson Education, Inc. All rights reserved.

Group Planning for Routines

Name of Group: _____

Week of: _____

Person(s) Completing This Form: _____

---

*Developing a caring community: Think about what is happening and what could happen
to develop a relationship-based program for children, families, and teachers.*

Routine	What is going well for the children and teachers?	What could we do to improve the experience for children, families, and the teachers?
Greeting time or good-bye time		
Feeding infants and toddler eating times		
Infant sleep and toddler nap time		
Diapering		
Toileting		
Play times		
Outdoor times		
Transitions		

Permission is granted by the publisher to reproduce this form for evaluation and record-keeping. From Donna S. Wittmer and Sandra H. Petersen, *Infant and Toddler Development and Responsive Program Planning: A Relationship-Based Approach* (3rd ed.). Copyright © 2013 by Pearson Education, Inc. All rights reserved.

References

AAP (American Academy of Pediatrics). (1997). Breastfeeding and the use of human milk. *Pediatrics, 100*(6), 1035–1039.

AAP (American Academy of Pediatrics). (1999). Newborn and infant hearing loss: Detection and intervention. *Pediatrics, 103*(2), 527–530.

AAP (American Academy of Pediatrics). (2004). U.S. government should ban baby walkers. Retrieved from http://www.aap.org

AAP (American Academy of Pediatrics). (2005a). AAP recommendations on SIDS 2005. Retrieved from http://www.aap.org

AAP (American Academy of Pediatrics). (2005b). The changing concept of sudden infant death syndrome: Diagnostic coding shifts, controversies regarding the sleeping environment, and new variables to consider in reducing risk. *Pediatrics, 116*(5), 1245–1255.

Acredolo, L., & Goodwyn, S. (1985). Symbolic gesturing in language development: A case study. *Human Development, 28,* 40–49.

Acredolo, L., & Goodwyn, S. (2002). *Baby signs: How to talk with your baby before your baby can talk.* New York: McGraw-Hill.

Adamson, L. B., Bakeman, R., & Deckner, D. J. (2004). The development of symbol-infused joint engagement. *Child Development, 75*(4), 1171–1189.

Adolph, K. E. (2008). Learning to move. *Current Directions in Psychological Science, 17,* 213–218.

Adolph, K. E., & Eppler, M. A. (2002). Flexibility and specificity in infant motor skill acquisition. In J. Fagan (Ed.), *Progress in infancy research* (Vol. 2, pp. 121–167). Mahwah, NJ: Erlbaum.

Ainsworth, M. D. S., Bell, S. M., & Stayton, D. J. (1971). Individual differences in the strange situation behavior of one-year-olds. In H. R. Schaffer (Ed.), *The origins of human social relations* (pp. 17–58). San Diego, CA: Academic Press.

Ainsworth, M. D. S., Blehar, M. C., Waters, E., & Wall, S. (1978). *Patterns of attachment: A psychological study of the strange situation.* Hillsdale, NJ: Erlbaum.

Als, H., Lester, B., Tronick, E. Z., & Brazelton, T. B. (1982). Towards a research instrument for the assessment of preterm infants' behavior (A.P.I.B.). In H. E. Fitzgerald, B. M. Lester, & M. W. Yogman (Eds.), *Theory and research in behavioral pediatrics* (Vol. 1, pp. 85–132). New York: Plenum.

Amato, P. R., & Rivera, F. (1999). Paternal involvement and children's behavior problems. *Journal of Marriage and the Family, 61*(22), 375–384.

(AMCHP) Association of Maternal and Child Health Programs. (2009). Supporting evidence-based home visiting. Retrieved from: http://supportingebhv.org/home-visiting-models.

American Academy of Pediatrics, American Public Health Association, National Resource Center for Health and Safety in Child Care. (2011). *Caring for our children: National health and safety performance standards for out-of-home child care programs* (3rd ed.). Elk Grove Village, IL: American. Retrieved from nrckids.org/CFOC3/

Annie E. Casey Foundation (2008). 2008 KIDS COUNT Data Book: State profiles of child well-being. Retrieved from www.aecf.org

Annie E. Casey Foundation (2012). 2012 KIDS COUNT Data Book: State trends in child well-being. Retrieved from www.aecf.org

Appleyard, K., Egeland, B., van Dulmen, M. H. M., & Sroufe, A. L. (2005). When more is not better: The role of cumulative risk in child behavior outcomes. *Journal of Child Psychology and Psychiatry, 46*(3), 235–245.

Arnett, J. (1989). Caregivers in child care centers. Does training matter? *Journal of Applied Developmental Psychology, 10,* 541–552.

Arnold, C. M., Aragon, D., Shepherd, J., & Van Sell, S. L. (2011). The coming of the blessing: A successful cross-cultural collaborative effort for American Indian/Alaska Native families. *Family & Community Health, 34*(3), 196–201.

Association of Maternal and Child Health Programs (AMCHP). (2009). Supporting evidence-based home visiting. Retrieved from http://supportingebhv.org/home-visiting-models

Astington, J. W., & Barriault, T. (2001). Children's theory of mind: How young children come to understand that people have thoughts and feelings. *Infants and Young Children, 13*(3), 1–12.

Baby Center. (2008). *Motor development: Ten red flags.* Retrieved from www.babycenter.com/0-motor-development-ten-red-flags_11640.bc

Bahrick, L. E. (1995). Intermodal origins of self-perception. In P. Rochat (Ed.), *The self in infancy: Theory and research advances in psychology* (pp. 349–373). Amsterdam: North Holland/Elsevier.

Bailey, T. M., & Plunkett, K. (2002). Phonological specificity in early words. *Cognitive Development, 17*(2), 1265–1282.

Baillargeon, R. (1993). The object concept revisited: New directions in the investigation of infant's physical knowledge. In C. Granrud (Ed.), *Visual perception and cognition in infancy* (pp. 265–315). Hillsdale, NJ: Erlbaum.

Baillargeon, R. H., Normand, C. L., Séguin, J. R., Zoccolillo, M., Japel, C., Pérusse,...Tremblay, R. E. (2007). The evolution of problem and social competence behaviors during toddlerhood: A prospective population-based cohort survey. *Infant Mental Health Journal, 28,* 12–38.

Baillargeon, R. H., Sward, G. D., Keenan, K., & Cao, G. (2011). Opposition-defiance in the second year of life: A population-based cohort study. *Infancy, 16*(4), 418–434.

Bandura, A. (1977). *Social learning theory.* Upper Saddle River, NJ: Prentice Hall.

Bandura, A. (1989). Social cognitive theory. In R. Vasta (Ed.), *Annals of child development* (Vol. 6). Greenwich, CT: JAI.

Bandura, A. (1997). *Self-efficacy: The exercise of control.* New York: Freeman.

Bandura, A. (2001). Social cognitive theory: An agentive perspective. *Review of Psychology, 52,* 1–26.

Barnes, M. W. (2011). When couples become parents: The creation of gender in the transition to parenthood. *Journal of Marriage and Family, 73,* 310–312.

Barrera, I., Corso, R., & Macpherson, D. (2003). *Skilled dialogue: Strategies for responding to cultural diversity in early childhood.* Baltimore: Paul H. Brookes.

Barrera, I., & Kramer, L. (1997). From monologues to skilled dialogues: Teaching the process of crafting culturally competent early childhood environments. In P. Winton, J. McCollum, & C. Catlett (Eds.), *Reforming personnel preparation in early intervention: Issues, models, and practical strategies* (pp. 217–252). Baltimore: Brookes.

Barrera, I., Kramer, L., & Macpherson, D. (2012). *Skilled dialogue. Strategies for responding to cultural diversity in early childhood* (2nd ed.). Baltimore: Paul H. Brookes.

Batya, L., Simoni, H., & Perrig-Chiello, P. (2008). Conflict between peers in infancy and toddler age: What do they fight about? *Early Years: Journal of International Research & Development, 28*(3), 235–249.

Bauer, P. J., Evren Güler, O., Starr, R. M., & Pathman, T. (2011). Equal learning does not result in equal remembering: The importance of post-encoding processes. *Infancy, 16*(6), 557–586. doi:10.1111/j.1532-7078.2010.00057.x

Baumrind, D. (1991). The influence of parenting style on adolescent competence and substance use. *Journal of Early Adolescence, 11*(1), 56–95.

Bayer, J. K., Sanson, A.V., & Hemphill, S. A. (2006). Parent influences on early childhood internalizing difficulties. *Journal of Applied Developmental Psychology, 27,* 542–559.

Beard, J. L., Connor, J. D., & Jones, B. C. (1997). Brain iron: Location and function. *Progress in Food and Nutrition Science, 17,* 183–221.

Begus, K., & Southgate, V. (2012). Infant pointing serves an interrogative function. *Developmental Science, 15*(5), 611–617.

Bellagamba, F., Camaioni, L., & Colonnesi, C. (2006). Change in children's understanding of others' intentional actions. *Developmental Science, 9*(2), 182–188.

Bellm, D., Whitebook, M., & Hnatiuk, P. (1997). *The early childhood mentoring curriculum: A handbook for mentors.* Washington, DC: National Center for the Early Childhood Work Force.

Belsky, J., & Fearon, R. M. P. (2002). Early attachment security, subsequent maternal sensitivity, and later child development: Does continuity in development depend upon continuity of caregiving? *Attachment and Human Development, 4,* 361–387.

Benenson, J. F., Tennyson, R., & Wrangham, R. W. (2011). Male more than female infants imitate propulsive motion. *Cognition, 121*(2), 262–267.

Berglund, E., & Eriksson, M. (2000). Communicative development in Swedish children 16–28 months old. The Swedish early communicative development inventory—words and sentences. *Scandinavian Journal of Psychology, 41*(2), 133–144.

Besag, F. M. (2002). Childhood epilepsy in relation to mental handicap and behavioural disorders. *Journal of Child Psychology and Psychiatry, 43,* 103–131.

Bettelheim, B. (1987, March). The importance of play. *Atlantic,* 35–46.

Biehle, S. N., & Mickelson, K. D. (2011). Preparing for parenthood: How feelings of responsibility and efficacy impact expectant parents. *Journal of Social and Personal Relationships, 28*(5), 668–683. doi:10.1177/0265407510385493

Blasco, P. M. (2001). *Early intervention services for infants, toddlers, and their families.* Boston: Allyn & Bacon.

Bloom, P. J. (2000). *Circle of influence: Implementing shared decision making and participative management.* Lake Forest, IL: New Horizons.

Bloom, P. J., Hentchel, A., & Bella, J. (2010). *A great place to work: Creating a healthy organizational climate.* The Director's Toolbox series. Lake Forest, IL: New Horizons. Available from NAEYC.

Bornstein, M., & Cote, L. (2005). Expressive vocabulary in language learners from two ecological settings in three language communities. *Infancy, 7,* 299–316.

Bower, T. G. R. (1977). *A primer of infant development.* San Francisco: Freeman.

Bowlby, J. (1969). *Attachment and Loss:* Vol. 1. *Attachment.* New York: Basic Books.

Bowlby, J. (1982). *Attachment.* New York: Basic Books.

Boyer, W. (2009). Crossing the glass wall: Using preschool educators' knowledge to enhance parental understanding of self-regulation and emotion regulation. *Early Childhood Education Journal, 37,* 175–182. DOI 10.1007/s10643-009-0343-y

Brannon, E. M. (2002). The development of ordinal numerical knowledge in infancy. *Cognition, 83,* 223–240.

Braungart-Rieker, J. M., Garwood, M. M., Powers, B. P., & Wang, X. (2001). Parental sensitivity, infant affect, and affect regulation: Predictors of later attachment. *Child Development, 72*(1), 252–270.

Brazelton, T. B. (1972). Implications of infant development among the Mayan Indians of Mexico. *Human Development, 15*(2), 90–111.

Brazelton, T. B. (1992). *Touchpoints: Your child's emotional and behavioral development*. Reading, MA: Perseus.

Brazelton, T. B., & Greenspan, S. I. (2000). *The irreducible needs of children: What every child must have to grow, learn, and flourish*. New York: Perseus.

Brazelton, T. B., & Sparrow, J. D. (2004). *Toilet training: The Brazelton way*. Cambridge, MA: Da Capo.

Brems, S., & Berg, A. (1988). *"Eating down" during pregnancy: Nutrition, obstetrics, and culture considerations in the third world*. Washington, DC: UN Advisory Group on Nutrition.

Breslin, D. (2005). Children's capacity to develop resiliency: How to nurture it. *Young Children, 60*(1), 47–57.

Bretherton, I. (1985). Attachment theory: Retrospect and prospect. *Monographs of the Society for Research in Child Development, 50*(1/2), 3–35.

Bretherton, I. (2010). Fathers in attachment theory and research: A review. *Early Child Development & Care, 180*(1/2), 9–23.

Bricker, D., & Squires, J. (2009). *Ages and Stages Questionnaires, Third Edition (ASQ-3). A parent-completed monitoring system*. Baltimore: Brookes.

Bromwich, R. (1997). *Working with families and their infants at risk*. Austin, TX: Pro-Ed.

Bronfenbrenner, U. (1979). *The ecology of human development*. Cambridge, MA: Harvard University Press.

Bronfenbrenner, U. (1986). Ecology of the family as a context for human development: Research perspectives. *Developmental Psychology, 22*(6), 723–741.

Bronfenbrenner, U. (1994). Who cares for the children. In H. Nuba, M. Searson, & D. L. Sheiman (Eds.), *Resources for early childhood: A handbook* (pp. 113–129). New York: Garland.

Bronfenbrenner, U. (Ed). (2004). *Making human beings human: Bioecological perspectives on human development*. Thousand Oaks, CA: Sage.

Bronson, M. B. (2000a). Recognizing and supporting the development of self-regulation in young children. *Young Children, 55*(2), 32–37.

Bronson, M. B. (2000b). *Self-regulation in early childhood: Nature and nurture*. New York: Guilford Press.

Bronte-Tinkew, J., Carrano, J., & Guzman, L. (2006). Resident fathers' perceptions of their roles and links to involvement with infants. *Fathering: A Journal of Theory, Research, & Practice About Men as Fathers, 4*(3), 254–285.

Brook, J. S., Zheng, L., Whiteman, M., & Brook, D. (2001). Aggression in toddlers: Associations with parenting and marital relations. *Journal of Genetic Psychology, 162*(2), 228–241.

Brooks, R., & Meltzoff, A. N. (2005). The development of gaze following and its relation to language. *Developmental Science, 8*(6), 535–543.

Brophy-Herb, H., Schiffman, R. F., Bocknek, E. L., Dupuis, S. B., Fitzgerald, H. E., Horodynski, M., ... Hillaker, B. (2011). Toddlers' social-emotional competence in the contexts of maternal emotion socialization and contingent responsiveness in a low-income sample. *Social Development, 20*(1), 73–92.

Brown, R. (1973). *A first language: The early stages*. London: Allen & Unwin.

Brown, G. L., Mangelsdorf, S. C., & Neff, C. (2012) Father involvement, paternal sensitivity, and father-child attachment security in the first 3 years. *Journal of Family Psychology, 26*(3), 421–430.

Brown University. (2006). Fussy babies and postpartum depression linked, study finds. *ScienceDaily*. Retrieved from www.sciencedaily.com/releases/2006/05/060502090732.htm

Brownell, C. A., & Carriger, M. (1990). Changes in cooperation and self-determination during the second year. *Child Development, 61*, 1164–1174.

Brownell, C. A., & Kopp, C. B. (2007). *Socioemotional development in the toddler years. Transitions and transformations*. New York: Guilford Press.

Brownell, C. A., Nichols, S. R., Svetlova, M., Zerwas, S., & Ramani, G. (2010). The head bone's connected to the neck bone: When do toddlers represent their own body topography? *Child Development, 81*(3), 797–810. doi:10.1111/j.1467-8624.2010.01434.x

Brownell, C. A., Ramani, G. B., & Zerwas, S. (2006). Becoming a social partner with peers: Cooperation and social understanding in one- and two-year-olds. *Child Development, 77*(4), 803–821.

Brownell, C., Svetlova, M., & Nichols, S. (2009). To share or not to share: When do toddlers respond to another's needs? *Infancy, 14*, 117–130.

Brownlee, J., & Bakeman, R. (1981). Hitting in toddler-peer interactions. *Child Development, 52*(3), 1076–1080.

Bruner, J. (1966). *Toward a theory of instruction*. Cambridge, MA: Harvard University Press.

Bruner, J. (1996a). *The culture of education*. Cambridge, MA: Harvard University Press.

Bruner, J. (1996b). What we have learned about early learning. *European Early Childhood Education Research Journal, 4*(1), 5–16.

Buell, M. J., Gamel-McCormick, M., & Hallam, R. A. (1999, December). Inclusion in a child development and education context: Experiences and attitudes of family child development and education providers. *Topics in Early Childhood Special Education, 19*, 217–224.

Burchinal, M. R., Howes, C., & Kontos, S. (2002). Structural predictors of child care quality in child care homes. *Early Childhood Research Quarterly, 17*, 87–105.

Burchinal, M. R., Roberts, J. E., Nabors, L. A., & Bryant, D. M. (1996). Quality of center child care and infant cognitive and language development. *Child Development, 67*, 606–620.

Bureau of Labor Statistics. (2012). Table 6. Employment status of mothers with own children under 3 years old by single year of age of youngest child and marital status, 2010–2011 annual averages. Retrieved from http://www.bls.gov/news.release/famee.t06.htm

Butterfield, P. (2002). Child care is rich in routines. *Zero to ThreeZEROZ, 22*(4), 29–32.

Byers-Heinlein, K., Burns, T. C., & Werker, J. F. (2010). The roots of bilingualism in newborns. *Psychological Science, 21*(3), 343–348. doi:10.1177/0956797609360758

Cabrera, N. J., Hofferth, S.L., & Chae, S. (2011). Patterns and predictors of father-infant engagement across race/ethnic groups. *Early Child Research Quarterly, 26*(3), 365–375.

Cacola, P., Gabbard, C., Santos, D., & Batistela, C. (2011). Development of the affordances in the home environment for motor development – Infant Scale. Pediatrics International, 53(6), 820–825.6),

Cahill, L. (2005). His brain, her brain. *Scientific American, 292*(5), 40–47.

Campbell, D. W., & Eaton, W. O. (1999). Sex differences in the activity levels of infants. *Infant and Child Development, 8*, 1–17.

Campbell, S. B. (1995). Depression in first-time mothers: Mother-infant interaction and depression chronicity. *Developmental Psychology, 31*(3), 349–357.

Camras, L. A. (1992). Expressive development and basic emotions. *Cognition and Emotion, 6*(3), 269–283.

Canterino, J. C., VanHorn, L. G., Harrigan, J., Ananth, C., & Vintzileos, A. (1999). Domestic abuse in pregnancy: A comparison of a self-completed domestic abuse questionnaire with a directed interview. *American Journal of Obstetrics and Gynecology, 181*(5), 1049–1051.

Capatides, J., Collins, C. C., & Bennett, L. (1996). *Peer interaction in toddlers: Parallel play revisited.* Paper presented at the conference "Ask the Child: Why, When, and How?" Teachers College Press, New York.

Carey, S. (1978). The child as word learner. In M. Halle, J. Bresnan, & G. A. Miller (Eds.), *Linguistic theory and psychological reality* (pp. 264–293). Cambridge, MA: MIT Press.

Carlson, M., & McLanahan, S. (2002). *Characteristics and antecedents of involvement by young, unmarried fathers.* (Working Paper #02-09-FF). Princeton, NJ: Princeton University, Center for Research on Child Wellbeing.

Carlson, M. J., Pilkauskas, N. V., McLanahan, S. S., & Brooks-Gunn, J. (2011). Couples as partners and parents over children's early years. *Journal of Marriage and Family, 73*(2), 317–334. doi:10.1111/j.1741-3737.2010.00809.x

Carmichael, S., De Moor, T., & van Zanden, J. L. (2011). "When the heart is baked, don't try to knead it": Marriage age and spousal age gap as a measure of female "agency." *Working Papers,* 0019, Utrecht University, Centre for Global Economic History.

Carter, M. (1992). Honoring diversity: Problems and possibilities for staff and organization. In B. Neugebauer (Ed.), *Alike and different: Exploring our humanity with young children* (Rev. ed.). Washington, DC: NAEYC.

Carter, M., & Curtis, D. (1998). *The visionary director: A handbook for dreaming, organizing, and improvising in your center.* St. Paul, MN: Redleaf.

Cartwright, K. B. (2012). Insights from cognitive neuroscience: The importance of executive function for early reading development and education. *Early Education and Development, 23*(1), 24–36.

Cartwright, S. (1999). What makes good preschool teachers? *Young Children, 54*(4), 4–7.

Caruso, D. A. (1988). Play and learning in infancy: Research and implications. *Young Children, 43*(6), 63–70.

Cassels, C. (2008). Widespread newborn screening for Fragile X under way. Retrieved from http://www.medscapre.com/viewarticle/579468

Castillo, J. T., Welch, G. W., & Sarver, C. M. (2012). Walking a high beam: The balance between employment stability, workplace flexibility, and nonresident father involvement. *American Journal of Mens Health, 6*(2), 120–131. doi: 10.1177/1557988311417612.

Cawlfield, M. E. (1992). Velcro time: The language connection. *Young Children, 47*(4), 26–30.

CCW (Center for the Childcare Workforce). (2004). *Current data on the salaries and benefits of the U.S. early childhood education workforce.* Washington, DC: Author.

CDC (Centers for Disease Control and Prevention). (2006) *Violence and reproductive health: Home.* Retrieved from http://www.cdc.gov/reproductivehealth/violence/

CDC (Centers for Disease Control and Prevention). (2011). National vital statistics reports, 60 (1). Authors Martin, J.A., et al. Retrieved from http://www.cdc.gov/nchs/data/nvsr/nvsr60/nvsr60_01.pdf

CDC (Centers for Disease Control and Prevention). (2012). Autism spectrum disorders: Data and statistics. Retrieved from http://www.cdc.gov/ncbddd/autism/data.html

CEC (Council for Exceptional Children). (2009). What every special educator must know—ethics, standards, and guidelines for special educators (6th ed.). Arlington, VA: Author.

CFF (Cystic Fibrosis Foundation). (2009). *What is cystic fibrosis?* Retrieved from http://www.cff.org/AboutCF/

Chang, A., & Aronson, S. (2002). Introduction. In American Public Health Association & American Academy of Pediatrics, *Caring for our children: National health and safety performance standards: Guidelines for out-of-home child care programs.* Washington, DC: APHA & AAP.

Chao, R. K. (1994). Beyond parental control and authoritarian parenting style: Understanding Chinese parenting through the cultural notion of training. *Child Development, 65*(4), 1111–1119.

Chen, X., French, D., Schneider, B.H., Ed. (2006). *Peer relationships in cultural context*. Cambridge, Cambridge University Press.

Chen, D., & Haney, M. (1999). *Promoting learning through active interaction. Project PLAI. Final report.* Northridge: California State University. (ERIC Document Reproduction Service No. ED432118)

ChildStats. (2011). America's children in brief: Key national indicators of well-being. Retrieved from http://www.child-stats.gov/americaschildren/glance.asp

ChildStats.gov. (n.d.). America's children in brief: Key national indicators of well-being, 2012. Retrieved from http://www.childstats.gov/americaschildren/glance.asp

Child Trends. (2002). *Databank*. Retrieved from http://www.childtrendsdatabank.org

Child Trends. (2010). *The compendium of quality rating systems and evaluations*. Washington, DC: Author.

Child Trends. (2011*)*. Children in poverty. Retrieved from www.childtrendsdatabank.org/?q=node/221

Child Trends (2012). Disadvantaged families and child outcomes. The Importance of Emotional Support. By bandy, T., Andrews, K.M., & Anderson, K. Retrieved from http://www.childtrends.org

Cicchetti, D., & Curtis, W. J. (Eds.). (2007). Special issue: A multilevel approach to resilience. *Development and Psychopathology, 19*(3).

Children's Defense Fund. (2006). *Annual report 2006.* Retrieved from http://www.childrensdefense.org/site/DocServer/2006_annual_report.pdf?docID=5141

Children's Defense Fund. (2011). Child poverty in America: 2011. Retrieved from http://www.childrensdefense.org/child-research-data-publications/data/2011-child-poverty-in-america.pdfChil

Child Welfare Information Gateway. (2008). *Parent education. Issue brief.* Retrieved from www.childwelfare.gov/pubs/issue_briefs/parented/

Chiriboga, C. A. (1991). Abuse of children: Fetal and pediatric AIDS, fetal alcohol syndrome, fetal cocaine effects, and the battered child syndrome. In L. P. Rowland (Ed.), *Merritt's textbook of neurology* (pp. 995–1000). Baltimore: Williams & Wilkins.

Chomsky, N. (1975). *Reflections on language*. New York: Pantheon Books.

Chrisler, J. C. (2012, Feb. 29). *Reproductive justice: A global concern.* Santa Barbara, CA: ABC-CLIO Praeger.

Chrisman, K., & Couchenour, D. (2003). Developing concepts of gender roles. In C. Copple (Ed.), *A world of difference* (pp. 116–117). Washington, DC: NAEYC.

Christie-Mizell, C. A., Peralta, R., & Laske, M. (2008, July). *Maternal depression and race: The consequences of neighborhood perceptions and neighborhood location*. Paper presented at the annual meeting of the American Sociological Association, Boston, MA, Retrieved from http://www.allacademic.com/meta/p241248_index.html

Chu, M. (2014). *Developing mentoring and coaching relationships in early care and education: A reflective approach.* Upper Saddle River, NJ: Pearson

Chugani, H. T. (1998). A critical period of brain development: Studies of cerebral glucose utilization with PET. *Preventive Medicine, 27,* 487–497.

Cicchetti, D., & Curtis, W. J. (Eds.). (2007). Special issue: A multilevel approach to resilience. *Development and Psychopathology, 19*(3).

Clark, R., & Fenichel, E. (2001). Mothers, babies, and depression: Questions and answers. *Zero to Three, 22*(1), 48–50.

Clarke-Stewart, K. A., Vandell, D. L., Burchinal, M., O'Brien, M., & McCartney, K. (2002). Do regulable features of child-care homes affect children's development? *Early Child Research Quarterly, 17,* 52–86.

CLASP. (2012). Early Head Start participants, programs, families and staff in 2011 by Stephanie Schmit. Retrieved from www.clasp.org/admin/site/publications/files/EHS-PIR-2011-Fact-Sheet.pdf

Clifton, R. K., Rochat, P., Robin, D., & Berthier, N. E. (1994). Multimodal perception in the control of infant reaching. *Journal of Experimental Psychology: Human Perception and Performance, 20*(4), 876–886.

Coleman, J. G. (1999). *The early intervention dictionary: A multidisciplinary guide to terminology*. Bethesda, MD: Woodbine.

Coley, R. L., & Chase-Lansdale, P. L. (1999). Stability and change in paternal involvement among urban African-American fathers. Journal of Family Psychology, 13(3), 416–435.

Coll, C. G., & Magnuson, K. (2000). Cultural differences as sources of developmental vulnerabilities and resources. In J. P. Shonkoff & S. J. Meisels (Eds.), *Handbook of early childhood intervention* (2nd ed., pp. 94–114). New York: Cambridge University Press.

Collier, A. M., & Henderson, F. W. (2000). Respiratory disease in infants and toddlers. In D. Cryer & T. Harms (Eds.), *Infants and toddlers in out-of-home care* (pp. 163–178). Baltimore: Brookes.

Colonnesi, C., Zijlstra, B. J. H., van der Zande, A., & Bögels, S. M. (2012). Coordination of gaze, facial expressions and vocalization of early infant communication with mother and father. *Infant Behavior and Development, 35*(3), 523–532.

Consumer Products Safety Commission. (2009). Nursery product-related safety injuries and deaths among children under five. Retrieved from www.cpsc.gov/library/nursery08.pdf

Cooper, P. J., & Murray, L. (1998). Postnatal depression. *British Medical Journal, 316,* 1884–1886.

Cooper, R. P., & Aslin, R. N. (1990). Preference for infant-directed speech in the first month after birth. *Child Development, 61*(5), 1584–1595.

Copple, C. (Ed.). (2003). *A world of difference: Readings on teaching young children in a diverse society.* Washington, DC: NAEYC.

Copple, C., & Bredecamp, S. (Eds.). (2009). *Developmentally appropriate practice in early childhood programs* (3rd ed.). Washington, DC: NAEYC.

Cote, S. M., Vaillancourt, T., LeBlanc, J. C., Nagin, D. S., & Tremblay, R. E. (2006). The development of physical aggression from toddlerhood to pre-adolescence: A nationwide longitudinal study of Canadian children (Clinical report). *Journal of Abnormal Child Psychology, 34*(1), 71–86.

Cowan, C. P., & Cowan, P. A. (1992). *When partners become parents.* New York: Basic Books.

Cox, M. J., Owen, M. T., Henderson, V. K., & Margand, N. A. (1992). Prediction of infant-father and infant-mother attachment. *Developmental Psychology, 28,* 474–483.

CQO Study Team. (1995). *Cost, quality, and child outcomes in child care centers.* Public report. Denver: University of Colorado–Denver.

Crais, E. R. (2009, March). *Early infant/toddler behaviors that may lead to a diagnosis of autism.* Presented at the annual Ohio Speech-Language-Hearing Association, Columbus, Ohio. Retrieved from www.ohioslha.org/pdf/Convention/2009%20 Handouts/Elizabeth%20Crais-Early%20Infant%20Toddler-Reduced.pdf

Creighton, A. (2011) Mother-infant musical interaction and emotional communication: A literature review. *Australian Journal of Music Therapy, 22,* 37–58.

Crick, N. R., Ostrov, J. M., & Kawabata. Y. (2007). Relational aggression and gender: An overview. In D. J. Flannery & A. Vazsonyi (Eds.), *The Cambridge handbook of violent behavior and aggression* (pp. 243–260). New York: Cambridge University Press.

Crittenden, P. (1995). Attachment and psychopathology. In S. Goldbert, R. Muir, & J. Kerr (Eds.), *Attachment theory: Social, developmental, and clinical perspectives* (pp. 367–406). Hillsdale, NJ: Analytic Press.

Crockenberg, S., Leerkes, E., & Lekka, S. K. (2007). Pathways from marital aggression to infant emotion regulation: The development of withdrawal in infancy. *Infant Behavior and Development, 30*(1), 97–113.

Cross, A. F., Traub, E. K., Hutter-Pishagi, L., & Shelton, G. (2004). Elements of successful inclusion for children with significant disabilities. *Topics in Early Childhood Special Education, 24*(3), 169–184.

Crowell, J. A., Treboux, D., & Brockmeyer, S. (2009). Parental divorce and adult children's attachment representations and marital status. *Attachment & Human Development, 11*(1), 87–101. doi:10.1080/14616730802500867

Cryer, D., Harms, T., & Bourland, B. (1988). *Active learning for threes.* Menlo Park, CA: Addison-Wesley.

CWIG (Child Welfare Information Gateway). (2001). Understanding the effects of maltreatment on early brain development. Retrieved from www.childwelfare.gov/edtoolkit/pdfs/earlybrain.pdf

CWIG (Child Welfare Information Gateway). (2004). How many children were adopted in 2007 and 2008? Numbers and trends. Retrieved from www.childwelfare.gov/adoption/intro.cfm

Cystic Fibrosis Foundation (CFF). (2009). What is cystic fibrosis? Retrieved from http://www.cff.org/AboutCF/

Damasio, A. (2003). *Looking for Spinoza: Joy, sorrow, and the feeling brain.* Orlando, FL: Harcourt.

Damasio, A., & Damasio, H. (1999). Brain and language. In *The Scientific American book of the brain,* by the editors of *Scientific American Magazine.* Guilford, CT: Lyons.

Darling, N. (1999, March). Parenting style and its correlates. *ERIC Digest* (ED427896). Champaign, IL: ERIC Clearinghouse on Elementary and Early Childhood Education.

DaRos, D., & Kovach, B. (1998). Assisting toddlers and caregivers during conflict resolutions: Interactions that promote socialization. *Childhood Education, 75*(1), 25.

de Boer, B., & Kuhl, P. K. (2003). Investigating the role of infant-directed speech with a computer model. *Acoustics Research Letters Online (ARLO), 4*(4), 129–134. Retrieved from scitation.aip.org/ARLO/top.jsp

DEC (Division for Early Childhood). (2009). *Code of ethics.* Retrieved from www.dec-sped.org/uploads/docs/about_dec/position_concept_papers/Code%20of%20Ethics_updated_Aug2009.pdf

DEC (Division for Early Childhood). (2013). Recommended practices. Retrieved from www.dec-sped.org/About_DEC/Recommended_Practices

DeCasper, A., & Fifer, W. (1980). Of human bonding: Newborns prefer their mothers' voices. *Science, 208,* 1174–1176.

DeCasper, A., & Spence, M. J. (1986). Prenatal maternal speech influences newborns' perception of speech sounds. *Infant Behavior and Development, 9,* 133–150.

Decker, C. A., & Decker, J. R. (2001). *Planning and administering early childhood programs* (7th ed.). Upper Saddle River, NJ: Merrill/Prentice Hall.

Degnan, K. A., Hane, A. A., Henderson, H. A., Moas, O. L., Reeb-Sutherland, B. C., & Fox, N. A. (2011). Longitudinal stability of temperamental exuberance and social-emotional outcomes in early childhood. *Developmental Psychology, 47*(3), 765–780.

Degotardi, S. (2010). High-quality interactions with infants: Relationships with early-childhood practitioners' interpretations and qualification levels in play and routine contexts. *International Journal of Early Years Education, 18*(1), 27–41. doi:10.1080/09669761003661253

de Groot Kim, S. (2010). There's Elly, It must be Tuesday: Discontinuity in child care programs and its impact on the development of peer relationships in young children. *Early Childhood Education Journal, 38*(2), 153–164. doi:10.1007/s10643-010-0400-6 de Hann, D., & Singer, E. (2003). Use your words: A sociocultural approach to the teacher's role in the transition from physical to verbal strategies of resolving peer conflicts among toddlers. *Journal of Early Childhood Research, 1*(1), 95–109.

DeHouwer, A. (1999, July). Two or more languages in early childhood: Some general points and practical recommendations. *ERIC Digest* (ED433697). District of Columbia: ERIC Clearinghouse on Languages and Linguistics.

Delamonica, E., & Minujin, A. (2007). Incidence, depth and severity of children in poverty. *Social Indicators Research, 82,* 361–374.

Delaney, C. (2000). Making babies in a Turkish village. In J. DeLoache & A. Gottlieb (Eds.), *A world of babies: Imagined child care guides for seven societies* (pp. 117–144). Cambridge, UK: Cambridge University Press.

DeLoache, J. (2000). Cognitive development in infants. In D. Cryer & T. Harmes (Eds.), *Infants and toddlers in out of home care* (pp. 7–48). Baltimore: Brookes.

DeLoache, J. S., Pierroutsakos, S. L. T., & Troseth, G. L. (1997). The three Rs of pictorial competence. *Annals of Child Development, 12,* 1–48.

DeLoache, J. S., Pierroutsakos, S. L., Troseth, G. L., Uttah, D. H., Rosengren, K. S., & Gottlieb, A. (1998). Grasping the nature of pictures. *Psychological Science, 9,* 205–210.

DeLoache, J. S., Strauss, M. S., & Maynard, J. (1979). Picture perception in infancy. *Infant Behavior and Development, 2,* 77–89.

Derman-Sparks, L., & The A.B.C. Task Force. (2003). Expanding awareness of gender roles. In C. Copple (Ed.), *A world of difference* (pp. 118–119). Washington, DC: NAEYC.

De Schipper, J., Tavecchio, L. C., & Van IJzendoorn, M. H. (2008). Children's attachment relationships with day care caregivers: Associations with positive caregiving and the child's temperament. *Social Development, 17*(3), 454–470. doi:10.1111/j.1467-9507.2007.00448.x

DeVries, R., & Zan, B. (1996). A constructivist perspective on the role of the sociomoral atmosphere in promoting children's development. In C. T. Fosnet (Ed.), *Constructivism: Theory, perspectives, and practice* (pp. 103–119). New York: Teachers College Press.

Dew, J., & Wilcox, W. B. (2011). If momma ain't happy: Explaining declines in marital satisfaction among new mothers. *Journal of Marriage and Family, 73*(1), 1–12. doi:10.1111/j.1741-3737.2010.00782.x

Dewar, G. (2011). Traditional Chinese parenting: What research says about Chinese kids and why they succeed. *Parenting Science.* Retrieved from www.parentingscience.com/chinese-parenting.html

de Wolff, M. S., & van IJzendourn, M. H. (1997). Sensitivity and attachment: A meta-analysis on parental antecedents of infant attachment. *Child Development, 68,* 571–591.

Deynoot-Schaub, M., & Riksen-Walraven, J. (2006). Peer contacts of 15-month-olds in childcare: Links with child temperament, parent-child interaction and quality of childcare. *Social Development, 15*(4), 709–729. doi:10.1111/j.1467-9507.2006.00366.x

Diamond, K. E. (2001). Relationships among young children's ideas, emotional understanding, and social contact with classmates with disabilities. *Topics in Early Childhood Special Education, 21,* 104–113.

Dicker, S., Gordon, E., & Knitzer, J. (2001). *Improving the odds for the healthy development of young children in foster care.* New York: National Center for Children in Poverty.

Diener, P. (1992). Family day care and children with disabilities. In D. Peters & A. Pence (Eds.), *Family day care: Current research for informed public policy* (pp. 129–146). New York: Teachers College Press.

Dietrich, S. L. (2005). A look at friendships between preschool children with and without disabilities in two inclusive classrooms. *Journal of Early Childhood Research, 3*(2), 193–215.

Dodge, D. T., Rudick, S., & Berke, K. (2011). *The Creative Curriculum for infants, toddlers, and twos,* Vol. 1: *The foundation.* Washington, DC: Teaching Strategies.

Donahoo, S. (2003, Spring). Single parenting and children's academic achievement. *NPIN Parent News.*

Dunfield, K., Kuhlmeier, V. A., O'Connell, L., & Kelley, E. (2011). Examining the diversity of prosocial behavior: Helping, sharing, and comforting in infancy. *Infancy, 16*(3), 227–247. doi:10.1111/j.1532-7078.2010.00041.x

Dunham, P., & Dunham, F. (1996). The semantically reciprocating robot: Adult influences on children's early conversational skills. *Social Development, 5,* 261–274.

EHSRE (Early Head Start Research and Evaluation Project). (1996–Current). Retrieved from www.acf.hhs.gov/programs/opre/ehs/ehs_resrch/index.html

Eaton, W. O. (2009). Motor activity level. Retrieved from home.cc.umanitoba.ca/~eaton/child-development-motor-activity-level.htm

Eckerman, C. O., & Didow, S. M. (2001). *Peer and infant social communicative development.* London: Blackwell.

Eckerman, C. O., Whatley, J. L., & Kutz, S. L. (1975). Growth of social play with peers during the second year of life. *Developmental Psychology, 11*(1), 42–49.

Edin, K. (2000). What do low-income single mothers say about marriage? *Social Problems, 47,* 112–133.

Edwards, C., Gandini, L., & Forman, G. (Eds.). (1998). *The hundred languages of children: The Reggio Emilia approach—Advanced reflections.* Greenwich, CT: Ablex.

Edwards, C., & Raikes, H. (2002). Extending the dance: Relationship-based approaches to infant/toddler care and education. *Young Children, 57*(4), 10–17.

Egeland, B., Weinfield, N., Bosquet, M., & Cheng, V. K. (2000). Remembering, repeating, and working through: Lessons from attachment-based interventions. In J. D. Osofsky & H. E. Fitzgerald, *WAIMH handbook of infant mental health.* Vol. 4,

Infant mental health in groups at high risk (pp. 35–90). New York: Wiley.

Eggbeer, L., Mann, T., & Gilkerson, L. (2003). Preparing infant-family practitioners: A work in progress. *Zero to Three, 24*(1), 35–40.

Eggbeer, L., Mann, T. & Seibel, N. (2007). Reflective supervision: Past, present, and future. *ZERO TO THREE, 28*(2).

EHSREP (Early Head Start Research and Evaluation Project). (2006). *Research to practice: Depression in the lives of Early Head Start families*. Retrieved from www.acf.hhs.gov/programs/opre/resource/depression-in-the-lives-of-early-head-start-families-research-to-practice

Eiden, R. D., Schuetze, P., Colder, C. R., & Veira, Y. (2011). Maternal cocaine use and mother-toddler aggression. *Neurotoxicology Teratology, 33*(3), 360–369.

Eiden, R. D., Schuetze, P., & Coles, C. D. (2011). Maternal cocaine use and mother-infant interactions: Direct and moderated associations. *Neurotoxicology Teratology, 33*(1), 120–128.

Eimas, P. D., & Quinn, P. C. (1994). Studies on the formation of perceptually based basic-level catagories in young infants. *Child Development, 65*, 903–917.

Eisenberg, N., Cumberland, A., & Spinrad, T. L. (1998). Parental socialization of emotion. *Psychological Inquiry, 9*(4), 241–273.

Ekas, N. V., Braungart-Rieker, J. M., Lickenbrock, D. M., Zentall, S. R., & Maxwell, S. M. (2011). Toddler emotion regulation with mothers and fathers: Temporal associations between negative affect and behavioral strategies. *Infancy, 16*(3), 266–294. doi:10.1111/j.1532-7078.2010.00042.x

Ellis, S., & Siegler, R. S. (1997). Planning as a strategy choice, or why don't children plan when they should? In S. L. Friedman & E. K. Scholnick (Eds.), *The developmental psychology of planning: Why, how, and when do we plan?* (pp. 183–208). Mahwah, NJ: Erlbaum.

Emde, R. N. (1988). The effect of relationships on relationships: A developmental approach to clinical intervention. In R. A. Hinde & J. Stevenson-Hinde (Eds.), *Relationships within families* (pp. 334–364). Oxford, UK: Clarendon.

Emde, R. N. (1994). Individuality, context, and the search for meaning. *Child Development, 65*, 719–737.

Emde, R. N. (1998). Early emotional development: New modes of thinking for research and intervention. *Pediatrics, 102*, 1236–1243.

Emde, R. N. (2001). Preface. In L. Gandini & C. Edwards (Eds.), *Bambini: The Italian approach to infant/toddler care* (pp. vii–xiv). New York: Teachers College Press.

Emde, R. N., Biringen, Z., Clyman, R. B., & Oppenheim, D. (1991). The moral self of infancy: Affective core and procedural knowledge. *Developmental Review, 11*, 251–270.

Emde, R. N., & Robinson, J. L. (2000). Guiding principles for a theory of early intervention: A developmental-psychoanalytic perspective. In J. P. Shonkoff & S. J. Meisels (Eds.), *Handbook of early intervention* (pp. 160–178). New York: Cambridge University Press.

Engel de Abreu, P., Cruz-Santos, A., Tourinho, C. J., Martin, R., & Bialystok, E. (2012). Bilingualism enriches the poor: Enhanced cognitive control in low-income minority children. *Psychological Science, 23*(11), 1364–1371.

Erikson, E. (1950). *Childhood and society.* New York: Norton.

Erikson, E. (1963). *Childhood and society* (2nd ed.). New York: Norton.

Erickson, M. F., & Kurz-Riemer, K. (1999). *Infants, toddlers and families: A framework for support and intervention.* New York: Guilford Press.

Eriksson, M., Marschik, P. B., Tulviste, T., Almgren, M., Pérez Pereira, M., Wehberg, S., ... Gallego, C. (2012). Differences between girls and boys in emerging language skills: Evidence from 10 language communities. *British Journal Of Developmental Psychology, 30*(2), 326–343.

Eshel, N., Daelman, B., de Mello, M., & Martines, J. (2006). Responsive parenting: Interventions and outcomes. *Bulletin of the World Health Organization, 84*(12), 991–998.

Esteve-Gibert, N., & Prieto P. (2012). Prosody signals the emergence of intentional communication in the first year of life: Evidence from Catalan-babbling infants. *Journal of Child Language,* 1–26. doi:10.1017/S0305000912000359.

Fabes, R. A., Eisenberg, N., Jones, S., Smith, M., Guthrie, I., Poulin, R.,...Friedman, J. (1999). Regulation, emotionality, and preschoolers' socially competent peer interactions. *Child Development, 70*(2), 432–442.

Fabes, R. A., Hanish, L. D., & Martin, C. L. (2003). Children at play: The role of peers in understanding the effects of child care. *Child Development, 74*(4), 1039–1044.

Fabes, R. A., Martin, C. L., & Hanish, L. D. (2004). The next 50 years: Considering gender as a context for understanding young children's peer relationships. *Merrill-Palmer Quarterly, 50*(3), 260–274.

Fattal-Valevski, A., Leitner, Y., Kutai, M., Tal-Posener, E., Tomer, A., & Lieberman, D. (1999). Neurodevelopmental outcome in children with intrauterine growth retarda-tion: A 3-year follow-up. *Journal of Child Neurology, 14*, 724–727.

Feigenson, L., Carey, S., & Spelke, E. (2002). Infants' discrimination of number vs. continuous extent. *Cognitive Psychology, 44*, 33–66.

Feldman, R., Greenbaum, C. W., & Yirmiya, N. (1999). Mother-infant affect synchrony as an antecedent of the emergence of self-control. *Developmental Psychology, 35*(1), 223–231.

Feldman, R., Eidelman, A., Sirota, L., & Weller, A. (2002). Comparison of skin-to-skin (kangaroo) and traditional care. *Pediatrics, 110*(1), 16–27.

Fenichel, E. (Ed.). (1992). *Learning through supervision and mentorship: A sourcebook.* Arlington, VA: ZERO TO THREE.

Fenichel, E. (2002). Relationships at risk: The policy environment as a context for infant development. *Infants and Young Children, 15*(2), 49–56.

Fernald, A. (1985). Four-month-old infants prefer to listen to motherese. *Infant Behaviour and Development, 8,* 181–195.

Fetal development. (2004, May 8). Retrieved from the *MedlinePlus Medical Encyclopedia,* an online service of the National Library of Medicine and the National Institutes of Health, www.nlm.nih.gov/medlineplus/ency/article/002398.htm

Field, T. (2010). Touch for socioemotional and physical well-being: A review. *Developmental Review, 30*(4) 367–383.

Field, T. (1998). Maternal depression effects on infants and early interventions. *Preventive Medicine, 27,* 200–203.

Field, T., & Brazelton, T. B. (1990). *Advances in touch.* Skillman, NJ: Johnson & Johnson.

Fitchen, J. M. (1995). The single-parent family, child poverty, and welfare reform. *Human Organization, 54,* 355–362.

Fitzsimons, G. M., & Finkel, E. J. (2010). The effects of self-regulation on social relationships. In D. Vohs & R. F. Baumeister (Eds.), *Handbook of self-regulation: Research, theory, and applications* (2nd ed., pp. 407–421). New York: The Guilford Press..

Flagler, B. (2010). Quality child care vital. *Atlanta Constitution.*

Flavell, J. H. (1977). *Cognitive development.* Upper Saddle River, NJ: Prentice Hall.

Flavell, J. H. (1996). Piaget's legacy. *Psychological Science, 7,* 200–203.

Forman, D. R., O'Hara, M. W., Larsen, K., Coy, K. C., Gorman, L. L., & Stuart, S. (2003). Infant emotionality: Observational methods and the validity of maternal reports. *Infancy, 4*(4), 541–565.

Fox, N. A., Rubin, K. H., Calkins, S., Marshall, T., Coplan, R., Porges, W., ... Stewart, S. (1995). Frontal activation asymmetry and social competence at four years of age. *Child Development, 66,* 1770–1784.

Fraiberg, S. (1996). *The magic years: Understanding and handling the problems of childhood* (Reissue ed.). New York: Fireside.

Frank, D. A., Jacobs, R. R., Beeghly, M., Augustyn, M., Bellinger, D., Cabral, H., et al. (2002). Level of prenatal cocaine exposure and scores on the Bayley Scales of Infant Development: Modifying effects of caregiver, early intervention, and birth weight. *Pediatrics, 110*(6), 1143–1152.

Frankel, L. A., Hughes, S. O., O'Connor, T. M., Power, T. G., Fisher, J. O., & Hazen, N. L. (2012). Parental influences on children's self-regulation of energy intake: Insights from developmental literature on emotion regulation. *Journal of Obesity,* 327259. doi:10.1155/2012/327259. Epub March 28, 2012. Retrieved from www.hindawi.com/journals/jobes/2012/327259/

Friedman, D. L. (2004). When teachers participate, reflect, and choose change. *Young Children, 59*(6), 64–70.

Gable, S., & Cole, K. (2000). Parents' child care arrangements and their ecological correlates. *Early Education and Development, 11*(5), 549–572.

Gaensbauer, T. (2004). Telling their stories: Representation and reenactment of traumatic experiences occurring in the first year of life. *Zero to Three, 24*(5), 25–31.

Galinsky, E., Howes, C., & Kontos, S. (1995). *The family child care training study: Highlights of findings.* New York: Families and Work Institute.

Galluzzo, D., Matheson, C., Moore, J., & Howes, C. (1990). Social orientation to adults and peers in infant day care. In N. A. Fox & F. Fien (Eds.), *Infant day care: The current debate* (pp. 183–192). New York: Ablex.

Gandini, L., & Edwards, C. (Eds.). (2001). *Bambini: The Italian approach to infant/toddler care.* New York: Teachers College Press.

Gandini, L., & Goldhaber, J. (2001). Two reflections about documentation. In L. Gandini & C. Edwards (Eds.), *Bambini: The Italian approach to infant/toddler care* (pp. 124–145). New York: Teachers College Press.

Garbarino, J., & Ganzel, B. (2000). The human ecology of early risk. In J. P. Shonkoff & S. J. Meisels (Eds.), *Handbook of early childhood intervention* (2nd ed., pp. 76–93). New York: Cambridge University Press.

Garcia, E. (1992). Effective instruction for language minority students: The teacher. *Journal of Education, 173*(2), 130–141.

Garcia-Sierra, A., Rivera-Gaxiola, M., Percaccio, C. R., Conboy, B. T., Romo, H., Klarman, L., ... Kuhl, P. K. (2011). Bilingual language learning: An ERP study relating early brain responses to speech, language input, and later word production. *Journal of Phonetics, 39*(4), 546–557. 2011; doi:10.1016/j.wocn.2011.07.002

Gartstein, M. A., Slobodskaya, H. R., Zylicz, P. O., Gosztyla, D., & Nakagawa, A. (2010). A cross-cultural evaluation of temperament: Japan, USA, Poland and Russia. *International Journal of Psychology and Psychological Therapy, 10*(1), 55–75.

Geist, E. (2003). Infants and toddlers exploring mathematics. *Young Children, 58*(1), 10–12.

Genesee, F., Nicoladis, E., & Paradis, J. (1996). Language differentiation in early bilingual development. *Journal of Developmental and Behavioral Pediatrics, 22,* 611–631.

George, S., Solomon, J., & McIntosh, J. (2011). Divorce in the nursery: On infants and overnight care. *Family Court Review, 49.*

George, C., & Solomon, J. (2003). Babies' attachment to parents affected by overnights. Retrieved from mentalhealth.about.com/cs/familyresources/a/attach403.htm

Gergely, G., Bekkering, H., & Király, I. (2002). Rational imitation in preverbal infants. *Nature, 415,* 755

Gesell, A. (1946). The ontogenesis of infant behavior. In L. Carmichael (Ed.), *Manual of child psychology* (pp. 295–331). New York: Wiley.

Gibson, J.J. (1977). The theory of affordances. In R. Shaw & J. Bransford (Eds.) *Perceiving, acting, and knowing: Toward an ecological psychology* (pp. 67–82). New York: John Wiley and Sons.

Gibson, E. J., & Pick, A. D. (2003). *An ecological approach to perceptual learning and development.* London: Oxford University Press.

Girolametto, L. (2000). Directiveness in teachers' language input to toddlers and preschoolers in daycare. *Journal of Speech, Languages, and Hearing Research, 43*(5), 1101.

Gloeckler, L., & Cassell, J. (2012). Teacher practices with toddlers during social problem solving opportunities. *Early Childhood Education Journal, 40*(4), 251–257. doi:10.1007/s10643-011-0495-4

Goffman, E. (1976). Replies and responses. *Language and Society, 5*(3), 257–313.

Golden, O., Hawkins, A., & Beardslee, W. (2011). Home visiting and maternal depression: Seizing the opportunities to help mothers and young children. *The Urban Institute.* Retrieved from www.urban.org/expert.cfm?ID=WilliamBeardslee

Goldman, B. D., & Buysse, V. (2007). Friendships in very young children. In O. Saracho & B. Spodek (Eds.), *Contemporary perspectives on socialization and social development in Early Childhood Education* (pp. 165–192). Charlotte, NC: Information Age Publishing.

Golub, M. S., Keen, C. L., Gershwin, M. E., & Hendrickx, A. G. (1995). Developmental zinc deficiency and behavior. *Journal of Nutrition, 125,* 2263S–2271S.

Goncu, A., & Gaskins, S. (Eds.). (2007). *Play and development: Evolutionary, sociocultural, and functional perspectives.* Mahwah, NJ: Erlbaum.

Gonzalez-Mena, J. (2001). *Multicultural issues in child care* (3rd ed.). Mountain View, CA: Mayfield Publishing Co.

Gonzalez-Mena, J. (2006). *50 early childhood strategies for working and communicating with diverse families.* Upper Saddle River, NJ: Merrill/Prentice Hall.

Gonzalez-Mena, J. (2008). *Diversity in early care and education: Honoring differences* (5th ed.). Washington, DC: NAEYC.

Gonzalez-Mena, J., & Eyer, D. W. (2001). *Infants, toddlers, and caregivers* (5th ed.). Mountain View, CA: Mayfield.

Gonzalez-Mena, J., & Eyer, D. W. (2009). *Infants, toddlers, and caregivers: A curriculum of respectful, responsive care and education* (8th ed.). Boston: McGraw-Hill College.

Goodnow, J. J., Cashmore, J., Cotton, S., & Knight, R. (1984). Mothers' developmental timetables in two cultural groups. *International Journal of Psychology, 19,* 193–205.

Goodwyn, S., Acredolo, L., & Brown, C. (2000). Impact of symbolic gesturing on early language development. *Journal of Nonverbal Behavior, 24*(2), 81–103.

Gopnik, A., Meltzoff, A. N., & Kuhl, P. K. (1999). *The scientist in the crib: Minds, brains, and how children learn.* New York: Morrow.

Gottlieb, A. (2000). Luring your child into this life: A Beng path for infant care. In J. DeLoache & A. Gottlieb (Eds.), *A world of babies: Imagined child care guides for seven societies* (pp. 55–90). Cambridge, UK: Cambridge University Press.

Gottlieb, G. (1992). *Individual development and evolution: The genesis of novel behavior.* New York: Oxford University Press.

Gottman, J. M., Katz, L. F., & Hooven, C. (1997). *Meta-emotion: How families communicate emotionally.* Mahwah, NJ: Erlbaum.

Gowen, J. W. (1995). The early development of symbolic play. *Young Children, 50*(3), 75–84.

Grabmeier, J. (1999). *Infants use sign language to communicate at Ohio State school.* Retrieved from researchnews.osu.edu/archive/signlang.htm

Greenman, J. (1988). *Caring spaces, learning places: Children's environments that work.* Redmond, WA: Exchange.

Greenman, J., & Stonehouse, A. (1996). *Prime times: A handbook for excellence in infant and toddler programs.* St. Paul, MN: Redleaf.

Greenman, J., Stonehouse, A., & Schweikert, G. (2008). *Prime times: A handbook for excellence in infant and toddler programs* (2nd ed.). Minneapolis, MN: Redleaf Press.

Greenspan, S. I. (1997). *The growth of the mind and the endangered origins of intelligence.* Reading, MA: Perseus Books.

Greenspan, S. I., & Greenspan, N. T. (1994). *First feelings: Milestones in the emotional development of your baby and child.* New York: Penguin. (Original work published 1985)

Griffin, A. (1998). Infant/toddler sleep in the child care context: Patterns, problems, and relationships. *Zero to Three, 19*(2) 24–29.

Gross, S. (1987). The power of purpose. *Child Care Information Exchange, 56.*

Gunnar, M., & Cheatham, C. L. (2003). Brain and behavior interface: Stress and the developing brain. *Infant Mental Health Journal, 24*(3), 195–211.

Gunnar, M. R., & Quevedo, K. (2007). The neurobiology of stress and development. *Annual Review of Psychology, 58*(1), 145.

Guralnik, M. J. (2000). The early intervention system and out-of-home child care. In D. Cryer & T. Harms (Eds.), *Infants and toddlers in out-of-home care* (pp. 207–234). Baltimore: Brookes.

Hackshaw, A., Rodeck, C., & Boniface, S. (2011). Maternal smoking in pregnancy and birth defects: A systematic review based on 173,687 malformed cases and 11.7 million controls. Oxford Journals, 17(5), 589–604.

Haith, M. M. (1980). *Rules that babies look by: The organization of newborn visual activity.* Hillsdale, NJ: Erlbaurn.

Hanna, E., & Meltzoff, A. N. (1993). Peer imitation by toddlers in a laboratory, home, and day-care contexts: Implications for social learning and memory. *Developmental Psychology, 4,* 701–710.

Harel, J., & Scher, A. (2003). Insufficient responsiveness in ambivalent mother-infant relationships: Contextual and affective aspects. *Infant Behavior and Development, 26*(3), 371–383.

Harmes, T., Cryer, D., & Clifford, R. M. (2006). *Infant/toddler environment rating scale.* New York: Teachers College Press.

Hart, B., & Risley, T. R. (1992). American parenting of language-learning children: Persisting differences in family-child interactions observed in natural home environments. *Developmental Psychology, 28,* 1096–1105.

Hart, B., & Risley, T. R. (1995). *Meaningful differences in the everyday experience of young American children.* Baltimore: Brookes.

Hart, B., & Risley, T. R. (1999). *The social world of children learning to talk.* Baltimore: Brookes.

Hast, F., & Hollyfield, A. (1999). *Infant and toddler experiences.* St. Paul, MN: Redleaf Press.

Hastings, P. D., Utendale, W. T., & Sullivan, C. (2007). The socialization of prosocial development. In J. E. Grusec & P. D. Hastings (Eds.), *Handbook of socialization: Theory and research* (pp. 638–664). New York: The Guilford Press.

Hawley, P., & Little, T. (1999). On winning some and losing some: A social relations approach to social dominance in toddlers. *Merrill-Palmer Quarterly, 45*(2), 185–214.

Hay, D. F., Payne, A., & Chadwick, A. (2004). Peer relations in childhood. *Journal of Child Psychology and Psychiatry, 45,* 84–108.

Head Start Early Childhood Learning and Knowledge Center. (2000). *National Head Start child development institute training materials (Multimedia kit).* Available from eclkc.ohs.acf.hhs.gov/hslc/hs/resources/ECLKC_Bookstore/Pub1100.htm

Head Start. (2013). FY 2013 Office of Head Start monitoring protocol. Retrieved from: eclkc.ohs.acf.hhs.gov/hslc/mr/monitoring

Helburn, S. W. (Ed.). (1995). *Cost, quality, and child outcomes in child care centers* [Technical report]. Denver: Department of Economics, Center for Research in Economic and Social Policy, University of Colorado–Denver.

Heller, S., & Gilkerson, L. (2009). *A practical guide to reflective supervision.* Washington DC: ZERO TO THREE.

Henderson, H. A., Marshall, P., Fox, N. A., & Rubin, K. H. (2004). Converging psychophysiological and behavioral evidence for subtypes of social withdrawal in preschoolers. *Child Development, 75,* 251–263.

HGP (Human Genome Project). (2008). Human Genome Project information. Retrieved from www.ornl.gov/sci/techresources/Human_Genome/home.shtml

HGP (Human Genome Project). (2011) Frequently asked questions about genetic disorders: What are genetic disorders. Retrieved from www.genome.gov/19016930

High/Scope. (2008). Assessment. Retrieved from www.highscope.org/Content.asp?ContentId=372

HighScope. (2012). Infants and toddlers. Retrieved from www.highscope.org/Content.asp?ContentId=62

Hinde, R. (1988). Introduction. In R. Hinde & J. Stevenson-Hinde (Eds.), *Relationships within families: Mutual influences* (pp. 1–4). Oxford, UK: Clarendon.

Hinde, R. (1992a). Developmental psychology in the context of older behavioral sciences. *Developmental Psychology, 28,* 1018–1029.

Hinde, R. (1992b). Ethological and relationship approaches. In R. Vasta (Ed.), *Six theories of child development: Revised formulations and current issues* (pp. 251–285). London: JKP Press.

Hinde, R., & Stevenson-Hinde, J. (1987). Interpersonal relationships and child development. *Developmental Review, 7,* 1–21.

Hines, M. (2011). Gender development and the human brain. *Annual Review of Neuroscience, 34,* 69–88. doi:10.1146/annurev-neuro-061010-113654

Hirsch, E. S. (1996). *The block book* (3rd ed.). Washington, DC: NAEYC.

Hirsh-Pasek, K., Golinkoff, R. M., Berk, L. E., & Singer, D. G. (2009). *A mandate for playful learning in preschool: Presenting the evidence.* New York: Oxford University Press.

Hodgkinson, H. (2003). Leaving too many children behind: A demographer's view on the neglect of America's youngest children. Retrieved from www.iel.org/pubs/manychildren.pdf

Hoff, E. (2006). How social contexts support and shape language development. *Developmental Review, 26,* 55–88.

Hofferth, S., & Goldscheider, F. (2010). Family structure and the transition to early parenthood. *Demography, 47,* 415–437.

Holdgrafer, G., & Dunst, C. J. (1990). Use of low-structured observation for assessing communicative intents in young children. *First Language, 10*(3), 243–253.

Honig, A. (1986). Tuning in to toddlers: A communication challenge. *Early Child Development and Care, 25,* 207–219.

Honig, A. (1993). Mental health for babies: What do theory and research tell us? *Young Children, 48*(3), 69–76.

Honig, A. (1994). Helping toddlers with group entry skills. *Zero to Three, 14*(5), 15–19.

Honig, A. (1995). Singing with infants and toddlers. *Young Children, 50*(5), 72–78.

Honig, A. (2000). Raising happy achieving children in the new millennium. *Early Child Development and Care, 163,* 79–106.

Honig, A. (2001). How infants and toddlers move through space. *Scholastic Early Childhood Today, 15*(7), 26–27.

Honig, A. (2002a). Choosing childcare for young children. In M. Bornstein (Ed.), *Handbook of parenting* (Vol. 4, pp. 411–435). Hillsdale, NJ: Erlbaum.

Honig, A. (2002b). Playing it out: The aftermath of September 11th in early care and education. *Zero to Three, 22*(3), 52.

Honig, A. (2002c). *Secure relationships: Nurturing infant toddler attachment in early care settings.* Washington, DC: NAEYC.

Honig, A. (2003a). Beauty for babies. *Scholastic Early Childhood Today, 17*(7), 22–25.

Honig, A. (2003b). Helping babies feel secure. *Scholastic Early Childhood Today, 18*(1), 27–29.

Honig, A. (2007). Choosing great books for babies: Helping children develop a love of reading. *Early Childhood Today (3), 21*(4), 24–26.

Honig, A. (2013). Infants & toddlers: Building intimacy. *Early Childhood Today.* Retrieved from www.scholastic.com/teachers/article/infants-toddlers-building-intimacy

Honig, H. S., & Brophy, H. E. (1996). *Talking with your baby: Family as a first school.* Syracuse, NY: Syracuse University Press.

Howarth, A. M., Swain, N., & Treharne, G. (2011). Taking personal responsibility for well-being increases birth satisfaction of first-time mothers. *Journal of Health Psychology, 16*(8), 1221–1230.

Howes, C. (1980). Peer play scale as an index of complexity of peer interaction. *Developmental Psychology, 16,* 371–372.

Howes, C. (1988). Peer interaction in young children. *Monographs of the Society for Research in Child Development, 53*(1), (Serial No. 217).

Howes, C. (1996). The earliest friendships. In W. M. Bukowksi, A. F. Newcomb, & W. W. Hartup (Eds.), *The company they keep: Friendship in childhood and adolescence* (pp. 66–86). Boston: Cambridge University Press.

Howes, C. (2000). Social development, family, and attachment relationships. In D. Cryer & T. Harms (Eds.), *Infants and toddlers in out-of-home care* (pp. 87–113). Baltimore, MD: Brookes.

Howes, C. (2009). Culture and child development in early childhood programs: Practices for quality education and care (early childhood education). New York: Teachers College Press.

Howes, C., & Farver, J. (1987). Toddlers' responses to the distress of their peers. *Journal of Applied Developmental Psychology, 8,* 441–452.

Howes, C., & Hamilton, C. E. (1992). Children's relationships with caregivers: Mothers and childcare teachers. *Child Development, 63,* 859–866.

Howes, C., & Hamilton, C. E. (1993). The changing experience of childcare: Changes in teacher and in teacher-child relationships and children's social competence with peers. *Early Childhood Research Quarterly, 8,* 15–30.

Howes, C., Hamilton, C. E., & Matheson, C. (1994). Children's relationship with peers: Differential associations with aspects of the teacher-child relationship. *Child Development, 65,* 253–263.

Howes, C., Matheson, C., & Hamilton, C. E. (1992). Sequences in the development of competent play with peers: Social and social-pretend play. *Developmental Psychology, 28,* 961–974.

Howes, C., Phillips, D., & Whitebook, M. (1992). Thresholds of quality: Implications for the social development of children in center-based child care. *Child Development, 63,* 449–460.

Howes, C., & Phillipsen, L. (1998). Continuity in children's relations with peers. *Social Development, 7*(3), 340–349.

Howes, C., & Smith, E. (1995). Relations among child care quality, teacher behavior, children's play activities, emotional security, and cognitive activity in child care. *Early Childhood Research Quarterly, 10,* 381–404.

Howes, C., Unger, O., & Seidner, L. (1989). Social pretend play in toddlers: Parallels with social play and with solitary pretend. *Child Development, 60,* 77–84.

Huda, S. N., Grantham-McGregor, S. M., & Tomkins, A. (1999). Biochemical hypothyroidism secondary to iodine deficiency is associated with poor school achievement and cognition in Bangladeshi children. *Journal of Nutrition, 129,* 980–987.

Hussey-Gardner, B. (2003). *Parenting to make a difference.* Palo Alto, CA: Vort.

Huttenlocher, J., Haight, W., Bryk, A., Seltzer, M., & Lyons, T. (1991). Early vocabulary growth: Relation to language input and gender. *Developmental Psychology, 27*(2), 236–248.

Huttenlocher, P. R. (1984). Synapse elimination and plasticity in developing human cerebral cortex. *American Journal of Mental Deficiency, 88,* 488–496.

IRSF (International Rett Syndrome Research Foundation). (2009). Retrieved from http://www.rettsyndrome.org/

Ilari, B., & Johnson-Green, E. (2002). Musical resources for children. *Zero to Three, 23*(1), 49–52.

Im, J. H., Osborn, C. A., Sánchez, S. Y., & Thorp, E. K. (2007). *Cradling literacy: Building teachers' skills to nurture early language and literacy from birth to 5.* Washington, DC: ZERO TO THREE.

Irwin, J., Carter, A. S., & Briggs-Gowan, M. I. (2002). The social-emotional development of "late-talking" toddlers. *Journal of the American Academy of Child and Adolescent Psychiatry, 41*(11), 1324–1332.

Irvine, J. T. (1978). Wolof "magical thinking": Culture and conservation revisited. *Journal of Cross-Cultural Psychology, 9,* 300–310.

Isbell, R., & Isbell, C. (2003). *The complete learning spaces book for infants and toddlers.* Beltsville, MD: Gryphon House.

Izard, C. E., & Malatesta, C. Z. (1987). Perspectives on emotional development: Differential emotions theory of early emotional development. In J. D. Osofsky (Ed.), *Handbook of infant development* (pp. 494–554). New York: Wiley.

Jablon, J. R., Dombro, A., & Dichtelmiller, M. L. (1999). *The power of observation.* Washington, DC: Teaching Strategies.

Jacobson, J., & Jacobson, S. W. (2002). Effects of prenatal alcohol exposure on child development. *Alcohol Research and Health, 26*(4), 282–286.

Jacobvitz, D., & Hazen, H. (1999). Developmental pathways from infant disorganization to childhood peer relationships. In J. Solomon & C. George (Eds.), *Attachment disorganization* (pp. 127–159). New York: Guilford Press.

Jeffer, F., Bakermans-Kranenburg, M. J., & van IJzendoorn, M. H. (2005). The importance of parenting in the development of disorganized attachment: Evidence from a preventive intervention study in adoptive families. *Journal of Child Psychology and Psychiatry, 46*(3), 263–274.

Jordan, K. E., & Brannon, E. M. (2006). The multisensory representation of number in infancy. *Proceedings of the National Academy of Sciences, 103,* 3486–3489.

Jorde-Bloom, P. (1995). *Circle of influence: Implementing shared decision making and participative management (director's toolbox).* Far Hills, NJ: New Horizons Press.

Jorde-Bloom, P. (1995). Shared decision-making: The centerpiece of participatory management. *Young Children, 50* (4), 55–60.

Kagan, J. (1997). Temperament and the reactions to the unfamiliarity. *Child Development, 68,* 139–143.

Kantor, D. (2006). *Rett syndrome—Overview.* Retrieved from www.umn.edu/ency/article/001536.htm

Kaplan Early Learning Company Catalog. (2013). Retrieved from www.kaplanco.com

Kaplan, H., & Dove, H. (1987). Infant development among the Ache of eastern Paraguay. *Developmental Psychology, 23*(2), 190–198.

Kaplan, L. (1978). *Oneness and separateness.* New York: Simon & Schuster.

Karrass, J., Braungart-Rieker, J. M., Mullins, J., & Burke Lefever, J. (2002). Processes in language acquisition: The roles of gender, attention, and maternal encouragement of attention over time. *Journal of Child Language, 29* (3), 519–543.

Katz, L. G. (1995). *Talks with teachers of young children: A collection* (ERIC Document No. ED380232). Norwood, NJ: Ablex

Katz, J. (2004). Building peer relationships in talk: Toddlers' peer conversations in child care. *Discourse Studies, 6*(3), 329–347.

Katz, J., & Snow, C. (2000). Language development in early childhood: The role of social interaction. In D. H. Cryer (Ed.), *Infants and toddlers in out-of-home care* (pp. 49–86). Baltimore: Brookes.

Katz, L. G. (1987). The nature of professions: Where is early childhood education? In L. G. Katz (Ed.), *Current topics in early childhood education* (Vol. 7). Norwood, NJ: Ablex.

Kearney, P., & Griffin, T. (2001). Between joy and sorrow: Being a parent of a child with developmental disability. *Journal of Advanced Nursing, 34*(5), 582–593.

Keenan, M. (1997). Shifting gears for infants and toddlers. *Child Care Information Exchange, 113,* 92–98.

Keenan, M. (1998). Making the transition from preschool to infant/toddler teacher. *Young Children, 53*(2), 5–11.

Keller, H., Lamm, B., Abels, M., Yovsi, R. D., Borke, J., Jensen, H., ... Chaudhary, N. (2006). Cultural models, socialization goals, and parenting ethnotheories: A multi-cultural analysis. *Journal of Cross-Cultural Psychology, 37,* 155–172.

Keller, H., & Otto, H. (2009). The cultural socialization of emotion regulation during infancy. *Journal of Cross-Cultural Psychology, 40*(6), 996–1011. doi:10.1177/0022022109348576

Kelley, S. A., Brownell, C. A., & Campbell, S. B. (200_ . Mastery motivation and self-evaluative affect in toddlers: Longitudinal relations with maternal behavior. *Child Development, _*(4), 1061–1071.

Kesner, J. E., & McKenry, P. C. (2001). Single parenthood and social competence in children of color. *Families in Society: The Journal of Contemporary Human Services, 82,* 135–143.

KIDS COUNT census data online. (2006). 2000 Census data—income and poverty profile for United States. Retrieved from http://www.kidscount.org/

KidsHealth. (2008). Abusive head trauma (shaken baby syndrome). Retrieved from www.kidshealth.org/parent/medical/brain/shaken.html

KidsHealth. (2009). *A primer on preemies.* Retrieved from health.msn.com/kids-health/articlepage.aspx?cp-documentid=100151172

Kim, Y. M., Sugai, G., & Kim, G. (1999). Early intervention needs of children at risk due to prenatal drug exposure: A survey of early childhood educators. *Journal of Research in Childhood Education, 13*(2), 207–214.

Kinch, A. F., & Schweinhart, L. J. (2004). Achieving high-quality child care: How ten programs deliver excellence parents can afford. Available from www.naeyc.org/ece/

Klinkner, J. M., Riley, D., & Roach, M. A. (2005). Organizational climate as a tool for child care staff retention. *Young Children, 60*(6), 90–95.

Klinnert, M., Emde, R. N., Butterfield, P., & Campos, J. J. (1986). Social referencing: The infant's use of emotional signals from a friendly adult with mother present. *Developmental Psychology, 22*(4), 427–432.

Kolata, G. (2012). Bits of mystery DNA, far from "junk," play crucial role. *New York Times.* Retrieved from www.nytimes.com /2012/09/06/science/far-from-junk-dna-dark-matter-proves-crucial-to-health

Konner, M. (1977). Infancy among the Kalihari Desert San. In P. H. Liederman, S. R. Tulin, & A. Rosenfeld (Eds.), *Culture and infancy: Variations in the human experience* (pp. 287–327). New York: Academic Press.

Kontos, S. (1988). Family day care as an integrated early intervention setting. *Topics in Early Childhood Special Education, 8*(2), 1–4.

Kontos, S., Howes, C., Shinn, M., & Galinsky, E. (1995). *Quality in family child care and relative care.* New York: Teachers College Press.

Kopp, C. B. (2000). Self-regulation in children. In J. J. Smelser & P. B. Baltes (Eds.), *International encyclopedia of the social and behavioral sciences.* Oxford, UK: Elsevier.

Krøjgaard, P. (2005). Infants' search for hidden persons. *International Journal of Behavioral Development, 29*(1), 70–79.

Kubicek, L. F. (2003). Fresh perspectives on young children and family routines. *Zero to Three, 22*(4), 4–9.

Kuhl, P. K. (2000). A new view of language acquisition. *PNAS, 97*(22), 11850–11857.

Kuhl, P. K. (2007). Is speech learning "gated" by the social brain? *Developmental Science, 10*(1), 110–120.

Kuhl, P. K., Conboy, B. T., Coffee-Corina, S., Padden, D., Rivera-Gaxiola, M., & Nelson, T. (2008). Phonetic learning as a pathway to language: New data and native language magnet theory expanded (NLM-e). *Philosophical Transactions of the Royal Society B, 363*(1493), 979–1000.

Kuhl, P. K., Stevens, E., Hayashi, A., Deguchi, T., Kiritani, S., & Iverson, P. (2006). Infants show a facilitation effect for native language phonetic perception between 6 and 12 months. *Developmental Science, 9*(2), 13–21.

Kuhl, P. K., Tsao, F. M., & Liu, H. M. (2003). Foreign-language experience in infancy: Effects of short-term exposure and social interaction on phonetic learning. *Proceedings of the National Academy of Sciences, 100*, 9096–9101.

Kuhl, P. K., Williams, K. A., Lacerda, F., Stevens, K. N., & Lindblom, B. (1992). Linguistic experience alters phonetic perception in infants by 6 months of age. *Science, 255*, 606–608.

Kumin, L. (1998). Comprehensive speech and language treatment for infants, toddlers, and children with Down syndrome. Retrieved from Down Syndrome: Health Issues Web site: www.ds-health.com/speech.htm

Kutner, L. (1993). *Pregnancy and the first year.* New York: Morrow.

LaFrenierse, P. J., & Sroufe, L. A. (1985). Profiles of peer competence in the preschool: Interrelations between measures, influence of social ecology, and relations to attachment history. *Developmental Psychology, 21*, 56–69.

Laible, D. J., & Thompson, R. A. (2002). Mother-child conflict in the toddler years: Lessons in emotion, morality, and relationships. *Child Development, 73*(4), 1187–1203.

Lally, J. R. (1995). The impact of child care policies and practices on infant/toddler identity formation. *Young Children, 51*(1), 58–67.

Lally, J. R. (2001) The art and science of child care. *Program for Infant Toddler Care.* Retrieved from www.pitc.org.

Lally, J. R. (2003). Infant-toddler child care in the United States: Where has it been? Where is it now? Where is it going? *Zero to Three, 24*(1), 29–34.

Lally, J. R., Griffin, A., Fenichel, E., Segal, M., Szanton, E., & Weissbourd, B. (1995). *Caring for infants and toddlers in groups: Developmentally appropriate practice.* Washington, DC: ZERO TO THREE.

Lally, J. R., Torres, Y., & Phelps, P. (1994). Caring for infants and toddlers in groups: Necessary considerations for emotional, social, and cognitive development. *Zero to Three, 14*(5), 1–8.

Lamb, M. E. (2004). *The role of the father in child development,* (4th ed.). New York: Wiley.

Lamb, M. (2010). *The role of the father in child development.* New York: Wiley.

Lamb, M. E., Bornstein, M. H., & Teti, D. (2002). *Development in infancy* (4th ed.). Hillsdale, NJ: Erlbaum.

Lawrence, R. A. (1997). A review of the medical benefits and contraindications to breastfeeding in the United States. *Maternal and child health: Technical information bulletin.* Washington, DC: National Center for Maternal and Child Health.

Lazarov, M., & Evans, A. (2000). Breastfeeding: Encouraging the best for low-income women. *Zero to Three, 21*(1), 15–23.

Lee, S. A., Davis, B., & Macneilage, P. (2010). Universal production patterns and ambient language influences in babbling: A cross-linguistic study of Korean- and English-learning infants. *Journal of Child Language, 37*(2), 293–318.

Legerstee, M., & Barillas, Y. (2003). Sharing attention and pointing to objects at 12 months: Is the intentional stance implied? *Cognitive Development, 18*(1), 91–110.

Lerner, C., & Dombro, A. (2000). *Learning and growing together: Understanding and supporting your child's development.* Washington, DC: ZERO TO THREE.

Lewis, M. L. (1993). Self-conscious emotions: Embarrassment, pride, shame, and guilt. In M. Lewis & J. M. Haviland-Jones (Eds.), *Handbook of emotions* (pp. 563–573). New York: Guilford Press.

Lewis, R. (2007). *Postural drainage.* Retrieved from Medline Plus Web site: www.nim.nih.gov/medlineplus/ency/imagepages/18084.htm

Lewkowicz, D. J., & Lickliter, R. (Eds.). (1994). *The development of intersensory perception: Comparative perspectives.* Hillsdale, NJ: Erlbaum.

Lick, D. J., Tornello, S. L., Riskind, R. G., Schmidt, K. M., & Patterson, C. J. (2012). Social climate for sexual minorities predicts well-being among heterosexual offspring of lesbian and gay parents. *Sexuality Research and Social Policy,* 1–14.

Lieberman, A. (1993). *The emotional life of a toddler.* New York: Free Press.

Liu, J., Leung, P., Sun, R., Li, H.-T., & Liu, J.-M. (2012). Cross-cultural application of Achenbach System of Empirically Based Assessment: Instrument translation in Chinese, challenges, and future directions. *World Journal of Pediatrics, 8*(1), 5–10. doi:10.1007/s12519-011-0329-x

Liu, C. H., & Tronick, E. (2011), Neurobehavioural development in infancy. In D. Skuse, H. Bruce, L. Dowdney, & D. Mrazek (Eds.), *Child psychology and psychiatry: Frameworks for practic,* (2nd ed., pp. 18–22). Chichester, UK: John Wiley & Sons.

Loman, S., Cellini, N., Johnson, M., & Hallett, E. (2009), Magical moments in movement: Antioch University New England dance/movement therapy and counseling students in the real world. *American Journal of Dance Therapy, 31*, 159–169.

Love, J. M., Kisker, E. E., Ross, C., Raikes, H., Constantine, J., Boller, K., …Vogel, C. (2005). The effectiveness of Early Head Start for 3-year-old children and their parents: Lessons for policy and programs. *Developmental Psychology, 41*(6), 885–901.

Lowenthal, B. (1995). Strategies that promote social skills in toddlers with special needs in the inclusive setting. *Infant-Toddler Intervention: The Trandisciplinary Journal, 5*(1), 15–22.

Lozoff, B., Klein, N. K., Nelson, E. C., McClish, D. K., Manuel, M., & Chacon, M. E. (1998). Behavior of infants with iron-deficiency anemia. *Child Development, 69,* 24–36.

Lu, M. (1998). Language learning in social and cultural contexts. *ERIC Digest* (ED423531). Bloomington, IN: ERIC Clearinghouse on Reading, English, and Communication.

Lu, M. (2000). Language development in the early years. *ERIC Digest* (ED446336). Bloomington, IN: ERIC Clearinghouse on Reading, English, and Communication.

Lussier, B. J. (1994). Effect of three adult interaction styles on infant engagement. *Journal of Early Intervention, 18*(1), 12–24.

Luthar, S. S. (2006). Resilience in development: A synthesis of research across five decades. In D. Cicchetti & D. J. Cohen (Eds.), *Developmental psychopathology,* Vol. 3: *Risk, disorder, and adaptation* (2nd ed., pp. 739–795). New York: Wiley.

Lutton, A. (Ed.). (2012). *Advancing the early childhood profession: NAEYC standards and guidelines for professional development.* Washington, DC: NAEYC.

Lynch, E. W., & Hanson, M. J. (1998). Steps in the right direction. In E. W. Lynch & M. J. Hanson (Eds.), *Developing cross-cultural competence: A guide for working with parents and families* (pp. 491–512). Baltimore: Brookes.

Maccoby, E. E. (1998). *The two sexes: Growing up apart, coming together.* Cambridge, MA: Belknap.

Maccoby, E. E., & Martin, J. A. (1983). Socialization in the context of the family: Parent-child interaction. In P. H. Mussen & E. M. Hetherington (Eds.), *Handbook of child psychology* (Vol. 4, pp. 1–102). New York: Wiley.

Magill-Evans, J., Harrison, M. J., Benzies, K., Gierl, M., & Kimak, C. (2007). Effects of parenting education on first-time fathers' skills in interactions with their infants. *Fathering, 5*(1), 42–57.

Mahler, M. S. (1975). *The psychological birth of the human infant.* New York: Basic Books.

Main, M. (2000). The organized categories of infant, child, and adult attachment: Flexible vs. inflexible attention under attachment-related stress. *Journal of the American Psychoanalytic Association, 48,* 1055–1096.

Main, M., & Cassidy, J. (1988). Categories of response with the parent at age 6: Predicted from infant attachment classifications and stable over a one-month period. *Developmental Psychology, 24,* 415–426.

Main, M., & Goldwyn, R. (1994). Adult attachment rating and classification systems. In M. Main (Ed.), *A typology of human attachment organization assessed in discourse, drawings, and interviews.* New York: Cambridge University Press.

Main, M., Kaplan, N., & Cassidy, J. (1985). Security in infancy, childhood, and adulthood: A move to the level of representation. In I. Bretherton & E. Waters (Eds.), *Growing points of attachment theory and research. Monographs of the Society for Research in Child Development, 50*(Serial No. 209), 66–104.

Malaguzzi, L., & Gandini, L. (1993). For an education based on relationships. *Young Children, 49*(1), 9–12.

Malina, R. M. (2004). Motor development during infancy and early childhood: Overview and suggested directions for research. *International Journal of Sport and Health Medicine, 2,* 50–66.

Mandler, J. M., & McDonough, L. (1996). Concept formation in infancy. *Cognitive Development, 8,* 291–318.

Mangione, P. L., Lally, R. J., & Signer, S. (1990). The ages of infancy: Caring for young, mobile, and older infants [Video magazine]. Sacramento, CA: CDE Press.

Marsden, D. B., Dombro, A. L., & Dichtelmiller, M. L. (2003). *The Ounce Scale user's guide.* New York: Pearson Early Learning.

Martinez, G., Daniels, K., & Chandra, A. (2012). Fertility of men and women aged 15–44 years in the United States: National survey of family growth, 2006–2010. *National Health Center Reports. Centers for Disease Control and Prevention.* Retrieved from www.cdc.gov/nchs/data/nhsr/nhsr051.pdf

Maslow, A. H. (1968). *Toward a psychology of being.* New York: Van Nostrand Reinhold.

Masten, A. S., & Motti-Stefanidi, F. (2008). Understanding and promoting resilience in children: Promotive and protective processes in schools. In T. Gutkin & C. Reynolds (Eds.), *The handbook of school psychology* (4th ed.). New York: Wiley.

Matthey, S., Barnett, B., Ungerer, J., & Waters, B. (2000). Paternal and maternal depressed mood during the transition to parenthood. *Journal of Affective Disorders, 60*(2), 75–85.

Maxted, A. E., Dickstein, S., Miller-Loncar, C., High, P., Spritz, B., Liu, J., & Lester, B. M. (2005). Infant colic and maternal depression. *Infant Mental Health Journal, 26*(1), 56–68.

Mayberry, R. I., Lock, E., & Kazmi, H. (2002). Linguistic ability and early language exposure. *Nature, 417*(6884), 38.

McCabe, J., Fairchild, E., Grauerholz, L., Pescosolido, B.A., & Tope, D. (2011). Gender in twentieth-century children's books: Patterns of disparity in titles and central characters. *Gender & Society, 25,* 197–226.

McCullough, A. L., Kirksey, A., Wachs, T. D., McGabe, G. P., Bassily, N. S., Bishry, Z., ... Jerome, N. W. (1990). Vitamin B-6 status of Egyptian mothers: Relation to infant behavior and maternal-infant interactions. *American Journal of Clinical Nutrition, 51*(6), 1067–1074.

McDevitt, T. M., & Ormrod, J. E. (2002). *Child development and education.* Upper Saddle River, NJ: Merrill/Prentice Hall.

McElwain, N. L., & Booth-LaForce, C. (2006). Maternal sensitivity to infant distress and non-distress as predictors of infant-mother attachment security. *Journal of Family Psychology, 20*(2), 247–255.

McElwain, N. L., Cox, M. J., Burchinal, M. R., & Macfie, J. (2003). Differentiating among insecure mother-infant attachment classifications: A focus on child-friend interaction and exploration during solitary play at 36 months. *Attachment & Human Development, 5*(2), 136–164.

McFarlane, J. (1975). Olfaction in the development of social preferences in the human neonate. In M. Hofer (Ed.), *Parent-infant interaction* (Ciba Foundation Symposium 33; pp. 103–113). Amsterdam: Elsevier.

McGaha, C.G., Cummings, R., Lippard, B., & Dallas, K. (2011). Relationship building: Infants, toddlers, and 2-year-olds. *Early Childhood Research and Practice, 13*(2). Retrieved from ecrp.uiuc.edu/v13n1/mcgaha.html

McLane, J. B., & McNamee, G. D. (1991). The beginnings of literacy. *Zero to Three, 12*(1), 1–8.

Mcquaid, N. E., Bibok, M. B., & Carpendale, J. I. M. (2009). Relationship between maternal contingent responsiveness and infant social expectations. *Infancy, 14*(3), 390–401.

Medicinenet.com (2012). Asthma in children. Retrieved from www.medicinenet.com/asthma_in_children/article.htm

Medline Plus. (2011) *Fetal development. US National Library of Medicine and the National Institute of Health*. Retrieved from: http://www.nlm.nih.gov/medlineplus/ency/article/002398.htm

MedlinePlus. (2012), TORCH screen. Retrieved fro: www.nlm.nih.gov/medlineplus/ency/article/003350.htm

Mehler, J., Jusczyk, P., Lambertz, G., Halsted, N., Bertoncini, J., & Ameil-Tison, C. (1988). A precurser of language acquisition in young infants. *Cognition, 29,* 143–178.

Meins, E. (1997). Security of attachment and maternal tutoring strategies: Interaction within the zone of proximal development. *British Journal of Developmental Psychology, 15,* 129–144.

Meins, E., Fernyhough, C., de Rosnay, M., Arnott, B., Leekam, S. R. & Turner, M. (2012). Mind-mindedness as a multidimensional construct: Appropriate and nonattuned mind-related comments independently predict infant–mother attachment in a socially diverse sample. *Infancy* 17(4): 393–415.

Meins, E., Fernyhough, C., Wainwright, R., Clark-Carter, D., Gupta, M. D., & Fradley, E. et al. (2003). Pathways to understanding mind: Construct validity and predictive validity of maternal mind-mindedness. *Child Development, 74,* 1194–1211.

Meisels, S. J., Dombro, A., Marsden, D. B., Weston, D. R., & Jewkes, A. M. (2003). *The Ounce Scale.* New York: Pearson Early Learning.

Meltzoff, A. N. (1995). Understanding the intentions of others: Reenactment of intended acts of others by 10-month-old children. *Developmental Psychology, 31,* 838–850.

Meltzoff, A. N., Kuhl, P. K., Movellan, J., & Sejnowski, T. J. (2009). Foundations for a new science of learning. *Science, 325,* 284–288. doi:10.1126/science.1175626

Meltzoff, A. N., & Moore, M. K. (1977). Imitation of facial and manual gestures by human neonates. *Science, 198,* 75–78.

Mennella, J. A., & Beauchamp, G. K. (2002). Flavor experiences during formula feeding are related to preferences during childhood. *Early Human Development, 68,* 71–82.

Mesman, J., Stoel, R., Bakermans-Kranenburg, M. J., van IJzendoorn, M. H., Juffer, F., Koot, H. M., & Alink, L. R. A. (2009). Predicting growth curves of early childhood externalizing problems: Differential susceptibility of children with difficult temperaments. *Journal of Abnormal Child Psychology, 37,* 625–636.

Meyers, A., & Chawla, N. (2000). Nutrition and the social, emotional, and cognitive development of infants and young children. *Zero to Three, 21*(1), 5–11.

Michigan State University (n.d.). American Sign Language browser. Retrieved from aslbrowser.commtechlab.msu.edu/

Milkie, M. A. (2011). Social and cultural resources for and constraints on new mothers' marriages. *Journal of Marriage and Family,73*(1),18–22.doi:10.1111/j.1741-3737.2010.00784.x

Miller, K. (1999). *Simple steps: Developmental activities for infants, toddlers, and two-year-olds.* Beltsville, MD: Gryphon House.

Milne, A. A. (1991). *Winnie-the-Pooh.* New York: Dutton. (Original work published 1926)

Minkler, M. (2002). *Grandparents and other relatives raising children: Characteristics, needs, best practices, & implications for the aging network.* Washington, DC: Administration on Aging, Department of Health and Human Services.

Miner, J. L., & Clarke-Stewart, K. A. (2008). Trajectories of externalizing behavior from age 2 to age 9: Relations with gender, temperament, ethnicity, parenting, and rater. *Developmental Psychology,44*(3), 771–786.

Miquelote, A. F., Santos, D. C. C., Caçola, P. M., Montebelo, M. I. de L., & Gabbard, C. (2012). Effect of the home environment on motor and cognitive behavior of infants. *Infant Behavior & Development, 35*(3), 329–334. doi:10.1016/j.infbeh.2012.02.002

Mischel, W. (1961). Father absence and the delay of gratification. *Journal of Abnormal and Social Psychology, 62,* 116–124.

MOD (March of Dimes). (2009a). *Cerebral palsy. Quick reference: fact sheets.* Retrieved from www.marchofdimes.com

MOD (March of Dimes). (2009b). *Genital herpes and pregnancy. Quick reference: fact sheets.* Retrieved from www.mofdimes.com

MOD (March of Dimes). (2009c). *Multiples: Twins, triplets, and beyond.* Retrieved from search.marchofdimes.com

MOD (March of Dimes). (2009d). *Preterm births rise 36 percent since early 1980s.* Retrieved from www.marchofdimes.com

MOD (March of Dimes). (2009e). *Sexually transmitted infections in pregnancy.* Retrieved from www.marchofdimes.com

Moher, M., Tuerk, A. S., & Feigenson, L. (2012). Seven-month-old infants chunk items in memory. *Journal of Experimental Child Psychology, 112*(4), 361–377. doi:10.1016/j.jecp.2012.03.007

Moller, L., & Serbin, L. (1996). Antecedents of toddler gender segregation: Cognitive consonance, gender-typed toy preferences, and behavioral compatibility. *Sex Roles: A Journal of Research, 34*(7–8), 445–461.

Moon, C., Cooper, R. P., & Fifer, W. P. (1993). Two-day-olds prefer their native language. *Infant Behavior and Development, 16*(4), 495–500.

Morasch, K. C., & Bell, M. A. (2012). Self-regulation of negative affect at 5 and 10 months. *Developmental psychobiology, 54*(2), 215–221. doi:10.1002/dev.20584

Morehouse, L. (2008). Supporting teachers: Resources for mentors. Retrieved from www.edutopia.org/mentor-teachers-resources.

Morgan, G. A., Harmon, R. J., & Maslin-Cole, C. A. (1999). Imitation of facial and manual gestures by human neonates. *Science, 198,* 75–78.

Morgan Stanley Children's Hospital of New York—Presbyterian. (n.d.). *Age Appropriate Vision Milestones.* Retrieved from childrensnyp.org/

Mother's day: More than candy and flowers, working parent's need paid time-off. (2002). Retrieved from http://www.childpolicyintl.org/issuebrief/issuebrief5.htm

Müller, E. (2007). *Collaborative partnerships between SEAs and Parent Training and Information Centers (PTIs).* Retrieved from http://nasdse.org/DesktopModules/DNNspot-Store/ProductFiles/21_c9ec21a1-3101-4d8f-bc7e-de63e88225df.pdf

Mulligan, S. (1997). Group activities: One child at a time. *Child Care Plus, 8*(1), 1.

Murphy, L. B. (1936). Sympathetic behavior in young children. *Journal of Experimental Education, 5,* 79–90.

Murphy, L. B. (1994). Hopping, jumping, leaping, skipping, and loping: Savoring the possibilities of locomotion. *Zero to Three, 15*(1), 27.

Murray, L., & Cooper, P. J. (1999). Effects of postnatal depression on infant development. *Archives of Disease in Childhood, 77,* 99–101.

NAEYC (National Association for the Education of Young Children). (2005). *Code of ethical conduct and statement of commitment.* Retrieved from www.naeyc.org/files/naeyc/file/positions/PSETH05.pdf

NAEYC (National Association for the Education of Young Children). (2006a). NAEYC accreditation. Assessment in the new NAEYC accreditation system. *Young Children, 61*(3), 60–62.

NAEYC (National Association for the Education of Young Children). (2006b). NAEYC early childhood program standards and accreditation criteria. Retrieved from www.naeyc.org/academy/primary/standardsintro

NAEYC (National Association for the Education of Young Children). (2009). Developmentally appropriate practice in early childhood programs serving children from birth through age 8. Retrieved from www.naeyc.org/files/naeyc/file/positions/PSDAP.pdf

NAEYC (National Association for the Education of Young Children). (2009). NAEYC standards for early childhood professional preparation. Washington, DC: NAEYC. Retrieved from www.naeyc.org/files/naeyc/files/2009%20Professional%20Prep%20stdsRevised%204_12.pdf

NAEYC (National Association for the Education of Young Children. (2011). 2010 NAEYC standards for initial and advanced early childhood professional preparation programs. Retrieved from www.naeyc.org/ecada/files/ecada/file/Standards/NAEYC%20Initial%20and%20Advanced%20Standards%203_2012.pdfNN

NAEYC (National Association for the Education of Young Children). (2012). Accreditation. Retrieved from www.naeyc.org/accreditation

NAFCC (National Association for Family Child Care). (2013). 2013 Accreditation updates. Retrieved from http://nafcc.org/

Nag, M. (1994). Beliefs and practices about food during pregnancy. *Economic and Political Weekly,* 2427–2438.

Namy, L. (2001). What's in a name when it isn't a word? 17-month-olds' mapping of nonverbal symbols to object categories. *Infancy, 2*(1), 73–86.

Namy, L., & Waxman, S. R. (1998). Words and gestures: Infants' interpretations of different forms of symbolic reference. *Child Development, 69*(2), 295–308.

National Early Childhood Technical Assistance Center. (NECTAC). (2012). Early intervention program for infants and toddlers with disabilities (Part C of IDEA). Retrieved from www.nectac.org/partc/partc.asp

National Fatherhood Initiative. (2012). The father factor: Data on the consequences of father absence. Retrieved from www.fatherhood.org/media/consequences-of-father-absence-statistics

National Heart, Lung, and Blood Institute (2012) *What is sickle cell anemia?* Retrieved from: www.nhlbi.nih.gov/health/health-topics/topics/sca/

National Scientific Council on the Developing Child (2004). *Young Children Develop in an Environment of Relationships: Working Paper No. 1.* Retrieved from www.developingchild.harvard.edu

National Scientific Council on the Developing Child. Center on the Developing Child. (2010a). *Early experiences can alter gene expression and affect long-term development: Working Paper No. 10.* Retrieved from http://www.developingchild.harvard.edu

National Scientific Council on the Developing Child. (2010b). *Persistent Fear and Anxiety Can Affect Young Children's Learning and Development: Working Paper No. 9.* Retrieved from www.developingchild.harvard.edu

National SIDS/Infant Death Resource Center. (2007). *Helping baby "Back to Sleep."* Retrieved from www.sidcenter.org/documents/sidrc/BackToSleep.pdf

NCCIC (National Child Care Information and Technical Assistance Center). (2009). *Child care technical assistance network.* Retrieved http:archive.acf.hhs.gov/programs/ccb/ta/cctan.htm

NCSBS (National Center on Shaken Baby Syndrome). (2009). *Physical consequences of shaking.* Retrieved from http://www.dontshake.org/

NCTM (National Council of Teachers of Mathematics). (2000). *Principles and standards for school mathematics.* Washington, DC: Author.

NDSS (National Down Syndrome Society). (2005). Available at the NDSS Web site, http://www.ndss.org

NECTAC (National Early Childhood Technical Assistance Center). (2012). *Annual appropriations and number of children.* Retrieved from http://ectacenter.org/partc/partcdata.asp

NECTAC (National Early Childhood Technical Assistance Center (2013). *Overview to the early intervention program for infants and toddlers with disabilities (Part C) under IDEA.* Retrieved from http://ectacenter.org/partc/Partc.asp - overview

Newman, R. S., & Hussain, I. (2006). Changes in preference for infant-directed speech in low and moderate noise by 4.5- to 13-month-olds. *Infancy, 10*(1), 61–76.

NFXF (National Fragile X Foundation). (2008). What is fragile X? Available at the NFXF Web site, www.fragilex.org

NICHD Early Child Care Research Network. (1996). Characteristics of infant child care: Factors contributing to positive caregiving. *Early Childhood Research Quarterly, 11,* 269–306.

NICHD Early Child Care Research Network. (1997). The effects of infant child care on infant–mother attachment security: Results of the NICHD study of early child care. *Child Development, 68,* 860–879.

NICHD Early Child Care Research Network. (1998). Relations between family predictors and child outcomes: Are they weaker for children in child care? *Developmental Psychology, 34,* 1119–1128.

NICHD Early Child Care Research Network. (2000a). Characteristics and quality of child care for toddlers and preschoolers. *Applied Developmental Science, 4*(3), 116–135.

NICHD Early Child Care Research Network. (2000b). The relation of child care to cognitive and language development. *Child Development, 71*(4), 960–980.

NICHD Early Child Care Research Network. (2001a). Child care and children's peer interaction at 24 and 36 months. *Child Development, 72*(5), 1478–1501.

NICHD Early Child Care Research Network. (2001b). Nonmaternal care and family factors in early development: An overview of the NICHD study of early child care. *Journal of Applied Developmental Psychology, 22,* 457–492.

NICHD Early Child Care Research Network. (2002a). Child care structure, process, outcome: Direct and indirect effects of child care quality on young children's development. *Psychological Science, 13,* 199–206.

NICHD Early Childhood Research Network. (2002b). The interaction of childcare and family in relation to child development at 24 and 36 months. *Applied Developmental Science, 6*(3), 144–157.

NICHD Early Child Care Research Network. (2003). Child care and mother–child interaction from 36 months through first grade. *Infant Behavior and Development, 26,* 345–370.

NICHD Early Child Care Research Network. (2004). Father's and mother's parenting behavior and beliefs as predictors of child social adjustment in the transition to school. *Journal of Family Psychology, 18*(4), 628–638.

Nicoladis, E., & Genesee, F. (1996). A longitudinal study of pragmatic differentiation in young bilingual children. *Language Learning, 46*(3), 439–464.

Nichols, S. R., Svetlova, M., & Brownell, C. A. (2009a). The role of social understanding and empathic disposition in young children's responsiveness to distress in parents and peers. *Cognition, Brain, Behavior, XIII*(4), 449–478.

Nichols, S., Svetlova, M., & Brownell, C. A. (2009b). Toddlers' understanding of peers' emotions. *Journal of Genetic Psychology, 171*(1), 35–53.

NIH (National Institutes of Health). (2000). *National Institutes of Health consensus development statement. Phenylketonuria: Screening and management.* Washington, DC: Author.

NTSADA (National Tay-Sachs & Allied Diseases Association, Inc.). (2009). What is Tay-Sachs disease? Retrieved from www.ntsad.org/

NWHIC (National Women's Health Information Center). (2009). Pregnancy and a healthy diet. Retrieved from www.4woman.gov/

O'Brien, M. (1997). *Inclusive child care for infants and toddlers: Meeting individual and special needs.* Baltimore: Brookes.

Ødegaard, E. E. (2006). What's worth talking about? Meaning-making in toddler-initiated conarratives in preschool. *Early Years, 26*(1), 79–92.

Oser, C., & Cohen, J. (2003). *America's babies: The Zero to Three policy center data book.* Washington, DC: ZERO TO THREE.

OTIS. (2005). DEET (N, N-ethyl-m-toluamide) and pregnancy. Retrieved from www.otispregnancy.org/pdf/DEET.pdf

Özçalışkan, Ş., & Goldin-Meadow, S. (2010). Sex differences in language first appear in gesture. *Developmental Science, 13*(5), 752–760. doi:10.1111/j.1467-7687.2009.00933.x

Ozonoff, S., Macari, S., Young, G. S., Goldring, S., Thompson, M., & Rogers, S. J. (2008). Atypical object exploration at 12 months of age is associated with autism in a prospective sample. *Autism: The International Journal of Research and Practice, 12*(5), 457–472.

Paintner, A., Williams, A. D., & Burd, L. (2012). Fetal alcohol spectrum disorders—Implications for child neurology, Part 2: Diagnosis and management. *Journal of Child Neurology, 27*(3), 355–362.

Pan, B. A., Imbens-Bailey, A., Winner, K., & Snow, C. (1996). Communicative intents expressed by parents in interaction with young children. *Merrill-Palmer Quarterly, 42,* 248–266.

Pan, B. A., Imbens-Bailey, A., Winner, K., & Snow, C. (1996). Communicative intents expressed by parents in interaction with young children. *Merrill-Palmer Quarterly, 42*, 248–266.

Parent to Parent USA (2012). Emotional and informational support for families of children who have special needs. Retrieved from www.p2pusa.org/

Park, K. A., & Waters, E. (1989). Security of attachment and preschool friendships. *Child Development, 60*(5), 1076–1081.

Parkinson, G. M. (2002). High incidence of language disorder in children with focal epilepsies. *Developmental Medicine and Child Neurology, 44*(8), 533–537.

Parlakian, R. (2003). *Before the ABCs: Promoting school readiness in infants and toddlers.* Washington, DC: ZERO TO THREE.

Parlakian, R., & Seibel, N. (2001). *Being in charge: Reflective leadership in infant/family programs.* Washington, DC: ZERO TO THREE.

Parten, M. B. (1932). Social participation among preschool children. *Journal of Abnormal and Social Psychology, 27*, 243–269.

Parten, M. B. (1933). Social play among preschool children. *Journal of Abnormal and Social Psychology, 28*, 136–147.

Patterson, C. (2006). Children of lesbian and gay parents. *Current Directions in Psychological Science, 15*(5), 241–244.

Pawl, J. H. (1995). The therapeutic relationship as human connectedness: Being held in another's mind. *Zero to Three, 15*(4), 1–5.

Pawl, J. H., & St. John, M. (1998). How you are is as important as what you do...in making a positive difference for infants, toddlers, and their families. Washington, DC: ZERO TO THREE.

Pearson, B. Z., Fernandez, S. C., Lewedeg, V., & Oller, D. K. (1997). The relation of input factors to lexical learning by bilingual infants. *Applied Psycholinguistics, 18*(1), 41–58.

Pearson, B. Z., Fernandez, S. C., & Oller, D. K. (1993). Lexical development in bilingual infants and toddlers: Comparison to monolingual norms. *Language Learning, 43*(1), 93–120.

Penn, H. (2005). *Unequal childhoods: Young children's lives in poor countries.* London: Routledge.

Perera, F. P., Illman, S. M., Kinney, P. L., Whyatt, R. M., Kelvin, E. A., Shepard, P., ... Raul, V. A. (2002). The challenge of preventing environmentally related disease in young children: Community-based research in New York City. *Environmental Health Perspectives, 110*(2), 197–204.

Perrin, E. C. (2002). Technical report: Coparent or second-parent adoption by same-sex parents. *Pediatrics, 109*(2), 341–344.

Perry, B. (1996). *Maltreated children: Experience, brain development, and the next generation.* New York: Norton.

Perry, B. (1999, July–August). Time is precious in early childhood development. *Good Health Magazine,* 1.

Perry, B. (2001, April). The importance of pleasure in play. *Scholastic Early Childhood Today,* 24–25.

Perry, B., & Pollard, R. (1997). Altered brain development following global neglect in early childhood. *Neuroscience.* Proceedings from the annual meeting, New Orleans.

Petersen, S. H., & Wittmer, D. S. (2013). *Endless opportunities for infants and toddlers: A relationship-based approach.* Upper Saddle River, NJ: Merrill/Prentice Hall.

Petitto, L.A., Berens, M.S., Kovelman, I., Dubins, M.H., Jasinska, K., & Shalinsky, M. (2012). The "Perceptual Wedge Hypothesis" as the basis for bilingual babies' phonetic processing advantage: New insights from fNIRS brain imaging *Brain and Language, 121*(2), 130–43.

Petitto, L. A., Katerelos, M., Levy, B., Gauna, K., Tetreault, K., & Ferraro, V. (2001). Bilingual signed and spoken language acquisition from birth: Implications for the mechanisms underlying early bilingual language acquisition. *Journal of Child Language, 28*(2), 453–496.

Pham, L. (1994). Infant dual language acquisition revisited. *Journal of Educational Issues of Language Minority Students, 14,* 185–210.

Phillips, D., & Adams, G. (2001). Child care and our youngest children. *The Future of Children Journal: Caring for Infants and Toddlers, 11*(1), 35–52.

Phillips, D., Crowell, N. A., Sussman, A. L., Gunnar, M., Fox, N., Hane, A., & Bisgaier, J. (2012). Reactive temperament and sensitivity to context in childcare. *Social Development, 21*(3), 628–643. doi:10.1111/j.1467-9507.2011.00649.x

Phillips, D. A., Fox, N. A., & Gunnar, M. R. (2011). Same place, different experiences: Bringing individual differences to research in child care. *Child Development Perspectives, 5*(1), 44–49. doi:10.1111/j.1750-8606.2010.00155.x

Piaget, J. (1952). *The origins of intelligence in children.* New York: Norton.

Piaget, J. (1954). *The construction of reality in the child.* New York: Basic Books.

Piaget, J., & Inhelder, B. (2000). *The psychology of the child.* New York: Basic Books. (Original work published 1969)

Pierroutsakos, S. L. (2000). Infants of the dreaming: A Warlpiri guide to child care. In J. DeLoache & A. Gottlieb (Eds.), *A world of babies: Imagined child care guides for seven societies.* Cambridge, UK: Cambridge University Press.

Pines, M. (1984). Children's winning ways. *Psychology Today,* 59–65.

PITC (Program for Infant/Toddler Care). (2012). *Program for infant/toddler care.* Retrieved from www.pitc.org

Plusquellec, P., Francois, N., Boivin, M., Perusse, D., & Tremblay, R. E. (2007). Dominance among unfamiliar peers starts in infancy. *Infant Mental Health Journal, 28*(3), 324–343.

Pons, F., Lewkowicz, D. J., Soto-Faraco, S., & Sebastián-Gallés, N. (2009). Narrowing of intersensory speech perception in infancy. *Proceedings of the National Academy of Science, 106*(26), 10598–10602.

Popenoe, D. (1999). Challenging the culture of fatherlessness. In W. F. Horn, D. E. Eberly, D. Blankenhorn, & M. B. Pearlstein (Eds.), *The fatherhood movement: A call to action* (pp. 17–24). Lanham, MD: Lexington.

Porter, C. L., & Jones, B. L. (2011). Does brief bradycardia at the onset of arm-restraint predict infants' emotional reactivity during restraint? *Infancy, 16*(2), 166–179.

Posner, M. I. (Ed.). (2011). *Cognitive neuroscience of attention* (2nd ed.). New York: Guilford Press.

Post, J. (2011). *Tender care and early learning: Supporting infants and toddlers in child care settings.* Ypsilanti, MI: HighScope Press.

Poulin-Dubois, D., Blaye, A., Coutya, J., & Bialystok, E. (2011). The effects of bilingualism on toddlers' executive functioning. *Journal of Experimental Child Psychology,108*(3), 567–579.

Prizant, B., Wetherby, A., & Roberts, J. (1993). Communication disorders in infants and toddlers. In J. Charles & H. Zeanah (Eds.), *Handbook of infant mental health.* New York: Guilford Press.

Program for Infant/Toddler Care. (2012). Retrieved from www.pitc.org

Pruden, S. M., Hirsh-Pasek, K., Golinkoff, R. M., & Hennon, E. A. (2006). The birth of words: Ten-month-olds learn words through perceptual salience. *Child Development, 77*(2), 266–280.

Quann, V., & Wien, C. A. (2006). The visible empathy of infants and toddlers. Retrieved from www.journal.naeyc.org/btj/100607/Quann709BTJ.asp

Radin, N. (1982). *Paternal involvement in child care index.* Ann Arbor: University of Michigan School of Social Work.

Raikes, H. (1993). Relationship duration in infant care: Time with a high-ability teacher and infant-teacher attachment. *Early Childhood Research Quarterly, 8,* 309–325.

Rakic, P., Bourgeois, J. P., & Goldman-Rakic, P. S. (1994). Synaptic development of the cerebral cortex: Implications for learning, memory, and mental illness. In J. van Pelt, M. A. Corona, H. B. M. Uylings, & P. H. Lopes da Silva (Eds.), *The self-organizing brain: From growth cones to functional networks* (pp. 227–243). Amsterdam: Elsevier Science.

Recchia, S. L. (2012). Caregiver-child relationships as a context for continuity in child care. *Early Years: An International Journal of Research and Development, 32*(2), 143–157.

Recchia, S. L., & Dvorakova, K. (2012). How three young toddlers transition from an infant to a toddler child care classroom: Exploring the influence of peer relationships, teacher expectations, and changing social contexts. *Early Education & Development, 23*(2), 181–201.

Recchia, S. L., & Loizou, E. (2002). Becoming an infant caregiver: Three profiles of personal and professional growth. *Journal of Research in Childhood Education, 16*(2), 133–147.

Redshaw, M., & Martin, C. (2011). Motherhood: A natural progression and a major transition. *Journal of Reproductive and Infant Psychology, 29*(4), 305–307.

Reese, E., & Fivush, R. (1993). Parental styles of talking about the past. *Developmental Psychology, 29*(3), 596–606.

Reindle, N. (2004). *The zone of proximal development in block play.* Paper and documentation panel presented in a University of Colorado–Denver course titled Advanced Developmentally Appropriate Practice.

Repacholi, B. M. (1998). Infants' use of attentional cues to identify the referent of another person's emotional expression. *Developmental Psychology, 33*(5), 1017–1025.

Restak, R. (2001). *The secret life of the brain.* Washington, DC: Joseph Henry Press.

Richardson, H. (1997). Kangaroo care: Why does it work? *Midwifery Today, 44,* 50–51.

Riley, E. P., Alejandra Infante, M. M., & Warren, K. R. (2011). Fetal alcohol spectrum disorders: An overview. *Neuropsychology Review, 21*(2), 73–80.

Rinaldi, C. (2001). Reggio Emilia: The image of the child and the child's environment as a fundamental principle. In L. Gandini & C. Edwards (Eds.), *Bambini: The Italian approach to infant care* (pp. 49–55). New York: Teachers College Press.

Rizzo, K. M., Schiffrin, H. H., & Liss, M. (2012, June). Insight into the parenting paradox: Mental health outcomes of intensive mothering. *Journal of Child and Family Studies.* doi10.1007/s10826-012-9615-z

Roberts, S. B., & Heyman, M. B. (2000). How to feed babies and toddlers in the 21st century. *Zero to Three, 21*(1), 24–28.

Robertson, A. S. (1998). The parenting education spectrum: A look at the scope of parenting programs that should be available within a community. *Parent News: National Parent Information Network.*

Robin, D. J., Berthier, N. E., & Clifton, R. K. (1996). Infants' predictive reaching for moving objects in the dark. *Developmental Psychology, 32,* 824–835.

Robinson, J. L., & Acevedo, M. C. (2001). Infant reactivity and reliance on mother during emotion challenges: Prediction of cognition and language skills in a low-income sample. *Child Development, 72*(2), 402–416.

Rochat, P. (2001). *The infant's world.* Cambridge, MA: Harvard University Press.

Rogoff, B. (2003). *The cultural nature of human development.* New York: Oxford University Press.

Roisman, G. I. (2007). The psychophysiology of adult attachment relationships: Autonomic reactivity in marital and premarital interactions. *Developmental Psychology, 43,* 39–53.

Roopnarine, J. L., & Field, T. M. (1983). Peer-directed behaviors of infants and toddlers during nursery school play. *Infant Behavior and Development, 6*(1), 133.

Ross, H. S., & Lollis, S. P. (1989). A social relations analysis of toddler peer relationships. *Child Development, 60*(5), 1082–1092.

Rothbart, M. K., & Bates, J. E. (1998). Temperament. In W. Damon (Ed.), *Handbook of child psychology,* Vol. 3: *Social, emotional, and personality development* (5th ed., pp. 105–176). New York: Wiley.

Rothbart, M. K., & Derryberry, D. (1981). Development of individual differences in temperament. In M. E. Lamb & A. L. Brown

(Eds.), *Advances in developmental psychology* (Vol. 1, pp. 37–86). Hillsdale, NJ: Erlbaum.

Rothbart, M. K., Sheese, B. E., Rueda, M. R., & Posner, M. I. (2011). Developing mechanisms of self-regulation in early life. *Emotion Review, 3*(2), 207–213. doi:10.1177/1754073910387943

Rouse, K. (1998). Infant and toddler resilience. *Early Childhood Education Journal, 26*(1), 47–52.

Rubin, K. H. (1998). Social and emotional development from a cultural perspective. *Developmental Psychology, 34*(4), 611–615.

Rubin, K. H., Bukowski, W., & Laurensen, B. (Eds.). (2008). *Handbook of peer interactions, relationships, and groups.* New York: Guilford.

Rubin, K. H., Bukowski, W., & Parker, J. G. (1998). Peer interactions, relationships, and groups. In W. Damon (Ed.), *Handbook of child psychology,* Vol. 3: *Social, emotional, and personality development* (5th ed., pp. 619–700). New York: Wiley.

Rubin, K. H., Burgess, K. B., Dwyer, K. M., & Hastings, P. D. (2003). Predicting preschoolers' externalizing behaviors from toddler temperament, conflict, and maternal negativity. *Developmental Psychology, 39*(1), 164–177.

Rubin, K. H., Burgess, K., & Hastings, P. (2002). Stability and social-behavioral consequences of toddlers' inhibited temperament and parenting behaviors. *Child Development, 73*(2), 483–496.

Rubin, K. H., & Coplan, R. J. (2004). Paying attention to and not neglecting social withdrawal and social isolation. *Merrill-Palmer Quarterly, 50*(4), 506–535.

Rubin, K. H., Coplan, R. J., & Bowker, J. C. (2009). Social withdrawal in childhood. *Annual Review of Psychology,* 60, 141–171.

Runyan, D. K., Hunter, W. M., Socolar, R. R. S., Amaya-Jackson, L., English, D., Landsverk, J., … Mathew, R. M. (1996). Children who prosper in unfavorable environments: The relationship to social capital. *Pediatrics, 101*(1), 12–18.

Ruzek E., Burchinal, M., Farkas, G, Duncan, G., Dang, T & Lee, W. (2011, March). *Does high quality childcare narrow the achievement gap at two years of age?* Presented at Society for Research on Educational Effectiveness, Washington, DC.

Saffran, J. R. (2002). Constraints on statistical language learning. *Journal of Memory and Language, 47,* 172–196.

Saffran, J. R., Loman, M. M., & Robertson, R. W. (2000). Infant memory for musical experiences. *Cognition, 77*(1), B15–B23.

Sameroff, A. J. (1998). Management of clinical problems and emotional care: Environmental risk factors in infancy. *Pediatrics, 102*(5), 1287–1292.

Sameroff, A. J., & Chandler, M. (1975). Reproductive risk and the continuum of caretaking casualty. In F. Horowitz, M. Hetherington, & S. Scar-Salaperk (Eds.), *Review of child development research* (Vol. 4, pp. 187–244). Chicago: University of Chicago Press.

Sameroff, A. J., & Feise, B. H. (2000). Transactional regulation: The development ecology of early intervention. In J. P.

Shonkoff & S. J. Meisels (Eds.), *Handbook of early childhood intervention* (2nd ed., pp. 135–159). New York: Cambridge University Press.

Sameroff, A. J., & MacKenzie, M. J. (2003). A quarter-century of the transactional model: How have things changed? *Zero to Three, 24*(1), 14–22.

Sánchez, S. Y., & Thorp, E. K. (1998a). Discovering meanings of continuity: Implications for the infant/family field. In E. Fenichel (Ed.), *Bulletin of Zero to Three: National Center for Infants, Toddlers, and Families, 18*(6), 1–5.

Sánchez, S. Y., & Thorp, E. K. (1998b). Policies on linguistic continuity: A family's right, a practitioner's choice, or an opportunity to create shared meaning and a more equitable relationship? In E. Fenichel (Ed.), *Bulletin of Zero to Three: National Center for Infants, Toddlers, and Families, 18*(6), 12–20.

Sánchez, S. Y., & Thorp, E. K. (1998c). The use of discontinuity in preparing early educators of culturally, linguistically, and ability-diverse young children and their families. In E. Fenichel (Ed.), *Bulletin of Zero to Three: National Center for Infants, Toddlers, and Families, 18*(6), 27–32.

Sano, Y., Smith, S., & Lanigan, J. (2011). Predicting presence and level of nonresident fathers' involvement in infants' lives: Mothers' perspective. *Journal of Divorce & Remarriage, 52*(5), 350–368. doi:10.1080/10502556.2011.586613

Santelli, B. (2003). *Parent to parent support.* Retrieved from www.nichcy.org/pubs/basicpar/bp2txt. htm

Santos, D., Cacola, P., Gabbard, C. P., & de Freitas, T., & Miquelote, A.F. (2011). Family socioeconomic status and affordances in the home for motor development. *Research Quarterly for Exercise and Sport, 82*(1), supplement, A-30.

Sapienza, J., & Masten, A. S. (2011). Understanding and promoting resilience in children and youth. *Current Opinion in Psychiatry, 24*(4), 267–273.

Sawyers, J. K., & Rogers, C. S. (2003). Helping babies play. [NAEYC resources in focus; selected excerpts.] *Young Children, 58*(3), 52–53.

Schaal, B., & Durand, K. (2012). The role of olfaction in multisensory development. In A. J. Bremner, D. J. Lewkowicz, & C. Spence (Eds.), *Multisensory development* (pp. 29–43). Oxford, UK: Oxford University Press.

Scarborough, H. S., & Dobrich, W. (1990). Development of children with early language delay. *Journal of Speech and Hearing Research, 33,* 70–83.

Schickedanz, J. A. (2003). NAEYC resources in focus: Creating a book nook for babies and toddlers. *Young Children, 58*(2), 61.

Schmuckler, M. A., Collimore, L. M., & Dannemiller, J. L. (2007). Infants' reactions to object collision on hit and miss trajectories. *Infancy, 12*(1), 105–118.

Schreiber, M. E. (1999). Time-outs for toddlers: Is our goal punishment or education? *Young Children, 54*(4), 22–25.

Sears, W., & Sears, M. (2001). *Attachment parenting: A common-sense guide to understanding and nurturing your baby.* New York: Little, Brown.

Segatti, L., Brown-DuPaul, J., & Keyes, T. (2003). Using everyday materials to promote problem solving in toddlers. *Young Children, 58*(5), 12–18.

Seidl, A. (2007). Infants' use and weighting of prosodic cues in clause segmentation. *Journal of Memory and Language, 57*(1), 24–48. doi:10.1016/j.jml.2006.10.004

Seifer, R., Sameroff, A. J., Baldwin, C. P., & Baldwin, A. (1992). Child and family factors that ameliorate risk between 4 and 13 years of age. *Journal of the American Academy of Child and Adolescent Psychiatry, 31,* 893–903.

Sevón, E. (2012). "My life has changed, but his life hasn't": Making sense of the gendering of parenthood during the transition to motherhood. *Feminism & Psychology, 22*(1), 60–80. doi:10.1177/0959353511415076

Shahaeian, A., Peterson, C. C., Slaughter, V., & Wellman, H. M. (2011). Culture and the sequence of steps in theory of mind development. *Developmental Psychology, 47*(5), 1239–1247.

Shalala calls for a new era of support to families with infants and toddlers. (1995). *Children Today, 23*(3), 4–5.

Shatz, M. (2007). Revisiting *A Toddler's Life for the Toddler Years*: Conversational participation as a tool for learning across knowledge domains. In C. Brownell & C. Kopp (Eds.), *Socioemotional development in the toddler years: Transitions and transformation* (pp. 241–260). New York/London: Guilford Press.

Shin, M. (2010). Peeking at the relationship world of infant friends and caregivers. *Journal of Early Childhood Research, 8*(3), 294–302.

Shirah, S., Hewitt, T., & McNair, R. (1993). Preservice training fosters retention: The case for vocational training. *Young Children, 48*(4), 27–31.

Shneidman, L.A., & Goldin-Meadow, S. (2012). Language input and acquisition in a Mayan village: how important is directed speech? *Developmental Science, 15*(5), 659–673.

Shoemaker, C. C. (2000). *Leadership and management of programs for young children* (2nd ed.). Upper Saddle River, NJ: Merrill/Prentice Hall.

Shonkoff, J.P. (2011). Protecting brains, not simply stimulating minds (2011). *Science, 333*(6045), 982–983.

Shonkoff J. P., & Garner, A. S. (and the Committee on Psychosocial Aspects of Child and Family Health; Committee on Early Childhood, Adoption, and Dependent Care; Section on Developmental and Behavioral Pediatrics). (2012). The lifelong effects of early childhood adversity and toxic stress. *Pediatrics, 129*(1), e232–246. Retrieved from www.ncbi.nlm.nih.gov/pubmed/22201156

Shonkoff, J. P., & Meisels, S. J. (2000). *Handbook of early childhood intervention* (2nd ed.). Cambridge, UK: Cambridge University Press.

Shonkoff, J. P., & Phillips, D. A. (Eds.). (2000). *From neurons to neighborhoods: The science of early development.* Washington, DC: National Academy Press.

Shore, R. (1997). *Rethinking the brain: New insights into early development.* New York: Families and Work Institute.

Siegel, A. C., & Burton, R. V. (1999). Effects of baby walkers on motor and mental development in human infants. *Journal of Developmental and Behavioral Pediatrics, 20,* 355–361.

Singer, E., & Hannikainen, M. (2002). The teacher's role in territorial conflicts of 2- to 3-year-old children. *Journal of Research in Early Childhood Education, 17*(1), 5–18.

Skeels, H. M., & Dye, H. B. (1939). *A study of the effects of diferential stimulation on mentally retarded children.* Proceedings and addresses of the American Association on Mental Deficiency.

Skinner, B. F. (1957). *Verbal behavior.* New York: Appleton-Century Crofts.

Small, M. F. (1998). *Our babies, ourselves: How biology and culture shape the way we parent.* New York: Anchor.

Smilansky, S., & Shefatya, L. (1990). *Facilitating play: A medium for promoting cognitive, socioemotional, and academic development in young children.* Gaithersburg, MD: Psychosocial and Educational Publications.

Smith, A. B., Dannison, L. L., & Vach-Hasse, T. (1998). When "Grandma" is "Mom": What today's teachers need to know. *Childhood Education, 75*(1), 12–16.

Smith, P. K., & Pellegrini, A. (2008). Learning through play. In R. E. Tremblay, R. G. Barr, R. deV Peters, & M. Boivin (Eds.), *Encyclopedia on early childhood development* (pp. 1–6). Montreal, Quebec: Centre of Excellence for Early Childhood Development.

Smith, P. M. (2003). You are not alone: For parents when they learn that their child has a disability. Kidsource Online. Retrieved from www.kidsource.com/NICHCY/parenting.disab.all.4.2.html

Soderstrom, M. (2007). Beyond babytalk: Re-evaluating the nature and content of speech input to preverbal infants. *Developmental Review, 27,* 501–532.

Solchany, J. E. (2001). *Promoting maternal mental health during pregnancy.* Seattle, WA: NCAST.

Soodak, L. C., & Erwin, E. J. (2000). Valued member or tolerated participant: Parents' experiences in inclusive early childhood settings. *Journal of the Association for Persons with Severe Handicaps, 25,* 29–44.

Sparks, T. A., Hunter, S. K., Backman, T. L., Morgan, G. A., & Ross, R. G. (2012). Maternal parenting stress and mothers' reports of their infants' mastery motivation. *Infant Behavior & Development, 35*(1), 167–173. doi:10.1016/j.infbeh.2011.07.002

Spectrum Health. (2009). Hearing milestones. Retrieved from https://www.spectrumhealth.org/

Spelke, E. S. (2002). Developmental neuroimaging: A developmental psychologist looks ahead. *Developmental Science, 5*(3), 392–396.

Spelke, E. S. (2005). Sex differences in intrinsic aptitude for mathematics and science: A critical review. *American Psychologist, 60,* 950–958.

Spelke, E. S., Breinlinger, K., Jacobson, K., & Phillips, A. (1993). Gestalt relations and object perception: A developmental study. *Perception, 22,* 1483–1501.

Spelke, E. S., & Kinzler, K. D. (2007). Core knowledge. *Developmental Science, 10*(1), 89–96.

Spelke, E. S., & Owlsley, C. (1979). Infants' intermodal perception of events. *Infant Behavior and Development, 2,* 13–17.

Spina Bifida Association. (2012). Important message on folic acid. Retrieved from: www.spinabifidaassociation.org/site/c.evKRI7OXIoJ8H/b.8029669/k.9884/Lower_the_Risk.htm

Spitz, R. A. (1945). Hospitalism: An inquiry into the genesis of psychiatric conditions of early childhood. *Psychoanalytic Study of the Child, 1,* 53–74.

Sroufe, E. A. (1990). The fate of early experience following developmental change: Longitudinal approaches to individual adaptation in childhood. *Child Development, 61,* 1363–1373.

Stacks, A.M., & Partridge,, T. (2011). Infants placed in foster care prior to their first birthday: Differences in kin and non-kin placements. *Infant Mental Health Journal, 32*(5), 489–508.

Stanford University Medical Center. (2007, July 30). Severe trauma affects kids' brain function, say researchers. *ScienceDaily.* Retrieved from www.sciencedaily.com/releases/2007/07/070726184910.htm

Stefani, L. H., & Camaioni, L. (1983). Effects of familiarity on peer interaction in the first year of life. *Early Child Development and Care, 11*(1), 45–54.

Stein, M. T., Colaruso, C., Mckenna, J. J., & Powers, N. G. (2001). Cosleeping (bedsharing) among infants and toddlers. *Pediatrics, 107,* 873–877.

Stephens, K. (1999). Toilet training: Children step up to independence. *Child Care Information Exchange,* 76–80.

Stern, D. (1995). *The motherhood constellation.* New York: Basic Books.

Stern, D. (2000). *The interpersonal world of the infant.* New York: Basic Books.

Stifter, C. A., Putnam, S., & Jahromi, L. (2008). Exuberant and inhibited toddlers: Stability of temperament and risk for problem behavior. *Development and Psychopathology, 20,* 401–421.

Stroud, J. E. (1995). Block play: A foundation for literacy. *Early Childhood Education Journal, 23*(1), 9–13.

Super, C. M., & Harkness, S. (1997). The cultural structuring of child development. In J. W. Berry, P. R. Dasen, & T. S. Saraswathi (Eds.), *Handbook of cross-cultural psychology,* Vol. 2: *Basic processes and human development* (pp. 1–39). Boston: Allyn & Bacon.

Susman-Stillman, A., Appleyard, K., & Siebenbruner, J. (2003). For better or worse: An ecological perspective on parents' relationships and parent-infant interaction. *Zero to Three, 23*(3), 4–12.

Sutherland, P. (1992). *Cognitive development today: Piaget and his critics.* London: Chapman.

Svetlova, M., Nichols, S. R., & Brownell, C. A. (2010). Toddlers' prosocial behavior: From instrumental to empathic to altruistic helping. *Child Development, 81,* 1814–1827. doi: 10.1111/j.1467-8624.2010.01512.x

Swain, I., Zelazo, P., & Clifton, R. (1993). Newborn infants' memory for speech sounds retained over 24 hours. *Developmental Psychology, 29,* 312–323.

Swingley, D. (2008). The roots of the early vocabulary in infants' learning from speech. *Current Directions in Psychological Science, 17*(5), 308–312.

Sylvester, K. (2001). Caring for our youngest: Public attitudes in the United States. *The Future of Children Journal: Caring for Infants and Toddlers, 11*(1), 53–61.

Szalavitz, M. (2010). Missing out on mother's day. Retrieved from www.thefix.com/content/mothers-day-addicted-pregnant-women-policy8710

Szanton, E. S. (2001). For America's infants and toddlers, are important values threatened by our zeal to "teach"? *Young Children, 56*(1), 15–21.

Tamis-LeMonda, C. S., Adolph, K. E., Lobo, S. A., Karasik, L. B., Dimitroupoulou, K. D., & Ishak, S. (2008). When infants take mothers' advice: 18-month-olds integrate perceptual and social information for guiding motor action. *Developmental Psychology, 44,* 734–746.

Tamis-LeMonda, C. S., & Cabrera, N. J. (2002). *Handbook of father involvement: Multidisciplinary perspectives.* Mahwah, NJ: Erlbaum.

Tarullo, A. R., Mliner, S., & Gunnar, M. R. (2011). Inhibition and exuberance in preschool classrooms: Associations with peer social experiences and changes in cortisol across the preschool year. *Developmental Psychology, 47*(5), 1374–1388.

Taylor, F., Ko, R., & Pan, M. (1999). Prenatal and reproductive health care. In E. Kramer, S. Ivey, & Y. W. Ying (Eds.), *Immigrant women's health: Problems and solutions* (pp. 121–135). San Francisco: Jossey-Bass.

Teaching Strategies for Early Childhood. (2012). Curriculum overview. Retrieved from www.teachingstrategies.com

The Division for Early Childhood. (2012). Recommended practices. Retrieved from www.dec-sped.org/About_DEC/Recommended_Practices

Thelen, E. (2000). Grounded in the world: Developmental origins of the embodied mind. *Infancy, 1,* 3–30.

Thelen, E., & Smith, L. B. (1996). *A dynamic systems approach to the development of cognition and action.* Cambridge, MA: MIT Press.

Thiessen, E. D., Hill, E. A., & Saffran, J. R. (2005). Infant-directed speech facilitates word segmentation. *Infancy, 7*(1), 53–71.

Thomas, A., & Chess, S. (1977). *Temperament and development.* New York: Brunner/Mazel.

Thomas, A., Chess, S., Birch, H. G., Hertzig, M. E., & Korn, S. (1963). *Behavioral individuality in early childhood.* New York: New York University Press.

Thomas, M. S. C., & Johnson, M. H. (2008). New advances in understanding sensitive periods in brain development. *Current Directions in Psychological Science, 17*(1), 1–5.

Thompson-Rangel, T. (1994). The Hispanic child and family: Developmental disabilities and occupational therapy intervention. *Developmental Disabilities Special Interest Newsletter, 16*(1), 2.

Tomasello, M. (1992). The social bases of language acquisition. *Social Development, 1,* 68–87.

Torelli, L., & Durrett, C. (2007). Landscape for learning: The impact of classroom design on infants and toddlers. Retrieved from www.spacesforchildren.com/impact.html

Tortora, S. (2004). Our moving bodies tell us stories, which speak of our experiences. *Zero to Three, 24*(5), 4–12.

Tremblay, R. E. (2004). Decade of behavior distinguished lecture: Development of physical aggression during infancy. *Infant Mental Health Journal, 25,* 399–407.

Tremblay, R. E., & Nagin, D. S. (2005). The developmental origins of physical aggression in humans. In R. E. Tremblay, W. W. Hartup, & J. Archer (Eds.), *Developmental origins of aggression* (pp. 83–106). New York: Guilford.

Troy, M., & Sroufe, A. (1987). Victimization among preschoolers: Role of attachment relationships. *Journal of the American Academy of Child and Adolescent Psychiatry, 1987 26*(2): 166–172.

UCP (United Cerebral Palsy). (2013). About Cerebral Palsy www.ucp.org/

Ulione, M. S. (1997). Health promotion and injury prevention in a child development center. *Journal of Pediatric Nursing, 12*(3), 148–154.

UNICEF. (2008). *The state of the world's children 2008.* Retrieved from www.unicef.org/publications/files/SOWC_2008_Exec_Summary_EN_042908.pdf

UNICEF. (2009). Convention on the Rights of the Child. Retrieved from www.unicef.org/crc/

U.S. Census Bureau (2004). *Living arrangements of children: 2004.* Retrieved from http://www.census.gov/prod/2008 pubs/p70-114.pdf

U.S. Census Bureau, American FactFinder. (2006). *Selected economic characteristics.* Retrieved from http://factfinder2.census.gov/

U.S. Census Bureau (2010a). *2010 poverty table of contents (Based on census 2010 population controls).* Retrieved from www.census.gov/hhes/www/cpstables/032011/pov/POV02_100.htm

U.S. Census Bureau. (2010b). *Who's minding the kids? Child care arrangements: Spring 2010—detailed tables.* Retrieved from http://www.census.gov/hhes/childcare/data/sipp/2010/tables.html

U.S. Census Bureau. (2011). Who's minding the kids? Child care arrangements. Retrieved from www.naccrra.org/about-child-care/child-demographics

U.S. Census Bureau (2012). Profile American facts for features. Retrieved from http://www.census.gov

U.S. Consumer Product Safety Commission. (2012). Proposed Collection of Information; Baby Bouncers, Walker-Jumpers, and Baby Walkers. Retrieved from www.cpsc.gov/

U.S. Department of Health and Human Services. (2001). Building futures: Head Start impact study frequently asked questions. Retrieved from www.acf.hhs.gov/

U.S. Department of Health and Human Services. (2012). The AFCARS Report. Retrieved from http://www.acf.hhs.gov/sites/default/files/cb/afcarsreport19.pdf

U.S. Department of Justice. (1997). Commonly asked questions about child care centers and the Americans with Disabilities Act. Retrieved from www.ada.gov/childq%26a.htm

Uzgiris, I. C., & Hunt, J. M. (1975). *Assessment in infancy: Ordinal scales of psychological development.* Urbana: University of Illinois Press.

Vallotton, C. D. (2009). Do infants influence their quality of care? Infants' communicative gestures predict caregivers' responsiveness. *Infant Behavior and Development, 32,* 351–365.

Vallotton, C., & Ayoub, C. (2011). Use your words: The role of language in the development of toddlers' self-regulation. *Early Childhood Research Quarterly, 26*(2), 169–181. doi:10.1016/j.ecresq.2010.09.002

Vandell, D., Belsky, J., Burchinal, M., Steinberg, L., Vandergrift, N., & the NICHD Early Child Care Research Network. (2010). Do effects of early child care extend to age 15 years? Results from the NICHD Study of Early Child Care and Youth Development. *Child Development, 81*(3), 737–756.

Vandell, D., & Wolfe, B. (2001). *Child care quality: Does it matter and does it need to be improved?* Washington, DC: U.S. Department of Health and Human Services.

Van De Zande, I. (1995). *1, 2, 3...The toddler years: A practical guide for parents and caregivers.* Santa Cruz, CA: Santa Cruz Toddler Care Center.

van Hoogdalem, A., Singer, E., Wijngaards, L., & Heesbeen, D. (2012). The role of familiarity and similarity in friendship relationships in toddlers in Dutch daycare centers. *European Early Childhood Research Journal, 20*(2), 189–204.

Van Hulle, C. A., Goldsmith, H. H., & Lemery, K. S. (2004). Genetic, environmental, and gender effects on individual differences in toddler expressive language. *Journal of Speech, Language, and Hearing Research, 47*(4), 904–1003.

Vernon, F. (2003, Spring). Sink play. *Focus on Infants and Toddlers, 15*(1), 5.

Verissimo, M., Santos, A. J., Vaughn, B. E., Torres, N., Monteiro, L., & Santos, O. (2011). Quality of attachment to father and mother and number of reciprocal friends. *Early Child Development and Care, 181*(1), 27–38.

Volling, B., Notaro, P. C., & Larsen, J. J. (1998). Adult attachment styles: Relations with emotional well-being, marriage, and parenting. *Family Relations, 47*(4), 355–367.

Vygotsky, L. S. (1962). *Thought and language.* Cambridge, MA: MIT Press.

Vygotsky, L. S. (1978). *Mind in society: The development of higher psychological processes.* Cambridge, MA: Harvard University Press.

Warneken, F., & Tomasello, M. (2007). Helping and cooperation at 14 months of age. *Infancy, 11,* 271–294.

Warneken, F., & Tomasello, M. (2008). Extrinsic rewards undermine altruistic tendencies in 20-month-olds. *Developmental Psychology, 44*(6), 1785–1788.

Warneken, F., & Tomasello, M. (2009). The roots of human altruism. *British Journal of Psychology, 100,* 455–471

Watamura, S., Donzella, B., Alwin, J., & Gunnar, M. (2003). Morning-to-afternoon increases in cortisol concentrations for infants and toddlers at child care: Age differences and behavioral correlates. *Child Development, 74*(4), 1006–1021.

Watemberg, N., Silver, S., Harel, S., & Lerman-Sagie, T. (2002). Significance of microcephaly among children with developmental disabilities. *Journal of Child Neurology, 17,* 117–122.

Watson, J. (1972). Smiling, cooing, and the game. *Merrill-Palmer Quarterly, 18,* 323–340.

Watson, M., & White, J. (2001). Accident prevention activities: A national survey of health authorities. *Health Education Journal, 60*(3), 275–283.

Waxman, S. R., & Markow, D. B. (1995). Words as invitations to form categories: Evidence from 12- to 13-month-old infants. *Cognitive Psychology, 29,* 257–302.

Weatherston, D. (2001). Infant mental health: A review of relevant literature. *Psychoanalytic Social Work, 8*(1), 39–69.

Weikum, W., M., Vouloumanos, A., Navarra, J., SotoFaraco, S., Sebastian-Galles, N., & Werker, J.F. (2007). Visual language discrimination in infancy. *Science, 316*(5828), 1159.

Weil, J. L. (1993). *Early deprivation of empathic care.* Madison, CT: International Universities Press.

Weinfield, N. S., Sroufe, A. L., Egeland, B., & Carlson, E. A. (2002). In J. Cassidy & P. R. Shaver (Eds.), *Handbook of attachment: Theory, research, and clinical applications* (pp. 68–88). New York: Guilford Press.

Weitoft, G. R., Hjern, A., Haglund, B., & Rosén, M. (2003). Mortality, severe morbidity, and injury in children living with single parents in Sweden: A population-based study. *Lancet, 361*(9354), 289–294.

Werker, J. F., Pons, F., Dietrich, C., Kajikawa, S., Fais, L., & Amano, S. (2007). Infant-directed speech supports phonetic category learning in English and Japanese. *Cognition, 103,* 147–162.

Westby, C. (1980). Assessment of cognitive and language abilities through play. *Language, Speech, and Hearing Sciences in Schools, 11,* 154–168.

Whaley, K., & Rubenstein, T. (1994). How toddlers "do" friendship: A descriptive analysis of naturally occurring friendships in a group child care setting. *Journal of Social and Personal Relationships, 11,* 383–400.

Whitebook, M., & Bellm, D. (1996). Mentoring for early childhood teachers and providers: Building upon and extending tradition. *Young Children, 52*(1), 59–64.

Whitebook, M., Howes, C., & Phillips, D. (1998). *Worthy work, unlivable wages: The national child care staffing study, 1988–1997.* Washington, DC: Center for the Child Care Workforce.

Whitehurst, G. J., Zenvenberger, A. A., Crone, D. A., Schultz, M. D., Velting, O. N., & Fischel, J. E. (1999). Outcomes of an emergent literacy intervention from Head Start through second grade. *Journal of Educational Psychology, 91,* 261–272.

Wickramaratne, P., Gameroff, M. J., Pilowsky, D. J., Hughes, C. W., Garber, J., Malloy, E., King, C., ... Weissman, M. M. (2011). Children of depressed mothers 1 year after remission of maternal depression: findings from the STAR*D-Child study. *The American Journal of Psychiatry, 168*(6), 593–602. doi:10.1176/appi.ajp.2010.10010032

Williams, M. N. (2011). The changing roles of grandparents raising grandchildren. *Journal of Human Behavior in the Social Environment, 21*(8), 948–962. doi:10.1080/10911359.2011.588535

Wittmer, D. (1991). *Toddlers with special needs as initiators and recipients of prosocial behaviors.* Denver: University of Colorado Junior Faculty Award Report.

Wittmer, D. S. (2008). *A focus on peers in the early years: The importance of relationships.* Washington, DC: ZERO TO THREE.

Wittmer, D., & Petersen, S. (1992). Social development and interaction: Facilitating the prosocial development of typical and exceptional infants and toddlers in group settings. *Zero to Three, 12*(4), 52–60.

Wittmer, D. S., & Petersen, S. H. (2009). Issues in infant/toddler programs. In S. Feeney, A. Galper, & C. Seefeldt (Eds.), *Continuing issues in early childhood education* (3rd ed., pp. 58–82). Upper Saddle River, NJ: Merrill/Pearson.

Wober, M. (1972). Culture and the concept of intelligence: A case in Uganda. *Journal of Cross-Cultural Psychology, 3,* 327–328.

Woodward, A. L., Markman, E. M., & Fitzsimmons, C. M. (1994). Rapid word learning in 13- and 18-month-olds. *Developmental Psychology, 30,* 553–566.

Wu, Y., Selig, J., Roberts, M., & Steele, R. (2011). Trajectories of postpartum maternal depressive symptoms and children's social skills. *Journal of Child & Family Studies, 20*(4), 414–423. doi:10.1007/s10826-010-9407-2

Wynn, K. (1992). Addition and subtraction by human infants. *Nature, 358,* 749–750.

Xu, F., & Carey, S. (1996). Infants' metaphysics: The case of numerical identity. *Cognitive Psychology, 30*(2), 111–153.

Yamaguchi, M., Kuhlmeier, V. A., Wynn, K., & vanMarle, K. (2009). Continuity in social cognition from infancy to childhood. *Developmental Science, 12*(5), 746–752. doi:10.1111/j.1467-7687.2008.00813.x

Yoshinaga-Itano, C., Sedey, A. L., Coulter, D. K., & Mehl, A. L. (1998). Language of early- and later-identified children with hearing loss. *Pediatrics, 102*(5), 1161–1172.

Zahn-Waxler, C., & Radke-Yarrow, R. (1990). The origins of empathic concern. *Motivation and Emotion, 14,* 107–130.

Zahn-Waxler, C., Radke-Yarrow, R., & King, R. A. (1979). Child rearing and children's prosocial initiations toward victims of distress. *Child Development, 50*(2), 319–330.

Zanolli, K. M., Saudargas, R. A., & Twardosz, S. (1997). The development of toddlers' responses to affectionate teacher behavior. *Early Childhood Research Quarterly, 12*(1), 99–116.

Zeanah, C. H. (2012). *Handbook of infant mental health* (3rd ed.). New York: Guilford Press.

Zeanah, C. H., Berlin, L. J., & Boris, N. W. (2011). Practitioner review: Clinical applications of attachment theory and research for infants and young children. *Journal Of Child Psychology & Psychiatry, 52*(8), 819–833. doi:10.1111/j.1469-7610.2011.02399.x

Zeanah, C. H., Boris, N. W., & Larrieu, J. A. (1997). Infant development and developmental risk: A review of the past 10 years. *Journal of the American Academy of Child and Adolescent Psychiatry, 36*(2), 165–178.

ZERO TO THREE. (2008). *Caring for infants and toddlers in groups: Developmentally appropriate practice* (2nd ed.). Washington, DC: ZERO TO THREE.

ZERO TO THREE. (2009). Brain development. Retrieved from www.zerotothree.

ZERO TO THREE. (2012). *Building a strong infant-toddler workforce.* Retrieved from www.zerotothree.org/

Zinner, S. H., McGarvey, S. T., Lipsitt, L. T., & Rosner, B. (2002). Neonatal blood pressure and salt taste responsiveness. *Hypertension, 40,* 280–285.

Ziv, Y., Aviezer, O., Gini, M., Sagi, A., & Koren-Karie, N. (2000). Emotional availability in the mother-infant dyad as related to the quality of infant-mother attachment relationship. *Attachment & Human Development. 2,* 149–169.

ZERO TO THREE. (2012). Choosing books for babies. Retrived from main.zerotothree.org/site/PageServer?pagename=ter_key_language_bookselection

Ziv, Y., Oppenheim, D., & Sagi-Schwartz, A. (2004). Social information processing in middle childhood: Relations to infant-mother attachment. *Attachment and Human Development, 6*(3), 327–349.

Zoglio, S. (1997). *Training program for teams at work.* Doylestown, PA: Tower Hill.

Zuckerman, B., Frank, D. A., Hingson, R., Amaro, H., Levenson, S. M., Kayne, H., ... Bauchner, H. (1989). Effects of maternal marijuana and cocaine on fetal growth. *New England Journal of Medicine, 320,* 762–768.

Name Index

Subject Index

for cognitive development and learning, 187
for enhancing emotional development, 127–133
for enhancing learning, 127–133
for infant-toddler professionals, 411–413
organization of, 412
relationship-based, 63, 290–296
shared decision making in, 412–413
theories in, application of, 62–63
proprioceptive system, 236
prosocial behaviors, 139
prosocial development
familiarity and, 151
friendships, development of, 151–153
in infants and toddlers, 148–153
prosody, 194
protective factors, 15–16, 35
protégés, 418
proximal development, zone of, 58, 180
proximal-distal, 235
proximal style, 28
pruning, 91
psychosocial development theory, 52–53
psychotherapy, insight-based, 128–129
PTIC. *See* parent training and information center (PTIC)

Q
quality
of child care, 129, 270–271
defined, 251–257, 410
of environment for centers and child care homes, 318–322
importance of, 251–257
laws supporting, 271–273
of life, 3
policies supporting, 271–273
process variables of, 256–257
structural variables of, 252–256
systems supporting, 271–273
quality rating systems, 273
questions, 218
quiet opportunities, 326

R
raking grasp, 238
ratio and group sizes, 252–253
rational imitation, 59
RDAs. *See* Recommended Daily Allowances (RDAs)
RDS. *See* respiratory distress syndrome (RDS)
reading, 219
real baby, 34
reasonable modifications, 395
rebozo, 234
receptive language, 194
reciprocal play, 147
reciprocal social play, 147
reciprocity, 48, 294
Recommended Daily Allowances (RDAs), 98
referral making, 394–395

reflection, 277, 303, 313, 325, 326
in professional relationship-based community, 414–416
relationship-based approach to guidance and, 352–354
relationship-based community, 414–416
reflective practice model, 416–417
reflective supervision, 417–418
reflexes, 229–231
Moro, 230
palmar grasp, 231
primitive, 229
rooting, 229
startle, 230
step, 231
sucking, 229
tonic neck, 230
Reggio Emilia, 345–346
regulation, 111–112
relationships and, 113–114
relate strategies, 354–355
relating, 277, 303, 313, 325, 326
relationship-based approach to guidance and, 354–363
relationship-based approach to guidance, 350–363
reflecting, 352–354
relating, 354–363
respect, 350–352
relationship-based community, 290
creating, 290
development of, 414–416
professional, 414–416
reflection in, 414–416
respect in, 414
responding to, 416
relationship-based curriculum, 344–346
Creative Curriculum for Infants, Toddlers & Twos, The, 344–345
on culturally sensitive care, 298–302
foundation for, 279–281
HighScope, 344
infant-toddler professional's role in, 289–298
adult-child interactions, 290–296
imitation, 297–298
interactions, 297–298
relationship-based community, 290
relationship-based programs, 290–296
special skills of, 289–290
learning, importance of, 281–289
development and learning process, 283–284
encouraging play, 287–289
integrated learning, 284–287
Program for Infant/Toddler Care (PITC), 344
Reggio Emilia, 345–346
relationship-based planning, 302–309
relationships with families, 298–302
responsive-based planning, 302–309

relationship-based model, 3–8, 61–62
on attributes, 5–6
on capacities, 5–6
defined, 3
ecology and, 5
research on relationships, 6–8
relationship-based planning, 302–309
relationship-based programs, 63, 290–296
relationship-based theory, 46–48
of child development, 46
defined, 46, 47
relationship factors, 16
relationship realignments, 363–372
biting, 366–371
responsive interactions, 365–366
separation anxiety, 363–364
tantrums, 364–365
toddler resistance, 364
toilet learning, 371–372
relationships. *See also* emotional relationships
adult, 30
capacities, effect on, 5–6
in child care, 220
cognitive development and learning in, 176–184
concepts of, 181–184
culture and, 176–177
tools of, 177–179
cultural differences in, 121
culturally sensitive care in, 298–302
emotional expression in, 121–125
with families, 298–302
in family, supporting, 355
human, 13–14
identity development in, 120–121
language development and learning in, 197–219, 205–214
bidialectical children and families, 200–205
bilingual children and families, 200–205
birth to 2 months, 206–207
culture and, 197–200
18 to 36 months, 212–214
8 to 12 months, 208–211
4 to 8 months, 207–208
prior to birth, 206
strategies for, 214–219
12 to 18 months, 211–212
2 to 4 months, 207
maternal depression, impact of, 125–126
motor development and learning in, 233–239
affordances for, 237–238
culture and, 233–234
motor development through relationships, 234–235
movement and, 235–237
principles of, 235
progression of, 235
professional development of, 413–419
regulation and, 113–114

U.S. Department of Agriculture (USDA),
269, 270
U.S. Department of Health and Human
Services (HHS), 272
unpaid leave, 20
USDA. *See* U.S. Department of Agriculture
(USDA)
use of space, 181, 182–183
use of tools, 181, 182
User's Guide, 80
utensils, safely handling, 268–269

V
values, 84, 411
core, 411
velcro time, 285

vestibular system, 236
vigilance, 373–374
violence, 92–93
vision, 410
vocabulary, 215, 358–359
vulnerability, 14–16

W
wait, ability to, 361
well-being, 3, 372
windows of opportunity, 11
"wiring the brain" phenomenon, 90
womb
birth defects in, structural/metabolic, 101
brain development, as environment for,
98–102

maternal infections in, 101
nutrition in, 98–99
prenatal testing in, 101–102
teratogens in, 99–101
toxins in, 99–101
working memory, 169
working sense of self, 283
writing opportunities, 333

Z
ZERO TO THREE, 187, 277, 339, 417
zone of proximal development, 58, 180